W9-AQK-065

Children's Literature Review

Guide to Gale Literary Criticism Series

When you need to review criticism of literary works, these are the Gale series to use:

If the author's death date is:	You should turn to:
After Dec. 31, 1959 (or author is still living)	***CONTEMPORARY LITERARY CRITICISM*** for example: Jorge Luis Borges, Anthony Burgess, William Faulkner, Mary Gordon, Ernest Hemingway, Iris Murdoch
1900 through 1959	***TWENTIETH-CENTURY LITERARY CRITICISM*** for example: Willa Cather, F. Scott Fitzgerald, Henry James, Mark Twain, Virginia Woolf
1800 through 1899	***NINETEENTH-CENTURY LITERATURE CRITICISM*** for example: Fedor Dostoevski, Nathaniel Hawthorne, George Sand, William Wordsworth
1400 through 1799	***LITERATURE CRITICISM FROM 1400 TO 1800 (excluding Shakespeare)*** for example: Anne Bradstreet, Daniel Defoe, Alexander Pope, François Rabelais, Jonathan Swift, Phillis Wheatley ***SHAKESPEAREAN CRITICISM*** Shakespeare's plays and poetry
Antiquity through 1399	***CLASSICAL AND MEDIEVAL LITERATURE CRITICISM*** for example: Dante, Homer, Plato, Sophocles, Vergil, the Beowulf Poet

---

Gale also publishes related criticism series:

CHILDREN'S LITERATURE REVIEW

This ongoing series covers authors of all eras. Presents criticism on authors and author/illustrators who write for the preschool through high school audience.

SHORT STORY CRITICISM

This series covers the major short fiction writers of all nationalities and periods of literary history.

ISSN 0362-4145

volume 15

Children's Literature Review

Excerpts from Reviews,
Criticism, and Commentary
on Books for Children
and Young People

Guest Essay, "Didacticism and Anarchy in Recent Children's Books from America and England," by Dennis Butts

Gerard J. Senick
Editor

Melissa Reiff Hug
Associate Editor

Gale Research Company
Book Tower
Detroit, Michigan 48226

STAFF

Library of Congress Catalog Card Number 75-34953
ISBN 0-8103-0319-1
ISSN 0362-4145

Computerized photocomposition by
Typographics, Incorporated
Kansas City, Missouri

Printed in the United States

CONTENTS

PREFACE

As children's literature has evolved into both a respected branch of creative writing and a successful industry, literary criticism has documented and influenced each stage of its growth. Critics have recorded the literary development of individual authors as well as the trends and controversies that resulted from changes in values and attitudes, especially as they concerned children. While defining a philosophy of children's literature, critics developed a scholarship that balances an appreciation of children and an awareness of their needs with standards for literary quality much like those required by critics of adult literature. *Children's Literature Review (CLR)* is designed to provide a permanent, accessible record of this ongoing scholarship. Those responsible for bringing children and books together can now make informed choices when selecting reading materials for the young.

Scope of the Series

Each volume of *CLR* contains excerpts from published criticism on the works of authors and illustrators who create books for children from preschool through high school. The author list for each volume is international in scope and represents the variety of genres covered by children's literature—picture books, fiction, folklore, nonfiction, poetry, and drama. The works of approximately fifteen authors of all eras are represented in each volume. Although earlier volumes of *CLR* emphasized critical material published after 1960, successive volumes have expanded their coverage to encompass criticism written before 1960. Since many of the authors included in *CLR* are living and continue to write, it is necessary to update their entries periodically. Thus, future volumes will supplement the entries of selected authors covered in earlier volumes as well as include criticism on the works of authors new to the series.

Organization of the Book

An author section consists of the following elements: author heading, author portrait, author introduction, excerpts of criticism (each followed by a bibliographical citation), and illustrations, when available.

- The **author heading** consists of the author's full name followed by birth and death dates. The portion of the name outside the parentheses denotes the form under which the author is most frequently published. If the majority of the author's works for children were written under a pseudonym, the pseudonym will be listed in the author heading and the real name given on the first line of the author introduction. Also located at the beginning of the introduction are any other pseudonyms used by the author in writing for children and any name variations, including transliterated forms for authors whose languages use nonroman alphabets. Uncertainty as to a birth or death date is indicated by question marks.

- An **author portrait** is included when available.

- The **author introduction** contains information designed to introduce an author to *CLR* users by presenting an overview of the author's themes and styles, occasional biographical facts that relate to the author's literary career, a summary of critical response to the author's works, and information about major awards and prizes the author has received. Where applicable, introductions conclude with references to additional entries in biographical and critical reference series published by Gale Research Company. These sources include past volumes of *CLR* as well as *Authors in the News, Contemporary Authors, Contemporary Literary Criticism, Dictionary of Literary Biography, Nineteenth-Century Literature Criticism, Something about the Author, Something about the Author Autobiography Series, Twentieth-Century Literary Criticism,* and *Yesterday's Authors of Books for Children.*

- **Criticism** is located in three sections: **author's commentary** and **general commentary** (when available) and within individual **title entries,** which are preceded by **title entry headings.** Criticism is arranged chronologically within each section. Titles by authors being profiled are highlighted in boldface type within the text for easier access by readers.

  The **author's commentary** presents background material written by the author or by an interviewer. This commentary may cover a specific work or several works. Author's commentary on more than one work appears after the author introduction, while commentary on an individual book follows the title entry heading.

The **general commentary** consists of critical excerpts that consider more than one work by the author being profiled. General commentary is preceded by the critic's name in boldface type or, in the case of unsigned criticism, by the title of the journal.

Title entry headings precede the criticism on a title and cite publication information on the work being reviewed. Title headings list the title of the work as it appeared in its country of origin; titles in languages using nonroman alphabets are transliterated. If the original title is in a language other than English, the title of the first English-language translation follows in brackets. The first publication date of each work is listed in parentheses following the title. Differing U.S. and British titles of works originally published in English follow the publication date within the parentheses.

Title entries consist of critical excerpts on the author's individual works, arranged chronologically by publication date. The entries generally contain two to six reviews per title, depending on the stature of the book and the amount of criticism it has generated. The editors select titles that reflect the entire scope of the author's literary contribution, covering each genre and subject. An effort is made to reprint criticism that represents the full range of each title's reception—from the year of its initial publication to current assessments. Thus, the reader is provided with a record of the author's critical history. Publication information (such as publisher names and book prices) and parenthetical numerical references (such as footnotes or page and line references to specific editions of works) have been deleted at the editor's discretion to provide smoother reading of the text.

Entries on authors who are also illustrators will occasionally feature commentary on selected works illustrated but not written by the author being profiled. These works are strongly associated with the illustrator and have received critical acclaim for their art. By including critical comment on works of this type, the editors wish to provide a more complete representation of the author's total career. Criticism on these works has been chosen to stress artistic, rather than literary, contributions. Title entry headings for works illustrated by the author being profiled are arranged chronologically within the entry by date of publication and include notes identifying the author of the illustrated work. In order to provide easier access for users, all titles illustrated by the subject of the entry will be boldfaced.

CLR also includes entries on prominent illustrators who have contributed to the field of children's literature. These entries are designed to represent the development of the illustrator as an artist rather than as a literary stylist. The illustrator's section is organized like that of an author, with two exceptions: the introduction presents an overview of the illustrator's styles and techniques rather than outlining his or her literary background, and the commentary written by the illustrator on his or her works is called illustrator's commentary rather than author's commentary. Title entry headings are followed by explanatory notes identifying the author of the illustrated work. All titles of books containing illustrations by the artist being profiled as well as individual illustrations from these books are highlighted in boldface type.

- Selected excerpts are preceded by **explanatory notes,** which provide information on the critic or work of criticism to enhance the reader's understanding of the excerpt.

- A complete **bibliographical citation** designed to facilitate the location of the original book or article follows each piece of criticism.

- Numerous **illustrations** are featured in *CLR.* For entries on illustrators, an effort has been made to include illustrations that reflect the characteristics discussed in the criticism. Entries on major authors who do not illustrate their own works may also include photographs and other illustrative material pertinent to the authors' careers.

Other Features

- A list of **authors to appear in future volumes** follows the preface.

- A **guest essay** appears before the first author entry. These essays are written specifically for *CLR* by prominent critics on subjects of their choice. Past volumes have included essays by John Rowe Townsend, Zena Sutherland, Sheila A. Egoff, Rudine Sims, Marcus Crouch, Anne Pellowski, Milton Meltzer, and Margery Fisher. Volume 15 contains Dennis Butts's "Didacticism and Anarchy in Recent Children's Books from America and England." The editors are honored to feature Mr. Butts in this volume.

- An **appendix** lists the sources from which material has been reprinted in the volume. It does not, however, list every book or periodical consulted for the volume.

- The **cumulative index to authors** lists authors who have appeared in *CLR* and includes cross-references to *Authors in the News, Contemporary Authors, Contemporary Literary Criticism, Dictionary of Literary Biography, Nineteenth-Century Literature Criticism, Something about the Author, Something about the Author Autobiography Series, Twentieth-Century Literary Criticism,* and *Yesterday's Authors of Books for Children.*

- The **cumulative nationality index** lists authors alphabetically under their respective nationalities. Author names are followed by the volume number(s) in which they appear. Authors who have changed citizenship or whose current citizenship is not reflected in biographical sources appear under both their original nationality and that of their current residence.

- The **cumulative title index** lists titles covered in *CLR* followed by the volume and page number where criticism begins.

Acknowledgments

No work of this scope can be accomplished without the cooperation of many people. The editors especially wish to thank the copyright holders of the criticism included in this volume, the permissions managers of many book and magazine publishing companies for assisting us in securing reprint rights, and the staffs of the Kresge Library at Wayne State University, the University of Michigan Library, the Detroit Public Library, and the Wayne Oakland Library Federation (WOLF) for making their resources available to us. We are also grateful to Bill Beem and Fred M. Meyer for their assistance with the L. Frank Baum entry and to Anthony J. Bogucki for his assistance with copyright research.

Suggestions Are Welcome

In response to various suggestions, several features have been added to *CLR* since the series began, including author entries on retellers of traditional literature as well as those who have been the first to record oral tales and other folklore; entries on prominent illustrators featuring commentary on their styles and techniques; occasional entries devoted to criticism on a single work by a major author; explanatory notes that provide information on the critic or work of criticism to enhance the usefulness of the excerpt; more extensive illustrative material, such as holographs of manuscript pages and photographs of people and places pertinent to the authors' careers; and a cumulative nationality index for easy access to authors by nationality.

Readers are cordially invited to write the editor with comments and suggestions for further enhancing the usefulness of the *CLR* series.

AUTHORS TO APPEAR IN FUTURE VOLUMES

Aardema, Verna (Norberg) 1911-
Adams, Harriet S(tratemeyer) 1893?-1982
Adams, Richard 1920-
Adler, Irving 1913-
Ahlberg, Janet 1944- and Allan 1938-
Anderson, C(larence) W(illiam) 1891-1971
Arrick, Fran
Arundel, Honor (Morfydd) 1919-1973
Asbjörnsen, Peter Christen 1812-1885 and Jörgen Moe 1813?-1882
Asch, Frank 1946-
Avery, Gillian 1926-
Avi 1937-
Aymé, Marcel 1902-1967
Bailey, Carolyn Sherwin 1875-1961
Ballantyne, R(obert) M(ichael) 1825-1894
Banner, Angela 1923-
Bannerman, Helen 1863-1946
Barrett, Judi(th) 1941-
Barrie, J(ames) M(atthew) 1860-1937
Baumann, Hans 1914-1985
Beatty, Patricia Robbins 1922- and John 1922-1975
Beckman, Gunnel 1910-
Behn, Harry 1898-1973
Belloc, Hilaire 1870-1953
Berenstain, Stan(ley) 1923- and Jan(ice) 1923-
Berger, Melvin H. 1927-
Berna, Paul 1910-
Beskow, Elsa 1874-1953
Bianco, Margery Williams 1881-1944
Bishop, Claire Huchet
Blake, Quentin 1932-
Blos, Joan W(insor) 1928-
Blumberg, Rhoda 1917-
Blyton, Enid 1897-1968
Bodecker, N(iels) M(ogens) 1922-
Bødker, Cecil 1927-
Bonham, Frank 1914-
Brancato, Robin F(idler) 1936-
Branscum, Robbie 1937-
Breinburg, Petronella 1927-
Bridgers, Sue Ellen 1942-
Bright, Robert 1902-
Brink, Carol Ryrie 1895-1981
Brinsmead, H(esba) F(ay) 1922-
Brooke, L(eonard) Leslie 1862-1940
Brown, Marc Tolon 1946-
Browne, Anthony (Edward Tudor) 1946-
Bryan, Ashley F. 1923-
Buff, Mary 1890-1970 and Conrad 1886-1975
Bulla, Clyde Robert 1914-
Burch, Robert (Joseph) 1925-
Burgess, Gelett 1866-1951
Burgess, Thornton W(aldo) 1874-1965
Burkert, Nancy Ekholm 1933-
Burnett, Frances Hodgson 1849-1924
Butterworth, Oliver 1915-
Caines, Jeannette (Franklin)
Carlson, Natalie Savage 1906-
Carrick, Carol 1935- and Donald 1929-
Chambers, Aidan 1934-
Chönz, Selina
Christopher, Matt(hew F.) 1917-
Ciardi, John (Anthony) 1916-1986
Clapp, Patricia 1912-
Clark, Ann Nolan 1898-
Clarke, Pauline 1921-
Cohen, Barbara 1932-
Colby, C(arroll) B(urleigh) 1904-1977
Colman, Hila
Colum Padraic 1881-1972
Cone, Molly 1918-
Conrad, Pam 1947-
Coolidge, Olivia E(nsor) 1908-
Coolidge, Susan 1835-1905
Cooney, Barbara 1917-
Courlander, Harold 1908-
Cox, Palmer 1840-1924
Crane, Walter 1845-1915
Cresswell, Helen 1934-
Crompton, Richmal 1890-1969
Cunningham, Julia (Woolfolk) 1916-
Curry, Jane L(ouise) 1932-
Dalgliesh, Alice 1893-1979
Daly, Maureen 1921-
Danziger, Paula 1944-
Daugherty, James 1889-1974
D'Aulaire, Ingri 1904-1980 and Edgar Parin 1898-1986
De la Mare, Walter 1873-1956
De Regniers, Beatrice Schenk 1914-
Dickinson, Peter 1927-
Dillon, Eilís 1920-
Dillon, Leo 1933- and Diane 1933-
Dodge, Mary Mapes 1831-1905
Domanska, Janina
Drescher, Henrik
Duncan, Lois S(teinmetz) 1934-
Duvoisin, Roger 1904-1980
Eager, Edward 1911-1964
Edgeworth, Maria 1767-1849
Edmonds, Walter D(umaux) 1903-
Epstein, Sam(uel) 1909- and Beryl 1910-
Ets, Marie Hall 1893-
Ewing, Juliana Horatia 1841-1885
Farber, Norma 1909-1984
Farjeon, Eleanor 1881-1965
Field, Eugene 1850-1895
Field, Rachel 1894-1942
Fisher, Dorothy Canfield 1879-1958
Fisher, Leonard Everett 1924-
Flack, Marjorie 1897-1958
Forbes, Esther 1891-1967
Forman, James D(ouglas) 1932-
Freeman, Don 1908-1978
Fujikawa, Gyo 1908-
Fyleman, Rose 1877-1957
Galdone, Paul 1914-1986
Gantos, Jack 1951-
Garfield, Leon 1921-
Garis, Howard R(oger) 1873-1962
Garner, Alan 1935-
Gates, Doris 1901-
Gerrard, Roy 1935-
Giblin, James Cross 1933-
Giff, Patricia Reilly 1935-
Ginsburg, Mirra 1919-
Goble, Paul 1933-
Godden, Rumer 1907-
Goodall, John S(trickland) 1908-
Goodrich, Samuel G(riswold) 1793-1860
Gorey, Edward (St. John) 1925-
Gramatky, Hardie 1907-1979
Greene, Constance C(larke) 1924-
Grimm, Jacob 1785-1863 and Wilhelm 1786-1859
Gruelle, Johnny 1880-1938
Guillot, René 1900-1969
Hader, Elmer 1889-1973 and Berta 1891?-1976
Hague, Michael 1948-
Hale, Lucretia Peabody 1820-1900
Haley, Gail E(inhart) 1939-
Hall, Lynn 1937-
Harnett, Cynthia 1893-1981
Harris, Christie (Lucy Irwin) 1907-
Harris, Joel Chandler 1848-1908
Harris, Rosemary (Jeanne) 1923-
Hayes, Sheila 1937-
Haywood, Carolyn 1898-
Head, Ann 1915-
Heide, Florence Parry 1919-
Heine, Helme

Heinlein, Robert A(nson) 1907-
Highwater, Jamake (Mamake) 1942-
Hoberman, Mary Ann 1930-
Hoff, Syd(ney) 1912-
Hoffman, Heinrich 1809-1894
Holland, Isabelle 1920-
Holling, Holling C(lancy) 1900-1973
Hughes, Langston 1902-1967
Hunter, Mollie 1922-
Hurd, Edith Thacher 1910- and Clement 1908-
Hyman, Trina Schart 1939-
Ipcar, Dahlov (Zorach) 1917-
Iwasaki, Chihiro 1918-1974
Jackson, Jesse 1908-1983
Janosch 1931-
Johnson, Crockett 1906-1975
Johnson, James Weldon 1871-1938
Jones, Diana Wynne 1934-
Judson, Clara Ingram 1879-1960
Juster, Norton 1929-
Kelly, Eric P(hilbrook) 1884-1960
Kennedy, (Jerome) Richard 1932-
Kent, Jack 1920-1985
Kerr, (Anne-)Judith 1923-
Kerr, M. E. 1927-
Kettelkamp, Larry (Dale) 1933-
King, (David) Clive 1924-
Kipling, Rudyard 1865-1936
Kjelgaard, Jim 1910-1959
Kraus, Robert 1925-
Krauss, Ruth (Ida) 1911-
Krumgold, Joseph 1908-1980
La Fontaine, Jean de 1621-1695
Lang, Andrew 1844-1912
Langton, Jane (Gillson) 1922-
Latham, Jean Lee 1902-
Lattimore, Eleanor Frances 1904-1986
Lauber, Patricia (Grace) 1924-
Lavine, Sigmund A(rnold) 1908-
Leaf, Munro 1905-1976
Lenski, Lois 1893-1974
Levy, Elizabeth 1942-
Lightner, A(lice) M. 1904-
Lipsyte, Robert 1938-
Lofting, Hugh (John) 1866-1947
Lunn, Janet 1928-
MacDonald, George 1824-1905
MacGregor, Ellen 1906-1954
Mann, Peggy
Marshall, James 1942-
Masefield, John 1878-1967
Mayer, Marianna 1945-
Mayne, William (James Carter) 1928-
Mazer, Harry 1925-
Mazer, Norma Fox 1931-
McCaffrey, Anne (Inez) 1926-
McGovern, Ann
McKee, David (John)
McKillip, Patricia A(nne) 1948-
McNeer, May 1902-
Meader, Stephen W(arren) 1892-1977
Means, Florence Crannell 1891-1980
Meigs, Cornelia 1884-1973
Merrill, Jean (Fairbanks) 1923-
Miles, Betty 1928-
Miles, Patricia Miles 1899-1986
Milne, Lorus 1912- and Margery 1915-
Minarik, Else Holmelund 1920-
Mizumura, Kazue
Mohr, Nicholasa 1935-
Molesworth, Mary Louisa 1842-1921
Morey, Walt(er Nelson) 1907-
Mowat, Farley (McGill) 1921-
Munsch, Robert 19??-
Naylor, Phyllis Reynolds 1933-
Neufeld, John (Arthur) 1938-
Neville, Emily Cheney 1919-
Nic Leodhas, Sorche 1898-1969
Nielsen, Kay 1886-1957
North, Sterling 1906-1974
Norton, Andre 1912-
Ofek, Uriel 1926-
Ormondroyd, Edward 1925-
Ottley, Reginald (Leslie) 1909-
Oxenbury, Helen 1938-
Parish, Peggy 1927-
Peck, Robert Newton 1928-
Perl, Lila
Perrault, Charles 1628-1703
Petersen, P(eter) J(ames) 1941-
Petersham, Maud 1890-1971 and Miska 1888-1960
Picard, Barbara Leonie 1917-
Pierce, Meredith Ann 1958-
Platt, Kin 1911-
Politi, Leo 1908-
Price, Christine 1928-1980
Pyle, Howard 1853-1911
Rackham, Arthur 1867-1939
Rawls, Wilson 1919-
Reiss, Johanna 1932-
Reeves, James 1909-1978
Richards, Laura E(lizabeth) 1850-1943
Richler, Mordecai 1931-
Robertson, Keith (Carlton) 1914-
Rockwell, Anne 1934- and Harlow
Rodgers, Mary 1931-
Rollins, Charlemae Hill 1897-1979
Ross, Tony 1938-
Rounds, Glen H(arold) 1906-
Salinger, J(erome) D(avid) 1919-
Sanchez, Sonia 1934-
Sandburg, Carl 1878-1967
Sandoz, Mari 1896-1966
Sawyer, Ruth 1880-1970
Scarry, Huck 1953-
Scoppettone, Sandra 1936-
Scott, Jack Denton 1915-
Sebestyen, Ouida 1924-
Seton, Ernest Thompson 1860-1946
Sewell, Anna 1820-1878
Sharmat, Marjorie Weinman 1928-
Sharp, Margery 1905-
Shepard, Ernest H(oward) 1879-1976
Shotwell, Louisa R(ossiter) 1902-
Sidney, Margaret 1844-1924
Silverstein, Alvin 1933- and Virginia B(arbara Opshelor) 1937-
Sinclair, Catherine 1800-1864
Skurzynski, Gloria (Joan) 1930-
Sleator, William (Warner) 1945-
Slobodkin, Louis 1903-1975
Smith, Jessie Willcox 1863-1935
Snyder, Zilpha Keatley 1927-
Spence, Eleanor (Rachel) 1928-
Sperry, Armstrong W. 1897-1976
Spykman, E(lizabeth) C. 1896-1965
Starbird, Kaye 1916-
Steele, William O(wen) 1917-1979
Stevenson, James 1929-
Stolz, Mary (Slattery) 1920-
Stratemeyer, Edward L. 1862-1930
Streatfeild, (Mary) Noel 1897-1986
Taylor, Sydney 1904?-1978
Taylor, Theodore 1924-
Tenniel, Sir John 1820-1914
Thiele, Colin 1920-
Thomas, Joyce Carol 1938-
Thompson, Julian F(rancis) 1927-
Titus, Eve 1922-
Tolkien, J(ohn) R(onald) R(euel) 1892-1973
Trease, (Robert) Geoffrey 1909-
Tresselt, Alvin 1916-
Treviño, Elizabeth Borton de 1904-
Turkle, Brinton 1915-
Twain, Mark 1835-1910
Udry, Janice May 1928-
Unnerstad, Edith (Totterman) 1900-
Uttley, Alison 1884-1976
Ventura, Piero (Luigi) 1937-
Vining, Elizabeth Gray 1902-
Waber, Bernard 1924-
Wahl, Jan 1933-
Ward, Lynd 1905-1985
Wells, Rosemary 1943-
White, T(erence) H(anbury) 1906-1964
Wiese, Kurt 1887-1974
Wilkinson, Brenda 1946-
Worth, Valerie 1933-
Wyeth, N(ewell) C(onvers) 1882-1945
Yates, Elizabeth 1905-
Yonge, Charlotte M(ary) 1823-1901
Yorinks, Arthur 1953-
Zemach, Harve 1933-1974 and Margot 1931-
Zion, Gene 1913-1975

Readers are cordially invited to suggest additional authors to the editors.

GUEST ESSAY

Didacticism and Anarchy in Recent Children's Books from America and England

by Dennis Butts

> "Mrs. Barbauld once told me that she admired "The Ancient Mariner" very much, but that there were two faults in it,—it was improbable, and had no moral. As to the probability, I owned that that might admit some question; but as to the want of a moral, I told her that in my own judgement the poem had too much— "
>
> (Samuel Taylor Coleridge, *Table Talk*)[1]

It is a commonplace in discussing American literature to draw attention to its moral seriousness, even when that literature appears to be at its most amoral and chaotic. Cooper's tales of Deerslayer and his Indian friends, Melville's exotic sea stories, and Hawthorne's romances of New England are all works to which Coleridge's own criticism of "The Ancient Mariner" might be applied, the weakness being not, as Mrs. Barbauld thought, the absence of any moral, but rather the presence of too much moral. The same can perhaps be said of many American writers. Is it any wonder, given this tradition, that Hemingway himself borrowed the titles for two of his best novels from the *Devotions* of John Donne and the *Book of Ecclesiastes*?[2]

This same tradition persists, I believe, among many recent American children's books where, despite the robust acceptance of a teenage society in which abortions, child abuse, and lesbian relationships are frankly dealt with, the thread of moral didacticism continues to run very clearly.[3]

The work of Betsy Byars is a case in point. Though her earlier books, such as *The Summer of the Swans* (1970) and *The 18th Emergency* (1974) have a delicate restraint and pleasing irony, some of her later works move a little nearer to bibliotherapy. *The TV Kid* (1976), for example, is a witty and accessible story about a boy, Lennie, whose mother runs the Fairyland Motel, where, because of his deep-rooted insecurity and loneliness, he spends most of his time watching TV at the expense of personal relationships and his schoolwork. He knows all the commercial jingles by heart, and makes up fantasies about winning quiz programs and buying a full-sized puppet for a companion. Behind the motel are some holiday houses which Lennie likes to visit in the autumn when the holiday-makers have left, and here one day he is bitten by a rattlesnake—a horrific experience—but saved by a passing policeman and taken to hospital. After a period of intense pain he begins to recover, but the experience has changed him. When a TV set is installed in his hospital room, he realizes that the programs present a very artificial view of life, and that the real things are his pain and his mother's love. He tells his mother about the science test he failed before his accident, and begins working on a new project to make up for it. The story ends with Lennie reading his project—the topic is rattlesnakes!—to two young girls whose parents are staying at the motel. For all the book's hardboiled witticisms and topical material, in other words, Betsy Byars is clearly a serious-minded writer concerned not only with the personality of the child but also with his need to integrate into the world around him. It is a sign of Lennie's progress that he is able to form relationships with the two young girls at the end of the story.

In *The Pinballs* (1977), to give another example, Betsy Byars portrays three children from disturbed backgrounds who are sent to a foster home. At first they have great problems relating to each other and the world outside. They are like the balls in a pinball machine, says Carlie, helplessly knocked about by everyone (she is in the home after being beaten up by her *third* stepfather). Gradually, however, the children learn to trust and love each other, and discover that life can be worthwhile. It is a lively story, and the tense relationships between the children are caught in some genuinely witty dialogue as they learn to live with each other. "I guess even a blind pig can come up with an acorn every now and then," Carlie tells her eight-year-old foster brother Thomas J. when he finds her missing earring.[4] But it is all a little too insistently didactic, too neatly packaged, right up to the statement of the moral at the end—"Pinballs can't help what happens to them and you and me can," says Carlie, just in case readers missed the importance of learning responsible and socially-aware behavior.[5]

Judy Blume's work is very similar [see entry beginning on page 57 of this volume]. Though her books are usually written both in the first person singular and in the colloquial idiom of American teenagers, the moral lessons are generally quite overt. Perhaps because it is more genuinely autobiographical, *Starring Sally J. Freedman as Herself* (1977) is freer of didacticism than Blume's other works. Examples of Blume's more typically didactic novels are *Then Again, Maybe I Won't* (1971), which details the problems of twelve year-old Tony Miglione as he gradually learns to cope with the strong feelings which threaten to make him ill, and *Blubber* (1974), which tells the story of a girl who unthinkingly participates in the bullying of a fat classmate until she finds herself victimized and learns the errors of her ways. Even *Forever* (1975), Blume's controversially frank treatment of teenage sexuality, puts enormous emphasis on personal and social responsibility and contains the description of a visit to a family planning clinic that is almost documentary in its effect (and intention?). As Patricia Craig has said, *Forever* has at times "a clinical, instructive quality."[6]

However, there is another tradition of writing in America connected, oddly enough, with the figure of Henry James, not perhaps the first novelist who comes to mind when thinking of children's books. In such stories as "The Lesson of the Master" (1888) and supremely in the novel *The Ambassadors* (1903), he came to question those austere values we associate with Puritanism and asserted the primacy of the joy of experience, even when this joy challenged conventional morality and seemed to threaten it with anarchy. Strether, the elderly and rather prim New England bachelor who is sent to Europe to bring his young friend Chad back to his business responsibilities, in Paris discovers the errors of his own unfulfilled life and urges Bilham not to make the same mistake—"Live all you can; it's a mistake not to. It doesn't so much matter what you do in particular, so long as you have your life. If you haven't had that what *have* you had? Do what you like as long as you don't make my mistake. For it was a mistake...Live!"[7] Readers of Mark Twain will recognize similar sentiments behind his "Notice" at the beginning of *The Adventures of Huckleberry Finn* (1884): "Persons attempting to find a motive in this narrative will be prosecuted; persons attempting to find a moral in it will be banished."[8]

Given the strength of the achievements of James and Twain, it is ironical that such categorical imperatives seem to have been observed more in the restrained and genteel pages of English children's books than in the open spaces and radical experiments of American fiction. The whole tradition of quasi-surrealistic fantasy, going right back to *Alice's Adventures in Wonderland* (1865)—and even earlier—is evidence of that, and the fact that this writing often takes the form of fantasy rather than realism suggests ways in which English culture needed to go underground (almost literally!) in order to articulate its own anarchical and subversive values in ostensibly nonserious ways. Who could regard a little girl's adventures with playing cards down a rabbit hole as a serious questioning of authority? But, as Juliet Dusinberre has recently pointed out, by the time Lewis Carroll died in 1898 *Alice* had quite supplanted John Bunyan's *Pilgrim's Progress* (1678), the great *moral* allegory, in the popular imagination.[9] And this kind of writing has been an important strand in English children's books ever since, and has produced a good deal of literature, often challenging authority, which emphasizes individual rather than social values and is comic, even farcical, in form.

Another nineteenth-century example of subversive literature is Rudyard Kipling's *Stalky & Co.* (1899), like *Alice* a parody of earlier didactic books, this time of such school stories as Thomas Hughes's *Tom Brown's Schooldays* (1857) and F.W. Farrar's *Eric; or, Little by Little* (1858). Where Hughes and Farrar uncritically praised manliness, muscular Christianity and the school spirit, Kipling's characters are admired for their independence and antiestablishment ingenuity, their skill, for example, at avoiding school games and going off for a quiet smoke. When reprimanded by a House Master for being unhygenic, they take their revenge by hiding a dead cat under the floorboards to stink the school out, and Kipling actually approves of this rebellious behaviour.

Richmal Crompton's *William* books continued that tradition in the 1920s. *Just—William* (1922), was the first of a series of over thirty books, and in the activities of William and his gang of Ginger, Douglas, and Henry, not forgetting the dog Jumbles, we see something of the same kind of cheerful anarchy found in *Stalky & Co.* as William, with ruffled hair and socks around the ankles as immortalized in the drawings of Thomas Henry, sides with tramps and jolly ladies and eccentrics against the world of parents and teachers and clergymen, and all the respectable, materialistic values of Violet Elizabeth Bott's bourgeois family.

Nearer to our own times is *The Bash Street Kids,* a comic strip created by Leo Baxendale and Ken Walmsley for the illustrated weekly children's magazine the *Beano* in 1953. Here is another group of children—Toots, Smiffy with protruding teeth and a nearly bald head, Plug with fang-like teeth—clearly in a contemporary urban setting, often a classroom which the mortar-boarded teacher, a nice anachronism, unavailingly tries to control. The comedy is blacker and the anarchy stronger than Richmal Crompton's, for this is a world where soot bombs explode and the kids use racing-pigeons to make pigeon pie. Raymond Briggs exhibits similarly cheerful anarchic values in his early picture books for young children. *Father Christmas* (1973) depicts a grumpy, swearing misanthropist rather than the usual sentimental stereotype, and *Fungus the Bogeyman* (1977) celebrates the lives of Fungus, Mildew, and Mould, who live underground (again!) in regions of filth and actually enjoy eating green eggs and washing in scummy water! (This is not far from the world of such popular BBC-TV comedy programs as *Monty Python's Flying Circus* and *The Young Ones,* of course.)

Gene Kemp's stories about Cricklepit Combined School share something of the same counterculture, I think, with their inclusion of bad language and bullying, and with jokes and riddles in practically every chapter. Indeed, Gowie Corby, the hero of *Gowie Corby Plays Chicken* (1979), commits all kinds of wild and unpopular offences simply because he enjoys being a loner. He trips up and injures the captain of the school football team, pours glue over another boy's briefcase, and constantly bullies his helpless deskmate, Heather. Child of a broken home, with one brother dead and another in prison, he rejoices in his independence in an aggressive *patois:*

> "Go and get knotted...I ain't done nuthin' for nobody 'cos nobody's done nuthin' for me. Not ever. And they never will. And I tell you this. You've gotter look after yourself in this stinkin' world, 'cos nobody else will, and anybody who tells you any different is talkin' crap..."[10]

Perhaps Gowie's violence frightened even Gene Kemp—he undergoes a most unconvincing reformation about two-thirds of the way through the book, rather as if Betsy Byars wrote the ending with its assertion of reintegrative values. But the damage has been done by then, I suspect, and it is the ball-of-fire Gowie of the first ten chapters who will live in most children's memories, not least because of the relish with which Gene Kemp records his exploits.

Tyke Tiler shows no such reformation in her last term at The Cricklepit Combined School, befriending the form idiot and potential thief instead of more socially acceptable children, falling into a pond in an attempt to reclaim a dead sheep's bones, stealing the examination questions, and finally climbing up the school tower and wrecking it on the last day of term. Again, like the Gowie Corby book, *The Turbulent Term of Tyke Tiler* (1977) is original and funny, catching the authentic noises of the classroom in ways that remind one of *The Bash Steet Kids,* and asserting the values of the child and his or her experiences against the adult hierarchy. It is no wonder that this book won the 1977 Carnegie Medal and also the Other Award given by the Children's Rights Workshop in the same year.

This kind of literature, I would suggest, has three characteristics which distinguish it from recent, more didactic stories, though the distinctions are not always precise. First, anarchical books depict a hero or heroine, with a group of like-minded companions, who refuses to go along with the values of the establishment. However, they are not necessarily reformers or revolutionaries, and usually accept the social structure as established fact; they simply don't find it particularly helpful nor seek to join it. What they want to do is to have a good time by asserting their own individuality, and to outwit the regime when it prevents this happening. This is why—and here is a second characteristic—the central protagonists usually enjoy life. They have adventures and get into scrapes which are exhilarating and amusing. These characters are the heroes and heroines of *comic* books. But, thirdly, these heroes do have values of their own: independence, initiative, originality, an unwillingness to conform, and a loyalty to others who share these values. These are their alternative values to those of the prevailing social system, and at times they threaten to subvert it.

Jan Mark's *Thunder and Lightnings* (1976), which also won the Carnegie Medal, is another example. It tells the story of Andrew, whose parents are relaxed, middle-class liberals, and of Victor, whose working-class mother is rigid and repressed, obsessed with neatness and tidiness. The novel has several themes: the problems of friendship across class barriers, the need to accept life as it is, and above all the integrity of the individual, whatever sort of society he lives in. It is Andrew, the clever boy going to university, who has to learn about courage and independence from Victor, the boy who can barely read. For when Andrew offers to teach Victor how to read, Victor rejects his well-meaning attempt in these terms:

> "That's no good you trying to teach me anything . . . If you start being good at something, people expect you to be even better and then they get annoyed when you aren't. That's safer to seem a bit dafter than you are."
>
> "But you're not daft," said Andrew. "I thought you were at first, till I knew you better. The same as the first time I saw you I thought you were fat. I didn't know you were dressed in layers. Why do you wear so many clothes? Don't you get hot?"
>
> "Now and again," said Victor, "but I don't care."

"But don't you care if people think you're stupid?"

"No I don't," said Victor. "Why be miserable just to make other people happy."[11]

This is the voice of the genuine child maverick, of course, one heard repeatedly in Jan Mark's work, notably in *Hairs in the Palm of the Hand* (1981), where a young girl hilariously disrupts the school system, confuses the teachers by giving a series of false names, and even contrives to stir up protests about sexist teaching and inadequate classrooms before revealing that she is not a pupil at the school anyway! And it's all very funny. "Why be miserable just to make other people happy." "Live all you can; it's a mistake not to."

For those who wonder if the anarchy of these books is irresponsible—and some readers, I know, have been embarrassed by the success of the *William* books, *The Bash Street Kids,* and Gene Kemp—it is important to recognize their popularity and to try to identify the reasons for it. Leo Baxendale, one of the originators of the anarchical *Bash Street Kids,* defended his creation in these terms:

> We live in a society that screws people up and screws people down. One section of the populace are selected to be a competitive ambitious elite, screwed up to go careering through life like demented clockwork toys. A larger section are screwed down to the floor, demoralised into acceptance of lives and jobs below their potential and hopes. If you consider that each person, to himself or herself, is the centre of the universe, this screwing of people's lives must lead to frustrations, resentments, anger, and feelings of inadequacy boiling away inside. And...these things feed my humour.[12]

This suggests very well how what looks like a peculiarly English response to a peculiarly English set of problems may have wider and political implications than first appears. For example, Robert Cormier's American school story *The Chocolate War* (1974) is about more than schoolboys, too, though its powerful and painful picture of school life might deceive some readers. What we are really offered is a vivid account of the working of a power structure led by an ambitious headteacher, and a sadistic elite of bullies who combine in order to make everyone conform in a deliberately systematic way. One either has to accept the regime or to rebel against it and then be destroyed, as Jerry, the defeated hero, is. There is no hope of the cheerful anarchy found in Kipling or Gene Kemp; and, though *Beyond the Chocolate War* (1985) offers some resistance, when Obie challenges Archie, the leader of the Vigils, he gets nowhere, and the story ends with Archie's successor firmly installed to extend the system and brutalize it further.

This account of some recent American and British children's books is inevitably limited. One could point to the presence of such didactic English works as Bernard Ashley's well-meant story of a black boy, *The Trouble with Donovan Croft* (1974), or Jan Mark's bleaker (and less successful?) science fiction, such as *The Ennead* (1978), as ways of qualifying the broad picture. But even so there does appear to be a greater interest in didactic forms among recent American children's books with their emphasis on maturity and social integration, and the persistence of more anarchic forms among British books with their emphasis on independence and nonconformity.

Whether this tells us something about British and American societies in the 1970s and 1980s is an interesting subject for speculation. But an extension of the subject matter and emphasis on didacticism in much American fiction, and a resurgence of vitality in the anarchic tradition in British writing seem to me two clearly defined features of the current literary scene, however much we may wish to qualify that broad generalization.

Perhaps, as Fred Inglis anticipated in his article "The Awkard Ages; or, What Shall We Tell the Children?," our writers are beginning to acknowledge the facts of "a changing fluid self and a society which we both create and are created by."[13] The definition of goodness itself may be changing in the changing moral landscape of the last decades of the twentieth century, and, if so, it is not surprising that writers are beginning to redefine our notions of personal integrity and social responsibility on both sides of the Atlantic.

It it, however, reassuring to know that we are not alone and that others have been this way before us. "He that kisses the joy as it flies/Lives in Eternity's sunrise," said William Blake nearly two hundred years ago,[14] and to remind ourselves that a cheerful and anarchic rejection of conformity cannot in the last analysis be narrowly ascribed either to English or American writers, let me end by quoting the last words of Mark Twain's great and subversive American classic *Huckleberry Finn:*

> "I reckon I got to light out for the Territory ahead of the rest, because Aunt Sally she's going to adopt and sivilize me, and I can't stand it. I been there before."[15]

Notes

1. Samuel T. Coleridge, *Table Talk,* in *Coleridge: The Clark Lectures 1951-52,* by Arthur Humphry House (London: Hart-Davis, 1969), 90.
2. Ernest Hemingway, *For Whom the Bell Tolls* (New York: Scribner's, 1940) and *The Sun also Rises* (New York: Scribner's, 1926).
3. See respectively Paul Zindel, *My Darling, My Hamburger* (New York: Harper, 1969); Betsy Byars, *The Pinballs* (London: Puffin, 1980); and Rosa Guy, *Ruby* (New York: Viking, 1976).
4. Byars, 18.
5. Ibid., 93.
6. Patricia Craig, *Twentieth-Century Children's Writers,* ed. D.L. Kirkpatrick, 2nd ed. (New York: Macmillan, 1983), 94.
7. Henry James, *The Ambassadors* (London: Dent, 1950), 129.
8. Mark Twain, *The Adventures of Huckleberry Finn* (London: Nelson, n.d.), i.
9. Juliet Dusinberre, *Alice to the Lighthouse: Children's Books and Radical Experiments in Art* (London: Macmillan, 1987), 1.
10. Gene Kemp, *Gowie Corby Plays Chicken* (London: Faber, 1981), 43.
11. Jan Mark, *Thunder and Lightnings* (London: Puffin, 1987), 150.
12. Leo Baxendale, *A Very Funny Business* (London: Duckworth, 1978), 136. For examples of Baxendale's work, see the annual publications of *The Beano Book* (London: Thomson, 1953—).
13. Fred Inglis, "The Awkward Ages, or What Shall We Tell the Children?" *Children's Literature in Education* 13 (March 1974): 30.
14. William Blake, *Complete Writings,* ed. Geoffrey Keynes (London: Oxford University Press, 1972), 179.
15. Twain, 373.

Bibliography

Ashley, Bernard. *The Trouble with Donovan Croft.* Illustrated by Fermin Rocker. London: Oxford University Press, 1974.

Blume, Judy. *Blubber.* Scarsdale, N.Y.: Bradbury, 1974.

______. *Forever. . . .* Scarsdale, N.Y.: Bradbury, 1975.

______. *Starring Sally J. Freedman as Herself.* Scarsdale, N.Y.: Bradbury, 1977.

______. *Then Again, Maybe I Won't.* Scarsdale, N.Y.: Bradbury, 1971.

Briggs, Raymond. *Father Christmas.* London: Hamilton, 1973.

______. *Fungus the Bogeyman.* London: Hamilton, 1977.

Bunyan, John. *Pilgrim's Progress from This World, to That Which Is to Come: Delivered under the Similitude of a Dream.* London: Ponder, 1678.

Byars, Betsy, *The 18th Emergency.* Illustrated by Robert Grossman. New York: Viking, 1973.

______. *The Pinballs.* New York: Harper, 1977.

______. *The Summer of the Swans.* Illustrated by Ted CoConis. New York: Viking, 1970.

______. *The TV Kid.* Illustrated by Richard Cuffari. New York: Viking, 1976.

Carroll, Lewis. *Alice's Adventures in Wonderland.* Illustrated by John Tenniel. London: Macmillan, 1865.

Cormier, Robert. *Beyond the Chocolate War.* New York: Knopf, 1985.

______. *The Chocolate War.* New York: Pantheon, 1974.

Crompton, Richmal. *Just—William.* Illustrated by Thomas Henry. London: Newnes, 1922.

Farrar, Frederick William. *Eric; or, Little by Little: A Tale of Roslyn School.* Edinburgh: Black, 1858.

[Hughes, Thomas]. *Tom Brown's School Days: By an Old Boy.* Cambridge: Macmillan, 1857.

James, Henry. *The Ambassadors.* New York: Harper, 1903.

______. *The Lesson of the Master, The Marriages, The Pupil, Brooksmith, The Solution, Sir Edmund Orme.* New York: Macmillan, 1892.

Kemp, Gene. *Gowie Corby Plays Chicken.* London: Faber, 1979.

______. *The Turbulent Term of Tyke Tiler.* Illustrated by Carolyn Dinan. London: Faber, 1977.

Kipling, Rudyard. *Stalky & Co.* London: Macmillan, 1899.

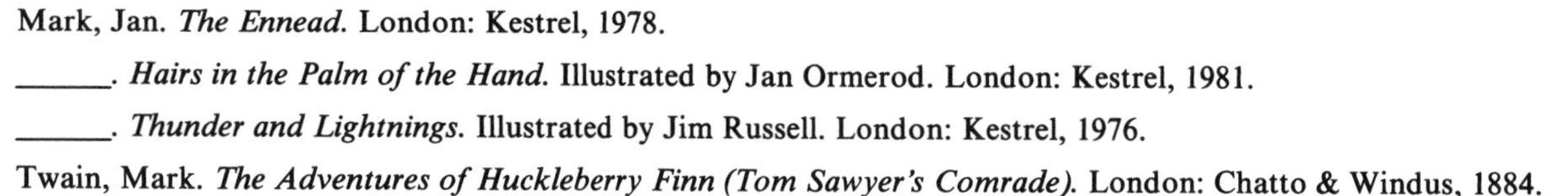

Mark, Jan. *The Ennead.* London: Kestrel, 1978.

______. *Hairs in the Palm of the Hand.* Illustrated by Jan Ormerod. London: Kestrel, 1981.

______. *Thunder and Lightnings.* Illustrated by Jim Russell. London: Kestrel, 1976.

Twain, Mark. *The Adventures of Huckleberry Finn (Tom Sawyer's Comrade).* London: Chatto & Windus, 1884.

Dennis Butts is an English author, critic, editor, and teacher. He is the author of the monograph *Robert Louis Stevenson* (1966) and study outlines for Charles Dickens's *Great Expectations* (1985) and *Bleak House* (1986), as well as the editor of the eighth volume of *Pergamon Poets* (1970), a selection of poems by Vernon Scannell and Jon Silkin; *Good Writers for Young Readers* (1977), a collection of critical essays on contemporary children's authors; and a critical edition of Frances Hodgson Burnett's *The Secret Garden* (1987). He has also been a contributor to such periodicals as *Children's Literature in Education, Signal,* and *The Use of English.* A founding member of the National Association for the Teaching of English, Butts is currently teaching in the master's degree program in children's literature at Bulmershe College of Higher Education, Reading. He has also served as a writer and broadcaster for the BBC on children's books and nineteenth-century literature.

Children's Literature Review

Jim Arnosky

1946-

(Born James Edward Arnosky) American author/illustrator and illustrator of picture books and nonfiction.

Combining skills as a naturalist and an artist, Arnosky creates informative, appealing picture books that inspire readers to become thoughtful observers of wildlife. He adopts an informal, anecdotal approach in his lyrical texts, which clearly present facts about such topics as fishing and the lifestyles of various animals. An autobiographical writer, Arnosky speaks from his own experience, sometimes using as his vehicle the characters of Crinkleroot, a grandfatherly woodsman, or Nathaniel, an everyday outdoorsman. The author of two wordless concept books featuring playful mice who teach youngsters how to make numbers and letters and do cursive writing, Arnosky is acclaimed for his more sophisticated how-to-draw books, *Drawing from Nature* (1982) and *Drawing Life in Motion* (1984). These works, which were the basis for a series of public television programs, contain attractive pencil sketches showing readers how to observe and draw various natural subjects. Employing such techniques as black-and-white line drawings, pencil, and watercolors, Arnosky utilizes whimsy and humor in his illustrations while consistently portraying the details gained from his hours of watchful study.

Critics praise Arnosky for his factual accuracy, lucid explanations, attractive drawings, and careful integration of text and pictures. While noting that some of his early works lack organization, reviewers are impressed with Arnosky's continuing ability to spark his readers' curiosity about wildlife and convey his deep appreciation for the natural world.

In addition to receiving several adult-selected awards, Arnosky won the Christopher Award in 1983 for *Drawing from Nature*.

(See also *Something about the Author*, Vol. 22; *Contemporary Authors New Revision Series*, Vol. 12; and *Contemporary Authors*, Vols. 69-72.)

Courtesy of Lothrop, Lee & Shepard Books

AUTHOR'S COMMENTARY

[*The following excerpt is from an interview by Kimberly Olson Fakih.*]

[Jim Arnosky] wants viewers to observe everywhere and anytime, without constraints or self-consciousness. . . .

[Of his books he says]: "The best nonfiction lets the reader knock on the door, and you let them in. Then you go away."

He might not be the best of technicians as an artist, he asserts, but he still can tell others "how to look at a tree," not as a biologist or a natural historian, but "just looking at this green stuff and enjoying things just by shape." And, in the spirit of a natural scientist, Arnosky asks, "How do you help others draw from nature without making 'stalkers' out of them?" He talks of accepting nature exactly as *he* sees it. He doesn't see animal stories as his vehicle ("I didn't care if the fox got the rabbit,") but sees himself reflected in nature. "I learn about water from the viewpoint of fishing and canoeing, and about a deer from looking at its tracks, to see where it's been." . . .

"When I'm fishing I'm totally a fisherman, and when I'm drawing I'm concentrating on my art. I fill myself on the world around me." . . . (p. 44)

Kimberly Olson Fakih, "Watching the Artist Watch Nature," in Publishers Weekly, *Vol. 231, No. 21, May 29, 1987, pp. 43-4.*

GENERAL COMMENTARY

KENNETH MARANTZ

Watching Foxes has large, full-colored pages on which four frisky pups are illustrated with precise attention to anatomy. [***Secrets of a Wildlife Watcher*** and ***Drawing Life in Motion***] guide our hands and eyes and educate our minds to the problems involved with drawing from nature. The author knows his animal subjects well and designs artistically conceived pages that pull the reader in. (p. 54)

Kenneth Marantz, in a review of "Watching Foxes," "Secrets of a Wildlife Watcher" and "Drawing Life in Motion," in School Arts, *Vol. 85, No. 6, February, 1986, pp. 53-4.*

C. C. GRAHAM

For those who love to draw or would like to learn, Jim Arnosky's ***Drawing from Nature*** and ***Drawing Life in Motion*** are superb. The sketching is simple and creative; the instruction is clear, forthright, and thought-provoking. Arnosky speaks to children with a great deal of dignity and caring.

C. C. Graham, "Activity Book Bag," in The Five Owls, *Vol. 1, No. 6, July-August, 1987, p. 92.*

I WAS BORN IN A TREE AND RAISED BY BEES **(1977)**

Like Crinkleroot, the Santa-like backwoodsman who guides kids through the seasons, Arnosky lives in the bush and wishes to share with children his delight in observing nature. But asking questions like "how many drones and worker bees can you count" (on a pictured honeycomb) is an uninspiring way to do it. Crinkleroot's tour mixes other hidden pictures with project suggestions (growing popcorn, tracing leaves), a mini-lecture on interdependence ("Try to figure out what food chain *you* belong to"), and random notes on everything from where different wild flowers grow to why owls keep turning their heads. The welcoming informality of the sketches suggest that Arnosky would make an agreeable trail companion, but children should expect something more than a cutesy rehash of other nature books from a canny old woodsman who claims to "speak caterpillar, turtle, and salamander too."

A review of "I Was Born in a Tree and Raised By Bees," in Kirkus Reviews, *Vol. XLIV, No. 23, December 1, 1976, p. 1261.*

The author's black-and-white drawings, occasionally washed in brown, are filled with details that often have to be searched for amid the woodland scenes. This is a good introduction for an aspiring naturalist that can lead to various nature study activities. However, city-dwellers, even those with a park close by, might have difficulty identifying with some of the material, which is found only in the country.

Barbara Dill, "Picturely Books for Children," in Wilson Library Bulletin, *Vol. 51, No. 6, February, 1977, p. 488.*

Crinkleroot is a backwoods gnome who introduces readers to simple nature information and experiences ("listen to the sounds"; "follow these tracks"; etc.). Unfortunately, his advice is misleading and full of non sequiturs. For example, directions for sprouting a corn kernel don't give any indications of how long it would take for popcorn to grow. Crinkleroot is a whimsical old geezer and Arnosky's puzzle-filled illustrations will intrigue readers, but this nature appreciation booster is without any real substance.

Susan Sprague, in a review of "I Was Born in a Tree and Raised By Bees," in School Library Journal, *Vol. 23, No. 7, March, 1977, p. 128.*

This delightful book combines solid factual information, whimsical drawings, sensitivity toward the outdoors and a chance for even the youngest readers to enter into a search for hidden animals. . . . The reader is drawn into an active part of the story as he or she is asked to find hidden animals, to tell what story has taken place by reading tracks in the snow and to be more aware of the natural environment. This book would be a valuable addition to school and classroom libraries.

Martha L. Sanders, in a review of "I Was Born in a Tree and Raised By Bees," in Science Books & Films, *Vol. XIII, No. 3, December, 1977, p. 164.*

OUTDOORS ON FOOT **(1978)**

Beginning with a look at different animals' feet, Arnosky then attempts to wander off in two directions at once, observing the world and its creatures on the one hand and "your" feet and footgear on the other—without much sense of purpose anywhere. First, "barefoot walking is a way to really feel the world" (gooey mud, still water, firm sand). So far so good, but autumn has you *sitting* on a rock and observing wildlife in your playshoes; in winter you make tracks and snowballs, pick up snow, and follow your footprints home; and in spring (wearing boots) you look for earthworms after a rain, or (clad perhaps in rubber waders) for frogs in the swamp. (Presumably, all of you live near beaches, woods, and swamps.) Arnosky's initial idea has possibilities but instead of shaping it up he barges off—on a trail that ends up nowhere.

A review of "Outdoors on Foot," in Kirkus Reviews, *Vol. XLVI, No. 3, February 1, 1978, p. 101.*

This isn't really about feet or about the outdoors. It's a hodgepodge (albeit a cheerful and nicely illustrated one) of things to do and look for in each season. From the beginning ("Could you grow webbed feet?") to the very end, the text falters for lack of organization. Arnosky's clever, sketchy, ink-and-wash drawings give a humorous and inviting appearance to the book and convey his appreciation of nature much better than his words.

Susan Sprague, in a review of "Outdoors on Foot," in School Library Journal, *Vol. 25, No. 1, September, 1978, p. 102.*

[There] is an interesting explanation of how the different parts of the foot work in walking. A brief review of the feet of ducks, beavers, raccoons, hares, sheep and goats is included, showing how each animal's feet are adapted for a specific purpose. All of this is illustrated by delightful drawings featuring a small girl and boy walking and exploring. This is a good book for reading aloud to a young child or for early readers to read to themselves.

Donald F. Logsdon, Jr., in a review of "Outdoors on Foot," in Science Books & Films, *Vol. XIV, No. 4, March, 1979, p. 233.*

NATHANIEL **(1978)**

While the Vermont woodsman, Nathaniel, is adventuring in the wordless stories here, he's entertaining. **"Gathering Wood"** is a series of handsome black-and-white drawings of a winter landscape, and of Nathaniel. Resting on a bearskin rug in his cabin, he notices his depleted woodpile and goes out to forage for kindling and logs. On his errand, Nathaniel is watched by wild creatures, all very appealing, and finally meets a huge black bear. The bear picks up the man and his load of wood and carries them to his cave where the hibernator lies down on them—poetic justice. The other entries are rather a mishmash, a letter and an excerpt from Nathaniel's diary, not particularly rewarding. Either he or his creator, Arnosky, could spell better.

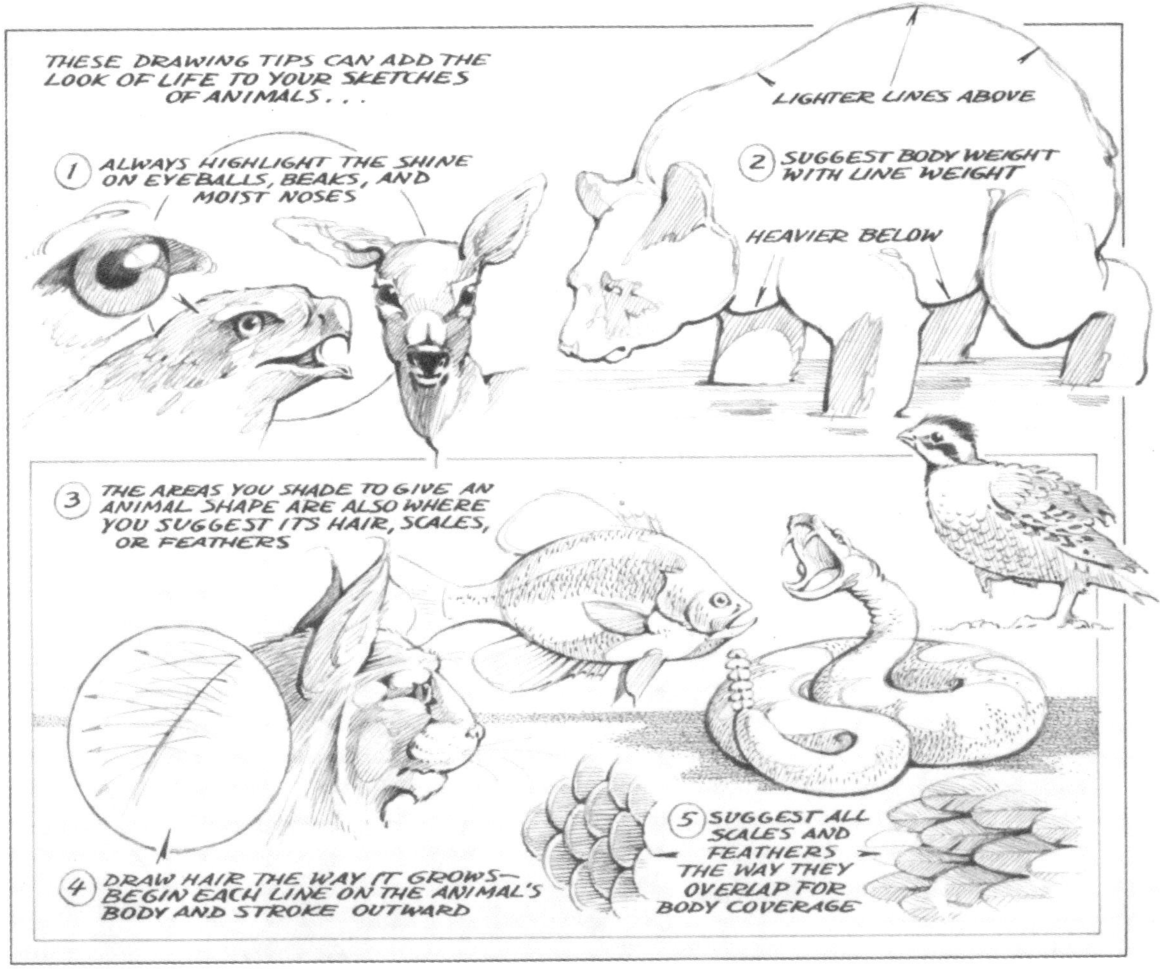

From Drawing from Nature, *written and illustrated by Jim Arnosky. Lothrop, Lee & Shepard Books, 1982. Copyright © 1982 by Jim Arnosky. All rights reserved. By permission of Lothrop, Lee & Shepard Books (A Division of William Morrow & Company, Inc.).*

A review of "Nathaniel," in Publishers Weekly, *Vol. 213, No. 13, March 27, 1978, p. 72.*

[Nathaniel] is the only element that is common to these five little numbers. In an unusual but awkward arrangement, two hand-lettered anecdotes—about chasing a bat and looking for a "lucky pipe," respectively—fill the spaces between three wordless picture stories. In **"Gathering Wood,"** Nathaniel *and* his armful of wood gets gathered up by a bear; in **"The Diary"** he tries slamming, nailing, and gluing closed the volume whose printed contents escape letter by letter whenever it's shut; and in the weakest, **"The Orphan,"** he adopts a young nestling who grows too big to keep. Both the bear bit and the diary conceit are mildly clever (though the latter seems out of place in the woodsy setting), but if they are too slight to stand alone, the rest is nothing but stretcher.

A review of "Nathaniel," in Kirkus Reviews, *Vol. XLVI, No. 7, April 1, 1978, p. 365.*

Line drawings that have a tinge of comic strip humor tell three wordless stories. . . . In addition, there are two hand-printed diary entries recounting some not very funny mishaps. There's little humor in the book, which has an air of cut-and-paste contrivance.

Zena Sutherland, in a review of "Nathaniel," in Bulletin of the Center for Children's Books, *Vol. 31, No. 11, July-August, 1978, p. 169.*

A gentle but silly wilderness resident is featured in three short, wordless stories which are oddly juxtaposed with two unrelated entries from his diary. . . . Arnosky's black-and-white illustrations do not tell the stories with ease, and Nathaniel in each of these situations does not come through as a strong enough character to unify the whole.

Michele Woggon, in a review of "Nathaniel," in School Library Journal, *Vol. 25, No. 1, September, 1978, p. 129.*

MUD TIME AND MORE: NATHANIEL STORIES (1979)

Four wordless episodes which find farmer *Nathaniel* more or less coping with the rigors of rural life. In the first, **"Mud Time,"** he turns to a cow for transport after his car sinks to the roof; in the second, he solves the problem of weather-vane birds that fly away, a weather-vane fish that leaps into a pond, by substituting an immobile weather-vane house. Numbers three and four involve him, less imaginatively, in picking apples and gathering eggs—in the latter instance, he's simply butted by an ornery ram. The drawings have a scraggly humor but that's about it.

A review of "Mud Time and More: Nathaniel Stories," in Kirkus Reviews, *Vol. XLVII, No. 7, April 1, 1979, p. 383.*

The overall effect is very low-key even when the subject matter isn't, due to the small format and the author's appealing but subdued black line drawings. An intended audience is hard to pinpoint, but this seems more an entertainment for adults than for children.

Corinne Camarata, in a review of "Mud Time and More: Nathaniel Stories," in School Library Journal, *Vol. 26, No. 1, September, 1979, p. 101.*

CRINKLEROOT'S BOOK OF ANIMAL TRACKS AND WILDLIFE SIGNS **(1979)**

Simpler by far than Mason's *Animal Tracks* or Webster's *Track Watching,* Arnosky's Crinkleroot, a sort of Grizzly Adams sans grizzly, gives a folksy introduction to the habits, habitats, and hoof-paw-claw prints of a variety of relatively common wild "critters"—beaver, otter, raccoon, bobcat, red fox et al.—plus a bird or two in illustrated mini-mysteries. There are lots of clear illustrations by the author washed in woodsy browns and greys. Sure to be useful to Den Mothers, and a pleasantly informative book for young readers.

Patricia Manning, in a review of "Crinkleroot's Book of Animal Tracks and Wildlife Signs," in School Library Journal, *Vol. 25, No. 9, May, 1979, p. 57.*

The chatty, wise fellow last seen in ***I Was Born in a Tree and Raised by Bees*** takes readers to the woods to discover the meaning behind wildlife signs. Crinkleroot covers a variety of animals from the beaver and otter to the owl and whitetail deer. Canny readers will find not only the tracks to be good identifying signs, but also other things animals leave behind, such as antlers, owl pellets, and even homes. There is just enough detail for an inexperienced nature tracker to get inspired. The diagrams and illustrations are clear, helpful, and pleasant to look at, too.

Judith Goldberger, in a review of "Crinkleroot's Book of Animal Tracks and Wildlife Signs," in Booklist, *Vol. 75, No. 17, May 1, 1979, p. 1359.*

This charming, beautifully designed book will appeal to any child interested in wildlife and the outdoors. Exceptional and profuse illustrations by the author are informative as well as appealing to the eye. The subject matter is clearly presented and is sufficiently detailed for young readers. . . . The author has provided a picture puzzle on each of the eight animals treated in depth. In order to solve these puzzles, readers must apply something they have learned. Illustrations of the footprints of 21 other mammals and birds also are included; nine of these animals are commonly found in urban environments. Highly recommended.

Fred Rasmussen, in a review of "Crinkleroot's Book of Animal Tracks and Wildlife Signs," in Science Books & Films, *Vol. XV, No. 3, December, 1979, p. 166.*

This book will be excellent at generating armchair enthusiasm and field frustration. The illustrations are delightful and usually accurate enough for the purpose. The author gives the reader a good handle on track sizes by comparing them to parts of his own body, or showing them full-sized in the rear two-page spread. He also does an excellent job of clarifying the difference between cat and dog tracks, dog and fox track patterns, and the track patterns of hopping and walking birds. Unfortunately, the author does not focus the novice on other basic diagnostic features in track and sign identification such as the numbers of toes, the differences between front and hind feet and the size, spacing and pattern of tracks. So after initial success with the dog and cat, the reader will be most likely to tackle squirrel and rabbit, only to find that although the otter gets a four-page treatment, the squirrel is represented by one lone print. And the novice will not recognize it as a left front which can not possibly be compared to the right rear shown for the cottontail. And his confidence, in self or the author, will be further shaken when he finds chewed twigs, which the book leads him to think are diagnostic of beaver, associated with his rabbit/squirrel tracks. The illustrations supply sufficient basis to make most of the points needed. It is too bad that the author did not follow them up to the text. (pp. 10-11)

Marion P. Harris, in a review of "Crinkleroot's Book of Animal Tracks and Wildlife Signs," in Appraisal: Children's Science Books, *Vol. 13, No. 3, Fall, 1980, pp. 10-11.*

A KETTLE OF HAWKS AND OTHER WILDLIFE GROUPS **(1979)**

As this is a direct descendant of Eve Merriam's *Gaggle of Geese,* and of all the word games about what groups of animals are called, there may be little need for yet another treatment of the subject. However, the combination of prose, brief poems, and handsome illustrations is a pleasure to leaf through, to pore over, and to read more than once. In concept and vocabulary the book may be beyond some readers—certainly the very young, but older ones (including adults) will enjoy it.

George Gleason, in a review of "A Kettle of Hawks and Other Wildlife Groups," in School Library Journal, *Vol. 26, No. 1, September, 1979, p. 126.*

In its own way, this is an inspirational work, one that should awaken or jog readers' curiosity about nature while goading them to seek further. The form is one repeated for each of six animals: a page of short, illustrated free verse followed by a few paragraphs of informational matter accompanied by one or two more pictures. Within his subject, Arnosky meanders from hawks to bees to fish and digresses from his explanations of how and why they group themselves to other aspects such as eating and migrating habits. In all, it's a quiet, watchful book with smooth text and well-executed etching-like pictures. There's not a lot of meat here, but it's well seasoned and arranged thoughtfully. Best for browsing or as a discussion sparker.

Judith Goldberger, in a review of "A Kettle of Hawks and Other Wildlife Groups," in Booklist, *Vol. 76, No. 1, September 1, 1979, p. 38.*

This is a handsome and fascinating book, simple enough for the young, yet rich in detail. . . . The text and illustrations are well integrated and beautifully designed, with a large yet elegant typeface and spacious layout. It's a pleasure to read a book such as this—a book conceived as a whole with text and pictures working magnificently in concert.

Carole Cochran, in a review of "A Kettle of Hawks and Other Wildlife Groups," in Appraisal: Children's Science Books, *Vol. 13, No. 1, Winter, 1980, p. 9.*

FRESHWATER FISH AND FISHING **(1982)**

Arnosky has gained a wide following among young nature lovers. Readers who learn from and enjoy his ***Outdoors on Foot, A Kettle of Hawks*** and other books will find the author-illustrator's latest exceptionally helpful as well as imaginatively written. The handsome drawings show in detail what's explained in the text: how to make a spoon lure, how to make knots for attaching a line to a hook or lure, how to catch and clean a fish, how to make fish prints. In addition there are color paintings of a variety of freshwater fish with information on where they're found, in all seasons. Arnosky doesn't stint a bit on any aspect of instructions necessary for the aspiring fisherman. He has even included alluring scenes of ponds, lakes and creeks along with advice on how to "reel in more nature than fish," making the adventure complete.

From Freshwater Fish and Fishing, *written and illustrated by Jim Arnosky. Four Winds Press, 1982. Copyright © 1982 by James Arnosky. All rights reserved. Reprinted with permission of Four Winds Press, an imprint of Macmillan Publishing Company.*

A review of "Freshwater Fish & Fishing," in Publishers Weekly, *Vol. 221, No. 12, March 19, 1982, p. 70.*

The illustrator of articles for *Fly Fisherman* and *Rod & Reel* has put together an attractive, informative book. With obvious respect for the natural surroundings, the author-artist shares his knowledge of "the fish, the fishing, and the wonders of the freshwater world." Opening with a double-page diagram of the parts of a typical fish, the book is divided into sections, such as "Trout" and "Perch & Pike"; information is given about each type of fish—including, of course, the best way to catch them. The author intersperses important advice throughout and stresses the necessity of learning the laws—the legal number and size of fish that may be taken—and of retrieving tangled line so wild creatures do not get snared. An abundance of attractive, detailed black-and-white illustrations of insects, waterfowl, and other wildlife that coexist with fish are carefully placed, and there are four full-color double-page spreads notable for both an underwater and above-water view of the habitat of each family of fish. Clear directions on tying a fly, making several kinds of lures, tying fishing knots, and cleaning the catch are enhanced by the drawings. Also included are instructions for making a print of that "special fish" before it goes into the frying pan.

Nancy Sheridan, in a review of "Freshwater Fish & Fishing," in The Horn Book Magazine, *Vol. LVIII, No. 3, June, 1982, p. 304.*

Detailed watercolors blend with lyrical text to impart solid information while evoking an appreciation for the serenity and beauty of nature that is the fisher's milieu. . . . By stressing observation of feeding and living habits, Arnosky makes fishing strategy logical. Casting techniques, equipment, and instructions on how to make simple ties and lures are reinforced by delicate black line drawings. . . . Though limited to freshwater fish, the text and careful illustrations go beyond the average how-to book to capture the mood of a nature retreat. A personal invitation, executed with care, that will interest both the fisher and the worm-wary.

Linda W. Callaghan, in a review of "Freshwater Fish & Fishing," in Booklist, *Vol. 78, No. 21, July, 1982, p. 1450.*

It is always a joy to read an information book for young children that not only presents facts accurately but also uses our language with skill and appreciation. Arnosky writes such books, and this one about freshwater fishing shows his appreciation for fishing and for the charm of the countryside as well as his skill with the intricacies of tying a fly and of attaching a fly line to a leader. He knows what kinds of bait work best for different fish, and he knows where those fish are. He includes information for making several flies out of rather ordinary materials: a cork, part of a balloon; he also includes easy-to-follow instructions for making a fish print at the site of your catch. . . . His black and white illustrations are integrated skillfully into the text so that instructions are easy to follow and techniques are made clear. (p. 11)

Information is so elementary and carefully presented that I think this book will appeal to a younger audience than suggested by the publisher. A table of contents, complete and easily readable, takes the place of an index. (p. 12)

Norma Bagnall, in a review of "Freshwater Fish and Fishing," in Appraisal: Children's Science Books, *Vol. 15, No. 3, Fall, 1982, pp. 11-12.*

***MOUSE NUMBERS AND LETTERS* (1982)**

In this wordless picture book/concept book, a masterful mouse first discovers the numbers 1-10 while on a cross-country excursion one afternoon—climbing "2" hills, flinging a stone "7" skips across the river, nearly being drowned under "8" enormous waves. He then proceeds to bend twigs, found on his journey, into the letters of the alphabet. The humorous cartoon illustrations are done in sparse line drawings, highlighted by a rust-red border and colored letters, numbers and objects representing each number. Because there are three or four cartoons on a page, sometimes more, the use of red accents the main objects immediately, and helps maintain an overall uncluttered, appealing effect. This is not a book for toddlers unfamiliar with numbers and letters, but rather a welcome new addition for the older preschool set, to be "read" independently.

Janice Springborn, in a review of "Mouse Numbers & Letters," in School Library Journal, *Vol. 28, No. 8, April, 1982, p. 55.*

The idea is clever, and the two-color illustrations are appealing. Two-, three-, and four-year-olds who previewed the book were enthusiastic, poring over details and requesting repeated readings.

Margo Showstack, in a review of "Mouse Numbers and Letters," in Children's Book Review Service, *Vol. 10, No. 14, August, 1982, p. 131.*

***DRAWING FROM NATURE* (1982)**

The well-known illustrator presents an excellent how-to book. In addition to his obvious artistic ability, Arnosky is skillful in explaining why and how to look at things and the reasons why an artist does what he does. In detailed, clearly labeled black-and-white drawings he shows the shapes of things we rarely think of noticing: drops of water, the banks of streams, the feathers of birds. The book is divided into four sections—water, land, plants, and animals—of which the first two are superior because there is so much more to be said about drawing plants and animals than can be included in a small book. A fine starting point for the young artist-naturalist—sensible, thoughtful, and inspiring.

Ann A. Flowers, in a review of "Drawing from Nature," in The Horn Book Magazine, *Vol. LVIII, No. 5, October, 1982, p. 527.*

At first glance this appears to be a "how-to" book, but in fact it is a great deal more—and a little less. Arnosky provides excellent pencil sketches from nature. . . . But there are very few of the block and round shapes that start the novice artist on his way. The author's pictures are full-blown, and what they teach is how to be observant rather than how to draw, per se. For instance, drops of water are shown coming out of a faucet. The first drop clings to the rim, the next has a teardrop shape, an egg shape on its way down, until it flattens into a splash. The text is as graceful as the art, and it is full of advice on sharpening awareness. The casual artist will be inspired by this book, but it will be of most use to those, young and old alike, who have already exhibited an inclination or definite talent for drawing. (pp. 364-65)

Ilene Cooper, in a review of "Drawing from Nature," in Booklist, *Vol. 79, No. 5, November 1, 1982, pp. 364-65.*

This is not a manual on how to draw step-by-step from nature, but a spiritual sharing of ideas and techniques by a gifted wildlife artist. Jim Arnosky takes his absolute love of nature and skill in putting it on paper that was earlier displayed in his book, ***Crinkleroot's Book of Animal Tracks and Wildlife Signs*** to a higher, more technical level. In this book, he shows how to draw land and water—both above and below the surface—how to draw snow, animal tracks in it and in mud, how to draw animals still and in motion, birds in flight and landing. He knows his subject inside out and his pointers reveal hours of careful study and observation. The novice wildlife artist will learn about drawing birds' beaks, feathers and feet, animals' coats wet, dry, long and short—to emphasize musculature. The key words here are "learn about" because Arnosky's aim is to show how to observe rather than teach step-by-step, line-by-line drawing. His technique still emphasizes all the best rules of drawing, including perspective, positive and negative space, mass with shadow and the changing role of light. Arnosky's goal seems to be to teach young readers how to see as an artist would, and observe as a naturalist would. He succeeds beautifully.

Patricia Homer, in a review of "Drawing from Nature," in School Library Journal, *Vol. 29, No. 5, January, 1983, p. 70.*

This is a delightful little book! Arnosky succeeds brilliantly on two levels. First, his notes on "Drawing from Nature" provide clear, concise instructions for the budding artist. I suppose that is the primary and most obvious function of the book.

But ***Drawing from Nature*** is also a masterful science text. In talking about art, Arnosky introduces dozens of bits of factual information about the natural world. The reader learns a good deal of natural history science background in a subtle, painless, indeed, intriguing way.

I'm charmed, pleased and impressed by this book, and I think your kids will be too.

David E. Newton, in a review of "Drawing from Nature," in Appraisal: Children's Science Books, *Vol. 16, No. 2, Spring-Summer, 1983, p. 13.*

***MOUSE WRITING* (1983)**

Engaging and eminently useful is Jim Arnosky's ***Mouse Writing.*** With its ice-blue cursive letters (capital and small) and matching page borders, it provides an ingenious introduction to penmanship. While mesmerized by the fancy figure-skating (really letter-skating) of two agile and extroverted mice, the young viewer can painlessly learn where first to put pen to paper, and what direction to follow in forming each letter of the alphabet. (pp. 38-9)

Selma G. Lanes, in a review of "Mouse Writing," in The New York Times Book Review, *October 9, 1983, pp. 38-9.*

What makes this different from other alphabet books is that the letters are in cursive. The pictures are simply drawn with black ink on white pages; blue provides emphasis, used only for finished letters and borders. The background details (the stones, fallen logs, mounds of snow and trees found at a skating pond in the woods) are interesting without being distracting. But the best part of the pictures are the three animals: Arnosky creates much expression (determination, humor, pride, joy, playfulness) as the mice go through the motions used to make letters. The pleasure of accomplishment will be transmitted to children who use this most effective book. (p. 52)

Lauralyn Levesque, in a review of "Mouse Writing," in School Library Journal, *Vol. 30, No. 4, December, 1983, pp. 51-2.*

The skaters' waltz of handwriting! . . .

The humorous ink sketches capture the impish spirit of the mice as they play tricks on each other. Bold blue borders frame each incident and heighten the frenzied action by placing a greater focus on the ice-etched script. The skill, determination, and overconfidence of the mouse duo endear them to the reader.

Although cursive warm-ups may not be necessary for children, they can relate to the full effort and concentration displayed by these alphabet-loving comrades. They too could become carefree calligraphers!

Ronald A. Jobe, in a review of "Mouse Writing," in Language Arts, *Vol. 61, No. 3, March, 1984, p. 291.*

***SECRETS OF A WILDLIFE WATCHER* (1983)**

"Joy in looking and comprehending is nature's most beautiful gift." This quotation from Albert Einstein is the philosophical foundation for this unique book. The author's enthusiasm sparks the text as he encourages readers to actively observe nature, to question and sharpen their skills of observation while experiencing the delight of watching animals in their natural unguarded moments. The text is divided into three major sections: "Finding," "Stalking" and "Watching," covering topics such as home ranges, night calls, camouflage, animal senses, blinds, grooming, warning signals, posturing and more. Two pages are devoted to drawings of animal tracks with measurements on the pages' edges to adjust for scale. The illustrations are outstanding; soft pencil drawings on cream-colored paper that encircle the text in a lovely dance of grace, energy and clarity. The different spirits and moods of the animals are captured and portrayed from fresh and sometimes humorous perspectives. Throughout the author has drawn himself (in pith helmet and moustache) when he requires a human figure to demonstrate a "watching" technique which adds to the intimacy of the animal secrets he has gleaned firsthand and now shares. This is a first choice selection; a rare combination: handsome in form, intriguing in fact and imbued with caring. (pp. 62-3)

Barbara Peklo Serling, in a review of "Secrets of a Wildlife Watcher," in School Library Journal, *Vol. 30, No. 4, December, 1983, pp. 62-3.*

With compelling intimacy, Arnosky draws the reader into his own fascination with wildlife and dares her to come along. Visually, the book is a joy, bordered with black and white illustrations carefully related to the text. . . . Loaded with practical advice on finding owls, turtles, deer, and other wild animals, the handbook also shares stalking and observation techniques. Arnosky's delight in wildlife, and the effectiveness with which he conveys it, conspire to lure the young naturalist, book in hand, out into the wild. The book's attention to detail and straightforward manner make it a fine choice for a beginner watcher of any age. (Its brevity prevents the lack of an index from being a major drawback.)

Carolyn Noah, in a review of "Secrets of a Wildlife Watcher," in Appraisal: Children's Science Books, *Vol. 17, No. 1, Winter, 1984, p. 7.*

When we have a skilled artist imbued with a naturalist's discerning eye, the result is a rare book—enjoyable from cover

From Mouse Writing, *written and illustrated by Jim Arnosky. Harcourt Brace Jovanovich, 1983.*

to cover by any lover of the out-of-doors. Jim Arnosky's notes on nature are accurate, lacking the flaws so common in many so-called nature books. Here is a writer who obviously knows and understands his natural surroundings.

Books of this nature are hard to come by these days; my advice is to read it, cherish it, and make it a part of your nature library for future reference. It is timeless.

Douglas B. Sands, in a review of "Secrets of a Wildlife Watcher," in Appraisal: Children's Science Books, *Vol. 17, No. 1, Winter, 1984, p. 7.*

[***Secrets of a Wildlife Watcher***] is a sheer delight! From the beauty of its binding to the freshness of its format, this is a book any budding naturalist would love to own. . . .

Just as important as the text . . . are the author's clear, skillful pencil sketches which form a frame around the outer edge of every page. This naturalist's-notebook style lends an informal, inviting feel to the book.

Secrets of a Wildlife Watcher, however, is more than just a collection of useful hints and attractive illustrations. It is an ardent attempt to nourish a child's interest in the world around him and is a fitting tribute to Einstein's words quoted in the epigraph: "Joy in looking and comprehending is nature's most beautiful gift."

Franja C. Bryant, "Animal Books for Information and Pleasure," in The Christian Science Monitor, *April 6, 1984, p. B6.*

DRAWING LIFE IN MOTION **(1984)**

By combining practical tips for making effective drawings from nature with observations of natural processes, the author-artist has produced a book which should be useful to aspiring young artists. Dealing with motion in both plants and animals, the author clearly demonstrates how a bold stroke can lend weight or thrust to an animal's movement or how the clinging tendrils of a vine contribute to its sense of surging growth. He explains how plants react to gravity and light and how their movements may be observed; and he emphasizes the care needed in choosing the exact pose which captures the fluid movement of a swimming otter and the pleasure to be found in watching the pattern of a falling leaf. Intended for artists with some experience, the book is not a step-by-step manual for beginners but, at all times, encourages young people to rely on their own observations. The fine black-and-white drawings greatly enhance a book that is both informative and attractive.

Ethel R. Twichell, in a review of "Drawing Life in Motion," in The Horn Book Magazine, *Vol. LX, No. 5, September-October, 1984, p. 604.*

Arnosky writes with the voice of the poet and observes life with the eyes of a naturalist who is also an artist. Do plants dance? If you doubt it, notice the curling, grasping movements of vine tendrils. . . . Curved lines and directional arrows show you the path of motion in the sketches. To view the world through Arnosky's eyes is to see a world dancing to its inner beat. Never again will you settle for a static drawing. Although this book is in picture book format, don't be misled into thinking it does not belong in a high school library. It is a book for all ages.

"See a World in a Grain of Sand," in Journal of Reading, *Vol. 28, No. 4, January, 1985, p. 373.*

Occasionally this artist's work had a slightly saccharine or Disneyesque quality that separates it from true scientific illustration. . . . Not so for this book! The line is fluid but sure. The interpretation from life is imaginative and interesting, but not overly fanciful or sentimental. . . .

This is definitely not a step-by-step instruction book. Instead, it offers an examination of nature close up, which both instructs the student and delights the browser.

Lavinia C. Demos, in a review of "Drawing Life in Motion," in Appraisal: Children's Science Books, *Vol. 18, No. 3, Summer, 1985, p. 12.*

This book is of much broader scope than the title implies, since it is about *seeing* and *movement* as well as about drawing.

Generally, we do not think of plants as moving. Yet they do, as a result of tropism—or involuntary orientation—to light, gravity, etc. We learn here why leaves and vine tendrils face or twine in certain directions; how tendrils "feel about" for something to grasp, and how by sketching different plants once each hour during an entire afternoon you will see how some plants move a great deal; while others move very little.

The book analyzes the way in which different animals perform numerous different push and pull movements in their locomotion, illustrating this with a raccoon, an inchworm, a toad, a lizard. The point is to show how an artist can best indicate this push and pull in a drawing (by drawing in the direction of the action).

Discussed also are such things as how to place shadow in your drawings, how a lighter line will suggest buoyancy while a heavier line will suggest the pull of gravity as well as the line of motion, and how even the movements of falling leaves are remarkably lively and varied.

There is in the book much of the richness and immediacy found in Mr. Arnosky's ***Secrets of a Wildlife Watcher.*** It is to be hoped that some general readers are not put off by the title, thinking it is a book solely for aspiring artists. For there is much of interest here even for those not in the least interested in drawing. (pp. 12-13)

Miriam Schlein, in a review of "Drawing Life in Motion," in Appraisal: Children's Science Books, *Vol. 18, No. 3, Summer, 1985, pp. 12-13.*

WATCHING FOXES **(1985)**

In a brief, full-color picture book based on his observations of a den of foxes, Arnosky makes us privy to the young foxes' morning of play. Mother Fox leaves. Her pups awake, watch a bee, scratch a flea, and find a twig and fight over it. Mother returns and nurses her babies in the sun. The story is slight, but engages our interest without humanizing the foxes at all. The illustrations—pencil sketches with watercolor washes—are attractive and appealing, their spacious, action-packed compositions an attention-grabber for youngest story sessions.

Carolyn Phelan, in a review of "Watching Foxes," in Booklist, *Vol. 81, No. 16, April 15, 1985, p. 1188.*

One or two brief sentences in large type accompany each pair of pages, but they offer little information that cannot be gleaned from the pictures themselves ("One pup pounces on the other three"). Apparently to maintain the rhythm of his text, the author has cropped one sentence unceremoniously short: "A tail gets bit'' weighs harshly on the readers' sensibilities. The illustrations, in color pencil and watercolor wash, are clear and attractive; they will be readily interpreted by the very young audience for whom they are intended. Despite the dust jacket hype, however, there is nothing presented here that warrants the adjective ''remarkable.''

Janet French, in a review of ''Watching Foxes,'' in School Library Journal, *Vol. 31, No. 10, August, 1985, p. 52.*

Both a lively and comforting book for young children, Jim Arnosky's colored pencil illustrations look as though they too have been warmed by the light of the sun. This is the simplest of the texts, concepts, and illustrations, but there comes from it a feeling of great satisfaction. Children can relate to the animals' behavior and might even be spurred to do their own observations, sitting quietly outdoors, as Jim Arnosky sat in the cornfield, drawing and writing about any creatures they can see.

Sarah Lamstein, in a review of ''Watching Foxes,'' in Appraisal: Children's Science Books, *Vol. 19, No. 3, Summer, 1986, p. 14.*

DEER AT THE BROOK (1986)

Arnosky's illustrations are everything here, amplifying the sparest of texts with dramatic scenes of deer coming to a woodland brook to drink, eat, play, and nap. The full-color pictures are soft and compelling, focusing on a doe and her two fawns, which are masterfully drawn and imbued with nearly as much presence as real-life creatures would have. Other wildlife are artistically integrated into the drawings. Children for whom such sights are a rarity will find this an excellent chance to observe and absorb the magic of the moment.

Denise M. Wilms, in a review of ''Deer at the Brook,'' in Booklist, *Vol. 82, No. 15, April 1, 1986, p. 1138.*

Told very simply in a few, well-chosen, melodic words, the book is ideal for beginning readers or for bedtime comfort.

Arnosky's pastel illustrations glow with well-drawn animals and undetailed but accurate flora. He has obviously observed deer; while their large and liquid eyes resemble Bambi's, their movements are authentic. He has a delicate sense of light, so that lambent colors tint other nearby surfaces: ''. . . a sparkling place,'' indeed. End papers realistically show the fresh track of a doe and fawns in the brookside sand.

A review of ''Deer at the Brook,'' in Kirkus Reviews, *Vol. LIV, No. 8, April 15, 1986, p. 633.*

Arnosky has created a simple volume for the very youngest nature lovers. The book's real lesson comes not from the sparse, descriptive text, but from the illustrations. Hoof prints on the inside cover and title page prepare children for the deer's appearance; close-ups of the deer provide an awesome treat. A singing thrush, soaring swallows, jeweled butterfly, leaping fish, spindly damselflies, nest-building sparrow—all appear in Arnosky's very realistic two-page softly colored pencil drawings. It's a nature lesson that's likely to be treasured by tots and parents, too.

Susan Scheps, in a review of ''Deer at the Brook,'' in School Library Journal, *Vol. 32, No. 9, May, 1986, p. 67.*

Though the text is sparse, the many illustrations of gentle, soft-eyed deer should fascinate very young readers. Colorful, realistic, and uncluttered, each drawing has little surprises to delight children, such as a frog peeking out of the reeds, a bird building a nest in a tangle of branches, or a fish snapping at a mayfly. Young children can learn much about the appearance and behavior of deer and the natural environment of a stream by viewing these beautiful drawings.

Janey N. Hoff, in a review of ''Deer at the Brook,'' in Science Books & Films, *Vol. 22, No. 2, November-December, 1986, p. 114.*

FLIES IN THE WATER, FISH IN THE AIR: A PERSONAL INTRODUCTION TO FLY FISHING (1986)

Blending the beauty of nature with the joy of sport, Arnosky leaves no doubt that fishing is an art form, a reverent pilgrimage in which the respectful and observant are rewarded. Each chapter opens with a full-page drawing facing a lyrical, descriptive paean to the natural world that reflects Arnosky's acute observation, appreciation for nature, and respect for the adversarial fish. His simple, flowing style quietly evokes the joy of the sport through anecdotes that subtly inform. Since fly fishing duplicates the insects fish feed on, Arnosky discusses the life cycle and behavior of mayflies, caddis flies, and other insects. Chapters discuss reading the terrain and water for signs of feeding fish, walking and wading, and using proper equipment, tackle, and ''flies.'' Soft pencil drawings swirl around the text, flowing down the margins and across the double-page spreads. All captions are as delicately lettered as the drawings, mirroring the author's quiet tone. A pleasure to the eye, the mind, and the soul.

Linda Callaghan, in a review of ''Flies in the Water, Fish in the Air: A Personal Introduction to Fly Fishing,'' in Booklist, *Vol. 82, No. 21, July, 1986, p. 1618.*

The author-artist of ***Freshwater Fish and Fishing*** has written a somewhat longer, more detailed book specifically about fly fishing. Lacing the narrative with facts and advice and snaring the reader's attention with his anecdotal style, he shares information with clarity and with a generosity uncharacteristic of many fishermen. In fact, the opening chapter on insects goes into even more detail than is necessary for an introductory book. In his discussion of the selection of equipment Arnosky is right on target, succinctly covering rods, reels, line and leaders and devoting an entire chapter to the all-important flies. Whether he is providing tips for moving through and reading the water or describing a favorite fly rod, the author writes knowledgeably and thoughtfully, communicating his respect for nature in both his prose and his numerous attractive pencil drawings. There is something so sincere, so down-to-earth, so quietly exuberant about the book that even the most marginally interested fly fisherman will surely snap the volume shut and head for the nearest body of water.

Karen Jameyson, in a review of ''Flies in the Water, Fish in the Air: A Personal Introduction to Fly Fishing,'' in The Horn Book Magazine, *Vol. LXII, No. 4, July-August, 1986, p. 464.*

Intended to introduce novices to all aspects of fly fishing, Arnosky's book is informative and fun to read. . . . A number of features separate this book from the average writings of this nature. Arnosky's text is full of anecdotes from his fishing outings which liven up the material. His background as a naturalist emerges in a number of instances. Probably the most outstanding feature is the numerous pencil drawings laced throughout the text, adeptly illuminating the author's points. Arnosky is careful to explain the technical jargon, but the absence of a glossary limits the book's reference value, as several terms which are explained once are then used repeatedly without explanation. This minor drawback aside, ***Flies in the Water, Fish in the Air*** is a quality work surpassing Du Broff's *Still Water Fly Fishing for Young People* in depth of coverage, quality of illustrations and reading enjoyment.

Tom S. Hurlburt, in a review of "Flies in the Water, Fish in the Air: A Personal Introduction to Fly Fishing," in School Library Journal, *Vol. 32, No. 10, August, 1986, p. 98.*

After an hour with this book, I felt calmer than when I opened it. I knew the life cycles of a dozen insects, the conformation of lake shores and stream beds, and the habits of many kinds of fish. Whether or not I ever choose to go fishing, I have an anticipation of visiting streams and renewing the experience Jim Arnosky provides with his compelling black-and-white sketches and his poetic, almost whispered, narrative. And when I do get to my next stream or lake, I will be looking not only for the various insects and their water larvae, the predictable water eddies around rocks, and the elusive trout that Arnosky makes so personal, but also for the pith helmet, moustache, and waders that Arnosky shows himself wearing while stalking a fishing site.

This small book reads like a novel, a biography, a nature study, a journal, and a tour guide. It is a treat for anyone, with so much lore packed into an afternoon's reading. Take it along wherever you go. You will experience Jim Arnosky's world as he spins his poetic science of flies in the water and fish going after them. Definitely, fly fishing is a quiet, contemplative, gentle sport enjoyed in beautiful places. Thanks for sharing it with us, Jim!

Ruth E. Symonds, in a review of "Flies in the Water, Fish in the Air: A Personal Introduction to Fly Fishing," in Appraisal: Children's Science Books, *Vol. 20, No. 1, Winter, 1986, p. 14.*

SKETCHING OUTDOORS IN SPRING **(1987)**

Arnosky is known for widening young readers' perceptions of the abundance of nature. Succeeding ***Drawing from Nature*** and ***Drawing Life in Motion,*** the author's third guide gently teaches children to see and record emerging life in March and April. Quick sketches and detailed drawings show budding wild flow-

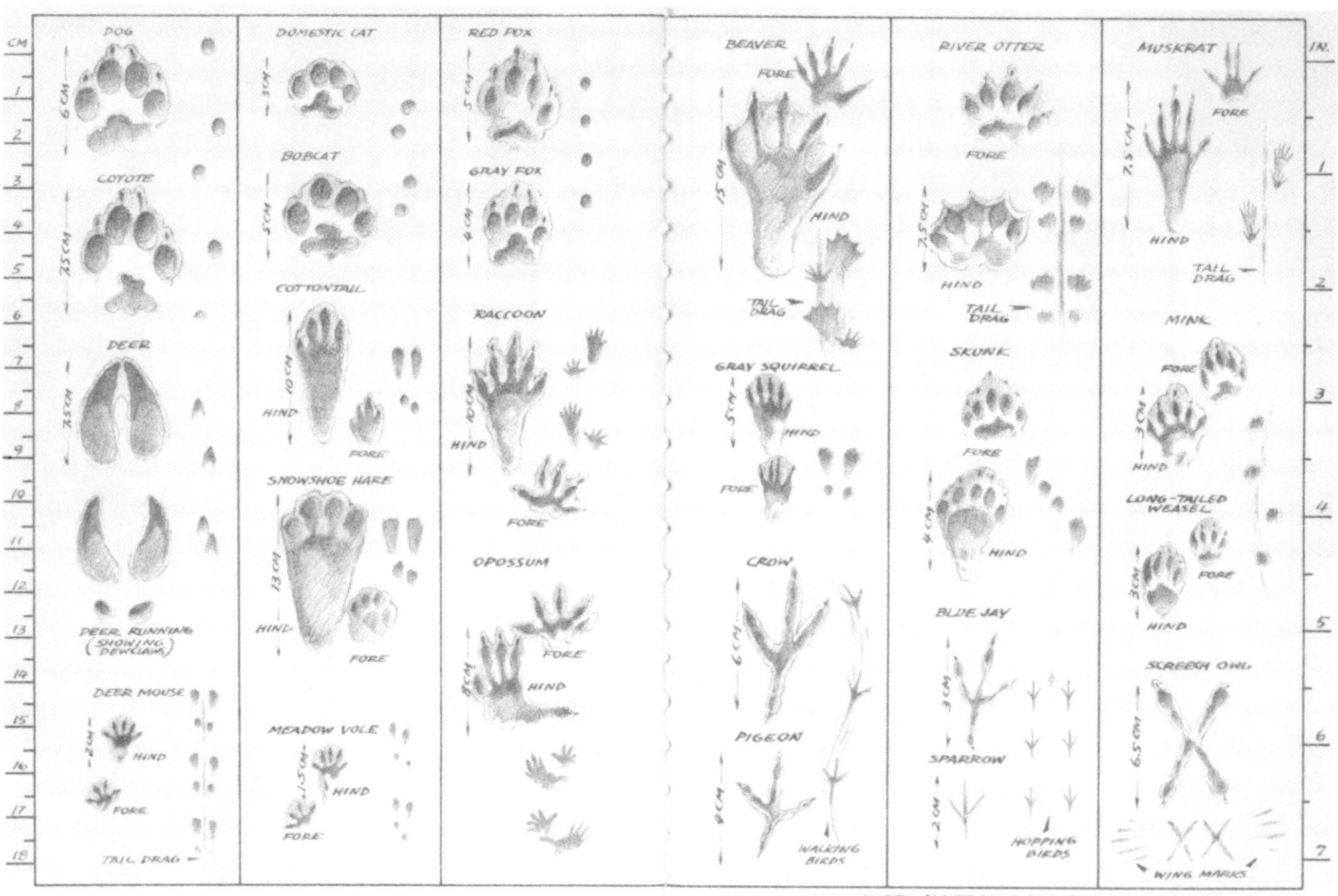

From Secrets of a Wildlife Watcher, *written and illustrated by Jim Arnosky. Lothrop, Lee & Shepard Books, 1983. Copyright © 1983 by Jim Arnosky. All rights reserved. By permission of Lothrop, Lee & Shepard Books (A Division of William Morrow & Company, Inc.).*

ers, birds, flowing streams and animals, and many other sights around Arnosky's rural home in Vermont. These vital scenes are accompanied by the artist's practical advice (take a minimum of supplies; wear gloves if it's cold), techniques and pointers that the writer's friendly, informal approach makes easy to grasp. There is further inspiration in descriptions of how and why each wonder commends itself to an artist's eye.

A review of "Sketching Outdoors in Spring," in Publishers Weekly, *Vol. 231, No. 11, March 20, 1987, p. 80.*

Another lovely book in which the artist-naturalist shares his pleasure in sketching the world around him. Two typefaces define the dual purpose of the book—large print paragraphs describe Arnosky's personal experience in sketching trees, brooks, emerging spring flowers, and woodland animals; small print notes give general suggestions on drawing technique. Like his earlier ***Drawing from Nature,*** the book successfully conveys the aesthetic pleasure of sketching and demonstrates how important a focused awareness of the observed world is to the artist. However, this book is less successful in describing the techniques which translate observation into a sketch. The drawing suggestions tend to be vague and subjective, so while this book can give readers a great deal of pleasure, it is not as successful at teaching drawing technique. Unlike other authors who teach simple tricks and patterns in drawing, Arnosky focuses on awareness and the connections that artists make to the objects they draw. He assumes a level of knowledge and experience beyond the scope of many young readers. While this limits the book's usefulness as a drawing book, the combination of text and beautifully executed drawings could inspire young readers, artists or not, to go into the spring woods and really look at the world around them. (pp. 105-06)

Eleanor K. MacDonald, in a review of "Sketching Outdoors in Spring," in School Library Journal, *Vol. 33, No. 8, May, 1987, pp. 105-06.*

Carrying a minimum of art supplies—two soft-leaded pencils, a sharpener, an eraser, and a pad of quality drawing paper—Jim Arnosky goes out to greet the spring, and in this intimate book he shares what he finds in the woods around him. The same marvel and wonder at looking at nature that characterizes ***Secrets of a Wildlife Watcher*** runs through this book. But ***Sketching Outdoors in Spring*** celebrates just as well the artist's craft and this artist's method of drawing what he sees. His notes reveal not only what has been happening in the broken maple trees but how he captures these trees, birds, flowers, ferns, and baby animals on paper. Each double-page spread is designed around a magnificent and expressive drawing or drawings. The movement and spontaneity that are such an exciting part of life drawing are evident throughout the book—like the tree roots which seem to dance and pulse with energy. Because most books for children present them with art that is much more refined and finished, the book is valuable for these sketches alone. But it is also a wonderful paean to the natural world. Short of taking a field trip in person with Roger Tory Peterson, sitting down with a book such as this one is the best way to discover the marvels of the natural world.

Anita Silvey, in a review of "Sketching Outdoors in Spring," in The Horn Book Magazine, *Vol. LXIII, No. 3, May-June, 1987, p. 355.*

RACCOONS AND RIPE CORN **(1987)**

On an autumn night, nature sends dry, yellow leaves and raccoons from a tree near the farm to the cornfield. The corn is ripe and the raccoons feast on the sweet kernels. The night passes, and the moon, an owl and the raccoons retreat before sunrise. Green husks, bare ears and half-eaten corn are left scattered among the fallen leaves. Arnosky's photograph-like depiction of nature allows the smallest of life-forms and the largest of natural phenomena to participate in one uniform process—earth and sky, autumn winds and nocturnal animals, hunger and eating are all parts of nature's weaving. Fall colors of brown and yellow take on a softened, pastel look in the realistic night setting, and accurate details (the moonlight reflected in raccoon eyes) give readers a good picture of one night's occurrence. But a question remains: Can a stalk of corn really support a small but weighty-looking owl?

A review of "Raccoons and Ripe Corn," in Publishers Weekly, *Vol. 232, No. 7, August 14, 1987, p. 101.*

It's another wonderful picture story of wildlife, carefully presented with accurate and loving detail. Perhaps the thin plot is not a source of worry for those paying $13.00, but more seems to have been going on in previous Arnosky books, such as ***Deer at the Brook*** or ***Watching Foxes.*** What sort of den did the racoons return to? Arnosky has spoiled us in the past.

A review of "Raccoons and Ripe Corn," in Kirkus Reviews, *Vol. LV, No. 16, August 15, 1987, p. 1235.*

This is definitely a mood piece whose success is dependent upon the power of the artist's pictures. . . . Arnosky's pictures have a way of making nature larger than life. His raccoons are a strong focus of attention, and the hushed nighttime mood is almost palpable. The nature lesson implicit in the depicted episode is not romantic; these raccoons are greedy and somewhat destructive. A close-up of one of them gnawing an ear of corn has an undercurrent of ferocity. The book reflects keen observation; youngsters not in a position to take in similar sights will find this slice of country life vivid and revealing.

Denise M. Wilms, in a review of "Raccoons and Ripe Corn," in Booklist, *Vol. 84, No. 1, September 1, 1987, p. 58.*

L(yman) Frank Baum

1856-1919

(Also wrote under pseudonyms of Floyd Akers, Laura Bancroft, Captain Hugh Fitzgerald, Suzanne Metcalf, and Edith Van Dyne) American author of fiction, short stories, and picture books; reteller; and poet.

From Dictionary of American Portraits. *Dover Publications, Inc., 1967. Courtesy of Fred Meyer.*

Baum is often considered the greatest and most controversial American writer of children's fantasy. He is best known as the creator of the magical land of Oz, an original and believable world through which Baum introduced a contemporary, specifically American flavor to the European-influenced fairy tale genre. Recognized by Edward Wagenknecht as "the first distinctive attempt to construct a fairy land out of American materials," *The Wonderful Wizard of Oz* (1900; later published as *The Wizard of Oz*) and the thirteen sequels written by Baum convey a uniquely American concept of Utopia. Presenting a series of adventures which focus on numerous protagonists in varied settings and scenarios, the Oz books include several characters which have become part of popular culture. Perhaps the most beloved are Dorothy Gale, a determined young girl from Kansas who is first taken to Oz in a cyclone, and the distinctive personalities she meets on her journey to see the Wizard and thus find her way back home: the Scarecrow, who seeks brains but actually manifests intelligence and wit; the Tin Woodman, who requests a heart but is inordinately kind and compassionate; and the Cowardly Lion, who asks the Wizard for courage but acts bravely throughout their experiences. Oz so captivated the public's fancy that a succession of writers, most notably Ruth Plumly Thompson, continued the series long after Baum's death. Yet for nearly thirty years critics, librarians, and educators ignored Baum's achievement. They dismissed his works as insignificant series books, considered his writing pedestrian, and deemed his humorous, sometimes irreverent approach unwholesome. In recent years, however, Baum has been the subject of much critical attention and is the inspiration for the International Wizard of Oz Club and its publication, the *Baum Bugle*.

Baum began his prolific writings for children with *Mother Goose in Prose* (1897), retellings of the nursery rhymes mainly significant for their drawings by Maxfield Parrish, and *Father Goose, His Book* (1899), a collection of original poems largely dependent for its success on the illustrator W. W. Denslow. With the publication of *The Wizard* in the following year, Baum produced his greatest work. The author's intent, as he stated in the book's introduction, was to write a "modernized fairy tale," a children's story without "the horrible and blood-curdling incidents" or the didactic themes of Hans Christian Andersen and the Brothers Grimm. Nevertheless, the Oz stories contain a number of gentle moral lessons as well as gruesome episodes. Baum's lasting achievement was in creating a fantasy land that is recognizably American in psychology and setting: the virtues of home and family are stressed, and the characters are self-reliant, forthright individuals full of optimism and the pioneer spirit. In addition, the topographical features of Oz parallel those of the United States, and the magic in Oz is generally produced by science and technology rather than by spells and witchcraft. Baum fashioned many of his characters, such as the Scarecrow and the Tin Woodman, out of real and familiar materials. A recurring theme of the Oz books—to find happiness, look no farther than your own backyard—is exemplified by the characters' search for qualities they already possess. Throughout the series, Baum upheld conventional morality by affirming individual freedom, reverence for life, and the senselessness of war. He emphasized tolerant, selfless, and humble behavior and ridiculed pseudo-intellectuals, the military, and figures who show greed or conceit.

More unconventionally, Baum was among the first American authors to stress entertainment rather than didacticism in his works. He also created far more female than male characters, and often invested them with strength, independence, leadership qualities, and positions traditionally assigned to men. With their numerous puns and telling observations on human nature, the Oz books appeal not only to children but to adults, who enjoy Baum's unsentimental, mildly satiric approach to his characters and their dilemmas.

Baum never intended *The Wonderful Wizard of Oz* to be the first of a series. After unsuccessfully attempting over a period of years to interest his readers in other adventures, he was induced by persistent popular demand and financial difficulties to write additional Oz books. Even the acclaim of the fantasies *Queen Zixi of Ix* (1905) and *John Dough and the Cherub* (1906) did not silence the public, nor did his scheme

to close off the land of Oz from all communication in *The Emerald City of Oz* (1910). By 1913, Baum resigned himself to producing an annual Oz book, doing so until his death in 1919. A voluminous author, he also wrote under various pseudonyms. As Laura Bancroft, Baum produced a series of nature fairy tales; as Floyd Akers, he created the "Boy Fortune Hunters" adventure series; and as Edith Van Dyne, he wrote the successful "Aunt Jane's Nieces" series, ten volumes of realistic fiction.

Critics commend Baum for creating some of the most memorable characters in children's literature and for skillfully interweaving the everyday with the fantastical. While acknowledging that he often used weak plots and wrote his books in a mediocre style, reviewers recognize Baum as a natural storyteller who gave children humor, action, and excitement in a noncondescending way. Brian Attebery has said, "Even with his weaknesses, he is our Grimm and our Andersen, the man who introduced Americans to their own dreams."

(See also *Twentieth-Century Literary Criticism*, Vol. 7; *Something about the Author*, Vol. 18; *Contemporary Authors*, Vol. 108; and *Dictionary of Literary Biography*, Vol. 22: *American Writers for Children, 1900-1960*.)

AUTHOR'S COMMENTARY

L. FRANK BAUM

[*The following excerpt is from an essay originally published in the August 19, 1909 issue of the* Advance.]

The earliest literature of which we have knowledge is that of fairy lore, and the fairy tale has survived through all the changing ages to this day, and is still as popular with childish minds as in the beginning. (p. 137)

[There] are many books to be had of the right sort; books that will entertain and delight your little ones without putting a single bad or repulsive idea into their heads. So I entreat parents, and those who present books to children, to be particular in selecting modern, up-to-date fairy tales, for in this way you will feed the imaginative instinct of the little ones and develop the best side of child nature. Glance into the book yourself, and see that the story is not marred by murders or cruelties, by terrifying characters, or by mawkish sentimentality, love and marriage. Because some fairy tales have these faults it would be folly to withhold all fairy tales from children. (p. 139)

It is folly to place before the little ones a class of literature they cannot comprehend and which is sure to bore them and to destroy their pleasure in reading. What they want is action—"something doing every minute"—exciting adventures, unexpected difficulties to be overcome, and marvelous escapes.

To my mind a good book of this sort is just as necessary to the proper promotion of a child's welfare as baths, exercise, or wholesome food. There is no danger of deceiving the little one, or giving it a false impression of life. The children know very well that fairies and fairylands are apart from human life, even if they believe for a time that such things really exist. The myth concerning Santa Claus deceives few modern children, but delights them all; and so it is with the fairies. Childhood loves the vivid interest of fairy tales and the glamor of fairyland . . . , and there is no particle of harm in the entertainment thus afforded them if proper care is taken in the selection of their books. (p. 140)

L. Frank Baum, "Modern Fairy Tales," in his The Wizard of Oz, *edited by Michael Patrick Hearn, Schocken Books, 1983, pp. 137-40.*

GENERAL COMMENTARY

THE DIAL

That dreamlike confusion of the actual and the impossible which was so peculiarly the invention of the late "Lewis Carroll" has its counterpart in many a volume put out this year. Mr. L. Frank Baum frankly acknowledges his obligations to his more original predecessor in ***A New Wonderland***. . . . But Mr. Dodgson had a real distinction of style which is wholly lacking here, though to be found in a chapter or two of Mr. Baum's other book, ***The Wonderful Wizard of Oz,*** which is remarkably illustrated by Mr. William W. Denslow, who possesses all the originality of method which has been denied his collaborator. This last book is really notable among the innumerable publications of the year, making an appeal which is fairly irresistible to a certain standard of taste.

A review of "A New Wonderland" and "The Wonderful Wizard of Oz," in The Dial, *Vol. XXIX, No. 347, December 1, 1900, p. 436.*

THE NEW YORK TIMES

L. Frank Baum is dead, and the children, if they knew it, would mourn. That endless procession of "Oz" books, coming out just before Christmas, is to cease. ***The Wizard of Oz, Queen Zixi of Ix, Dorothy and the Wizard, John Dough and the Cherub,*** there will never be any more of them, and the children have suffered a loss they do not know. Years from now, though the children cannot clamor for the newest Oz book, the crowding generations will plead for the old ones.

Baum brought the fairy tale up to date. . . . Nevertheless, the modern fairy tale, even Baum's, is not a real fairy tale. . . . For a fairy story has to be written by one who believes in fairies; and they who write them nowadays . . . do not believe in fairies. . . .

Baum did not believe in his Tin Woodman and his Scarecrow; behind the scenes you could see the smile of the showman. . . .

[The Brothers Grimm] had the child heart, just as Baum had it, and they were able to conceal any skepticism about the truth of what they wrote, which he was not and which no fairy-tale writer since has been able to do. . . .

"The age of chivalry is dead." Is the age of fairy-tale writing? Not so long as men like Baum can counterfeit it.

"Fairy Tales," in The New York Times, *Section 3, May 11, 1919, p. 1.*

EDWARD WAGENKNECHT

[It] is in ***The Wizard of Oz*** that we meet the first distinctive attempt to construct a fairyland out of American materials. Baum's long series of Oz books represents thus an important pioneering work: they may even be considered an American utopia. (p. 17)

[These] are *American* fairy tales. By this I do not mean that Mr. Baum has used no European materials. He . . . used very freely whatever suited his purpose from older literatures and from older cultures. Indeed had he not done this, his output could hardly have been recognized as wonder tales at all. The greatest villian in all the Oz books is the Nome King—the

"G" is left out because the children cannot pronounce it!—the ruler of an underground nation of elves, as old as fairy lore itself. Again, we have Polychrome, the Rainbow's daughter, a character surely with nothing distinctively American about her, and in ***Dorothy and the Wizard in Oz*** there is a thrilling fight with the gargoyles, taken posthaste from mediaeval cathedrals.

These, however, are not the distinctively "Ozzy" characters. Suppose we look at the Scarecrow and the Tin Woodman. In ***The Wizard of Oz,*** Dorothy finds the Scarecrow, newly-made, with a bean pole up his back, in the middle of a corn field. She lifts him down and they go to the Emerald City together, where Dorothy plans to ask Oz to send her home to Kansas while the Scarecrow wants brains instead of straw in the painted sack that serves him for a head. The next addition to their party is the Tin Woodman whom they find rusted in the woods and who cannot go along with them until they oil his joints so that he may walk. The Tin Woodman was once a man of flesh and blood, one Nick Chopper, in love with a pretty Munchkin girl. But a wicked witch enchanted his ax, so that as he was working in the forest he cut himself to pieces. Fortunately Nick Chopper had among his friends a very wonderful tinsmith who, as soon as any part of Nick's body had been cut off, would replace it with tin, until at last the man was wholly tin and as good as new. Only one thing was lacking: he had no longer a heart and accordingly he did not care whether he married the pretty Munchkin girl or not. The Tin Woodman therefore goes along with Dorothy and the Scarecrow to the Emerald City in the hope that the Wizard may give him a heart. Now who but an American—in a country overrun with mechanical skill—could ever have dreamed of a creature like that?

Other, similar characters are introduced in later volumes. (pp. 23-5)

The use of machinery in the Oz books is also characteristically American. In general, magic may be said to inhere not in persons but in things. Whoever has the magical instrument can perform magic deeds. Continually, the forces of Nature, as we know them in America, are used for purposes of conveyance. In ***The Wizard of Oz,*** it is a Kansas cyclone which carries Dorothy and her house over the desert and deposits them in the Land of Oz. In ***Ozma of Oz,*** Dorothy is shipwrecked. In ***Dorothy and the Wizard in Oz,*** Dorothy, in California, is swallowed by an earthquake and carried down into the center of the Earth, from whence she makes her way to Oz. (pp. 27-8)

Indeed the United States is well represented in Oz. Dorothy is from Kansas; the Shaggy Man comes from Colorado; and Betsy Bobbin's home is Oklahoma. The Wizard of Oz himself is a native of Omaha. There he was connected with Bailum and Barney's Consolidated Shows, and his magic was, all of it, pure fake. . . . It is not until later in his career when the Wizard becomes a pupil of the great sorceress, Glinda the Good, that he learns something about real magic.

Now what is the significance of all this? Not surely that American magic is any better than French magic or German magic. No. Simply that Mr. Baum has enlarged the resources of fairyland. He has not destroyed European magic: he has simply added to it. And he has done one thing more. He has taught American children to look for the element of wonder in the life around them, to realize that even smoke and machinery may be transformed into fairy lore if only we have sufficient energy and vision to penetrate to their significance and transform them to our use. (pp. 28-9)

It is not healthy—and it is not true—for children to be made to feel that romance belongs only to the past, and that everything in America today is drab, uninteresting, and businesslike. . . . Thus Mr. Baum's work is primarily significant because it has pointed in the right direction: it has helped to teach us how to find wonder in contemporary American life.

I have spoken of the Land of Oz as an American utopia. By this I do not mean that the Oz books are full of social criticism. Since they were written for children, this is obviously not the case. Yet the utopia element in them is strong, and if the children do not forget it all by the time they grow up, perhaps it is not too fantastic to imagine that it may do some good. It would not be a bad thing if American lawmakers and executives were to imbibe a few of the ideals which actuate the lovely girl ruler of the Emerald City—Ozma of Oz. (p. 30)

All in all, there is much fuller command over nature in Oz than we enjoy in any country yet known. Animals can talk and mingle with human beings on terms of equality. Even flies are considerate and kindly: if one alights on you, you do not kill it: you simply request it politely to move on, and it complies with your request. Many of the inhabitants of the country, not being made of flesh and blood, do not need food, sleep, drink, or clothes. Those who feel that misery and imperfection are necessary to interest either in literature or in life may find some comfort in the fact that around the Emerald City itself the country is so peaceful that no adventures are possible. Consequently all the Oz books take you off to some obscure corner of Oz which has not yet been cultivated and where the sway of the Queen is only nominal.

Best of all, there is no army in Oz. Ozma refuses to fight even when her kingdom seems in danger of invasion. "No one has the right to destroy any living creatures, however evil they may be, or to hurt them or make them unhappy. I will not fight—even to save my kingdom." For the safety of the world's future, the children could not well learn any more wholesome doctrine than that.

(Is it becoming clear, then, why so many of those who are well satisfied with the established order will have none of the Oz books?)

There is one element in the Oz books that the children probably do not get, and that is the element of satire. You will remember how in ***The Wizard of Oz,*** Dorothy, the Scarecrow, and the Tin Woodman travel to the Wizard because they want, respectively, to get home to Kansas, to receive some brains, and to be given a heart. The fourth member of the party is a Cowardly Lion, who wants courage. He is a most ferocious fighter in the jungle, but he is much concerned over the fact that whenever there is danger he is terribly afraid. . . . So he goes to Oz to ask for courage. Mr. Baum makes the whole journey a sermon on the text: "Man does not live by bread alone but principally by catchwords." All through the journey, the Lion is the valiant protector of the party, and whenever any particularly difficult problem comes up, it is the Scarecrow who solves it. Once the Tin Woodman accidentally steps on a beetle and kills it. Greatly distressed over this act of clumsiness, he weeps bitter tears. . . . The point is, of course, that all these creatures, except Dorothy, are already in possession of that of which they are going in search. Yet because they lack the name, the fact that they are in actual possession of the thing itself wholly eludes them. (pp. 32-5)

There are numerous other examples of satire. . . . The absurd conceit of the Scarecrow after he gets his brains, the outrageous sentimentality of the Tin Woodman—these are notorious and delightful. . . . The Donkeys of Dunkiton think that donkeys are the wisest and most beautiful of all human creatures. They do not need to go to school. The worrying fraternity are made fun of in the Flutterbudget incident of ***The Emerald City of Oz,*** and here Mr. Baum has skilfully chosen exactly the absurd sort of thing that nervous, imaginative children do worry about. Sometimes the satire strikes a deeper note as in the incident of the Woggle Bug having reduced all knowledge to pills, so that the students in his college do not need to spend any of their valuable time in studying but may be free to devote it all to such important things as football and other outdoor sports. (pp. 36-7)

The Oz books are "popular" in character. That admits, of course, of no dispute. In distinction of style they are utterly lacking and often in imaginative distinction as well. Nobody could possibly write fifty volumes of fairy tales and keep the whole up to a high level of imaginative power. In this respect the series may be said to have declined notably as commercial considerations made it necessary to string it on indefinitely. (p. 37)

As popular literature then, and along the lines indicated in this essay, I think the Oz books deserve consideration. They are an American phenomenon. It would be calamitous if children were to read them only and were therefore to stop reading Perrault and Madame D'Aulnoy and the Brothers Grimm. Nevertheless they have their place. And it is undeniable that literature conceived in terms of our own life and thought must have always a certain vividness for us which other, sometimes much finer, literature does not possess. This too has been illustrated in the experience of American children with the Oz books. (pp. 37-8)

Someday we may have better American fairy tales but that will not be until America is a better country. (p. 40)

Edward Wagenknecht, in his Utopia Americana, *University of Washington Book Store, 1929, 40 p.*

JAMES THURBER

I have been for several weeks bogged in Oz books. It had seemed to me, at first, a simple matter to go back to the two I read as a boy of ten, ***The Wizard of Oz*** and ***The Land of Oz,*** . . . and write down what Oz revisited was like to me now that my life, at forty, has begun again. I was amazed and disturbed to discover that there are now twenty-eight different books about Oz. . . . The thing is obviously a major phenomenon in the wonderful land of books. I began my research, therefore, not by rereading the two Oz books I loved as a child (and still do, I was happy to find out later) but with an inquiry into the life and nature of the man who wrote the first fourteen of the series, Mr. L. Frank Baum. . . .

When he was about ten he became enamoured of (if also a little horrified and disgusted by) the tales of the Grimm brothers and of Andersen and he determined that when he grew up he would write fairy tales with a difference. There would be, in the first place, "no love and marriage in them"; . . . furthermore, he wanted to get away from the "European background" and write tales about fairies in America. . . . There was also another significant change that he wanted to make in the old fairy tales. Let me quote from his own foreword to the first Oz book, ***The Wizard*** [see Author's commentary for *The Wonderful Wizard of Oz* (1900)]: ". . . the time has now come for a series of newer 'wonder tales' in which the stereotyped genie, dwarf and fairy are eliminated, together with all the horrible and blood-curdling incident devised by their authors to point a fearsome moral. . . . ***The Wizard of Oz*** aspires to be a modernized fairy tale in which the wonderment and joy are retained, and the heartaches and nightmares left out." I am glad that, in spite of this high determination, Mr. Baum failed to keep them out. Children love a lot of nightmare and at least a little heartache in their books. I know that I went through excruciating lovely nightmares and heartaches when the Scarecrow lost his straw, when the Tin Woodman was taken apart, when the Saw-Horse broke his wooden leg. . . .

In all, [Baum] wrote about fifty books, most of them for children. He was forty-three in 1899 when he did ***The Wizard of Oz,*** which to him was just another (the twentieth or so) book for children. It sold better than anything he had ever written. The next year he wrote a thing called ***Dot and Tot of Merryland.*** But his readers wanted more about Oz. . . . He ignored the popular demand for four years, meanwhile writing a book called ***Baum's American Fairy Tales. . . .*** He must have been hurt by its cold reception. Here he was, nearing fifty, trying to be what he had always fondly wanted to be, an American Andersen, an American Grimm, and all the while American children—and their parents— would have none of it, but screamed for more about Oz. His American fairy tales, I am sorry to tell you, are not good fairy tales. The scene of the first one is the attic of a house "on Prairie Avenue, in Chicago." It never leaves there for any wondrous, faraway realm. Baum apparently never thoroughly understood that fatal flaw in his essential ambition, but he understood it a little. He did another collection of unconnected stories but this time he placed them not in Illinois but in Mo. ***The Magical Monarch of Mo*** is not much better than the American tales; but at least one story in it, **"The Strange Adventures of the King's Head,"** is a fine, fantastic fairy tale. The others are just so-so. On went L. Frank Baum, grimly, into the short tales making up ***The Enchanted Island of Yew;*** but the girls and boys were not interested. Finally, after four years and ten thousand letters from youngsters, he wrote ***The Land of Oz. . . .***

The first two, ***The Wizard*** and ***The Land*** are far and away the best. Baum wrote ***The Wizard,*** I am told, simply as a tour de force to see if he could animate, and make real, creatures never alive before on sea or land. He succeeded, eminently, with the Scarecrow and the Tin Woodman and he went on to succeed again in the second book with Jack Pumpkinhead, the Saw-Horse and the Woggle Bug. After that I do not think he was ever really successful. (p. 141)

I think the fatal trouble with the later books (for us aging examiners, anyway) is that they became whimsical rather than fantastic. They ramble and they preach . . . , they lack the quick movement, the fresh suspense, the amusing dialogue and the really funny invention of the first ones. They dawdle along like a class prophecy. None of their creatures comes to life for me. I am merely bored by the Growleywogs, the Whimsies, the Cuttenclips, the Patchwork Girl, Button-Bright, the Googly-Goo, and I am actually gagged by one Unc Nunkie. Mr. Baum himself said that he kept putting in things that children wrote and asked him to put in. He brought back the Wizard of Oz because the children pleaded and he rewrote the Scarecrow and the Woodman almost to death because the children wanted them. The children should have been told to hush up and go back to the real Wizard and the real Scarecrow and the real Woodman. They are only in the first two books. (pp. 141-42)

James Thurber, "The Wizard of Chittenango," in The New Republic, *Vol. LXXXI, No. 1045, December 12, 1934, pp. 141-42.*

ROLAND BAUGHMAN

A little more than half a century ago a story for children was written which not only completely captivated its juvenile audience but found its way into the hearts of numberless older readers as well. In ***The Wonderful Wizard of Oz,*** . . . the author's purpose was simply to give pleasure to children of his day by means of a fairy tale of contemporary flavor. . . . Instead of the traditional props of fear and evil destiny he supplied humor and kindly philosophy. He was by no means the first man in the world to think of children's stories as properly concerned with gladness rather than discipline, but there was a timely element about Baum's approach which neither children nor adults could resist; there was moreover an indigenous quality that had never before been written into an American fairy story.

Whether Baum meant at first to write for older readers as well as for youngsters we may never be quite sure, but certainly he wrote for himself. Over and over again he included wisdom in his stories that must have largely eluded his younger audience. Perhaps he never intended them to take it in, which may be why he insisted so positively that his stories carried no moral. (pp. 15-16)

The nature of Baum's special contribution is a subject that has lain neglected too long. And there are some even more pointed questions to which a lot of authors would like to know the answers—how Baum was able almost without realizing it to capture at one stroke the imaginations of children all over the world, to make himself and his stories so vivid to them that he became the recipient of thousands of letters from his readers, and to hold that popularity long after his life was done. For once Baum had published ***The Wizard of Oz*** he was never again his own master; try as he would to interest his following in other kinds of fairy tales, he was invariably driven back to the original theme by demands from chlildren all over the country for "more about Oz!" . . . [It] is entirely fitting that the name of L. Frank Baum came to represent Oz and only Oz to a whole generation of children, to be identified with a particular type of fantasy, and to become the hall-mark of an unique humor and a wise and convincing philosophy.

No more decisive example of Baum's wisdom comes to mind than the underlying theme of the saga of ***The Wonderful Wizard of Oz.*** (pp. 16-17)

[The] lesson that "we get what we have" may be the most elaborate one to be found in the long series of Oz books that flowed from Baum's pen during two decades, but it is by no means the only one. "Banter" is perhaps a safer term than "satire" for most of the oblique remarks that he made about human frailties which he never took more than half seriously. In any event there is small reason to think that he meant his comments for tender ears alone. There is something to be gained by every reader, of no matter what age, because Baum was adept at reducing humanity's shortcomings to absurdities. (p. 18)

[No] matter how mature an idea Baum sought to illustrate, he never failed to keep his language simple, so that it rests with the reader whether or not the double meaning is found. Baum's sarcasms are usually by-plays; undertones are there, but the incidents are amusing enough in themselves to carry one's interest. (p. 20)

Roland Baughman, "L. Frank Baum and the 'Oz Books'," in Columbia Library Columns, *Vol. IV, No. 3, May, 1955, pp. 15-35.*

BERNARD M. GOLUMB

I can no longer bear in silence the profession-wide disdain for the Oz books. . . . What is wrong with the Oz books? Well, they are "negative." Of the terms evasive of exact meaning, negative seems to me to be one of the foremost. They are negative to what "positive?" . . . [The] Oz books are unrealistic fantasy. We live in a practical age and fantasy should not be encouraged. For that reason most libraries stock the realistic *Freddie, the Pig*. From these books twentieth century minds learn how our pig friend learns to fly or how he acts in conjunction with the "baseball team from Mars." Since few of our little ones see pigs in their urban lives, this presentation of the noble animal cannot be considered amiss.

The chief professional criticism, taught in our seminaries, the library schools, is that all series are bad. Oz books are undoubtedly a series. (p. 137)

Perhaps the most popular juvenile author today is Walter Farley, whose "Black Stallion" is the hero of countless junior horse lovers. (pp. 137-38)

These (Farley) books are written in unimpeachable literary style, veritable Miltonian prose. They present accurate material on the nature of horses. We don't mind that they seem to be a series. . . . Why should the Oz books be singled out as unacceptable? Who says one has to have all of them if one has

Baum as a twelve-year-old military academy cadet.

any? . . . How many of our children's librarians or their little evaluation groups have taken the opportunity to judge each title on its own merits?

I have read and re-read the Oz books at least five times each. That is, those by Thompson and Baum. The others have no charm for me. I read almost nothing else from the age of seven to ten. I read Oz books periodically until I entered the army. That my reading for three years was so limited is not the fault of the books but of the library and its librarians. I could have been better directed, perhaps.

Nevertheless, I was the best reader in the class. I developed the literary habit. My vocabulary was better than most of my classmates, my grades as good. I continued by series through Edgar Rice Burroughs, Sabatini, Rohmer, Altsheler, Cooper, and finally "good books". During the time that my playmates found other things to do, including car stealing, the pleasure that I had gotten from the Oz books persistently drew me back to the library. I find that I am as well read and frequently better read than my fellow professional librarians. Having read the Oz books did not harm me. I submit that they probably did me a world of good. I shall read them to my children who I think will enjoy them immensely. Then I shall donate them to some good public library. (p. 138)

Bernard M. Golumb, "A Defense of the Oz Books," in Junior Libraries, *an appendix to* Library Journal, *Vol. 4, No. 2, October, 1957, pp. 137-38.*

RUSSEL B. NYE

In his tales, Baum wrote in the preface to ***The Wizard of Oz,*** "The stereotyped genie, dwarf, and fairy are eliminated, together with all the horrible and bloodcurdling incident . . ." [see Author's Commentary for *The Wonderful Wizard of Oz* (1900)]. His were to be "modernized" fairy stories, "in which the wonderment and joy are retained, and the heartaches and nightmares left out." "Modern education," he wrote, "includes morality; therefore the modern child seeks only entertainment in its wonder-tales." His stories would be stripped of "fearsome" morality at least, and aimed simply to "excite laughter and gladden the heart."

Fortunately for three generations of children, Baum never fully succeeded in attaining all of his objectives. He drew freely on the past, and his books are far more derivative than possibly he realized. The Oz books conform to the accepted pattern far more often than they deviate. Elves, gnomes, wizards, beasts, dragons, princesses, witches, sorcery, all the conventional machinery of ancient folk and fairy tale appears in Oz, with Baum's own clever twists and adaptations. His strength as a storyteller for children lay in his unique ability to implement and adapt the familiar apparatus of the older tale by reworking old materials into new forms. He worked within the framework of the Grimm tradition despite his disavowal of many of its elements, constructing out of essentially traditional materials a fresh new gallery of characters and a group of delightfully varied plots. The changes he rang on the traditional fairy story, not his rejection of that tradition, account to a great extent for his effectiveness. A great part of the perennial attraction of the Oz books lies in the child's recognition of old friends in new roles and costumes.

The "horrible and bloodcurdling incident" to which Baum objected in the Grimms, of course, appears nowhere in Oz. Here Baum followed out his original intentions. There are excitement and danger in his stories, but violence is absent and evil under control. The witches may enchant Dorothy; they never threaten to eat her or bake her in an oven, and the bad wizards and witches who threaten Oz are frustrated creatures whom one could never imagine victorious. The Nome King, though obviously a thorough villain, is given to temper tantrums and capricious mischief much like a spoiled child, but no more dangerous and almost as easily disciplined. The Wicked Witch is defeated by a stout heart and a pail of water. The Hungry Tiger wants to eat a fat baby but his love for children won't let him—thus Baum tenderizes the tigers of folklore. Missing too are the "heartaches" of the Tin Soldier and Thumbelina, the bittersweet sentiment of Andersen, for Oz is a land of laughter, not tears, as Baum intended it to be.

In his effort to create an American *genre,* Baum had least success and more or less gave up the attempt. The tremendous popularity of ***The Wizard*** surprised him. He had held really higher hopes for his next book, ***Baum's American Fairy Tales: Stories of Astonishing Adventures of Boys and Girls with the Fairies of their Native Land,*** which appeared in 1901. These "American" tales, laid in American locales, were lost in the instant popularity of the Oz stories, and Baum's attempt to create a native *genre* simply did not come off. Clever, inventive, with a substratum of very shrewd satire, the stories fail to measure up to the standard set by the Wizard and his crew. Nor could Baum quite keep Oz out of the book; the most effective stories in the collection are those dealing with the kingdom of Quok (another version of some of the wildly wonderful realms of the later Oz books) and with the doings of the Ryls (blood brothers of Munchkins and Gillikins).

The ***American Fairy Tales*** were good stories, far better than most run-of-the-mill "educational" tales for children, but in the majority of them Baum failed to observe the first rule of the wonder-tale—that it must create a never-never land in which all laws of probability may be credibly contravened or suspended. When in the first story the little girl (Dorothy by another name) replies to a puzzled, lost genie, "You are on Prairie Avenue in Chicago," the heart goes out of the story. It is only in Quok, or in Baum's zany version of the African Congo, or among the Ryls, that the book captures the fine free spirit of Oz. The child could see Chicago (or a city much like it) with his eyes; Oz he could see much more distinctly and believably with his imagination. Baum nevertheless clung for a few years to the belief that he could make the United States an authentic fairyland. "There's lots of magic in all nature," he remarked in ***Tik-Tok of Oz,*** "and you may see it as well in the United States, where you and I once lived, as you can here." But children could not. They saw magic only in Oz, which never was nor could be Chicago or Omaha or California or Kansas. (pp. 1-3)

The Oz books became classics, . . . not because Baum succeeded in writing a new kind of Americanized fairy story, but because he adapted the fairy tale tradition itself to twentieth-century American taste with imaginative ingenuity. There are in the Oz books a number of references to American locale, and Dorothy herself, of course, comes to Oz via a prairie twister. But beyond such casual references Oz has no real relation to the United States—it is fundamentally the out-of-time, out-of-space fairyland of tradition. Working from the midst of older materials, Baum's clever and occasionally brilliant variations on traditional themes are marks of craftsmanship and creativeness of a high order. It is not solely in their "Americanism," nor in their avoidance of the "horrible and bloodcurdling," nor in their rejection of moralism (which Baum did not wholly reject), nor in their pure entertainment value (which Baum did maintain), that the power of the Oz books lies. It stems rather from Baum's success in placing his work directly in the stream of the past, in his assimilation into Oz of the ageless universals of wonder and fantasy. What Baum did was to enlarge the resources of the European inheritance by making it possible to find the old joy of wonderment in the fresh new setting of Oz, creating a bright new fairyland in the old tradition. (p. 4)

Whatever Baum's original disclaimer, the strain of moralism is strong in the Oz books. They are not simply pure entertainment, devoid of any lesson, for as Baum once admitted, he tried to hide "a wholesome lesson" behind the doings of his characters. The child (or adult, for that matter) who reads the Oz books for a second or third time can usually find its hiding place, and one of the pleasures of reading Baum lies in its discovery. Baum's "wholesome lesson" is particularly evident in his creation of characters whose function is fully as much didactic as dramatic. The lesson of the Woodman, the Scarecrow, and the Lion in ***The Wizard of Oz*** is clearly a moral one. (p. 5)

The Wizard of Oz himself is perhaps the best example of Baum's method of indirect teaching by characterization. A gentle, inoffensive little man, the Wizard's magic is strictly of the side-show variety. . . . There is something of Colonel Sellers the salesman in the Wizard, a trace of P. T. Barnum and the "sucker born every minute" philosophy, without cruelty or intent to defraud. . . . [There] is no malice in him, and for his well-intentioned humbuggery he is rewarded by learning real sorcery from Glinda. To the child the meaning of the Wizard's story comes clear. How silly it is to turn to humbuggery to get something false, when you can have the true!

Baum had, too, a well-developed sense of satire, though satire is probably too strong a term for what Baum did. He was never zealous or intense in his attitude toward people, for his aim was amusement and not criticism. "Chaff," or "banter," describes more accurately Baum's manner of poking gently at those human frailties and foibles that the child reader could observe for himself in the world about him. (p. 6)

One of Baum's major contributions to the tradition of the fantasy tale is his recognition of the inherent wonder of the machine, his perception of the magic of *things* in themselves. In the Oz books he expanded the resources of the fairy tale to include, for the first time, the mechanical developments of the 20th century, when every child saw about him—in the automobile, the dynamo, the radio, the airplane, and the rest—the triumph of technology over distance, time, and gravity. . . . The mechanical marvels of Oz fitted exactly the technological pattern of American life, its consciousness of machinery, its faith in the machine's seemingly unlimited potential. Kipling, of course, had experimented before Baum with tales of technology, but from a much more mature and sophisticated point of view. Tom Swift, the boy's version of peculiarly American Edison-Ford myth, also made machines that outstripped reality (but not by much), but Tom's creations were always presented as real, just-around-the-corner inventions, far removed from fantasy. Baum, in a burst of inspiration, moved the machine into the child's world of imagination, endowed it with life and magic, and made it the ally of all the forces of good and justice and well-being in Oz.

The machines of Oz are magician's creations, with the white magic of the sorcerer clinging to them. By transforming the talking beasts of ancient folktales into talking machines, Baum grafted twentieth-century technology to the fairy tale tradition. . . . At no time did Baum allow the machines of Oz to get out of control. They are always under orderly discipline; they never exceed their limitations; they act always in harmony with the desires of those who use them. . . . And there are in Oz certain limits beyond which technology cannot go, however skillful the technician and powerful his magic. Ku-Klip the Tinsmith, who built the Tin Woodman and the Tin Soldier, fails dismally when he tries to construct a flesh-and-blood creature, producing only the characterless Chopfyte, who is "always somebody else." And in the end, the most ingenious mechanics of all, Smith and Tinker, overreach themselves. One paints a lake so realistically that he drowns in it; the other builds a ladder to the moon and is so fascinated by the misty, unreal Moon Country that he refuses to leave it. Thus Baum comments on technological overdevelopment, which may undo the unwary in America as it does in Oz.

The Oz books are permeated by an authentic, persistent strain of humor that is one of Baum's most easily recognized characteristics. They are fundamentally "funny" books from the child's point of view, for Baum was able, as few men are, to translate himself without condescension into the child's world. He put into the Oz books his own recognition of the incongruities of human nature, accurately catching and emphasizing some of the absurdities of life. Baum was no Swift nor Twain, but he belonged in the same tradition and his wit is (on a lesser level) astonishingly subtle and ingenious. The pertinent but unexpected association of the apparently unrelated, the joy of novelty, the pleasure of recognition of the obvious in new form, the surprise at the perception of qualities previously unseen, the shift in an accustomed framework of values—all the classic elements of the humor tradition appear in the Oz books.

Baum's wit, though, is geared to the child's pace. It is wit a child can understand and appreciate, since it deals with concepts within the circle of his experience and those which are applicable to his own sphere of action. Baum's skill in evoking a humorous response from a child is real and expert; he locates quickly and unerringly those areas of incongruity and absurdity that are recognizable to a child and subject to his judgment. There are witty bits in the Oz books that children may miss the first time, but if adults can be prevented from explaining the joke . . . they can have the wonderful pleasure of finding it the second or third time.

The humor of Oz lies in the interaction of character and situation, in the genuinely humorous creations who get into equally humorous predicaments because they are what they are. Sometimes the humor is broad and obvious—such as the Kingdom of Utensia, populated by kitchenware, whose King Kleaver often makes cutting remarks to Captain Dip of the Spoon Brigade. . . . At other times Baum's strokes are somewhat more delicate, as with Ann Soforth, the ambitious young queen who sets out to conquer the world with sixteen officers and one private, or with Diksey the jokester, who once made such a bad joke it led to war—both witty commentaries on military motivations. . . . The best illustration of all, however, is probably H. M. Woggle-Bug, T. E., a masterpiece of humorous creation. . . . H. M. Woggle-Bug, T. E., struts his way self-importantly through various adventures, the very symbol of ostentatious erudition. All this, and much more like it, is genuine humor, touched now and then with genius.

Beyond humor, or moral lessons, or adventure, the heart of the Oz books lies in the Land of Oz itself, which, as others have pointed out, is really an American Utopia. (pp. 7-10)

The First Law of Baum's Utopia of Oz, the rule that inspires its harmonious order, is Love. This theme, on which Baum played constant and subtle variations, binds all the Oz books together as a moral unit. Love in Oz is kindness, selflessness, friendliness—an inner check that makes one act decently toward human beings, animals, plants, fairies, machines, and even one's enemies. (pp. 10-11)

The theme of selflessness as the cardinal principle of love runs through all the Oz books, forming the thread that binds them together. In Baum's world of Oz Bad = Selfishness, Good = Selflessness, Love = Happiness, Hate = Evil and Unhappiness. Those who use power for selfish ends, are Bad, and are punished in proportion to their crime. (p. 11)

Oz is a family-style Utopia, phrased in terms and placed in a framework the child can understand. It is simply the perfect home, built on love, permeated by happiness, filled with a big loving family. (p. 12)

Oz is a fairyland small-town or suburban home, tailored to the pattern of a little girl's dream.

For Oz is beyond all doubt a little girl's dream-home. Its atmosphere is feminine, not masculine, with very little of the rowdy, frenetic energy of boys. There is no consistent father-image in Oz, or brother-image, to correspond to Ozma and Glinda. Dorothy brings Aunt Em and Uncle Henry from Kansas to Oz after her fourth trip, but they are merely the kindly farm relatives every little girl desires. Nowhere in Oz does Father appear. . . . The Land of Oz, where Dorothy is a Princess in her own right, is all that a girl could ask for in a dream home, just as Dorothy is Baum's picture of the daughter he never had. A coolly levelheaded child in whom a refreshing sense of wonder is nicely balanced by healthy common sense, there is nothing fey or magic about her, nothing of the storybook princess. A solid, human, child, Dorothy takes her adventure where she finds it, her reactions always generous, reasonable, and direct.

The few boys in Oz are girls' boys, drawn as little girls assume boys should be. Baum could not make Oz fit boys, nor was he capable of making boys who could fit easily and naturally into Oz society. There are no Huck Finns or Tom Sawyers in Oz, but rather a somewhat bloodless group of younger Prince Charmings. (pp. 12-13)

Surprisingly enough, despite the tremendous sale of Oz books during Baum's lifetime and after, neither he nor Oz received more than casual mention in contemporary surveys of children's literature, of which there were dozens published in the magazines at Christmas time. From 1900 to 1919, the years during which Baum was producing almost a book a year to the plaudits of children in the hundreds of thousands, none of his books received a review in a major journal. (pp. 13-14)

Part of the answer lies, no doubt, in the fact that Baum set his sights (by adult critical methods) fairly low, aiming at a maximum of enjoyment with a minimum of admonition. The Oz books provided only a sketchy pattern for behavior, and in comparison to Little Lord Fauntleroy, for example, gave parents very little help in their job of adjusting and civilizing the young. This lack of overt moralizing bothered the educators and the critics of Baum's time. (p. 14)

Modern critical studies of children's literature still maintain silence concerning the Oz books. The most recent and definitive study, *A Critical History of Children's Literature,* contains no mention of Baum. Entries on juvenile literature in the leading encyclopedias fail to list his name. No magazine article on Baum has ever appeared, with the exception of a short piece by James Thurber nearly twenty years ago [see excerpt dated 1934]. *Twentieth Century Authors* contains a short, inaccurate biography of Baum which includes this estimate: "The [Oz] books were lacking in style and imaginative distinction." In general, modern critics of children's literature, while admitting the appeal of the Oz books, tend to class them as popular but not worth bothering about.

It is true that the Oz books do not have the depth of Howard Pyle's re-tellings of the Robin Hood and King Arthur stories, or Kipling's Jungle Books, or the books of Kenneth Grahame or A. A. Milne. Baum's work, in the opinion of the critics, lacks literary quality. He tells his stories simply and directly, contributing little to the child's sense of language or to his awareness of its potentialities; they do not read aloud well, except with the youngest, for Baum is in no sense a stylist. There is in the Oz stories no more than a trace of fun with ideas nor any of the multilevelled nonsense of Lear and the logical lunacy of Lewis Carroll. And there are, however much one enjoys Baum, occasional dead spots in the action of some of the later stories.

Yet one suspects, after attempting to read Carroll or Lear to a modern American child, that Baum knew better than his critics what children enjoy and understand. The nightmarish episodes, the complex paradoxes, and the logical and mathematical implications of the *Alice* books neither fit nor satisfy the child's needs and desires, however attractive they may be to mature readers. The cloying sentimentality and obsolescent vocabulary (what child of today can identify *treacle* or a *match girl*?) of many of the nineteenth century juvenile classics simply puzzle a modern youngster and leave him cold. The Wonderful Land of Oz, by contrast, is as real to him as his own neighborhood; the Scarecrow, the Woodman, and the Lion are old storybook acquaintances in new dress, familiar, friendly, and vividly alive.

It is manifestly unfair to Baum to criticize his work for its lack of those qualities, desirable as they may seem to adults, found in the great British writers of children's books. The votes of a million children who have read his books with fascination and enjoyment should most certainly be counted in the verdict. The Oz stories, as the critics must admit, fulfill all that a child may ask of a story—they are exciting, humorous, filled with fresh invention and swift action, sustained throughout by imaginativeness of a high order. Though he may have failed to create a specifically American fairyland quite as he wished, Baum's books have an indigenous flavor, reflecting American attitudes and ideals with as much accuracy and validity as the English classics reflected England's. The virtues of Oz are the homely American virtues of family love, friendliness for the stranger, sympathy for the underdog, practicality and common sense in facing life, reliance on one's self for solutions to one's problems. Dorothy, in the midst of strange and disconcerting events, retains a natural, direct approach that has an authentic American ring. No one has ever tried to interview the Wizard of Oz; Dorothy does, and neatly punctures the whole illusion. Throughout the Oz books the "good" characters maintain their self-integrity, finding their answers within themselves—an echo, perhaps of the Franklin tradition of self-help. There is no whisper of class consciousness in Oz (as there is in Alice's Wonderland) or any of the overtones of snobbery that nineteenth century juvenile fiction sometimes had. The whimsicality of the British that balances on the edge of preciousness (as in A. A. Milne) is not present in Baum, nor is the insipidity of the

Milne imitators. The Oz books do have their subtleties, but the whimsy is broad and the caprice is brushed in sweeping strokes.

Baum's work does not deserve the critical neglect with which it is still treated. He wrote American tales for twentieth-century American children in an American vein, and by this he should be judged. He had his weaknesses (some of them the result of fourteen Oz books), but he had his undeniable strengths. No one can accuse him of failure to provide full measure of plot, character, and action. His plots are usually exciting, humorous, imaginative, and highly inventive. The feeling of active peril and its inevitable resolution, so essential to successful children's stories, appears in all the Oz stories as Baum sensed they must; Oz is a land of persistent danger (though not very dangerous danger) in exactly the proper degree. The perils produce no nightmares, the injustices bring no tears. The solutions satisfy the child's sense of right and justice, for Baum knew that justice put aright was the clearest principle of the child's creed and the deepest into morality that the child's tale may safely go.

In the creation of character Baum displayed his greatest mastery. Here he need bow to no one. The Tin Woodman, the Scarecrow, and the Cowardly Lion, among others, have long since secured permanent places in the gallery of great creations, and are as well known to American children as Mother Goose and Reynard the Fox. After fifty years the Land of Oz is still familiar territory; its population still provides friends and playmates for millions of children. Baum could enter into the child's world on the child's terms, create and preserve its delightful atmosphere, and tell his story with the genuine sincerity of a believer. (What child can resist an attempt to pronounce Bini Aru's unpronounceable magic word, PYRZQXGL, just to see what might happen if he *did* succeed in pronouncing it correctly? Things like this are tributes to Baum's real genius for creating belief.) Baum had the child's heart, and the child's love of the strange and beautiful and good, with the ability to bring them all alive. For this gift he deserves recognition. (pp. 14-17)

Russel B. Nye, "An Appreciation," in The Wizard of Oz & Who He Was *by L. Frank Baum, edited by Martin Gardner and Russel B. Nye, Michigan State University Press, 1957, pp. 1-17.*

MARTIN GARDNER

America's greatest writer of children's fantasy was, as everyone knows except librarians and critics of juvenile literature, L. Frank Baum. His ***Wonderful Wizard of Oz*** has long been the nation's best known, best loved native fairy tale, but you will look in vain for any recognition of this fact in recent histories of children's books. . . . By and large, the critics have looked upon Baum's efforts as tawdry popular writing in a class with Tom Swift and Elsie Dinsmore; certainly not to be compared with such classic "children's" fantasies as *Pilgrim's Progress* or *Gulliver's Travels*.

Fortunately, children themselves seldom listen to such learned opinion. . . . [Half] a century after they were written, children turn the pages of Baum's Oz books with passionate delight. Surely it is only a matter of time until the critics develop sufficient curiosity to read the books themselves. When they do they will be startled to find them well written, rich in excitement, humor, and philosophy, and with sustained imaginative invention of the highest order. (pp. 19-20)

After the success of ***The Wonderful Wizard,*** Baum . . . began work in earnest on other books for children. Three were published in 1901, none about Oz. ***Dot and Tot of Merryland*** is a full length fantasy for very young readers. ***The Master Key,*** for older boys, is a science fiction story about the wonders of electricity. The third volume, ***Baum's American Fairy Tales,*** deserves special mention because it marks the first appearance in American letters of fairy tales of merit that have the United States as a setting.

In 1902 Baum published ***The Life and Adventures of Santa Claus,*** a warm, moving story told in almost Biblical prose and involving an elaborate Dunsany-like mythology. (pp. 25-6)

[A] theme of tolerance runs through all of Baum's writings, with many episodes that poke fun at narrow nationalism and ethnocentrism. In ***John Dough and the Cherub,*** for example, we encounter the Hilanders who are tall and thin, their country separated by a stone wall from the Lolanders who are short and fat. A law observed in both regions forbids anyone to ask questions of strangers or of inhabitants on the opposite side of the wall. As a consequence, neither country knows anything about the other, regarding its own area as a paradise and inhabitants on the other side as barbarians. (p. 30)

Eccentric as Baum's "meatless" characters are, they have a consistency of personality and behavior that makes them very real to the mind of a child. . . . Baum was a natural storyteller and even his most outlandish characters seem always to move about with a life of their own.

In spite of the fact that he continued to receive hundreds of letters . . . from children who wanted to hear more about Oz, Baum's interests still lay in fairy tales of other sorts. His ***Enchanted Island of Yew,*** 1903, is not a bad story (the chapter on Twi, a land where everything exists in double form, is an amazing *tour de force*) but it did not sell well, and it is marred by unpleasant psychological undertones.

Finally, in 1904, Baum yielded to the persistent demands of his readers. He wrote ***The Marvelous Land of Oz*** (later retitled ***The Land of Oz***). . . . It is his only Oz book in which Dorothy does not appear. (pp. 30-1)

Many new and entertaining "meatless" characters are introduced in the story. Jack Pumpkinhead is an awkward wooden figure whose head is a pumpkin carved in an eternal grin. A wooden sawhorse is brought to life, much to its own astonishment. And of course we must not fail to mention Professor H. M. Woggle-Bug, T. E.

The Woggle-Bug is Baum's caricature of the over-educated pedant. . . . The Woggle-Bug is addicted to using big words and has to be rebuked occasionally for his tendency to indulge in bad puns. This is partly a satire on Baum himself, for the Oz books abound in puns. They reach a crescendo in a later book when Dorothy visits the Kingdom of Utensia where all the citizens are pieces of kitchenware. In eight pages of text Baum manages to introduce no less than fifty puns! (p. 31)

Certainly one reason for the immense popularity of the Oz books is the fact that they are told with such a wealth of detail that a strong sense of reality is created. These details range from such trifling observations as the fact that the Scarecrow has difficulty picking up small objects with his padded fingers, to important data about the history, geography, and customs of Oz. There is even a map of Oz, drawn by Professor Woggle-Bug. (p. 35)

It is a rare occasion when Baum describes a scene that might frighten a sensitive child. Only a morbid adult could object to a wicked witch melting away or Jack Pumpkinhead carving a new head for himself to replace a former one that has spoiled. Baum's intention, stated in the preface of ***The Wizard,*** to leave out the "heartaches and nightmares" was amply fulfilled. You have only to glance through Grimm and Andersen, *Pinocchio,* or many another classic fairy tale to realize how skillfully Baum managed in contrast with these works, to retain the excitement and avoid the violence and tears. . . . It is true that Baum occasionally forgot his promise, especially in ***Dorothy and the Wizard in Oz*** where an atmosphere of violence and gloom hangs over a large part of the tale, and in the macabre episode (in a later book) of the Tin Woodman's conversation with his former head. But on the whole his books are singularly free of shocking scenes and the spirit of Oz is a happy, sunny one. There are only two references in all of Baum's Royal History to its having rained in Oz.

Literary masterpieces are often written with astonishing carelessness of detail. . . . Like the Baker Street Irregulars who delight in inventing plausible explanations for Watson's memory lapses, a group of Oz enthusiasts can spend many pleasant hours suggesting ways for harmonizing similar contradictions in the Royal History.

The Land of Ev, for example, lies just across the Deadly Desert. But in what direction? You can find a basis for placing it to the north, south, east, or west of Oz. The early history of Oz, before the Wizard arrived in his balloon, is riddled with difficulties. There is reason to believe that grass takes on the color of each region in Oz and equally good reason to think it doesn't. Exactly what happens when a Nome touches an egg? Does he wither away or turn into a mortal? Why do the Shaggy Man and Polychrome, the Rainbow's daughter, act like strangers when they meet (in ***Tik-Tok of Oz***) for the second time? These are only a fraction of the tantalizing problems that face the student of Oz.

An equally fascinating pastime is to speculate on how Baum arrived at the names of various characters and countries. In many instances the basis is obvious. For example, Princess Langwidere is a haughty woman with a "languid air." General Jinjur is a girl with lots of "ginger." But what about Woot the Wanderer, protagonist of ***The Tin Woodman of Oz***? Did Baum take the initials of the tin man's title then switch the "T" from front to back?

The word Oz itself has been the subject of much speculation. The most popular theory is that Baum, searching for a name, looked up at a filing cabinet and saw the words "From O to Z." Another is that it came from "Boz," the nickname of Charles Dickens, one of Baum's favorite authors. And someone has pointed out that Job lived in the land of Uz. The late Jack Snow advanced a captivating theory in the preface of his monumental *Who's Who in Oz*. Baum once wrote that he had always enjoyed stories that cause the reader to exclaim with 'Ohs" and "Ahs" of wonder, and Mr. Snow points out that Oz can be pronounced either "Ohs" or "Ahs." (pp. 36-8)

Ray Bradbury has spoken many times of the influence of Oz on his career as a popular author of fantasy and science fiction. His story "The Exiles" pictures a future in which the psychologists have succeeded at last in destroying all books of fantasy. The narrative closes with the collapse of the Emerald City as the last Oz book goes up in flames.

But I do not think the Emerald City will collapse for a long, long time. A child's love of fantasy is too healthy a love. (p. 41)

Martin Gardner, "The Royal Historian of Oz," in The Wizard of Oz & Who He Was *by L. Frank Baum, edited by Martin Gardner and Russel B. Nye, Michigan State University Press, 1957, pp. 19-46.*

DICK MARTIN

[The wonder of Oz consists of] the magnificent combination of old-world fantasy and new-world enterprise, blended in a happy, rollicking yarn. It is this eclectic quality (which, strangely enough, so annoys the critics) that characterizes Baum's writing. We find ancient folk-tale conventions, archaic pomp and ceremony and medieval black magic juxtaposed with Yankee colloquialisms, cracker-barrel philosophy and the latest electrical machinery—all in harmonious medley.

All Baum's fantasies have a gentle, Golden Rule philosophy—"sentimental" sometimes, and regrettably, "impractical" in our sorry world—but surely not "unwholesome." True, some of his later books occasionally boggle down in sticky sentimentality, but even these are relieved by unexpected and surprisingly tart observations. (In the ***Wizard,*** and many of the rest of the series, there is a pungent vein of extremely adult social criticism.) Another refreshing aspect of his stories is that even the most sweetly idealistic characters sometimes show unsuspected traits of cold-blooded practicality. By way of contrast, his worst villains (notably the peevish Nome King, who keeps turning up like a bad penny) have all-too-human quirks and weaknesses that give them an engaging charm.

The chief criticism of Baum's books is that they are "utterly lacking in literary distinction." This is not strictly true. Although his ***Wizard*** and his other books are not masterpieces of literary style, he possessed a flawless command of English, and his narratives are written with a dignity, grace and ease not often found in children's books.

The man was, first and foremost, a story-teller, and he told his stories well. He never "talked down" to his audience. Children are quick to recognize that quality of over-simplification and silliness . . . , and they resent it. Baum didn't hes-

Baum's wife Maud and sons Robert, Harry, Kenneth, and Frank J. Baum. Mother Goose in Prose *(1897), Baum's first children's book, was prompted when the boys asked their father to tell them stories about the nursery rhyme characters.*

itate to use four- and even five-syllable words; hence many adults read his books, too.

He had an uncanny ability to instill an utterly realistic atmosphere in even his wildest fantasies. This effect was created at least in part by his scrupulous attention to small detail. The geography of the Land of Oz and its four kingdoms is minutely defined; the economic system and government are precisely established. Occasional footnotes of Ozian historical data give the chronicles a further note of convincing actuality. (pp. 107-08)

With only a few lapses, there has been a new Oz book every year, from 1900 to 1951. . . .

Unfortunately, this staggering collection has produced a certain amount of poorly conceived, carelessly written stuff—as much of it by Baum as by his successors, Thompson, Neill, et al. Undoubtedly, if there had been fewer Oz books, they would have been better; and consequently, less vilified by the librarians and critics of juvenile literature. (One wonders how much of the disrepute of ***The Wizard of Oz*** stems from the superfluity of its sequels.) . . .

[After] nearly sixty years the tale of the little Kansas Girl, the Scarecrow, the Tin Woodman and the Cowardly Lion still sparkles with succinct observations on human nature, wise and kindly philosophy, superb imagination, and an appreciation of the wonders of the real world about us. (p. 108)

Dick Martin, "The Wonderful World of Oz," in Hobbies, *Vol. 64, No. 3, May, 1959, pp. 106-09.*

S. J. SACKETT

I choose here . . . to consider the Oz books as examples of Utopian fiction. Certainly they represent an ideal country, even though their creator never indicates how it would be possible to bring the ideal conditions to actual existence, or even whether it would be desirable so to do. Certainly they have influenced the generations of children who have read them in certain attitudes toward government and society.

The Land of Oz, after Princess Ozma came to the throne, was a confederation of four separate kingdoms. That of the Winkies, to the west, was ruled over by Nick Chopper, the Tin Woodman; that of the Munchkins, to the east, by a mysterious king who was never a figure in the stories about Oz; that of the Gillikins, to the north, by the good witch whom Dorothy Gale met when she first came to Oz but who had no further role in the history of Oz; that of the Quadlings, to the south, by the benign sorceress Glinda the Good. Over them all ruled Ozma.

Oz was never a thoroughly civilized and mapped country; it always had a permanent frontier in the form of vast unexplored areas where no one ever traveled and where all sorts of strange beings might (and did) live. To a certain extent this condition was owing to a philosophy of *laissez-faire* on the part of Ozma and the other administrative officials. . . . Neither Ozma nor anyone else wanted to meddle in the affairs of the citizenry, who were free, within extraordinarily broad limits, to do anything they wanted to.

That the individual citizen was so free as this is more surprising in view of the tremendous power which Ozma herself, to say nothing of her counselors Glinda the Good and the Wizard of Oz, could wield. As one reads the chronicles of Oz, however, one is struck by the fact that Ozma seems almost deliberately to have refrained from exercising her vast powers. She came to the throne, it is true, only in 1904; and the last book by the first Royal Historian of Oz appeared in 1921. From this it might be argued that Ozma had had by that time only seventeen years to function effectively as a ruler. On the other hand, she was an absolute monarch with unlimited power and no restraint except self-restraint; and viewed from that standpoint, in those seventeen years she had done remarkably little. A few bridges are mentioned in later books over streams which had had no bridges in earlier books, and presumably Ozma had wished these into existence with her magic belt; yet even by 1921 many of the main thoroughfares of Oz were broken by unbridged rivers. Apparently one of the earliest acts was the abolition of money, for the use of money is referred to in the first two books and is not mentioned, except occasionally as something that the inhabitants of Oz knew about, after 1904. Aside from these two matters, Ozma's reign has been, by the standards of the outside world, a do-nothing reign. (pp. 275-76)

The limits imposed on the broad freedom enjoyed by the citizens of Oz were really only two. First, individual communities, which had by our standards a startling degree of independence from the central government, were not to fight each other, as the Flatheads and Skeezers once did (***Glinda of Oz***) and as the Horners and Hoppers seemed to do almost perennially (e.g., in ***The Patch-work Girl of Oz***). Secondly, no unauthorized person could make use of magic. Violations of this rule were recounted in ***The Patch-work Girl of Oz, The Lost Princess of Oz,*** and ***The Magic of Oz.*** Aside from these two restrictions, everything else was legal.

People in Oz were suspicious of laws. The Tin Woodman once remarked, ". . . laws were never meant to be understood, and it is foolish to make the attempt" (***The Land of Oz***). But if Oz had had a constitution, it probably would have been expressed in one sentence: Do what you like, unless it hurts somebody else. (The reason why magic was prohibited was that so many people, like Ugu the Shoemaker, used magic for evil instead of for good.)

The reason for so much freedom is that life is more fun if you are free to do whatever you want. Absolute freedom, however, has its drawbacks, as the King of Bunnybury discovered in ***The Emerald City of Oz.*** The King was weary of taking responsibility and wanted to be free of it; but he learned that responsibility brings with it so many privileges that it is far wiser to live with responsibility than to live in the irresponsibility of anarchy. If freedom is essential, but absolute freedom is disastrous, then the solution to the problem of government must be in a *via media* of voluntary acceptance of responsibility. And this, in effect, is the principle which underlies government in Oz. (pp. 276-77)

While royalty was necessary for the maintenance of authority—and, one suspects, because Baum was working in the tradition of the European fairy tale—it was a highly democratic royalty. Even the aristocratic Princess Langwidere of Ev darned her own socks (***Ozma of Oz***); and Ozma, the supreme ruler of Oz, was really a merry little girl who enjoyed playing with her commoner girlfriends.

Under Ozma's beneficent rule, based as it was on as much absence of law as possible, there were of course very few criminals. How can you break a law when there are no laws to break? For this reason crime and delinquency were not problems in the Oz state. But when laws were broken, the inhabitants of Oz had a philosophy ready to meet the problem. (pp. 277-78)

[The] dominant philosophy of penology in the Land of Oz is that progressive one which holds that it is more important to rehabilitate the criminal and restore him to a productive place in society than it is to inflict on him society's vengeance for his act.

One of the reasons why there is no crime in the Land of Oz is that there is no money and therefore no temptation to rob anyone. The trouble with money, as the Shaggy Man once remarked, is that it "makes people proud and haughty; I don't want to be proud and haughty. All I want is to have people love me. . . ." (***The Road to Oz***). And fittingly the medium of exchange in the Land of Oz is love. . . . The only way to acquire goods or services, then, is to be so lovable that other people want to give them to you. True, you might steal goods (though you cannot under this system compel services); but there is no need to steal goods when one has only to be loved and they will be given to him. (pp. 279-80)

It is true that Oz was not a heavily industrialized nation. It was chiefly agricultural, with only one city (its capital, the Emerald City); there were a few towns and villages scattered over the countryside, but the bulk of the land—that of it at least that was not wilderness—was under cultivation, and the bulk of the inhabitants were farmers. Most of them were self-sufficient; they raised their own food, spun their own cloth and made their own garments, and built their own houses. In a society like this there is little need for money anyway. . . .

Most Utopias imply a wish to implement them in the real world; and while there is no doubt that L. Frank Baum would have agreed to the general proposition that the real world would be a better place if it were more like his agrarian paradise, there is real reason to doubt that he ever seriously thought that the world could ever be made more Oz-like except perhaps in small details like the adoption of progressive prison reform. And, in truth, one might well scoff that the Utopia of Oz was made possible by the existence of magic and that human nature is too corrupt for so perfect a fairyland. (p. 280)

And so far as the unchangeability of human nature is concerned, Baum has provided us with an answer for that, too. The key to the problem is epistemology. You must assume with Locke that the mind at birth is a *tabula rasa,* an empty page; that there are no innate ideas, no Jungian archetypes or other inherited memories. According to this theory the individual's environment will completely mold his personality, for he has no inherited psychological characteristics. . . . The only reason, according to this theory, that human nature is what it is is that the Utopian environment has never been tried. By establishing a Utopian environment, you change human nature.

It is not far-fetched to say that in the Oz books Baum subscribed to this theory. (pp. 280-81)

Two more points need to be made here concerning the reasons why the social structure of Oz worked as well as it did. The first is that the inhabitants subscribed to a philosophy given verse form by Johnny Dooit:

> The only way to do a thing,
> Is do it when you can,
> And do it cheerfully, and sing
> And work and think and plan.
> The only real unhappy one
> Is he who dares to shirk;
> The only really happy one
> Is he who cares to work.

(***The Road to Oz***)
(p. 282)

The last point that should be made about the success of the unique socio-economical system of Oz is that it was based upon a set of values which are totally foreign to us. We measure success . . . in money. Ozma, however, very early in her reign established a whole new standard: "the only riches worth having," she said, are "the riches of content" (***The Land of Oz***). That man who is most contented is most wealthy. (p. 283)

Thus far we have been discussing the general principles upon which the Utopia of Oz was founded. It is time now to take up a few of the specific principles of the Utopia.

To begin with, nonconformity was prized, as might be expected in so free a society. . . .

The status of women was at one time at least, prior to Ozma's accession to the throne, a major issue. Jinjur's successful rebellion, recounted in ***The Land of Oz,*** was a rebellion of the women against the men. While there is no question that the Royal Historian deprecated the act of rebellion, it is also clear that he sympathized with the impulse behind the revolutionaries, that of bettering woman's lot—though he felt that Jinjur had gone too far. (p. 284)

War was never much of a problem in Oz, and there was not a military tradition. The customary pattern for military organization, however, was to have several officers and only one private; this was the pattern followed both in the Royal Army of Oz itself (***Ozma of Oz***) and in the Army of Oogaboo (***Tik-Tok of Oz***). Part of the reason was that, because of the freedom of the entire society, the individuals who entered these armies were free to select their own rank. Since the privates did the actual fighting, there were very few who were willing to accept a private's job; the titles and uniforms of the officers' ranks, however, as well as their comparative safety, attracted many to the upper echelons of military life. This suggests that if, in the outside world, those who are in a position to cause a war were also under the obligation of fighting it, there would be many fewer wars; whereas the attractions of militarism are such that men can always be found to embrace it so long as they are under no necessity to face the unpleasant realities of warfare. (p. 285)

Perhaps the greatest problem in the Land of Oz was education. Some there were, including Ozma herself, who doubted the value of education at all, suspecting that the search for education was only an excuse used by those who wished to evade responsibility outside the academy. "You see," Ozma once explained to Dorothy, who had asked her about Professor Woggle-Bug's College, "in this country are a number of youths who do not like to work, and the college is an excellent place for them" (***Ozma of Oz***). . . .

It is probable that the low repute of learning in Oz, in some circles at least, was owing to the excessive pedantry and incomprehensibility of the members of the learned professions. (p. 286)

[Perhaps] the central philosophical problem in the Land of Oz was whether the intellect or the emotions were more desirable attributes. Certainly it was the many long disagreements which they had over this issue, some of the most interesting of which were reported in ***The Wizard of Oz,*** which paradoxically made the Scarecrow and the Tin Woodman such firm friends. (Their friendship, by the way, may suggest that the Royal Historian felt that the best answer to the problem was the uniting of the intellect and the emotions in a harmonious relationship.). . .

The Scarecrow's problem really was that he confused knowledge with intellect. Knowledge is an accumulation of facts; intellect is the ability to accumulate facts and to use them to solve problems. The Wizard of Oz himself explained this distinction to the Scarecrow: "A baby has brains," Oz said, "but it doesn't know much. Experience is the only thing that brings knowledge, and the longer you are on earth the more experience you are sure to get." Thus the Scarecrow, even before the Wizard supplied him with brains, was intelligent; he merely lacked knowledge. (p.287)

It was because he felt that he had no brains that the Scarecrow directed all his attention to intellectuality and was on the verge of becoming an unemotional thinking machine. Similarly, the Tin Woodman, who felt he had no heart, directed all of his attention to the life of the emotions and was on the verge of becoming excessively sentimental. . . .

That emotions are desirable things to have we learn from the Scarecrow's case as well as the Tin Woodman's. The latter's own argument for benevolence and kindheartedness actually is weak: "you must acknowledge that a good heart is a thing that brains cannot create, and that money cannot buy." While this is true, it still does not establish benevolence as a desirable characteristic. This is done rather by the whole moral tendency of the Oz stories, which are set in a benevolistic framework much like that found in the sermons of the seventeenth-century English latitudinarians, Barrow, South, and Tillotson, whose philosophy remained popular well into the nineteenth century. (p. 288)

If a great deal of attention was paid in Oz to the problems of the intellect versus emotion, very little was given to artistic problems. In the preface to ***The Wizard of Oz*** the Royal Historian pointed out the superiority of fairy tales which are not gory to fairy tales which are [see Author's Commentary for *The Wonderful Wizard of Oz* (1900)]; and that was the extent of the literary interests shown in the Oz books. None of the little girls who are the heroines of most of the Oz series—Ozma, Dorothy, Betsy Bobbin, and Trot—spend much time reading; their favorite recreations are listening to stories, talking with each other, going to parties, and playing games. (pp. 288-89)

The important thing, the matter which I set out to consider, is how American young people would have been affected by their exposure to the chronicles of [the Utopia of Oz]. I leave aside matters of morality; the morality of Oz was a conventional one with no startling innovations to offer, the general tendencies of which were benevolent, and we can say simply that children who read the Oz books would be influenced to be good children in the conventional sense of the word, with an especial disposition toward charitable or benevolent actions. But we can say also that they would have been influenced to believe in the freedom of the individual, in the voluntary acceptance of responsibility, in progressive prison reform, in the proposition that money is relatively unimportant in life, in the possibility of making a better world, in the pleasures of work, in the significance of contentment, in nonconformity, in the superiority of man to machine, in the need for permitting both sexes to share equally in the good life, in the folly of war, in reverence for life, in a truly substantial education, and in the need for the intellect and the emotions to be brought into harmony.

If we had enough people who believed in these things, our world would be almost as good for us as the Land of Oz was for its inhabitants. The attitudes listed above are all positive ones, and among them you can find practically the complete roll call of the attitudes desirable to insure the continuance of democracy, of civilization, of life—of everything that we in the United States hold valuable. A third generation of American children is now having the Oz books read to it or is reading them for itself. We can all say, "Thank God." (pp. 289-90)

S. J. Sackett, "The Utopia of Oz," in The Georgia Review, *Vol. XIV, No. 3, Fall, 1960, pp. 275-91.*

OSMOND BECKWITH

What made Oz so popular? The books stand out as the only juvenile "series" to please successive younger generations. . . . (p. 19)

Creating robots and automata would seem automatically to place Baum as a forerunner in the United States' growing concern with science-fiction and scientific fantasy. . . . Yet, to an unprejudiced adult, re-reading the Oz books will disclose little likeness to modern science-fiction. Rather the resemblance is to those English Christmas pantomimes in which the role of "principal boy" is traditionally played by a girl (in Oz, however, the principal boy always wears skirts). . . .

There are strong similarities between ***The Wonderful Wizard of Oz*** . . . and another more universally-acknowledged children's classic: Lewis Carroll's *Alice in Wonderland*. . . . (p. 20)

Both *Alice* and ***The Wonderful Wizard*** are fables of innocence and experience. Both have as "hero" a little girl. Both are packed as full as puddings of unconscious distortions and symbolizations. The differences between them, including basic differences in literary ability, are biographical, or, if you like, indigenous.

Carroll's Alice drops down the rabbit hole unharmed and unharming; she even replaces the crockery examined on her way, so as not to hurt anybody; but Baum's Dorothy enters Oz with a death, her cyclone-carried house killing an old woman. An atmosphere of delicacy, of social contretemps, embarrassing situations, tiffs and misunderstandings accompanies Alice throughout her long dream—which is always identified as a dream—the only situation that seems likely to become serious is ended by her awakening. It is quite different with Dorothy. Her adventures not only include attacks by mythical beasts but by lions, wolves, bees, monkeys, and creatures who snap their heads like hammers. She is overcome by poison gas, and almost by chapter threatened with death in various forms.

The motivating force in both books is a search; but while Alice looks for the lovely garden she has glimpsed in her first hour in Wonderland, Dorothy, surrounded by all the beauty of a fairy kingdom, only wants to go home. Alice travels alone; Dorothy makes friends, but what sort of friends?—a straw-stuffed scarecrow, a woodchopper who having chopped himself to bits is now completely artificial, and a lion afraid of his own roar. (Three different ways of writing eunuch.) Searching for the wonderful wizard who is to heal them and give each his heart's desire, the friends reach the emerald city of Oz, but must be blinkered in order to enter. Aloof and terrifying, the Wizard refuses his help unless Dorothy kills off still another old woman, the powerful Witch of whom he lives in constant fear. In attempting this exploit the Scarecrow is eviscerated, the Tin Man scrapped, the Lion captured, and the girl enslaved.

Carroll tells his tale by puns, parodies, and witty transsubstantiations of harsh reality. The word "death," if I am not mistaken, occurs only once in his entire book. But Baum's approach throughout is literal and matter-of-fact. He doesn't suggest that his horrors might not exist; he spares no detail to increase their vividness. (pp. 20-1)

The Land of Oz, Baum's second Oz book, offers no points of comparison with Carroll's sequel but is a fable of sex warfare, in which a palace revolt led by a strong-minded girl calling herself General Jinjur unseats King Scarecrow. (p. 22)

Ozma of Oz re-introduces Dorothy, washed ashore in a floating chicken coop with a talking yellow hen, on the beach of the land of Ev (perhaps Eve?). . . . Ev turns out to be the familiar Baum matriarchal fairyland. . . .

The fourth book is the first to introduce a boy—that is, a boy who stays boy. Whether or not he is responsible, ***Dorothy and the Wizard in Oz*** is one of the most gloomy and depressing of the series. Most of the action takes place underground, and a steady succession of horrible characterizations express the most implacable hatred of anything fertile or human. (p. 23)

[The] first four books contain the meat of Baum's message. The later stories merely dilute and conventionalize this strong original flavor.

In these books Baum has found a surprising number of ways to vary his message; or, as a psychoanalyst might say, his neurosis has found a variety of outlets. In the analyst's terminology again, everything is "over-determined." Nothing is ever simply demonstrated once.

Very particularly in ***The Wonderful Wizard of Oz,*** the most artistic as it is the most honest of the series—for only there are we occasionally allowed to glimpse the pathos of his condition—has Baum set out, almost as a real artist might, to personalize all his anxieties.

He is by definition Dorothy, an innocent child, who through no fault of her own (but very luckily nevertheless) kills her mother as she is born. It is all for the best, everyone assures her, but still she is guiltily anxious to get out of a world where such things happen. She goes to look for her father, who can, perhaps, *send her back.* Her innocence is complemented and balanced by the innocence of the Scarecrow (Baum again) who has just been born and is therefore of the same age as Dorothy. A love affair is indicated, and of course Dorothy does love the Scarecrow best of all, but after all he is only a man stuffed with straw, he is an intellectual who only wants brains. As might be expected, the Scarecrow is never of any use to Dorothy in physical difficulties: he gives good advice, but is always getting knocked over or punched flat when the fighting begins. So the Woodchopper is required. He has *once* been a real man who has loved a woman, but an older woman has been jealous—not of him, but of his beloved who lives with her, in just what relationship is not explained—and by magic the Woodchopper's axe has repeatedly slipped until he is cut to pieces: a friendly tinsmith supplying prosthesis. The woodman still loves until his *heart* is cut through; but then he ceases to love. He means to ask Oz for a *heart* and afterward to return and ask the girl to marry him, when he can love her again. (He forgets all about this, incidentally, after he gets the heart, but maybe that is because it is really a heart that Oz gives him. The Woodman is a very delicate person and would be unlikely to call things by their proper names.)

There is a great deal of fine characterization in the Woodman, who of course is Baum again at a more advanced stage. He is depressed, weeps easily, avoids stepping on insects and hurting people's feelings, and is pathetically grateful for Dorothy's ministrations. He is of tin—the ridiculous metal. The terrible "chopper who chops off your head" is armed with a gleaming axe which he uses for nothing except to cut down trees (until later; Baum's characterizations do not hold very long). He is a nightmare de-glamorized. All good so far.

The Lion is Baum again as in man's conventional sexual role What is the point of being king of beasts, he seems to be saying, and come roaring out of the forest, if I am full of inward doubts and fears, and can be stopped by a slap on the nose? What is the use of a thick beard and big teeth and loud voice, if they cannot even get me a mate (as they apparently have not)? Better if I turned into a little dog and ran at this girl's heels—because that's what I want to do, if the truth were known. And so another nightmare is tamed.

It should not pass unnoticed that Baum, while satisfying himself, has also satisfied the canons of conventional romance by surrounding his heroine not only with protectors but with guardians. What was usually accomplished by relationship or senescence—and the 19th century made great play with uncles and grandfathers—he accomplishes by emasculation, not only once but three times.

However the attitude so far (and Baum is one-third through his book) is not unhealthy. Three objects of greater fear to a child than a Lion, a Scarecrow, and a Chopper (who is also a Cripple), could not easily be named, and yet Baum has kept them all gentle and touching. He has pumped them full of himself, and since he is a harmless and pathetic fellow, he is saying in substance to the child, "And so are your fears!"

But he has gone as far as he can on that line. Ten pages after the fake-Lion he introduces the Kalidahs, terrifying invented animals. The childish reader invariably trembles at this point, puzzling the adult, to whom the Kalidahs do not seem that terrible. But the child is right. There are other terrors in the world then besides "men," he feels; the Kalidahs are *real.* They are all the more real because they are made-up. There is no chance of them ever turning back into Daddy. We are in the world of nightmare, of fever dreams, where a pet grows the "body of a bear and the head of a tiger."

Baum is now definitely committed to a tale of adventure, and little more healthy can occur. The Emerald City ought by right to be a vast fake, because its people are compelled to wear green glasses, but actually it is a fake-fake and the emeralds are real. The Wizard plays out all over again the Baum "appearances": he is a Head, a beautiful Lady, and a horrible Beast. His ultimate exposure is long deferred. For the story he is a father-figure who instead of being tender and loving, or even weak and pathetic, is suspicious and implacable. Instead of consoling and comforting his daughter, he ridicules her fears; and tells her she can only win his love by killing again. Even in the conventional story-book sense the Wizard is a horrible man. He insists that the Witch is evil, but admits she has never harmed him; it is only because she *might* that he wishes Dorothy to kill her; he is too cowardly to do so himself. He is Baal or Moloch, immolating children to placate the elements; and this aspect of his character is suggested by his fourth appearance, as a flaming ball of fire.

No one could ever possibly like the Wizard after this self-indictment; and yet his subsequent devaluation is only used to humanize him, even to justify him: fear makes us do anything! "I think you are a very bad man," Dorothy says; "Oh no, my dear," he replies, safely complaisant now that his arch-enemy is liquidated, "I'm really a very good man; but I'm a very bad Wizard, I must admit." Dorothy is not quite reassured. When he satisfies her friends, however (which is not very hard to do), she allows herself to be appeased. Poor Dorothy! Her history is that of a gradual reconciliation.

Glinda, the Good Witch, must not be taken as a mother-symbol. The mothers are all ugly old women, who get it in the neck deservedly. Glinda is eternally young and eternally beautiful. She has never married; she could hardly be a mother! Glinda, in boarding-school terminology, is Dorothy's *ideal*. There is no man good enough for her. To emphasize this point, a long story is told about one of Glinda's remote ancestresses and her difficulties in choosing a husband. True love, in Oz, is love between girls, when one is a little older than the other, innocent, sterile, and uncompetitive. Glinda thinks only of what Dorothy wants. . . . Kindliness repays adoration, for Glinda. The sixth form puts the third form on to the ropes, and all ends happily at Prize-Day.

Oz revenges as many old injuries as it invents fantastic fulfillments: the chief resentment apparently, next to having been brought into the world in the wrong form, is for having been brought into the world at all. Though "mothers" are worse than "fathers" in the Oz world, both are preferably extinct altogether. In no other American children's books, even Horatio Alger's, are there so many orphans. No human Oz-star has both parents at once. Only the supers have a normal and usually comic family life. The animals fare no better: there are no records of the parentage of the Cowardly Lion, the Hungry Tiger, or Jim the Cab-horse. Eureka the cat is a foundling. Billina is presumably immaculately hatched and brought up by a farmer boy who (to make the double point) never knew until too late whether she was a hen or a rooster. But the horrible Dragonettes have a horrible mother.

Baum's fondness for automata and magically-created beings is of course due to this same rejection or exclusion of natural begetting. Only the Tin Woodman, who we already know to be the most honest and touching of the Ozian creatures, is allowed mention of a real father and mother, though both are long dead. The Scarecrow is the contrivance of two farmers (male), and Tik-Tok the invention of two inventors (male). Tip by himself, while still male, gives life to the Gump and the Saw-horse, but these are very lumpish productions, almost stillbirths; it would seem, in Oz as in the real world, that two progenitors are really necessary. Mombi and Tip's creation of Jack Pumpkinhead seems to be an uglified travesty of birth (as Tip's later transformation is a sweetened travesty of emasculation). After the boy has laboriously worked to make his man, the old woman comes along and sprinkles it with the powder of life, quickening it for her own nefarious purposes. . . . The solemn Jack Pumpkinhead insists on addressing Tip as "Father"; and since Tip is a little boy who is really a little girl, the confusions and insults appear deliberately multiplied.

The drama of decapitation (in the psychoanalytic vocabulary, decapitation and castration are synonyms) is played over and over and again as entr'acte. The Tin Woodman, who has once chopped off his own head, chops off the head of a hunting Wildcat. Oz first appears as an enormous Head, hairless, armless and legless. The Lion kills his opponent, the spider-monster, by striking off its head. The Scarecrow twists the necks of the Crows. The Scarecrow's head is also removable (he tells Oz: "You are quite welcome to take my head off, as long as it will be a better one when you put it on again"); and this is only one of a selection of demountable, retractable and replaceable heads that culminate in Langwidere's gallery of thirty. The Hammerheads use their heads like battering-rams; the Scoodlers theirs as missiles. The Gump is all head. Jack Pumpkinhead deserves his name: he is in continual fear lest his head rot off. And so on. The *conversations* about decapitation recall that other humorous work *The Mikado*.

Billina the hen is Oz's final topsy-turvy insult to injury. On the surface a "sensible" young female, she will have nothing to do with love, which like the suffragettes of Jinjur's army she sees only as masculine presumption ("Do you think I'd let that speckled villain of a rooster lord it over *me*?"). She lays eggs and has, apparently, hatched them, but she never mentions the offspring of this incubation; the barnyard role of the mother-hen is not for her. She speaks of "thirteen" as a suitable clutch to illustrate, presumably, her real feelings about this unlucky necessity. Laying to her is a sanitary habit ("I feel better since I laid my morning egg"), and she is only concerned with the freshness (infertility) of her product. She connives in the use of her eggs as poisonous weapons; in fact suggests it. Though she frees the Queenmother of Ev and her children, it is not out of maternal concern: she derides the Queen's anxiety and tells her sarcastically, "Don't worry. Just at present they (the lifeless children) are out of mischief and perfectly safe, for they can't even wiggle. Come with me, if you please, and I'll show you how pretty they look." Billina's reward, "a beautiful necklace of pearls and sapphires" is, like Ozma's new clothes, the typical material reward of the spoilt-child gold-digger—and should be contrasted with the merely appetitive fudge and chocolates awarded Jinjur and her suffragettes.

Sociologically viewed, the Oz myth as Baum created it is a vast transvaluation of juvenile romantic values. Boys' adventures become girls' adventures; girls' humiliations become boys' humiliations; boys' affairs with older boys become girls' affairs with older girls; and the mother is the villain instead of the father. It is a transvaluation because the values remain the same: traveling, fighting and killing achieve the rewards, and the punishments are subordination and domesticity. (It should be remembered that the Wicked Witch "tortures" Dorothy by making her do housework!) The arena is no longer the social one of Louisa May Alcott but the transvestite one of a boy-turned-girl. Baum has kissed his elbow; Tip has put on women's clothes; but it is only to breed more girls-turned-boys. (In this connection it may not be insignificant to note that the "L." in L. Frank Baum stood for "Lyman." Only a determination to expunge the "man" from his name would seem to explain this amputation of his signature, so important to a writer.)

Baum's frantic popularity really requires no further explanation. Most of his readers were young girls. This audience, if not completely understanding, could appreciate his idolization of an immature and impubescent femininity. The combination of innocence with authority that produced all these girlish brows wrinkling over problems of finance and policy, these girlish arms driving chariots of state or extended imperiously, these girlish feet in the silver of safety or the satin of luxury, had the attraction, to them, of a mirror of Narcissus. (pp. 24-30)

Osmond Beckwith, "The Oddness of Oz," in Kulchur, *No. 4, Fall, 1961, pp. 19-30.*

MARIUS BEWLEY

[*The following excerpt is taken from an essay originally published in the* New York Review of Books *on December 3, 1964.*]

The considerable imaginative achievement represented by the fourteen Oz books has been ignored for well over half a century.

Publicity poster for Baum's children's books dated 1901.

Even those critics who have recognized their classic status have hesitated to approve their style; but Baum was always a satisfactory writer, and at his best his prose reflects themes and tensions that characterize the central tradition of American literature. Since he wished to create in Oz a specifically American fairyland, or Utopia, it is not particularly surprising that at first his writing was influenced by the comparatively new school of realists and naturalists. The description of the grimly impoverished Kansas farm of Dorothy Gale's aunt and uncle with which ***The Wonderful Wizard of Oz*** begins is a very good example of writing in this genre. . . . But Baum soon moved on to more distinguished models in the same mode, and in at least one instance, surprising as it may seem, he appears to have been strongly influenced by Stephen Crane. (pp. 255-56)

[Crane's] short story "The Open Boat," published in 1897, has been described by more than one eminent critic as the best short story in English up to the time of its publication, which is nonsense of course. In 1907 Baum published his third Oz book, ***Ozma of Oz.*** The opening chapter of this book, "The Girl in the Chicken-Coop," is so close to Crane's story in theme, imagery, and technique that it is impossible to imagine, on comparing the two in detail, that the similarity is wholly, or even largely, accidental. (pp. 256-57)

Perhaps it was the nature of the land whose history he was writing that drew Baum's style away from literary realism. At any rate, after several more books, one becomes aware of allegorical themes and attitudes that put one in mind of Hawthorne's short stories. In ***The Scarecrow of Oz*** Baum tells the story of a Princess whose heart was frozen by witchcraft so that she could no longer love. . . . (p. 259)

It is possible that Jack Pumpkinhead was suggested to Baum by Hawthorne's "Feathertop: A Moralized Legend," but he draws nearest to Hawthrone in his treatment of certain themes that, without breaking the frame of a children's story, explore the heart and personality with a good deal of subtlety. In ***The Tin Woodman of Oz*** Baum searches into the ambiguities of identity and one's relation to one's own past in a remarkable episode. The Tin Woodman, whose man's body was gradually replaced by tin parts as his limbs, torso, and head were successively severed by an enchanted ax, sets out in this book to recover his past and to rectify certain sins of omission of which he had been guilty in his youth. In a remote part of the Munchkin country he comes face to face with his severed but still living head. . . . (pp. 259-60)

A pilgrim in search of his own past, its recovery proves impossible for the Tin Woodman, and he and his former head remain strangers without a common ground of meeting. The pilgrimage back through time to one's origins and source was a favorite theme of many American writers. . . . Baum, who handles the theme expertly enough on his own level, also finds that the past cannot be repeated, or even rediscovered in any satisfying way.

Probably Baum never tried to incorporate a consistent meaning or set of values in his books, yet a significant pattern of values does exist in them. We know, for example, that General Jinjur, who captures the Emerald City with her army of girls in ***The Land of Oz,*** is an extended satire on the suffragette movement; and Baum's deep affection for monarchy and the trappings of royalty that runs through all the books reflects a facet of sensibility shared by many nineteenth-century Americans. Baum created a land so rich in palaces, crowns, costume, heraldry, and pomp that he had no grounds for complaining, as [Henry] James had done, of the poverty of the American environment in supplying the writer with material. Yet Oz remains unmistakably an *American* fairyland. In nothing is this more apparent than in the way Baum transforms magic into a glamorized version of technology and applied science. (pp. 260-61)

[The] tension between pastoralism and technology is one of the things the Oz books are about, whether Baum was conscious of it or not. . . . It is a distinguishing mark of the Oz books that a satisfactory resolution of the tension is achieved in them, and the Munchkins on their small farms in the East continue down to the time that Baum wrote of them to exemplify an agrarian ideal. (p. 262)

[Magic] is the science or technology of Oz. (p. 264)

The Ozites understood the necessity of bringing this source of energy and power under the control of the central government, and only Glinda the Good, the Wizard, and Ozma herself were entitled to practice magic legally. By this prohibition, which placed government restrictions on promiscuous and uncontrolled "technological" experimentation, Oz retained her pastoral landscape and guaranteed her people's happiness. There were of course criminal practitioners of magic—particularly in the still wild Gillikin Country in the north—but one of the principal functions of government in Oz was to keep these enemies of order under control. There were machines in Oz, but as with Tik-Tok, the clockwork man, they tended to be thoroughly humanized. (p. 265)

Selflessness and loving kindness constitute the very air of Oz. . . .

One has to bear in mind that love in Oz is a value actively present in the stories, dramatized in the action, and realized in the characters. There is nothing self-conscious, sentimental, or priggish about it. It is the imaginative element in which Dorothy, Ozma, Glinda, the Tin Woodman, the Scarecrow, the Cowardly Lion, and all the rest exist and have their meaning. As [Russel B.] Nye points out, the most evil character in all the Oz books is the ruler of the Phantasms, whose title is the First and Foremost. That beautifully sinister title sums up the final meaning of Oz history. The aggrandizement of the individual and private self at the expense of others is the root of all evil. (p. 266)

[Oz] was a world in which magical technology was strictly controlled, and in which perfect selflessness and love was the element of life. It was, in short, the Great Good Place. (p. 267)

Marius Bewley, "The Land of Oz: America's Great Good Place," in his Masks & Mirrors: Essays in Criticism, *Atheneum, 1970, pp. 255-67.*

FRED ERISMAN

Students of American progressivism generally agree that one of the difficulties of the Progressive leaders was their inability to adapt essentially rural ideals to a complex urban society. . . . [The] Progressives, despite their predominantly urban upbringing, were largely committed to a rural ethos. From this commitment came their dedication to the ideals of the Founding Fathers, their simplistic attitude toward many of the problems of the city, and their firm belief in simplicity and individual responsibility. From these beliefs, in turn, came the idealistic tone characteristic of Progressive reform. . . . [Most] Progressives seemed to feel that the old, absolute ways were the best—if only they could be reestablished.

An unusual and suggestive dramatization of this problem occurs in the works of L. Frank Baum . . . [Baum] is best known for his series of fantasies set in the magical Land of Oz. These fantasies, when examined in conjunction with one of his lesser-known series (the "Aunt Jane's Nieces" books, which Baum began in 1906 as "Edith Van Dyne"), reveal one man's reaction to the Progressive dilemma. Although Baum usually avoided overly political comments in his published writings, these books nonetheless illustrate one American's commitment to the older value system, his tacit recognition of the dilemma posed by this commitment, and the resolution that he evolved for himself and for his readers.

On the surface, the Oz stories and the Aunt Jane's Nieces books seem far apart. The fantasies tell of a utopian fairyland inhabited by talking animals, pleasant people and benevolent monarchs. Life is tranquil: the country is agrarian by nature, evil is almost completely absent and death is unknown. In contrast, the Aunt Jane's Nieces series tells of life in contemporary America, complete with political chicanery, slums, snobbery and war. Although each series contains characters who speak for the traditional ideals of America, the characters themselves function differently. Dorothy Gale . . . tests rural ideals against the fairyland's magic; John Merrick and his three nieces . . . provide a traditional point of reference in the changing world of 20th century America. All of these characters embody what Baum considers the ideal; from their adventures and reactions in the worlds they meet comes his picture of American life.

Even more striking than the books' differences, however, are their similarities. Both series, like Progressivism, are grounded in the traditional ideals of an unsophisticated America. Consider, for example, the virtue of generosity. In the Land of Oz, generosity is the basis of the entire economy. . . . It is an economy in which money is unnecessary, for generosity is shared by all. The same attitude in a modern setting appears in the accounts of Aunt Jane's Nieces; though money is much in evidence, selfishness is considered bad, generosity good. (pp. 616-17)

Simplicity also unifies the two series. Despite the opulence of Oz, the inhabitants relish simplicity. In fact, Baum's belief in American simplicity wins Dorothy Gale royal status in Oz. . . . Merrick and the nieces also revere simplicity. Patsy Doyle, one of the nieces, is described approvingly as "so absolutely unaffected that she won all hearts." Even John Merrick, despite his riches, is untainted. . . . To Baum, sophistication implies something undesirable; in his scheme of things, only the simple people are worthy.

An even more obvious unifying factor in the two sets of books is individualism. Baum gives to the people of Oz an unfailing respect for the individual. Early in the series, the Scarecrow remarks that "The only people worthy of consideration in this world are the unusual ones. For the common folks are like the leaves of a tree, and live and die unnoticed." (p. 618)

John Merrick and his wards share this belief. Patsy Doyle, though relishing the gifts showered upon her by her wealthy uncle, is disturbed by "the loss of her independence."... To Merrick (and, therefore, to Baum), [establishing the girls as newspaper publishers] is a source of many virtues. Above all, it impresses upon the nieces the importance of self-reliance, originality and resourcefulness. Baum calls these the attributes of the true individual.... (pp. 618-19)

Perhaps the most notable of the qualities shared by Oz and America is a firm belief in the virtues of industry. This is particularly striking in Oz, because Baum creates a magical world in which work is unnecessary. Nonetheless, the people of Oz revel in work.... Baum's views on the virtue of work are clear: work is an end in itself, and its chief benefits come as much from the effort as from the achievement.

The same attitude toward the redeeming nature of work permeates the world of Aunt Jane's Nieces. Here, too, Baum repeatedly extols the beauties of work. (pp. 619-20)

At this point, the similarities in Oz and America end, for Oz is everything that the nieces' America is not. In Oz, Baum has created a world in which the professed, rural ideals of America are actualities. Ozians practice the ideals of generosity, simplicity, individualism and industry as part of their daily lives. They know no other way, and the result is a pastoral utopia. The nieces, however, live in another world entirely. As they, like the Progressives, attempt to live by rural values in an urban world, they move from one predicament to another—predicaments caused by their own innocent and trusting natures. The ideal individual, Baum seems unconsciously to say, cannot function in the real world.

This inability has many expressions. ***Aunt Jane's Nieces At Work,*** for example, tells how the nieces support the political campaign of a close friend (who is running on a reform ticket), only to be stymied by the machinations of their Democratic opponents.... And, in ***Aunt Jane's Nieces On Vacation,*** the nieces' newspaper rouses the ire of a village mill-owner, brings about a strike at his plant, and puts the girls in severe danger. In each case, the characters find themselves in a situation in which neither Merrick's wealth nor their own innate goodness is of the least use. This in many ways parallels the plight of the Progressives: their old beliefs are unsuited to the new world.

The failure of Merrick and the nieces to adapt to 20th century complexity is a suggestive failure, particularly when paralleled with the carefree world that Baum presents in Oz. In both series, Baum advances a value system that he feels is good. Only in the imaginary world, though, is this system viable. In the real world, it breaks down, forcing Baum to introduce a character antithetical to everything that he believes in. He recognizes that the old ways are inadequate; rather than compromise the standards of his central characters, he creates a non-ideal character who brings the stories to a satisfactory ending.

This character is Quintus Fogerty, a private detective of superlative ability who clears up the election . . . and breaks the strike. But, though his ability is great, Fogerty is very much a person of the real world.... His regard for established authority goes only so far; when it suits his purposes, he freely violates the restrictions of urban life. "Never mind the speed limit," he snarls to a taxi-driver; "No one will interfere with us. I'm Fogerty." (pp. 620-21)

Despite his personal unpleasantness, however, Fogerty is Baum's conception of the "new American" that the urban world will require. He is not bound, as are the central characters, by the traditional ways of achieving good; he is free to use even the forces of evil (e.g., deceit or willful lawbreaking) to attain his goal. (p. 621)

Baum's use of Fogerty to resolve the Aunt Jane's Nieces books provides a key to the significance of both that series and the Oz tales. When he began each series . . . , Baum was a man of mature years. Born in 1856, he had by 1900 presumably committed himself to a definite system of values. These values, though, are those of an earlier time, and Baum had to reconcile them with the demands of the modern world. Significantly, he could not. What remains is an insoluble conflict between a value system no longer applicable (but held too firmly to be given up) and the recognition that new ways are needed.

This conflict appears explicitly in the parallel development of the two series. As the difficulties of Aunt Jane's Nieces become more and more complex, Oz becomes more and more idyllic.... The course of the books suggests that as Baum saw his ideals crushed by the urban world, his delineation of Oz became more perfect. Confronted at last by the ultimate manifestation of the new world, modern war (as presented in ***Aunt Jane's Nieces in the Red Cross,*** 1915), he gave up entirely. With the exception of one abortive series, the "Mary Louise" books, he wrote nothing after 1915 except Oz tales. Seemingly aware at last of his inability to reconcile his beliefs with the modern world, aware at last that he could never become the "new man" personified by Fogerty (and aware that he would not care to), Baum turned to the fantastic world of Oz. Here, in an admittedly unrealistic land, he was able to achieve the realization of his ideals that was impossible in the world of reality. He had found, for himself, an answer to the problems of Progressivism.

It is perhaps asking too much of Baum to call his works a parable of Progressive reform idealism, but the notion is a tempting one. In the two series, he establishes the dichotomy that appears throughout the entire Progressive movement—on the one hand, the vision of an ideal state in which the law is supreme and the people are the law, and on the other, the bleak realization that his ideal state must be built with the clay and straw of 20th century America. (pp. 621-22)

Baum (like the nieces) failed in his quest for an ideal America. Both Baum and the Progressives were faced with the inadequacy of traditional values in the modern world. The Progressives, like Fogerty, by flexibility, by adaptation and in great part by luck saw many of their goals become reality. Baum, on the other hand, clung rigidly to his convictions. (pp. 622-23)

And yet, Baum may well have achieved a success not immediately apparent from a consideration of his works. Both series, Oz and Aunt Jane's Nieces, depend upon the question "what if." The adventures of Merrick and the nieces are, in their own way, fantastic: they record what might happen should a few people try to practice traditional ideals in a modern context. But the fantastic world of Oz builds upon a slightly different question—"What if everyone practiced these ideals?" Baum's success does not lie in his own answer to the question, for his answer is impossible. Instead, his success and his vindication lie in the audience of whom he asks the question.

Baum wrote for children—children who would become the adults of the next generation. He presents to them a twofold picture of the world: in one form it is flawed, but still possesses, in the traditional values, the seeds of perfection; in the other, it is perfect. . . . If Baum's generation failed in applying these values to the modern world, perhaps the next generation would succeed.

Baum's failures parallel the failure of the Progressives to adapt completely to modern needs; they are all the more striking for the intensity of his belief. His success, in the utopia of Oz, looks ahead to the possible successes of the future. If enough people realize that the old ways are still viable, he suggests, and if enough people make a conscious attempt to practice them, the ideal America may yet become a reality. Indeed, though one cannot say so with certainty, it is possible that Baum, by suggesting to the children of the early 20th century what might be achieved, helped to preserve American idealism through the reality of a depression and two world wars. If so, his success is not a minor one. (p. 623)

Fred Erisman, "L. Frank Baum and the Progressive Dilemma," in American Quarterly, *Vol. XX, No. 3, Fall, 1968, pp. 616-23.*

C. WARREN HOLLISTER

[*The following excerpt is from an essay that originally appeared in the Christmas 1971 issue of the* Baum Bugle.]

A few years ago Martin Gardner made the provocative statement, "America's greatest writer of children's fantasy was, as everyone knows except librarians and critics of juvenile literature, L. Frank Baum" [see excerpt date 1957]. Whatever one may think of Mr. Gardner's judgment of Baum, he is on the mark in suggesting that few librarians and children's literature critics are Oz enthusiasts. What do they have against the Oz books?

Martin Gardner suggests several possibilities: that the Oz books are too popular and librarians get tired of checking them in and out, that the books are poorly bound, that they are illustrated in an unfashionably realistic style. I can't believe that these are the reasons.

I think the answer is perfectly straightforward: The fourteen Oz books of L. Frank Baum fall short of many other children's fantasies when measured by the four criteria which critics usually apply to children's fiction: *theme, characterization, plot,* and *style*. "We have nothing against Baum," the critics would say. "It's only that there are so many *better* writers of fantasy—Carol Kendall, Lloyd Alexander, Alan Garner, Tove Jansson, P. L. Travers, Mary Norton, Lucy Boston, Kenneth Grahame, on and on." (p. 192)

The difference between [***The Wizard of Oz*** and Ursula K. Le Guin's *A Wizard of Earthsea*] is striking. Le Guin's *Wizard of Earthsea* is a deeply intelligent, sensitive, imaginative fantasy that excels in all four criteria: it has a great underlying theme (coming of age), rich characterization, a tight plot, and a lean, rhythmic style. Baum's ***Wizard of Oz*** doesn't measure up. It appears to have no underlying theme—no unity of conception. Its characterizations seem shallow. Dorothy has no inner problems, doesn't develop, doesn't grow. Oz never really changes. As for plot, it rambles. There is a pointless story within a story in Chapter 14, and the last seven chapters, involving a long journey to the Quadling country, are anticlimactic. The style, which has been described, unfairly, as "sentimental" is, in fact, straightforward but undistinguished, lacking in sparkle and in witty, surprising turns of phrase.

So much for ***The Wizard of Oz.*** Baum's other Oz books yield to much the same criticisms. Why bother with them at all?

The difficulty is, we can't really avoid them. For the past seventy years children have persisted in loving Oz. (p. 193)

Oz is uniquely popular, intellectually influential, and seemingly timeless—yet mediocre with respect to theme, characterization, plot, and style. Obviously something is badly out of focus. The critics would argue that popularity is irrelevant, standards are everything. . . .

In continuing to insist on uncompromising, adult-imposed library norms, we may lose much of what remains of our child audience. This may well be the cost of paying too much attention to good but narrow standards, too little to what children love. (p. 194)

My plea, then, is not to redeem L. Frank Baum (who hardly needs it) but to achieve something much more basic: a long-needed critical reexamination of the four criteria. . . . What critics must do, for their own good health and professional credibility, is to stop telling us why Oz is bad and start figuring out why Oz is great; not "Down with Oz—it fails to meet our criteria," but "Where have our criteria gone wrong?" This is their job—their profound obligation to the field of children's literature and to themselves.

As a beginning, I offer this suggestion. I propose the addition of a fifth criterion—the most important of them all for children's fantasy—*three-dimensionality*. By three-dimensionality I don't mean simply the old cliché, "willing suspension of disbelief." That negative, vapid phrase would far better be expressed positively: "the compulsion to believe." But three-dimensionality means still more. It is the magical tugging of the child-reader through the page into the story—into the other world. You not only suspend disbelief in Oz; you not only positively, ardently believe in Oz; you are there!

Three-dimensionality is, I suggest, the secret of Oz's astonishing popularity, just as it is the secret of the more recent popularity of C. S. Lewis's Narnia stories, particularly among English children, and of Tolkien's adult fantasy, *The Lord of the Rings*. By comparison, Ursula Le Guin's *Wizard of Earth-*

Baum's library at Ozcot, his home in Hollywood, California. Many of the Oz books were written here.

sea, Lloyd Alexander's *High King,* and most other distinguished modern fantasies are two-dimensional. Beautifully plotted, written, charactered, and themed, they lack the special magic of Oz. They lack that beguilement, utterly transcending the four criteria, which brings joyous intoxication to the child-reader and, afterward, a memory that never passes—a recollection of the taste of joy, the three-dimensional experience of going into another universe where everything is brighter and more fragrant, more dangerous, and more alive—a world of intensely satisfying unexpectedness—a real journey— . . . and with a happy ending always.

This longing for a journey into elsewhere runs deep in the human psyche. (pp. 194-95)

Many children's critics—puritans at heart—suspect a book such as ***The Wizard of Oz*** that does nothing for the child but give him joy. It teaches him very little, doesn't preach, doesn't improve his literary taste. But joy has its uses, too. No child can make the journey to Oz without acquiring in the process a fascination for books, a realization that reading needn't always be the sour, educative, edifying medicine it sometimes seems in school. Reading becomes an exciting quest for other books touched with the same enchantment as the Oz books.

What a pity that this touch of enchantment, so real to children, is invisible to so many adult critics. Perhaps it is because adult critics were themselves invisible to Baum, who wrote exclusively for children. His stories draw the child in, carrying him to Oz as effectively as did Ozma's magic belt. But the critic is usually left behind. To him, the pages of the Oz books are opaque—two-dimensional. The critic reads what is on the page, but can't see through the page—or pass through the page—to Oz. So he is bewildered: he wonders that it's all about—weak plot, shallow characters, no theme, pedestrian style. Dorothy is superficial? Rather she is broadly sketched so that children can *become* Dorothy for a time, ride the cyclone with her, walk in her silver shoes down the Yellow Brick Road as they could not if Dorothy had hated her father or been astigmatic or had an I.Q. of 156, or were tormented by oncoming puberty. The critic asks, why don't Oz characters ever develop and mature? Every child knows the answer: nobody grows older in Oz. Why aren't the Oz plots more unified? Real adventures in magical lands are, as children know, tantalizingly open-ended. Why isn't Baum's style more glittering? Because glitter gets in the way. To pass through the page into the other world, the words must be as nearly *invisible* as possible. They should merely carry the story, as Baum's words do effectively, unpretentiously. Where is the theme? The theme is Oz.

If critics recognized this fifth criterion—three-dimensionality—Oz would enter our libraries not begrudged but warmly welcomed. The critics and librarians who have given their lives—and their love—to children's books would at last discover the very books that American children have always loved most of all. More than that, critics and librarians would learn the secret that three-dimensionality is more than a mere criterion. It is a kind of magic that carries one between worlds—that has transported countless children to Glinda's castle, the Nome King's caverns, the Emerald City. It might carry librarians and critics there too, if only they understood what so many of our children know—that there really is a way to Oz. (pp. 195-96)

C. Warren Hollister, "Oz and the Fifth Criterion," in The Wizard of Oz *by L. Frank Baum, edited by Michael Patrick Hearn, Schocken Books, 1983, pp. 192-96.*

RAY BRADBURY

[The following excerpt is from an essay dated 1973.]

Let us consider two authors whose books were burned in our American society during the past 70 years. Librarians and teachers did the burning very subtly by not buying. And not buying is as good as burning. Yet, the authors survived.

Two gentlemen of no talent whatsoever.

Two mysteries of literature, if you can call their work literature.

Two men who changed the world somewhat more than they ever dreamed, once they were in it, once their books came to be published and moved in the minds and blood of 8 year olds, 10 year olds, 12 year olds.

One of them changed the future of the entire world and that Universe which waited for Earthmen to birth themselves in space with rockets.

His name: Edgar Rice Burroughs. (p. xi)

The second man, also a "mediocre" talent, if you can believe the teachers and librarians of some 70 years, created a country, Oz, and peopled it with not one influence, but several dozens.

His name: L. Frank Baum.

And once you begin to name his people in his country, it is hard to stop: Dorothy, Toto (indeed a very real person), The Tin Man, The Scarecrow, Tik-Tok, Ozma, Polychrome, The Patchwork Girl, Ruggedo, Prof. Wogglebug, Aunty Em, The Wicked Witch of the ——. You see how easily the names pop out, without having to go look them up! . . .

Let us get on with the mystery of L. Frank Baum, that faintly old-maidish man who grew boys inward to their most delightful interiors, kept them home, and romanced them with wonders between their ears. . . .

[Baum is the] man who wanted to work magic but, oh dear, not *hurt* anyone along the way. He is that rare chef who would never dream to yell at his cooks, yet got results anyway: a bakery-kitchen full of valentines, sweet-meats, dragons without teeth, robots with feelings, Tin men who were once real (to reverse the Pinocchio myth), and girls who are so toothsome and innocent that if you nibble them at all, it would only be their toes, ears, and elbows. (p. xii)

[Baum is] a man who set out, unknowingly, to slaughter his own best talents, but was saved by a mob of strange creatures from another land who knew better than he that they needed to be born. And in birthing themselves insured the miraculous fact that if we all went to the nearest travel agency tomorrow and were asked if we wanted to go to Alice's Wonderland or The Emerald City, it would be that Green Place, and the Munchkins and the Quadlings and all the rest, every time!

It is fascinating to compare memories of Dorothy and Oz and Baum with Alice and the Looking Glass and the Rabbit Hole and Lewis Carroll, who made out better with librarians and teachers.

When we think of Oz a whole mob of incredibly lovely if strange people falls across our minds.

When we think of Alice's encounters we think of mean, waspish, small, carping, bad-mannered children ranting against *going* to bed, refusing to get *out* of bed, not liking the food, hating the temperature, minding the weather out of mind.

If Love is the lubricant that runs Oz to glory, Hate is the mud in which all sink to ruin inside the mirror where poor Alice is trapped.

If everyone goes around democratically accepting each other's foibles in the four lands surrounding the Emerald City, and feeling nothing but amiable wonder toward such eccentricities as pop up, the reverse is true when Alice meets a Caterpillar or Tweedledum and Tweedledee or assorted knights, Queens, and Old Women. Theirs is an aristocracy of snobs, no one is good enough for them. They themselves are crazy eccentrics, but eccentricity in anyone else is beyond comprehension and should best be guillotined or grown small and stepped on.

Both books, both authors, stay in our minds, for mirror-reversed reasons. We float and fly through Oz on grand winds that make us beautiful kites. We trudge and fight our way through Wonderland, amazed that we survive at all.

Wonderland, for all its fantasy, is most practically real, that world where people have conniption fits and knock you out of line on your way onto a bus.

Oz is that place, ten minutes before sleep, where we bind up our wounds, soak our feet, dream ourselves better, snooze poetry on our lips, and decide that mankind, for all it's snide and mean and dumb, must be given another chance come dawn and a hearty breakfast.

Oz is muffins and honey, summer vacations, and all the easy green time in the world.

Wonderland is cold gruel and arithmetic at six a.m., icy showers, long schools.

It is not surprising that Wonderland is the darling of the intellectuals.

It is similarly not surprising that dreamers and intuitionists would reject the cold mirror of Carroll and take their chances on hotfooting it over the forbidden desert which at least promises utter destruction for purely inanimate reasons (the desert, after all, is not alive and doesn't know whom it is destroying), heading for Oz. Because in Oz of course reside amiable villains who are really not villains at all. Ruggedo is a fraud and a sham, for all his shouts and leaping about and uttering curses. Whereas Wonderland's Queen of Hearts really *does* chop off heads and children are beaten if they sneeze.

Wonderland is what we Are.

Oz is what we would hope and like to be.

The distance between raw animal and improved human can be measured by pegging a line between Alice's Rabbit Hole and Dorothy's Yellow Brick Road. (pp. xiii-xv)

I would like to believe Alice puts antibodies in our blood to help us survive Reality by showing us as the fickle, reckless, abrupt and alarming children we are. Children, of course, recognize themselves in the mostly bad-mannered grotesques that amble, stalk, and wander up to Alice.

But mean and loud and dreadful make for high tea lacking vitamins. Reality is an unsubstantial meal. Children also recognize a good dream when they see it, and so turn to Mr. Baum for the richer cake rather than the swamp gruel, for the mean-spirit that is really Santa Claus pretending at horrible. Children are willing to risk being smothered in true marmalade and saccharine. Mr. Baum provides both, with some narrow escapes from the maudlin and the things we damn as sentimentality. (p. xv)

Oz has not fallen, has it? Even though legions of bright people with grand good taste, and thousands of librarians have fired cannonades in tandem with hosts of sociologists who fear that the mighty Wizard will pollute their children, Baum, across the years, simply reaches in his pocket and produces, Shaggy Man that he is, the Love Magnet.

And if he is not the Shaggy Man, which he surely is, he is the Pied Piper who takes the adoring children away from their dull and unappreciative parents. Let the older folk survive into starvation with their algebra breakfasts, mathematical luncheons, and computer-data-fact dinners. To the children, Baum cries, "Let them eat cake!" but *means* it, and delivers.

In a story of mine . . . , *The Exiles,* fine fantasists like Poe and Hawthorne, along with Dickens, and Baum, find themselves shunted off to Mars as the non-dreamers, the super-psychological technicians, the book burners of the future, advance through towns and libraries, tossing the last of the great dreams into the furnace.

At the finale of my story, a rocket arrives on Mars, bearing with it the last copies in existence of Poe and Dickens and Baum. The captain of the ship burns these books on a dead Martian sea-bottom, and Oz at long last crashes over into ruins. . . . (pp. xvi-xvii)

I do not for a moment believe that day will ever come. The fight between the dreamers and the fact-finders will continue, and we will embody both in equal proportion, or risk all men singing *castratto* soprano for the literary popes. (p. xvii)

Baum is a small and inconsequential flower blooming in the shade of Shakespeare. . . . But both lived inside their heads with a mind gone wild with wanting, wishing, hoping, shaping, dreaming. There, if no other place, they touch fingertips.

In a world where books are machine-made for "age groups" and pass through dry-parchment analysts' hands before being pill-fed to kids, . . . Baum is needed. When the cities die, in their present form at least, and we head out into Eden again, which we must and will, Baum will be waiting for us. And if the road we take is not Yellow Brick why, damn it, we can imagine that it is. . . . (p. xviii)

Ray Bradbury, "Because, Because, Because. . . . ," in Wonderful Wizard, Marvelous Land *by Raylyn Moore, Bowling Green University Popular Press, 1974, pp. xi-xviii.*

RAYLYN MOORE

In general, . . . in Baum's best work, either the magic is restricted to the exotic locale or, if it occurs in a non-fairyland, it [is] made strikingly appropriate to its location. Dorothy might well fall into a cleavage in the earth during a quake if she were in California early in the century. So with the funnel-shaped windstorm on the Great Plains. Furthermore, it is plausible that Dorothy's house should be picked up and whirled away—half a mile or a thousand, what's the difference? Even adults can willingly accept the initial premise; children will not balk at the next, that the house comes down on a wicked witch. For the second premise is appropriate to the new locale, if not the old.

In the classic fairy tale, into which category several of Baum's non-Oz books fall, ***Queen Zixi*** in particular, the reader is not presented with this step-by-step chance to accept the improbable; the whole mythos is revealed immediately: take it or leave it. In the Oz series, on the other hand, Baum tested and found valid the rule that latter-day fantasy depends far more than other genres upon Coleridge's "willing suspension of disbelief." In most cases its plausibility (and acceptability) depends upon this same acceptance of an initial hypothesis not repugnant to credulity, which may or may not proceed to another more or less acceptable hypothesis. Just as in Oz, the reader is never given the chance to exclaim, with Alice, "Why you're only a pack of cards!"

It seems very likely, in fact, that in any ultimate assessment of Baum's books for children, his greatest strength and the source of his endurance will be seen to stem from the fundamental appeal of his mythic themes, combined with this imaginatively maintained high degree of conviction.

Beside these qualities even his other virtues seem overshadowed, though they should not be ignored. He was indeed wonderfully inventive. Like Lewis Carroll he understood how to write for young people without "talking down." Though he was never guilty of the kind of auctorial moralizing which characterizes the Charles Kingsley school of children's literature, his work does offer guidance painlessly stated and demonstrated which is at best useful and at worst inoffensive. And he could hold the attention of adults while speaking more directly to younger readers. . . . (pp. 149-50)

Not to be neglected either is the fact that Baum stories move briskly, and while there are occasional Pickwickian pauses for the story-within-the-story, the insertions are always as action-filled as the mainline adventure.

Baum is occasionally congratulated as well upon his clarity, and for the most part it is true that his language constructions are straightforward and that he avoids the alien expression and the polysyllabic word. This makes the more remarkable his occasional use of a word such as "retroussé."

But there is a misapprehension about Baum which deserves mention if only because it has been several times repeated. He is said by some to have ". . . possessed a flawless command of English," while in actuality, as any close reader of Baum knows, he was a master of the dangling modifier who also excelled at the frequent redundancy and the occasional solecism, hazards which could all have been avoided, incidentally, had he only been blessed with responsible copy editors. (pp. 150-51)

There remains to be mentioned a major flaw in flawless Oz, one that can be viewed both as a conscious, workaday problem of a series writer, and as an inherent failure of the golden-age archetype itself.

One of the primary objections of children's librarians and critics to series books in general is that while the original stories may be acceptable, the succeeding ones utilizing the same characters and settings tend to depend less on literary merit than on wilder, and consequently "thinner," variations on a single tested theme. Thus the child reader, for whom every book should open a new world and so extend his experience, is led time and again over the same known ground which annually grows more barren as the writer's imaginative faculty declines.

Baum is certainly not immune to this charge. The real difference between him and other series writers for children seems to be one of degree. For he managed to produce more than the usual number of creditable stories before the supply of creativity began to run low. The point is that it did run low. (pp. 152-53)

The Wizard is the best of all Oz books. Action is constant, the characters live, the plot is tightly managed, and the outcome immensely satisfactory. Above all, the allegory is sustained throughout.

Beside ***The Wizard,*** even ***The Land of Oz*** must take second place, although it too is a well conceived adventure, with allegorical overtones and a convincing set of characters. ***Ozma of Oz*** is less original; perhaps its best points are the introduction of two new characters (Tik-Tok and Billina) who come up in nearly every way to the standards of the earlier ones, and one of Baum's happier applications of the death-rebirth theme, in the descent to the underworld and return. In ***Dorothy and the Wizard*** this descent is abused by its very length and the near-horrors provided by purely evil enemies, while ***The Road to Oz*** errs in the other direction: it is little more than a casual excursion which ends in a party, to which Baum invites many of the characters from all his other fairy-tale books. While the quest pattern, now familiar, is preserved, there seems insufficient motivation for the sparse action here.

As if to make up for this very flaw, ***The Emerald City*** employs a double-quest plot; while the invaders of Oz are proceeding toward the city to destroy it, Dorothy and her party are junketing about Oz in an attempt to show Aunt Em and Uncle Henry the wonders. The stories are told in alternating chapters and suspense is sustained because the excursionists are happily oblivious to their danger until the last possible moment.

A more formal employment of the pattern appears in ***The Patchwork Girl.*** The reason for Ojo's long and trouble-fraught journey to the Emerald City is a valid one: he wants to save his uncle's life, and he exhibits the same sort of courage and resourcefulness shown by Dorothy in the first book. The Patchwork Girl herself is probably the last of Baum's truly successful inventions in the weird-character department. And these items may add up to making this the last of the really successful Oz books.

Probably because it was conceived first as a stage musical, ***Tik-Tok*** is little more than a reworking of the tailings of Baum's earlier and more successful "strikes." It begins with shipwreck, as does ***Ozma;*** the people of Oogaboo pick everything they need from trees, as do the people of Mo (and as Dorothy picks the dinner pails in ***Ozma;*** McKinley's slogan in the election campaign of 1900 had been "the full dinnerpail"). . . . As in ***Dorothy and the Wizard,*** the protagonists pick a ruler from a plant in a vegetable kingdom. And once again there is the descent to the underworld to rescue someone imprisoned there (Offenbach's *Orpheus in Hades* was very popular at the time) as there had been in ***Ozma.***

The other six books trail off into various degrees of paleness. ***Rinkitink*** is a fairy story which has practically nothing to do with Oz (some sources say it was an earlier story pulled into the series with minor rewriting), but this is no failing in either ***John Dough*** or ***Queen Zixi;*** both are imaginative and humorous. And this is probably the root of the problem: as we have seen, in the later books both the imagination and the humor have worn out.

Further, Oz-as-eden can now be seen to be Baum's greatest strength and greatest weakness. So long as the paradise remains in its prelapsarian state, the mother-goddess reigns unchallenged; it is only after the Fall that Eve becomes subject to her husband and the patriarchal Judeo-Christian cycle begins, with its consequent sorrows and responsibilities. And yet to remain in the Garden, never to emerge, is never to grow; it is recounting the myth (life to death) and leaving out half the story (death to rebirth). Any return to the womb is a regress to death, any attempt to exist in the static atmosphere of a state of perfect existence leads inevitably to tedium and nothingness. Where there can be no growth in any direction, there can be no freshness or change. Dorothy, because she could not grow up, could only deteriorate; Oz, always green, can never provide the cyclical miracle of the seasons. (pp. 168-71)

Playing the game of "if" is not always productive. And yet *if* Baum had stood by his original intention of making the ***Wizard*** a story without sequel, the result might have solved the problem of a bleak and changeless immortality. For Dorothy completes the cycle in that tale and returns to Kansas renewed, reborn, ready to grow up at last. On the other hand, such an early cut-off on Oz would have denied us ***Ozma of Oz*** and ***The Emerald City.*** (p. 172)

Perhaps in the end the real wonder of L. Frank Baum is that, of the hundreds of things he wrote, under pressure and otherwise, as many as six or seven books have proved so durable. And promise to go on enduring. (p. 173)

Raylyn Moore, in her Wonderful Wizard, Marvelous Land, *Bowling Green University Popular Press, 1974, 213 p.*

RUTH PLUMLY THOMPSON

[Thompson was an American author of children's books, journalist, playwright, and editor who continued writing the Oz series following Baum's death. Between 1921 and 1939, she created nineteen Oz books. Since the actual date of the following excerpt is unknown it is here dated 1976, the year of Thompson's death.]

In 1492 Christopher Columbus discovered America. In 1900 L. Frank Baum discovered Oz, the first American fairyland, a land whose characters like Mary Martin's famous song in *South Pacific* are "wholesome as blueberry pie," "corny as Kansas in August"—so utterly *us* and U.S.A., small wonder they have become a part of our language and folklore. . . . [Baum created a] *believable* unbelievable country.

This he could well do, being an imaginative realist, a distinctly American characteristic he shares with most of our boys and girls, past and present. True, they are dreamers, but active fun-loving dreamers—practical, too. In this merry plausibly plotted country, Baum gives them a land they can not only dream of but completely visualize, enter into, and enjoy. With little shrieks of laughter and vociferous cries of welcome and recognition, they have taken Oz to their collective hearts and claimed it for their own. (p. 176)

Quickly and concisely, Baum sketches in his geozofy as we travel along, touching briefly but with a nice attention to detail on the history and curious customs of this singular land. So deftly does he mix plausibility with implausibility, we never know where one begins and the other leaves off. (p. 177)

A child who may not be able to name offhand the capital of Nebraska or Montana, can tell you in a flash the capital of Oz and is often more familiar with its principal rivers, mountains, rulers, points of interest, and historical landmarks than with those of his native state—perhaps because he considers Oz his native state. In Oz, Baum actually added another state to the Union. To you it may be a state of mind, but to the boys and girls it is as definite and existent as Kansas or Maine. And woe—black woe to the author, dramatist, picture maker, or editor who dares to tamper with the cherished characters, geography, traditions, or laws of Oz! (p. 178)

Like all children born and growing up in the nineteen hundreds, I fell hungrily upon each new Oz book as it appeared and waited with breathless impatience for the next. All unconscious and unaware of the part Oz would play in my future and the many ways it would color and complicate my literary life, I chuckled with delicious abandon over the further adventures of the Scarecrow and his merry clan. And I assure there is many a chuckle in store. Baum not only loved and understood children, but talked to them on a comradely level with no condescension or ponderous moral in mind. Though each adventure had a gentle underlying lesson and purpose, none ever impinged on the story. Above all Baum had a sly sense of fun that delights children from six to sixty and makes the reading of Oz books to the small fry a treat, shall we say, instead of a treatment. (p. 179)

Ruth Plumly Thompson, "Concerning 'The Wonderful Wizard of Oz'," in The Wizard of Oz *by L. Frank Baum, edited by Michael Patrick Hearn, Schocken Books, 1983, pp. 176-79.*

GORE VIDAL

Like most Americans my age (with access to books), I spent a good deal of my youth in Baum's land of Oz. I have a precise, tactile memory of the first Oz book that came into my hands. It was the original 1910 edition of ***The Emerald City.*** . . . I also remember that I could not stop reading and rereading the book. But "reading" is not the right word. In some mysterious way, I was translating myself to Oz, a place which I was to inhabit for many years. . . . With ***The Emerald City,*** I became addicted to reading.

By the time I was fourteen, I had read Baum's fourteen Oz books as well as the nineteen Oz books written after his death in 1919 by . . . Ruth Plumly Thompson. . . .

Recently I was sent an academic dissertation. Certain aspects of Baum's ***The Land of Oz*** had reoccurred in a book of mine. Was this conscious or not? It was not. But I was intrigued. I reread ***The Land of Oz.*** Yes, I could see Baum's influence. I then reread ***The Emerald City of Oz.*** I have now reread all of L. Frank Baum's Oz books. I have also read a good deal of what has been written about him in recent years. Although Baum's books were dismissed as trash by at least two generations of librarians and literary historians, the land of Oz has managed to fascinate each new generation and, lately, Baum himself has become an OK subject if not for the literary critic for the social historian.

Even so, it is odd that Baum has received so little acknowledgment from those who owe him the most—writers. After all, those books (films, television, too, alas) first encountered in childhood do more to shape the imagination and its style than all the later calculated readings of acknowledged masters. . . . Lack of proper acknowledgment perhaps explains the extent to which Baum has been ignored by literary historians, by English departments, by. . . . As I write these words, a sense of dread. Is it possible that Baum's survival is due to the fact that he is *not* taught? That he is not, officially, Literature? If so, one must be careful not to murder Oz with exegesis. (p. 10)

. . . . .

I have reread the Oz books in the order in which they were written. . . . I was struck by the unevenness of style not only from book to book but, sometimes, from page to page. The jaggedness can be explained by the fact that the man who was writing fourteen Oz books was writing forty-eight other books at the same time. Arguably, ***The Wizard of Oz*** is the best of the lot. . . . Yet, as a child, I preferred ***The Emerald City, Rinkitink,*** and ***The Lost Princess*** to ***The Wizard.*** Now I find that all of the books tend to flow together in a single narrative, with occasional bad patches. . . .

[In ***The Wizard of Oz,*** the] house crosses the Deadly Desert and lands on top of the Wicked Witch of the West who promptly dries up and dies. Right off, Baum breaks his own rule that no one ever dies in Oz. I used to spend a good deal of time worrying about the numerous inconsistencies in the sacred texts. From time to time, Baum himself would try to rationalize errors but he was far too quick and careless a writer ever to create the absolutely logical mad worlds that Lewis Carroll or E. Nesbit did. . . .

The style of the first book is straightforward, even formal. There are almost no contractions. Dorothy speaks not at all the way a grownup might think a child should speak but like a sensible somewhat literal person. There are occasional Germanisms (did Baum's father speak German?): "'What is that little animal you are so tender of?'" Throughout all the books there is a fascination with jewelry and elaborate costumes. Baum never got over his love of theater. . . .

Baum's passion for the theater and, later, the movies not only wasted his time but, worse, it had a noticeably bad effect on his prose style. . . . ***The Wizard of Oz*** is chastely written. ***The Land of Oz*** is not. Baum riots in dull word play. There are endless bad puns, of the sort favored by popular comedians. There is also that true period horror: the baby-talking ingenue, a character who lasted well into our day in the menacing shapes of Fanny (Baby Snooks) Brice and the early Ginger Rogers. Dorothy, who talked plainly and to the point in ***The Wizard,*** talks (when she reappears in the third book) with a cuteness hard to bear. Fortunately, Baum's show-biz phase wore off and in later volumes Dorothy's speech improves.

Despite stylistic lapses, ***The Land of Oz*** is one of the most unusual and interesting books of the series. (p. 38)

Essentially, Baum's human protagonists are neither male nor female but children, a separate category in his view if not in that of our latter-day sexists. Baum's use of sex changes was common to the popular theater of his day, which, in turn, derived from the Elizabethan era when boys played girls whom the plot often required to pretend to be boys. . . .

Today of course any sort of sexual metamorphosis causes distress. . . . But, surely, for a pre-pube there is not much difference between a boy and a girl protagonist. After all, the central fact of the pre-pube's existence is not being male or female but being a child, much the hardest of all roles to play. During and after puberty, there is a tendency to want a central character like oneself. . . . Nevertheless, what matters most even to an adolescent is not the gender of the main character who experiences adventures but the adventures themselves, and the magic, and the jokes, and the pictures.

Dorothy is a perfectly acceptable central character for a boy to read about. She asks the right questions. She is not sappy (as Ozma can sometimes be). She is straight to the point and a bit aggressive. Yet the Dorothy who returns to the series in the third book, ***Ozma of Oz,*** is somewhat different from the original Dorothy. She is older and her conversation is full of cute contractions that must have doubled up audiences in Sioux City but were pretty hard going for at least one child forty years ago. (p. 39)

[In ***Ozma of Oz***] I found the changing of heads fascinating. And puzzling: since the brains in each head varied, would Langwidere still be herself when she put on a new head or would she become someone else? Thus Baum made logicians of his readers. (p. 40)

Although Baum's powers of invention seldom flagged, he had no great skill at plot-making. Solutions to problems are arrived at either through improbable coincidence or by bringing in, literally, some god (usually Glinda) from the machine to set things right. Since the narratives are swift and the conversations sprightly and the invented characters are both homely and amusing (animated paper dolls, jigsaw puzzles, pastry, cutlery, china, etc.), the stories never lack momentum. Yet there was always a certain danger that the narrative would flatten out into a series of predictable turns. (p. 41)

To the extent that Baum makes his readers aware that our country's "practical" arrangements are inferior to those of Oz, he is a truly subversive writer and . . . of course, he is brave and affirmative. . . .

[The] Oz books continue to exert their spell. "You do not educate a man by telling him what he knew not," wrote John Ruskin, "but by making him what he was not." In Ruskin's high sense, Baum was a true educator, and those who read his Oz books are often made what they were not—imaginative, tolerant, alert to wonders, life. (p. 42)

Gore Vidal, "The Wizard of the 'Wizard'" and "On Rereading the Oz Books," in The New York Review of Books *, Vol. XXIV, Nos. 15 and 16, September 29, 1977 and October 13, 1977, pp. 10, 12, 14-15, 38-42.*

DAVID L. GREENE AND DICK MARTIN

The Wonderful Wizard of Oz is America's greatest fairy tale, and Oz is its best-loved fairyland. . . . Oz and its inhabitants

Baum telling Oz stories, circa 1909.

have become a part of American vocabulary; every public figure from William Randolph Hearst to Everett Dirksen seems to have been likened at one time to the humbug Wizard, while the word "Oz" itself has becomes synonymous with wondrous, faraway places. Dorothy and her comrades are immortals, existing independently of the book in which they first appeared, and for countless readers, the fairyland through which they journey is a very real place, certainly no less real for being imaginary. (p. v)

The Wonderful Wizard of Oz is a deceptively simple story. (p. 11)

[The plot], like most of Baum's plots, is seriously flawed: the journey to Glinda is anti-climactic. What, then, gives ***The Wizard*** greatness? Most fairy tales are universal because they occur in distant times and places. Baum achieved universality by combining the folk tale with elements familiar to every child—cornfields, things made of tin, circus balloons. Dorothy is an especially fine creation: a simple child who in the midst of wonders goes matter-of-factly about her business. (p. 12)

The Scarecrow and the Tin Woodman are among the greatest grotesques in American literature. They are made human by their very human desires, and Baum supplies many details to render them even more "real." A prime example is the Tin Woodman's tale of how he became tin. . . . Other small touches, like the Tin Woodman's tendency to rust and the Scarecrow's difficulty in picking berries with his padded fingers, help the reader to accept the two characters. (p. 13)

The Marvelous Land of Oz was recognized by the early reviewers as a fine book. Many said that it was as good as ***The Wizard*** itself. . . . The major flaw in ***The Marvelous Land of Oz*** comes from Baum's plans to turn it into a stage play. Unlike the reviewer in the Cleveland *Leader* for November 6, 1904, most modern readers aren't bothered by the fact that "General Jinjur and her soldiers are only shapely chorus girls. We can see their tights and their ogling glances even in the pages of the book." But it comes as a jolt that Tip is changed into a girl at the end of the book. (p. 18)

Especially noteworthy among the many virtues of the book are the grotesques. In his stupidity, Jack Pumpkinhead is appealing, and even the Sawhorse is given personality. Mr. H. M. Woggle-Bug, T.E. . . . is one of Baum's comic masterpieces. . . . (p. 19)

Ozma of Oz is one of the finest of the Oz books; it adds important new characters and develops important new themes. . . . The best new character . . . is the Nome King . . . , and the most complex of the themes centers on his great fear of eggs. (p. 27)

The next two Oz books, unfortunately, are poorer than the first three, perhaps because Baum was spending more energy on various stage projects. . . . (pp. 27-8)

[***Dorothy and the Wizard in Oz***] is the shortest of Baum's Oz titles and shows signs of having been written quickly. . . . It has been criticized because it is so gloomy, but children can take that better than some adults. ***Dorothy and the Wizard*** is, in fact, a fascinating failure.

The reviewers greeted ***Dorothy and the Wizard*** cordially, referring to Oz, after eight years and four books, as a "perennial favorite." (p. 28)

The 1909 title, ***The Road to Oz,*** is the poorest Baum book in the series. The plot . . . quickly becomes tedious. . . . (p. 29)

The Emerald City was favorably reviewed, although comments were sometimes perfunctory; the annual addition to the Oz canon was no longer especially newsworthy. (p. 32)

The Patchwork Girl of Oz is the first really excellent Oz book after ***Ozma of Oz.*** (p. 35)

Baum's amazing facility in creating grotesques was never greater than in ***Patchwork Girl***. . . . The greatest of them, and one of the great American fantasy characters, is Scraps the Patchwork Girl. . . . (p. 37)

Tik-Tok of Oz is interesting for its themes. As in ***Ozma of Oz,*** the Nome King is defeated by eggs, and the Nomes turn another symbol of life and growth into the beautiful but sterile Metal Forest. War, the greatest of all destructive forces, is made much more ridiculous than it was in ***Ozma of Oz.*** (p. 40)

[***The Scarecrow of Oz***] is not a bad book, and it was Baum's own favorite among his Oz titles. (p. 41)

For his next Oz book, Baum decided to use his unpublished manuscript *King Rinkitink,* which appeared in 1916 as ***Rinkitink in Oz. Rinkitink*** is essentially the story of Prince Inga of Pingaree, an island in the Nonestic Ocean. . . . [Inga] sets out to rescue his parents and the other islanders, all of whom have been carried off into slavery by marauders.

The book leaves one with a sense of pleasure that Baum found a way of publishing such a fine fantasy, and disappointment that he had to pull Dorothy into it at the end and conclude the book in the Emerald City. Why, most readers have asked themselves, couldn't Inga, who does so much, ultimately free his parents? In the original manuscript, he probably did. (p. 47)

[Baum's] final four Oz books . . . are, with the possible exception of ***The Tin Woodman of Oz,*** among the best in the long series. (p. 48)

The Lost Princess of Oz is a satisfying Oz mystery, with interesting characters and well-developed suspense. The giant Frogman . . . is yet another notable addition to the gallery of grotesques. . . . Ugu is one of Baum's best villains. He possesses a drive for power with which the reader is forced to sympathize. The end of the book is particularly satisfying: Ugu repents his wickedness and decides to remain a dove. (pp. 48-50)

The Tin Woodman centers on questions of identity. Who is Chopfyt? How are he and his two donors related to each other? What is the relationship between Nick and his severed human head, with which he holds a conversation in Ku-Klip's workshop? Neither tin man has ever questioned his own identity before; now they are forced to do so. It is a humbling experience.

Despite its provocative theme, . . . ***The Tin Woodman*** is the most flawed of Baum's later Oz books. Much of it is spent in an episodic tour of Oz, without any real connection with the quest and without any particularly interesting episodes or characters. (p. 51)

[***The Magic of Oz*** and ***Glinda of Oz***] mark an important change in the series. They are more somber than any other Oz title except ***Dorothy and the Wizard in Oz.*** (pp. 51-2)

The Magic of Oz is an important book for several reasons. As C. Warren Hollister has suggested, the revolt of the animals is probably a parody of the Russian Revolution, which had occurred two years before the book was published. . . . Trot and Cap'n Bill, who literally take root on an enchanted island . . . and start to shrink, face the most frightening fate in all the Baum Oz books. By being lured nearly to destruction by beauty, they place ***The Magic of Oz*** in one of the oldest mythic traditions. And the Lonesome Duck, who provides Trot and Cap'n Bill with magic toadstools to sit on, anticipates the modern preoccupation with alienation: it can bear the company of no other creature. (pp. 54-6)

[***Glinda of Oz***] is the most tightly plotted of all of Baum's books. It is also as somber as ***The Magic of Oz.*** Its villains are proud, cruel and vindictive, without any of the comic touches that make us laugh at the Nome King. Magic is more mechanistic than it is in any other Oz book: the most important magic is no longer a simple device, but a complex machine, and the machine is more important than the person who makes it function. Even in a fairyland, technology, like war, can dehumanize. . . .

[Baum's] last two Oz books were published posthumously. News of his death was telegraphed around the world, and newspapers of every size and type, from the *New York Times* to small country weeklies, eulogized America's greatest writer of fairy tales and praised his creation. The Land of Oz was a real place to millions of children and adults, and to many, Baum had seemed a personal friend. Now Baum was dead; Oz, of course lives on. (p. 56)

David L. Greene and Dick Martin, in their The Oz Scrapbook, *Random House, 1977, 182 p.*

ROGER SALE

A good deal of the best American children's literature . . . enchants by its ease, its unselfconsciousness, its naïveté. And the first to achieve this, and still the best, is Baum. (p. 225)

[Until] we understand the way he loved and hated writing Oz books we will not be able to account for the careless, slapdash writing that mars and even destroys some of the Oz books, and, more important, we will not understand why, despite all that is wrong, the Oz books have rightly gained for Baum a permanent place in the minds of those who love him.

We might begin with a look at the figures who provide the easy and pleasant solutions that . . . [are] part of the standard furniture of American children's literature. The most famous of these is the Wizard himself, but there are also the Shaggy Man and Cap'n Bill; they are all older men, dry and sexless, and they accompany Dorothy and other young heroines on their journeys to Oz. They seem types of Baum himself, and the rule about these figures is that the less one sees of them the better they appear. (p. 227)

These men can for a moment or two fill up a scene as though it were all there was, as though there were no impinging past or future, and it is that which makes them impressive, more than their practical know-how. That it is the presence and not the expertise that counts is what the consistently enchanting Oz figures, Dorothy and Tip and the other children, show us. They cannot build boats in two minutes, or know when or how to whistle their way past the encircling trees. They must rely on their native sense of themselves and let that be enough. The fact that what is magical about them is their spirit and their presence and not their knowledge gives us the clue to Baum's achievement. They do not fuss, they immerse themselves in the present, which makes them children, to be sure, but it also makes them important. We are inclined to think Baum works better with girls than with boys, but Baum in fact is an almost totally sexless author and our impression is created by Dorothy alone. The other girls, Betsy Bobbin and Trot, have nothing like Dorothy's stature, and three of the boys, Tip, Inga, and Evric, have some very fine moments. But it is nonetheless Dorothy who is most impressive. . . . (p. 229)

[In ***Ozma of Oz,***] people go to sleep, in the dark they look for light, in the morning they search for food, when a door appears in a rock they look for a key, when they find a disused mechanical man they wind him up. Baum moves totally without self-consciousness from a real world to an improbable world to a magic world. The sentences come easily and imply they were no harder to write than it would be to take the journey they describe. Dorothy commands a presence just by responding to and accepting each detail with the same equipoise and easy curiosity with which she faced the last. It is precisely the atmosphere of Baum's writing not to be atmospheric, or faerie, or involving, or mysterious; his "new wonder-tale," free of morals and disagreeable incident, is free of all that as well. He genuinely accepts Dorothy and never tries to create a storyteller's manner that is any different from hers. That way he can imply what is obviously true: he could do no better at taking these journeys than she does. (p. 231)

The extraordinary freshness of the writing lies in Dorothy's never thinking about how she got where she is, or how she is going to get away, or how she might have done differently or have avoided danger. . . .

In Thoreau's terms, Dorothy is fully awake. She does not worry or fret or plan, and so everything can be fully itself. The smallest details can be memorable, even though Baum seldom offers full descriptions. (p. 232)

[A sense of situation], and Dorothy's ability to accept her presence in some strikingly strange ones, is and must be closely related to Baum's sense of plot or story. . . . [In Kipling, we see] how skillfully and tactfully he employed a loose plot in *Kim* so as to hold a large book together without sacrificing his investment in the immediate situations. So too with Baum. After one moment we have another, and we move without feeling we are going deeper or farther into some mystery; in a strong narrative we are always remembering the past and anticipating the future, and Baum works against those feelings. To feel one is getting deeper into something, getting closer to the heart of a mystery, is to diminish the desire to live totally now. Thus what Baum lacks is also the source of his way of being enchanting. Dorothy talks to the hen, flees from the Wheelers, rescues Tik-Tok from his cave, defies Langwidere and is imprisoned, is herself rescued by Ozma. Each event is complete in itself, and what holds the sequence together is only a very loose sense of narrative, one that does not impinge on Dorothy's allowing every action to be entered into for itself alone and not for what it allows one to go from or toward. The young son of a friend of mine complains that the Oz books are "too cinchy," because Baum's storytelling is transparent and naïve; one can easily find tales that are less "cinchy," but they cannot do what Baum's can. (pp. 233-34)

It is the child's journey to a magic country that Baum does best, because this gives us both the enchanting present and just the right amount of narrative sequence. He does occasionally try to link events causally and tightly in some of his books, and thus create suspense and strong narrative motion, but he does not usually do this well. He more often falls into a fully disparate series of events, a journey from this to that to the other place without any narrative tissue, and the results can be unfortunate because the emphasis is taken away from the child making the journey and put onto the odd things she meets, and so we feel we are wandering around in a zoo, locked into the present all right, but without the central presence to enchant us. But the trip to the magical country offers just the right sense that we are going somewhere, but without cause or guide or map, so that Dorothy or some other child must respond freshly, with the sense that each moment is different, and a challenge, and itself. (pp. 234-35)

[It] is in the early Oz books, when there are still fresh journeys to Oz to be taken, that Baum is at his very best. After Dorothy moves to Oz permanently as part of Baum's strategy for writing no more Oz books, she loses a good deal of her sparkle. . . . The later books often . . . show a marked falling off in quality. ***Tik-Tok*** is almost entirely a reworking of old materials; ***The Patchwork Girl*** has Ojo, the least interesting of Baum's children, and is constantly marred by some of Baum's worst punning and horseplay; ***The Scarecrow*** begins well with Trot and Cap'n Bill getting to Oz but then dwindles into wooden romance; ***The Tin Woodman*** and ***The Magic*** are almost grotesquely tired; the last book, ***Glinda,*** had to be padded with census taking of all the old Oz characters in order to be made into one of the shortest books in the series. Furthermore, nothing in these books matches the great opening journeys in ***The Land, Ozma,*** and ***The Road.***

This way of arguing the case, however, distorts Baum's talents and achievements even if it does isolate his very best things. Baum wrote quickly and never seems to have worried if he could sustain his interest for the length of a whole book. He seems to have known when he began a book how he wanted it to start, and perhaps where he wanted it to end, but he left the middle to be contrived as he went along. . . . The second Oz book, ***The Land,*** and the fifth, ***The Road,*** are wonderful for a hundred or more pages, but then fade, while the fourth, ***Dorothy and the Wizard,*** and the sixth, ***The Emerald City,*** are among the weakest in the series. We can't, thus, imagine Baum doing wonderfully well with Oz until he lost interest because he was always capable of losing interest, of falling into slapdash writing, easy satire, or trivial zoo-keeping inventiveness. Furthermore, two of the later books, ***Rinkitink*** and ***The Lost Princess,*** though they take no journey to magic lands and therefore lack some of the moment-to-moment sparkle of some of the early books, are very good at sustaining their narrative propositions through to the end; and the last book, ***Glinda,*** has a fine central situation and . . . one spectacular stretch.

The essence of Baum is his restless, careless ease, his indifference to the complexities of life, his eagerness to describe what enchanted him without ever exploring or understanding it. . . . [When his plots went] wrong, Baum found it hard to do more than plunge ahead, which seldom worked well; conversely, however, once set right, he tended to be able to invent and plot with ease and grace. But his attention span . . . seems to have been no longer than that of an intelligent child. As a result there is no one Oz book to which one can point as clearly the best, the one for skeptics to begin with; ***Ozma of Oz*** for me does more good things for the whole stretch of the book than any other, but it would be unfair to it, and to the series as a whole, to call it Baum's masterpiece. He wrote too much, too quickly, and too restlessly to have a single book as his masterpiece. He tired of many individual books before they were ended, and he tired of the series as a whole before it was ended, yet he kept on with it, and some of the characters and incidents his admirers remember best come in odd places in otherwise not very good books. (pp. 236-39)

Baum's was such a rare gift that it seems almost impertinent to ask how good he is, or how much he achieved, or to try to assess his books with great soberness. He was careless of his art and he seldom wrote as well as he could; he never thought hard about life or grasped its complexities; he could not, even at his best, convey sadness or fear or deep joy. He has always been scorned, or guardedly admired, by the traditional custodians of children's literature, so he has had to find his audience in spite of teachers and librarians, for the most part. Yet his audience is still extremely large long after he and his naïve view of life have departed. The virtues of which these many apparently crushing limitations are only the defects are virtues of the sort we believe to exist in life far more than we ever expect to see in literature, and so Baum is rightly treasured more than many who seem to have a better claim on our respect and on our imagination. . . .

[The] magic itself . . . is not the important quality in the Oz books; it exists mostly as validation of that other magic that is the child's wonderful acceptance of situation, self, and journey. That validation is total, and so the child and Baum's readers are never deceived, never shown anything they cannot trust or whose motives are ulterior; they need never be suspicious or mistrustful, never be grown up, and the readers can envy the child without folly or other penalty.

As a guide to life it is as naïve as it is essential. To be free of self and of the nagging necessities of maturity is usually to be irresponsible and wasteful, but on the roads to Oz it is truly liberating and enchanting, the challenge and promise of the morning. (p. 243)

Roger Sale, "L. Frank Baum and Oz," in his Fairy Tales and After: From Snow White to E. B. White, *Cambridge, Mass.: Harvard University Press, 1978, pp. 223-44.*

BRIAN ATTEBERY

The Wizard of Oz is an American fairytale. . . . Somehow L. Frank Baum put together a fairyland, like none before it, that we recognize as our own. . . . (pp. 83-4)

Before 1900 there was no coherent American fantasy world; afterward there was. . . . Baum, unlike his predecessors, created a fairyland with such solid outlines that it remains recognizable in reproduction after reproduction, like a drawing still clear after a thousand tracings. (p. 84)

Oz is America made more fertile, more equitable, more companionable, and, because it is magic, more wonderful. What Dorothy finds beyond the Deadly Desert is another America with its potential fulfilled: its beasts speaking, its deserts blooming, and its people living in harmony.

If Oz is America, then Dorothy is its Christopher Columbus. ***The Wizard of Oz*** is primarily a story of exploration, and one of its principal strengths is the feeling of "wild surmise" that Keats ascribed to Cortez and his men. Dorothy is the discoverer who opens up the newest new world; later she and other children . . . chart the unknown regions remaining in Oz and the lands around it. All of the stories are based on movement. They whisk one away from known lands with a dizzying swoop, proceed over land, water, and air toward a brief action, then take off again for home. In ***The Road to Oz,*** indeed, there can be said to be no plot at all except the journey of Dorothy, Button Bright, Polychrome, and the Shaggy Man to Oz. The journey motif owes something to traditional fairy tale structure . . . but it owes as much or more to an American tradition of restlessness and curiosity. Happily, the discovery of Oz undoes some of the evils that accompanied the discovery of

America. The natives accept the invaders, who, in turn, leave them in possession of their lands. Profit and progress are firmly excluded, and Oz remains the sleepy paradise it began.

Selma Lanes points out in her essay on "America as Fairy Tale" that the discovery of Oz coincided with a change in America's image of itself. Not until we realized that we were not living in a fairyland of peace and plenty could we begin to draw upon the power of that archetype in our fictions. (p. 87)

Oz is at the turning point. It could only have been invented by someone who, like Baum, personally felt the gap between American ideals and American life. (pp. 87-8)

The successful creation and immediate acceptance of Oz indicates that Americans by 1900 had finally begun to feel the need of an ideal world apart from America itself, as it was believed to be or as it was expected to become. . . . ***The Wizard of Oz*** reveals a shift toward introspection and the redefinition of values.

That is not to say that Americans, including Baum, immediately and totally transferred their allegiance from this world to various Others. The perfections of Oz would not be so poignant if they did not so strongly suggest qualities of American life at its rare best. In this respect, I would say that the primary source of secondary belief taken advantage of by Baum is the powerful but receding faith in the American Dream, rather than any corpus of supernatural legend. That faith has not yet left us entirely (it is kept alive partly by having been realized imaginatively in Oz) so that if Kansas, for example, is proven to be a part of the fallen world, there is still a glimpse of earthly paradise farther on, in California or Alaska or on the moon. (p. 88)

Oz is not a utopia, though it has many utopian elements. It is something more lasting, a fairyland. The difference is that Oz, like any fantasy world, allows for—rather, demands—the existence of the impossible. How does Baum integrate the impossible into a setting derived from pragmatic American experience? The best way to point out his techniques is to look at . . . [four] earmarks of fantasy: narrative structure, hero, nonhuman characters, and a coherent system of magic and significance. The fact that Baum's work, American as it is, lends itself to analysis along these lines, which were drawn originally from the British fantasy tradition, is a sign of his unprecedented entry into the mainstream of fantasy after our hundred or so years of apprenticeship.

The land of Oz is a constant throughout the series, and so may be described as if all fourteen volumes were one evolving work. But there is no overall story structure to the set; each book must be considered individually. The most important story, and the most highly structured, is that of ***The Wizard of Oz***. . . .

Baum was probably unaware of most of the scholarly work being done in his time by folklorists, and in any case he lived before the important analyses of the folktale . . . had been made. If his story corresponds in any significant measure to the traditional structure, it indicates not a studied imitation but an intuitive grasp of the fundamental dynamics of the folktale. And ***The Wizard*** does, indeed, follow the traditional pattern, with the additional multiplication of elements and overlaying of action we expect of a written work. . . . (p. 91)

Baum not only intuitively understood fairy tale structure, but he was also able to adjust it at will to fit his needs. The sharp break between the opening segment and the ensuing action, for example, he made serve as a crossing of the threshold into another world. By doubling and tripling certain elements he was able to take advantage of his major strengths as a writer, the portrayal of movement and the quick and comical delineation of character. The embedded plot is neatly introduced by having one character, the Wizard, take on two functional roles. The Wizard is also placed in a central position in the book, structurally and geographically, with the result that at the heart of fairyland we find Omaha-born Oz Diggs, a reminder of the opening scene of the book and a forecast of its end. Baum's skill in handling the fairy tale story line—in making it his own—surpasses, I believe, that of any of the imitators of European style fairy tales . . . , just as his grasp of American character and landscape surpasses that of all his predecessors in the native, fairies-in-America line. (p. 93)

As Baum continued to write "modernized" tales, he grew bolder in his treatment of the fairy tale structure. ***The Land of Oz*** has an unconventional ending: the boy hero is revealed at last to be, not a king in disguise, but a queen, transformed by witchcraft into male form. In ***Ozma of Oz*** and several of the later Oz books, Dorothy becomes a sort of heroine errant, performing quests not for her own sake but for other, lesser characters; the hero role is broken up, that is, into an active but unconcerned protagonist and one or more passive but needy companions. ***The Scarecrow of Oz*** contains a fairy tale in burlesque, the "hero" of which is the most ineffectual character in the story. Some of the books, like ***Dorothy and the Wizard in Oz*** and ***The Road to Oz,*** suppress all phases of the fairy tale morphology except the quest-journey, but they still follow the proper sequence for that segment of the full structure. In others, like ***The Emerald City of Oz, Tik-Tok of Oz,*** and ***Glinda of Oz,*** a rival story line of conquest and siege all but overpowers the individualistic fairy tale development, perhaps reflecting America's growing awareness of international strife up to and during World War I. But the underlying pattern remains constant and occasionally, as in ***Rinkitink in Oz,*** reappears in classic form. (pp. 94-5)

An important literary source for ***The Wizard,*** and probably the primary inspiration for Dorothy herself, is Lewis Carroll's *Alice in Wonderland*. . . . [For] Baum, who was considering it as a source book, the important thing about *Alice* is not its discovery of the absurd but its development of the fairy tale hero into a distinctive, perceiving individual. (pp. 95-6)

Baum threw away offhand everything but the spirit of *Alice in Wonderland*. . . . Dorothy and Alice are two of the most likeable heroines in literature, two witty and contemporary character sketches of the sort one finds in the best domestic comedies. Carroll discovered that such a character could be removed from the social world into the world of dream, and Baum took things one step further (in terms of violations of reality) into a world of waking marvels.

Though Alice and Dorothy are both portraits of believable, modern-day children, there are important differences between them. Dorothy, unlike Alice, never wonders who she is, where she is going, or why the world has suddenly turned upside down. (p. 96)

Alice is English; Dorothy is aggressively, triumphantly American. As the primary link between the naturalistically portrayed Kansas of the beginning and the transmogrified America that is Oz, she must be able to make explicit the comparisons between the two, and to do so she must be accepted by the reader as a valid representative of all things American. Therefore, Dorothy is not merely a fairy tale heroine, or a believable child, she is also heir to an American conception of character, especially of its own character. And what is the essential American character? Often it is the explorer, the wanderer, who penetrates ever wilder regions of the world or the mind and comes back relatively unscathed. (pp. 96-7)

Since Dorothy is female and a Westerner, she suggests one other category of character, another peculiarly American one: the pioneer woman. There are two classes of pioneer women in the popular imagination. One is faded and bleak and particularly appealing to local color writers with a naturalistic vision. That is Aunt Em. The other is lively and attractive, drawing her strength from the earth she lives so close to. That is, of course, Dorothy, who is to some degree a forerunner of the Nebraska heroine in Willa Cather's *My Ántonia*. Throughout ***The Wizard,*** Dorothy gives her comrades guidance and encouragement, like a little mother. . . . She does an admirable job of keeping herself and Toto provided for on an arduous journey. Nurture, comfort, and guidance: these, in mythology, are the functions of the Earth Mother. If Dorothy were allowed to mature, we might imagine her something like the grown-up Ántonia, full-figured, sun-burned to earth colors, radiating order, contentment, and fertility.

She does not grow up, however. An adult heroine would . . . bring back all those troublesome questions of belief and reason that drove Poe's heroes mad. So Baum imposed on Oz an end to aging, and Dorothy, rather than maturing, began to fall into a rather gushing girlishness. That is one of the primary weaknesses of the later books, so important is Dorothy's earthiness to the fantasy. . . .

If the fairy tale gave Baum an outline for his main character, one might say that Lewis Carroll taught him how to draw in features and make them appear three-dimensional. (p. 98)

With an outline and a set of features, Dorothy still needed color. It is not enough to say, "I will create a character who seems to be a living, breathing American child." One must have some notion of what it means to be such a creature. Part of what it meant to Baum is to be healthy, confident, exploratory, and full of pioneer spirit, to the point of invoking the quasi-mythic conception of frontier womanhood. This side of Dorothy's character reveals Baum's regional-minded optimism: what wonderful children we are raising in the West, he is saying; they are the hope of the country. . . . In the matter of character, as in setting, Baum is all the more an American writer for being a regional one as well.

What about the characters around Dorothy? Just as she is the essential tie with the familiar, they are the wonder-working helpers and adversaries who must carry us into the marvelous. How does Baum stand up on our [third] element of fantasy, the assortment of nonhuman characters? Excellently, for the most part. From the Good Witch at the beginning of ***The Wizard*** to the fascinating Yookoohoo in ***Glinda of Oz,*** his last book, Baum produced with seeming ease a host of vivid, unquestionably magical beings: he brought a scarecrow to life, made an engaging eccentric out of an insect, revealed a common tramp to be a wonder worker, and made witches seem like his own invention. (p. 99)

What kind of world view does Baum express through his use of magic?

The answer is, a limited one. Baum does adopt [Nathaniel] Hawthorne's system of symbolization, so that in whatever points a character differs physically from the norm, he is also likely to illustrate a moral issue. Jack Pumpkinhead has something to say about the pumpkin-headedness of us all, and so on for each speaking creature in Oz. But Baum's introduction of characters was haphazard and frequently dictated by his impatience with the progress of the plot. Enduring characters like Jack begin, through simple accretion, to take on some philosophical complexity, but his one-shot, ad hoc creations—the Fuddles of Fuddlecumjig are a good example, being nothing more than a literalization of the phrase "to go all to pieces"—can hardly be said to be artistic examinations of the problems of life. Nor are they meant to be. In the often quoted phrase that became the title for the standard biography of Baum, he wrote "to please a child." It is for children, not for critical adults, that he upholds such uncontroversial virtues as kindness, generosity, and self-reliance. Ambivalence and sin, with their meatier dramas, he leaves to Hawthorne.

If there is a grander scheme of philosophy in the workings of Oz, it will show up in the essential rules of magic within which Baum operates, rather than in his piecemeal inventions. The following seem to me to be the fundamental magical operations throughout the series: animation, transformation, illusion, disillusion, transportation, protection, and luck. Now these are not unusual operations; they are found throughout fairy legend and *Märchen*. But Baum has set them up in a rudimentary system, and that is an important distinction between imitation of folk forms and creative fantasy.

Animation comes in several forms in the Oz books. . . . [The] Scarecrow's unexplained awakening and Jack Pumpkinhead's

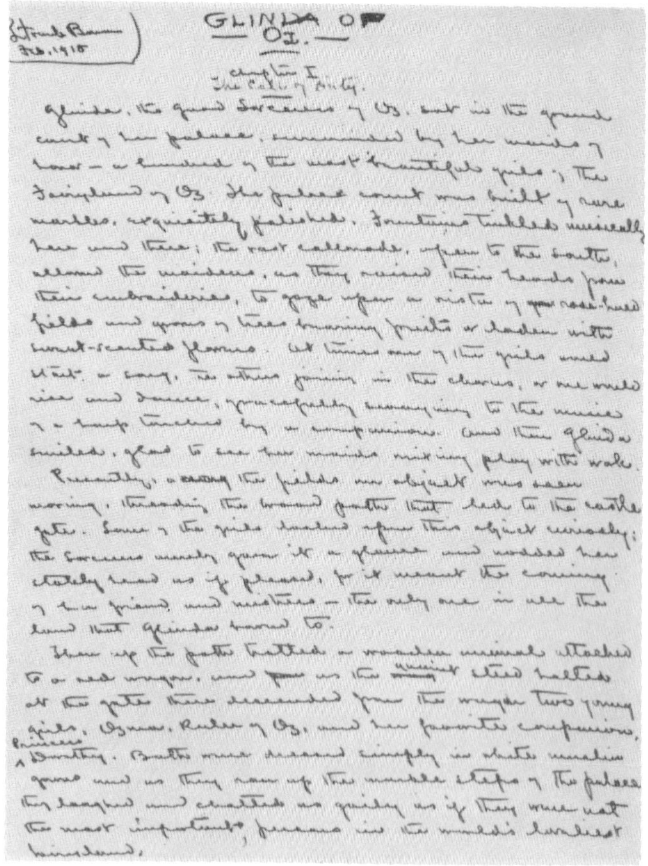

First page of the manuscript for Glinda of Oz *(1920), Baum's last published Oz book.*

birth under Mombi's cackling midwifery [are examples]. (pp. 104-05)

Things always seem to be springing to life in Oz. . . . [It] is a remarkably fertile place. But what is the end result of all this magical procreation? It is almost always to the good. By this means Oz has been provided with some of its most valuable and colorful citizens. No one could wish the Scarecrow still hanging lifeless on his stake, or Jack Pumpkinhead rotting on a compost heap. Not everyone is a fan of the talking phonograph, the vain glass cat, or the unpleasantly floppy bear rug, but all three have their uses. The principle here seems to be that it is better to exist than not, no matter what your form or foibles. These animations are part of a general tendency toward increasing richness of life; they represent a universe slanted toward Becoming. (p. 105)

[Some] characters are created for questionable reasons or by downright wicked characters like Mombi. But in every case, things turn out for the best. It is never wrong, in Baum's view, to create, and, indeed, it is difficult to help it.

Transformation is another matter. There are many people in Oz and its environs capable of transforming objects. . . . It would seem that transformation is a neutral art, usable for either good or evil ends. But there are two quite different sorts of transformation in Oz. What Mombi and her fellow villains do is to impose a new shape on an unwilling victim, or on themselves for evil purposes. What Dorothy and her friends do is to restore victims to their original form. (pp. 105-06)

In a sense, transformation is the opposite of animation. To desire to change the people and objects around one is to deny their intrinsic importance, to wish them, as it were, unmade. The archetype of all transformations is that fearful operation, threatened by Mombi and performed accidentally by the ambiguous Crooked Magician, petrifaction. Turning someone to stone is the ultimate denial, and of course in Oz it must eventually be undone by the affirmative act of reanimation. . . .

Illusion and disillusion form another couplet like transformation and animation. Once more, the operation that denies reality is evil, and that which restores it is good. The implication is that reality is more wonderful than any obscuring of it, in fairyland or in the real world, a belief which would not seem to lead naturally into fantasy except for the fact that, for Baum, it never hurts to add to the store of existence through imagination. Generally the same people practice illusion as indulge in transformations. But anyone with a little insight can undo an illusion, simply by ignoring it. Several times Baum has his characters pass a seeming obstacle by closing their eyes and walking through, or poking it with a pin, or making friends with what appeared to be an enemy. (p. 106)

Transportation has no particular moral value in Oz, but it does act as a sign that anything in the world is possible and within reach. Dorothy's cyclone, the enchanted road in ***The Road to Oz,*** Ozma's magic carpet, and so on are simply variations of the traditional seven-league boots, which carry their owner to fame and fortune. Most of the modes of transportation to and within Oz are natural objects, rather than conscious agents. They represent the unpredictability of nature, which to Baum is rarely hostile but always amazing.

Protection and luck are really two views of the same thing. Glinda's spell of invisibility over Oz, the Good Witch's protective kiss, and the Shaggy Man's love magnet are the same as Ojo the Lucky's good fortune in ***The Patchwork Girl.*** The only difference is that luck is a more mysterious, pervasive thing, not traceable to any knowable cause. Both operations stress, again, the benevolence of the world. It is as if there were watchful parents everywhere, some visible and some invisible. (p. 107)

[These basic principles] do not make up a very new or rigorous philosophy. It is a child's vision that Baum is presenting, and so he shies away from any more darkness or complexity than he felt a child would be prepared to deal with. Writing for children freed Baum's imagination . . . , but the boon was also a limitation. We have no proof that Baum *could* have written a more mature work of fantasy than Oz, with a more demanding and rewarding reordering of the world's laws, but he certainly could not do so as long as he conceived of fairy tales as the province primarily of children. So we have the Oz books: simple, sunny, utterly delightful, but narrow in their range of emotion and significance.

Yet the barrier had been broken, effortlessly punctured like a wall of illusion. Baum proved, without doubt, that an American writer could write fantasy from American materials, even if those materials were significantly unlike the well-developed tales and legends available to European collectors and storytellers. Other writers could build on his accomplishment, as he built on the efforts of those before him, could gradually bring into their American fairylands those questions he left out. Even with his weaknesses, he is our Grimm and our Andersen, the man who introduced Americans to their own dreams. (pp. 107-08)

Brian Attebery, "Oz," in his The Fantasy Tradition in American Literature: From Irving to Le Guin, *Indiana University Press, 1980, pp. 83-108.*

JUSTIN G. SCHILLER

[Schiller is a noted collector of antiquarian children's books who founded the International Wizard of Oz Club in 1957 when he was twelve years old. The club publishes the Baum Bugle, *a journal specializing in popular and scholarly articles about Oz and its creators.]*

Oz remains an unique wonderland of fantasy, adventure, and escape, beautifully buoyed by optimism even when there appears no obvious solution, but always encouraging to a young reader because everything unravels logically one step at a time. Oz lives, and will continue to do so for many generations. It is not simply a Victorian children's book, by now outdated and old-fashioned as some critics would have us believe. It is a pioneering adventure about a wanderer who explores uncharted shores, having much in common with those who built America itself. Through her gentle good manners and optimistic spirit, Dorothy fulfills her objective. . . .

As readers, we join the explorers along the Yellow Brick Road, safely protected from each obstacle they encounter by the knowledge that this is only a story. Gradually we come to appreciate the wisdom, kindness and bravery of the modest troupe long before they themselves discover it. And once back in Kansas, both we and Dorothy retain the happy memory of Oz. That is the heritage L. Frank Baum has given us, perhaps personifying the essence of what makes America such a land of opportunity and fulfillment. We come to equate personal achievement with genuine perseverance, a formula that anticipates the building of a healthier future. (p. 267)

Justin G. Schiller, in an appreciation to The Wonderful Wizard of Oz *by L. Frank Baum, University of California Press, 1986, pp. 256-68.*

THE WONDERFUL WIZARD OF OZ **(1900; also published as *The New Wizard of Oz* and *The Wizard of Oz*)**

AUTHOR'S COMMENTARY

[*Baum wrote the following essay in April 1900 as his introduction to* The Wonderful Wizard of Oz.]

Folk lore, legends, myths and fairy tales have followed childhood through the ages, for every healthy youngster has a wholesome and instinctive love for stories fantastic, marvelous and manifestly unreal. The winged fairies of Grimm and Andersen have brought more happiness to childish hearts than all other human creations.

Yet the old-time fairy tale, having served for generations, may now be classed as "historical" in the children's library; for the time has come for a series of newer "wonder-tales" in which the stereotyped genie, dwarf and fairy are eliminated, together with all the horrible and blood-curdling incident devised by their authors to point a fearsome moral to each tale. Modern education includes morality; therefore the modern child seeks only entertainment in its wonder-tales and gladly dispenses with all disagreeable incident.

Having this thought in mind, the story of ***The Wonderful Wizard of Oz*** was written solely to pleasure children of today. It aspires to being a modernized fairy tale, in which the wonderment and joy are retained and the heartaches and nightmares are left out.

L. Frank Baum, in an introduction to his The Wonderful Wizard of Oz,*University of California Press, 1986, p. iv.*

In ***The Wonderful Wizard of Oz*** the fact is clearly recognized that the young as well as their elders love novelty. They are pleased with dashes of color and something new in the place of the old, familiar, and winged fairies of Grimm and Andersen.

Neither the tales of Aesop and other fableists, nor the stories such as the "Three Bears" will ever pass entirely away, but a welcome place remains and will easily be found for such stories as ***Father Goose: His Book, The Songs of Father Goose,*** and now ***The Wonderful Wizard of Oz,*** that have all come from the hands of Baum and Denslow.

This last story of ***The Wizard*** is ingeniously woven out of commonplace material. It is of course an extravaganza, but will surely be found to appeal strongly to child readers as well as to the younger children. . . .

The drawing as well as the introduced color work vies with the texts drawn, and the result has been a book that rises far above the average children's book of today, high as is the present standard. Dorothy, the little girl, and her strangely assorted companions, whose adventures are many and whose dangers are often very great, have experiences that seem in some respects like a leaf out of one of the old English fairy tales that Andrew Lang or Joseph Jacobs has rescued for us. A difference there is, however, and Baum has done with mere words what Denslow has done with his delightful draughtsmanship. The story has humor and here and there stray bits of philosophy that will be a moving power on the child mind and will furnish fields of study and investigation for the future students and professors of psychology. Several new features and ideals of fairy life have been introduced into the ***Wonderful Wizard,*** who turns out in the end to be only a wonderful humbug after all. A scarecrow stuffed with straw, a tin woodman, and a cowardly lion do not at first blush promise well as moving heroes in a tale when merely mentioned, but in actual practice they take on something of the living and breathing quality that is so gloriously exemplified in the "Story of the Three Bears," that has become a classic.

The book has a bright and joyous atmosphere, and does not dwell upon killing and deeds of violence. Enough stirring adventure enters into it, however, to flavor it with zest, and it will indeed be strange if there be a normal child who will not enjoy the story.

A review of "The Wonderful Wizard of Oz," in The New York Times Book Review, *September 8, 1900, p. 605.*

The Wonderful Wizard of Oz, described by its publishers as a modern fairy story, fairly sustains the claim put forth for it that it is something new. Besides this it is very attractive, not only by reason of the story, . . . but also through its profuse illustrations in color by W. W. Denslow. . . . The story tells the adventures of a little girl who is carried by a cyclone from her home on the Kansas prairie to a strange country. On the way she meets a cowardly lion, a tin woodman, and a scarecrow, and the conversations maintained by these four comrades and their curious experiences constitute the tale. It is not lacking in philosophy and satire which will furnish amusement to the adult and cause the juvenile to think some new and healthy thoughts. At the same time it is not objectionable in being too knowing and cannot be fairly charged with unduly encouraging precocity. The average modern child will understand that it is not a true or possible story without at all losing interest in it.

A review of "The Wonderful Wizard of Oz," in Book News, *Vol. XIX, No. 218, October, 1900, p. 84.*

The Wizard of Oz is no masterpiece of literary style, or even of literary invention. It does not rank with the "Alice" books, with *Peter Pan,* or with the fairy tales of such masters as Andersen and Grimm. Its author does not even play in the same league as the authors of those greater classics.

But it is a friendly, kindly book, and it is no small thing for a writer to have created figures of fantasy that live as surely, on whatever level, for millions of his countrymen, as these absurd, ingratiating puppets of our popular pantheon. (p. 14)

Vincent Starrett, in a review of "The Wizard of Oz," in Chicago Sunday Tribune Magazine of Books, *May 2, 1954, pp. 2, 14.*

The Wonderful Wizard of Oz has been immensely popular, providing the basis for a profitable musical comedy, three movies and a number of plays. It is an indigenous creation, curiously warm and touching, although no one really knows why. . . . But its uniqueness does not rest alone on its peculiar and transcendent popularity. (pp. 47-8)

Baum stories often include searching parodies on the contradictions in human nature. The second book in the series, ***The Marvelous Land of Oz,*** is a blatant satire on feminism and the suffragette movement. In it Baum attempted to duplicate the format used so successfully in ***The Wizard,*** yet no one has noted a similar play on contemporary movements in the latter work. Nevertheless, one does exist, and it reflects to an astonishing degree the world of political reality which surrounded Baum in 1900. In order to understand the relationship of ***The Wizard*** to turn-of-the-century America, it is necessary to first know something of Baum's background. . . . [Baum] journeyed to Aberdeen, South Dakota, in 1887. Aberdeen was a little prairie town and there Baum edited the local weekly until it failed in 1891. . . .

While Baum was living in South Dakota not only was the frontier a thing of the past, but the Romantic view of benign nature had disappeared as well. The stark reality of the dry, open plains and the acceptance of man's Darwinian subservience to his environment served to crush Romantic idealism. (p. 48)

Baum's stay in South Dakota also covered the period of the formation of the Populist party. . . . Western farmers had for a long time sought governmental aid in the form of economic panaceas, but to no avail. The Populist movement symbolized a desperate attempt to use the power of the ballot. In 1891 Baum moved to Chicago where he was surrounded by those dynamic elements of reform which made the city so notable during the 1890s.

In Chicago Baum certainly saw the results of the frightful depression which had closed down upon the nation in 1893. Moreover, he took part in the pivotal election of 1896, marching in "torch-light parades for William Jennings Bryan.". . . No one who marched in even a few such parades could have been unaffected by Bryan's campaign. Putting all the farmers' hopes in a basket labeled "free coinage of silver," Bryan's platform rested mainly on the issue of adding silver to the nation's gold standard. Though he lost, he did at least bring the plight of the little man into national focus. (p. 49)

The Wizard of Oz has neither the mature religious appeal of a *Pilgrim's Progress,* nor the philosophic depth of a *Candide.* Baum's most thoughtful devotees see in it only a warm, cleverly written fairy tale. Yet the original Oz book conceals an unsuspected depth, and it is the purpose of this study to demonstrate that Baum's immortal American fantasy encompasses more than heretofore believed. For Baum created a children's story with a symbolic allegory implicit within its story line and characterizations. The allegory always remains in a minor key, subordinated to the major theme and readily abandoned whenever it threatens to distort the appeal of the fantasy. But through it, in the form of a subtle parable, Baum delineated a Midwesterner's vibrant and ironic portrait of this country as it entered the twentieth century. (p. 50)

[The plight of the Tin Woodman in losing his human body shows how] Eastern witchcraft dehumanized a simple laborer so that the faster and better he worked the more quickly he became a kind of machine. Here is a Populist view of evil Eastern influences on honest labor which could hardly be more pointed.

There is one thing seriously wrong with being made of tin; when it rains rust sets in. Tin Woodman had been standing in the same position for a year without moving before Dorothy came along and oiled his joints. The Tin Woodman's situation has an obvious parallel in the condition of many Eastern workers after the depression of 1893. (p. 52)

Dorothy is Baum's Miss Everyman. She is one of us, levelheaded and human, and she has a real problem. Young readers can understand her quandary as readily as can adults. She is good, not precious, and she thinks quite naturally about others. For all of the attractions of Oz Dorothy desires only to return to the gray plains and Aunt Em and Uncle Henry. . . . Dorothy sets out on the Yellow Brick Road wearing the Witch of the East's magic Silver Shoes. Silver shoes walking on a golden road; henceforth Dorothy becomes the innocent agent of Baum's ironic view of the Silver issue. Remember, neither Dorothy, nor the good Witch of the North, nor the Munchkins understand the power of these shoes. The allegory is abundantly clear. On the next to last page of the book Baum has Glinda, Witch of the South, tell Dorothy, "Your Silver Shoes will carry you over the desert. . . . If you had known their power you could have gone back to your Aunt Em the very first day you came to this country." Glinda explains, "All you have to do is to knock the heels together three times and command the shoes to carry you wherever you wish to go." William Jennings Bryan never outlined the advantages of the silver standard any more effectively. (pp. 52-3)

The Lion represents Bryan himself. In the election of 1896 Bryan lost the vote of Eastern labor, though he tried hard to gain their support. In Baum's story the Lion, on meeting the little group, "struck at the Tin Woodman with his sharp claws." But, to his surprise, "he could make no impression on the tin, although the Woodman fell over in the road and lay still." Baum here refers to the fact that in 1896 workers were often pressured into voting for McKinley and gold by their employers. Amazed, the Lion says, "he nearly blunted my claws," and he adds even more appropriately, "When they scratched against the tin it made a cold shiver run down my back." The King of Beasts is not after all very cowardly, and Bryan, although a pacifist and an anti-imperialist in a time of national expansion, is not either. The magic Silver Shoes belong to Dorothy, however. Silver's potent charm, which had come to mean so much to so many in the Midwest, could not be entrusted to a political symbol. Baum delivers Dorothy from the world of adventure and fantasy to the real world of heartbreak and desolation through the power of Silver. It represents a real force in a land of illusion, and neither the Cowardly Lion nor Bryan truly needs or understands its use. (pp. 53-4)

Those who enter the Emerald City must wear green glasses. Dorothy later discovers that the greenness of dresses and ribbons disappears on leaving, and everything becomes a bland white. Perhaps the magic of any city is thus self imposed. But the Wizard dwells here and so the Emerald City represents the national Capitol. The Wizard, a little bumbling old man, hiding behind a facade of papier mâché and noise, might be any President from Grant to McKinley. He comes straight from the fair grounds in Omaha, Nebraska, and he symbolizes the American criterion for leadership—he is able to be everything to everybody.

As each of our heroes enters the throne room to ask a favor the Wizard assumes different shapes, representing different views toward national leadership. To Dorothy, he appears as an enormous head, "bigger than the head of the biggest giant." An apt image for a naive and innocent little citizen. To the Scarecrow he appears to be a lovely, gossamer fairy, a most appropriate form for an idealistic Kansas farmer. The Woodman sees a horrible beast, as would any exploited Eastern laborer after the trouble of the 1890s. But the Cowardly Lion, Like W. J. Bryan, sees a "Ball of Fire, so fierce and glowing he could scarcely bear to gaze upon it." (p. 54)

The Wizard has asked them all to kill the Witch of the West. . . . The Witch of the West uses natural forces to achieve her ends; she is Baum's version of sentient and malign nature. . . .

Baum makes [the Witch's] Winged Monkeys into an Oz substitute for the plains Indians. Their leader says, "Once . . . we were a free people, living happily in the great forest, flying from tree to tree, eating nuts and fruit, and doing just as we pleased without calling anybody master." "This," he explains, "was many years ago, long before Oz came out of the clouds to rule over this land." But like many Indian tribes Baum's monkeys are not inherently bad; their actions depend wholly upon the bidding of others. (p. 55)

Dorothy presents a special problem to the Witch. Seeing the mark on Dorothy's forehead and the Silver Shoes on her feet, the Witch begins "to tremble with fear, for she knew what a powerful charm belonged to them." Then "she happened to look into the child's eyes and saw how simple the soul behind them was, and that the little girl did not know of the wonderful power the Silver Shoes gave her." Here Baum again uses the Silver allegory to state the blunt homily that while goodness affords a people ultimate protection against evil, ignorance of their capabilities allows evil to impose itself upon them. The Witch assumes the proportions of a kind of western Mark Hanna or Banker Boss, who, through natural malevolence, manipulates the people and holds them prisoner by cynically taking advantage of their innate innocence.

Enslaved in the West, "Dorothy went to work meekly, with her mind made up to work as hard as she could; for she was glad the Wicked Witch had decided not to kill her." Many Western farmers have held these same grim thoughts in less mystical terms. If the Witch of the West is a diabolical force of Darwinian or Spencerian nature, then another contravening force may be counted upon to dispose of her. Dorothy destroys the evil Witch by angrily dousing her with a bucket of water. Water, that precious commodity which the drought-ridden farmers on the great plains needed so badly, and which if correctly used could create an agricultural paradise, or at least dissolve a wicked witch. Plain water brings an end to malign nature in the West.

When Dorothy and her companions return to the Emerald City they soon discover that the Wizard is really nothing more than "a little man, with a bald head and a wrinkled face." (pp. 55-6)

"It was a great mistake my ever letting you into the Throne Room," the Wizard complains. "Usually I will not see even my subjects, and so they believe I am something terrible." What a wonderful lesson for youngsters of the decade when Benjamin Harrison, Grover Cleveland and William McKinley were hiding in the White House. Formerly the Wizard was a mimic, a ventriloquist and a circus balloonist. The latter trade involved going "up in a balloon on circus day, so as to draw a crowd of people together and get them to pay to see the circus." Such skills are as admirably adapted to success in late-nineteenth-century politics as they are to the humbug wizardry of Baum's story. A pointed comment on Midwestern political ideals is the fact that our little Wizard comes from Omaha, Nebraska, a center of Populist agitation. (p. 56)

The Silver Shoes furnish Dorothy with a magic means of travel. But when she arrives back in Kansas she finds, "The Silver Shoes had fallen off in her flight through the air, and were lost forever in the desert." Were the "her" to refer to America in 1900, Baum's statement could hardly be contradicted.

Current historiography tends to criticize the Populist movement for its "delusions, myths and foibles," Professor C. Vann Woodward observed recently. Yet ***The Wonderful Wizard of Oz*** has provided unknowing generations with a gentle and friendly Midwestern critique of the Populist rationale on these very same grounds. Led by naive innocence and protected by good will, the farmer, the laborer and the politician approach the mystic holder of national power to ask for personal fulfillment. Their desires, as well as the Wizard's cleverness in answering them, are all self-delusion. Each of these characters carries within him the solution to his own problem, were he only to view himself objectively. The fearsome Wizard turns out to be nothing more than a common man, capable of shrewd but mundane answers to these self-induced needs. Like any good politician he gives the people what they want. Throughout the story Baum poses a central thought; the American desire for symbols of fulfillment is illusory. Real needs lie elsewhere.

Thus the Wizard cannot help Dorothy, for of all the characters only she has a wish that is selfless, and only she has a direct connection to honest, hopeless human beings. Dorothy supplies real fulfillment when she returns to her aunt and uncle, using the Silver Shoes, and cures some of their misery and heartache. In this way Baum tells us that the Silver crusade at least brought back Dorothy's lovely spirit to the disconsolate plains farmer. Her laughter, love and good will are no small addition to that gray land, although the magic of Silver has been lost forever as a result.

Noteworthy too is Baum's prophetic placement of leadership in Oz after Dorothy's departure. The Scarecrow reigns over the Emerald City, the Tin Woodman rules in the West and the Lion protects smaller beasts in "a grand old forest." Thereby farm interests achieve national importance, industrialism moves West and Bryan commands only a forest full of lesser politicians.

Baum's fantasy succeeds in bridging the gap between what children want and what they should have. It is an admirable example of the way in which an imaginative writer can teach goodness and morality without producing the almost inevitable side effect of nausea. Today's children's books are either saccharine and empty, or boring and pedantic. Baum's first Oz tale—and those which succeed it—are immortal not so much because the "heart-aches and nightmares are left out" as that "the wonderment and joy" are retained. (pp. 57-8)

The Wizard has become a genuine piece of American folklore because, knowing his audience, Baum never allowed the consistency of the allegory to take precedence over the theme of youthful entertainment. Yet once discovered, the author's allegorical intent seems clear, and it gives depth and lasting interest even to children who only sense something else beneath the surface of the story. (p. 58)

Henry M. Littlefield, "'The Wizard of Oz': Parable on Populism," in American Quarterly, *Vol. XVI, No. 1, Spring, 1964, pp. 47-58.*

No children's book of the twentieth century has proven to be as popular or as controversial as ***The Wizard of Oz.*** When Bobbs-Merrill issued their first edition in 1903, a reviewer remarked: "Mr. L. Frank Baum's last delicious bit of nonsense is amusing to the little people, and even more so to their elders. It is no small gift to write a juvenile which is not inane, and this gift Mr. Baum possesses to a degree which is almost monopoly." Nearly sixty years later when the first paperback editions of the Oz books were being published, another reviewer, noting "the genius of this American author," said, "Frank Baum had a flow of imagination, a depth of humor, a sense of character and narrative control rare in writers of fantasy.'' The first book of the long Oz series is one of the fifteen best-selling books of the twentieth century and remains as popular with children today as when it was first published. . . . Although there remains some resistance on the part of educators and librarians, ***The Wizard of Oz*** is a major American work of juvenile literature. (pp. 11-12)

[A] reason for the success of ***The Wizard of Oz*** was Baum's awareness of what a child likes. His chapters are full of comic and casual conversations, quite different from the stilted language usual in children's books of the period. He was not interested in being didactic; his work is free of the cloying sentimentality and moralizing of much of the now forgotten but once popular children's literature of the last century. . . . Rarely were children given books ''just for fun.'' One of Baum's aims was to fill this void with entertaining tales of magic lands. (pp. 37-8)

With the simplest use of detail and emphasis Baum was able to create both the atmospheric and physical sense of a locale, whether imaginary or real. The first few paragraphs of ***The Wizard of Oz*** demonstrate this power to create a concrete reality through the barest means. Baum was interested in telling a good story so he worked hard on a strong plot in all his stories. . . . Baum wrote for children, but never down to them. he was also writing to please himself. He wanted to entertain, but he did not think it below him to insert a lesson if he could. (p. 38)

Of course, his story is not intended to have an overriding and didactic moral, as in the fables of Aesop and the tales of Perrault. Baum was creating a personal mythology, although intended for children, in which many truths of the world could be expressed. The characters and incidents in his book can be viewed as symbolic, and a symbol can represent many things at the same time. For example, besides possessing the qualities of courage, intelligence, and kindness, Dorothy's three companions also embody the three states of nature—animal, vegetable, and mineral. . . .

One cannot overemphasize Baum's conscious development of the ''modernized'' or ''American'' fairy tale. Earlier American writers had explored the possibilities of fantasy in the New World. In the short tales of Washington Irving and Nathaniel Hawthorne can be seen the origins of the search for a mythology of the American people. Baum was, however, neither concerned with the preservation of folk traditions as was Irving nor with great metaphysical morality as was Hawthorne. Baum was concerned with the interests and objects familiar to a child of that time. He did not feel a need to imitate the folktales of Grimm (as Howard Pyle did) to tell a wonder story; he did not have to return to the Greco-Roman tradition (as Hawthorne did) to understand mythology. As Baum mentions in his introduction to ***Baum's American Fairy Tales*** (1908), his stories ''bear the stamp of our own times and depict the progressive fairies of today.'' (p. 39)

Baum never, however, succeeded in creating a purely ''American'' fairy tale; he borrowed freely from European fairy-tale forms so that witches and wizards, magic shoes and caps exist in the same world with scarecrows, patchwork girls, and magic dishpans. . . .

Still more reason for the popularity of the book was its appeal to adults. Although juvenile literature is written for children, adults buy it. Both Denslow's pictures and Baum's text were sophisticated enough to amuse the turn-of-the-century mind. His characters were the result of a mature mind, no matter how they entertained children. Baum slipped many bits of wit and wisdom into his narrative; often those who read the book as children discover these subtleties upon rereading it as adults. (p. 40)

The author of ***The Wizard of Oz*** was . . . well read in the occult sciences. (p. 69)

The belief that everything is composed of ''elementals,'' or the four building blocks from which all matter is made is of the Aristotelian tradition. . . . Paracelsus, the sixteenth-century Swiss alchemist and physician, divided all spirits into four categories: Air, sylphs; Water, nymphs or undines; Earth, gnomes; Fire, salamanders. These could be expanded to the ancient idea of the four states of matter—gas, liquid, solid, and energy. . . . A quick glance at Baum's fairy tales reveals that he wrote about each Paracelsian classification of spirits. His sylphs are the ''winged fairies'' (Lulea of ***Queen Zixi of Ix,*** Lurline of ***The Tin Woodman of Oz***); the undines are the mermaids (Aquareine of ***The Sea Fairies,*** the water fairies of the first chapter of ***The Scarecrow of Oz***); the gnomes are the Nomes (the Nome King of ***The Life and Adventures of Santa Claus*** and ***Ozma of Oz***); and the salamanders are the fairies of energy (the Demon of Electricity of ***The Master Key,*** the Lovely Lady of Light of ***Tik-Tok of Oz***). Baum seems to have created a highly sophisticated cosmology by interpreting this theory of spirits or ''elementals'' in terms of traditional fairies.

This is basically a religion of Nature. Modern science itself has its origins in the occult sciences, in the search for the secrets of Nature. . . . It is not by mistake that the Shaggy Man in ***The Patchwork Girl of Oz*** refers to Oz as being a fairyland ''where magic is a science.'' Both science and magic have the same ends. (pp. 70-1)

[A] frequent complaint of librarians and critics is that ***The Wizard of Oz*** is poorly written. This would seem to be a matter of taste rather than of criticism. Baum was not a stylist as were many writers of juvenile literature. . . . Baum's main concern was in telling a good story, but his style is generally good and without the archaisms and long descriptive passages that, though of interest to an adult, sometimes confuse a child. It is also free of the sentimentality and class consciousness that mar many juvenile books of the nineteenth century. As with all great works of fantasy its style and mood are timeless; it reads as well today as when it was first written.

The Wizard of Oz is also well structured. Dichotomy is important. The first and last chapter take place in Kansas; the loss of home is comfortably restored. Dorothy is befriended by two good witches; in the second chapter the Good Witch of the North presents her with a pair of Silver Shoes, in the next to the last chapter the Good Witch of the South discloses their power. The center of the book is the Discovery of Oz, the Terrible. Dorothy is disappointed twice by the Wizard; first, after she kills the Wicked Witch of the East and he appears as a great head; second, after she kills the Wicked Witch of the West and he escapes in his balloon. The second half of the story reflects the first. The first concerns the discovery of intelligence, kindness, and courage; after the brain, heart, and courage are received, their qualities, embodied now with outer symbols, must be put into practice in the second half. There are conscious rephrasings of conversations of the first part in the second. In Chapter 18 the discussion about Glinda the Good reflects one in the second chapter between Dorothy and the Good Witch of the North about the Wizard. Within this framework Baum has created several of the most memorable characters in children's literature. The Scarecrow, Tin Woodman, and Cowardly Lion in their search for a brain, heart, and courage are today as much a part of the child's world as any traditional nursery characters. (pp. 76-7)

Michael Patrick Hearn, in an introduction to The Annotated Wizard of Oz: The Wonderful Wizard of Oz *by L. Frank Baum, Clarkson N. Potter, Inc., 1973, pp. 11-81.*

Ann (Sager) Blades

1947-

Canadian author/illustrator and illustrator of picture books.

Considered one of the most outstanding contemporary creators of Canadian picture books, Blades is recognized for helping to develop a nationalistic juvenile literature by providing children in rural areas with books about themselves. She is noted for the empathy, directness, and lack of sentimentality of her regional stories as well as for the fresh beauty of her watercolors. Combining such themes as compassion and personal courage with larger social issues like the effect of progress on tradition, Blades presents young readers with authentic depictions of northern Canada and its culturally diverse peoples. As a nineteen-year-old school teacher in Mile 18, an isolated Mennonite community in British Columbia, she saw the need for more appropriate books for her pupils and created her first and best-known book, *Mary of Mile 18* (1971), to fill the gap. Basing her main character on a child in her class, Blades describes how a lonely girl is allowed to keep a half-wolf puppy as a pet despite her family's objections. The story, which contrasts the warmth of human contact against the coldness of the environment, conveys a strong sense of hope despite the bleakness of the setting. Blades found the model for her second book, *A Boy of Taché* (1973), when teaching at a wilderness school on a Carrier Indian reservation in British Columbia. Portraying the heroic journey of a young Indian boy who seeks help for his stricken grandfather, she addresses themes of self-reliance and maturity, raises ecological concerns, and demonstrates the past and present-day customs of the Carrier Indians. Blades is also the author and illustrator of *The Cottage at Crescent Beach* (1977), a picture book which recreates her childhood summers, and *By the Sea: An Alphabet Book* (1983), which is both an ABC book in the classic tradition and the story of a day's adventures on the beach. She has contributed illustrations to several works by other authors, chiefly Betty Waterton's award-winning *A Salmon for Simon* (1978), in which a small Indian boy helps a salmon escape to the sea. A self-taught artist, Blades initially utilized a primitive, spontaneous style to create her watercolor illustrations, which are painted in soft, rich colors and include rudimentary human figures. Her later works show an increased use of perspective, expression, and detail while retaining the naive charm, excellence of design, and capacity to evoke place, season, and feeling that characterize all of Blades's art.

Critics praise Blades for the veracity, understatement, and optimism of her writing as well as for her ability to capture landscape and mood in vivid yet unpretentious illustrations. She is also acclaimed for the universality of her works despite their emphasis on locale and for the originality of *Mary of Mile 18*. Although some reviewers believe that Blades's pictures overshadow her narratives and that her illustrations for works by other authors are occasionally inconsistent with the texts, most agree that her memorable stories and striking paintings have made a significant contribution to Canadian children's literature.

Mary of Mile 18* won the Canadian Library Association Book of the Year Award in 1972 and the German and Austrian National Book Award Honorable Mention in 1976. *A Boy of

Photograph by Joan Malcolmsen. Courtesy of Ann Blades.

***Taché* received the Canadian Library Association Honorable Mention in 1974. *A Salmon for Simon* won both the Canada Council Children's Literature Award for Illustration and the Amelia Frances Howard-Gibbon Illustrator's Award in 1979. The first Elizabeth Mrazik-Cleaver Canadian Picture Book Award was presented to Blades for *By the Sea* in 1987.**

(See also *Something about the Author*, Vol. 16; *Contemporary Authors New Revision Series*, Vol. 13; and *Contemporary Authors*, Vols. 77-80.)

GENERAL COMMENTARY

JEAN McLAREN

[***A Boy of Taché*** is] set in the North, and as in ***Mary of Mile 18*** the setting is intrinsic and decisive. In both the harshness of the country makes survival difficult; failure is an ever present possibility and death comes easily. That is why Mary's father will not let her keep the puppy she finds since the household can only support animals that work or give food. It is only when the puppy proves his worth as a guard dog that he is given to Mary. Similarly in ***A Boy of Taché*** the land determines events in the characters' lives. The low key text tells of Charlie, an Indian boy who goes into the wilderness with his old grandparents, Za and Virginia, to trap beaver. Za develops a "cold sick'' which quickly turns to pneumonia in spite of Virginia's brew of ''the balsam bark, the spruce bark, the rock plant & the branch of the cranberry tree'' and it seems likely he will die. Although Charlie has never taken the riverboat up the dangerous Taché he must make the trip alone to the nearest settlement to summon help, knowing that if he touches the river bottom or hits a log the plane will not come and Za will die. In spite of the difficulties he succeeds and Za is saved. Thus the book ends on a positive note, for although Za will not be able to hunt or trap again Charlie is now strong enough and mature enough to carry on for him.

A Boy of Taché is as good a book as ***Mary of Mile 18*** is, and for the same reasons: both are entirely credible and both describe difficult situations with sympathy but without sentimentality. It is possible that children will respond more readily to ***Mary of Mile 18***—after all, it is hard to beat the emotional impact of a child/dog story—but the theme of courage and responsibility found in ***A Boy of Taché*** should attract older and more sensitive children.

In both books the drawings are primitive in style but there is a noticeable difference in their execution. The pictures in ***Mary of Mile 18*** are big and bold with people, houses, animals and machinery dominating the landscape. In ***A Boy of Taché*** the drawings are more delicate and detailed and the landscape predominates. Because ***A Boy of Taché*** is set in the spring the country also seems lovelier than in the harsh winter setting of ***Mary of Mile 18***. The soft blues and greens of rivers, lakes and trees and the oranges and reds of the sunsets give one a feeling for the beauty of the North.

This is a worthy successor to ***Mary of Mile 18*** and a must for all children's libraries. (pp. 28-9)

Jean McLaren, in a review of ''A Boy of Taché,'' in In Review: Canadian Books for Children, *Vol. 8, No. 2, Spring, 1974, pp. 28-9.*

LEONARD R. MENDELSOHN

[The following excerpt is taken from a speech delivered at the MLA Seminar on Children's Literature in 1974.]

A quiet but pleasant triumph of the interplay between image and text may be seen in ***Mary of Mile 18***, winner of the 1972 [Book of the Year Award], Canadian equivalent of the Newbery Award. Ann Blades, for one year an elementary school teacher in a Mennonite community eighteen miles to the east of mile 73 along the Alaska highway, found the faces of the children and the stark beauty of the surroundings crying out for a narrative. Her paintings contrast the harshness of subarctic life with the intimacy of the family. Like the pictures, the story is simple but satisfying, perhaps in this way capturing the lifestyle of these gentle but hardy people. The following year Ann Blades served in a school on an Indian reserve at Stuart Lake in the British Columbia wilderness. Her desire to provide these isolated school children with a book about themselves led to ***A Boy of Taché***, an understated account of the heroism of an Indian lad on a trapping expedition. The two volumes show that regionalism may be an asset, at least on the artistic level if not on the economic one, and they demonstrate that good images can make good narratives, even out of the most unpretentious plots. (pp. 145-46)

Leonard R. Mendelsohn, ''The Current State of Children's Literature in Canada,'' in Children's Literature: Annual of the Modern Language Association Seminar on Children's Literature and The Children's Literature Association, *Vol. 4, 1975, pp. 138-52.*

MARY RUBIO

Children fortunate enough to have been given Ann Blades' ***Mary of Mile 18*** and ***A Boy of Taché*** have acquired gifts that will both give pleasure and increase in value: I have little doubt that first editions of these two books will be valuable collector's items someday. Both of them, milestones in the production of quality Canadian children's literature, herald what I hope will be a unique contribution by Canada to the international body of children's literature—the contemporary realistic ethnic story. But more about that later. The best news is that Ann Blades, whose youthful work ***Mary of Mile 18*** received much attention as winner of the Book of the Year Award, has increased her reputation as a truly gifted author and primitive artist in ***A Boy of Taché***, and the public can only hope that she will give us more books of the same calibre.

Most librarians, teachers, and people interested in Canadian children's books know ***Mary of Mile 18*** and the story of its genesis: how its author created the plainly spoken, beautifully illustrated record of her experience with the children and scenery in that small Mennonite farming community in northern British Columbia so that her students would have a story about themselves. The plot is simple: little Mary Fehr, one of the several children of a kind but unsentimental homesteader, finds a puppy; her father voices the practical pioneer attitude that ''our animals must work for us or give us food.'' Her acceptance of her father's austerity makes highly poignant the pup's proving himself useful and Mary's subsequent joy when her father permits her to keep him.

Mary of Mile 18 is much more than plot, however. The text conveys extremely well the detail and quality of Mary's life through descriptive phrase and understatement. We are presented with details of living in cramped, primitive quarters where one goes into sub-zero weather to the outhouse and where one brings in snow to melt for water; we also see that the warmth of the woodburning stove and the smell of baking bread offset these hardships. We are given insight into that paradoxical loneliness and isolation which a sensitive child in a large family often experiences. And we find ourselves being led to feel compassion for a gruff, inarticulate father once Mary's mother explains to her, ''Your father gives you everything he can. When you ask for more, it hurts him to refuse. That is why he gets angry.''

The story's major artistic tension is symbolized by the cold, unfriendly, flashing Northern lights of the first page which serve as contrast to the warmth within a loving and lonely child's heart as she finally snuggles into bed with her new pet at the end of the story. Each symbol is beautifully illustrated by Blade's full page paintings of Mary, her family, the community, and the natural scenery.

A Boy of Taché, written about Ann Blades' experiences teaching the following year in the Indian reserve of Taché in northern British Columbia, has received less attention to date. This is unfortunate, I think, because it is as good—if not better—as an artistic production.

The book's design is similar to ***Mary of Mile 18***: large multicolor primitive paintings accompany each page of her text. However, an elementary school librarian has pointed out one possible difficulty caused by the format: because it uses the picture book format like ***Mary of Mile 18***, it will normally be shelved in the picture book section, yet the story—which is printed in much smaller type, incidentally—is more appropriate for intermediate level children because of its level of com-

From Mary of Mile 18, *written and illustrated by Ann Blades. Tundra Books, 1971. © 1971, Ann Blades. Reproduced by permission of the publisher.*

plexity. The teacher-librarian should be aware of this potential problem so that she will call the book to the attention of the older students who will enjoy it.

Children do not readily notice those literary techniques which give a work depth and power, but they are quite susceptible to their effects. The story of ***A Boy of Taché*** communicates with the reader on many verbal levels, both literal and symbolic, as well as visually through the illustrations whose rich colours present the seasonal cycles which figure so prominently in the work. The story itself is built on the simple, classic theme of a young boy achieving maturity, but the action is set within cycles of seasons and climatic forces which orchestrate human activity. When the story begins on a spring morning, Charlie, a young Indian boy of Taché, excitedly watches the past winter's ice break up. As it does, he and his grandparents, Za and Virginia, go through the spring ritual of preparing boats and supplies for the journey to northern trapping grounds. Once they begin the trip north, Blades skillfully begins to foreshadow themes which are later developed: passing one settlement, Charlie remembers that an old man of Taché was taken ill suddenly last year and died before a plane could come to take him to a hospital. We watch Charlie and his grandparents pass a construction camp of men who are clearing a track for a railroad; we hear Charlie reflect upon his father's occupation, that of being a guide to the hunters and fishermen who come here in spring, summer, and fall; finally, we see Charlie and Za watch a beautiful, powerful eagle circling in freedom overhead. "Not many left now," says Za. "Long ago he was all over. Now we see one, maybe two." Yes, there is an ironic undercurrent: as railroads and civilization encroach, nature and a way of life will die. But these reflections are subtly understated by Miss Blades; the focus of the story is on Charlie's growth into a man. With frightening speed, Charlie's grandfather Za catches a "cold-sick" which develops into pneumonia. Rushing against time, but mature enough to realize that haste may result in incapacitating his motor boat in the river, Charlie goes to get help for the rapidly weakening Za. Supporting the text, the last illustration shows two people, Charlie and an older man, watching the rescue plane carrying Za to a hospital; the airplane is flying West, into a glorious sunset. The white-haired friend reassures Charlie, "Za will get better . . . He never gives up. But this will be his last trip. You will hunt and trap for Za and Virginia now." Though Za will recover from this illness, the story contains his metaphorical death: the winter-spring cycle is complete, and Charlie, through his involvement in the cycle, has been born into manhood.

We feel relief that the grandfather will recover, yet joy that Charlie has grown to replace him. Likewise, we are strangely suspended between relief that the white man's hospitals are there and regret that progress is encroaching upon the natural world to which these Indians are so well attuned and which has so much meaning to them. (If we have missed the point, the editor's postscript tells us that the 1600 Indians in Taché in the 1880's have dwindled to a mere 300 in 1969.) Truly Charlie has grown to manhood, and we see that the Indian way is passing into the sunset along with Charlie's grandfather. The story is remarkable because, while it operates on so many levels, it is at the same time so simple. I loved it, and so did my six and nine-year-old children, both girls, when I read it to them.

Each of these Ann Blades' books in representative of what I hope will become one of Canada's strengths: the contemporary realistic ethnic story. Canada, because of her mosaic-like composition, is in a remarkable position to create a vital and distinctive children's literature of this type—stories which give a perceptive insider's presentation of the quality of human life within one of the specific cultural traditions of contemporary Canada. (pp. 77-9)

Mary Rubio, "Pictorial and Narrative Realism," in Canadian Children's Literature: A Journal of Criticism and Review, *Vol. 1, No. 1, Spring, 1975, pp. 77-9.*

CALLIE ISRAEL

"Yes, Mary is a real little girl" answers Ann Blades to the question most asked of her about her book ***Mary of Mile 18.*** Although she is shy and rather inarticulate, Ann's eyes light up when she talks about Mary and about her experiences as a teacher in North British Columbia. . . .

Out of her experiences there and her love for the people who faced their hardships with such courage, grew her desire to create a story which would show them and the rest of Canada that dignity and a brave spirit could dwell anywhere.

Ann has always liked to paint and although the illustrations for ***Mary of Mile 18*** have been described as naive and primitive, they show an eye for the emotional effect of colour and a flair for design. Above all, Ann has succeeded in capturing the stark beauty of Canada's north, and as one reviewer says "in any place in the world, you'd know the book for one of ours." That the illustrations were done with a child's water paints on ordinary paper seems appropriate to the simple story.

When Ann and her husband left Mile 18 for a teaching assignment at the Taché Indian Reservation the book was not yet completed. But, when it was finished and submitted to Tundra Books in Montreal, its charm and vitality sparked an instantly happy response. . . . (p. 16)

The Blades's experiences at Taché impressed Ann so much that her second story, ***A Boy of Taché,*** demanded telling. It tells of Charlie, a young Indian boy who lives with his grandparents, and how he ultimately saves his grandfather's life. The reconciliation of the old ways of hunting and fishing with the new way of life on the Reserve is the theme of the book. Again soft watercolours in the primitive style are just right to illustrate the story. Both pictures and words convey a vivid portrait of contemporary Indian life, a theme so much needed in books for Canadian children. . . .

A great deal has happened to Ann Blades since she wrote her stories of Mary and Charlie. Along with her artistic growth as a writer and painter has come an increasing social awareness and a firm determination to become involved with people. This led to her enrollment in a nursing course, and upon graduation, Ann worked for a time at the Vancouver General Hospital. . . .

The strength and artistry of her books come so deeply from her past adventures in living that whatever the future holds for her, these experiences are sure to be reflected in more exciting books for children by Ann Blades. (p. 18)

Callie Israel, "Anne Blades," in Profiles, *edited by Irma McDonough, revised edition, Canadian Library Association, 1975, pp. 16-18.*

SHEILA EGOFF

Ann Blades' watercolour illustrations of life in the far northern Mennonite and Indian communities of Mile 18 and Taché have a dream-like calm. In ***Mary of Mile 18*** and ***A Boy of Taché*** which she both wrote and illustrated, there is an effect of poignant clumsiness in her asymmetrical compositions—as if life has been caught and held in the primitive toy world of childhood art: houses look like toy boxes, children like wooden dolls. But if the figures are posed, geometrically stiff as statues or dolls, the subtle texture of layered washes, the wet and dry brush techniques, the rich, pebbly watercolour paper, the skilful blending of colours and tonal variations all convey a remarkable impression of weather, seasons, night and day in the lonely northern landscape. (p. 264)

. . . . .

Very few picture-storybooks achieve any kind of memorability; they come and go like the average best-seller, their fall as rapid as their rise. Two Canadian picture-storybooks will probably have more staying power—Ann Blades' ***Mary of Mile 18*** and William Kurelek's *A Prairie Boy's Winter*—chiefly because of their intense and loving portrayal of the Canadian landscape.

Mary of Mile 18 reveals the daily life of a little Mennonite girl in northern British Columbia (north on the Alaska highway for 73 miles then right for 18). It is a monotonous, hard-working existence whose pattern is broken only when she acquires a wolf-pup for a pet. Mary is an earnest miniature adult going about the serious business of living—all work and little play. The simple text has an inner rhythm that supports full-page watercolours that are warm, still, unsentimental evocations of a bleak yet glowing northern scene.

> One clear night in February the temperature drops to forty degrees below zero and the northern lights flash across the sky. Mary Fehr gets out of bed and goes to the window to watch and listen. She hears a crackling sound and smiles, excited. Mary likes to pretend that if she hears the music of the lights, the next day will bring something special.

In both the text and illustrations of ***Mary of Mile 18*** the simplicity achieved is perfectly suited to the subject. Blades' ***A Boy of Taché*** strives for the same quality in the text but it lacks polish, while the inherent dramatic possibilities in the little plot are not fulfilled. On an Indian reserve in northern British Columbia a young boy is preparing to accompany his grandfather on the annual hunt to trap beaver. The grandfather falls ill with pneumonia and Charlie goes for the help that will summon a rescue plane. While the illustrations show Ann Blades' great talent as a landscape artist and as an interpreter of Indian life, the text is little more than short, jerky sentences put together in 'readerlike' fashion:

> Camille turns to Charlie. 'Za will get better, Charlie. He never gives up. But this will be his last trip. You will hunt and trap for Za and Virginia now. I know you can do it, Charlie.'

As a teacher in the communities she describes, Ann Blades intended to give the children she knew a book about themselves; but the children in her book emerge as little stereotypes of social history rather than as characters that other children will take to their hearts. Her illustrations are a great contribution to the Canadian picture-storybook, however; the picture in ***Mary of Mile 18*** of the girl trudging through the silvery northern woods is memorable.

So far Ann Blades and William Kurelek have shown themselves as artists rather than as writers, but they both have the saving grace of unpretentiousness that allows their art to play upon the imagination. (pp. 280-81)

Sheila Egoff, "Illustration and Design" and "Picture-Books and Picture-Storybooks," in her The Republic of Childhood: A Critical Guide to Canadian Children's Literature in English, *second edition, Oxford University Press, Canadian Branch, 1975, pp. 255-70, 271-91.*

MURIEL WHITAKER AND JETSKE SYBESMA-IRONSIDE

Six Darn Cows [which was written by Margaret Laurence and illustrated by Blades] is a curiously old-fashioned book. With its pattern of misdemeanour . . . , atonement, and reconciliation, it is moral in a nineteenth century way. . . . Jen Bean and Tod Bean are "farm kids". Their parents have tried to instill in them the precept that "on a farm everyone helps." The children's particular job is bringing home the cows, a chore that they find time-consuming and boring. One day they carelessly leave the field gate open. The cows get out and the children with their faithful hound Zip must go into the dark woods to find them. The quest is accomplished with a minimum of suspense and with predictable success. Returning home with the six darn cows, the kids meet their mother who states the moral of the tale, or one of the morals, at any rate:

> All of us get fed up from time to time . . . I'm proud of you. You went into the woods to find the cows. You did what you thought was best. I think you are brave kids.

But do the author and artist really create the sense of courageous adventure that this maternal praise implies? In myth and folklore, entering the forest is a conventional way of demonstrating heroic attributes. (p. 59)

We would expect that Margaret Laurence, whose novels convey such a strong sense of locale, and Ann Blades, whose ***Mary of Mile 18*** was marked by a vivid revelation of northern landscape, would have been able to do rather well in the spine-tingling line. But neither represents the archetype adequately. It is true there is a passing reference to a wolf, but that is quickly counterbalanced by "Then they heard soft wings and a bird call. Thank goodness! It was only an owl that lived in the woods." The illustration shows a small orange bird perched like a stuffed toy on a high branch. The trees in the Dark Woods are tall and their bleak colour evokes a haunting mood but this feature is overpowered by the boring manner in which they are painted. Furthermore, the darkness is not convincingly created. A clearly lit foreground is combined with a dark sky in the background, while the children's clothes are as bright as they would be in daylight. There is inconsistency, too, between the artist's leafless trees and shrubs and the author's concluding remark: "And the next day it was still summer."

Some of the book's characteristics may be explained by the fact that ***Six Darn Cows*** is part of the Kids of Canada Series. Aiming, perhaps, at "comprehensive coverage," it comes close to being a unisex book. Nothing in the text distinguishes Jen and Tod—not even the assignment of guilt for leaving the gate open. They speak the same way; they feel the same way—"Me too"; and they are depicted visually with "twin" expression and "mirror-image" poses. (pp. 59-61)

Betty Waterton's ***A Salmon for Simon*** is also a story that teaches a lesson though in this case the theme is ecological as well as moral. Simon lives on an island near the west coast of Canada. His greatest desire is to catch a salmon with the fishing rod that his father has given him. But even though it is September, when the salmon are running, he is unsuccessful until an eagle drops a fish into a clam hole that the boy has dug. But "Sukai" is so beautiful that Simon has no wish to kill it. Rather he determines to find a way of returning the salmon to the sea. His plan requires long, hard work. His hands become blistered and his feet grow cold. But he is "warm inside. And happy." (p. 61)

Ann Blades' illustrations complement this text so superbly that she was awarded the Amelia Frances Howard-Gibbon Illustrators' Award for the best illustrated book published in Canada in 1978. She causes the observer's viewpoint to alternate in an imaginative way, so that the anxieties or joys of the boy are expressed in the varied space relationships used in the paintings: the eagle carrying the salmon flies high up—far away from Simon who is seen as a tiny speck on the shore. The

From A Boy of Taché, *written and illustrated by Ann Blades. Tundra Books, 1973. © 1973, Ann Blades. Reproduced by permission of the publisher.*

boy's diminished size makes one perceive the great distance between the eagle and Simon. At the same time, the close-up of the bird evokes a sense of excitement by the proximity to the onlooker of this dangerous creature.

In contrast to this use of space is the space relationship found in the illustration of the salmon swimming in the clam hole. Blades composes the scene as if the boy were seeing his own toes while looking down at the beautiful salmon. The observer identifies with Simon in perceiving this fish.

With regard to form, the draughtmanship in ***A Salmon for Simon*** is more successful than that in ***Six Darn Cows.*** The lonely figure of Simon on the title page, for instance, captures the gestalt of the boy in a far more convincing manner than is achieved by the quite formless cows and dog on the cover of ***Six Darn Cows.*** On both covers Blades uses simple forms, typical of her style, but the dark and clearly contoured boots of Simon remain in their stylization a strong form, while the equally black shape of the dog in the center of the Laurence book cover is formless in spite of being patched up with a weakly drawn contour which tries to assist us in reading this shape as "a dog." In several instances the proportions of the animals in ***Six Darn Cows*** are disturbingly awkward; this is not the case in the illustrations for ***A Salmon for Simon.***

At the same time, the children in the Laurence book lack variation in their movement and their stereotyped poses are repetitive compared with Simon's. Another point of comparison, the representation of night, is also expressed more sensitively in the Waterton book where the consistent use of muted tones in the illustration of Simon's return to the lamp-lit homes makes us "feel" the darkness. In short, the sensitive realism of the text in conveying both the exterior and interior world of the child, together with the formal strength of the illustrations, produces an impression of rich human experience that is strangely absent from ***Six Darn Cows.*** (pp. 61-4)

Muriel Whitaker and Jetske Sybesma-Ironside, in a review of "Six Darn Cows" and "A Salmon for Simon," in Canadian Children's Literature: A Journal of Criticism and Review, *No. 21, 1981, pp. 58-65.*

JON C. STOTT

While Ann Blades is a competent writer, the success of her books results mainly from her watercolor illustrations, which are the appropriate vehicle for the dominant subject of her works: the simple lives of children who are in harmony with those around them and who learn to adapt to their environments.

Because they deal with emotions of children in real life situations, Blades' books are enjoyed by early elementary aged children. These children can be invited to discuss how they would have reacted in similar situations and can examine how Blades makes use of different colors to suggest a variety of emotions. (p. 38)

Jon C. Stott, "Ann Blades," in his Children's Literature from A to Z: A Guide for Parents and Teachers, *McGraw-Hill Book Company, 1984, pp. 37-8.*

MARY OF MILE 18 **(1971)**

AUTHOR'S COMMENTARY

[*The following excerpt is from an interview by Eleanor Wachtel.*]

[Books in Canada]: How did ***Mary of Mile 18*** come to be written?

[Ann Blades]: When I was 19, I taught grades one to three at Mile 18, a small farming community just off the Alaska Highway, 50 miles outside of Fort St. John in northern B.C. It was a real shock to be thrown out into the bush with 22 kids and three grades after one year of teacher training with almost no classroom experience. I started the drawings during the Easter holidays. I was just beside myself because I hadn't gone out of Mile 18 the whole year and there was absolutely no social outlet for me at all. The men in the community could go hunting together, while the women stayed indoors and did their housewife things. I had nothing in common with 45-year-old housewives. So really it was something to occupy my time. That was the main thing. It was also prompted by the fact that there were no books, well—few books that were suitable for kids in a rural setting. So many books that are published in Toronto or New York are intended for urban kids and have very little meaning in Mile 18.

BiC: Do you work from sketches?

Blades: I sketched Mary. They didn't know I was doing the book and neither did I. I just knew I had to sketch her. I took photographs too, and partly it was just from memory. I did the story and one set of illustrations while I was at Mile 18, but I did the illustrations that appear in the book the following year when I was teaching on a northern Indian reserve at Taché. (p. 32)

Ann Blades and Eleanor Wachtel, in an interview in Books in Canada, *Vol. 8, No. 10, December, 1979, pp. 32-3.*

Mile 18 is a real place, a little, remote Mennonite community in Canada, and Mary was a real child, one of the students in the Mile 18 school where the author taught. While the book has a fairly patterned plot (Father refuses to let Mary keep a half-wolf cub until it gives warning of a coyote) the story's major appeal is in the picture it gives of the hardworking, almost self-sufficient lives of the families of Mile 18 and of the frigid and beautiful country in which they live. The paintings have a primitive sturdiness and naive charm that is reminiscent of the work of Grandma Moses.

Zena Sutherland, in a review of "Mary of Mile 18," in Bulletin of the Center for Children's Books, *Vol. 25, No. 9, May, 1972, p. 135.*

[A] recent book and one about contemporary life, ***Mary of Mile 18,*** of course is the direct result of the author's intimate involvement in a small out of the way community. Ann Blades was part of it as a teacher, and totally aware of the realities of life in the British Columbia backwoods where the people accept their fate and make the best of it. She accepts the objective facts, but she also knows that human beings need the promise of hope, however small that hope must be. In its own way this beautiful story recreates one definite response to Canadian conditions of life, but it stirs only sympathy and admiration, not criticism. (p. 7)

Irma McDonough, "Canadian Identity in Children's Books," in In Review: Canadian Books for Children, *Vol. 7, No. 4, Autumn, 1973, pp. 5-8.*

[*The following excerpt is from a talk by Blades's publisher, May Cutler, the founder and president of Tundra Books. Her speech was given at the first Pacific Rim Conference on Children's Literature, which was held 10-15 May 1976.*]

From A Salmon for Simon, *written by Betty Waterton. Illustrated by Ann Blades. Douglas & McIntyre, 1978. Text copyright © by Betty Waterton, 1978. Illustrations copyright © by Ann Blades, 1978. All rights reserved. Reproduced by permission of Douglas & McIntyre Ltd.*

[A book close] to my heart, because it cost me so much, is Ann Blades' ***Mary of Mile 18***. It changed my attitude, I suppose. If I am very anti-nationalistic, and very resentful of many of my fellow publishers, and especially of the Canada Council, it is associated with the production of this one book. It moved me far out of nice Canadianism (which means doing everything sweetly and kindly), into doing what I believed was excellent. And I was determined to do it. Ann Blades had sent ***Mary of Mile 18*** to most of the publishers in Canada before it came to Tundra Books. After all, we were barely in existence at the time, and one of the last one would normally think of. I was so delighted with the book that I felt I had to find a way to publish it. I applied to the Canada Council . . . for help, because it was a color book and very expensive. Their anonymous readers sent back a letter saying, "Isn't it a pity that there are so few children's books coming out in Canada, and that we can't do better than this?" So I was turned down, but I decided somehow or other to publish that book. I did, finally, and in the first year it sold only fourteen hundred copies. Last year it sold thirty-five thousand.

It is a very special book, and it is a book I am proud of because it is unique and unrepeatable. Even Ann Blades herself could never repeat it, because the whole tension and excitement came from her particular effort and love in one particular situation. She is not a school-trained artist, but by God, she conveyed what she felt. Of course, that is part of the charm of naive or primitive painting, the painting of untaught or self-taught artists. When it reaches her particular dimension, such as doing it for the children in her class, it comes through. That is the most important thing, not the fact that it was chosen as the Canadian Book of the Year for Children the following year. (pp. 213-14)

It is a specialized book and it is very hard for people to imagine what was involved in selecting it. It is not hard now: somebody looked at it the other day and said, "Oh, well, anybody can see that's a great book." And I said, "Yes, that's nice," since nobody could see it six years ago. ***Mary of Mile 18*** is one book which I do believe will be around twenty, thirty, or forty years hence. Most of all because the children, who are the final arbiters, the last (often the last thought of, I am afraid, in all of these matters) to judge, love it. (p. 214)

May Cutler, "Ah, Publishing!" in One Ocean Touching: Papers from the First Pacific Rim Conference on Children's Literature, *edited by Sheila A, Egoff, The Scarecrow Press, Inc., 1979, pp. 212-20.*

Reminiscent of Kurelek's *Lumberjack*, [***Mary of Mile 18***] . . . glorifies the spartan life. . . . Blades' appreciation of the Canadian wilderness and of those who eke out a living there is apparent in her richly colored and textured primitive watercolors. Providing a breathtaking backdrop to the story, they contrast the stark frozen landscape with the cozy warmth of the seven-member Fehr family inside their rustic farmhouse.

Leah Deland Stenson, in a review of "Mary of Mile 18," in School Library Journal, *Vol. 23, No. 6, February, 1977, p. 54.*

This simply-told tale of a child's longing for a pet is truly delightful. Narrated in a style as crisp and clear as its Canadian frontier setting, the story conveys, by its careful choice of detail, the feel of life as experienced by the child Mary and her homesteading farm family.

The author excels in transmitting psychological as well as physical messages. For example, the scene in which the mother mediates between father and child is exquisitely, even inspirationally, done: "Your father gives you everything he can. When you ask for more, it hurts him to refuse. That is why he gets angry." The word images are beautifully complemented by eighteen colorful illustrations, matched in their primitive style to the tone of story and scene.

Perhaps the book's most unique contribution is the basic, hardworking, family-centered life style which it portrays. This provides the modern, urban parent and child with a refreshingly different experience than that encountered in their daily existence—an experience similar in idea and tone to the ever-popular *Little House* series by Laura Ingalls Wilder.

Diane A. Parente, in a review of "Mary of Mile 18," in Best Sellers, *Vol. 36, No. 12, March, 1977, p. 385.*

This book gives a vivid description of the day-to-day life of a modern pioneer family. Blades' close attention to small details—such as the way the children dress, and the plumbing and heating systems in a house with wood-burning stoves and no running water—makes the story realistic. The vocabulary and sentence structure are suitable for readers between the ages of 6 and 10. However, even small children can understand Mary's desire for a puppy of her own and her feelings of disappointment and injustice when her father refuses to let her keep the wolf pup. The ultimate happy ending always pleases children.

Ann Blades' simple, colourful illustrations complement her text. They realistically portray a winter day in northern B.C. including icicles, northern lights and frosty forests. The wood heater made from an oil barrel and the outhouse of Mary's yard are authentic touches.

The descriptions of Mary's life contain many elements familiar to northern children, many of whom still go to bush camps in the spring and summer, where wood must be cut and buckets of water carried. They know what it's like to wear many layers of clothing, and tie "scarves over their heads and across their faces to protect them from the cold." Children who live in regions where the temperature falls below minus 40° for weeks at a time can easily imagine Mary's physical discomfort when walking home from the Bergen farm:

> As she runs home in the cold night her toes and fingertips sting and the air burns her throat.

Blades' attention to detail in both text and illustration, and her understanding of Mary's feelings make the book believable for primary school children. While the story has a northern setting, Mary's dreams and desires are universal. (p. 143)

Mary Ellen Binder, "Northern Children," in Canadian Children's Literature: A Journal of Criticism and Review, *Nos. 39-40, 1985, pp. 141-43.*

A BOY OF TACHÉ **(1973)**

Based on an episode which occurred while the author was teaching at the remote Indian reserve of Taché in northern British Columbia, this is a moving story about a young Indian boy. Charlie and his grandparents set out on the annual beaver hunt, journeying over land and water until they reach their cabin. There, the 74-year-old grandfather, Za, wakes up one morning with a "cold sick" and develops pneumonia. Charlie must follow the same route in reverse to get help at the nearest hospital. The text is overly wordy, but Blades' folk-primitive watercolor illustrations are as distinctive as those in her acclaimed ***Mary of Mile 18.*** While not as appealing as its predecessor, the simple recreation of this tribe's speech and way of life will be useful for units on Indians.

Marilyn McCulloch, in a review of "A Boy of Taché," in School Library Journal, *an appendix to* Library Journal, *Vol. 20, No. 8, April, 1974, p. 55.*

A view of life in British Columbia different from last year's ***Mary of Mile 18,*** this one reads more naturally as there is no conventional story imposed on the material. Here the scene is Taché, a Carrier Indian reservation where Charlie lives with his grandparents Za and Virginia. . . . [When] Za catches "a cold sick," Virginia fears it's pneumonia, and Charlie has to go phone for an ambulance plane from a distant camp. None of this is dramatized and, like her narrative, Blades' naive watercolors avoid closeups of Charlie. If neither is involving—or as sharp as the details of harsh living in ***Mary***—both text and pictures have the certain authenticity that makes the visit worthwhile.

A review of "A Boy of Taché," in Kirkus Reviews, *Vol. XLV, No. 4, February 15, 1977, p. 159.*

Set in 1969, this story of Charlie . . . is really a vehicle for gently evoking a contemporary tribal life-style. Amidst the understated exposition there's enough drama to keep young listeners hooked. . . . The northern locale shows through in Blades' serene, earthy-hued watercolors that feature birch-covered fields, rough cabins, and open sky. Loving and matter of fact, with the same quiet respect that characterized the author's earlier ***Mary of Mile 18***. . . .

Denise M. Wilms, in a review of "A Boy of Taché," in Booklist, *Vol. 73, No. 16, April 15, 1977, p. 1262.*

The story gives a strong sense of the continuity of a cultural pattern, of ways that are tempered but not changed by progress. The writing is direct and simple, placed in a column of unfortunately small print at the side of the full color painting on each page: the paintings have a sturdy, primitive quality that is an effective foil for the delicacy of subtly colored skies and the patterns of trees.

Zena Sutherland, in a review of "A Boy of Taché," in Bulletin of the Center for Children's Books, *Vol. 30, No. 10, June, 1977, p. 154.*

The fine, slightly primitive watercolors showing magnificent skies and a striking prevalence of white birches are superbly evocative of the simple life of the Indians. Signs of modern life are subtle: motors on the boats, Za's remark about the eagle as a vanishing species. The book is both a believable adventure story and a sympathetic portrait of the Indians of Taché. A map and a description of life among the Carrier Indians in the 1880s and of their subsequent population decline are added.

Ann A. Flowers, in a review of "A Boy of Taché," in The Horn Book Magazine, *Vol. LIII, No. 5, October, 1977, p. 530.*

From By the Sea: An Alphabet Book, *written and illustrated by Ann Blades. Kids Can Press, 1985. Copyright © 1985 by Ann Blades. All rights reserved. Reproduced by permission of the publisher.*

THE COTTAGE AT CRESCENT BEACH **(1977)**

While this book doesn't have the drama or tension of ***Mary of Mile 18*** or ***A Boy of Taché,*** it does illustrate Ann Blades' feeling for landscape and her ability to capture not only the details of a scene but the emotions associated with it. This book, which is a loving reminiscence of Ann Blades' childhood summers, is in the tradition of Robert McCloskey's ***A Time of Wonder,*** being a book with no plot as such, but with a unity provided by a natural rhythm. For McCloskey, the rhythm is that of the entire summer season; for Ann Blades it's the cycle of a day. We follow the young Ann, and her friend Marjorie as they pursue their daily activities. The climax of the day is a visit to a local haunted house, the conclusion a wiener roast. This book may not attract as many readers as did ***Mary of Mile 18,*** but it is a very good book and it marks an advance in Ann Blades' career.

Jon C. Stott, in a review of "The Cottage at Crescent Beach," in The World of Children's Books, *Vol. III, No. 1, 1978, p. 55.*

A SALMON FOR SIMON **(1978)**

[A Salmon for Simon *was written by Betty Waterton.*]

A dedicated fisher, Simon becomes disgusted when he fails to catch a salmon and decides to dig for clams instead. Fortuitously, a high-flying eagle, excited by some screeching seagulls, loses its grip on a fish and drops it into Simon's clam hole. At last he has a salmon; but the boy, seeing at close range the beauty of the creature and its dependence on him for life, devises a way to get it back to the sea—and freedom. The small boy's recognition of nature in its own element, his confrontation with a life-and-death situation, and his determination to do something on his own are perceptively and warmly told in spite of the contrived appearance of the fish. The deep blues, greens, and browns of the full-page watercolor paintings not only expand the cool, uncrowded atmosphere and meld the sea and land of the Pacific Coast of Canada but also strengthen the foundation of decision—and the solitary, resolute way in which it was made.

Barbara Elleman, in a review of "A Salmon for Simon," in Booklist, *Vol. 76, No. 17, May 1, 1980, p. 1300.*

Simon is a west-coast Canadian Indian—which, happily, one gathers only from the pictures and by inference. Another pleasant difference from the norm is the fate of the coveted salmon that finally lands, thanks to a passing eagle, in a clam hole, now filled with water, at Simon's feet. In time-honored fashion Simon yearns, now, to return the big silvery salmon to the sea; but it's "too big and heavy and slippery for him to pick up" (though the pictures, unfortunately, don't really show it so). So Simon digs "a channel for the salmon to swim down to the sea"—and the sight of that salmon entering the channel (to the words "cold sea water flowed into it") and proceeding toward the sunset and the red-streaked sea is one that few youngsters (or adults) will soon forget. The text, though slightly wordy, has some resonant lines too—making this altogether one of those almost-ordinary books that unobtrusively gets under the skin. (pp. 579-80)

A review of "A Salmon for Simon," in Kirkus Reviews, *Vol. XLVIII, No. 9, May 1, 1980, pp. 579-80.*

The book won the major Canadian prize for illustration, and the soft watercolors that fill, but do not crowd, the pages are attractive in their simple composition and the subdued use of color that accentuates the mood of solitary activity . . . [The] chief appeal [lies] in the response of a small Canadian Indian boy to the beauty of another creature.

Zena Sutherland, in a review of "A Salmon for Simon," in Bulletin of the Center for Children's Books, *Vol. 33, No. 11, July-August, 1980, p. 225.*

The sweeping, flowing lines and deep, warm watercolors convey the majesty of the west coast of Canada and the touching appeal of the sturdy, resolute little Indian. This is a harmonious blend of picture and text, a truly lovely little book.

Linda Haag, in a review of "A Salmon for Simon," in Catholic Library World, *Vol. 52, No. 4, November, 1980, p. 191.*

BY THE SEA: AN ALPHABET BOOK **(1985)**

An ABC book may seem to be the simplest kind of picture book. In fact, it challenges the artist to do something interesting with the random structure provided by the alphabet while helping a child absorb the order, shapes, and sounds of the letters. . . .

[Ann Blades] has met this challenge admirably with ***By the Sea.*** She has combined a clear, basic approach to the alphabet with a fresh look at a day at the beach.

As a pure ABC book, ***By the Sea*** is the classic kind. A is for airplane, B is for ball, C is for crab—each item named is distinctly shown in a full-page painting. At the bottom of the page is the letter in upper and lower case and the relevant word. The connection between the letter, the word, and the picture could not be more straightforward.

But the pictures do much more than teach the alphabet. They show 26 aspects of a day at the beach in clear, pale colours that create the feeling of a cool breeze off the sea. The perspective shifts from wide views (as in K for Kite) to closer looks (D for Dog). This is an uncrowded beach, and the two children who appear in most of the pictures find plenty of room to play in the beach grass, eat ice cream, and sit bundled in their towels or jackets, gazing out to sea. The lines in the paintings flow so that even though the figures are rather flat and simplified, there is an ease and a sense of relaxation throughout the book.

As an ABC and as a book about a day at the beach, this book can be looked at, talked about, and enjoyed many times.

Celia Lottridge, in a review of "By the Sea: An Alphabet Book," in Quill and Quire, *Vol. 51, No. 8, August, 1985, p. 37.*

Ann Blades lives just a block away from Crescent Beach near Vancouver and this lovely ABC is a collection of the people, the animals and the vistas which are to be seen where sea, sand and mountain meet along the Pacific coast of Canada. The watercolours are gentle yet vivid in their evocation of Ann Blades' seashore experiences—crabs, eagles, fish, kites, and sand castles. Each letter in the alphabet is matched to a single word, and the selection is clear, obvious and above all, pleasant to behold.

A review of "By the Sea—An Alphabet Book," in Children's Book News, *Toronto, Vol. 8, No. 3, December, 1985, p. 3.*

[Alphabet] books have become the ultimate illustrator's exercise, not just pedagogical tools. Even those children who know their ABCs will want to read Ann Blades's ***By the Sea.*** The West Coast artist's beautifully muted and moody watercolors take a brother and sister through a day at the beach. As they gambol over the sandbars, the two discover a multitude of seaside delights. Unlike the rambling style of most alphabet books, the children's reactions weave a dramatic thread from play and wonderment to daydream and finally exhaustion. And Blades does not have to strain the theme to illustrate difficult letters: ''X'' stands for drawing Xs in the sand; ''Y'' is for yawn; ''Z'' is for falling asleep on a beach blanket at sunset. (p. 45)

John Bemrose, Marni Jackson, and Ann Walmsley, ''A Treasury of Children's Books,'' in MacLean's Magazine, *Vol. 98, No. 49, December 9, 1985, pp. 44-5.*

Judy (Sussman) Blume (Cooper)

1938-

American author of fiction and picture books.

Perhaps the most popular contemporary author of works for upper elementary to junior high school readers, Blume is the creator of frank, often humorous stories which focus on the emotional and social concerns of suburban adolescents. Recognized as a pioneer for her candid treatment of such topics as menstruation, masturbation, and premarital sex, she is also considered a controversial and provocative figure by those critics and librarians who object to her works as overly explicit and harmful, and denounce her for not taking a moral stand on the actions of her protagonists. However, Blume has won the devotion of an extensive and loyal youthful following, as evidenced by the record sales of her books and the thousands of letters she receives regularly from children; as critic Naomi Decter observes, "there is, indeed, scarcely a literate girl of novel-reading age who has not read one or more Blume books." Blume deals with issues that are significant to the young, such as friction between parents and children, friendship, peer group approval, divorce, social ostracism, religion, and death, as well as sexuality. Combining intimate first-person narratives with amusing dialogue supplemented by familiar everyday details, her books reveal Blume's East Coast upper-middle-class Jewish background while describing the anxieties of her protagonists, characteristically female preteens and teenagers who encounter problematic situations and survive them. Despite the fact that she often ends her works on a note of uncertainty, Blume consistently underscores her books with optimism about the successful adaptability of her characters.

Photograph by George Cooper. Courtesy of Judy Blume.

Although Blume is best known for her fiction for adolescents, she began her career by writing books for younger children, an audience she still continues to address; *Tales of a Fourth-Grade Nothing* (1972) and *Superfudge* (1980), two entertaining tales about ten-year-old Peter and his incorrigible baby brother, Fudge, are especially popular with readers. *Are You There, God? It's Me, Margaret* (1970) depicts eleven-year-old Margaret's apprehensions about starting her period and choosing her own religion. At the time of the book's publication, Blume was praised for her warm and funny recreation of childhood feelings and conversation, but was criticized for her forthright references to the human body and its processes. *Margaret* is now considered a groundbreaking work due to the candor with which Blume presents previously taboo subjects. *Forever* (1975), in which Blume relates the particulars of her eighteen-year-old heroine's initial sexual experience, created an even greater furor. Despite the fact that it was published as an adult book, protestors pointed out that Blume's name and characteristically uncomplicated prose style attracted a vulnerable preteen audience who could be influenced by the intimate details of the novel. In *Tiger Eyes* (1981), Blume relates the story of how fifteen-year-old Davey adjusts to her father's murder. Hailed by many critics as Blume's finest work for her successful handling of a complex plot, *Tiger Eyes* includes such issues as alcoholism, suicide, anti-intellectualism, and violence. *Letters to Judy* (1986) was prompted as a response to the voluminous amount of mail that Blume receives from her readers. Selecting a number of representative letters to reprint anonymously with accompanying comments, she created the book for a dual purpose: to enable children to see that they are not alone and to make parents more aware of their children's needs.

Reviewers commend Blume for her honesty, warmth, compassion, and wit, praising her lack of condescension, superior observation of childhood, and strong appeal to children. Critics are strongly divided as to the success of Blume's plots, characterization, writing style, and nonjudgmental approach; they object to her uninhibited language and permissive attitude toward sexuality, and complain that her cavalier treatment of love, death, pain, and religion trivializes young people and the literature written for them. However, most commentators agree that Blume accurately captures the speech, emotions, and private thoughts of children, for whom she has made reading both easy and enjoyable.

Blume has won approximately fifty national and international child-selected awards for her various works.

(See also *CLR*, Vol. 2; *Contemporary Literary Criticism*, Vols. 12, 30; *Something about the Author*, Vols. 2, 31; *Contemporary Authors New Revision Series*, Vol. 13; *Contemporary Authors*, Vols. 29-32, rev. ed.; and *Dictionary of Literary Biography*, Vol. 52: *American Writers for Children since 1960: Fiction*.)

AUTHOR'S COMMENTARY

[The following excerpt is taken from an interview by Norma Klein with Blume, who comments on the way censorship has affected her literary career.]

I am finding more editorial resistance today to language and sexuality in books for young people than I did when I began to publish, eleven years ago. In ***Tiger Eyes,*** the novel I have just finished, my editor asked me to take out a short paragraph in which a fifteen-year-old girl masturbates for the first time since her father's death. We agreed that it was psychologically sound behavior, a beginning in terms of being able to feel again, after having been numb for many months from the trauma of the tragedy. So I was somewhat disappointed at my editor's suggestion, but I understood. That paragraph wasn't worth the censor's wrath. It wasn't what the book is all about. And both of us want the book to get to the kids.

Masturbation, more than sexual intercourse, has become a no-no in books for young people. I find this difficult to explain and more difficult to accept, but there it is. In a recent book banning, outside of Phoenix, Arizona, I participated by phone in a radio interview with the three mothers who brought the complaint against my books to the school board. One woman said, "Judy Blume tells our children that it's all right to masturbate, that nothing bad will happen to them if they do. But we teach our children that it's harmful and sinful to touch their bodies and they will be punished for it."

I can't help wondering, if I were writing ***Deenie*** today, whether the scenes dealing with the discussion of masturbation would be editorially censored. The answer is probably yes, although my editor has been my supportive ally over the years, a true friend, and he has fought on my behalf over countless issues in my books. This is not an easy time for him, either. To be forced into keeping an eye on the censors, to be forced into taking them seriously, is painful for all of us.

If I were writing ***Forever*** today, it would have to be published as an adult novel. And that's a sad twist. I don't feel I can write realistically about today's teenagers, in their own language, and publish it as a book for young people. Ten giant steps backward.

Next to sexuality, language is a major cause of book banning. And so, our editors and publishers are wary. In ***Tiger Eyes,*** I was asked to rewrite heated argumentative scenes without using language that my editor considered inflammatory to the censors. It was difficult for me to rewrite those scenes but I finally solved the problem by writing, "I called him every name in the book." Not exactly the emotional impact I was after but I assume my readers will understand.

This climate of fear is contagious and dangerous. The censors are crawling out of the woodwork. The publishers are in business to sell books. The writers want their books to be published. We're caught in a no-win situation. One side of me says, "Don't give in, Judy! Fight for what's important to you—honesty and reality for kids." The other side says, "Accept the fact that this may not be the right time." What's the answer? Do we wait it out? Do we bang our heads against the wall? I don't know. The only thing I am sure of is this: the battle isn't doing the kids any good. And somebody has to stand up for their rights. If it comes down to taking sides, I'm with them. (pp. 139-40)

Norma Klein, "Some Thoughts on Censorship: An Author Symposium," in Top of the News, *Vol. 39, No. 2, Winter, 1983, pp. 137-53.*

GENERAL COMMENTARY

RICHARD W. JACKSON

[At the time he wrote the following excerpt, Jackson was vice-president and editor-in-chief of Bradbury Press as well as serving as Blume's editor.]

Judy Blume's books talk to kids. Hundreds of letters tell us so. For one thing, her stories sparkle with kids' talk. Her dialogue seems to be theirs, not so much written as overheard. But few people can know the part that talk plays while Judy is creating her books.

Early in her career Judy Blume found a writing style exactly right for her stories (and her readers,) and she's perfected it. Style is the one aspect of the writer's art that she and I don't talk much about; her style is *there;* editing it would just be fussing. But we do talk about plot, structure, character, pacing. And after such talks new scenes, new characters come spinning out of her imagination; she always knows more about her people, kids or adults, than she shows in the early versions of the manuscripts we see. Talking somehow releases what she knows, frees ideas that were inside a story and inside her head, just waiting. Since our first meeting about ***Iggie's House,*** Judy's first novel for children, we have spent literally weeks talking.

I usually see a new manuscript from her in its third draft, that is, after she has written the book out and polished it twice. The manuscript always arrives with a handwritten covering letter; for instance, this one: "Here's Margaret! I can hardly stand parting with her. She's become my very good friend." Readers of the book, which became ***Are You There God? It's Me, Margaret,*** will know what Judy meant. My partner, Bob Verrone, and I read the script that came with the letter . . . and started talking immediately. "True," "honest," "funny," "needed," "controversial" were some of the words we used. . . . We talked, off and on, for a couple of weeks.

Talking with Bob helps me crystalize my thinking before I start making notes for Judy. These are most often written in the margins of the manuscript during my second reading. They may take me another couple of weeks.

Judy then comes in to Bradbury to talk. . . . The manuscript sits between us . . . , and we go through it page by page. We may spend an hour talking about a single point in one paragraph because such a point often draws to itself many other strands from elsewhere in a book. Sometimes I've made suggestions about moving a chapter from one place to another or even deleting it, or amplifying a line or a short scene from which Judy may create a new chapter completely. Sometimes we discuss recutting chapters, that is, starting and stopping them in different places—it's remarkable what an effect she can achieve by ending a chapter in the middle of an event rather than at its resolution. For instance, the break between chapters 4 and 5 in ***Are You There God?*** is effective because it suspends Margaret Simon between first-day-at-a-new-school feelings and anticipation about joining her new friends' secret club.

A lot of our talking is questions and answers. . . . Here's an example. In ***Are You There God?,*** Nancy Wheeler, one of Margaret's friends, goes on a weekend trip to Washington, D.C. with her family. While she's away she drops Margaret a postcard with three words on it: "I got it!" (she refers to getting her period for the first time). Margaret reads what Nancy has written, is furious and rips up the card. On the manuscript alongside the message I wrote: "Is Nancy telling the truth?" There was something in her character that made me suspect she was lying. The question surprised Judy, who was thinking about Margaret more than she was about Nancy, but it released something too. It turned out that Nancy *was* lying. That fact, and Margaret's reaction to learning about it later on, is very important to the story.

Judy is naturally a first-person writer, she's most comfortable expressing her main character's point-of-view. In first-person books the speaker plays a literary role, but he or she must always be "in character." For this reason, first-person writing is tricky. Judy and I had one of our best editorial conferences on this point about Tony Miglione in ***Then Again, Maybe I Won't.*** In order to organize my thinking I had written out a report and sent it to Judy before she came in for our second talk on the script; these quotes come from that written report: "What is Tony writing this book about? Not about 'values' (which might summarize for adults the theme of *your* book), but about himself and the world of his life: family, friends, moving, school, doctors, etc. Yet the sound of what he tells us is objective rather than intimate. . . . You've given him, at the beginning of the book, a reporter's role.

"You are a writer, so you are mindful of keeping us informed; the trick will be to inform us but not to appear that you're doing so, because Tony is *not* a writer. . . .

"It suddenly strikes me what it is about the Jersey City sequence that isn't right. It is a *sequence* of observed details of the Migliones' life there, the trappings, but most of it is from the outside. The present chapter one springs to life through Tony as a person: once when he is speculating on whether his father is a spy, and again at the end, when the meaning of the move to Rosemont crashes in on the kid and he bawls.

"The description of moving is so 'thing-bound.' Could moving be portrayed subjectively from Tony's insides by means of a scene about some loved article of his that Mama wants to leave behind in Jersey City?"

Judy went home to think about it. By the end of the next week, the loved article had become a school pennant—and the scene that had grown in the center of the second chapter showed us naturally a kid's feelings about moving from a familiar house to a strange new one. The feelings had been there all along; the question had merely nudged them into the light.

Because of our talks, ***Then Again*** grew by thirty manuscript pages, its characters grew fuller, its pacing between serious and comic more complex. When the final manuscript arrived, Judy enclosed a note: "It's been great fun to work on but I'm afraid if I hang on to it any longer I'll do too much to it. . . . Hope it all goes together right—I can't tell any more." Of all Judy's books, ***Then Again*** is my favorite—perhaps because of the good work on it I shared in.

With one exception, all of Judy's manuscripts have grown longer during editing. The exception is ***It's Not the End of the World,*** from which Judy cut several sequences and one character between the third draft and the final. Originally, Karen Newman's father met and fell in love with a young woman after he'd moved out of the family house. She was the antithesis of Karen's mother, and naturally enough Karen, who tells the story, didn't like her one bit. But the woman was a true-to-life character in a divorce situation. In the third draft of the book Karen's father remarried and his three kids attended the wedding with very mixed feelings. The scene was excellently done, but the remarriage issue took the focus off Karen (as the narrator she couldn't know anything that happened out of earshot, couldn't express anyone's emotions except her own; the result was that only dislike for the woman came across, making her a "heavy" and Karen's father appear unsympathetic, as if the divorce were his fault). Judy's story concerns a twelve-year-old girl and her family. She doesn't take sides in the divorce question—in fact, she set out to show us two decent parents caught by their situation rather than a bad scene caused by one or the other. We talked about it. Judy decided that for Karen's sake in the story she should cut out the remarriage issue. I agreed with her; the decision grew out of her feeling for Karen.

It's Not the End of the World presented a plotting challenge: a chronology imposed by the legalities of divorce proceedings. Judy's solution was Karen's "Day Book" which unobtrusively dates events throughout the last half of a school year, and—more noticeably—allows Karen complete and often desperate honesty in a situation in which honesty is difficult. (On March 2 Karen writes in the Day Book: "Divorce . . . it's the end of the world." On May 9 she writes to her grandfather: "Daddy and Mom are definitely going to get divorced! I've tried hard to get them back together. Honest! But nothing works. I have discovered something important about my mother and father. When they are apart they're not so bad, but together they are impossible!" During those three months Karen has sensed how difficult adults find being honest with children; she comes to accept what she can't change.) To me, ***It's Not the End of the World*** is about honesty as a kid experiences it, rather than divorce.

But the novel is often described as Judy Blume's "divorce book." We don't consider any of her books by their apparent subject matter—for menstruation (***Are You There God?***), wet dreams (***Then Again***) or divorce (***It's Not the End***) are not the subjects of any of these books. To us the books belong to the kids who people them. As a writer, Judy's means of showing us kids in all their quirkiness is *situational*. Each of her main characters faces a problem, but none of her books is about the problem; each is about a kid or kids in a real situation, facing it in his or her own way.

So our editorial talks turn again and again, page after page, to kids. Some of Judy's clearest appear in her newest book, ***Deenie.***

Deenie Fenner is a beautiful girl, almost thirteen, who seems destined to become a model. Her mother pushes and pushes, though Deenie would rather be having fun with her friends than traipsing around to modeling agencies. A perceptive gym teacher notices something odd about Deenie's posture during a cheerleading tryout, and eventually Deenie is told by doctors that she has scoliosis, a gradually progressing curvature of the spine which, if untreated, will cause pain and permanent deformity. Treatment is either an operation or a brace which has to be worn for four years. The book is very recently published, so I won't spoil it by giving the story away. But the outcome of the final scene surprises even Deenie herself.

The *editorial* surprise was not Deenie at all. It was her friends, Janet and Midge. From the beginning, Deenie was a jaunty, outgoing kid, and she was right in the center of the book, but as a character she had nowhere to go. The situation stopped her from growing literarily, just as scoliosis was stopping her spine from growing straight. Suddenly it struck us (in a telephone conversation, I think) that Janet and Midge were the answer. Deenie *did* have somewhere to go in her relationship with these kids, from whom she decides to keep the truth about her illness. Judy called me up in great excitement about how a revision of Janet and Midge was coming along. When they hear, finally, that Deenie is to have an operation, they take her for a day on the town, and buy her a nightgown for the hospital. The nightgown, an ordinary enough article, like Tony Miglione's school pennant, symbolizes a situation and expresses with simplicity a range of feelings in the story. And it becomes an element of the plot.

Judy was pleased with Janet and Midge. But in ***Deenie*** she was most pleased with a couple of pigeons. In chapter 16, Deenie is called to the Vice-Principal's office at school. She doesn't know why, and she's nervous. She describes the scene: "I opened the door. Mrs. Anderson was smiling. I've heard she always does, even when she's punishing kids. Her desk was in front of a big window but she sat with her back to it so she couldn't see the pigeon standing on the ledge. Ma says pigeons are dirty birds with lots of germs and I should stay away from them." Further in the scene, after Mrs. Anderson has told her that she's eligible to ride the special bus for handicapped children, Deenie tells us: "All of a sudden there was a big lump in my throat. I had to look out the window so Mrs. Anderson wouldn't notice. Another pigeon was on the ledge and both of them were walking back and forth looking at me." Two weeks later Deenie is called to the office again, on the same matter. "'Oh that . . .' I looked out the window but no pigeons were on the ledge. I tried to think of what to say . . ." Those pigeons, which Deenie first sees when, in consternation, she looks away from Mrs. Anderson, which then seem to be dumbly confirming Deenie's oddity as someone handicapped, and which later have flown off, express deftly the progression of Deenie's fears and feelings about herself. A small touch, to be sure, but the kind of detail which in its rightness gives a writer joy.

Has the joy in writing come through in this appreciation? Perhaps writing appears to be just work, work, work, for editor as well as author. I hope that's not the impression I give. Writing *is* work, no doubt about it: saying what you mean is difficult, and the pressure to grow from book to book is sometimes immobilizing. But Judy Blume, for one, has been rewarded with great popularity. She does receive hundreds of letters.

> Nothing pleases me more (she has written us) than having one of my young readers ask, "But how do you know all our secrets?" I try to explain that when I write it is the child I *was* speaking but kids find that very hard to believe.
>
> I really do remember everything that's happened to me from third grade on. I know just how I felt and exactly what I was thinking. When I hear the phrase Now Child I say to myself . . . Oh, that was me in 1950. Yet it also describes my daughter today. And fifty years ago it was my mother, writing secret thoughts in her diary.
>
> The middle years of childhood are tough and just getting through the day is a full time job for most kids. That's the way it's always been and the way it's always going to be. Growing up is no picnic. No kid gets by without a few scars; most wind up with more than that . . . and a first experience is still a first, whether it's a kiss, a menstrual period, or a punch in the nose. There will always be fear and hope, love and hate, jealousy and joy . . . because feelings belong to everyone. They are the link between the child of today and the children we were.

Judy Blume takes joy in her books. And it shows. From the first idea to the final touch the books bloom steadily, warming to the objective light we cast during the editorial (talking) process. But the Blumes the world loves are Judy's. Editors do not write the books they publish, and though their influence in a book and over a writer may be strong, the writer is the originator, who has the first and the last word. (pp. 779-83)

Richard W. Jackson, "Books That Blume: An Appreciation," in Elementary English, *Vol. 51, No. 6, September, 1974, pp. 779-83.*

INTERRACIAL BOOKS FOR CHILDREN BULLETIN

The message of most of the Blume books is, simply stated: Even if your parents get divorced, your sibling gets a lot of attention, you get scoliosis or you haven't gotten your period yet, it doesn't mean that your parents don't love you, that you can't make it. Living is a difficult task, but nothing is cut and dried; time heals much and you can work through, overcome or learn to live with such difficulties.

However, it is precisely because Blume pretends to a socially conscious perspective and wants her characters to come to grips with life's problems, that most of her books are disappointing. Too often she poses difficult "problems" and then proceeds to end her stories in confusion, ambivalence and inadequate problem-solving (although it must be noted that having the child's ambivalence be the resolution—which Blume sometimes does—is an OK approach as long as it does not leave the reader ambivalent).

In ***Tales of a Fourth Grade Nothing,*** Peter lives in the shadow of his mischievous brother, Fudge, who gets most of their parents' time and attention. By focusing heavily on the humorous aspects of Fudge's behavior, Blume neglects Peter. Thus, when Peter's parents finally give him overdue attention at book's end—sufficient enough for Blume—it seems to the reader like too little, too late. One senses that despite the author's intentions, Peter will continue to feel like a "nothing" way past the fourth grade.

In ***Otherwise Known as Sheila the Great,*** another book which is funny at times, we have a frightened ten-year-old girl whose insecurity manifests itself in chronic lying, boasting and competitiveness. Unfortunately, the book never rises above being a chronicle of Sheila's dissembling and ends with the girl's unpleasant character virtually intact. One wonders what the point is, and the mind boggles to find a reviewer in *Publishers Weekly* calling ***Sheila*** and "absolute lark of a book" (Aug. 14, 1972).

Blubber, the most poorly resolved story of the lot, also features an obnoxious, nasty hero. This time it is fifth grade Jill Brenner who, along with her school friends, guiltlessly harasses and terrorizes a fat girl they have dubbed "Blubber." In the confusing and unreal ending, Jill comes to Blubber's defense only because another harasser is threatening to dominate the group, not because harassment as such is inhumane. The pack then turns on Jill, who glibly out-talks them, imparting the lesson that if you have a quicker lip than everyone else you can survive and keep the pack off your back. If not, watch out. Most unsatisfactory reading.

In addition, these three stories offer a picture (present as well in some of the other books) of terrific competitiveness between children—friends, siblings, schoolmates and sexes. While Blume undoubtedly wishes to tell-it-like-it-is and capture what she probably views as the reality of kids' competitive drives, something is way off. The implication is that competition and even misogyny are natural, universal, even sort of "cute" childhood traits. Many in our society mistakenly assume that these forms of behavior are universal "truths of human nature." In fact, they are not necessarily basic to all children, and it has been demonstrated that in some societies such behavior is actually considered abnormal. While Blume does, at times, present children as loving and supportive, a more politically conscious or understanding writer would have proceeded differently. Bent on creating new kinds of anti-competitive, anti-sexist, loving children, the writer would not create such mean characters without somehow making clear to readers that competitiveness is destructive and unnecessary for survival. Not to do this seems irresponsible, giving children a go-ahead to be smart-alecky and nasty.

Another area in which Blume must be faulted concerns feminism, or rather her lack of it. Despite her "timely" subject matter and "progressive" treatment of sex and body functions, in other respects Blume seems quite conventional and outdated. With the exception of ***Deenie,*** her perspective seems to be virtually untouched by the women's movement.

Although six of Blume's eight main characters are girls, not one fights the feminist fight—that is, struggles consciously to change the second-class status of her girlhood. Only in ***Deenie*** is there any clear feminist sentiment, expressed (for example) in the hero's unequivocal support of her tough girl friend who would rather "be on the football team than cheer for it," and who intends to sue the school if not given the chance. In general, the girl characters are more or less 1950's types—cute, sometimes tom-boyish, smart-alecky, precocious. They are not girls who are bent on changing the society in which they live, or who want to take new, assertive, out-front postures in life. (The one exception here is Winnie of ***Iggie's House,*** who single-handedly, albeit ineptly, tries to fight racism in her neighborhood.)

Sex roles are rarely questioned. One of the few instances occurs in ***Deenie,*** when the hero consciously rejects the housewife role and wishes, instead, to be a doctor or lawyer. There is no question, for example, that the mother rather than the father will keep the kids after divorcing in ***It's Not the End of the World***; it is "cute" when Peter Hatcher's father is totally inept at caring for his kids while his wife is away and "cuter" still when he plots to leave all the dishes for his wife's return. And Winnie's mother—unchallenged by author Blume—won't take out the garbage because it's a "man's job." Finally, despite Blume's frank handling of sexuality, even this seems dated. Girl characters are into such things as shaving their legs and cosmetics (***It's Not the End of the World***) or are obsessed with bras and developing breasts like those of *Playboy* bunnies (***Are You There, God? It's Me, Margaret***).

Blume's treatment of ethnic and racial issues is equally wanting and limited in scope. The Miglione family of ***Then Again, Maybe I Won't*** is Italian, and the Garbers who move into ***Iggie's House*** are Black, but the only other ethnic representations are half-Jewish Margaret, Deenie's Jewish girl friend and the Chinese American girl friend in ***Blubber.***

In ***Iggie's House,*** Blume makes her one and only attempt at an anti-racist statement by having Winnie start a one-girl crusade against her neighborhood's racist reaction to new Black neighbors. However, a confused picture is presented as to what is racist and what isn't. Winnie's parents, for example, are very racist and spend a large portion of the book trying to "make up their minds" whether or not to sign a petition against the Black family. Although they are never seriously forced to confront and deal with their own racism, Blume nevertheless portrays them as likeable, positive people. When Winnie, a confused "liberal" herself on the race issue, defers to her family in the final scene, readers might easily deduce that the parents' racist position is really OK after all. Moreover, the Black viewpoint, though represented to some extent through the character of a Black boy, is not strong enough to provide real illumination of the issues for readers.

The class setting of Blume's books is usually middle and mostly suburban. Only Deenie's family and the Migliones in ***Then Again, Maybe I Won't,*** are working class, and the latter is the only Blume book to discuss class issues. While the author shows that a rise in class status can mean a lowering of humanitarian impulses, one questions why the author chose a working-class family of Italian descent to make her point.

Judy Blume is obviously concerned about focusing, in her work, on the real interests, needs and experiences of children in reality-oriented situations. The popularity of her books attests to the fact that, overall, she has caught the tempo of contemporary pre-teen attitudes and behavior. However, while a first reading of her books is, in many cases, a "fun" experience, questionable hidden messages become perceptible the second time around. We must, therefore, regretfully conclude that notwithstanding her writing skill, keen wit and effective handling of sexual material, her social consciousness is largely underdeveloped. (pp. 8-10)

"Old Values Surface in Blume Country," in Interracial Books for Children Bulletin, *Vol. 7, No. 5, 1977, pp. 8-10.*

R. A. SIEGEL

Like Cuisinart and fast food franchises, Judy Blume goes marching on. Onwards through sibling rivalry, divorce, menstruation, teenage sex, and ethnic upward mobility. One hesitates to speculate on what the theme of the next book for the pre-adolescent market will be for a writer whose muse seems to be Haim Ginott rather than Calliope. One can be assured, however, that it will mirror what people have been talking about lately in Darien and Short Hills and San Fernando, that it will be rendered with a cheerful, reassuring suburban sameness, and that it will have the same relationship to a truly significant exploration of social problems that a Stanley Kramer film does.

It's no secret that kids like Blume books—boxed paperback sets were a big seller last Christmas—but it's doubtful that the novelty of her themes alone is responsible for her popularity. After all, this kind of "realism" has become the cliched substance of Norman Lear situation comedies, and Judy Blume's books are really old-fashioned by comparison with, say, Norma Klein. In spite of the many, tiresome allusions to Bloomingdale's, these are not really trendy books and the values they promote are very much those of mainstream, Middle America.

Nor does it seem that Blume's books, or any other "problem" novels, ought to be discussed and evaluated on the basis of what they teach children about handling specific social or personal problems. Though books of this type may sometimes be useful in giving children a vehicle for recognizing and ventilating their feelings, they are, after all, works of fiction and not self-help manuals. Their success depends on the author's handling of narrative techniques and their meaning and educative value is embedded in those same techniques. To discover the key to Blume's popularity, one has to look beyond the realistic trappings and didactic intentions of the "problem" book to a closer study of why her narrative techniques work especially well with children. To understand what her books really teach children, one has to understand the way in which these techniques are used to communicate a style of experiencing and perceiving the self and the world and a definition of what it means to be a pre-adolescent child in suburban America.

As is often the case with popular fiction, Blume's books are successful for what they *are not* as much as for what *they are*. That is, her books are not very demanding and they make for the kind of easy, rapid reading that children like to relax with. Since all her books are told through the voice of a child narrator, the vocabulary is necessarily limited and the sentence construction basic and repetitious.

Her plots are loose and episodic: they accumulate rather than develop. They are not complicated or demanding and the pace is sometimes sloppy, as in ***Blubber,*** where Jill's change of heart seems too sudden and contrived. She has a repertoire of stock minor characters—the annoying older or younger sibling, the steadfast friend—who can be counted on as plot machinery or for comic effects. In the tradition of children's books, parents are kept harmlessly out of the way. And in the vein of recent American children's books, these parents are usually well-meaning but ineffectual characters whose efforts at communication are often comic failures.

On the other hand, Judy Blume is a careful observer of the everyday details of children's lives and she has a feel for the little power struggles and shifting alliances of their social relationships. She knows that children can be cruel to one another and that they are deeply concerned with peer group judgments. She can be funny in a broad, slapstick way, as in ***Tales of a Fourth Grade Nothing,*** but her humor is more often based on regarding her characters with cloying adult irony. For example, there is the scene in ***Are You There, God? It's Me, Margaret*** where Janie and Margaret, with much self-consciousness and embarrassment, purchase a package of sanitary napkins and Margaret incredulously observes the clerk's blase attitude: "That was all there was to it! You'd think he sold that kind of stuff every day in the week."

Blume's most characteristic technique and the key to her success is the first-person narrative: through this technique she succeeds in establishing intimacy and identification between character and audience. All her books read like diaries or journals and the reader is drawn in by the narrator's self-revelations. Creating the illusion that one is having an intimate conversation with a close friend, the first-person narrative succeeds especially in children's books because children enter so readily into a partnership with fictional narrators and because they tend to experience books as extensions of other types of personal relationships. (pp. 72-4)

What strikes one immediately about Blume's narrators is the sameness of voice. Listen, for example, to these two passages from ***Blubber*** and ***Then Again, Maybe I Won't***:

> By lunchtime, it was easy to tell that Wendy and Laurie were going to be best friends and so were Donna and Caroline. Some people are *always* changing best friends. I'm glad me and Tracy aren't that way. Still, it's nice to have a regular friend in your class, even if it's not a best friend. I ate lunch with Rochelle again. She's kind of quiet but I get the feeling that a lot goes on inside her head.
>
> I thought, maybe that's the trouble. Maybe kids don't always want you to give them everything. I looked at Ralph. I can do that without hating him now. I can say, okay, you're just ordinary but I can't do anything about it. I'm trying to understand his feelings about wanting his kids to have everything.

The odd thing is that, although the verbal patterns are the same in these passages, they presumably represent the thoughts of an eleven-year-old, middle class girl from a Philadelphia suburb and a thirteen-year-old, Italian boy whose roots are in Jersey City. Essentially the same voice speaks to the reader in ***Deenie*** and ***Margaret,*** in all of Blume's books, in fact, and the effect of this sameness on the child reader is probably reassuring, like discovering an old friend in a new neighborhood.

Blume's choice of first person narrative and her didactic intentions make it imperative that her characters be perceptive and self-conscious and that they continually draw conclusions from their experience. The above passages are once again characteristic: the narrator observes someone else's behavior and then leaps toward a generalization about that behavior. Blume's narrators are always cogitating, earnestly trying to be honest to their own feelings and to discover meaning and truth in the world: one has the sense that they will grow up to be characters in a John Fowles novel.

None of this can be taken very seriously as an accurate description of the mental processes of pre-adolescent children: kids of this age are beginning to become self-aware but this is too formulated, too pat, and thought crystallizes too readily into truism to be convincing. What seems important to note here, however, is that self-consciousness is offered as a model for children to identify with and that self-awareness and the awareness of other people's feelings are presented as goals in themselves.

Self-consciousness and self-awareness, however, can turn rapidly into self-absorption. Blume's books are remarkable in the number of narcissistic incidents they portray: Margaret examining herself in a mirror, Tony's masturbation, and so on. The pattern of such incidents suggests that they are fundamental to Blume's conception of the pre-adolescent child's nature.

One of the disturbing results of this preoccupation with the self is the loss of tangible intimacy with any concrete thing or object: the texture of lives lived in a specific, particular place is missing. Although the geography of the world of Blume's books is rather limited—Jersey City, Radnor, the urban or suburban Northeast—these places exist only as proper nouns, generalized abstractions. For all the reader knows about the sights and sounds and smells of these places, they might as well be Omaha or Anaheim. To put it another way, Blume makes Any Place into No Place, a talent which should not be confused with that of, say, E. B. White, who can turn Any Place into Every Place, an idealized but vividly realized setting.

It can be argued that Blume is holding up a mirror to the suburban milieu that is the setting of her novels. In ***Are You There, God? It's Me, Margaret,*** Margaret comments on the sameness of suburbia: "Every house on our new street looks a lot the same. They are all seven years old. So are the trees." In ***Then Again, Maybe I Won't,*** Tony watches as his family becomes assimilated to their new suburban neighborhood by slavishly imitating the materialistic habits of their new neighbors. In the end, though, Judy Blume's books are impoverished because she fails to establish a vital relationship between place and character. She creates no place for her characters to inhabit except the self, and more importantly, no world for her readers to live in. Things are not encountered by her characters; they are understood through intellection and rationalization.

In traditional children's literature, characters went out into the world, encountered it on non-subjective terms, and came to self-awareness in situations and through social actions which were meaningful in themselves. In Blume's novels, the quest turns inward, self-awareness becomes a goal and not a product, and actions are valuable only in so far as they authenticate the feelings of the narrators. This may be good training for life in narcissistic, self-absorbed, suburban America but, in the long run, it is poor nourishment for the imagination of children. (pp. 74-6)

R. A. Siegel, "Are You There, God? It's Me, Me, ME! Judy Blume's Self-Absorbed Narrators," in The Lion and the Unicorn, *Vol. 2, No. 2, Fall, 1978, pp. 72-7.*

NANCY CHAMBERS AND LANCE SALWAY

[*The first excerpt in this section is by* Signal *editor Nancy Chambers from her letter to critic Lance Salway; the second is his reply.*]

Britain is rather late in Blume-ing—she was absolutely top of the pops in the U.S. in the early seventies, I seem to remember. But then, we didn't get *Harriet the Spy* for over a decade. Didn't you turn down a Blume or two when who were a children's book editor a few years back? Would you now? Idle question, but interesting. I hadn't read any of the younger Blumes until this spring bunch. Knowledgeable friends in the States were so dismissive of her, I just assumed that her books would be as inconsequential as her enormous sales indicated they had to be. In fact, I was quite bowled over by her expertise. Not only does she write about real kids in a way that undoubtedly means something to them but she can encapsulate an emotion or a perception in a single sentence that makes the reader know it for himself as well as knowing it for the character in the book. Literary writers would linger over such points, but Blume whacks it down and gets it through to her audience with a childlike minimum of fuss. True, all her books seem to have the same narrator, whether male or female; the sound is the same, no matter what the setting. But I'll bet it'd be the rare child who would ever be bored by a Blume. (pp. 171-72)

. . . . .

I think your estimate of Judy Blume's skills is exactly right. She really does know how children feel and think and react. I found this particularly true of ***Otherwise Known as Sheila the Great,*** the story of Sheila Tubman's summer stay in a small town and how she succeeds in mastering her fear of dogs and water and other things. Blume is so good on the petty worries and humiliations of childhood, the complicated verbal sparring that happens when children meet for the first time and feel their way towards friendship, the ridiculous lies that they tell to impress others and bolster their own self-confidence. I think that Sheila Tubman *is* a distinctive narrator, though what you say about a similarity of narration certainly applies to the 'problem' novels. There *isn't* much difference between Tony Miglione in ***Then Again, Maybe I Won't*** and Karen Newman in ***It's Not the End of the World,*** apart from their particular hang-ups. I didn't care much for ***Tales of a Fourth Grade Nothing,*** mainly because I didn't find the lively little brother—Fudge the Pest?—as endearing as Blume clearly hoped I would. But ***Otherwise Known as Sheila the Great*** is a delight, and ***It's Not the End of the World*** is the only children's book about divorce I know that seems to ring true. Judy Blume's books deserve the same popularity here as they enjoy in the States. (p. 173)

Nancy Chambers and Lance Salway in their letters, in Signal, *No. 30, September, 1979, pp. 171-76.*

NAOMI DECTER

Miss Blume's works offer a child's-eye view of the trials and tribulations of life, and cover just about every social and emotional problem her readers are likely to encounter. . . .

[Most] of her books are in one way or another about sex. Her characters discuss their own sex lives or their parents'; they masturbate and menstruate; they worry about the size of their breasts and about kissing; they have wet dreams and they even have intercourse.

Given the sophistication of Miss Blume's material, her style is surprisingly simple. She writes for the most part in the first person: her vocabulary, grammar, and syntax are colloquial; her tone, consciously or perhaps not, evokes the awkwardness of a fifth-grader's diary. . . .

If the prose often seems at odds with the subject, however, it is perfectly suited to Miss Blume's imagination and characterization. Plot in the Blume books follows a rather strict pattern. There is, first of all, a "problem"—social or emotional; then, a hero or heroine to define, and other children to participate in, the problem; parents to pay the bills, drive the cars, and occasionally give a word of advice; the odd troublesome sibling or doting grandparent. The problem is resolved through the child's own experience, and the book ends.

Miss Blume's stock melodramas are staffed by stock characters—the Right People (from the author's point of view) and the Wrong People. The Right People do and think the Right Thing, the Wrong People the Wrong Thing. One Right Person is virtually indistinguishable from another, and Wrong Persons bear a striking resemblance to other Wrong Persons.

Children, for example, who are interesting—i.e., eat only peanut butter, quote the *Guinness Book of World Records,* or know how to do fancy embroidery—tend to learn the right lessons, while uninteresting children seem to be bullies, thieves, or liars. Mothers who work are wise, helpful, and even fun, while mothers who stay at home and spend their time cleaning the house tend to nag and whine. Grandmothers who dress well and, perhaps, belong to Planned Parenthood are lively and warm, while Grandmas with ugly black old ladies' shoes are cold and forbidding—and seek in vain for childish affection. Parents who respect their children's judgment—and their privacy—are rewarded with filial love and respect, while parents who insist on dictating "life-styles" court disaster—even suicidal children. Teachers who encourage the creative impulses of their students preside over a happy and stimulating learning environment, while teachers who concentrate on the dull facts elicit boredom and fidgeting. (p. 65)

[***Blubber, Deenie,*** and ***Forever***] are a perfect, if pint-sized, literary embodiment of contemporary enlightenment. They preach all the modern pieties and strike all the fashionable poses. They do so, moreover, with the rigidity of vision—and the social snobbery—that is the hallmark of their creed. There is in them no room for complexity of character, for conflicting emotions, or even for moral regeneration. Miss Blume's heroes never have an unacceptable thought; her villains, having once deviated from orthodoxy, are condemned absolutely to their villainy. And underlying everything is the sense that—whatever the issue—villainy is just the tiniest bit tacky.

All this, and sex to boot: Miss Blume has obviously found a winning combination. Her books not only cater to and reinforce the prejudices of her audience, they also answer a need peculiar to that community. For, quite apart from arousing and satisfying her young readers' prurient interest, the Blume books offer an ideal solution to the liberated parent who wonders how best to fulfill the uncomfortable duty of teaching his child sexual freedom. Judy Blume can safely be trusted to explain that *everyone* masturbates, and that it's the healthiest thing in the world—fun, too; that restrictions on youthful sexuality (especially female) are unhealthy relics of a repressed past; and that sexual intercourse is simply pleasurable and without consequence—as long as one is on the Pill.

The Blume ethic does not stop at erotic casualness. Miss Blume is as much a creature of her times and class spiritually as she is sexually. The consistent and overriding message of her books—for which, predictably enough, she has received the greatest acclaim—is that the proper focus of one's curiosity and concern is oneself. Everywhere Miss Blume garners high praise for her "respectful," "realistic," and "accurate" depiction of children's preoccupation with themselves.

Realistic, respectful, and accurate she is—with a vengeance. So respectful is she that not a childish thought or feeling is too pedestrian to merit her attention; so realistic that not a detail of a child's life—from breakfast menu to sleepwear fashions—is too tedious to go unrecorded; so accurate that an afternoon with Katherine, Deenie, or Jill must seem to her readers like a few hours alone in front of the bathroom mirror.

That a few more hours in front of the mirror is the last thing a young girl needs is a thought that does not seem to have occurred to Miss Blume or her army of fans. Yet the happiest magic of children's literature has always resided in its ability to burst the narcissistic bubble. One can, and does, learn any number of things from the March family, from Tom Sawyer, and even from Nancy Drew—for all their retrograde sociology. One learns to recognize and respect courage and honor; one learns the value of humor; at the very least, one learns to appreciate and emulate the spirit of adventure. Above all, one learns that life is full of things one has never seen; one learns the habit and the rewards of lifting one's eyes from one's own navel to look out upon the world.

Miss Blume finds the navel a much more worthy object of contemplation than the world—which is clearly why, in a narcissistic age, her limiting and narrowing vision should be heralded for its honesty and praised for its realism. (pp. 66-7)

Naomi Decter, "Judy Blume's Children," in Commentary, *Vol. 69, No. 3, March, 1980, pp. 65-7.*

JOHN GARVEY

At her best Judy Blume is a kind of training bra for Ann Beattie; at her worst she reads like Woody Allen without the humor. ***Forever*** features a grandmother who sends Katherine the following letter:

> "I hear you and Michael are officially *going together*. Thought these might come in handy. And remember, if you ever need to talk, I'm available. I don't judge. I just advise. Love, Grandma."

This grandma is nothing like mine, who found the Andrews sisters risqué. This grandma sent Katherine "a whole bunch of pamphlets from Planned Parenthood on birth control, abortion, and venereal disease. At first I was angry. Grandma is jumping to conclusions again, I thought. But then I sat down and started to read. It turned out she had sent me a lot of valuable information. . . ."

An ideology is on the prowl here, meaning well every inch of the way. This preachiness can also be found in Norma Klein's books. . . .

A book called *Freddy's Book,* by John Neufeld, tells about a little boy's frustrating attempts to find the meaning of the mysterious word "fuck." (What a distance this is from a search for the Grail!) Finally his kind older friend David tells him what it means and concludes, "If you're lucky all your life, Fred, that's what fucking will be: making love with someone you love."

Is it really *luck,* or does some sort of commitment have something to do with love? These books say next to nothing about choice and commitment, but they are full of feelings and the right attitudes towards feelings, and the tricks chance can play on children who would rather their parents stay together than get divorced. The main work of these books is teaching children to cope. There is something dismal about teaching children to cope, where in previous generations books for children encouraged a larger imagining, a thrill at the size of the universe they might encounter. In these books there is at best a small satisfaction: you learn to line up with the Right Attitudes.

Now it can be argued that some things ought not to be dealt with in children's books, but as soon as I try to think of something that shouldn't be dealt with I think of exceptions. . . . The landscape of children's literature is broad and wild and sometimes horrifying. The robber girl in Hans Christian Andersen's The Snow Queen is wilder than anything Judy Blume could imagine. Blume would have a counselor—a sensitive one—deal with Huck Finn.

The prose in these books reminded me of the Reverend Raymond J. O'Brien, who wrote books for Catholic kids several decades ago. I remember two titles, *Nice Going, Red* and *Brass Knuckles*. His books were first-person narratives, usually, about confused kids who were surrounded by Bad Companions. There was not always a clear reason for their being Bad; in this, Fr. O'Brien was close to traditional story-telling (which knows that evil is interesting in itself) and far from Judy Blume, who has reasons for everything: for her, an unpleasant child must have an unhappy home life, and could never be simply a pain in the ass. Fr. O'Brien's kids always encountered wise adults, often in the form of priests, who helped them out. Judy Blume's planned parenthood grandma may be less traditional than Fr. O'Brien's helpful priests, but she is certainly intended to be just as didactic.

It is important for adolescents to understand that feelings which are demanding and confusing are also quite normal; and if parents and schools won't tell their children about sex, better they should learn from Judy Blume than not learn at all. But more than information is being delivered here; a point of view is being urged on kids. The assumptions which saturate these books are the assumptions of upper-middle-class white liberals. They seem so self-evidently right to the authors that I am sure they don't see what an orthodoxy they have accepted. No doubt they think of their attitudes as simply true, and of more traditional attitudes as reactionary or unenlightened. The same point of view is shared by many of the educators who have pushed "values clarification" in the schools: people can find their own values, they assume, as if values were innate things. You go through your feelings and reactions—it is like looking for lice—until you find your values; they are in there somewhere, covered over with hang-ups and insensitivities. (pp. 392-93)

[The] fundamentalists have perceived one thing clearly: there is a new orthodoxy. It is being pushed in some schools, on television, and in a lot of children's literature. A few school boards have tried to make this fundamentalist objection to certain texts and library books look like the inquisitors versus us non-judgmental professionals, but frequently that isn't the case at all. The problem is that here one orthodoxy confronts another. (p. 393)

John Garvey, "The Voice of Blume: An Orthodoxy That Doesn't Recognize Itself," in Commonweal, *Vol. CVII, No. 13, July 4, 1980, pp. 392-93.*

DAVID REES

Perhaps the best thing to do with Ms. Blume would be to ignore her altogether; she is so amazingly trivial and second-rate in every department—the quality of her English, her ability to portray character, to unfold narrative—but that is impossible: she is "controversial" on both sides of the Atlantic, and her work is read and discussed not only by the young but by those adults who have a serious concern for children's literature. (p. 173)

What sort of picture would a being from another planet form of teenage and pre-teenage America were he able to read ***Are You There, God? It's Me, Margaret*** and ***Forever***? He would imagine that youth was obsessed with bras, period pains, deodorants, orgasms, and family planning; that life was a great race to see who was first to get laid or to use a Tampax; that childhood and adolescence were unpleasant obstacles on the road to adulthood—periods (sorry!) of life to be raced through as quickly as possible, to be discarded as casually as Michael in ***Forever*** throws away his used contraceptive. He would discover that the young have almost no intellect and very few feelings; that falling in love is not a matter of complex emotions that seem at the time to change one's perception of people—indeed the whole world—out of all recognition; but that it is simply a question of should one go on the pill or not, swapping partners quite heartlessly, and whether one is doing it right in bed. He'd realize, with some surprise, that sex isn't even very erotic: that it's just clinical.

Adolescents do of course have period pains and worry about the size of their breasts or penises; they fall in love and some of them sleep together. There should obviously be a place for all these concerns in teenage novels; but to write about them, as Judy Blume does, to the exclusion of everything else is doing youth a great disservice. She succeeds quite magnificently in trivializing everything, particularly young people themselves. She would appear not to know that they do find time, whatever their emotional and sexual preoccupations may be, to be interested in and participate in a very wide spectrum of human existence. To serve them up the kind of stuff of which ***Forever*** consists is to underestimate totally their ability to think and to feel, not only about themselves but about the whole complexity of living that goes on around them.

Nor is that Judy Blume's only major fault. ***Forever*** has a bad taste, a want of sensibility, a heavy-handed clumsiness that is breath-taking. The reader's reaction is laughter—anything from an embarrassed snigger to falling out of a chair with hilarity—when he ought to feel moved or excited or enthralled. Instead of enjoying one of the most rewarding of experiences, that of being so wrapped up in reading a novel that one loses, for a while, all form of engagement with anything outside the book, one is irresistibly urged to read the next excruciating paragraph aloud to family or friends so that they can all join in the fun.

Consider the artless banality of this: "I came right before Michael and as I did I made noises, just like my mother." It's the same sort of language as "I went into the kitchen and fixed myself a cup of coffee." Most writers are aware that human activity is enormously rich and varied, and to give value to that variety, what is linguistically apt for one thing is inappropriate to another. But not so Judy Blume. She has no sense of the incongruous, not even a sense of humor. There may be people who use after-shave lotion in the manner Kath suggests to Michael—on his balls—but were such a topic to arise in conversation, either in real life or in a novel, it would usually be treated as something grotesque or, at the very least, amusing; not by Judy Blume, however: it's done in the same tone as everything else in the book. Of course it makes the reader laugh, but that is something one assumes she didn't intend to do—and it isn't the kind of laughter she would like.

One could go on with other examples, but it hardly seems worth it. It's enough to say that the triviality of her thinking is matched by the sheer shoddiness of her English. She employs the usual sub-Salingerese American first-person narration, but so unmemorably that it makes Paul Zindel's use of the technique look like startling originality. There is absolutely nothing in Judy Blume's style that defines it as specifically hers. Nicholas Tucker, in a review of ***Forever*** in the *Times Literary Supplement* [see excerpt dated October 1, 1976 for ***Forever***], said that "talking straight from the adolescent's mouth can act as camouflage for slack writing"—indeed it all too often does—and added that Judy Blume's prose was "of the same soggy consistency as the used tissues that play such an important part in Kath's and Michael's post-amatory techniques." There is an implication here that the English has a built-in throw-away quality to it, that it is as disposable as the used tissue itself. Nicholas Tucker is right; Judy Blume's novels are the ultimate in the read-it-and-throw-it-away kind of book. They seem to be saying that when you've read the text you'll be equipped to do the real thing and you won't have to bother with the tedious business of coming back to a story to find out what it's like. In other words, they are not only short-changing the young; they are short-changing literature.

Jill Paton Walsh when asked on one occasion why she didn't write a novel on a subject such as a girl having her first period, replied somewhat testily that she wouldn't dream of doing any such thing: It would be a very bad book. Fiction, she said, quite rightly, had its origin in something rather more complex than a given subject, that its genesis was so complex that it was ultimately indefinable. It was certainly not just a matter of one conscious preoccupation, but of all sorts of subconscious concerns of which the author was not fully aware and over which he had little control. However, Judy Blume in ***Are You There, God? It's Me, Margaret*** rushed in where Jill Paton Walsh very wisely refused to tread, and produced exactly what Jill Paton Walsh foresaw: a very bad book. It's as throwaway as ***Forever.*** The young reader learns about how to wear a bra and what it's like to have a period, and nothing else is offered that could induce her (a boy is unlikely to find anything in the story of any interest) to return to it and re-open its pages. As for the adult, it's a bore and an embarrassment, a complete waste of one's time.

The trouble stems primarily from thinking that issues—such as how to get laid or what to do when you have your first period—are starting points for creative writing. They are not, and never can be. ***Otherwise Known as Sheila the Great*** is a marginally better book than ***Forever*** or ***Are You There, God? It's Me, Margaret*** because the issues—Sheila Tubman's various phobias about water and dogs—are made secondary considerations to the story, thin though the narrative is. ***Tales of a Fourth Grade Nothing*** should also be more interesting for the same reasons, though any attraction it may have is cancelled out by the wretched young brother, a character the author clearly finds very appealing but who comes over to the reader as extremely tiresome. He's a common enough figure in many second-rate children's books; a similar version of the type surfaces in Constance Greene's *I Know You, Al,* another non-novel, or ''issue'' book, which is also about having one's first period, and, in case that is not enough, divorce as well, with problems looming so large that they squeeze out everything else—story-line, characterization, even good English. Judy Blume's ***It's Not the End of the World*** is also about divorce, which is certainly a more interesting subject than menstruation. Clash of personalities, disruption of lives, emotional crises, are implicit in the material. It's probably her best book, though what I really mean is that it isn't as bad as the others. Certainly the reactions of the central character, Karen, to the break-up of her parents' marriage seem to ring true. Her sad attempts to bring the adults together again, and her facility for blaming herself when what happens isn't her fault at all, are characteristic of young children who have to suffer in such situations. Authentic, too, is her misunderstanding of trivial actions: she misinterprets them as being of great significance—imagining, for instance, that because her mother has gone to see the same lawyer twice she must be going to marry him. The inability of even the most well-meaning adults to explain what is going on when a marriage collapses, in terms that a child can comprehend, is also well done. But this is not sufficient. The narrator (it's yet another first-person story) sounds as if she is exactly the same person as the narrators in all Judy Blume's books; it could easily be Kath or Margaret, or Vic of ***Then Again, Maybe I Won't.*** There's an astonishing incapacity to show that people are different from one another in the way they think and feel and talk: it isn't good enough to suggest that they only differ in their actions. And there is the same entirely forgettable, drab, flat prose. . . . (pp. 173-78)

Then Again, Maybe I Won't is yet another non-novel, the problem this time being what happens if your father suddenly becomes very rich and the whole family moves out of a friendly close-knit lower-middle-class environment to an exceedingly well-to-do suburb, with different rituals, mores, and customs. It isn't a problem that many children are likely to face, but maybe the intention here is to say that life in the smart, private swimming-pool set is so awful in the way it corrupts Mum and Dad that would-be readers will stop hoping their fathers will suddenly find endless riches at their disposal. Whatever the intention is, and it isn't very clear, existence in the upper income bracket really isn't much like this. The *nouveaux riches'* treatment of Grandma, for example, is so callous as to be quite unbelievable, especially when the family background is Italian and Italians are noted for their close-knit family life style. The next-door neighbors are a pretty unattractive crowd, and are so obviously unpalatable to both the reader and the narrator, that it is not easy to see why Vic's mother should wish to imitate them so slavishly. (pp. 178-79)

[Another] ''problem'' in ***Then Again, Maybe I Won't*** is twelve-year-old Vic's developing sexuality; he's worried that he doesn't have wet dreams and the other fellows do—presumably what Judy Blume feels is the masculine equivalent of having one's first period. Vic's feelings about wet dreams and Margaret's feelings about periods in ***Are You There, God? It's Me, Margaret*** are more or less identical, but these two bodily functions are profoundly different, psychologically, and Judy Blume is mistaken in leaving the reader with the impression that they are similar. That, and other elementary considerations—that writing about such topics so obsessively may cause hang-ups in the child reader where none existed previously—seem to escape the notice of her advocates.

In talking about the sexual development of young people Judy Blume is at her most insensitive, which is why ***Forever*** is easily her worst book. She has little idea, it seems, of what really occurs, emotionally, in adolescent sexual relationships, either in real life or in the teenage novel. (pp. 179-80)

Adults should be very sure they know what they are doing before they start writing about young love in novels intended for a teenage readership. The two most important things to avoid are, firstly, relying on their own memories, because everything—social behavior, sexual mores, language, relationships with parents and teachers—has changed out of all recognition; and, secondly, allowing their own prejudices and didactic intentions, conscious or unconscious, to fill the pages, whether those feelings be in favor of keeping the young out of each other's beds, as in *Looking for a Wave,* or of getting them to leap in as quickly as possible, as in ***Forever.*** One turns back gratefully to Jill Chaney. Or to Ursula Le Guin, for it is interesting to see how the greatest living exponent of the myth-and-legend story handles the teenage love affair: in *Very Far Away from Anywhere Else* she might almost be making an explicit criticism of books like ***Forever***. . . . Surely all that's finest in all of us struggles to be what Owen wants to be—an individual, mature, and capable of choice—and what's timid, immature, and self-destructive in us wants to be what Kath and Michael are in ***Forever***: conformist, safe, only capable of boasting that they're doing exactly what everybody else boasts of doing.

Ursula Le Guin one can read again and again. Not so Judy Blume. For me it isn't a question of forever or not: her novels don't even make a pleasurable one-night stand. (pp. 182-83)

David Rees, ''Not Even for a One-Night Stand,'' in his The Marble in the Water, *The Horn Book, Inc., 1980, pp. 173-84.*

JUDITH M. GOLDBERGER

The name Judy Blume has become a byword to millions of young readers. During the last ten years, her books have attained unprecedented popularity among eight-to fourteen-year-olds; her readership spans cultural, sexual, and racial boundaries; and the loyalty she inspires is fierce. Yet, so too is criticism of her books, which also comes from a broad range of sources.

While the storm rages around them, Blume and her fans enjoy the quiet warmth of good communication. She writes to children about love, jealousy, and the many fears of growing up. They write to her and say, "You don't know me, but you've written this book about me." The bond is strong, the relationship between writer and reader confident and relaxed. As one teenager, speaking about Blume's young adult novel put it, "If I wasn't meant to read ***Forever,*** Judy Blume wouldn't have written it."

Today, many books for young readers deal directly with the everyday problems of growing up. But in the early 1970s, Judy Blume was a pioneer, breaking barriers of silence with novels such as ***Are You There, God? It's Me, Margaret,*** which relates a young girl's most private thoughts about the onset of her sexual maturity and her acceptance by a new peer group. In 1972, Blume wrote about a family in the throes of divorce, from the viewpoint of the adolescent daughter. In 1975, ***Forever,*** which plots a contemporary teenage love relationship, appeared. These and others of her novels have won the loyalty of young readers through her obvious identification and ability to communicate with her audience, and an outspoken mode of writing.

Judy Blume writes for and about today's children. And, because she writes about children's feelings, the honesty of her books is a key factor to her. Her allies—millions of juvenile (and adult) fans—would probably agree that it is her honesty which is a large part of what makes her so good to read. But it is also her honesty that makes her opponents so angry with her.

Blume's books definitely treat subjects that make parents nervous, subjects many adults have a great deal of trouble talking to youngsters about in any but strictly clinical terms. But an adult's agony over discussing these matters with children is nothing when compared to the personal agony the young experience when faced with the actual situations. And that is one reason why young people devour Judy Blume's books. They deal with matters of primary concern to their readers, with which many of those readers' parents can't or won't help them. Often, rather than talking *with* their children about touchy subjects, parents talk *at* them. Or they don't talk at all.

No doubt the largest group (or non-group, really) of critics are the parents of children who read, or try to read, Blume's novels—parents who do not always write articles or join protesting organizations, but who feel very strongly that their children will suffer from reading Blume's books. Their opinions might best be characterized by these statements, made by two different mothers: "There's no moral tone." "The more you talk about something, the more you think about it, and the more you think about it, the more you do it." What many parents fear is that, in writing about the way a group of fifth graders cruelly taunt an obese classmate, or in describing a seventeen-year-old girl's private vacillations and eventual decision to have sex with her boyfriend, Judy Blume will make her readers feel that such activities or decisions are good and right.

There is no punishment in store for a Judy Blume character who masturbates to comfort herself, or for one who sleeps with her boyfriend and, after several months, ends the relationship. Some parents who are disgusted with or shocked by the content of Blume's books want statements of condemnation, or moral definition; others would rather these delicate subjects not be touched on at all. And the strong words her critics use to describe Blume's novels are testimony to their fear of the harm they believe the books might do. (p. 57, 61)

Viewing the controversy without reading the books, one gets a lopsided version of what is, after all, at the heart of the matter. What are Judy Blume's books really about? Listening to her critics, or opening the books to certain selected pages, one could say that ***Are You There, God? It's Me, Margaret*** is about a girl who wants a bra and worries at length about when she will get her period. Similarly, at the other end of the age spectrum of Blume's juvenile titles, ***Forever*** is about losing one's virginity.

Then, one reads the books from cover to cover and gets an understanding of the misunderstanding, a sense of the irony of what is happening. A primer course in adolescent psychology is more than ample basis to make clear that Margaret's concerns are classic identity-finding worries—normal, common, and universal in the sense that rules may come and rules may go, but having a group alliance and grappling with the onset of sexual maturity is everyone's worry at some time. ***Margaret*** is not about a girl who wants a bra, any more than *Hamlet* is about a man who is in love with a woman who goes crazy.

The heroine of ***Forever,*** seventeen-year-old Katherine, certainly thinks about having sex, for the first time, with the boy with whom she is in love. And passages of ***Forever*** are definitely bedroom scenes. These have been described as "explicit" and "vulgar," but compared to parallel scenes in adult novels, they are discreet, brief, and personal, as opposed to removed and sensationalist. More to the point, the focus of the book, and of Katherine's thoughts which she shares with readers, is her relationship with Michael, in *all* of its complexity. Katherine thinks a lot more about whether she will spend her summer with Michael and why her parents are upset about her going steady than she does about birth control methods.

Thus, ironically, concerned parents and critics read Judy Blume out of context, and label the books while children and young adults read the whole books to find out what they are really about and to hear another voice talking about a host of matters with which they are concerned in their daily lives. The grown-ups, it seems, are the ones who read for the "good" parts, more so than the children.

In spite of her critics, Judy Blume thinks there is nothing one shouldn't or can't tell a child. And, although the manner of telling is something which requires care, it is not, for Blume, a question of how moral a stand to take on delicate subjects. Indeed, Judy Blume insists she purposely takes *no* moral stand, that the danger in moralizing in a realistic story is that there usually are no purely "right" answers. To claim that there are is to set guidelines that may not stand up to the test of reality.

When asked whether she had received any complaints from children, Blume explained that "one or two" young people had written to tell her that they found ***Forever*** "gross." She replied by counseling them to wait until they were a little older and to read ***Forever*** again. "Kids are their own best censors," says Blume. "They won't read what is over their heads." It is this faith in her readers that enables Blume to establish the kind of trust she and her fans have for each other.

Blume does not see herself in the role of superparent-as-writer, nor as champion of sexual or social exploration. She says it is not a "conscious effort" for her to come up with an idea for a book. She writes, remembering her own adolescent curiosities and concerns—the childhood of a white, middle-class woman—and no doubt, her own great need to understand and to know at that time in her life. If she allies herself with a cause, it is that of the child's right to know. "If they ask," says Blume, "they're entitled to an answer." (p. 62)

The issue, according to Judy Blume, is control. If critics would have her change the content of her books, adding moral judgments, or even altering racial, sexual, or economic class backdrops, they would deny the writer's right to speak personally, and hence, from the heart, without didacticism of orthodoxy. And, if they would have books about real adolescent concerns denied to adolescents, they would also deny the right of young people to seek and obtain support in working out their problems. "These people want to go back to not being honest with children," says Blume. "But, you can't go back, and you can't make the rest of the world go back with you." Moreover, she sees efforts to control children's reading taking a turn for the worse. The results of the last presidential election, Judy Blume believes, gave a lot of people the sense that they had the right to take repressive public stands.

In their undaunted enthusiasm for self knowledge, young people today are no different from those of any other time. Many of today's children have found a source of learning in Judy Blume. She speaks to children, and, in spite of loud protests, her voice is clear to them. She tells them there is a time at which each person must decide things for him or herself. In that sense, she carries an ageless message about the sanctity of individual rights. (p. 81)

Judith M. Goldberger, "Judy Blume: Target of the Censor," in Newsletter on Intellectual Freedom, *Vol. XXX, No. 3, May, 1981, pp. 57, 61-2, 81-2.*

FAITH McNULTY

On my first exposure to Blume, a few years ago, I turned out to be immune to Blume fever. Her realism struck me as shallow, and I was put off by her knack for observing unpleasant details. Recently, I read her again, determined to find her magic formula, and I am now ready to amend my views. In a Judy Blume book, realism is everything. True, it has no great depth, but it is extraordinarily convincing. True, she includes unpleasant details—things we all notice but usually don't mention—yet they increase the credibility that is the source of her magnetic power. Blume's technique might be compared to *cinéma vérité*. She writes as though filming the landscape of childhood from the eye level of a child. She focusses on nearby objects and immediate events with a child's intense gaze, picking out details that evoke instant recognition. As in a play, dialogue carries the story along. It is colloquial, often funny, and always revealing. Blume doesn't waste words. Her stories are told in the first person—sustained soliloquies that are prodigies of total recall. Each book begins on a note of candor. We have the feeling of reading a secret diary—something the writer intended only for himself. Thus, it seems natural when usually private matters are included. Often, they are things that have to do with the dawning of sex, and though most are quite innocuous it is a shock to see them suddenly exposed in print. The effect is a mesmerizing intimacy, which convinces Blume's readers that she writes the whole truth about what kids think and feel. (pp. 193-94)

[***Are You There, God? It's Me, Margaret*** discloses a] twelve-year-old secret—curiosity about the opposite sex. In Margaret's bedroom, with the door closed and a chair shoved in front of it, [she and the other three members of a secret club] examine a purloined copy of an anatomy book. They open it to a diagram of the male body:

> "Do you suppose that's what Philip Leroy looks like without his clothes on?" Janie asked.
>
> "Naturally, dope!" Nancy said. "He's male, isn't he?" . . .
>
> "Turn the page, Gretchen," Nancy said.
>
> The next page was the male reproductive system. None of us said anything. We just looked until Nancy told us, "My brother looks like that."
>
> "How do you know?" I asked.
>
> "He walks around naked," Nancy said.
>
> "My father used to walk around naked,"
>
> Gretchen said. "But lately he's stopped doing it."
>
> "My aunt went to a nudist colony last summer," Janie said. . . .
>
> "What do you suppose they do there?" Gretchen asked.
>
> "Just walk around naked is all. My aunt says it's very peaceful."

This scene and others like it are funny to us but strong stuff to a child reader—the junior equivalent of the tough, tell-it-like-it-is prose of countless adult novels today. It is easy to imagine the surprise of twelve-year-old readers as they recognize themselves caught doing and thinking things they usually conceal from adults. They must feel a chill go up their spine as they wonder "How on earth did she know?" Scenes like these shock some adults, too, who complain that sexuality pervades Blume's books. It does—but only to the degree that it enters most young minds. Except perhaps in ***Forever,*** Blume imparts no illicit knowledge but merely fills in an area of adolescent experience usually left blank in print. And she does it with a bland openness that allows her to retort to critics, "*Honi soit qui mal y pense*."

Blume is versatile. Her realism serves equally well for comic effect in ***Tales of a Fourth Grade Nothing***. . . . Kids always find breaking taboos and mentioning embarrassments immensely funny. (pp. 195, 198)

Superfudge is a compendium of small-boy humor. The high point may be an episode concerning a lady who is willing to pay Peter for collecting worms. She offers five cents a worm. Peter and his partner in the worm business speculate on what the lady does with them. Worm soup? Worm stew? Worm-and-cheese sandwiches? By the time they get to worm ice cream, they are doubled over with laughter. Worm jokes are not new, but they're surefire, and Blume seems to have a limitless store of similar touchstones of childhood. However, ***Superfudge*** is better than a mere joke book. The fun lies in Peter's dry wit, yet beneath his veneer of cynicism the reader can detect a warm emotional message as Peter unconsciously reveals his growing fondness for both little pests.

No report on Blume is complete without a look at ***Forever,*** the book for which some critics have not forgiven her. ***Forever*** is the case history of a teen-ager's affair, in which Katherine, seventeen, deludes herself that she is truly in love and sleeps with Michael, also seventeen. Blume's description of what Katherine and Michael do in bed, and what Katherine feels, is a carefully worded answer to questions hygiene manuals fail to address. The affair ends when Katherine falls out of love and realizes emotions can be unreliable. I found the encounter one of the dullest on record, but it is easy to see that a naïve reader must find it fascinatingly revealing. It is equally obvious that such a book could kick up quite a storm.

Without the revelations of ***Forever*** and the small, stunning shocks that Blume sprinkles through her other books like nuts in a brownie, she might not have lured so many millions of readers, but she has also won her audience through honest work, superior craftsmanship, and a talent for recreating an evanescent period of life—the years from nine to thirteen. She writes about the loneliness of being young; about youthful secrets—fear, anxiety, longing, guilt. It is rough being a kid, she often says. Her kids are swept along by capricious currents. They struggle to keep their sense of humor, and to keep their heads above water. At the end of the story, they find their feet for a moment of equilibrium as they contemplate the next stage of life. I sympathize with the librarians who hate to see *Tom Sawyer* and the rest of the books we have all loved shoved off the shelves, but the times, not Blume, are to blame for that. I find much in Blume to be thankful for. She isn't scary or sick. She writes clean, swift, unadorned prose. She has convinced millions of young people that truth can be found in a book and that reading is fun. At a time that many believe may be the twilight of the written word, those are things to be grateful for. (pp. 198, 201)

Faith McNulty, "Children's Books for Christmas," in The New Yorker, *Vol. LIX, No. 42, December 5, 1983, pp. 191-95, 198, 201.*

LYNNE HAMILTON

[Throughout] Blume's novels the age-old image of the female, a dependent, ineffectual creature whose importance can only be derived from a man, remains drooped over its pedestal. Conservative watchdogs accuse Blume of iconoclasm; but in fact her portrayal of young women helps perpetuate both the female stereotype and the status quo. Her adolescents may sprout breasts, but in a more fundamental sense they do not develop. Bland, passive, and unfocused, they are locked in Neverland where the future is a dirty word. (p. 88)

Lynne Hamilton, "Blume's Adolescents: Coming of Age in Limbo," in Signal, *No. 41, May, 1983, pp. 88-96.*

JON C. STOTT

The reason for the popularity of Judy Blume's books among young readers is not difficult to discover. They seek neither to sermonize nor to educate; rather they present the world as it appears to a specific young person. Generally a story is narrated by the central character so that the reader focuses on his perceptions. The hero's concerns are those that are most important to children from the ages of eight or nine to fifteen or sixteen: parents, peer group pressures, awakening sexuality, death, and religion. These are treated without condescension. No firm conclusions are reached; adaptability and greater understanding are the usual results for the characters. (p. 42)

In spite of their tremendous popularity—perhaps, in part, because of it—Judy Blume's works have often been criticized by adults. It has been said that she gives young readers what they

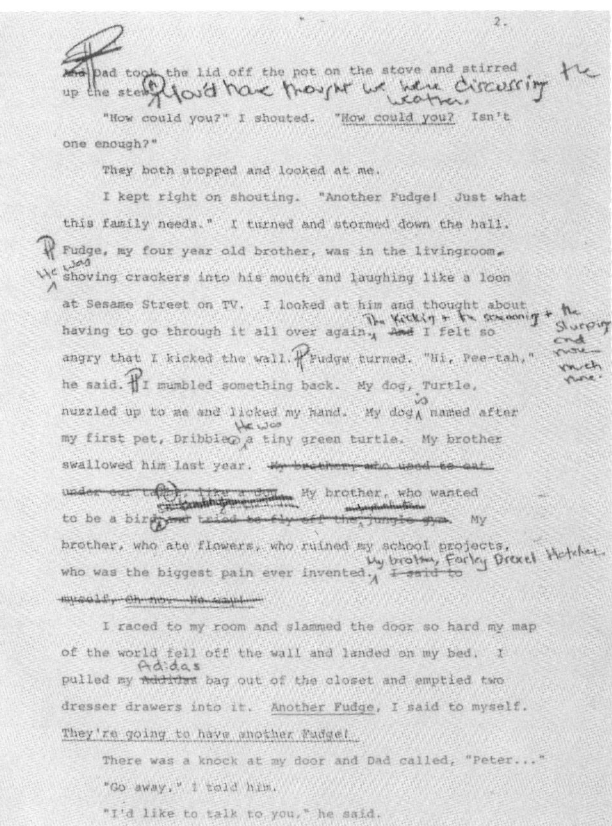

2.

Dad took the lid off the pot on the stove and stirred up the stew. You'd have thought we were discussing the weather.

"How could you?" I shouted. "How could you? Isn't one enough?"

They both stopped and looked at me.

I kept right on shouting. "Another Fudge! Just what this family needs." I turned and stormed down the hall.

Fudge, my four year old brother, was in the livingroom. He was shoving crackers into his mouth and laughing like a loon at Sesame Street on TV. I looked at him and thought about having to go through it all over again. The kicking + the screaming + the slurping and more—much more. I felt so angry that I kicked the wall. Fudge turned. "Hi, Pee-tah," he said. I mumbled something back. My dog, Turtle, nuzzled up to me and licked my hand. My dog is named after my first pet, Dribble. He was a tiny green turtle. My brother swallowed him last year. My brother, who wanted to be a bird. My brother, who ate flowers, who ruined my school projects, who was the biggest pain ever invented. My brother, Farley Drexel Hatcher.

I raced to my room and slammed the door so hard my map of the world fell off the wall and landed on my bed. I pulled my Adidas bag out of the closet and emptied two dresser drawers into it. Another Fudge, I said to myself. They're going to have another Fudge!

There was a knock at my door and Dad called, "Peter..."

"Go away," I told him.

"I'd like to talk to you," he said.

Page from a draft of Superfudge *(1980).*

want rather than need; that she doesn't challenge them. She has also been accused of shaping her plots to meet bibliotherapeutic ends. Perhaps most significantly, her use of the first person narrator has been criticized as limiting the scope of her vision; the reader is not given other points of view. Judy Blume has admitted this limitation of her work, but has then remarked that she aims to present honestly the particular point of view of a specific central character. She has noted that, were she to write about another character in the same book, a totally different approach might be taken.

"I think," she has remarked, "my only responsibility is to be truthful to the kids." While her books are unlikely to become classics, they are, in their honest portrayal of the children who are the characters and in their honesty to the children who are readers, significant children's novels of the 1970s. (pp. 42-3)

Jon C. Stott, "Judy Blume," in his Children's Literature from A to Z: A Guide for Parents and Teachers, *McGraw-Hill Book Company, 1984, pp. 40-3.*

JACK FORMAN

Judy Blume is probably the most popular author of novels today for older children and younger teenagers—for good reason. Writing with an attractive simplicity and a very natural sense of humor, she touches strong chords of identity in preteens and teenagers. At the same time, she has been successful in breaking down barriers which hitherto had prevented young adult authors from treating topics such as divorce, sexual feelings and activity, and death. True, she has been criticized on a number of counts, but much of the animosity towards her books has been based on adult fear and uncertainty. In one respect, however, criticism of her books is justified. Judy Blume promotes an attitude toward very serious topics which can best be described by one of her own titles—***It's Not the End of the World.*** Her characters almost always survive heavy personal, family, and school problems by turning to their own internal resources, absorbing any temporary discomfort or hurt, and getting on with their lives. They learn from their mistakes and become more self-reliant. Very little attention, however, is given to how others are affected by the resolution of problems, and rarely does Blume confront the lingering pain and hurt which characters might feel after resolving the problems. For instance, in ***Forever*** Katherine becomes sexually involved with Michael, and it is her first sexual encounter. Initially, she's confused and afraid, but she is told by Michael—her *very* good friend—that sex is healthy and natural. Later, when she loses her feeling for him, she tells herself it's healthy and natural to fall out of love. Breaking up, after all, is not the end of the world. So far, so good. But what about Michael's feelings? And, is Katherine really able to break off her relationship with so little emotional repercussion?

Unquestionably, children and teenagers need to believe in themselves and carve a niche for themselves in their society; they need the reassurance of a life after problems. Judy Blume gives them this. But they also need to know that there are consequences to their actions affecting other people and that there is a price paid for their mistakes—even if they learn the right lessons. (pp. 85-6)

Jack Forman, "Young Adult Books: 'Watch Out for #1'," in The Horn Book Magazine, *Vol. LXI, No. 1, January-February, 1985, pp. 85-7.*

JOHN GOUGH

Judy Blume is commonly regarded as that trivially popular writer of simple children's books on taboo problem topics such as puberty and sex. Her style is considered feeble, her characterisation shallow, her plots boring and didactic; and, anyway, those sorts of topics are just unacceptable. I do not believe this. Judy Blume's enormous commercial success, her prolific output and her easy-to-read stories distort and conceal her real achievement. She is an under-rated writer, critically abused or neglected, who deserves close attention and stands up to critical scrutiny very well.

Let's begin with setting. Judy Blume writes about what she knows. This happens to be middle-class East Coast children and teenagers, usually from a Jewish background, living in city apartments or well-appointed suburban villas. Her characters are not particularly clever or intellectual, not highly articulate or desperately sensitive, not talented or eccentric. They are pretty ordinary people. Most of the famous modern teenage characters in children's books are not ordinary. They *are* extremely bright or talented or difficult or sensitive or tough or eccentric. Consider the characters of Alan Garner, Paul Zindel, Jane Gardam, S. E. Hinton, Betsy Byers, Ursula Le Guin. These characters are very easy to be interested in; but we should not rush to dismiss more ordinary characters, such as Blume's. They are human, too, and probably more like most readers than their more extreme and critically acceptable counterparts. Give yourself a chance to know Blume's characters: give yourself a hard look in a mirror.

What about the action? Well, not much happens. No ancient stone axes are discovered, there are no crazy parties, no secret machine guns, no plotting by secret police, no ghosts, murder or incest, no crippling psychopathic trauma. Judy Blume's novels are filled with everyday events. Is this necessarily grounds for criticism? (p. 100)

Nicholas Tucker and David Rees claim that Judy Blume's writing style is 'slack', with the 'soggy consistency' and 'built-in throw-away quality' of the 'used tissues that play such an important part in Kath's and Michael's post-amatory techniques' in ***Forever.* . .** [see excerpt dated October 1, 1976 for ***Forever.* . .** and excerpt dated 1980 in General Commentary]. . . . But what is Blume's style really like?

Two of Blume's novels are fairly plain third-person past-tense narratives: ***Iggie's house*** and ***Starring Sally J. Freeman as herself.*** But this is deceptive. ***Iggie's house*** is her first full-length novel, written chapter by chapter, week by week, in a university course on 'how to write for children' to satisfy the course teacher. But even there Blume introduces a stylistic subtlety. As Winnie tries to cope with her best friend, Iggie, having moved away, and with the tensions that result from a black family moving into Iggie's house, Winnie writes letters to Iggie. At least she tries to write letters about the situation. But each letter, except the very last one, remains incomplete and unsent. Letter by letter we see Winnie's *own* incomplete view of the situation presented within the impartial third-person narrative. An ironic dialogue is set up in the reader's mind between the letters, or Winnie's self, and the narrative. Nothing startling as a literary device, but satisfying.

Blume uses letters in a similar way in most of her books. . . . She also uses Margaret's direct remarks to God (***Are you there God? It's me, Margaret***), Karen's diary entries (***It's not the end of the world***), foreshadowing chapter headings (***Blubber***), and Sally's imaginary films (***Starring Sally J. Freeman as herself***) as a way of commenting on the action and thoughts of the main character.

Apart from these two books and ***Tiger Eyes,*** all of Blume's novels are written in a fairly simple first-person past tense. But even here there are subtleties. For example, at moments of crisis the straightforward retelling of what happened breaks into a vivid, here-and-now present tense, as when Tony wakes up after his first wet dream, panic-stricken (***Then again, maybe I won't***). Sometimes the dominant past tense gives way to a present tense, as the main character reflects on what has been happening. It is what the character is thinking at the time, rather than after the events of the book. For instance, in ***It's not the end of the world,*** Karen tells us the aftermath of her attempt to get her parents back together:

> I got back into bed . . . all set to cry . . . I must have been a crazy person to think that my silly diorama could work magic. Now I know the truth . . . Well, I'm through fooling myself . . . I rolled over.

Again, this gives the reader a sense of immediacy and involvement; but it also allows Blume, as author behind the character's telling, to establish an ironic view of the action. We all know the pitfalls that lie ahead of someone who thinks she is through with fooling herself.

Such concealed irony occurs in ***Are you there God? It's me, Margaret,*** when Margaret, in her search for religious allegiance, has gone to synagogue, and done nothing more than count different coloured hats. Her father, an unbeliever raised as a Jew, married to a lapsed Christian, and estranged from his intolerant Christian parents-in-law, remarks that he too used to count hats. Despite this, and here is Blume's irony, Margaret remarks to God: 'I'm really on my way. By the end of the school year I'll know all there is to know about religion.'

The same kind of irony happens in ***Forever*. . . .** For example, Kath's parents talk about themselves having once gone steady with other boyfriends and girlfriends, clearly implying that Kath and Michael may be in the same situation. But Kath thinks to herself, 'It's not just some fifties fad, like going steady . . . with us it is love—real, true honest-to-god love'. The reader realises that love is not always what people, such as Kath, think it is. Blume's irony clearly shows us this.

Tiger Eyes is written in first-person *present* tense. The opening sentence plunges the reader into what is happening: 'It is the morning of the funeral and I am tearing my room apart, trying to find the right kind of shoes to wear.' The present tense heightens suspense as the facts of and feelings about the death are slowly revealed and gradually coped with. . . . [This] is Blume's best book so far, strongly written, strongly plotted, and full of character and dramatic clashes. ***Tiger Eyes,*** however, is unusual in that its driving force comes from the father's death. He was casually murdered in an armed hold-up. This is not quite Blume's usual ordinary everyday topic, though violent crime is increasingly 'everyday', and murder is as American as apple pie. This is not a book for young children but for young people: the main character is nearly sixteen.

Tiger Eyes, like Blume's other books, does not deal with only one aspect of one problem situation. Several situations, including alcoholism, suicide, racism, childlessness, peer-group pressures, and jealous guilt are introduced and shown from different points of view. Davey's, the main character's, grief is paralleled by her mother's grief, as well as by her aunt's. Later the aunt suffers again when Davey's family relinquishes her comforting to resume their own life. The murder is mirrored by Davey's uncle being a weapons researcher at Los Alamos. Davey begins to come to terms with her father's death only when she nurses a terminally ill old man. As the seasons move through a year, from a claustrophobic summer to the spring when the lizards run again, the many threads of the novel form a dense texture of image and feeling.

All of Blume's books are about coping with difficult situations. In seven of them families move home, forcing the main characters to make new friends and redefine themselves. Other difficult situations include changes in parents' lifestyles, separation and divorce, changes in allegiance to and from friends, peer-group pressures, the beginnings of puberty and sexual awareness, sibling rivalry, phobias, the death of relatives, and the tensions of family relationships. Again and again Blume's characters find that something as simple as waking up in the morning and getting on, however unwillingly or unhappily, with the day's tasks, can help adjust to a new and unpleasant situation. Survival can be a matter of just hanging on. Karen, in ***It's not the end of the world,*** changes her mind about divorce. At first she says in her diary, with much feeling and childish misunderstanding: 'Divorce . . . it's the end of the world.' Later she understands that none of her schemes, nor even her brother running away, can repair her parents' relationship. Eventually she finds she can accept that her parents are better apart, and she can have B-plus days again.

Consider ***Then again, maybe I won't,*** notorious for its thirteen-year-old hero who begins to have wet dreams and who secretly watches his neighbours' sixteen-year-old daughter undressing at night. In fact, only a few pages mention wet dreams, spying or related sexual matters, and these things *are* only mentioned, not described in detail. Far more attention is given to thirteen-year-old Tony's family: his older brother killed some years before in Vietnam; his father whose invention has made them newly rich; his sister-in-law who gets pregnant, then has a baby girl; his grandmother who is left mute after a larynx operation and is forced out of the family kitchen by the new maid; his status-seeking mother who buys a grand piano, though no one in the family plays. And Tony himself, seeing through the phoney values of wealth, agonising over his grandmother's unhappiness, jealous of the sixteen-year-old and her youth group leader boyfriend, suffering stomach pains of anxiety when he sees his friend Joel shoplifting. There's a lot more going on in this book than a little bit of anxious puberty.

At the end, though his family have not changed, Tony has survived. He knows himself better. He is beginning to come to terms with his developing sexuality, enjoying his dreams, and finding that the skinny girl his own age who likes him is also likeable. There are no easy solutions or happy endings. Tony's grandmother still locks herself away from the rest of the family in protest at being banished from the kitchen. The family's new wealth tempts his school-teacher brother into a pointless job in the firm. Tony bursts into tears, seeking comfort from his grandmother, realising they both 'have a lot in common', being 'outsiders in [their] own home'. Joel is not sent to the Juvenile Detention Centre, but to a military school to get the discipline his family do not have and cannot teach him. And Tony realises, 'it was funny. Funny and sad both'.

Tony is typical of Blume's heroes and heroines: human, confused, not arriving at clear-cut conclusions, but persisting, trying to understand, trying to be honest with himself. Kath, in ***Forever . . . ,*** is another archetypal Blume main character. Behind the few honest pages that describe Kath's developing sexual relationship with Michael, plainly written, and roundly damned by the critics, is a story of a girl trying to come to terms with independence and adulthood. Kath struggles to redefine her friendship with her schoolfriend Erica, as she grows closer to Michael. Kath and her parents muddle their way towards recognising and accepting Kath's coming independence, at a new stage in their parent-daughter relationship. Kath comes to rely on her up-to-date grandmother, and grieves when her grandfather dies. She realises that love and sex are only part of her friendship with Michael: 'besides everything else he is really my best friend now'. But she learns that love and friendship are not necessarily 'forever', that she is not always in control of situations, and not always blameless. She knows that the end of the relationship, and Michael's pain, is her fault, even if she could not help it. The reality she is growing into is adult, complex, and not easy. Blume does not trivialise her characters or subject-matter.

It might be objected that Judy Blume puts sex in her books in an exploitative, almost pornographic, way. Certainly ***Wifey,*** her adult novel, spares no four-letter words or intimate details. . . . What about the children's novels? Maybe she puts the sex in to titillate and make the books sell? I do not think so. . . . There is a consistency of characterisation, theme and treatment in all her novels (including ***Wifey***) that leads me to conclude that she is seeking honest discussion of ordinary lives in her books. (pp. 101-05)

Judy Blume is concerned to describe characters surviving, finding themselves, growing in understanding, coming to terms with life. This is apparent in the endings of Blume's novels. There are no grand resolutions, no happy tying-up of loose ends, no miraculous solutions to problems. Some insight is achieved, and then new problems await to be confronted. Margaret realises that religious belief cannot simply be chosen. Tony's last words are typically equivocal, 'Then again, maybe I won't.' Kath wants to tell Michael:

> I will never be sorry for loving him. That in a way I still do. . . . Maybe if we were ten years older it would have worked out differently. Maybe. I think it's just that I'm not ready for forever . . . all I could manage to say was, 'See you around . . .'

Davey, coming to terms with her father's murder, realises that, 'you can't go back. Not ever. You have to pick up the pieces and keep moving ahead.'

Such conclusions may not be original or profound; but neither are they trivial. The high sales of Blume's books are testimony to the fact that what she has to say is said well and is well worth saying. (pp. 105-06)

John Gough, "Growth, Survival and Style in the Novels of Judy Blume," in The School Librarian, *Vol. 35, No. 2, May, 1987, pp. 100-06.*

THE ONE IN THE MIDDLE IS THE GREEN KANGAROO (1969)

The traditional squeeze-play of the middle child is handled lightly but quite effectively here, as a small boy accomplishes something that neither his older brother nor his younger sister can. Freddy, a second-grader, felt that life was made up of hand-me-down clothes, a brother that was always ahead of him, and a small sister who not only was cute but couldn't even be retaliated against when she provoked trouble. He was delighted to accept the role of the Green Kangaroo in a play put on by the fifth and sixth grades. The story of his nervous flutters before the curtain goes up, his subsequent wallowing in the part (chiefly jumping) and the appreciation of his family is amusing; Freddy's own complacence at just being himself—an actor—makes him expansively tolerant about being the middle child. While the book treats the problem at a superficial level, it does treat a real problem in a believable way, and as a story it is satisfying.

Zena Sutherland, in a review of "The One in the Middle Is the Green Kangaroo," in Bulletin of the Center for Children's Books, *Vol. 23, No. 8, April, 1970, p. 125.*

FRECKLE JUICE (1971)

Envious of freckle-faced Nicky, second-grader Andrew pays 50 cents for a secret freckle juice formula hawked by an enterprising classmate, Sharon. The concoction made from Sharon's recipe fails to hit the spot—Andrew turns green but remains unfreckled. The next day he goes to school dotted with blue magic marker and receives a magic freckle remover (soap and water variety) from his teacher. Though long, this convincing small boy adventure proceeds smoothly to a satisfying conclusion in which Andrew realizes that Nicky, the object of his admiration would like to change his spots and is thus fair game for Sharon who is now selling a secret freckle removing recipe. The conniving little girl, understanding teacher, and feckless, freckleless boy are amusingly depicted . . . in the story which is especially suited for reading aloud to second- and third-graders.

Alice Adkins, in a review of "Freckle Juice," in School Library Journal, *an appendix to* Library Journal, *Vol. 18, No. 5, January, 1972, p. 50.*

Children in the seven to nine age range are likely to gravitate towards this bright and attractive book initially because it is so captivating to look at. In addition, what they discover to their delight is a well written short story that is both amusing and fascinating. . . .

Freckle Juice is another of [Judy Blume's] stories that explores an issue which may appear trivial to adults but is of important concern to children. . . .

There is no need to worry over the few Americanisms. Children seem to understand their usage and find them less irritating than adults do. The writing is well structured and helpful to children who are beginning to enjoy the reading of a complete book.

Ron Morton, in a review of "Freckle Juice," in Books for Your Children, *Vol. 19, No. 3, Autumn-Winter, 1984, p. 29.*

FOREVER . . . (1975)

One of the biggest gaps between adult and child understanding has always been in the area of sex and passion. Not so much in their existence and vocabulary, or in the various techniques for fulfilling them—most school playgrounds can be reasonably well-informed on these scores today. Rather, it arises from ignorance of the motive force that drives on the feelings and the acts, which a child cannot really find reflected in his own passions at the time, however generally curious he may be about such things. . . . Small wonder that when sex is explained to younger children at various intervals, it is received not so much with awe, disgust or technical discussion as sheer hilarity—why should adults, from the monarchy downwards, wish to behave in such bizarre ways, except perhaps for the sole clinical purpose of propagating children? In this sense, romance that deals with passion outside and beyond marriage is bound to appear even more baffling than most.

When children's writers have played down this passion in the past, therefore, it has not always been because of squeamishness—there is also the problem of being able to carry your audience with you. On the other hand, once this audience has passed into adolescence and understands these things rather better, there may then be good reasons for telling them how it really is, and an equally powerful wish to be told. Now that novels can be increasingly frank and still make the school or junior public library, we can expect growing numbers of books on this score, making up for some of the inhibitions of the past, where taboo titles might once be carefully guarded in the "For adults only" section of the librarian's shelf. And of such books, few have yet been quite so outspoken as Judy Blume's ***Forever***. . . .

This is a story as told by the adolescent heroine, about an affair with another seventeen-year-old that germinates, burgeons and finally goes to seed. As a narrative technique, talking straight from the adolescent's mouth can also act as camouflage for slack writing, not entirely avoided here. Although it may be in character for the narrator to rhapsodize about eyes that are "very dark, with just a rim of green and other times they sparkle and are greenish-gray all over", it is still no less tedious to read. So if the author does manage to catch the almost inexorable egotism of some adolescents at this age, it is at the cost of producing a dull novel about two very dull young people, told in prose of the same soggy consistency as the used tissues that play such an important part in the couple's post-amatory techniques.

But it is just in this area, perhaps, that the book either justifies itself or not; if it is sex that is wanted, there is plenty of it here. Mutual masturbation . . . and later intercourse play leading roles supported by a full cast of lesser objects and functions, from rubbers, the pill and Planned Parenthood to "breaking your cherry" and vaginal discharge. . . . Yet even as a fictionalized sex manual, ***Forever*** is nowhere near as explicit as other material available for everyone today, nor is it as erotic as, for example, that "jolly little story" *Fanny Hill.* In fact, it is not erotic at all: its protagonists couple and separate like two well-lubricated automata, and if this novel is remarkable for anything, it is in its ability to trivialize sex, something that so far no puritan has ever managed to, perhaps even intended to do. There is an absence of poetry or passion about this couple; an emotional impotence in the midst of perfect physical health. The characters are so flat one might almost be in a sexed-up Enid Blyton plot—*Five go on an orgy,* perhaps. But at least Enid Blyton sometimes dealt with feeling; a better analogy might be a so-far missing link in the Janet and John reading scheme: *Come and have sex!*

Nicholas Tucker, "Bedtime Stories," in The Times Literary Supplement, *No. 3890, October 1, 1976, p. 1238.*

Maintaining a strictly neutral moral tone, unless acceptance is synonymous with approval, this story of young love is surely the frankest exposition we have yet had from America. True, it is "a novel for young adults" and the protagonists are in their later teens, but it will without doubt be pored over (or pawed over) by younger readers.

This is no chaste hold hands and snatched kiss romance but a modern party-to-bed affair. Katherine meets Michael on New Year's Eve; a week or so later he asks her whether she is a virgin and, though she holds out for a time, soon the two seventeen-year-olds are progressing through masturbation to copulation. There is no pussyfooting in Judy Blume's account: four-letter words, intimate details, uninhibited discussions will ensure the attention of young readers.

Katherine's parents are superficially disapproving but do little to minimise temptation; unknown to them, a go-ahead grandmother sends Katherine planned parenthood pamphlets which inspire her to visit a birth control clinic. Her affair with Michael ends when she goes off to a summer camp and meets Theo: as the story closes he is obviously in line for Katherine's next round of sex. And, one is tempted to ask, after him, someone else?

Judy Blume's aim is serious and responsible enough and her revelation of young love is probably typical of many relationships today: the tone of the book is clear from the first sentence—"Sybil Davison has a genius I.Q. and has been laid by at least six different guys". The associated elements are not unexpected: Sybil has a baby, Artie attempts suicide, Michael and Erica get drunk, Sharon and Ike smoke "grass", Michael admits he contracted VD in an earlier liaison. But, however sympathetic towards adolescent problems Judy Blume is, I am left wondering how ***Forever . . .*** will really help its readers. The young tend to follow the life-style of their peers: will Katherine and Michael's affair help to impose yet another imprimatur on casual sex? It may well minimise a sense of guilt but will it encourage the need for firm and satisfying relationships? Perhaps the final irony is in the title of the book itself. . . .

G. Bott, in a review of "Forever. . .", in The Junior Bookshelf, *Vol. 41, No. 1, February, 1977, p. 49.*

As both an illustration of the love-romance and a demonstration of how little the pattern has changed over the past three-and-a-half decades, we will compare Maureen Daly's *Seventeenth Summer* (1942) to Judy Blume's ***Forever*** (1975). Both of these books have been, and continue to be, extremely popular. Although their titles appear to be opposite in meaning, they really say the same thing because "forever" carries with it an understood negation. The point of Blume's book is that the love affair is not "forever," just as Daly's point is that the romance is only for one significant summer.

Both books are about a quest. In ***Forever*** it begins when Katherine meets Michael symbolically on New Year's Eve, and in *Seventeenth Summer* it begins when Angie meets Jack "at the very beginning of the summer." It is part of the pattern that the important positive events in the stories are set in idyllic surroundings. Jack has his boat and the beach house at the lake. Michael is a skier, and the first time he and Katherine make love is when they go to his sister's ski cabin in Vermont with "beautiful fresh snow everywhere and miles and miles of woods."

Both Jack and Michael are in the vanguard of what was considered socially acceptable when the books were written. Jack smokes a pipe and drinks beer. For 1942, this was almost revolutionary in a teenage book. What Blume does to characterize Michael as more "worldly" than Katherine is to show that in the past Michael smoked pot but has made a decision against it for the future. Another indication of Michael's worldliness is the fact that he has had VD, which he got from a girl in Maine. Because it is important in wish fulfillment that the girl be the first one the boy has ever loved, Blume is careful to show that this was purely a physical thing. Michael did not even know the girl's name, so he couldn't get in touch with her to let her know she had it. The girls are portrayed as being more innocent because they are the real protagonists, and it is important that they embody the virtues held noblest by society.

Few boys have read *Seventeenth Summer;* more have read ***Forever,*** but it too is basically a girl's book. When it became a best seller, many adult males in the profession: librarians, high-school English teachers, and college instructors of adolescent literature read it. For some of them it was the first love-romance they had read seriously, and their reactions to the individual book were tied in with reactions to the genre or type. It made many of them feel uncomfortable and they snickered about it at professional meetings. One frequently quoted comment was, "The only character whose name I can remember is a penis called Ralph."

The stories are definitely female oriented. It is not just a coincidence that the protagonists in both *Seventeenth Summer* and ***Forever*** have only sisters, no brothers. The little sisters represent what Angie and Katherine used to be. Angie's older sisters and Katherine's two friends, Sybil and Erica, are foils in the stories. Their experiences with boys make the protagonists' romances seem so much better in contrast. The fathers in each family play very small roles. In contrast, the mother-daughter relationships are rather fully developed as warm and mutually supportive. Interestingly, Judy Blume dedicated her book to her daughter, and Maureen Daly dedicated hers to her mother.

About the only characters with whom male readers can identify are the boyfriends, and there are cultural attitudes that make this less than desirable. As already shown, Daly and Blume were careful to characterize the boys as "good catches." The crux of the problem is that people don't want to be "caught" or "hooked." For a teenage boy this is a disquieting idea, but for a girl the daydream of having a boy "fall" for her is the modern day counterpart to having a fairy godmother come and grant three wishes. As Angie explains:

> It's funny what a boy can do. One day you're nobody and the next day you're the girl that some fellow goes with and the other fellows look at you harder and wonder what you've got and wish that they'd been the one to take you out first. And the girls say hello and want you to walk down to the drugstore to have Cokes with them because the boy who likes you might come along and he might have other boys with him. Going with a boy gives you a new identity—especially going with a fellow like Jack Duluth.

In both books the girls are the ones to initiate the end of the romance. In *Seventeenth Summer,* Angie has always planned to leave and go to college at the end of the summer; in ***Forever,*** Katherine meets Theo and in a relatively painless fashion transfers her affections from one boy to another. In spite of this independence on the part of the girls, they have only the vaguest of goals for their own lives. When Angie is talking to Jack, trying to instill in him a greater ambition, she encourages him to "read a lot," but her only suggestion for herself is that, "I could brush my hair every night." And at Michael's family graduation party, when one of his uncles asks Katherine what she wants to do with her life, all she can answer is that she wants to be happy "and make other people happy too." (pp. 214-15)

Kenneth L. Donelson and Alleen Pace Nilsen, "The Old Romanticism: Of Wishing and Winning," in their Literature for Today's Young Adults, *Scott, Foresman and Company, 1980, pp. 205-27.*

Warren Johnson identifies three basic approaches to the sexuality of the young: eliminating it, accepting it, and cultivating it. The first he sees as the traditional approach; the second he finds increasingly prevalent, covering a range of adult behaviours from indifference or resignation to a concern with developing in the young a sense of responsibility and an understanding of the appropriateness of time and place. The third, cultivation, implying as it does the positive encouragement of sexual discovery and experimentation, is perhaps the most advanced but probably the least popular of the three approaches. (pp. 48-9)

All of the novels discussed so far in this section [Philippa Adams's *Nine Months,* Josephine Kamm's *Young Mother,* Paul Zindel's *My Darling, My Hamburger,* and Elizabeth MacIntyre's *It Looks Different When You Get There*] share a common characteristic, namely their avoidance of any description of the sex act. This 'frontier' in controversial subject matter is pushed back by two writers, Judy Blume and Aidan Chambers, but in very different ways. If one were to locate Blume on Warren Johnson's continuum of adult approaches to young people's sexuality, her novel ***Forever. . .*** would probably place her somewhere in between the 'acceptance' and 'cultivation' approaches, encouraging happy and safe teenage sex through fiction. ***Forever. . .*** is about Katherine and Michael, who are attracted to each other on first meeting at a party, make friends, move on rapidly to heavy petting, and ultimately decide to have sexual intercourse. The book charts their progress from initial blundering attempts to successful union. Thereafter little changes except the location of their sexual adventures and the positions that they choose.

Michael Schofield's research demonstrated that a majority of young people have their first experience of sexual intercourse in the home of their own or their partner's parents. The intimacy between Katherine and Michael certainly begins in the home of Katherine's parents, and gradually deepens and flourishes in the homes of Michael's sister and his parents. Indeed, Katherine's parents are at the start extremely acquiescent about the relationship, her mother only pointing out the commitment that a sexual relationship demands. As if to assure the reader that Katherine's mother is a caring parent and not merely indifferent or irresponsibly progressive, the author tells us that she is a librarian in charge of the children's room at the public library. The initial permissive approach does not last, however, and Katherine is suddenly forced to separate from Michael for a long holiday. Her parents' action, clearly designed to cool the romance, seems manipulative and heavy-handed, though it works for them: Katherine is attracted to another man and breaks her bond with Michael.

Blume makes her messages abundantly plain: first, that sex is an enjoyable experience that is enriched by affection and commitment; second, that one should not be misled into thinking that sexual harmony is the same as everlasting love; and third, that it is worthwhile to listen to one's parents as they may be right. In the book's favour, it does treat sex in an honest and realistic way. For example, in line with Schofield's finding that many teenagers are disenchanted with their first experience of sex, Michael and Katherine are by no means immediately successful in their love-making. Honesty and realism do not, however, counteract two major handicaps: the shallowness of characterization and the rather cosy approach to the sex theme. The personalities of Katherine and Michael are very superficially drawn. Their increasing sexual intimacy is plotted with chatty openness and painstaking physical detail so that there can be little mistaking how it is done. What is lacking is any great emotional depth: Blume's insistence on providing full factual information, right down to the last detail of Katherine's gynaecological tests, works against the portrayal of rounded characters and deep human feeling. (pp. 53-4)

Susan Thompson, "Images of Adolescence: Part I," in Signal, *No. 34, January, 1981, pp. 37-59.*

Popularity is the kiss of death, as far as literary critics are concerned. Judy Blume has sold more than twenty million paperback copies. Critically, she was dead long ago. But it is not just the popularity that infuriates critics. They can't stand Blume's plain talk about everyday things. Having a period was bad enough, in ***Are You There, God? It's Me, Margaret.*** Having wet dreams and liking to watch girls undressing was worse still, in ***Then Again, Maybe I Won't.*** But Blume really blew it, in ***Forever. . . ,*** with teenage petting and intercourse. Teenagers aren't supposed to be able or allowed to read about such things, at least not the way Blume tells them. Outrage, horror and condemnation! Anyway, every thinking person knows best-sellers must be trash.

But there is a danger of letting personal moral judgements interfere with less personal literary judgements. Just how bad is Blume? Let's reconsider the case against Blume by looking at ***Forever. . .***, the book that has attracted the most violent criticism. (p. 29)

Can anything good be said about ***Forever. . .***? To begin with, the critics are wrong to suggest that ***Forever. . .*** is only about a first sexual experience. Certainly the heroine, Kath, loses her virginity, but a lot more happens in the book that deserves serious attention. Kath is a young woman at a point of transition, of several transitions. School is finishing. Soon she will leave home and go to college. She is becoming increasingly independent of her parents. As her interest in Michael becomes more and more serious, she finds her school girl friendship with Erica is changing, and Michael becomes not just Kath's lover, but her best friend. Kath works as a voluntary aid in the geriatric ward of the local hospital. This is partly out of guilt for her negative reaction in childhood to her paternal grandmother's old age, and partly as a way of learning to care for her maternal grandfather who is recovering from a stroke and who Kath now feels close to. She is starting to take charge of her own life.

Kath's friends are also in transition. Erica is eager to 'get laid', and at first seems willing to lose her virginity, just for the experience, and to get it over and done with. But she decides eventually to wait to have that experience within a strong emotional relationship. This contrasts with her cousin Sybil who 'has a genius I.Q. and has been laid by at least six different guys . . . because of [her] fat problem and her need to feel loved—the getting laid part, that is'. Sybil gets pregnant, chooses not to have an abortion but to give birth 'for the experience', and then has the baby adopted. But she finds 'the whole experience was more than she bargained for'. Erica is emotionally involved with Artie, a fellow student with a gift for acting that his parents won't accept. They refuse to let him go to a drama academy, and his depression leads to a suicide attempt and psychiatric hospitalisation. Artie is also troubled by uncertainty about his own sexuality and impotence.

Other issues are raised briefly such as teenage drinking and smoking pot. It is interesting that, in a book which allegedly takes a very frank and perhaps even permissive attitude towards premarital sex, Kath strongly disapproves of the drunkenness of her friends. However she has tried pot once, herself. But because Kath felt sick she chose not to continue with it. Her attitude to drinking and smoking is admirably conservative: 'I don't like to lose control of myself.' There is also a brief reference to Michael having caught VD from another girl. Unfortunately the book suggests that modern antibiotics are an easy cure for this side-effect of sexual adventure that was decidedly casual: 'She was just somebody [Michael] met on the beach'.

But these issues are very minor. More important is Kath's slow realization that she is becoming an adult, becoming a person like her parents. She realizes also that the teenage experiences she is going through are not different from her parents' teenage years. Kath's maternal grandparents also become more significant to her as she grows out of childhood. Kath is very upset, then, by her grandfather dying after a second stroke.

Even in her relationship with Michael, what really matters is not their sexual life, but their affection for each other. The main action of the book is Kath's discovery that, despite her love for Michael, she is also attracted to another, older man. The love that was to be 'forever' is seen to be a changing part of growing up. In fact the title ***Forever . . .***, is seen to be an ironic comment on Kath's emotional uncertainty.

It is a major achievement that Blume presents the heroine as the one who takes initiative, the one whose heart changes. This is unlike earlier naively sentimental books of first love, such as Beverly Cleary's *Fifteen,* or Marjorie Stolz's *Goodbye My Shadow,* which end with unquestionably permanent true love burning in the happy couples' eyes. Cleary goes so far as to end *Fifteen* saying, 'She was Stan's girl. That was all that really mattered'—a view that now seems unacceptably male-dominated and unliberated.

Perhaps this might all seem like a rather breathless teenage soap opera. Inevitably any combination of drugs, drinking, suicide, VD, abortion, sex, love and death may seem trendily melodramatic. But most of these are really peripheral to the main theme in ***Forever . . .*** of directing one's life and accepting the consequences—friendship, love, pain, guilt and loss. There is also a subtlety of characterization and narrative that raises ***Forever . . .*** well beyond mere formula stories and soapies.

The characters are not cut-out stereotypes. They are changeable, ambivalent and at times self-contradictory. They are human. Kath is sometimes unsure of herself:

> It's true that I come on strong with my sarcastic act sometimes, but only when I'm interested in a guy. Otherwise I can be as nice and friendly as they come. Erica says that means I'm insecure. Maybe she's right—I just don't know.

Kath admires her younger sister's artistic and musical talent, but also at times is jealous, even though she can console herself that her sister is not as well physically coordinated. As Kath's affection for Michael grows, she endangers it with petty jealousy and silly jokes.

Kath's father objects to her relationship with Michael, because of a reasonable expectation that it will not last, and because of an irrational unwillingness to admit that Kath is no longer a dependent daughter. Yet, ironically, his possessiveness serves to drive Kath to greater independence.

Michael is very sensitive. He is the first to speak of being in love, while Kath hesitates, unsure. But he has a quick temper, that sits uneasily with his usually gentle nature. At the end, faced with Kath's divided affections, he is the one who calls an end to the affair, and leaves Kath with the hurtful suggestion that he had not been faithful to her, anyway. Neither Kath nor Michael are yet mature enough to continue with friendship once they stop loving.

At midpoint Kath is sure that her love is 'not just some fifties fad, like [her parents] going steady. That with us it is love—real, true honest-to-god love'. (Certainly Blume intends this as narrative irony. The reader knows that Kath's naive enthusiasm is only ordinary human feeling.) But by the end Kath realises that 'it's just that I'm not ready for forever'—this is painful self-knowledge. Kath is barely able to face Michael, and unable to talk with him. There can be no doubt that Kath and Michael are suffering. It is 'a big deal', contrary to [Lynne] Hamilton's superficial judgement. Only courage and persistence, her parents' support and her own growing maturity help Kath survive, despite the pain and guide.

All of this is told directly and deftly in Kath's first-person narrative. The style is personal, vernacular, and simple. But there are subtleties. The language slips from past tense, telling what happened, to a present tense that lets Kath say what her feelings and points of view are at the time of the events. This gives a strong feeling of immediacy, a sense of a real person speaking to us intimately. For example note the slide of tenses in the following short extract:

> It occurred to me in the middle of the night that Michael asked me if I was a virgin to find out what I expected of him. If I hadn't been one then he probably would have made love to me. What scares me is I'm not sure how I feel about that.

Another stylistic subtlety occurs near the end of the story. The final events are rapidly outlined by a series of letters that Kath and Michael write to each other when they are separated by their summer vacation jobs, Michael in a lumber yard and Kath at a tennis camp. There are letters also between Kath and Erica, adding other points of view. As Kath finds herself attracted to the older man, and emotionally confused, there is considerable ironic tension between what the reader knows is happening and what Kath is willing to admit in her letters to Michael. The last letter ends fragmentarily:

> I don't know how this happened or why. Maybe I can get over it. Do you think you can wait—because I don't want you to stop loving me. I keep remembering us and how it was. I don't want to hurt you . . . not ever. . . .

It is a letter which Kath rips up, unable to send it. Kath's love, that was to last 'forever', and her need for love changes, even in the course of this letter, into '. . . not [hurting you] ever . . .' This is something very different, and, again, the reader has ironic forewarning that the worst pain is still ahead of her. Inevitably she will hurt Michael, and herself, very badly.

Blume's prose style, like her realistic subject, is matter-of-fact, but powerful. Simple words and sentences, real-sounding dialogue, can be very effective, and at times very funny. (pp. 31-4)

Any book can seem dull if it is read superficially, or with inappropriate expectations. It is an unfortunate fact that the books for teenagers which receive critical approval are nearly all concerned with extreme characters and extreme situations. Most teenage fictional characters are extremely intelligent, or sub-criminal, or full of hate or extremely depressed, or bizarrely eccentric. They are facing up to intense parental conflict, life-or-death threats, war, gang violence or other extreme situations. Perhaps jaded critical appetites need such stimulus to produce a response. This is unfortunate because it results in quiet books about ordinary people in everyday situations being undervalued. Judy Blume is in fact one of the writers whose critical reputation suffers from a failure, or a refusal, to live up to artificially heightened critical expectations of personality and plot.

Perhaps teenage readers are attracted to the sensational scenes in ***Forever. . . .*** But I do not think so. It is, as [Nicholas] Tucker noted, in fact surprisingly inexplicit, for all its mention of 'penis', 'intercourse' and 'coming' [see excerpt dated October 1, 1976]. The real facts of the hygiene manuals, the details of human plumbing, of who does what to whom with what, are simply not in the book or are glossed over. But it is not the sex scenes which give ***Forever . . .*** its teenage popularity. Teenagers who want to read that sort of stuff can get it readily elsewhere. What attracts them is the fact that, thanks to Blume's vivid and honest writing, they can find *themselves* truthfully presented, undistorted, not *in extremis*—just ordinary life and its awful emotions.

Kath and Michael are ordinary people. Their falling in love and fumbling together and falling out of love is an ordinary situation. In itself this is no reason to condemn ***Forever . . .***, or any other book about ordinary life, except, perhaps, that for adults such things are not new, and they have been lived through and coped with.

If critical adults remember in their hearts the joy, pain, hope and anguish of teenage years, their view of ***Forever . . .*** might be less jaundiced. They might then be able to see the real literary qualities of ***Forever . . .*** as well. (pp. 34-5)

John Gough, "Reconsidering Judy Blume's Young Adult Novel 'Forever . . .'," in The Use of English, *Vol. 36, No. 2, Spring, 1985, pp. 29-36.*

***STARRING SALLY J. FREEDMAN AS HERSELF* (1977)**

Blume here paints a dull still life of growing up in 1947. Sally is a young Jewish girl from New Jersey, spending a school year in Miami with her mother and her older brother, who is recovering from nephritis. There is little plot and even less point to the story; the writing lacks the wit and insight of her earlier books, and the rare moments of humor are aimed at adults. Sally's obsession with Hitler, while certainly plausible and understandable, does not fit smoothly into the context of the book, and is often unnecessarily violent in its expression. For example, one of Sally's daydreams goes as follows, "Hitler . . . gets his knife and slowly slashes each of her fingers . . . her blood drips onto his rug . . . 'Look what you've done, you Jew bastard,' Hitler cries hysterically. 'You've ruined my rug!'" It seems almost painfully obvious that this is autobiographical, but in exorcising the demons of her youth, Blume is ignoring her eager audience and forgetting what she does best.

Diane Haas, in a review of "Starring Sally J. Freedman As Herself," in School Library Journal, *Vol. 23, No. 9, May, 1977, p. 59.*

Interestingly, Mrs. Blume herself has become a much discussed subject of the sub-teen culture she writes about. Kids read her books with a blushing curiosity once reserved for certain words in the dictionary, parts of the Bible and naughty passages in Hemingway. They know they will find some frank discussion of prurient matters like breasts and menstruation. Some of her readers may also have read *Fear of Flying,* yet they reread ***Are You There God? It's Me, Margaret.*** It's evident her appeal goes beyond sexual frankness: She must be conveying a certain emotional reality that children recognize as true. Portnoy may complain all he wants, but kids will go right on needing reassurance that there is a time of slow awakening, of normal curiosity and confusion about what they are learning and feeling. And this is soft at the core, not hard.

While Mrs. Blume's book is teeming with social value, its redeeming literary qualities are less conspicuous. Her characters are so recognizable they don't matter. She describes the 40's in a banal shorthand that misses a good chance to describe what it was really like growing up then. Just as my generation thinks of the 20's as bathtub gin and Clara Bow, I worry that the next generation can be bought off with Margaret O'Brien and Murphy beds.

Julia Whedon, "The Forties Revisited," in The New York Times Book Review, *May 1, 1977, p. 40.*

In introducing her 'most autobiographical novel', Judy Blume says 'In a way, I think the character of Sally explains how and perhaps why I became a writer'. Always good at recreating the mind and speech of adolescent girls, she certainly conveys most convincingly the whole atmosphere of a Jewish family after the Second World War, still stunned by the horrors of the holocaust, though the (amusingly detailed) American setting means that for 10-year-old Sally, there is little resemblance to reality in her imaginings about Lila the beautiful dead aunt of the photograph, and Hitler who, she becomes convinced, is alive and well in Miami. . . . The half-understood snippets of information from older girls going out with boys, the little tragedies and excitements of growing up, and the puzzles of adult behaviour, in particular the strains put on her parents' marriage by the long separation, are vivid and authentic. Sally learns to adjust to the apparent awfulness of her new school and classmates largely through Ma Fanny, her grandmother, a lovely portrait of a Jewish matriarch. This is not the Miami of the playboys, but a close-knit supportive Jewish community within the wider one, where joys and sorrows are shared, willy-nilly. The story moves at a good pace with lively humour, in a mixture of narrative, Sally's stories, her correspondence with her father, and the letters (undelivered) to 'Hitler-in-disguise'. It is easy to believe the characters are drawn from real life. (pp. 169-70)

M. Hobbs, in a review of "Starring Sally J. Freedman as Herself," in The Junior Bookshelf, *Vol. 47, No. 4, August, 1983, pp. 169-70.*

***SUPERFUDGE* (1980)**

No one knows the byways of the under-twelves better than Blume and that alone puts her ahead of the competition. Sixth-grader Peter Hatcher . . . plays likable straight man to his irrepressible little brother, Beezus to Fudgie's Ramona. Fudge won't budge from the bathroom the day Peter overindulges in Island Punch. Fudge papers baby Tootsie with green stamps ("I want to trade her in for a two-wheeler"). His first day at kindergarten Fudge kicks and name-calls his uptight teacher. For this he gets an on-the-spot transfer—to with-it Ms. Ziff. Ramona (. . . *the Brave*) had to stick out all of first grade with dull Mrs. Griggs. Blume lets her heroes off easy. Peter, who packs his Adidas bag in protest over a trial move from New York to (Princeton) New Jersey, is brushed, not bruised, by new experiences. The Hatchers (and supporting cast) don't have dimensions; they have attitudes. Smooth and easy to swallow, ***Superfudge*** is like a lemon meringue pie—without the lemon. (pp. 60-1)

Pamela D. Pollack, in a review of "Superfudge," in School Library Journal, *Vol. 26, No. 10, August, 1980, pp. 60-1.*

A problem with reviewing ***Superfudge*** was getting the book to stay still long enough to read it. The bush telegraph of 8- and 9-year-olds somehow got the word that Fudge was back. Peter Hatcher and his impossible kid brother have friends and fans everywhere: the children who empathized and chuckled their way through ***Tales of a Fourth Grade Nothing,*** as Peter's comfortable life in the Hatcher's Manhattan apartment was turned upside down by a living 2-year-old tornado known as "Fudge." They had groaned and gasped when the ultimate happened—Fudgie *ate* his brother's adored pet turtle—and now they couldn't wait to see how Peter had survived another year in the Hatcher household. Many of them found out before I did, but when finally the door was locked and the book in hand, Peter was discovered entering sixth grade. He has moved, at least for a year, to the suburbs—Princeton in fact.

Judy Blume, however, knows better than to let Peter spend a quiet year breathing cleaner air. Mrs. Hatcher produces ("How could you?" cries Peter) a second sibling known as Tootsie, Mr. Hatcher tries to write a book, and Peter goes into the worm business with his new friend, Alex.

Judy Blume's books for younger readers are funny, in just the outrageous way that appeals to the broad humor of 8- to 10-year-olds, but even more important to children is the clear knowledge that Blume is on their team. She doesn't tell them about Mommies who must work to fulfill themselves or parents who know it all or that one must be patient with pesky smaller kids. Peter is often driven to exasperation at the denseness of his grown-ups: no one seemed to care about the fate of his turtle as they waited at the hospital . . .

This subversive position enslaves children. Adult readers find it cute in books about 8- and 9-year-old urchins, but Blume's reputation—or notoriety—is so bound up with her novels for teenage girls that many forget she can create good clean fun. Peter is preoccupied with his turtle, selling worms and persuading Fudge to come down from the top of the kindergarten closet. Margaret of ***Are You There God? It's Me Margaret*** is 14 not 10, a girl not a boy, and is therefore more preoccupied with grow-bras and the onset of menstruation. The furor about novels like ***Margaret*** and ***Blubber*** (children do persecute overweight contemporaries whether or not Judy Blume writes about it) assuredly hasn't decreased her audience. There is no more determined reader than he or she who has been forbidden a certain volume, and no underground distribution network works like that of the playground. All the same, ***Superfudge*** will come as a relief to those who are made nervous by the very sound of the name Judy Blume.

Superfudge suffers from many of the problems typical of sequels. Its hard to top Fudge's exploit of eating the turtle, Fudge himself is older and the helpless Tootsie isn't yet very interesting—in fact on occasion the intrepid Peter seems almost to fall prey to her innocent charms, to forget that this bundle is an embryo Fudge. Fudge himself does acquire a most talkative mynah bird called Uncle Feather who helps the action along, but on the whole this is a book for the friends of Peter Hatcher—and they are legion.

Brigitte Weeks, "The Return of Peter Hatcher," in Book World—The Washington Post, *November 9, 1980, p. 12.*

Judy Blume is immensely popular with children, and it's easy to see why. She's a very good comic writer who does not condescend, and ***Superfudge*** is a genuinely funny story rather in the Erma Bombeck vein, dealing with the kinks and knots of modern family life. And except for a gratuitous but harmless toilet episode, its various scenes are as pure as the youngsters who animate them. By that I mean that Mrs. Blume understands the real nature of children's purity, which is in fact not precisely what it has been cracked up to be by some of our more wishful colleagues. This honesty is obviously refreshing to young readers. They love every minute of it.

Natalie Babbitt, in a review of "Superfudge," in The New York Times Book Review, *November 23, 1980, p. 36.*

***TIGER EYES* (1981)**

The murder of an Atlantic City 7-Eleven store owner might have been an outrageous basis for a teen-age novel a few years ago. But today the idea—think of all those brief and matter-of-fact stories in the newspaper—seems almost commonplace. We read that somebody is shot and dies, that he had a family, that the unknown assailant or assailants escaped with $50 in cash (which is what happens in ***Tiger Eyes,*** Judy Blume's latest book), and we finish our coffee or put out the cat and go on with our lives.

"Newspapers are very big on facts. I think," muses Davis (Davey) Wexler, the 15-year-old daughter left behind after her father was shot in the chest. "But not on feelings. Nobody writes about how it *feels* when your father is murdered."

Judy Blume does. And even if your father hasn't been murdered, even if you're no longer 15, and even if you'd rather think about something else, she puts you inside that girl: a luminous-eyed (thus the title) brownette, built like a swimmer, at once achingly vulnerable, funny and tough. In the proper cadence of grief—paralysis, anger, catharsis, gradual acceptance—you know how it feels, slowly, excruciatingly, over a school year's time. And maybe that's why kids like Blume's writing so much. You can cry with a friend, and then when you can't stand any more, she'll poke you in the ribs with a joke. Blume's often cynical, staccato style works splendidly as the voice of a child, who does not yet know enough to round out—and even forgive—adult idiocies.

Because Davey . . . er, Blume . . . talks to us in such a taut and dreamlike way, giving us images bit by bit, you'll keep reading to piece together the facts. For example, you'll know she had spinach pie the night her father died but you'll only get hints for a long time about where she was.

Davey's real thoughts come to the surface—as if from a very savvy teen-ager's diary—in the midst of some terrible ironies. The most overt is that Davey, her mother and 7-year-old brother are struggling to come to grips with a decimating, anonymous violence while seeking security in Los Alamos (The Atomic City). They've gone to live there temporarily with Uncle Walter, a physicist "thinking up new ways," as Davey says, "to kill people," and Aunt Bitsy, who leads bomb museum tours and is inclined toward saying things like, "She made her bed, now let her lie in it."

Davey, with the acute eye of the young, is disdainfully aware of the hypocrisy of among other things, a middle class which designs bombs during the week and worships on Sundays. "There are more churches in Los Alamos than I have ever seen anywhere . . . I don't know if it's because scientists pray more than other people, or what. Maybe they have more guilt and fear."

She is lectured by her uncle, in one wrenching scene, about the trappings of a "*better* man," a definition which her father—a high school graduate who sketched family portraits and listened to classical music in his 7-Eleven—does not fit. Her father, she knows, may have housed his family above the store, but he paid attention to them, and she longs for the feel of his hand smoothing the hair away from her face. She meets a girl whose father's success has won them a mansion, but he hasn't noticed that his daughter is drunk all the time.

In Los Alamos the people with whom Davey, white and part Jewish, finds the most comfort are a well-educated and sensitive Hispanic boy named Wolf—assumed by Aunt Bitsy to be a maintenance man—and his father, who although dying was "full of life and full of love."

Blume, the best-selling author of children's fiction in the country, touches lightly on most teen-age issues: misunderstandings with adults, drinking, drugs, dating, a girl's crushes and conflicts about depending on a boyfriend. As for sex, there's only, parents might be relieved to know, some heavy necking (if kids still call it that).

What parents might find more disturbing is the realization that it's the little, special things about themselves that their children will remember and that will carry them through the toughest adversity. Davey's father had a warm and homey ritual—which I won't give away here—but her reenactment of it is one of the most poignant and healing scenes in the book.

Judy Blume's ***Blubber*** provoked some controversy in Montgomery and Fairfax counties last year because some parents and school book review boards saw it as being cruel to fat children without, as one parent said, any "moral tone" from an adult or another child.

There's no hit-them-in-the-head moralizing in ***Tiger Eyes*** either, probably another reason why kids like Blume. Davey does, however, remind them subtly of their own good sense and remarkable resiliency. "Each of us must confront our own fears, must come face to face with them," she says. "How we handle our fears will determine where we go with the rest of our lives." (pp. 9-10)

Margaret Mason, "Judy Blume: Growing Up with Grief," in Book World—The Washington Post, *September 13, 1981, pp. 9-10.*

This is a masterly novel, not to be dismissed as simply another treatment of death and violence. The reader empathizes not only with the heroine but with all the other characters. Each has his own story, and each lights up some aspect of the American scene. Take Uncle Walter, for instance, who spends his days making atom bombs yet misses the irony in his overprotection of Davey; he's so sensitive to danger that he won't let her take Driver's Ed. Surely ***Tiger Eyes*** belongs at the top of Judy Blume's list. (p. 58)

Jean Fritz "The Heroine Finds a Way," in The New York Times Book Review, *November 15, 1981, pp. 56, 58.*

The last time a group of librarians moaned over my pronouncement that Judy Blume was the most influential novelist in America, one of them later ambushed me outside the convention hall to whisper: "It's awful, but you're right. In my children's section, when we're out of Judy Blumes, we're out of books."

If librarians had to deal only with readers, they would appreciate Blume as much as I do. Kids gorge on Blume. They stay up all night to read ***It's Not the End of the World*** or ***Are You There God? It's Me, Margaret*** with a flashlight under the covers. They gossip in the schoolyard about Deenie and Fudge and Sally J. Freedman. Best of all, thousands of growing fingers that seemed destined only to flip channels have been hooked by Blume into the habit of turning pages. Even non-Blume pages. Sometimes my pages.

But that's not the only reason for my enthusiasm. Blume explores the feelings of children in a nonjudgmental way. The immediate resolution of a problem is never as important as what the protagonist, usually a white, middle-class girl, will learn about herself by confronting her life. The young reader gains from the emotional adventure story both by observing another youngster in a realistic situation and by finding a reference from which to start a discussion with a friend or parent or teacher. For many children, talking about a Blume story is a way to expose their own fears about menstruation or masturbation or death.

Unfortunately, librarians and teachers must respond to their nonreading constituencies as well, and, in the case of books for children and adolescents, the nonreaders are more powerful than the readers. The Far Righteous has made Blume a special target of book-banning crusades since she asks more questions than she answers, gently nudging her readers toward a healthy skepticism. Even many liberal parents, teachers and librarians have their qualms about her open, seemingly off-hand treatment of sexuality. In many so-called "problem" juvenile novels, the wages of sin are abortions, V.D., suicide or at least a heavy guilt trip. Not so in Blume's books. The sexual humor in her 1975 best seller, ***Forever,*** compounded the outrage over the explicit sex play. A featured character was a penis named Ralph, and the book's opening line was this blunt narrative hook: "Sybil Davison has a genius I.Q. and has been laid by at least six different guys."

Blume's new book, ***Tiger Eyes,*** should slip past the censors. There is no explicit sex and there are no objectionable words. It is her finest book—ambitious, absorbing, smoothly written, emotionally engaging and subtly political. It is also a lesson on how the conventions of a genre can best be put to use.

The plot of ***Tiger Eyes*** is a staple of juvenile novels. A family member dies and the survivors must reconstitute themselves. Standard props are used: A lovable cat and a comical younger brother pop up from time to time to loosen the tension. Textbook suspense is created early: A mysterious paper bag and a romantic young stranger are left unexplained for many pages.

Thus the reader, perhaps 11 years old, is comfortable in TV sitcom territory. Even the opening chapter, in which a 15-year-old girl is searching for shoes to wear to the funeral of her father, shot during the robbery of his 7-Eleven store, is out of Eyewitness News.

But the story deepens, takes turns. Davey Wexler, her mother and her 7-year-old brother flee Atlantic City for the Los Alamos, New Mexico, home of the dead man's older sister, a rigid, domineering clubwoman, and her husband, a fearful, insular weapons scientist. In the oppressive atmosphere of Bomb City, the childless couple attempt to take control of the lives of the three visitors.

Davey's brother quickly attaches himself to his aunt and uncle. Davey's mother, drugged on headache pills, sinks into a depression. But Davey, a typically smart, assertive, spunky Blume heroine, never stops struggling for her independence—sometimes foolishly (by refusing to wear a bicycle helmet on a mountain ride), sometimes heroically (by forcing herself to face repressed fears and guilts).

Tiger Eyes never falters, never slides into melodrama or preachment. Blume is a crisp and often funny stylist with a gift for defining character through snappy dialogue. She is unafraid of emotion. And she offers no final answers. No one in ***Tiger Eyes*** changes forever, or emerges sadder but wiser, or even learns her lesson well. Rather, a girl and her mother weather a crisis, often helped and hindered by the same well-meaning, mean-spirited people, and now must go forward with their lives.

No wonder Blume is currently the most popular writer of Young Adult novels, a genre supposedly aimed at 12-to 18-year-olds. Actually, I suspect that most Y.A. readers are in the fifth, sixth and seventh grades, which would make them about 10 to 13 years old. Some Blumes appeal to younger children, while the Y.A. novels of Robert Cormier *(The Chocolate War, After the First Death)* are for older, more sophisticated readers who would also enjoy *Lord of the Flies* and *The Catcher in the Rye,* quintessential Y.A. novels, although, like Cormier's work, they transcend any marketing label.

This Y.A. market has been defined and vigorously cultivated for less than twenty years, although books for and about teenagers have a long and fascinating history. . . . The current wave of Y.A. books began in the late 1960s with the novels of Paul Zindel *(The Pigman),* Maia Wojciechowska *(Tuned Out),* John Donovan *(I'll Get There. It Better Be Worth The Trip.)* and S. E. Hinton *(The Outsiders),* among others, which pushed aside the prom and the big game as important literary concerns to make room for drug abuse, alienation and the problems of death and divorce.

The genre expanded in the 1970s with such writers as M. E. Kerr *(Dinky Hocker Shoots Smack),* Norma Klein *(Mom, the Wolfman and Me),* Isabelle Holland *(The Man Without a Face),* Alice Childress *(A Hero Ain't Nothin' but a Sandwich)* and Robin Brancato *(Blinded by the Light).*

Of course, this is an incomplete list. The number and variety of Y.A. titles is staggering, and the range in quality of books marketed for young readers is wide. (pp. 551-52)

If there is a common denominator among the best of the Y.A. books, it is probably the writers' passion to point out new directions and overlooked possibilities for this vulnerable, needy audience, to offer hope and the message "You're not alone."

The teachers and the librarians who use these books also find that they provide a bridge of words that can carry a child into a lifetime of reading. Too many kids have been turned off reading for pleasure by well-intentioned adults who assigned the classics too early.

Which brings us back to Judy Blume. Thousands of kids who have never read a book for pleasure before will find their way to ***Tiger Eyes*** through word of mouth, and then, out of Blumes, will ask for something more. (pp. 552-53)

Robert Lipsyte, "A Bridge of Words," in The Nation, *New York, Vol. 233, No. 17, November 21, 1981, pp. 551-53.*

Judy Blume's invariable method is to make a series of simple, unequivocal statements about her characters, and the result has often been slick and superficial. The subject of ***Tiger Eyes*** seems to have imposed on her a stronger discipline; she has certainly made a determined attempt to describe, through dialogue and confrontations, the effect of a man's death on his wife, daughter and young son. Davey . . . tells the story herself, and the degree of candour she shows varies from one moment to another; this allows the author to reserve part of the argument to the end of the book and the reader realises Davey's feelings gradually, in a true-to-life way. Then, too, Judy Blume's sharp evocation of domestic scenes is at its best in the picture of the house at Los Alamos where Mrs. Wexler and her children take refuge with relations: the background of atomic research and its dire problems, the possessive kindness of Mrs. Wexler's sister-in-law and her husband, emerge naturally in the comments of a girl who is young enough to see adults as gaolers as she pursues her own fantasies but old enough to perceive something of their point of view as well. This workmanlike tale has moved some way on from the generalised smoothness of ***Forever.***

Margery Fisher, in a review of "Tiger Eyes," in Growing Point, *Vol. 21, No. 2, July, 1982, p. 3926.*

A nagging feeling of familiarity dogged me while reading this absorbing story. I think I may have identified it. This is the kind of story which appears, in picture-strip form, in adolescent girls' magazines. Judy Blume, of course, is far more literate and she has much deeper penetration, but there is the same simplistic philosophy, the same picture of a world operating by clichés. Miss Blume has lots of sympathy for the young, and she knows all about adolescence, at least in its American manifestation, but does she really present a true three-dimensional portrait of her heroine? I doubt it. Her narrative, despite the irritating historic-present in which most of it is written, is thoroughly readable, but I fancy that girls in this country, if they have grown beyond the picture-story stage, will find this presentation of their problems less than convincing; if not, they will hardly want to grapple with all these words. (pp. 194-95)

M. Crouch, in a review of "Tiger Eyes," in The Junior Bookshelf, *Vol. 46, No. 5, October, 1982, pp. 194-95.*

THE PAIN AND THE GREAT ONE (1984)

Ink and watercolor illustrations [by Irene Trivas] that have considerable vitality and humor extend a text that is based on part of *Free to Be . . . You and Me,* by Marlo Thomas and others. Blume adds insight and wit in this fresh and wistfully funny adaptation; in separate monologues, a boy of six (The Pain) is described by his sister, two years older (The Great One) and he offers his scathing opinion of her in the other. What emerges is a perfect picture of sibling rivalry and jealousy, and both monologues end with "I think they love her/him better than me." In both cases, this gloomy suspicion is preceded by a hearty "YUCK!" as a climax to the listing of the most grievous sins of the other. Right on target and very amusing.

Zena Sutherland, in a review of "The Pain and the Great One," in Bulletin of the Center for Children's Books, *Vol. 38, No. 3, November, 1984, p. 40.*

I have not always cared for Judy Blume's supercharged adolescent stories, but she certainly knows her small kids. This picture-book is really the same story twice over, once from the viewpoint of the sister (the Great One), once from that of the younger brother (the Pain). Although the thoughts are much the same, the tone is nicely modulated to suit the speaker. The real voice of childhood is here, with no hint of adult intervention.

M. Crouch, in a review of "The Pain and the Great One," in The Junior Bookshelf, *Vol. 50, No. 1, February, 1986, p. 13.*

[***The Pain and the Great One***], illustrates the problem of the problem picture book. Dedicated to "the original Pain and Great One with love", it explores an elder sister's jealous resentment of her younger brother and vice versa: the droopy illustrations of peeved stares and sulky mouths bear out the message that what each child wants is, in Auden's phrase, "not universal love / but to be loved alone". But there is no story, no development, no structure beyond a fearfully obvious symmetry of her tale and his: the narrative vacancy swallows up the book's cathartic intentions.

Blake Morrison, "The Age of Anxiety," in The Times Literary Supplement, *No. 4324, February 14, 1986, p. 174.*

LETTERS TO JUDY: WHAT YOUR KIDS WISH THEY COULD TELL YOU (1986)

It is almost impossible to be a parent in this country without eventually knowing about Judy Blume. She is the phenomenally successful author of over a dozen books that have found their way into the hands of a readership which, until Blume more or less pre-empted the field, had gone without a spokesman—your children. Over 30 million of them have taken comfort from her words.

The characters in her stories are too fat, too unpopular, or too meanly treated by their best friends. They want to know about sex, with specifics, but are too embarrassed to ask. They live with parents who are getting divorced, favor their younger brother, or don't understand anything. Judy Blume does. She is one of those adults who forgot to forget what childhood is all about.

Now comes Blume with a book that flowed right out of her mailbox. Based upon the nearly 2,000 letters she receives every month from her mostly young readers, ***Letters to Judy: What Your Kids Wish They Could Tell You*** is an attempt, heartrendingly successful, to give parents a keyhole glimpse into the world their children inhabit. It is not a pretty place.

Take Molly, age 11. She comes to school one day and finds out that all her friends are ostentatiously crossing her name off their notebook covers. "It's Donna," (confides Molly to Blume) who has turned the class against her. They proceed to call her "Brace Face," "Tinsel Teeth," and "The Ratty Redhead." Molly's mother, sounding eerily like Everymother, tells her that "she's sick of this 'ganging up' thing, and would I please try to find some new friends."

Molly, attempting to confide in a teacher, is told to ignore the situation; it doesn't work. Weeks of social ostracism ensue. "I really need help. Last night I was in hysterics. I grabbed at my carpet and screamed very loudly. I thought of running away and also of commiting suicide . . . Then I thought of you and I knew you would understand. Please, please help me!"

We don't know what happened to Molly. As she does with all her correspondents, Blume answered her letter but none of her replies are included in the book. In fact, if there is any flaw in ***Letters to Judy,*** it is the fact that so many children are left floating in our minds, somewhere "out there" as they deal with situations, many of which are far worse than Molly's.

Blume hears from children whose stepfathers have sexually abused them, who are handicapped, have brothers in jail, are being torn by bloody divorces, and are struggling with the ramifications of living with retarded siblings. (p. 3)

Reading ***Letters to Judy*** with a slightly commercial eye, it is clear that Blume has a gold mine of new plots arriving in her mail on a daily basis. But far clearer is the urgent need of children to articulate their fears, anxieties and real problems. It is Blume's intention in this book to give parents a few hints as to how to ease their children's minds and hearts, based upon her own experience. Interspersed between the letters (divided into various categories) are snatches of autobiographical commentary from Blume's life as a child and parent which address various issues, such as divorce.

Throughout ***Letters,*** Blume inserts her own trials and errors where appropriate, giving form and overview to what might otherwise have been a book too full of "cries and whispers" from anonymous children to endure.

It is not all woe. "Dear Judy," writes Melanie, age 11, "How does a girl kiss a boy—arms around the neck or waist? Also, do you squeeze the lips real hard and are the girl's lips placed exactly on the boy's or is the girl's upper lip above the boy's upper lip or what?"

Whether the advice Blume gives to parents is advice you have already taken is a question only you can answer after reading the book. That reason for buying ***Letters*** is sufficient in itself. But the children Blume introduces are such radiantly candid and innocent human beings that we cannot help but look at our own children with a deeper understanding and compassion. Blume's correspondents quite effortlessly outshine the author which I rather suspect she is happy to allow. Letting them have center stage gives credit to the director. This is a generous book. (pp. 3-4)

Phyllis Theroux, "Judy Blume Listens to Her Young Readers," in Book World—The Washington Post, *April 27, 1986, pp. 3-4.*

When a ten-year-old child wrote to ask her to "write a book for adults about our problems to open their eyes," Blume realized that underlying many letters was the plea: "Help me tell my parents." Believing strongly in her responsibility to those who see her as confidante, Blume wrote ***Letters to Judy*** to share kids' letters with other kids to let them know they are not alone, and to let their parents know what kids cannot seem to tell them directly.

As she addresses the whole family, Blume is remarkably successful in her dual purpose. Chapters are arranged by subject, covering family relationships, friendship, disability and illness, coping with divorce or death and new family structures resulting, the facts of life, runaways, rape, incest, child abuse, drug and alcohol abuse, depression and suicide. Actual letters appear in the text with Blume's comments, sometimes specifically addressed to "kids" or "Parents", often tying in anecdotes from her own and her children's lives. Her tone is one of warm support and encouragement, without specific advice beyond urging young people to communicate with their families or other adults nearby, seeking professional help when necessary. Stating that she is not a psychologist, Blume acts instead as a facilitator or mediator in family communications. The letters themselves, from children as young as nine all the way through the teens (and some from adults) give clear, sometimes heartbreaking testament to the urgent need for better exchange within families. (pp. 171-72)

Readers of all ages will benefit from Blume's insight and concern, for by listening and caring, she inspires others to do so. An extensive resource list by subject incorporates agency referrals and book annotations, helping readers put new understanding into practice. Included is a plug for libraries and librarians, with Blume's conviction that books help solve problems, both nonfiction for facts and fiction for feelings. This excellent, ground-breaking new approach to family self-help belongs in all libraries and homes. (p. 172)

Cathi Edgerton, in a review of "Letters to Judy: What Your Kids Wish They Could Tell You," in Voice of Youth Advocates, *Vol. 9, Nos. 3 & 4, August-October, 1986, pp. 171-72.*

Every voluntary reader of fiction is no doubt self-searching to some degree, but the adolescent reader is particularly so. Provided it is open-minded, such reading entails deep imaginative contact. If a book isn't felt as some kind of personal, emotional discovery, it isn't read, but dead. . . .

Modern children for whom *Macbeth* doesn't quite fill the bill may turn to ***Blubber*** or ***Are you there, God? It's me, Margaret*** by Judy Blume, the American writer whose emotional "how-to" books for the under-sixteens are extremely popular on both sides of the Atlantic. Such books may require no great imaginative efforts from their readers, but they are far from stupid or dishonest. They faithfully re-create the realities of school and family life in good, brisk, colloquial prose. Anxieties are sensitively explored, and if the context is generally optimistic, it nevertheless retains a sense of uncertainty and flux as well as possibility; the false pink glow of happily-ever-after is usually nicely muted, if not avoided altogether.

All this began in the 1970s (and derives from 1960s barricade-storming as plainly as the surveys of Masters and Johnson do); by now it has become a minor industry. Two recent heirs are Paula Danziger and Norma Klein. . . . The woe that is in marriage, and family life in general, comes through relentlessly in the work of both these authors, the mother's struggle for her own growth and autonomy often providing an interesting extra dimension. . . . I wonder, though, if they speak as intimately to their young readers as those of Blume.

Letters to Judy spells out the extent, and the pathos, of the response. "Some of your books almost tell my life" writes Emma, a black girl bullied by her white class-mates; "I feel you're writing about me" is indeed the refrain, and on both sides of the Atlantic. But of course this isn't simply a collection of fan-mail; invariably, the correspondents go on to describe problems of their own, adding that they "can't talk" to their parents. It appears that, while teenagers have always tended to suffer crises of one sort or another, the modern two-generation family structure cruelly intensifies their sense of isolation. Parents are more likely to change partners, too, emerging from unassailable but comforting distance to become their children's sexual equals and rivals. None of the problems described could be termed trivial, least of all from the child's point of view, but some are more extreme than others, however casual the phrasing: "My mother was arrested for child abuse. She beat me and my heart stopped."

A number of the children suggest plots for further books, with touching apologies for "being pushy"; but of course the real need is to tell their own stories to a trusted listener. ("I will keep writing to you . . . will tell you one problem per letter.") Judy Blume, who trained as a teacher before she became a writer, makes a sensible and friendly guru. A trace of encounter-group jargon does not exceed the acceptable and the references to her own experiences as a child, a mother and a twice-divorced wife are easy and candid. Though she does not include her answering letters, the tone of her comments suggest their character, its genuine concern. . . . [The] writer is always alert to an emergency, urging counsellors and suicide hotlines if necessary. . . .

This book is very much the product of a problem-solving society, imbued with its optimism and naivety. Most European writers, apart from the professional agony aunts, would probably feel like scurrying back to their ivory towers at even a trickle of such letters. While admiring the openness and human decency that sits down and replies in person to each *cri de coeur,* I feel a certain unease that a writer should be under such pressure, that huge social obligations should be raising their shark-like fins under the frail craft of fictional integrity. It is an expression of the utmost democracy; and yet, strangely enough, it suggests the kinds of demands made on writers in societies that are anything but democratic, where, though books are read, the literary imagination is all but dead.

Carol Rumens, "Adolescent Appeal," in The Times Literary Supplement, *No. 4365, November 28, 1986, p. 1342.*

This is an extraordinary book: disturbing, moving, sometimes funny— but always immensely readable. I couldn't put it down. It is addressed to everyone in the family and can be read alone or together. . . . Most of the letters are from normal children; this is not a compilation of missives from the disturbed.

Reading this book made me remember things half-forgotten about my own period of growing up. I realized that those concerns were not unique to me but shared by many like-minded children. I hope therefore that other adults will hear their own inner voices as they read and take stock of their attitudes to one another and children and grant them the rights they feel are justly their own. (p. 68)

Elizabeth McCardell, in a review of "Letters to Judy: What Kids Wish They Could Tell You," in Reading Time, *Vol. 31, No. 3, 1987, pp. 68-9.*

JUST AS LONG AS WE'RE TOGETHER (1987)

Stephanie Hirsh, an eternal optimist, is looking forward to starting junior high. It bothers her that her father has to be on the West Coast until Thanksgiving, but at least she's home with her mom; her engaging younger brother, Bruce; and her best friend, Rachel Robinson. When Stephanie meets Alison Monceau, the Vietnamese daughter of an American actress, she happily incorporates the girl into her circle. But events are changing in Stephanie's life without her really being aware of them. Her father's absence turns out to be a marital separation from her mother, and Stephanie is inducted into the world of holidays split between parents, "flings," and adults caught up in their own lives. Moreover, Stephanie and Rachel have a falling out, and all of Stephanie's problems lead to a significant weight gain. It's been a while since Blume has written for this age group [grades six to eight], and she shows the same easy touch that has endeared her to so many children. Unfortunately, it's hard to be an innovator when one has so many imitators—this predictable though likable story nestles right into the first-person genre. Conversations about first periods, career mothers, and boy-girl relationships abound, but the serious problems, such as what it means to be overweight in a fanatically thin society, are never really addressed. While her plotting slides a bit, Blume's characters are engaging, and fans of the author will be happy to spend time with this winsome group. (pp. 1741-42)

Ilene Cooper, in a review of "Just as Long as We're Together," in Booklist, *Vol. 83, No. 22, August, 1987, pp. 1741-42.*

The relationships within the story—among the three friends, and between Steph and her parents—are complicated, and Blume handles this aspect realistically and with great ease. The plot resolution, though carefully handled, is curiously flat. Despite this weakness, the story is lively, moves quickly, and captures the nutty, poignant world of very young teenagers.

A review of "Just as Long as We're Together," in Publishers Weekly, *Vol. 232, No. 7, August 14, 1987, p. 105.*

Though occasionally sensational or awkward, [Judy Blume's] fiction is grounded in honesty, a quality that gets her books simultaneously bought and banned.

Just as Long as We're Together, her first novel in five years, looks at first like a Blume medley, with strains of earlier stories wound together. There are no new, big issues here; the main theme is friendship—how it is tested and how it endures. There is a muted, mellow tone to the story, and Blume fans looking for "the good parts" to dogear will find few. They may even get the feeling they have read this book before: Stephanie Hirsch, seventh grader, moves to a new neighborhood; tries to keep her best friend and make a new one at the same time; confronts the separation of her parents; gets fat; gets her period; gets a boyfriend; turns 13, and is finally O.K. in spite of it all. Peripheral problems include nuclear dreams, adoption, racial difference and famous-parent syndrome.

But the most interesting twist is that the Hirsches' attempt to protect their daughter from the truth succeeds only in crippling her. She doesn't realize for quite some time that they have separated, even though her father has moved to the West Coast. She thinks he is there on business. So when her parents finally decide she is ready to hear the truth, Stephanie is, ironically, not ready at all. She overeats, in despair and spite. Bitterness replaces her natural optimism, and she hides the family disintegration from her best friends even while demanding truthfulness from them.

The appeal of the Blume novels is in the recognition they engender, the feeling of "Yes, that's what it's really like!" But fiction also needs a sense of wonder, a hint of the unrecognizable, even in the suburbs, even in the seventh grade. The narrative tone here is flat and defensive, minimizing or deflecting emotion in the same way that cartoons do.

Another worrisome hitch is the ending. Like many children of divorce, Stephanie schemes to bring her parents together again. Incredibly, her effort *works,* and by book's end, chances for a reconciliation look good. "Don't get your hopes up," her mother says, but clearly the possibility exists. Although hope is surely not one of the dangers that children should be protected from, to offer *this* hope, here, is hardly consistent with the honest realism for which Judy Blume is known.

Josephine Humphreys, "Fat, 13 and Basically O.K.," in The New York Times Book Review, *November 8, 1987, p. 33.*

W(illiam) W(allace) Denslow

1856-1915

American author/illustrator of picture books, illustrator of fiction and verse, reteller, poet, playwright, and cartoonist.

Denslow is considered one of the most distinguished illustrators of children's books of the early twentieth century. He is credited with being the first American to create picture books in the aesthetic tradition of English illustrators Walter Crane, Kate Greenaway, and Randolph Caldecott and the first to combine color with a sense of design. Almost completely forgotten until recent years, due largely to the lack of distinction of his collaborators and the much-imitated use of his style, Denslow is now acknowledged as the definitive illustrator of L. Frank Baum's *The Wonderful Wizard of Oz* (1900; later published as *The Wizard of Oz*). Characteristically using color, expression, action, and humor in his drawings, Denslow successfully elevated the standards of the American picture book by conceiving each work as an artistic whole. He initially composed his pictures in black india ink and then worked closely with the printer to achieve the desired hues. Denslow's most frequent method of drawing was a bold, colorful poster style reminiscent of Japanese prints, in which his figures, often anthropomorphic animals, move within a two-dimensional space against a background of solid color. Adjusting the complexity of his illustrations to the age of his audience, Denslow drew simple pictures with skillfully placed spots and masses of color for the very young and added more figures and detail for older children. He often appended his Japanese-inspired stylized seahorse monogram to his works, which led to his nickname "Hippocampus Den." Also a prolific and leading artist of color comics for children, Denslow was perhaps the originator of the story strip, a feature in which the story line is continued from week to week.

Following employment as a designer of theatrical posters and costumes, an illustrator of books and book covers, and an artist for the *Chicago Herald,* Denslow was approached by Baum to illustrate *Father Goose, His Book* (1899), a collection of original light verse. Denslow's pictures include friezes of characters marching across the bright, poster-style page and active, individualized comic figures who sometimes escape their black borders. The work was a phenomenal success due mainly to Denslow's drawings, and it established Baum and Denslow as the most exciting contemporary team in American children's literature. With *Father Goose,* the artist established a style of design that influenced children's book illustration for two decades. For *The Wonderful Wizard of Oz,* Denslow was challenged not only to give visual conception to Baum's often strange, imaginary characters, but to portray an original fairyland in detail. He frequently incorporated new concepts not found in Baum's text, such as giving human characteristics to the buildings in the Emerald City. Quaintly charming and endearing, the over one hundred text illustrations and twenty-four color plates are now considered as inseparable from *The Wizard* as Sir John Tenniel's pictures are from *Alice in Wonderland.* Denslow's third and last book with Baum was the fantasy *Dot and Tot of Merryland* (1901), in which the illustrator used a decorative art nouveau style. Following the production of this book, the partnership dissolved in bitterness over financial concerns and Denslow's assumption of the credit for some of Baum's creations and ideas.

Prior to finishing *Dot and Tot,* Denslow published his first solo work, *Denslow's Mother Goose* (1901), which featured a double-page spread for each verse. Utilizing Baum's belief that children's books should have no violence or terror, he rewrote the familiar poems where necessary to achieve this goal and added colorful, dynamic pictures which are simplified to suit a young audience. The success of this book inspired Denslow to produce his well-received drawings for *Denslow's Night before Christmas* (1902), which illustrates Clement Clarke Moore's poem and includes some characters from *The Wizard.* In 1903 and 1904, the artist created a series of eighteen pamphlets known collectively as *Denslow's Picture Books,* which consist of traditional fairy tales and rhymes as well as original stories. One of the most popular was *Denslow's Scarecrow and the Tin-Man* (1904), based on the disillusionment of the characters with Baum's 1902 adult musical play *The Wizard of Oz.* Considered some of Denslow's best illustrative work, the brightly colored *Picture Books* contain lively figures, inventive drawing, and broad comedy. However, the texts—mainly expurgated retellings—are not as well received because they lose much of the drama of the traditional tales.

Denslow's successive books are considered largely forgettable because their texts are seen as uninspired. Together with Paul

West, Denslow created *The Pearl and the Pumpkin* (1904). The crowded plot concerning attempts to learn a boy's secret of growing pumpkins was Denslow's literary contribution. His illustrations depict realistic scenes of Bermuda as well as authentic representations of buccaneers. Both *The Pearl* and *Billy Bounce* (1906), written with Dudley A. Bragdon, were adapted into plays for which Denslow receives credit as coauthor. The main character of *Billy Bounce,* an original fairy tale about an orphaned messenger boy with an inflatable suit, first appeared in Denslow's popular 1901-02 comic strip "Billy Bounce." Following his well-designed illustrations for Isabel M. Johnston's fantasy *The Jeweled Toad* (1907), Denslow wrote and illustrated his last book, *When I Grow Up* (1909). This collection of short verses concerning a child's dreams of future careers was originally published in the children's magazine *St. Nicholas* and is illustrated in what is generally considered an inferior fashion.

Critics commend Denslow as a highly talented illustrator and book designer who successfully adapted the complexity of his illustrations to the age of his audience and excelled in his use of color. However, they generally find that his retellings lack excitement, that his plots are unstructured and inconsequential, and that he was a poor judge of the writing skills of his collaborators. While much of Denslow's work is unknown to audiences of today, he is recognized by many authorities as among the greatest American illustrators of children's books, one whose lasting achievement is the visual representation of the characters and land of Oz.

(See also *Something about the Author,* Vol. 16).

GENERAL COMMENTARY

L. FRANK BAUM

[The following is a poem composed at a party on January 1, 1900. Baum inscribed it in the guest book belonging to Denslow and his wife Ann Waters.]

Our Den once made a picture—"What's the Use?"
Which filled us with dejection and with sorrow.
And then he illustrated Father Goose—
That he who sighed today might laugh tomorrow.
Which proves the use of Father Goose
And makes me bold to mention
There's *no* excuse for "what's the use"—
A misanthrope's contention.
It needs no art to limn the guile
Of vain Ambition; yet
The man who coaxed the world to smile
Has made the world *forget.*
Then here's to joy and merriment—
They're Pleasure's fairest daughters—
And here's to Hippocampus Den,
And here's to dear Ann Waters.

L. Frank Baum, in a poem in The Best of the Baum Bugle, 1963-1964, *The International Wizard of Oz Club, 1975, p. 52.*

J. M. BOWLES

In no other field has the real fitness of things to their uses been so flagrantly disregarded as in the making of books for children. The educators were the first to discover this remission and brought about a reform in the text, at least for that period of childhood that comes under their care. . . . Then came a great innovation in the decoration and illustration. . . . The greatest illustrators turned their attention to this field and the result was that a whole school of illustration for children arose in England, many brilliant men engaged in this work in France, Germany, and America, and we now have a few little masterpieces from each of the countries here named.

Nearly every child's classic has been put into attractive form, and many special endeavors have been made in them to put forth works of art for the delectation of the child mind. (p. 377)

But a most important point in educational method has been missed in these art attempts for children—that the art must be reduced to the child's understanding to be of any real value or enjoyment to him.

Very few people realize that the great majority of illustrations in the books of this class are not for children, but of children. It takes some thinking for the average person to comprehend that this applies to even such exquisitely artistic books as those of Boutet de Monvel, one of the pioneers of the new movement, and still its leader in France. These are most admirable effects for a developed sense for exquisite form and refined color in a grown person of cultivated tastes. But have they the power of going straight to the heart of a child? (p. 378)

Many of the rich decorative compositions in illustration of child legends and fairy tales as done by the English group of designers of children's books are stunning phantasms of the complex imagination of maturity, the outgrowth of years of worldly observation and scientific unfoldment, but what does the child feel from conceptions which must seem to him the very outcome of subliminal and occult knowledge, even though it is expressed in a coarse and strong "wood-cut line," which attempts childish simplicity by imitating the crude early illustrated books? All this does not prevent the work of these men from being genuine, artistic, and valuable contributions to the world's store of treasures, but do children really enjoy them? In part it is the old question of the subject in art, Why are all the pictures of children, simply because of their subject, assumed to be attractive to children?

The child's taste is made up of strict embryonic logic, and extreme narrow experience and readiness to exult and expand by recognition of its little knowledge. In educating it, the only natural plan to follow is the line of its pleasure, with an extra touch of strange knowledge for his surprise and exuberance that will lead the experience a little further. But always must the new touch be a logical outgrowth of what he knows and loves, and always must the old be known to be what he does impulsively love, not what it seems to us he should. (pp. 378-79)

All children love color and humor. These are the first faculties he uses in looking at a book, and he undoubtedly prefers vivid colors to soft tones. But let no one imagine . . . that the principles of good color composition can be neglected. He prefers vivid and striking colors, but in order that he or any one else may get the full effect of a brilliant spot or mass, it must be intelligently placed; not haphazardly in the midst of other strong colors, but with a full knowledge of the use of grays and the law of contrast. It takes as much experience and knowledge to be truly simple for a child's mind and eye as to be architecturally simple in a Chavannes mural painting. (pp. 379-80)

To offer a child the old monstrosities of picture-books, many of which are still on the market, is to insult him, and to endanger the education of his eye. They are of no use one way or the other, for the crowding together of primary colors not only

"Father Goose" comic page from the New York World, *January 21, 1900.*

outrages the color sense, but is not practical, for he cannot see one color for another. Bad art, if there is such a thing, is worse than no art. It simply implants something that must be uprooted later. The grotesque wit in these infantile "penny dreadfuls" overshoots the mark, and he cannot understand. He believes what he can verify in his experience, or accept intuitively by his joy, nothing else. To overpower him, disgusts him, and in no sphere is clearness of perception so essential to the clearness of thought as in the pictured wit in his nursery books. Clear English is good English, and genuinely clear fun and color is good art. Since the aim of childish wit is to start thought through the imagination, great pains must be given that the humorous expressions are natural and logical, else if they reach his mind at all, it will be to make him ask, "Why?" (pp. 380-81)

In the child's first books color and wit should go hand in hand. His eye and his joyousness are the eminent signs of his intellect at this period, and the decorator who puts them forth most simply, and plausibly, and amusingly, and correctly gets the child public, and the one who either chooses one period of childhood to work for, and works within these childish limits, or else who follows the growth of a child through his various phases of growing mentality, thus working progressively in both art and nature, still keeping strictly within the boundaries of the child's world, is the one who is and will be a public benefactor of children. (p. 381)

Art for young babies is another problem, but of equal importance to any one who has watched a baby's mind unfold, nothing can be too good for these precious first impressions. This is the period, of course, where color does its single office, as the baby snatches at that alone. But a book rightly prepared should be able to serve from infancy to probably five years, without changing its point of view. However, it is not possible for an artist to make such a book unless he comprehends all the gradual and essential movements of the child mind, and most of all the spiritual thread that holds him consistently from the cradle to his enfranchisement into full speech—that is, the wit of his little life. And the wit seems to be from perennial times, the making of things to perform antics before him.

Such an artist, it seems to me, is W. W. Denslow, the subject of this paper, and the cause of all these speculations. He has a consistent, serious theory under which he works, and a strong personality to back it, both of which are well worth considering, especially as he is achieving great practical success. . . . [There are] cleverly disposed spots and masses of color scattered throughout the Denslow books. I have seen a baby of twelve months beam with delight as some of these pages were turned, and fairly jump at color deliberately placed by the crafty Mr. Denslow, who knows how to arouse these little emotions. The baby is not aware of it, but a wide knowledge of reproductive color processes, and a strict watch of the mechanical work on his books, especially for purity of color in inks used, plays a great part in Denslow's ability, as does his acquaintance with value of white paper upon which he does not print at all. This is a means of gaining an effect which less practical artists neglect. Were the baby or young child able to analyze and explain to us the causes of his delight in color, it might reason as follows: "Den's panels, circles, and spots, and his solid pages of gorgeous hues with perhaps one tiny figure or object in a lower corner are simply baits to catch my attention through my eye, which as yet gets only general impressions. In other words, my friend Mr. Denslow is an impressionist for babies. He omits all but fundamentals and essentials. He leaves out of his books everything except things that exist in our own little world of fact."

In more technical terms, first come the extreme color simplicities, the primary colors used strictly within the laws of harmony—unlike the usual run of toy books—and both modified and intensified by a knowing use of grays. No patterned backgrounds distract the eye, or are allowed to conflict with the main impression of the design, a point not always observed in Mr. Walter Crane's superb tapestry-like compositions for his toy children's books.

The expression of humor in this first period would be the animal joy of child action, or the grotesqueness of animals acting like a child, or at least like the comprehended actions of "big people." The examples of this in Denslow's [new series of booklets entitled ***Denslow's Picture Books***] are almost innumerable; the tea-drinking tiger . . . , the cow . . . astonished and horrified at being sold for a hatful of beans, the crow . . . eating his corn with salt and butter, the reckless-looking dancing lynx . . . , and the worried goat that has apparently lost something . . . as good in its way as anything of Sir John Tenniel's in *Alice in Wonderland*. I remember a walrus on an end-paper of one of the newest books which is a masterpiece, with some of "Den's" sly, sardonic touches in his make-up and surrounding, a sly reading between the lines, as it were, introduced without making it one whit the less a child's picture, a side-splitting cat in ***Old Mother Hubbard,*** a flute-playing dog taking himself quite too seriously in the same book, three comic bears dancing against a crimson background, and a little bear tobogganing, with each particular hair flying behind in the wind, in ***The Three Bears***; a porcupine, apparently Irish, and of the laboring class, nonchalantly smoking a clay pipe, and a page full of animals at afternoon tea in ***The Zoo,*** containing a social satire. And I cannot forget the end-paper showing Mary's lamb sitting shivering and miserable in a woolen bath-robe just after being sheared. In none of these is the point of similarity with the child forgotten which enables him to get his feeling focused with his knowledge; Denslow knows the baby mind.

In the second period of taste, the grotesque action in his books may become even more vagarious, even extreme, as the child has advanced to the realization that many actions and things lie out of his possibility, and it amuses him to see them appear within the child power. He also recognizes animals and inanimate objects doing things outside their province, such as the polite bowing egg in ***Humpty Dumpty*** . . . , and he is greatly pleased at the fun as well as morally awakened to sympathy. And the corresponding advancement artistically is his being cognizant, and enjoying the breaking up of color into designs. Here Denslow's work is superb.

In the third period, the humor of differentiation is carried still further with the creation of impossible personages, such as Denslow's conceptions of the tin-woodman, and the scarecrow, in ***The Wizard of Oz,*** . . . the fun of the thing for the child lying in making them plausible by relating them to daily life.

And after this period of love for the grotesque, the imagination of a child begins to be independent, to go to regions that he never tells of, and here may come the help in pictures of varied and soaring details that in themselves stimulate the imagination to knowledge and flight. (pp. 381-85)

By this time the child has reached a place where certain portions of great works having topics that appeal to a child may be shared with him. The time has come when he can appreciate books of children as well as books for children.

Mr. Denslow's theory and practice in this regard bears out from all these periods many points in the old nursery classics which have become so familiar to us that we no longer notice them. They have become as much a matter of course as war among Christian nations, capital punishment, and other relics of barbarism. He has actually had the audacity, from deep conviction, to *expurgate* "Mother Goose," and all fairy stories containing bloodshed, cruelty, coarseness, in fact, any episodes which might frighten children. And when one comes to think of it, these "yarns of a past age" abound with recitals of actual crime. Let Mr. Denslow give an instance: "See what a perfectly outrageous thing is Jack and the Bean-Stalk. A lad gains admittance to a man's house under false pretense, through lying and deceit, imposing on the sympathy of the man's wife, then he commits theft upon theft. He is a confidence man, a sneak-thief, and a burglar. After which, when the man attempts to defend his property, he is slain by the hero, (?) who not only commits murder, but mutilates the corpse, much to the delight of his mother." Probably to not one mother in a thousand has the idea occurred that perhaps it would be just as well to modify these legends as well as some of the Old Testament stories, yet the point is an important one, and not only for especially sensitive children, for every child mind is sensitive in the beginning.

Mr. Denslow does not bring about his reforms in a namby-pamby, bungling way, but sails around this dangerous literary corner in a delightfully humorous fashion. The giant in ***Jack and the Bean-Stalk*** (no longer "Jack the Giant-Killer") turns out to be not so terrible after all, but as good-natured as giants usually are. Jack tames him thoroughly and he does useful odd jobs, such as shingling the cottage without using ladders. At last he lands in a side-show where with Jack on his knee he sells his photographs at ten cents each. The wolf in ***Little Red Riding-Hood*** also becomes domesticated, and there is no eating of grandma. Reformed, and with a white tie about his neck, he becomes an invaluable watch-dog. Even ***Baby Bunting*** does not escape Mr. Denslow, as witness his new version, accompanying a picture of a disconsolate hunter looking after a rabbit disappearing in the distance.

> By, baby bunting,
> Daddy's gone a-hunting,
> He'll never get this rabbit's skin
> To wrap the baby bunting in!

"Color, fun, and action" are Denslow's watchwords, and the color is good, especially in the later books, action there certainly is in abundance, as an instance the inimitable liveliness in the drawing of the man springing out of bed "to see what was the matter" in ***The Night before Christmas.*** As for the fun it is exuberant and pervasive, from ***Father Goose*** and ***Mother Goose*** to the new series. . . . One often wishes for more correctness in the drawing, and a lack of academic training is often evident, but the man starts out for certain original, definite ends and gains them. . . . Perhaps a strict course before the cast and the life model would have thwarted some of his ideas, and dampened some of his enthusiasm. And perhaps not—who can tell? The covers, though doubtless practical, are often not as artistic as could be desired for these important positions, nor as truly decorative as Mr. Denslow can be, for instance in many of his end-papers. But Mr. Denslow gets his public, holds his public, and does it by the good blood of his art. There is a distinct philosophy of decoration to follow the philosophy of the texts put before a child. The artist who makes books for children, not of children, has a great problem confronting him, for after all there is nothing more limited than a child's understanding, which pedagogy keeps within, and yet behold the wonders of individuality there. The artist who chooses to work for children must abide within the same boundary, yet must he have the same wealth of imagination. This is where his liberty lies. And great artists usually ask no other freedom. (pp. 385-87)

J. M. Bowles, "Children's Books for Children," in Brush and Pencil, *Vol. XII, No. 6, September, 1903, pp. 377-87.*

THE DETROIT NEWS

[William Wallace Denslow] has spent a good part of his life trying to find out how to make the children happy—and has succeeded. . . .

When "Den" was a boy . . . he noticed that there weren't many good books for children, and that those printed especially for boys were based largely upon the innate love of cruelty supposed to slumber in the boyish breast. It is possible that his impulse to get up books for children had its beginning then.

As he likes the pencil better than the pen, he doesn't write, but draws his books, selecting not brand-new topics, as the manner of some is, but old standbys, such as **"Jack and the Beanstalk," "Humpty Dumpty," "Old Mother Hubbard," "Mary Had a Little Lamb,"** and the like. Under his magic touch these veteran stories take on new aspects, for his treatment is as fresh and novel as the stories are old. And note this—for it is one of the most important points in his creed as a maker of children's books—in his versions the cruelty is left out. "Den" believes that he can interest the little ones without telling brutal tales of bloodshed, and his popularity with the children shows that his belief is correct.

Not all the children's books of other days relied upon an appeal to the childish love of cruelty. There were plenty of volumes given over to all sorts of goody-goodiness and priggishness, but there was no joy in any of them. These suited "Den," the small boy, no better than the cruel ones.

"There was precious little printed then for a boy to laugh at," he said to the writer not long ago, "and I made up my mind that some day I'd furnish the laugh material to them."

"To make children laugh," he went on, "you must tell them stories of action. They aren't really fascinated by cruelty—it's action they want. The trouble is that their desires have been misunderstood. I tell my stories with pictures, and I can often indicate action by expression. Action and expression, then, are two of my mainstays, and when you add the incongruous you have the triad that I rely upon."

Incongruity is generally at the bottom of the humorous, as the analysis of most jokes will show. "Den" gets incongruous effects by the simplest means imaginable, more often, perhaps, through the use of an animal's face to show emotions that are supposed to be felt by human beings only than by any other method. His use of animals in this way is really his strong suit.

"The bear's face," he says, "is by long odds the most adaptable to my purposes." . . .

Only the elephant exceeds the bear in good sense, says he; both have the perception of humor highly developed, and fortunately each has a face that lends itself admirably to the expression of the emotions. The elephant's face is next to the bear's in the way of good material for the artist, but the face of nearly every animal that ever lived can be drawn so as to suggest joy, grief, comfort, pain, laughter or tears.

Most folk think the monkey's face is most like the man's, and so it may be on the surface, but the bear's beats it when you analyze it. The face of that curious creature, the chameleon, is another that resembles the human countenance more than one person in a thousand ever suspected. The face of the pig and that of the cat are both good ones, and so are the faces of most birds; the parrot's and the hen's particularly.

Like most effective drawings, Denslow's impress one as being done with great facility, and perhaps they are now, but every one of them stands for an almost endless amount of labor.

The little tricks by the use of which he places a broad grin or a lugubrious look upon the face of a wolf or a horse appear simple, and, in truth, are simple, but it took years of study and experiment to learn them. At the beginning he could do them sometimes, but it was mostly a matter of guessing. But guessing won't do in work of this sort; you must be certain that what you set out for you are going to do.

Denslow found this out when he was only a boy, and later he learned that he must study the animals he wished to make use of, not only by sketching them, but anatomically. It thus happens that he knows more about the bones and joints and muscles of animals than most folk. He is also well up in comparative anatomy, and knows thoroughly the differences that exist between the structure of men and the inferior animals. He has put more study on the anatomy of the face than any other part of the body, of course, and could probably draw a detailed diagram of almost any animal's facial muscles.

"A Lover of Children Who Knows How to Make Them Laugh," in The Detroit News, *September 13, 1903, p. 3.*

MARTIN GARDNER

[John Rea Neill] illustrated all of Baum's Oz books except the first one. . . . Whatever one may think of Neill's pictures as works of art, there is no denying that he caught the full flavor of Baum's text, and his illustrations have exactly the sort of color and realism that Oz books require. Denslow's drawings for ***The Wizard*** possess a quaint wooden charm, but I have yet to meet an Oz enthusiast who regrets that Denslow did not carry on with the series. (p. 41)

Martin Gardner, "The Royal Historian of Oz," in The Wizard of Oz & Who He Was *by L. Frank Baum, edited by Martin Gardner and Russel B. Nye, Michigan State University Press, 1957, 208 p.*

FRED M. MEYER

[The following excerpt is taken from an essay originally published in the Autumn 1963 issue of the Baum Bugle.*]*

Title page to the first edition of The Wonderful Wizard of Oz *(1900).*

So closely associated were W. W. Denslow and L. Frank Baum during the days of greatest creation for both that a study of one would be incomplete without at least some consideration of the other. ***Father Goose: His Book, Dot and Tot of Merryland,*** and greatest and most incomparable of all, ***The Wonderful Wizard of Oz,*** were the happy result of a partnership which made "Oz" almost a household word in America and known internationally. . . .

It was Denslow who gave visible form to the curious places and characters envisioned by Baum. The Scarecrow, the Tin Woodman, Mr. Split, and countless others came to life under his pen. An amusing device he employed occasionally was a frieze of several characters across a page, each differing only slightly in detail and performance from the others. It was Denslow who gave the face-like characteristic to Oz houses, and, in the opinion of this writer, no artist has excelled his concept of the Emerald City for sheer beauty and magnificence. Now, many years after publication of ***The Wonderful Wizard of Oz,*** the Denslow illustrations have acquired a quaint charm and seem somehow especially suited to the story. It is to Denslow's credit that the book with his pictures still competes successfully with more modern versions of the characters.

Fred M. Meyer, "The Forgotten Man of Oz," in The Best of the Baum Bugle, 1963-1964, *The International Wizard of Oz Club, 1975, p. 21.*

MICHAEL PATRICK HEARN

Although nearly everyone knows that L. Frank Baum wrote ***The Wizard of Oz,*** few people know anything about its first illustrator, W. W. Denslow. Yet, Denslow's drawings are as inseparable from ***The Wizard of Oz*** as John Tenniel's are from *Alice in Wonderland* and were in part responsible for the initial success of the book. Numerous artists have tried to picture Dorothy and her friends, but none has surpassed the original illustrations.

Once a prominent and influential illustrator of children's books, Denslow is now largely forgotten. . . . Although childless himself, he chose in middle age to devote the rest of his life to the creating of children's books characterized by "action, color, expression, and clean, wholesome fun for the little ones." (p. 40)

For [***Father Goose: His Book***] Denslow adapted his successful poster style with its bold black line and limited but strong use of color.

His way of working was not unusual; all of his drawings were in black india ink, with some dry brush, on lightweight bristol board, but he worked carefully with his printers in choosing the colors. Although ***Father Goose*** was printed in yellow, red, and gray, only the red was colored on the original drawings; the rest were evidently indicated by overlay notations to the engravers. Through subtle changes in the arrangement of these few colors, Denslow made the finished product a bright and lavishly illustrated book. (p. 43)

To illustrate [***The Wonderful Wizard of Oz***] Denslow drew 24 full color plates and countless text illustrations in two colors, which change as the story progresses from one area to another of the multi-colored Land of Oz. This format was not as congenial to Denslow's style as was the picture book, but Denslow however surpassed himself in the illustration of ***The Wizard of Oz.*** It was not only one of the earliest extensive uses of color in an American children's book, but also was Denslow's first assignment in full color. Again, the original drawings were done in ink and the colors chosen by the artist and his printers. To decrease the cost of the printing, only three colors and no black plate were used; through the overlapping of the colors and the varying of tones through fine parallel lines and cross-hatching, he and his engravers and printers produced a most attractive book. (pp. 43-5)

Denslow, now established as a leading illustrator of children's books, tried his hand at a traditional work and produced the ambitious ***Denslow's Mother Goose.*** Returning to the format of ***Father Goose,*** he expanded the broadly humorous style of this earlier work with a new color sense. For each illustration he prepared two drawings, the first in india ink and the other in pencil and watercolor on tinted paper to indicate the colors to the printer. Each page of verse was hand-lettered by Frederick Goudy, the noted type designer. By adopting Baum's policy of eliminating all references to cruelty in his children's books, Denslow edited and expurgated the old rhymes. ***Denslow's Mother Goose*** created a sensation, and he followed it with a companion volume, ***Denslow's Night Before Christmas.*** (p. 45)

For the Sunday comic supplement of *The New York Herald,* Denslow drew four **"Christmas Tales,"** published in 1902. The following year these four became the first of the eighteen-pamphlet ***Denslow's Picture Books.*** These were expurgated adaptations of traditional fairy tales and rhymes written and illustrated by Denslow. With this series he had great freedom;

as one reviewer noted, he drew his books rather than wrote them, again with a great concern for all aspects of each picture book's design. (pp. 45, 71)

Denslow was clearly the first American illustrator to concede the importance of both the pictures and story in a child's book in the tradition of the great English illustrators Walter Crane, Kate Greenaway, and Randolph Caldecott. (p. 71)

[His series of] picture books proved to be almost as lasting as his work for ***The Wizard of Oz***. . . . The effects of Denslow's picture books can be seen in elements of the work of as diverse contemporary American illustrators as Dr. Seuss and Maurice Sendak. (pp. 71-2)

His next works, however, were not of the same quality as his picture books. He revived the format of ***The Wizard of Oz*** with ***Pearl and the Pumpkin*** and ***Billy Bounce,*** but these lack both the originality of his drawings for ***The Wizard*** and the exuberance of his picture books. Somewhat better is his work for Isabel Johnston's ***The Jeweled Toad,*** another full-length fairy tale. . . . His last book, ***When I Grow Up*** (a collection of poems that first appeared in *St. Nicholas* magazine, 1908-1909), failed to keep the high standard of his other picture books. (p. 72)

Although a highly gifted illustrator, Denslow was careless with his career. With the exception of Baum, he never had a collaborator of the first rank. Most of his work is now known only to the collectors of early children's books. Only one of the books he illustrated is still in print—***The Wizard of Oz.*** Even his work for this book was unavailable for nearly 40 years. . . . Fortunately, in the last 10 years several facsimiles of the first edition have been published. Perhaps now his work may again receive the recognition it deserves. (p. 73)

Michael Patrick Hearn, "W. W. Denslow: The Forgotten Illustrator," in American Artist, *Vol. 37, No. 370, May, 1973, pp. 40-5, 71-3.*

DOUGLAS G. GREENE

W. W. Denslow was one of the most important illustrators of children's books of the early twentieth century. In making the elaborately illustrated children's book characteristic of publishing from about 1900 to 1920 he occupies a place in America similar to Kate Greenaway and Arthur Rackham in England. There had been earlier American illustrators, such as Howard Pyle, who had produced beautifully decorated volumes, and anonymous artists had contributed color plates to the poorly printed McLoughlin Brothers books. But not until Denslow illustrated ***Father Goose, His Book*** and ***The Wonderful Wizard of Oz*** did American illustrators combine color with a sense of design. Surprisingly little, nevertheless, has been written about Denslow, perhaps because he worked with mediocre authors whose books have justifiably been forgotten. Even L. Frank Baum, for whom Denslow illustrated three books including the first volume of the Oz series, has long been considered a minor writer of potboilers. But with the growing critical acceptance of Baum and with the recent discovery of several important contemporary articles about Denslow, it is time to recount and evaluate Denslow's career. (p. 86)

[That ***Father Goose***] was the surprise success of 1899—eventually selling more than one hundred thousand copies—must be due more to Denslow's pictures than Baum's verses. In ***Father Goose*** many of Denslow's early developments as an artist reach fruition. The work is of a sure hand, the humor is broad, the designs are carefully conceived and executed. He effectively uses friezes of characters marching across the page.

Illustration from The Wonderful Wizard of Oz *(1900).*

Although the colors seem subdued to the modern eye—yellow, orange, black, and gray—it is almost ablaze with color when compared to the usual children's book of the day. Denslow could now draw graceful pictures, but he purposely returned to his early woodenness for decorative and humorous effect. Denslow's work in ***Father Goose*** created a pattern for children's books of the next two decades. Some picture books were slavish imitations of ***Father Goose,*** as is obvious by their titles: *Mr. Bunny, His Book* (1900), *Baby Goose, His Adventures* (1900), *The Rejuvenation of Papa and Mama Goose* (1917). Other illustrators simply utilized Denslow's bold and colorful poster style.

The 1900 Baum-Denslow book, ***The Wonderful Wizard of Oz,*** was an even greater triumph for both men. Baum's story of Dorothy, the Scarecrow, the Tin Woodman, and the Cowardly Lion has become an American classic. . . . The initial success of the book, however, owed much to Denslow's illustrations. The book is riotous in color with the pictures cutting into and sometimes literally obscuring the text. The color plates are decorative and perfectly complement the story.

Baum and Denslow collaborated on only one other book, the almost plotless ***Dot and Tot of Merryland.*** In the preface, Baum complimented "Mr. Denslow's quaint and merry pictures, which, I think, in this book excel all his previous work;" but the illustrations are, in truth, disappointing. Denslow excelled in the use of color, but ***Dot and Tot*** has no color plates. Technically, few would criticize his drawings, but they are somewhat too decorative. At his best, Denslow combined decorativeness with action; nothing seems to happen in his ***Dot and Tot*** pictures. He was not entirely at fault, for little occurs in Baum's story either. ***Denslow's Mother Goose,*** which appeared the same year, more than makes up for the disappointment of ***Dot and Tot of Merryland.*** Like his work in ***Father Goose*** and the ***Wizard,*** his pictures are funny and carefully executed. ***Mother Goose,*** however, is far more colorful than his earlier works, and Denslow ignores borders, allowing his colors to bleed to the edges of the pages. ***Denslow's Mother Goose*** is not only his finest illustrated book, it is also one of the most attractive collections of nursery rhymes ever published.

By the end of 1901, Baum and Denslow were on difficult terms. Why the two men ended their partnership is not definitely known. Russell P. MacFall, in his biography of L. Frank Baum, presents evidence that there was some friction over the musical extravaganza version of ***The Wizard of Oz,*** produced in 1902. Baum wrote the typescript and, as author of the book, believed that he had sole interest in the play. Denslow, however, shared the copyright of the book and insisted that he be involved in the production of, and the profits from, the musical. Finally, it was agreed that he design the costumes and the sets, and apparently he did an excellent job. Another reason for their separation may have been that the two men had little in common besides their books. Baum's interests were centered in his family, while Denslow was a Bohemian with a roving eye. (pp. 91-2)

Probably more important to Baum than disputes over the musical and different attitudes toward family life was the fact that Denslow claimed credit for their books. Denslow illustrated independently two ***Father Goose*** comic pages, one of which does not even mention Baum. On the earlier page, Denslow asserted that he was the "creator" of ***Father Goose.*** Baum responded by describing himself as "the original Father Goose" in the newspaper syndication of his ***American Fairy Tales.*** When Denslow decided to move to New York City about 1902, he and Baum ended their cooperation, but Denslow still shared the copyright of their books, and around 1903, George W. Ogilvie and Company published a rare pamphlet entitled ***Pictures from the Wonderful Wizard of Oz*** "by W. W. Denslow" with no mention of Baum. In 1904, Denslow wrote and illustrated a pamphlet about two characters invented by Baum, ***Denslow's Scarecrow and the Tin-Man,*** and about the same time he published a series of newspaper stories with the same title. Denslow even went so far as to claim, in his list of accomplishments sent to the editors of *The Artist's Year Book* (1905), that he had "originated the characters of Scarecrow and Tin Woodman" in the *Wizard* musical comedy. Baum was well aware of Denslow's activities. On 10 August, 1915, he wrote to his publishers, Reilly & Britton of Chicago, that "Denslow was allowed to copyright his pictures conjointly with my claim to authorship . . . and, having learned my lesson from my unfortunate experiences with Denslow, I will never permit another artist to have an interest in the drawings he makes of my described characters, if I can help it." But Baum was a generous man and he realized that Denslow was a fine illustrator. A month later, he wrote that "I used to receive many compliments on Denslow's pictures when he was illustrating my books, from children and others." Much of the material we have already examined confirms Baum's opinion about Denslow. Personally, Denslow was not very honorable, but artistically, he was one of the great illustrators of his age. (pp. 92-3)

[Denslow] was a prolific illustrator of color comic supplements for newspapers. Besides drawing the **"Scarecrow and the Tin-Man"** pages, he wrote and illustrated episodes about **"Billy Bounce," "Mother Goose," "Peter and Mike the Monk," "Strenuous Bobby,"** and **"Santa Claus in the Glad Lands."** In addition, he continued illustrating books. In 1902, the Dillingham Company of New York published his beautiful edition of Clement Clarke Moore's ***Night Before Christmas.*** In some of the pictures in this book, incidentally, Denslow inserted characters from ***The Wonderful Wizard of Oz*** and ***Denslow's Mother Goose.*** The following year, Dillingham published twelve pamphlets under the general title, ***Denslow's Picture Books.*** This series, written and illustrated by Denslow, was expanded to eighteen titles in 1904. Particularly interesting are his illustrations for the pamphlet ***Tom Thumb*** which combine graceful *art nouveau* linework with his typical stiff figures. The texts are bowdlerized versions of traditional nursery tales, with, for example, Humpty Dumpty saving himself from breaking by becoming hard-boiled. Denslow had adopted Baum's belief that children's books should not be horrifying. Denslow wrote to *The Artist's Year Book* that he hoped "to make books for children that are replete with good clean wholesome fun, and from which the coarseness and vulgarity are excluded."

Denslow's goals may have been laudable, but he was mistaken in his belief that he was an accomplished author. Perhaps this was the reason that, after he separated from Baum, his career slowly declined. . . . Denslow was never again associated with an important author. He was co-author with Paul West of ***The Pearl and the Pumpkin*** (1904), a rather rambling fairy tale. ***Billy Bounce*** (1906), by Denslow and Dudley A. Bragdon, has even less plot, probably because it was an outgrowth of Denslow's newspaper episodes. In 1907, he finally decided to illustrate someone else's book, Isabel Johnston's ***The Jeweled Toad,*** but Miss Johnston was almost as bad a writer as Denslow himself. Denslow's illustrations remained excellent, especially his use of color in ***The Jeweled Toad,*** but these books have long been forgotten; the stories are simply too uninspired.

Probably because of his connection with such mediocre books, Denslow's commissions began to fall off. His reputation may have been further damaged by his last book, ***When I Grow Up*** (1909). Denslow's verses, about dreams of future careers, are forgettable, and his pictures do not have the bright, flat colors that are characteristic of his best work. (pp. 93-4)

Since Denslow's death, his work has fallen into obscurity. In 1893, he wrote that for him "the world is . . . built upon the joke principle;" probably the cruelest jest of all is that his influence on the design of children's books has seldom been recognized. It may have been, however, less the "world" than his own vanity which was at fault. If he had not fancied himself a writer and so often associated his pictures with unreadable stories, he would certainly be classified with such important artists as Reginald Birch and Maxfield Parrish. But as more is known about his pictures it becomes apparent that he belongs in the ranks of America's greatest illustrators of children's books. (p. 95)

Douglas G. Greene, "W. W. Denslow, Illustrator," in Journal of Popular Culture, *Vol. VII, No. 1, Summer, 1973, pp. 86-96.*

BARBARA BADER

"Such books as ***Denslow's Mother Goose*** . . . with a score of others of the comic poster order, should be banished from the sight of impressionable small children," wrote Anne Carroll Moore, then at the Pratt Institute Free Library, soon to organize children's work at the New York Public Library, and long to be "the yea or nay on all children's literature" in America. On the other hand, Miss Moore greatly admired the work of Leslie Brooke which began to appear at this time [approximately 1905]. . . . Denslow's animals are no more caricatured than Brooke's, nothing about his interpretation is vulgar or malicious, where he differs from Brooke is in style.

Why then the aversion to his work which was almost universal among those professionally connected with children's books? The sway of the naturalistic aesthetic is the only possible explanation, the equation of artistic quality with the faithful representation of nature, and the consequent dismissal of anything else as 'primitive' or 'degenerate.' Denslow's figures prance about on the picture plane: there is no space, no 'atmosphere.' The contour lines are heavy, the interiors absolutely flat: the forms are blatantly unshaded. The coloring is brash, arbitrary—in the sense of just so many inks—and abstracted, suggesting but not copying nature, and not aiming to. Thus the crux of Denslow's offense: in the face of five hundred years of Western painting, and of the Darwinian boost to belief in the progressive development of art, he and his fellows—Will Bradley was another—went their own way.

Denslow reigns today as the first and best illustrator of ***The Wizard of Oz,*** and his picturebooks—toy-books in format, twelve in 1903, six in 1904—were not unappreciated in their time. But they failed [in Mary Hazeltine's words] "to preserve the traditions of perspective, color values, forms and proportions" (without which children would "gain false notions of things") and librarians and educators scorned them. (pp. 7-8)

Barbara Bader, "Starting Points," in her American Picturebooks from Noah's Ark to the Beast Within, *Macmillan Publishing Co., Inc., 1976, pp. 2-12.*

DOUGLAS G. GREENE and MICHAEL PATRICK HEARN

In his collaborations with L. Frank Baum and in the picture book series which he edited himself, Denslow adopted the English toybook style to his own ideals for children's stories and pictures. He wrote that his "aim is to make books for children that are replete with good, clean, wholesome fun and from which all coarseness and vulgarity are excluded." He did more than prepare beautifully designed picture books; he carefully chose, and sometimes expurgated, the texts. "To make children laugh," he explained, "you must tell them stories of action. They aren't really fascinated by cruelty—it's action they want. The trouble is that their desires have been misunderstood" [see excerpt dated September 13, 1903]. With his sense of action and his broad humor, Denslow created the earliest and still some of the finest American picture books in color. (p. 2)

The finished volume [of ***Father Goose***] was a brilliant achievement in book design. Before ***Father Goose,*** few children's books published in America were printed in color, and those that did have some color plates, such as the cheaply lithographed McLoughlin Brothers books, were illustrated by mediocre artists with little sense of design. Most major artists drew for reproduction in black and white. Even such imaginative story books as Howard Pyle's *Pepper and Salt* and *The Wonder Clock* and Palmer Cox's *The Brownies: Their Book* used color only on the covers. American children had to rely on British imports for fine color pictures, most notably in the books engraved by Edmund Evans. He took great care in the production of his exquisitely printed volumes, and in a large measure he deserves credit for the distinguished careers of the great triumvirate of the illustrated children's book—Walter Crane, Kate Greenaway, and Randolph Caldecott.

Denslow's approach toward illustrating ***Father Goose*** closely resembled that of Crane. As Crane had done in 1877 with one of the first modern picture books, *The Baby's Opera,* Denslow conceived of the book as an artistic unit, with the cover, endpapers, title page, and text pages complementing each other. Moreover, Denslow did not merely draw pictures for Baum's verses; each page was carefully designed so that the lettering, pictures, and colors would make an harmonious whole. The result was to make ***Father Goose*** seem like a series of art posters bound together.

As in his book covers and posters, Denslow was restricted in his use of colors. Because Baum and Denslow had to pay for the printing plates of ***Father Goose,*** they limited the color scheme to yellow, red, gray, and black. But with subtle changes in the arrangements of these colors from one page to the next, Denslow produced a bright book; he was able to give ***Father Goose*** the appearance of having more colors than were actually printed. To heighten the effect of the color, he used a bold black or red outline to enclose the picture, but so that this effect would not become monotonous, he sometimes allowed a figure or a letter of the text to break through the border. Within this outline are wide areas of solid flat color against which the figures are placed. The flat two-dimensional space is seldom relieved even by an horizon line. In his use of space, line and color, Denslow effectively employed the style of the Japanese prints; his figures seem to exist within the "floating world."

Illustration from Denslow's Night Before Christmas *(1902).*

Furthermore, the pages of ***Father Goose*** adapt to the picture book the oriental use of calligraphy, in [Ralph Fletcher] Seymour's bold printing and Denslow's stylized seahorse monogram. Seymour's lettering perfectly harmonizes with Denslow's line, and makes the pages easy to read, a rare quality in children's books of that time.

Denslow was interested not only in the total design of the page, but also in the appearance of each individual figure. A little more than three years later, his friend Charles Waldron wrote of the care which Denslow always took with his figures. "He would have a different sketch tacked on to different boards, with his box of colors handy at his right hand. . . . When one drawing became tiresome he would work on another. In order to get the right action . . . the figure might have as many as six different legs, four heads, and as many arms. When the right ones were selected . . . they would be drawn in with ink and the others erased." . . . Even after he had completed his drawings, he occasionally made corrections by painting out portions of the design with Chinese white. All of the ***Father Goose*** drawings are in black India ink with some details in red. Denslow later said that the book consumed "six months at hard labor"; the result of this painstaking attention to detail was to make each figure remarkably active, individualized, and comic. From his successful covers and posters, Denslow adopted the decorative technique of parading friezes of characters across the page, each figure looking like its neighbor but distinguished by a slight change in dress or expression. This device creates a liquid movement from figure to figure, and page to page. (pp. 84-6)

In some drawings, Denslow's humor relied too heavily on the grotesque with crude results. ***Father Goose*** was not meant to be a pretty book, and it does not appeal to everyone's tastes. But nothing Denslow had done previously can compare in sense of design with ***Father Goose: His Book.***

Baum was delighted with the ***Father Goose*** pictures, and in a copy of the book which he presented to Denslow he wrote the following doggerel:

Dear Den: Within my chiffonier
Are many drawers; yet I fear
No drawer there can hope to beat
The pictures that you drew so neat
For dear old ***Father Goose: His Book***—
Unless I'm very much mistook.
There's better things (this goes to show)
In some old drawers that we know,
And even I shall draw in time
A check to pay me for my rhyme,
Which proves that both of us can draw—
You with your paw—I with my jaw.

Most reviewers were just as enthusiastic. . . . The critical response was almost uniform: ***Father Goose*** was one of the finest American picture books, and Baum and Denslow were the most important new team in children's literature. The Chicago *Journal of Fine Arts* commented, "As was Cruikshank to Dickens, so is Denslow to Baum." "Mr. Denslow is in truth a genius," wrote a reviewer in Boston *Ideas*. "Man and animal alike respond and express volubly whatever trait or quality the verses may suggest. . . . Humor is apparent everywhere, in all the subtle strength which highest art knows how to contribute." Probably most gratifying was a comment from Mark Twain. Ann Waters [Denslow's second wife] had sent him a copy of ***Father Goose,*** and Twain quickly replied that it marked a new era in nursery books. He would, he said, "usurp ambassadorial powers" and thank Baum and Denslow "in the name of the child world for making it. . . . Father Goose has a double chance to succeed: parents will buy him ostensibly for the nursery so that they may privately smuggle him out and enjoy him themselves." (pp. 86-8)

Denslow took great care in developing his interpretations of Baum's inventions [for ***The Wonderful Wizard of Oz***]. A particularly difficult challenge was making the Scarecrow and the Tin Woodman believable. "I made twenty-five sketches of those two monkeys before I was satisfied with them," Denslow told an interviewer. "You may well believe that there was a great deal of evolution before I got that golf ball in the Scarecrow's ear or the funnel on the Tin Man's head. I experimented and tried out all sorts of straw waist-coats and sheet-iron cravats before I was satisfied." Denslow not only had to picture the strange characters of Baum's imagination; he had to illustrate all the minute details of an original fairyland. . . . Denslow had to give life to this wild, uncharted landscape of deadly poppies, jeweled cities, and magic forests of fighting trees. He had to fill the air with winged monkeys and the forests with fabulous beasts. He had to give character to the architecture and native dress of the peoples. Sometimes he went far beyond Baum's words in depicting the fairyland. For example, he gave human characteristics to the buildings of the Emerald City and the land of the Munchkins; his Munchkin farmhouse smiles and his great gates of the Emerald City glower at approaching visitors.

One of the most original aspects of the landscape of ***The Wizard*** is its color scheme. Each section of the fairyland has its own distinct color: blue in the East, yellow in the West, red in the South, and green in the center, with brown marking the borderlands. Author and illustrator decided that the textual illustrations would be in black and a second color which varied according to changes in the setting of the story. Denslow drew more than one hundred illustrations for the text. His pictures often cut into the words, and sometimes the colors are actually printed over the type. The Detroit *Journal* noted the book's exceptional appearance: "the pages are cut up in all manner of ways, the illustrations are sandwiched in the queerest kinds of designs, and the whole ensemble is one of delightful irregularity."

Besides the text illustrations, ***The Wizard*** contains twenty-four full-color plates, which Denslow drew in black ink on white paper. He indicated with overlays and notes in pencil how the black drawing would be broken down into color. To contrast with the wild irregularity of the text illustrations, he planned the full-page plates to be rigid, almost static. In ***The Wizard*** the influence of the Japanese print on Denslow's art reached full fruition. Against a flat field of solid color, his figures move within a two-dimensional space. Seldom did Denslow suggest traditional western perspective; he generally omitted the horizon line, and when he included the barest elements of landscape and still-life, he was indicating setting rather than space. The figures are in bold outline, with no secondary linework to denote modeling. The colors of the figures are bright and solid, and each scene seems to be flooded with an artificial light. The effect is of characters posing on a stage, with a solid-colored backdrop behind them, and a bright spotlight illuminating the entire scene. As he had done in ***Father Goose,*** Denslow enclosed each full-color picture in a frame, but in opposition to traditional western picture space, his figures and objects often spill out of the frame or even sit upon it. Denslow's pictures give ***The Wizard*** an energetic, adventurous appearance, which still startles and fascinates by its originality. As many of the drawings act only as decorations, the book cannot be called "illustrated" in the traditional sense—in giving character and place to an episode of text. Denslow was as interested in purely visual effects as in picturing the events of the story. The entire volume is carefully designed; the covers, endpapers, headpieces, chapter titles, color plates, all combine to make the book a total work of art.

The critics were fascinated by ***The Wonderful Wizard of Oz.*** Praise again was lavished on "those two quaint and whimsical geniuses," Baum and Denslow. An Illinois paper noted that Baum possessed a "quaint philosophy that fits like a glove to the skilled hand of Denslow. These two artists work together with marvelous felicity and the productions of their meditations are destined to have a permanent place in the child's literature of the world." Almost all reviews praised Denslow's work, sometimes at great length. Although one paper claimed that he could not draw a "child-like child," the superlatives were generally unrestrained. The Grand Rapids, Michigan, *Herald* was particularly forceful in its enthusiasm: "the book is fearfully and wonderfully made. For strange vagaries of illustrations and wild riots of color there is nothing to surpass the pictures by W. W. Denslow, which are scattered in lavish profusion throughout the book. [It] is a revel of the imagination; the pictures are commingled visions of multifold opium dreams. It is the most fantastically delightful children's book of the year." Other reviewers did not come so close to the language of the *fin de siecle* decadents, but they were just as delighted with Denslow's art: "To the illustration of this charming text, Mr. Denslow brought all the power of his mature genius, all his quaint imaginings, all the strong forceful handling of brush and pencil as well as his extensive knowledge of the bookmaker's art. The result is a work that will prove a joy to children the world over." (pp. 91-4)

[Denslow] brashly named his [next book] ***Denslow's Mother Goose.*** Not even the great nineteenth century illustrators of nursery rhymes had so audaciously attached their names to Mother Goose. Walter Crane called his work *The Baby's Opera* and Kate Greenaway's collection was simply *Mother Goose, or the Old Nursery Rhymes*.

Like Crane, Greenaway, and Randolph Caldecott, Denslow chose the verses to illustrate. He was not, however, content merely to select the old texts; he also carefully edited some of them. (p. 97)

> I don't always adhere to the text of the familiar nursery rhymes. I believe in pure fun for the children, and I believe it can be given them without any incidental gruesomeness. In my ***Mother Goose*** I did not hesitate to change the text where the change would give a gentler and clearer tone to the verse. The comic element isn't lost in this way. . . . So when I illustrate and edit childhood classics I don't hesitate to expurgate. I'd rather please the kids than any other audience in the world. If I can reach them, as the sale of my books would indicate I have, I ask for little more.

There is a thin line between improving nursery classics and bowdlerizing them, but on the whole Denslow's changes are laudable. Few would object, for instance, to his decision to have the Old Woman Who Lived in a Shoe kiss her children rather than beat them all soundly before putting them to bed. Rather than rewrite the verses, however, Denslow usually preferred to choose rhymes which already met his high ideals. Most of the old favorites—**"Humpty Dumpty," "Mary Had a Little Lamb," "Peter Pumpkin Eater"**—are included, as well as several less known nursery rhymes and even one limerick. In his overall selection of rhymes Denslow demonstrated a sophisticated sense of not only the least offensive but also the most entertaining to children.

Denslow was also exceptionally sensitive in preparing illustrations which appeal to children. Each verse has a double-page spread: the left for the illustrated text, the right for a full-page design. . . . Instead of using a flat wash to indicate the background color, he sketched on colored paper. He then finished the pencil drawing with water colors. Next, he drew the same picture in black ink to be photographed and printed; the printers were to add the colors from the water color sketch. Unfortunately, the result was not completely successful, for the McClure printers chose rather dull, cream colors for the published book. The inks are of equal tonal value so that the fresh contrasts of the original water colors were lost.

Because ***Denslow's Mother Goose*** was intended for very young children, Denslow simplified his drawing. In comparison with ***Father Goose*** and ***The Wizard,*** his line is heavier with a stronger emphasis on round, simple forms. He did not even enclose the pictures in borders; the background colors "bleed" to the edges of the page, and the figures seem almost pasted against flat, two-dimensional space. This flatness is emphasized by the use of large solid panels, circles, hearts, of contrasting color. The individual pages are simple and dynamic in their directness; no detail is unnecessary, no gesture useless.

Denslow looked upon the original verses as the framework for elaborate stories, and he provided the details through his pictures. In his drawing for **"The Man in the Moon Came Down too Soon,"** he put a "To Let" sign on the moon. He carefully placed bottles of catsup and pepper sauce on the table to show how the Man in the Moon "burnt his mouth eating cold pease porridge." (pp. 97-9)

The popularity of ***Denslow's Mother Goose*** led to a commission from the McClure newspaper syndicate. . . . As Denslow was now considered the leading comic artist for young children, T. C. McClure asked him to prepare a comic page for the supplement.

Beginning on November 5, 1901, Denslow received one hundred dollars a page for a weekly comic called **"Billy Bounce."** Denslow's work significantly differed from earlier cartoon series, such as R. F. Outcault's "The Yellow Kid" and Rudolph Dirks' "The Katzenjammer Kids." These comics kept the same characters each week, but there was no continuity of story. Each episode was built around a joke, either social as in "The Yellow Kid" or slapstick as in "The Katzenjammer Kids." Denslow, on the other hand, conceived his **"Billy Bounce"** as a narrative, a weekly fairy tale. Denslow, in fact, may have been the originator of the story-strip.

Billy Bounce is an orphaned messenger boy whose fairy godfather has given him a magic, inflatable suit. The editor of the newspaper for which Billy works sends him to the North Pole to gather pictures. On inflating his suit, he resembles an enormous rubber ball which can travel a mile in one bounce. His adventures take him to many marvelous places inhabited by strange creatures. At Christmas time, when McClure and the artist were promoting ***Denslow's Mother Goose,*** installments based on the book alternated with **"Billy Bounce."** The villain becomes Simple Simon's pieman, whom Denslow clearly considered unsympathetic to children. As the series progressed into the next year, Denslow created the **"Billy Bounce Circus and Zoo, the Greatest Show on Earth,"** and the story concerns Billy's search for unusual animals for his show.

The early episodes of Denslow's comic are wonderfully alive and inventive. Before **"Billy Bounce,"** comic pages generally had either a single large panel as in the early "Yellow Kid" or rows of rectangular panels as in "The Katzenjammer Kids." Denslow apparently was the first artist to break away from this rigid form. He had the entire back page of McClure's supplement to experiment with a wide variety of circles, squares, and rectangles. His balloons for speech and the running captions are carefully arranged for decorative effect. No other artist for comic supplements showed quite the same inventive understanding of the page until Winsor McCay and his classic "Little Nemo in Slumberland" (1905). Unfortunately, the later episodes of **"Billy Bounce"** are far less imaginative than the earlier ones. After the series was limited to half a page, Denslow stopped experimenting with the comic strip form and used the standard arrangement of rectangular panels; as he lost interest in the art, he dropped the continuing narrative and depended primarily on gags. He may, in short, simply have become tired of drawing the same characters over and over again. (pp. 100-01)

With the popularity of **"Billy Bounce"** and ***Denslow's Mother Goose,*** Denslow had demonstrated that he was not dependent

Illustration from Denslow's Scarecrow and the Tin Man and Other Stories *(1904), one of eighteen pamphlets that are part of the* Denslow's Picture Book *series.*

on Baum. But there was one more 1901 project in which Denslow was involved and its success or failure would determine whether he would continue collaborating with Baum. Until ***Mother Goose*** was published, Denslow could not be certain that his books would sell without Baum. People commonly spoke of "Baum-Denslow books" as though the two men were permanently united. . . . Consequently, while working on his ***Mother Goose,*** Denslow was also illustrating Baum's ***Dot and Tot of Merryland.***

Baum's low-keyed story concerns a journey of a boy and girl through a magical land of seven valleys of toys and candy. Like the pictures in most other travelogues, Denslow's work emphasizes the strange and the marvelous. Because Baum was brief and inspecific in his descriptions, Denslow had the freedom to create his own portrayals of the characters and settings. The dolls, clowns, toy soldiers, mechanical toys, and the other unusual inhabitants of Merryland are given distinct personalities in Denslow's pictures. Conscious of the cutting remark that he could not draw "a child-like child," he took great care in picturing Dot and Tot. The drawing is precise in every detail to depict child-like and attractive children.

Dot and Tot of Merryland is the most decorative of all Denslow's books for children. The individual pages are beautifully designed. As in ***Denslow's Mother Goose,*** he greatly simplified his style. Backgrounds are generally broken down into their most fundamental forms, often just solid blocks of color. Especially effective are the friezes of characters. The introductory leaves are filled with marvelous designs; the copyright notice is among Denslow's most artistic uses of the page. Each chapter has a headpiece made up of a long thin panel which is beautifully contrasted with the delicately decorative lettering of the chapter titles.

Dot and Tot is a tightly planned work of art. Instead of color plates which might have interrupted the fluid movement from page to page, Denslow had the text illustrations printed in black line supported with cocoa brown and vermilion. This elegant combination of colors perfectly complements the sensuous, simplified forms appearing in profusion throughout the book. The binding is as attractive as the contents: yellow cloth, stamped in dark brown, red, and gold. The finished work is sophisticated and attractive, one of the finest examples of the *art nouveau* book for children. (pp. 102-03)

Despite its beauty, ***Dot and Tot*** did not sell well. The reviewers did not pan the book; they generally ignored it. (p. 103)

Why ***Dot and Tot of Merryland*** did not repeat the success of the previous Baum-Denslow books is not clear. One reason may have been that Hill did not purchase much advertising space. Because of the novelty of ***Father Goose*** and ***The Wizard,*** the press had given Baum and Denslow much free publicity; but that was not the case in 1901. Perhaps, moreover, the exquisite design of the book, though pleasing to adults, did not excite the more primitive tastes of children. Baum's writing is sweet and Denslow's drawings are pretty, but consequently they lack the frantic energy of ***Father Goose*** and ***The Wizard.*** (p. 104)

Denslow continued working on several projects. Besides the **"Billy Bounce"** comic, he was preparing his 1902 book, ***Denslow's Night Before Christmas,*** as a companion volume to his ***Mother Goose*** in artistic style and format. In reillustrating (and retitling) Clement C. Moore's "A Visit from St. Nicholas," Denslow had a formidable task, for the poem was closely identified with the pictures by the great cartoonist, Thomas

Nast. It was not certain that the public would purchase a copy of the poem with drawings by any other illustrator. Once or twice Denslow's work in his ***Night Before Christmas*** is reminiscent of Nast's drawings, but for the most part he devised his own interpretations of the characters. Denslow's Santa Claus, in his fur-lined suit and carefully trimmed beard, is more urbane than Nast's conception. Instead of the traditional red, Denslow dressed Santa in a green costume, which contrasts beautifully with the background colors. Much as Nast had done, Denslow included references to other children's books in his drawings. Nast put pictures from Aesop on the chimney-tiles and a copy of Crane's *The Baby's Opera* in Santa's hand; Denslow was more self-serving and wanted to promote his own books. Peering out of the saint's sack is a toy Tin Woodman and on the floor smiles a wooden Mother Goose. Santa's sleigh even sports a goose-head. All of these details are carefully placed, for Denslow was again concerned with the complete design of the book. With its pages filled with an array of comic animals and toys (resembling those in ***Dot and Tot of Merryland***), ***Denslow's Night Before Christmas*** is a child's delight. (p. 109)

In September, 1902, he signed an agreement with the Dillingham Company to prepare a series of toybooks [***Denslow's Picture Books***]. . . . In August, 1903, Dillingham published the first group of twelve picture books in individual sixteen page pamphlets and collected in two clothbound volumes. The series was a great success. . . . (pp. 114-15)

As with ***Father Goose*** and ***Mother Goose,*** Denslow worked within the English picture book tradition. Walter Crane's great series of toybooks, first printed by Edmund Evans, was gradually being reissued by John Lane of London and Randolph Caldecott's picture books, also originally engraved by Evans, were available through Frederick Warne. No American artist until Denslow had tried to produce a similar series. In one respect Denslow was more ambitious than the English artists: he completed eighteen pamphlets in two years, but Caldecott and others were required to prepare only two a year. Unlike the English toybooks, Denslow's series was consistently meant to appeal to children. Caldecott's pamphlets, for instance, contain Goldsmith's *Elegy on the Death of a Mad Dog,* and *Mrs. Mary Blaize*—hardly poems for the average child. Crane illustrated "My Mother" and other sentimental verses. Denslow avoided some of the eccentric goals of the two English artists. Caldecott's art recalled the age of Rowlandson in its Georgian pastoral scenes; his robust drawings probably appealed more to nostalgic adults than to children. Crane often overlooked the tastes of his young audience in order to educate grown-ups on his opinions about artistic furniture and dress. Denslow, however, designed his books for children. He told an interviewer that "it has been my experience that when you can reach the youngster you can reach their elders too. From the kids you can always get unbiased criticism. They don't play favorites, and there is no way you can tamper with the witnesses. They like a thing or they don't. And if they like it they demand more of it." (p. 115)

Denslow invented the stories of some of the pamphlets such as ***Zoo, One Ring Circus, Scarecrow and the Tin-Man***) entirely himself, but the majority are retellings of nursery classics. The series is similar to ***Denslow's Mother Goose*** in that all horrifying episodes are omitted. . . . Not all of Denslow's revisions are effective; the drama of the originals is often lost and there is no feeling of true villainy or menace. Moreover, Denslow's prose style is at best only adequate, and at worst stiff and lifeless. On the whole the most successful of the booklets are those (***5 Little Pigs, Animal Fair, Simple Simon, House that Jack Built***) which retain the original verses without revision.

The texts of Denslow's picture books are uneven, but the illustrations are consistently high in quality. He drew the originals in black and white often with an even briefer line than in ***Mother Goose*** and ***Night Before Christmas.*** He was able to indicate the texture of an object merely by drawing its edge. For the almost endless variety of animals, for example, Denslow used a very simple outline yet successfully depicted many different types of furs and skins. Denslow varied his style according to the complexity of the stories. In those pamphlets with very short texts—only one sentence a page in ***5 Little Pigs***—he used an extremely broad black line which properly matches the weight of the hand-lettering. Undetailed pictures illustrate the pamphlets intended for the youngest children—***5 Little Pigs, Simple Simon, Old Mother Hubbard.*** In marked contrast are Denslow's drawings in the more elaborate tales like ***Jack and the Bean-stalk, Tom Thumb,*** and ***One Ring Circus,*** containing more figures and greater detail. In all of the pamphlets, Denslow effectively used flat background colors held by black borders. The figures leap, dance, and are even thrown from the picture space. The panels are as imaginative as those in the **"Billy Bounce"** comic page. The entire eighteen volume series is marvelously inventive, free from the repetitiousness that often damages such sustained efforts. (pp. 116-17)

In his picture books, . . . Denslow tried to please the very young with his purity of line, bright, solid colors, and broad comic sense. (p. 117)

Denslow's comic animals avoid the extremes of Beatrix Potter on the one hand, and later of Walt Disney on the other. Despite their human clothing, Potter's sweet rabbits and squirrels remain entirely animals; Disney's Donald Duck and Mickey Mouse are hardly animals at all—there is little ducklike or mouselike about them. Denslow's beasts continue to look like animals, but they are pictured in human situations displaying human emotions. The unexpected appears on page after page of his picture books—a hippopotamus with a flowered hat and a coy expression dancing with a polar bear, a crocodile delicately putting sugar cubes in tea, a tiger removing the cap from a soda bottle, and a lamb having its wool curled. Denslow's ability to give life to these creatures came not only from his understanding of comparative anatomy but also from his handling of gesture and broad slapstick. . . . With action, expression, incongruity, and above all his inventive drawing, Denslow created the first distinctive American series of picture books in color.

Noteworthy among the 1904 picture books was ***Scarecrow and the Tin-Man.*** With the great success of *The Wizard of Oz* musical extravaganza, it was likely that both Baum and Denslow would attempt to publish about the two stars of the show, the Tin Woodman and the Scarecrow. . . . [The pamphlet] is a dull tale of how the two friends, bored with their life in the musical extravaganza, decide to run away; after several slapstick and rather pointless adventures, they are captured in time for the evening performance. Clearly, Denslow wanted to establish a claim as part creator of the famous characters.

Soon, the competition between Baum and Denslow spread to the Sunday comics. To promote *The Marvelous Land of Oz,* Baum and cartoonist Walt McDougall syndicated "Queer Visitors from the Marvelous Land of Oz," a series of stories beginning in August, 1904. Denslow followed on December 10, 1904, with his own series syndicated by McClure. **"Den-**

slow's Scarecrow and the Tin-Man" is a beautifully drawn comic page, but Denslow's accompanying stories, about a journey of the characters through the western hemisphere, are only mildly amusing. Probably his major reason for drawing the series was to emphasize his claim as the originator, through his illustrations, of the Tin Woodman and the Scarecrow. In New York, the heroes meet their "fairy godfather" who is probably Denslow, and when they are shipwrecked in Bermuda, they meet Denslow again; the artist pictured himself shaking the Scarecrow's hand. Denslow's comic page lasted only seventeen installments. The distribution was poor and the competition with Baum's series likely cut into his profits. (pp. 118-20)

In the summer of 1903, while making random sketches, Denslow first had the idea for a play and a full-length novel for children entitled ***The Pearl and the Pumpkin.*** He later explained to a newspaper interviewer that when he drew two rather grotesque characters (probably the Corn Dodger and the pumpkin-boy of the book), the story began to form in his head. He had worked out a fairly comprehensive plot when he realized that he lacked the skill to write both a lengthy book and a stage script. He therefore brought in Paul West, a successful songwriter and long Denslow's friend. (p. 121)

During the spring of 1904, while West did the actual writing of the book, Denslow began the illustrations in Bermuda. Many of the pictures show Bermuda scenes, including his island and house. . . . "This summer has not been a play time for me," he wrote to the editor of a Maine newspaper, "but a summer of hard work, for I have in three months completed the illustrations of ***The Pearl and the Pumpkin.*** I did 125 pictures for it, superintending the engraving and approving at long range." When he was not at his drawing board, he searched for authentic descriptions of Blackbeard, Captain Kidd, and other buccaneers who were to appear in the book. (pp. 122-23)

Unfortunately, all of this effort did not produce a very good story. Although Paul West did most of the writing, Denslow was responsible for devising the crowded but inconsequential plot. A boy named Joe Miller has discovered the secret of growing huge pumpkins. Among those anxious to learn his secret are John Doe, the village pieman (borrowed from the **"Billy Bounce"** comic page), and Ike Cannem ("my motto is—'I can!'"), a Bermuda canner. Joe's fame has reached even Davy Jones's locker and its pie-loving pirates, who send the Ancient Mariner, assisted by Mother Carey "who is a sort of fairy godmother to everyone under the sea," to discover Joe's secret. In the most effective scene of the book, Joe is ducking for apples at a Hallowe'en party hosted by his friend Pearl Pringle when the Ancient Mariner, complete with albatross and crossbow, pops up in the middle of the ducking barrel.

The story becomes increasingly confused, as the Ancient Mariner conspires with the canner and the pieman to kidnap Joe and obtain his pumpkin growing secret. They ask the assistance of the Corn Dodger, the sprite who rules all things growing in the ground. He enchants Joe so that the boy will become anything he wishes to be at midnight. Meanwhile, the cast has become even more cluttered with the appearance of Mother Carey "surrounded with a circle of green light." Although she had previously assisted the Ancient Mariner, she warns Joe against him and promises to help the boy whenever he calls on her.

That midnight, while Joe is carving a large pumpkin, he wishes (for a reason which is at best obscure) to be a pumpkinhead, and immediately he is transformed into a strange creature looking like an entire pumpkin patch. The Ancient Mariner the next evening coaxes them all to a magic spring, then leaps in with Joe, Pearl, and the pieman. The ground closes over them as they head toward the ocean. At Davy Jones's Locker, Joe's pumpkin brain cannot remember the formula for growing pumpkins, so the pirates plan to make him into a pie. Then the characters start dashing all over the place. Joe escapes with the help of Mother Carey but is recaptured; the Corn Dodger and the canner show up—the latter from inside an oyster shell (how he got there is never explained); King Neptune saves Joe from becoming a pie; but Joe cannot be restored without the Corn Dodger, who has been captured by Ike Cannem and carried to Bermuda to be canned.

As might be expected, all these events take a while to be absorbed by the main characters. When everything has been sorted out, the entire cast heads to Bermuda. A final complication arises. Bermuda is suffering from a pumpkin shortage, and a hotel proprietor wants to serve Joe to his patrons. The pieman, who has not previously played much of a role except to be the brunt of some bad puns, captures Joe and gives him to the hotel man, who makes his body into pies and tosses his jack o'lantern head into Hamilton Harbor. Happily, this is not the end of Joe, for Mother Carey brings the pumpkin head to shore and the Corn Dodger (who has just been rescued from the canner) changes it back into Joe Miller. Joe then remembers his secret and tells Davy Jones's pirates and the Bermudians how to grow pumpkins.

It is painfully apparent that neither Denslow nor West was skillful at handling a plot. The story is overly complex and the motivations of the principal characters are weak and inconsistent. In the hands of talented writers, all the havoc wrought for the sake of pumpkin pie might have been used for ironic effect; in ***The Pearl and the Pumpkin*** the extreme value placed on pie is merely ludicrous. After a slow start, however, the book moves along with such pace that many of its deficiencies are not apparent. In general, ***The Pearl and the Pumpkin*** received good reviews, as readers were pleased with a "story which teems with action." At least one newspaper thought that it "will rival *Alice* and ***The Wizard*** in popularity." But Denslow's illustrations were the main reason for the book's success.

In ***The Pearl and the Pumpkin,*** Denslow returned to the format of ***The Wonderful Wizard of Oz:*** a novel-length fairy tale illustrated with full-color plates and many text pictures. The total work, however, is not so successful as the Baum book. Denslow's line is heavier and obviously more rushed, and the figures lack the lighter touch of his many picture books. ***The Pearl and the Pumpkin*** is, nonetheless, an attractive book. The chapter headings have something of the decorative quality of those for ***Dot and Tot of Merryland,*** and the text illustrations occasionally are dynamic in their use of the page. In addition, many of Denslow's pictures of individual characters are wildly imaginative. His pumpkin-boy is a marvelous conception: a huge pumpkin body, with leaves and vines for his limbs and a jack o'lantern head. The Corn Dodger is shaped like a great ear of corn with a fantastic flurry of cornsilk for his hair. Each pirate is a distinct character; Davy Jones's crew sports a variety of costumes and expressions. Particularly inventive is Denslow's depiction of fish who replace his more usual comic animals. The fish act as messengers, servants, jesters. Without question, Denslow had the ability to invent and picture memorable characters. Unfortunately, he lacked a collaborator who had the writing ability to bring them to life.

Denslow at his desk.

Most of these eccentric personalities—possibly even including the fish—were more effective on stage than in a children's book. West was principally responsible for the script of the play, and Denslow designed the costumes and sets. (pp. 123-25)

When the syndication of the Kahles version of the **"Billy Bounce"** comic page ended Denslow decided to revive interest in his old character by writing the script for a play, ***Billy Bounce and Boogieman*** with a new collaborator, Dudley A. Bragdon, an undistinguished writer of theatrical sketches. Again, he drew watercolor studies of the principal characters to interest producers.

As with ***The Pearl and the Pumpkin,*** Denslow prepared a children's book based on his play. ***Billy Bounce,*** by Denslow and Bragdon and published by Dillingham in 1906, was a much less successful collaboration than ***The Pearl and the Pumpkin.*** The authors had high intentions; the book begins with a restatement of Denslow's opposition to horrifying and strongly moralistic tales. Their purpose, the authors wrote, is "fun for the 'children between the ages of one and one hundred.'" . . . By removing most frightening incidents from their book, Denslow and Bragdon restricted the possibilities of dramatic action; neither author was gifted enough to overcome this limitation.

Billy Bounce is the worst children's book of Denslow's career. The tale is so unstructured that it is nearly impossible to retell the plot or even to sort out all the incidents. The individual episodes are characterized by forced puns and the "Broadway gags" that Denslow once abhorred. The story is only slightly related to the original comic strip: Billy Bounce, the orphan messenger boy with an inflatable suit, is again the hero, but only one or two of the cartoon's characters are retained in minor roles. (pp. 132-33)

Some of Billy's adventures form a moralistic allegory—a poorly-executed pilgrim's progress—teaching him not to fear shams, mirages, superstitions, and spooks. Other episodes, however, have no point at all except to pad this overlong comic strip.

The story improves when Billy reaches the town of "Never Was," the home of Boogie Man. Its dark, empty, shadowy streets are described with great sensitivity. (p. 134)

Denslow's pictures for this strange mishmash are little better than the text. He seems, in fact, to have been more interested in sketching theatrical costumes for his eccentric characters than in designing a book or even providing finished pictures. Denslow did not try to make the volume an artistic unit. There are no head or tailpieces to set off the chapters, and the title page is one of his weakest drawings. ***Billy Bounce*** contains fewer textual pictures than any previous Denslow fairy tale, and they are printed entirely in black and white. Most contain only a single figure with no background whatever, not even the solid backdrops of the Floating World. Denslow seems to have dashed off his drawings, using a heavy, clumsy line. The sixteen color plates brighten the work, but they suggest more the garish Sunday comic strip than the well-printed picture book. Not all the pictures are equally disappointing; one or two, such as the color plate of the Singing Tree, are attractive. But the few skillful drawings do not counteract the clumsiness of most of the pictures. (p. 135)

During 1907, Denslow and Bragdon copyrighted ***Billy Bounce and Boogieman,*** but they failed to find a producer.

Denslow apparently did not realize that his career was being damaged by his association with books prepared primarily for the theater, and his 1907 book followed the pattern set by ***The Pearl and the Pumpkin*** and ***Billy Bounce.*** Due to the success of ***The Wizard of Oz*** . . . , the Bobbs-Merrill Company of Indianapolis published a series of children's fairy tales in the same format as ***The Wizard,*** based upon forthcoming musical extravaganzas. Among them were Emerson Hough's *The King of Gee-Whiz,* Curtis Dunham's *The Golden Goblin,* and the next book illustrated by Denslow, ***The Jeweled Toad*** by Isabel Johnston. In June, 1902, Mrs. Johnston had copyrighted "an extravaganza in 5 acts, based on the Kingdom of Wonderland and the loss of the jewel of knowledge." She could not find a producer for her play so she rewrote it as a children's story. Denslow, as illustrator, shared the copyright of the book, but fortunately he was not co-author. Although because of its musical comedy origins some of the scenes have the same farcical nonsense that debilitated ***Billy Bounce,*** the story as a whole is charming, with its fairy woods, castles, court intrigues, and talking animals. Certainly, ***The Jeweled Toad*** captured Denslow's imagination.

The Jeweled Toad is a beautifully designed book; in it Denslow recovered the ability which he appeared to have lost in ***Billy Bounce.*** There are not many pictures but they are carefully designed. Except for the decorations on the preliminary pages, the only textual illustrations are chapter headings, long narrow panels tightly yet delicately executed. These pages, printed in two colors which vary from chapter to chapter, create a rhythm which breaks up the monotonous appearance of text pages. The color plates are designed with a skill lacking in ***Billy Bounce.*** Denslow carefully placed his black line against bright, flat colors. The individual portrayals of children and animals rank with his finest work. But despite the beauty of ***The Jeweled Toad,*** it did not sell. (pp. 135-36)

Possibly by 1907, Denslow's name had become so associated with mediocre stories that buyers did not look closely at ***The Jeweled Toad.*** He would have been wise to continue illustrating nursery classics like ***Mother Goose*** and ***Night Before Christmas,*** but he believed himself a writer. The expurgations of old classics in his 1903-1904 picture books and the original full-length fairy tales, ***The Pearl and the Pumpkin*** and ***Billy Bounce,*** prove that he was neither a skillful constructer of plots nor a master of prose style. His assumption that to succeed one must have "pure wit and clean fun" eliminated tension and excitement which are often based on the menacing. Moreover, since the break with Baum, Denslow had been careless in his choice of collaborators. He generally worked with friends whose ability to write for children was untested—in the event, only Isabel Johnston produced a good story. His intentions for children's books were praiseworthy, but he and his co-authors, West and Bragdon, lacked the ability to give his ideas proper form.

Beginning in 1904, he had directed his books toward future stage presentation and thus had been too dependent on the topical and temporarily novel. He sometimes included characters and scenes in his children's books solely for their eventual use in the theater. What was amusing on the stage was often boring in books. For example, when Denslow was working on ***Billy Bounce,*** he had the startling idea of dressing an actor as a fried egg. Because he was to appear in the play, "White Wings the Fried Egg" dutifully shows up in the book; but he has no purpose in the narrative and has nothing clever to say or do. The creation of White Wings was probably typical of the composition of ***Billy Bounce*** and to a lesser extent ***The Pearl and the Pumpkin.***

As ***The Jeweled Toad*** had proven, Denslow had lost none of his abilities while straddling the conflicting worlds of the Broadway comedy and the children's book trade, but he was out of touch with developments in publishing. Printers began to use a sophisticated photo-reproduction process that was especially effective with complex shades and tiny details. The more prestigious firms published elegantly printed and bound gift books with reproductions of Maxfield Parrish's thinly glazed oil paintings and Arthur Rackham's transparent watercolors. In comparison, Denslow's once distinctive style seemed commonplace. So many artists had imitated him that his style appeared in varying quality in all forms of commerical art, from the garish Sunday comic supplements to uninspired standard cuts used by many printers. The vogue for his work created by ***Father Goose*** had passed. Denslow would illustrate only one more book. (pp. 137-38)

During 1908, Denslow received his last major commission. *St. Nicholas,* the most important children's magazine of its day, purchased a series of verses and drawings by Denslow, under the collected title ***When I Grow Up.*** The editors aggressively promoted the episodes: "of all the artists who have made illustrations for young folks," their advertisements read, "there is probably no other who combines in equal degree with Mr. Denslow the gifts of abounding humor, bold and masterly skill

Denslow and the Scarecrow, a self-portrait.

in drawing, and a genius for decorative effect.'' Denslow's series was the magazine's first extensive use of full-color lithographs. ***When I Grow Up*** appeared in twelve successive issues of *St. Nicholas,* beginning in November, 1908; and in September of the next year, the Century Company published the entire collection (with the addition of ten episodes that did not appear in the magazine) as a clothbound book.

Each verse, with its accompanying illustrations, describes a child's daydreams of a future career. Denslow's text is pleasant doggerel; the following lines are typical:

> A roving life's the one for me,
> Aboard a merry whaler;
> I'd dance and sing and have my fling
> I'd be a jolly sailor.

Denslow's illustrations are generally inferior to those in his earlier picture books. The lively black line and contrasting flat colors, which were the principal strengths of his previous designs, were lost in the color lithographs and black and white half-tones of ***When I Grow Up.*** The color printing is in an uneven gray-toned scheme, lacking the brightness of his Dillingham books. Moreover, it was already apparent in the 1890's that the black and white half-tone process was not well suited to Denslow's style. In ***When I Grow Up,*** the black and white wash drawings are muddy and dreary.

Even if the printing had been better, however, the book would not rank with Denslow's finest work, for the drawing is surprisingly unskillful. His line lacks sureness: individual figures have clumsy, heavy outlines, and they are cluttered with fussy, secondary details. Each drawing appears to have been conceived without regard for the total design of the page. In ***When I Grow Up,*** Denslow was more interested in the caricatural than in the purely illustrative. Personality dominates style, with a resulting imbalance between the central figure and the rest of the drawing. The pictures contain caricatures of contemporary figures: Teddy Roosevelt represents the soldier, William Jennings Bryan the orator, and Denslow himself the fisherman. Without the bite of his cartoons in *The Philistine* and *The Erudite,* these drawings are merely grotesques which seldom harmonize with the entire design. (pp. 139-40)

As the years passed, his accomplishments as an illustrator were almost forgotten. He is not mentioned in any important book on American illustrators for children. *The Junior Book of Authors* and *Illustrators of Children's Books* ignore Denslow while devoting entries to such artists as Will H. Bradley, who illustrated only one children's book, and Charles Dana Gibson and Aubrey Beardsley, who never designed any books for children. (p. 165)

Perhaps Denslow was partly at fault for the lack of critical recognition of his work. He did not always choose wisely which books to illustrate. His younger contemporaries, Arthur Rackham, Edmund Dulac, and Maxfield Parrish, often reillustrated old classics. Since the texts were established literature, these gift books need be judged only on their artistic merits and could remain in print for years without being dated. Except for his editions of ***Mother Goose*** and ***Night Before Christmas,*** Denslow illustrated original texts written by himself or his friends. Because they depended on topical humor, their popularity was brief. Of the original tales which he illustrated, only ***The Wonderful Wizard of Oz*** has survived and become established as a modern classic. But being associated with Baum did not help Denslow's reputation; only recently has Baum been recognized as one of America's most important authors of children's books. Many of Denslow's books remained in print more than a decade after his death, but they were so altered that his sense of design and color were lost. (pp. 165-66)

By the early 1920's, the plates [for ***The Wizard of Oz***] were so worn that a new edition was issued; color was dropped from the text and instead of reproducing the pictures from Denslow's original drawings, Bobbs-Merrill had another artist prepare clumsy copies of them. The publishers realized, nevertheless, that Denslow's conceptions of the characters were as much a part of ***The Wizard*** as Tenniel's were for *Alice in Wonderland.* They briefly toyed with the idea of having the Baum book reillustrated by the great English artist, Arthur Rackham, but they decided that no other illustrator could replace Denslow in children's affection. When the 1939 MGM *Wizard of Oz* movie was released, however, readers accepted other interpretations of Baum's characters, and in the 1940's Bobbs-Merrill issued a new edition with pictures by Evelyn Copelman. According to the title page, the artist based her drawings on Denslow's work, but it is clear that her main inspiration was the movie characterizations. All of Denslow's books were now out of print, and the pessimism of his print, **"What's the Use?"**, seemed to summarize his career.

Recently, however, interest has revived in Denslow's work. As L. Frank Baum began to receive critical recognition, several publishers reissued ***The Wonderful Wizard of Oz*** in facsimiles of the first edition. The sense of design and color of this book alone has gone far to establish Denslow as an important figure in the history of children's books. Appreciations of Denslow have recently appeared in scholarly and popular journals; his far-reaching contributions to the development of American illustrations are now being recognized. He was the first American to create picture books in the aesthetic tradition of Walter Crane, Kate Greenaway, and Randolph Caldecott. Sixty years after his death, **"Victory"** rather than **"What's the Use?"** describes his career; not the hollow victory of Denslow's popular print, but the victory of accomplishment. (pp. 166-67)

Douglas G. Greene and Michael Patrick Hearn, in their W. W. Denslow, *Clarke Historical Library, 1976, 225 p.*

DAVID L. GREENE AND DICK MARTIN

In the words of Bobbs-Merrill's promotion for its 1939 reissue of ***The Wizard,*** ''W. W. Denslow was the perfect collaborator for L. Frank Baum. His pictures could no more be separated from the text than Gilbert's words could be taken from Sullivan's music.'' Even in 1900, when the book was first published, reviewers remarked that it would be difficult to decide whether the artist drew the pictures to illustrate the tale or the author wrote the story to describe the pictures. Denslow's drawings are as much a part of ***The Wizard*** as Tenniel's are of *Alice,* Shepard's of *Winnie the Pooh,* or Cruikshank's of *Oliver Twist.* (p. 84)

In the first edition of ***The Wonderful Wizard of Oz*** Denslow established for all time the appearance of the Scarecrow, the Tin Woodman and the Cowardly Lion, and he was marvelously successful in endowing them with the attributes described by the author. They are by turns funny, absurd, pathetic, courageous, dignified, even noble—and at all times endearing. He was equally successful with almost all the other characters: the Wizard, the Guardian of the Gates, the Green-Whiskered Soldier, Dorothy's little dog, Toto. His Glinda has an Art Nouveau graciousness, and his villains are properly frightening. The Wicked Witch of the West is ugly, menacing and absurd, with her eye patch, spats, umbrella and three pigtails, each tied with a bow; his Winged Monkeys look dangerously mischievous. When Metro-Goldwyn-Mayer filmed ***The Wizard*** in 1939 it wisely, though somewhat freely, based its characters upon Denslow's concepts. (Visually, however, Judy Garland was a distinct improvement on Denslow's drawings of Dorothy; in 1900 reviewers had already pointed out one of Denslow's few flaws: he could not draw a childlike child.) (pp. 86-8)

Today Denslow is firmly established as the definitive illustrator of ***The Wizard of Oz***. . . . (p. 100)

David L. Greene and Dick Martin, in their The Oz Scrapbook, *Random House, 1977, 182 p.*

THE WONDERFUL WIZARD OF OZ **(1900; also published as *The New Wizard of Oz* and *The Wizard of Oz*)**

[The Wonderful Wizard of Oz *was written by L. Frank Baum.*]

In ***The Wonderful Wizard of Oz*** the fact is clearly recognized that the young as well as their elders love novelty. They are pleased with dashes of color and something new in the place of the old, familiar, and winged fairies of Grimm and Andersen.

Neither the tales of Aesop and other fableists, nor the stories such as the "Three Bears" will ever pass entirely away, but a welcome place remains and will easily be found for such stories as ***Father Goose: His Book, The Songs of Father Goose,*** and now ***The Wonderful Wizard of Oz,*** that have all come from the hands of Baum and Denslow.

This last story of ***The Wizard*** is ingeniously woven out of commonplace material. It is of course an extravaganza, but will surely be found to appeal strongly to child readers as well as to the younger children. . . .

The drawing as well as the introduced color work vies with the texts drawn, and the result has been a book that rises far above the average children's book of today, high as is the present standard. Dorothy, the little girl, and her strangely assorted companions, whose adventures are many and whose dangers are often very great, have experiences that seem in some respects like a leaf out of one of the old English fairy tales that Andrew Lang or Joseph Jacobs has rescued for us. A difference there is, however, and Baum has done with mere words what Denslow has done with his delightful draughtsmanship.

"A New Book for Children," in The New York Times Book Review, *September 8, 1900, p. 605.*

The Wonderful Wizard of Oz, described by its publishers as a modern fairy story, fairly sustains the claim put forth for it that it is something new. Besides this it is very attractive, not only by reason of the story, which is by L. Frank Baum, but also through its profuse illustrations in color by W. W. Denslow. These gentlemen will be remembered as the author and illustrator respectively of ***Father Goose,*** and Mr. Denslow has managed to maintain the reputation for originality that he earned in his former pictures. Besides originality, the drawings have life, action, and humor.

A review of "The Wonderful Wizard of Oz," in Book News, *Vol. XIX, No. 218, October, 1900, p. 84.*

The Wonderful Wizard of Oz is remarkably illustrated by Mr. William W. Denslow, who possesses all the originality of method which has been denied his collaborator. This . . . book is really notable among the innumerable publications of the year, making an appeal which is fairly irresistible to a certain standard of taste.

A review of "The Wonderful Wizard of Oz," in The Dial, *Vol. XXIX, No. 347, December 1, 1900, p. 436.*

(Albert) Sid(ney) Fleischman

1920-

American author of picture books, fiction, and nonfiction; and scriptwriter.

Recognized as a master of the tall tale, Fleischman is one of America's most popular humorists for children. Noted for his colloquial vocabulary and inventive, action-filled plots, Fleischman generally writes short, funny, and exciting stories particularly recommended for reading aloud and for enticing the reluctant middle-grade reader. His memorable characters—often folk-style heroes and villains—reveal his understanding of human nature, positive attitude towards life, and belief in such values as loyalty, perseverance, and courage. Focusing on subjects and settings as diverse as the gold rush in California, piracy on the high seas, and rural life from Ohio to Vermont, Fleischman shows his penchant for exhaustive historical research and his enthusiasm for nineteenth-century folk language. His entertaining novels have been compared to the writings of Mark Twain and Charles Dickens for their effective recreation of dialect and period. Formerly a professional magician, Fleischman began his literary career at the age of nineteen by publishing a book on magic; he has frequently included magicians and tricks in his more than thirty works. Best known for his comical McBroom series, which depicts an Iowan farmer, his wife, and eleven resourceful children on their amazingly productive one-acre farm, Fleischman regales his readers with a succession of imaginative impossibilities told in the straightforward but exaggerated manner of traditional tall tales. He has also written a compendium of McBroom's droll advice using elaborate wordplay in almanac format. In his highly acclaimed *The Whipping Boy* (1986), Fleischman portrays the spoiled Prince Brat and his stoical whipping boy, Jemmy. Through lively adventures, complete with kidnapping, treachery, mistaken identity, and narrow escapes, they learn about trust, friendship, and the importance of education. Fleischman departs from his customary approach and topics with his series of easy-to-read mysteries about the Bloodhound Gang. Featuring a trio of multiethnic, urban junior detectives, the books were adapted from scripts he wrote for the television show "3-2-1 Contact."

Critics admire Fleischman for his ingenious wit, vigorous style, polished craftsmanship, and meticulous research. Although some reviewers find the Bloodhound Gang series lacking in credibility and characteristic humor, they agree that Fleischman's exuberant works are an ideal introduction to independent reading and that his tall tales have contributed richly to American folk literature.

Fleischman has received numerous adult- and child-selected awards for his works. *McBroom Tells the Truth* won the Lewis Carroll Shelf Award in 1969, and *Humbug Mountain* was both a National Book Award finalist and the *Boston Globe-Horn Book* Award recipient in 1979. *The Whipping Boy* won the Newbery Award in 1987.

(See also *CLR*, Vol. 1; *Something about the Author*, Vol. 8; *Contemporary Authors New Revision Series*, Vol. 5; and *Contemporary Authors*, Vols. 1-4, rev. ed.)

AUTHOR'S COMMENTARY

Paul Hazard once wrote, "England could be reconstructed entirely from its children's books."

I wish the same observation could be made about our own country in this Bicentennial year. I'm afraid that a key shard of American life would turn up missing. Except for the works of Mark Twain it would be almost impossible to reconstruct the American sense of humor.

Laughter is the natural sound of childhood, but one would hardly suspect it from reading children's literature. I am reminded of a comedy sketch performed by the late Ernie Kovacs. Browsing silently along a library shelf, he pulled out *Camille* and opened it. The sound of coughing arose as if from the pages. He moved on to *The Three Musketeers*. The clank and clash of a sword fight was heard. And so on.

Can you imagine yourself browsing through the children's room of any library and opening books for the sound of laughter? One would go to the C's, obviously, for Clemens. And Cleary. To the K's for Konigsburg. The R's would yield Raskin. There are others (and I would hope you'd have some luck in the F's). But, by and large, it would be an exercise in futility.

The reason, at first glance, seems obvious. Laughter, surely, cannot be taken seriously—more about that in a moment. It is frivolous and confectionary and it belongs in the nursery.

Mother Goose is rich in broad comic images: a woman living in a shoe; a cow jumping over the moon; blackbirds flocking out of a pie. My earliest literary memories are funny ones. I remember most vividly the woodman's wife with the link sausages attached to her nose in "The Three Wishes." That had me rolling in the aisles—or on the living-room carpet. A little later came Lewis Carroll's Cheshire Cat and the mad Hatter.

Contemporary comic talent in the picture-story field comes easily to mind—Maurice Sendak, Arnold Lobel, Don Freeman, Bill Peet, David McPhail, Judith Viorst. But once we leave the nursery behind we are expected to shelve childish laughter like outgrown toys. Novels in the eight-to-twelve group seem to tell us that it is time to face real life. And if you remember your Longfellow you know what *that* is. "Life is real!" he wrote, complete with exclamation points in case you weren't paying attention. "Life is earnest!"

These were certainly the academic mantras of my boyhood. I was assigned "Evangeline" and not long after, *Silas Marner* and *Ivanhoe*. If you can find a laugh in any of these works, you have a better sense of humor than I. I was almost fully grown before I discovered that real life may also wear baggy pants and carry a slapstick.

But the writer offers this view of reality at his own risk. Comedy is easily misread as the mere vaudeville of literature. Mark Twain was routinely passed over for the Nobel Prize. Rarely since the 1920's and *Dr. Dolittle* have the Newbery judges given recognition to humor. In *Newbery and Caldecott Medal Books 1966-1975,* John Rowe Townsend, the English critic, writes, "One lack is very evident in children's books generally. . . . That is the absence of fine, sustained comic writing."

The trouble, I think, is that laughter is not quite respectable—a little vulgar, perhaps. That was certainly the stately view of George Meredith, who felt uneasy at anything above a smile. Walter Kerr has said that Meredith was "distressed that Oliver Goldsmith should have stooped so low to conquer" with "'an elegant farce for a comedy.'" Perhaps that's why Goldsmith is still read and Meredith merely quoted. And not very often at that.

I had better confess that I conceived ***Jingo Django*** as a dark and earnest novel. It was time to become respectable, I thought; I still accepted the majority view that comedy was the lesser of the Greek masks. In this story I was going to deal with a child ruthlessly abandoned by a truly sinister father. Oedipal hatred, orphan house cruelty, a painful and mysterious problem of identity—what raw materials could be more serious?

But a funny thing happened on the way to the typewriter. My resolve gave way to one caprice after another. Only after finishing the novel—it turned out to be a broad, farcical adventure—did I discover for myself the Great Truth. Comedy is tragedy; but it is tragedy in motley.

A stunning example of this is cited by Charles Chaplin in his autobiography. Perhaps the funniest scene ever put on film occurs in *The Gold Rush* when the starving Chaplin and a fellow miner dine on a hob-nailed shoe. Then his table companion hallucinates, seeing Chaplin as a huge, plump chicken to be similarly parboiled. The inspiration for this scene, as Chaplin reveals it, is a hair-raiser. He had been reading about the snow-trapped Donner Party driven by starvation to eating its footgear and to cannibalism.

Comedy, then, is alchemy; the base metal is always tragedy. War has excited the comic imagination from Aristophanes to Joseph Heller. It was only while preparing this paper that I realized, having written such tall tales as ***McBroom's Ghost*** and ***The Ghost on Saturday Night,*** that the ludicrous subject was death itself.

It was no accident that the tall tale flourished on the frontier, providing me with the raw material for the various McBroom stories. In laughter, pioneers found a way of accommodating themselves to the agonies that came with the land. Bitter cold? Even words froze in the air. Blowtorch summers? Chickens laid hard-boiled eggs. Raging winds? To pluck a chicken, hold it out a window. Tornadoes, plagues of grasshoppers, swarms of mosquitoes—all were natural subjects for tall-tale humor.

I have found that writers of comedy don't like to probe too deeply into their elusive and sometimes mysterious sources. They are in the position of the centipede asked by an admiring frog how he (she?) moved all those legs with such grace and precision. Since it came naturally, the centipede had never before given the matter a thought. Trying to figure out which leg to move when, the centipede entirely lost the fine art of walking.

But I will take a limited risk. I know where some ideas in my books come from. I remember my surprise, after writing ***By the Great Horn Spoon!,*** at being credited with the most outrageous imagination when I served up the notion that the forty-niners shipped their starched shirts to China for laundering. I thought everyone knew that. It's true. While saloons were in ample supply in boom-town San Francisco, no one felt a special calling to go into the laundry business. In due time a few Cantonese sailed to California and the source of the soiled haberdashery; others followed, and I suspect that out of this historical fluke arose the stereotype of the Chinese laundryman.

I had always regarded history as dignified as all get-out, but with this incident I discovered that the past assays out fairly rich in comic ore. In an old copy of the *Missouri Historical Review* I sifted out an incomparable petty schemer, a man caught stealing his neighbor's land by moving the rail fence at night, a few inches at a time. He became a key, though off-stage character, in ***Jingo Django,*** when Jingo and Mr. Peacock-Hemlock-Jones go tumbling across the country in search of a cache of Mexican gold coins buried under a fence post. You can imagine what happens and why, when my heroes go rooting around in *that* post hole.

In the last century the Missouri River jumped its bank in an act of pure comedy. A thriving tavern on the Missouri side awoke to find itself in dry Kansas. This provided me with the first faint stirrings of ***Humbug Mountain***. . . . I have enlarged upon the incident, cross-pollinating it with the history of mad speculation on town-building and lot-selling on the frontier. As you might guess, my raffish entrepreneur makes the mistake of staking out his rip-roaring metropolis-to-be on the Missouri. At the moment he's still trying to unload those cursed dry Kansas lots.

Folklore is rich in humor. The old belief that one born at midnight has the power to see ghosts set me on this train of thought. What if pirates threw their murdered captain into the same pit with buried treasure? What if they lost the map? It's another superstition that the murdered rest uneasy and walk their grave sites until avenged. Now I had it. What if my young hero were born at the stroke of midnight? Using his ghost-seeing gift, the pirates would know where to dig for the lost treasure. The result of this assortment of folklore and "what ifs" was ***The Ghost in the Noonday Sun.***

My favorite scene in ***Chancy and the Grand Rascal*** occurs when my heroes come across a chuck-wagon cook about to drown a sack of kittens. Uncle Will, the grand rascal, declares that one can tell the time by reading a cat's eyes. This is a folklore belief. The cook is persuaded and holds out one kitten as a timepiece. But what of the rest of the litter? The grand rascal advises the man to hang on to the entire litter. "I've known cats to run slow and run fast," he says.

Folklore once again provided me with the basic idea for ***Longbeard the Wizard,*** a picture book. I was reading a museum-published biography for an exhibit of the paintings of Chaim Soutine. A sentence leaped out at me. Soutine was affected by a folk belief that we are born to speak a certain and unknown number of words; when we use them up, we die. An irresistible idea. Enter Queen Gibble-Gabble, unaware that she is chattering her way into a sudden grave. Trivia? I think not. The magic power of words runs through all cultures.

It is American folklore that betrays our unconscious rather than our formal literary taste. I find that this common lore breaks down into three general areas—the supernatural; hero tales; and, writ especially large, HUMOR. And these are the delights of childhood. To be safely frightened. To identify with larger-than-life heroes. To laugh. Curiously, tragedy in tragic terms is dealt with almost exclusively in ballads. John Henry, for example, and Casey Jones.

Why, then, has there been so little laughter in children's books? The trouble seems to stem from a traditional judgment that humor is umpredictable. What some find funny, others may not. That's true, of course, But the premise is faulty. Why must we like the same books, the same paintings, the same music—the same humor? I was recently told of a boy, somewhat miffed and insulted by one of my McBroom tall tales. "If that story is true," he protested, "I'm stupid."

I am happy to be able to say that, while I have not been beating a dead horse, it appears to be a moribund one. If my mail is any indication, editors are now actively seeking out humor. In some schools in California, and perhaps elsewhere, a unit on tall tales is being taught as a legitimate aspect of frontier social history. And last year [1975] the National Council of Teachers of English/Children's Book Council joint conference in San Diego scheduled a session on humor in children's books. (pp. 465-70)

Sid Fleischman, "Laughter and Children's Literature," in The Horn Book Magazine, *Vol. LII, No. 5, October, 1976, pp. 465-70.*

GENERAL COMMENTARY

CHARLOTTE S. HUCK AND DORIS YOUNG KUHN

[Sid Fleischman is] becoming a master at creating modern tall tales. ***Chancy and the Grand Rascal*** is the story of a young orphan who sets out to find his brothers and sisters but first meets his uncle, the Grand Rascal, who can out-talk, out-laugh, and out-fox any man on the river. Uncle Will accompanies Chancy on his search, and what hilarious adventures they have! The free and easy style of this tale is exemplified by the Grand Rascal's account of his winter in Dakota. . . . Fleischman has also written ***McBroom Tells the Truth,*** a tall tale about a wonderful one-acre farm in Iowa that produces several crops daily. Once the owners had to wait as long as three hours for the field to produce a shade tree from an acorn! This tall tale is told in a matter-of-fact manner that contrasts superbly with the gross exaggerations of the story. (pp. 337-38)

Charlotte S. Huck and Doris Young Kuhn, "Modern Fantasy and Humor: New Tall Tales," in their Children's Literature in the Elementary School, *second edition, Holt, Rinehart and Winston, Inc., 1968, pp. 337-38.*

RUTH HILL VIGUERS

The main characters of Sid Fleischman's ***Mr. Mysterious and Company*** are an ingenious family who travel across badlands and prairies, through cactus, mesquite, and greasewood in a red covered wagon, putting on magic shows whenever they stopped at a town. They coped successfully with marauding Indians, an outlaw, and a band of ruffians, and they gave pleasure and met new friends wherever they went. In ***By the Great Horn Spoon!*** Praiseworthy, an urbane butler, traveled with Jack, his employer's son, on a fifteen-thousand-mile voyage—which they started as stowaways because their passage money had been stolen—to reach the gold fields of California. These and other books by Mr. Fleischman have a tall-tale quality, and situations recounted with skill, liveliness and great good humor. (pp. 487-88)

Ruth Hill Viguers, "Golden Years and Time of Tumult, 1920-1967: Quests, Survival, and the Romance of History, Adventure Tale and Historical Fiction," in A Critical History of Children's Literature *by Cornelia Meigs and others, edited by Cornelia Meigs, revised edition, Macmillan Publishing Company, 1969, pp. 484-510.*

MYRA POLLACK SADKER AND DAVID MILLER SADKER

Sid Fleischman has become outstandingly adept in his ability to relate tall tale adventures. . . .

[In ***Mr. Mysterious and Company***], the outstanding figure is Pa, kindly, and able to handle every situation no matter how difficult or dangerous. ***By the Great Horn Spoon*** . . . presents an even grander tall tale hero, Mr. Praiseworthy, the butler, who is indeed a man for all times and all seasons. (p. 327)

In Fleischman's ***The Ghost in the Noonday Sun*** . . . the competent hero is Oliver Finch, a young lad who, shanghaied by the dreadful Captain Scratch, has the unenviable task of uncovering the elusive ghost of the pirate, Gentleman Jack. The adventure is heightened by a band of cutthroat pirates who are equally ready to walk the plank, mutiny, or leave Oliver stranded on a tropical isle. Shysters and tall tale tellers emerge in ***Chancy and the Grand Rascal*** . . . , in which orphaned Chancy sets off to find his long lost sister, Indiana. Along the way he runs into his Uncle Will and a series of marvelously improbable adventures.

In his stories about McBroom and his amazing one-acre farm, Fleischman has created a tall tale hero who delights younger independent readers and also provides a grand vehicle for storytelling and reading aloud. The McBroom farm must combat grasshoppers who would eat anything green, including McBroom's socks, a wind so powerful that it blows McBroom's eleven children into the sky, and a winter so cold that sounds freeze and are not heard until they thaw out in the spring. (pp. 327-28)

Myra Pollack Sadker and David Miller Sadker, "Room for Laughter," in their Now upon a Time: A Contemporary View of Children's Literature, *Harper & Row, Publishers, 1977, pp. 318-59.*

SYBIL S. STEINBERG

Sid Fleischman was well into his career as a writer of books for adults and screenplays for Hollywood before he wandered into the children's book field by accident. "My kids (he has three) didn't understand what I did for a living. So one day I sat down and wrote a story for children and read it to them," he told [*Publishers Weekly*]. . . .

The book "sat around for a while," until Fleischman, who knew nothing about the children's book field, finally sent it off to his agent. Atlantic/Little, Brown published the story in 1962 as ***Mr. Mysterious and Company,*** and since then Fleischman has produced about 20 books in a comic vein for an enthusiastic young audience.

The ***McBroom*** series—tall tales about an Iowan farmer with incredibly fertile land—was another lucky accident. Fleischman's book ***Chancy and the Grand Rascal*** needed two tall tales, and the first one he dreamed up so tickled him that he ripped it out of ***Chancy*** and turned it into ***McBroom Tells a Lie.*** Though he didn't originally intend to do another story about fecund Josh McBroom (who has 11 euphoniously named offspring), Fleischman found himself captivated by his hero, and a steady crop of tall tales ensued. . . .

Fleischman says he doesn't approach humorous writing consciously. "When I sit at the typewriter, amusing notions come into my head," he told us, his voice conjuring up the image of a lively personality. But writing humor takes a knack and experience, he conceded. "You learn to balance a sentence, to end it with the right choice of words that makes it funny.

"Actually, my books are very serious," he said. . . . "It's only the surface that's humorous. Usually I take a frightening situation and deal with it in comic terms." ***Humbug Mountain*** . . . is about death and resurrection, "Yet it's a very funny book," Fleischman says.

A villainous character appears in all of Fleischman's stories. "I feel secure when I have a good comic villain who is also threatening. A cunning but lovable con man gives me situations I can work with, by using sleight-of-mind. Sometimes I have to spend a long time thrashing a way out of a situation."

The skill Fleischman calls "sleight-of-mind" is a residue from days spent as a magician, touring with a magic show. Born in Brooklyn and raised in San Diego, Fleischman says his travels took him into just about every small town in the country, and "in every one I heard folk speech and stories," grist for the writer's mill.

Fleischman says he detects a more open reception for humor in children's books in the last few years, and he's happy to spot the trend. "Humor is a marvelous way of introducing reading to children. What they like to do is laugh. So humorous books have a tremendous value." (p. 88)

Sybil S. Steinberg, "What Makes a Funny Children's Book?: Five Writers Talk about Their Methods," in Publishers Weekly, *Vol. 213, No. 9, February 27, 1978, pp. 87-90.*

EMILY RHOADS JOHNSON

At Ben Franklin School in Grand Forks, North Dakota, Sid Fleischman held a group of children spellbound for nearly an hour with feats of magic and intriguing glimpses into his life as a writer. When he stopped and asked for questions, a hand spiked the air. "But is it *fun* to write books?" a dubious fourth grader wanted to know.

"Yes it *is* fun," Mr. Fleischman replied, bending forward in a characteristic posture of enthusiasm. "Even when you're miserable, it's fun. It is endlessly interesting and endlessly exciting."

Like a child perched on the edge of a chair, this gentle, soft-spoken man anticipates life's adventures with a sense of wonder and a hungry delight. Not the slightest detail escapes his attention: the inflection in a stranger's voice, a distant train whistle, a new tidbit of information, the wistful expression on a child's face, a turn of phrase he has never heard before. Like the magician he is, he tucks these impressions away in the corners of his consciousness, then pulls them out at the exact moment they are needed in the process of creating a book.

Albert Sidney Fleischman was born in Brooklyn on March 16, 1920, but spent his growing-up years in San Diego, California. His Russian father was a good storyteller with a natural sense of pace, pause, and dramatic effect; and he remembers his mother reading him *Aesop's Fables* and *Uncle Tom's Cabin.* The book that affected him most profoundly, however, was *Robin Hood* "my first great reading experience, and my favorite of those early years."

As part of a tiny Jewish minority in San Diego, Fleischman had to learn to deal with the judgment of people who regarded Jews as social inferiors. During this time of a still active Ku Klux Klan, the anti-semitic fulminations of Henry Ford and Charles Lindbergh and the rise of Naziism in Germany, he came to terms with those feelings ("chucking them"), but out of it all grew an identification with the underdog. "I can see this in the dynamics of my choice of characters to write about," he says. "The butler (victim of the class system) in ***By the Great Horn Spoon!*** The gypsies in ***Jingo Django.*** And children, of course, are every generation's underdogs."

As a child Mr. Fleischman's fervent interest was not so much in books as it was in magic. After reading all the books on magic that the library could offer and perfecting a repertoire of tricks to perform before audiences, he decided, at age seventeen, to write his own book on magic. . . . The book was first printed in 1939 and is still in print today. Fleischman writes, "When I saw my name on the cover, I was hooked on writing books." (pp. 754-56)

[After World War II], he began writing adult detective and suspense novels, which developed and sharpened his fiction writing skills. "I learned to keep the story pot boiling," he says, "to manage tension and the uses of surprise." . . .

Mr. Fleischman was forty-two years old . . . when his first children's book, ***Mr. Mysterious and Company,*** was published. In it he put his wife, his children, their dog, and even himself. Now, twenty years and thirty-one books later, . . . he sticks to much the same schedule he has always followed. . . . "Like most professional writers, I work seven days a week. It's like being a juggler: you can't stop or you'll drop the pieces."

Mr. Fleischman is a painstaking writer who composes slowly, preferring to think out each sentence carefully before committing it to paper. As he hinted to the fourth grader who asked, "Is it fun?", writing sometimes makes him miserable. (p. 756)

But it is the burning desire to find out what will happen next in whatever he is writing that keeps Sid Fleischman returning to his desk each morning. "I don't like to know how a story ends," he admits. "Getting my characters into terrible fixes and not knowing how to get them out again sustains my interest."

When his children were young, he used to read them his books, chapter by chapter, then ask them for notions of what might happen next or how the story characters might get themselves out of their predicaments. His son Paul, now himself an author of children's books, delighted his father by giving him gifts of original similes or passing along a good name when he heard one.

Since Mr. Fleischman's longer novels have historical settings, he must do a tremendous amount of research before starting the actual writing. ***By the Great Horn Spoon!,*** for instance, is so steeped in authentic details and little known lore about the California Gold Rush that it would make superb supplementary reading in any elementary school classroom. And chances are, it would provide more information on the subject than most textbooks.

In addition to interesting details, Mr. Fleischman hunts for amusing bits of history that have slipped through the cracks of textbooks and formal histories.

> I gobble up town histories and diaries—if slightly illiterate, so much the better. . . . I discover interesting regional language and self-made imagery and folklore beliefs. These often give me scenes—as in ***Chancy and the Grand Rascal*** (the belief that the time of day can be read in a cat's eyes)—or a turn of phrase, such as having "the dry wilts" which I loved so much I almost overdid it in ***Humbug Mountain.*** When my stories take place in the past, I don't find it useful to visit the locale I'm using. I can't psyche myself into the past with McDonald's golden arch staring at me, the Taco Bells, the Kentucky Fried Chickens, the freeways, the motel strips, the highrises. My creative juices rise out of research almost entirely—that's where my imagination rummages around and is freed. The past is very much like fantasy since I can't really see or touch it except by leaps of imagination.

Anyone who can dream up characters like Cut-Eye Higgins, Quickshot Billy Bodeen, Hawg Pewitt, and an outlaw named Shagnasty John, who "wore a mangy old bearskin coat and was big around as a sauerkraut barrel," has got to have a peculiarly keen and colorful sense of humor, and Sid Fleischman has indeed produced some of the funniest books ever written for children. Eleanor Cameron, in *The Green and Burning Tree,* lists his books among those with "the childlike humor we find rib-tickling and genuine. . . . I believe this element of humor in children's literature to be one of the supreme tests of a writer—whether he is or is not truly and deeply remembering his childhood, truly and deeply being a child again."

Humor, like laughter, is difficult to define; but lying at the heart of Sid Fleischman's humor are two essential ingredients: a profound understanding of human nature, and the elusive element of surprise. Being caught off guard makes readers laugh, and it happens over and over again in Fleischman's books. In the opening paragraph of ***Humbug Mountain,*** for example, Glorietta bursts through the door, yelling to her brother, "They've got Mr. Johnson by the neck!" But not until the reader turns the page does he learn that the unfortunate Mr. Johnson is not a man, but a goose.

Likewise, in ***McBroom's Ghost,*** after being led to believe that McBroom's farm is haunted by a noisy ghost, readers discover on the last page that all those scaresome sounds were caused by frozen noises thawing out in the spring.

Surprises abound, too, in Fleischman's descriptions:

> —Mr. Chitwood went slinking off like a rained-on dog.
>
> —Mrs. Daggett was big as a skinned ox.
>
> —He had such a long jaw he could eat oats out of a nose bag.
>
> —Captain Scratch ripped open the buttons of his greatcoat and squeezed the rain out of his flaming beard as if he were wringing a chicken's neck.

Another dimension can be added to the pleasure of Mr. Fleischman's books by reading them aloud. His words don't just sit there on the page; they leap and cavort, turn somersaults, and sometimes just hang suspended, like cars teetering at the top of a roller coaster. What marvelous fun it is to bump into words like *sniggle* and *flamigigs, wrathy, muckworm, buffle-brained,* and *slickens!*

Fleischman's plots are masterful weavings of mystery, adventure, puzzle, and legend. Highly popular among younger readers are the McBroom books—rollicking tall tales about Josh McBroom and his one-acre farm, with soil so fertile that short nails grow into long nails, marbles expand into boulders, and corn planted in the morning can be harvested the same day. But Fleischman's stories, particularly the longer ones, consist of more than knee slaps and belly laughs. In quests for land or treasure or missing relatives, the heroes meet up with every imaginable kind of trouble, usually in the form of villains and cutthroats, imposters and fingle-fanglers. There are stories within stories, and the kind of action that keeps readers turning the pages. And at the heart of the stories, moving pluckily through the outlandishness, are sensitively drawn characters with whom young readers can easily identify.

In ***Humbug Mountain,*** thirteen-year-old Wiley Flint and his sister Glorietta set out in a horse-drawn wagon with their parents to track down their grandfather and the town of Sunrise, which they understand he has founded somewhere along the banks of the Missouri River. Some of the scoundrels and outrageous dilemmas they encounter along the way may be pure fantasy, but Wiley's troubles with his sister are as real as a stubbed toe. (pp. 757-58)

Not only do Mr. Fleischman's characters squabble realistically, they also care deeply about one another; and this, I feel, is what gives his books their substance and strength. To know Sid Fleischman, in person or through his work, is to experience an affirmation of life. (p. 759)

Emily Rhoads Johnson, "Profile: Sid Fleischman," in Language Arts, *Vol. 59, No. 7, October, 1982, pp. 754-59, 772.*

PAUL FLEISCHMAN

[Fleischman is the son of Sid Fleischman and the author of several books, including the 1983 Newbery Honor Book Graven Images: Three Stories.]

The scene was repeated all through my growing-up. I'd be dimly aware that my father had been typing. His study door would open and close. My mother would call my two sisters and me, the whole family gathering in the living room, my father always at the table in the corner. Everyone got comfortable. The phone was entreated not to ring. A brief recap of the story was given. Then he read aloud the chapter he'd just finished.

"The sun came up hot and clear," he might begin, "as if it had been cut out of a prairie fire with a pair of scissors."

Or, "Sometime during the night Cut-Eye Higgins left Hangtown for parts unknown."

Or, "At first light, Captain Harpe was up and shouting. 'Rise up gents! To the oars, my lazy mud turtles!'"

Or, "It was a week before we got out the next issue of *The Humbug Mountain Hoorah*. First we had to dig up the petrified man."

We were transported at once to the Old Post Road, to the decks of an Ohio River raft, to Hangtown or Matamoros. Part yarn-spinning session, vaudeville act, history lesson, and magic show, these readings transmitted, aside from their stories, so much of what I associate with my father.

First and foremost, we imbibed his love of language. We grew up knowing that words felt good in the ears and on the tongue, that they were as much fun to play with as toys. How could we help it, following the adventures of characters whose names were such fun to say: Pitch-pine Billy, Micajah Jones, Jingo, Hawg Pewitt, Billy Bombay, not to mention the McBroom family's children, Will*jill*hester*chester*peter*polly*tim*tom*mary*larry*andlittle*clarinda*. Characters whose speech made you wish you'd been born a century earlier if only so that you, too, could shout, "By the eternal!" or "Hoolah-haw!" or "Hackle me bones!" or "Don't that bang all!"

His description was equally colorful. I feel safe in claiming that you won't find a single cliché in all my father's books. What you will find is lots of rich, visual imagery. A character wasn't simply thin. He was thin enough to take a bath in a shotgun barrel or to fall through a stovepipe without getting sooty. We never had trouble imagining the scene my father was reading. It takes a lot longer to write this way—especially when, after a long career, you're faced with your tenth or eleventh skinny character to describe. With more than thirty children's books behind him now, he still, somehow, managed to fill ***The Whipping Boy*** with plenty of fresh imagery.

I said that these readings were part history lesson. Weeks before my father actually began writing, stacks of research books would be brought from the library, piling up on the piano and eventually making their way into his study. I remember as a child being fascinated flipping through the notebook in which he kept his research. There were sections on food, clothing, language, prices of things, and various other subjects, filled with his penciled notes. I was hooked and years later would find myself filling similar notebooks of my own.

Despite his books' historical accuracy, listening to them read aloud was not at all like attending a classroom lecture. Here was history brought to life, the history that rarely gets into textbooks: gold miners sending their clothes all the way to China to be laundered, sailors' fear of ghostlike "dredgies," Gypsy signs and lingo, goose pulls. The dusty corners and vivid details of history have always attracted my father. Walking into his study when he was out, I would find myself wanting to read all those strange-sounding books on his shelves: *33 Years Among Our Wild Indians, Hawkers & Walkers in Early America, Extraordinary Popular Delusions and the Madness of Crowds*. A few years back we gleefully joined in combing the used bookstores in search of all four volumes of Henry Mayhew's *London Labour and the London Poor,* a book he eventually drew on for ***The Whipping Boy.***

In grammar school my father became interested in magic, learned the tricks of the trade—inventing quite a few along the way, the subject of his first published book—and after high school, during vaudeville's last days, toured the country with Mr. Arthur Bull's Francisco Spook Show. This experience came out in his books, several of which involve magic or adventuresome journeys or both. I suspect that his stage experience influenced his writing methods as well. He's an improviser and likes to keep himself as interested and in the dark about what's going to happen next as his readers. When he sits down at the typewriter in his silent study, he might as well be a comic stepping on stage in a noisy nightclub, trying to get a read on his audience, always thinking on his feet.

His reading aloud, likewise, partook of the stage. We four were his New Haven. He could tell from our reactions if a scene had worked or if it needed work. Our opinions were asked for. I remember being proud when my suggestion that Mr. Mysterious and his family get lost turned up in the following chapter. My younger sister, a little jealous, had less success with her proposal that their family piano ought to burn down.

These readings were live literature. Live like an old-time radio show, with the attendant tingle of excitement and the necessity of imagining the action. It's perhaps not surprising that we're all fans of "A Prairie Home Companion" and of the British radio game show "My Word." Or that I went on to write two books of poems designed to be performed aloud by two readers.

My father's specialty in magic is sleight of hand. No birthday party was complete without a few tricks; likewise, these days, no school visit, when my father, reenacting his past, takes his act on the road each spring and fall. This style of magic is reflected in his writing. When he gave up being a professional magician, he became instead a prestidigitator of words, palming plot elements, making villains vanish, producing solutions out of thin air. He knows how to keep an audience guessing, how to create suspense, how to keep readers reading. A sleight-of-hand artist must be skilled at misdirection, keeping his audience's eyes away from the real action. My father is a master at doing the same with words, stealthily slipping in a clue, unnoticed by the reader, that will reappear in the book's climax, just as he used to miraculously pull nickels and dimes out of our ears.

His adult characters are also sleight-of-hand men of a sort. Mr. Mysterious, Uncle Will, Praiseworthy, Mr. Peacock-Hemlock-Jones are all tall, strong men. They rely, however, on their cleverness. They're quick with their wits, magicians at manipulating a villain through his vices. Though Praiseworthy throws a notable punch at one point, these figures are advertisements for the superiority of brains to brawn.

As much as his use of language and history and clever plotting, it's those irresistibly appealing adult characters, I suspect, that explain why his books are nearly all still in print and that the letters from children continue to pour in. How wonderful to imagine yourself out adventuring—but with an Uncle Will to watch over you. Someone who respects you yet protects you as well. Someone brave, big-hearted, never discouraged, whose mere presence reassures you that everything will work out. With so many children growing up away from their fathers these days, it's no wonder that the warmth and security offered by these figures has a strong appeal. My sisters and I were lucky. Sitting in the living room, ruminating on the chapter just read, we knew we had exactly such a figure—for a father. (pp. 429-32)

Paul Fleischman, "Sid Fleischman," in The Horn Book Magazine, *Vol. LXIII, No. 4, July-August, 1987, pp. 429-32.*

McBROOM AND THE BIG WIND (1967)

Always there is a request from parents for books for the boy who doesn't like to read. Always the best answer is to give them a tall tale, or a funny one. Always you can count on Sid Fleischman to give them a story that combines the best features of both. He comes through again, with McBroom again. (Surely you remember his ***McBroom Tells the Truth***.) McBroom's tall tale this time around is the tale of a big wind (and *he* should know).... [His] wild wind spins up and away and over the prairies to bring laughs and giggles to all who are lucky enough to get in its way.

A review of "McBroom and the Big Wind," in Publishers Weekly, *Vol. 191, No. 21, May 22, 1967, p. 64.*

McBroom Tells the Truth was a challenge along the lines of Can You Top This? Sid Fleischman makes a good try at it himself, and if there were any readers of the first book who didn't boggle over the spectacular productivity of McBroom's super topsoil, try them on this new one with the prairie wind that blew a black bear into McBroom's back yard, McBroom's 11 children out the chimney, and McBroom himself across country.... [The text] should serve as excellent storytelling fodder for seven- and eight-year-olds, who can read it themselves.

Elinor Cullen, in a review of "McBroom and the Big Wind," in Library Journal, *Vol. 92, No. 12, June 15, 1967, p. 2444.*

McBROOM'S EAR (1969)

Sid Fleischman has scored again with his consistently humorous tall-tale technique. In this saga, McBroom and his family—already old friends to fun-loving children who've read ***McBroom Tells the Truth*** and ***McBroom and the Big Wind***—spend their time trying to outwit a plague of grasshoppers which threatens to devastate their incredibly fertile one-acre farm. Their efforts to save a gigantic, prize-winning ear of corn for entry in the county fair make a hilarious adventure.... The author's knowledge of what turns young readers on has made him a favorite of young library patrons who will welcome this new offering.

Pat Byars, in a review of "McBroom's Ear," in School Library Journal, *an appendix to* Library Journal, *Vol. 16, No. 6, February, 1970, p. 78.*

A third tall tale about the McBroom farm in Iowa, told with well-matched exaggeration in words and [Kurt Werth's] drawings. For those who delight in this gusty form of humor, the story offers a richness of comedy indigenous to hot corn-growing country in grasshopper season.

Virginia Haviland, in a review of "McBroom's Ear," in The Horn Book Magazine, *Vol. XLVI, No. 2, April, 1970, p. 157.*

Another blithe tall tale about the marvelous McBroom farm, where instantaneous growth from superfertile soil and blazing Iowa sun provide magnificent crops of food and stories.... Adults should enjoy reading the book aloud or using it for storytelling, and independent readers are already a captive audience.

Zena Sutherland, in a review of "McBroom's Ear," in Bulletin of the Center for Children's Books, *Vol. 23, No. 9, May, 1970, p. 143.*

LONGBEARD THE WIZARD (1970)

There's this boy-king Sandor who's supposed to be poor, but he can pluck coins from the air when he's playing the Wizard; and he plays the Wizard to combat being unhappy, which he shouldn't be since he administers a happy kingdom. Sandor/Longbeard can only work that magic when it suits the story, since when this other king's henchmen capture him he's at a loss. Nevertheless he does enrich his subjects soon by putting one over on this queen who talks too much.... And the next (and the last) thing you know he plucks crows from a hat, which hasn't any more to do with anything than anything else has.... Even nonsense is better than no sense; this is a synthetic composite of both.

A review of "Longbeard the Wizard," in Kirkus Reviews, *Vol. XXXVIII, No. 13, July 1, 1970, p. 677.*

Sid Fleischman, surely one of the wittiest writers of tall tales around today, has come up with a fairy tale that rings with laughter—a lusty tale of magic and poor young princes and rich, greedy kings and queens who never stop yapping.

A review of "Longbeard the Wizard," in Publishers Weekly, *Vol. 198, No. 11, September 14, 1970, p. 70.*

McBROOM THE RAINMAKER (1973)

McBroom is back with another tall tale—this time about how he broke the Big Drought. It seems the local mosquitoes (so large they were often mistaken for woodpeckers) hungrily attack anything red. Crafty McBroom devises a plan to grow a few gargantuan red onions ("larger 'n washtubs") which will attract the mosquitoes. When the insects have gathered in the field, McBroom shoots the onions full of buckshot which releases their pungent aroma, causing the mosquitoes to shed enough tears to irrigate his property. McBroom's folksy narrative makes this a delight to read aloud and the humorous and colorful illustrations [by Kurt Werth] of the McBroom clan will add to the enjoyment for independent readers. (pp. 96-7)

Alice Ehlert, in a review of "McBroom the Rainmaker," in School Library Journal, *an appendix to* Library Journal, *Vol. 20, No. 7, March, 1974, pp. 96-7.*

THE GHOST ON SATURDAY NIGHT (1974)

As Great Aunt Etta, Opie's guardian, has promised to buy him a horse with her 1877 bank-deposited penny as soon as he saves up enough for a saddle, Opie who can streak (his word) through town with his eyes closed goes into the fog business as a guide in order to earn the necessary $17.59. And earn it he does, though not as expected; he receives the saddle as a reward for catching a bank robber. For Opie, alerted when an itinerant, fraudulent ghost raiser pays him for an errand with Aunt Etta's rare penny—guides the culprit, who asks on a foggy Saturday night to be steered out of town, straight into the arms of the sheriff. Another successful Fleischman concoction of flimflam and smart footwork.

A review of "The Ghost on Saturday Night," in Kirkus Reviews, *Vol. XLII, No. 10, May 15, 1974, p. 535.*

Opie discovers that the bank has been robbed, and he triumphantly brings Professor Pepper and his cigar-smoking, toad-faced, creepy assistant almost literally into the arms of the law. The short scenario, illustrated [by Eric von Schmidt] with figures as overstated and caricatured as those in the text, is filled with the same kind of hyperbole, piquant phrasing, and bravura that have made the author's other books so delightful and so much fun to read.

Anita Silvey, in a review of "The Ghost on Saturday Night," in The Horn Book Magazine, *Vol. L, No. 4, August, 1974, p. 379.*

A blithe and tallish tale is set in a west coast town at some time in the past. . . . The style is admirable: light, breezy, convincingly that of a child of ten; the author deftly puts into a quite short story just the right balance of action, humor, and quick characterization.

Zena Sutherland, in a review of "The Ghost on Saturday Night," in Bulletin of the Center for Children's Books, *Vol. 28, No. 4, December, 1974, p. 61.*

MR. MYSTERIOUS'S SECRETS OF MAGIC (1975)

Mr. Mysterious, the hero of Fleischman's novel ***Mr. Mysterious and Company,*** presents 21 miscellaneous easy tricks that will reward both audience and performer. Instructions for card, mind-reading, and disappearing-object tricks are clear. . . . General tips on doing magic tricks run throughout the text. An enjoyable, unintimidating introduction or additional resource.

A review of "Mr. Mysterious's Secrets of Magic," in The Booklist, *Vol. 72, No. 1, September 1, 1975, p. 39.*

It was probably inevitable that the celebrated Mr. Mysterious would one day share some of his magic tricks with his young admirers. And to those who know the well-loved story of which he is the ingenious hero, it was also inevitable that the descriptions of his tricks would be clear and good-humored. Twenty-one sleight-of-hand procedures are helpfully presented under such attractive titles as **"Frankenstein's Toothache," "The Witch's Foot,"** and **"The Invisible Man's Money."** [Eric von Schmidt's] offhand, free-and-easy sketches add their own light-heartedness, and explicit diagrams by the wizard himself elucidate the text.

Ethel L. Heins, in a review of "Mr. Mysterious's Secrets of Magic," in The Horn Book Magazine, *Vol. LI, No. 5, October, 1975, p. 477.*

Twenty-one illusions for beginning magicians. The tricks are so deceptive and yet simple to perform that illusionists may end up fooling themselves. The diagrams clarify the methods and the patter that Fleischman suggests enables kids to cover up the occasional slip-up. . . . Although some of the tricks are presented in other books on the subject (notably Bill Severn's numerous works), the fresh format and easy instructions make this the best choice for youngsters.

Everett C. Sanborn, in a review of "Mr. Mysterious's Secrets of Magic," in School Library Journal, *Vol. 22, No. 3, November, 1975, p. 77.*

McBROOM TELLS A LIE (1976)

A conveyance that runs on popcorn power and frozen sunlight, tomatoes that grow overnight, jumping-bean-eating chickens whose eggs flip over when fried, and hens that glow in the dark from consuming too many lightning bugs? Add to these ingredients a tricky Heck Jones, who plots to steal the McBroom one-acre farm, and an ingenious counterplot devised by the McBrooms and their eleven children—Will*jill*hester*chester*peter*polly*tim*tom*mary*larry*andlittle*clarinda*—and the resulting tall tale will keep children chuckling to the end. The lie? Well, McBroom does admit to exaggerating about Princess Prunella the cow—she didn't freeze to death in the popcorn; she only caught a very bad cold! Fleischman uses an easy down-home style that is just right for this spoof. . . . A fun way to introduce a tall-tale unit.

Barbara Elleman, in a review of "McBroom Tells a Lie," in Booklist, *Vol. 73, No. 2, September 15, 1976, p. 174.*

In ***McBroom Tells A Lie,*** McBroom is a verbose farmer who disregards hard-core fact the way kids disregard carrots. Some of the tales he tells are so tall you have to stand on a ladder to finish the book. And be careful—if you let too much jiggly laughter inside the pages of the book, the covers won't close when you're finished.

All in all, Sid Fleischman may have one of the best book ideas since my uncle Fred put out an edible cook book. . . .

Guernsey LePelley, "Where Have All the Trolls and Ogres Gone?" in The Christian Science Monitor, *November 3, 1976, p. 26.*

HERE COMES McBROOM (1976)

Children may find . . . difficulty with ***Here Comes McBroom!*** . . . , three short stories of a very shaggy dog nature which are a sequel to a previous collection, ***McBroom's Wonderful One-Acre Farm.*** The problem is the American vocabulary, very much of the "Tarnation! Goldarnit! Those pesky critturs!" variety, which may seem too foreign to some English readers, though the tall story humour is universal. **"McBroom the Rainmaker"**, the second tale, has a neat topicality, being concerned with a drought so severe that a cow will only give powdered milk and even the leather of shoes shrinks through lack of moisture. McBroom's answer is to grow onions so gigantic that the tears produced by the eyes of mosquitoes near by are sufficient to water the soil. Water Boards, please take note.

David Rees, "Wits of the Wild West," in The Times Literary Supplement, *No. 3890, October 1, 1976, p. 1239.*

The charming and delightfully zany activities of McBroom are illustrated by Quentin Blake whose scrabbly off-beat style just matches the writing. The two combine to make a delicious confection of tomfoolery. (p. 326)

D. A. Young, in a review of "Here Comes McBroom!" in The Junior Bookshelf, *Vol. 40, No. 6, December, 1976, pp. 325-26.*

If, like me, you had missed the earlier stories of Josh McBroom's wonderful one-acre farm, now is the time to remedy the omission. McBroom's farm is so 'amazing rich' that he can plant and harvest two/three crops a day—but his main output is tall tales, big windies, whizzers and whoppers. . . .

I can only endorse what others said about the earlier book. Here is zany ingenuity and full-blown humour packed onto the page. . . .

C. E. J. Smith, in a review of "Here Comes McBroom!" in The School Librarian, *Vol. 25, No. 1, March, 1977, p. 40.*

ME AND THE MAN ON THE MOON-EYED HORSE (1977; British edition as *The Man on the Moon-Eyed Horse*)

The master of the tall tale offers a non-stop, mirthful adventure—just the thing to chase anyone's blues. . . . Clint is a boy who lives with his Gramps, railroad telegrapher, and his sister, Elvira, in Furnace Flats, Arizona. The town is so dull that betting on the way tumbleweeds will blow is the chief entertainment. Then Gramps gets the warning that Step-and-a-Half Jackson, so called because he's always a step and a half ahead of the law, is threatening to wreck the circus train. The desperado shows up on his moon-eyed horse and gets the drop on Gramps, Clint and Elvira. Just when all seems lost, Clint outwits Jackson. The plot is a dilly, enchanced by the author's marvelous way with words.

A review of "Me and the Man on the Moon-Eyed Horse," in Publishers Weekly, *Vol. 211, No. 20, May 16, 1977, p. 63.*

When it comes to telling whopping tall tales, no one can match Sid Fleischman. . . . There's a cleverly engineered and *very* funny slap-stick finale; some inspired nutty touches (notably Gramp's ability to click out Morse Code with his false teeth); and several dithery drawings [by Eric von Schmidt] that gamely keep up with the breakneck pace of Fleischman's comedy.

Jane O'Connor, in a review of "Me and the Man on the Moon-Eyed Horse," in The New York Times Book Review, *September 11, 1977, p. 32.*

Humorous tales for children are always difficult to find and stories from America do not always make the Atlantic crossing successfully. ***The man on the moon-eyed horse*** falls into both categories, tries hard and almost succeeds. Like most books in dialect it will succeed better if read aloud. . . . The story is told in a rollicking style, full of Americanisms, 'tumbleweed', for example, which could detract from the pace of the story if they have to be explained. A useful book for the less able reader of ten to fourteen and a good story to read aloud to seven to tens.

Janet Fisher, in a review of "The Man on the Moon-Eyed Horse," in The School Librarian, *Vol. 29, No. 2, June, 1981, p. 132.*

McBROOM AND THE BEANSTALK (1977)

McBroom enter the World Champion Liar's Contest at the county fair? "Never and no sir!" he claims. "Why, hair'll grow on fish before I trifle with the truth." But a bean seed, planted by the McBroom children to lure down the giant who they're convinced is responsible for the huge footprint in the yard, sprouts the next day. The "rambunctious" vine grows and grows and heads straight for town, where it charges through a barber shop, slithers up the hotel, and rams through the bank, collecting two strangers and dumping them into jail. Fearful of what it might do next, McBroom races to the fair grounds and breathlessly tells his tale. The judges are unbelieving but impressed, and they award McBroom top prize. The surprise, however, is on them—and on McBroom's rival, Heck Jones, who started the whole thing. Fleischman overlays his tongue-in-cheek story with ridiculous nonsense that is giggle-inducing from beginning to end.

Barbara Elleman, in a review of "McBroom and the Beanstalk," in Booklist, *Vol. 74, No. 18, May 15, 1978, p. 1492.*

Fleischman's telling is surehanded, and the story is sure to produce sidesplitting laughter in middle-graders who, we all know, tickle easily. [Walter] Lorraine's illustrations reinforce the zaniness of the tale.

Ann Boes, in a review of "McBroom and the Beanstalk," in School Library Journal, *Vol. 25, No. 1, September, 1978, p. 108.*

HUMBUG MOUNTAIN (1978)

Dime novels are Wiley's oases of fantasy wherein he dreams of becoming a hero like Quickshot Billy Bodeen. Moving from place to place with his family at the turn of the century . . . , life begins to imitate art. Wiley finds himself in the midst of outlaws and con-men in what his grandfather has said is a prosperous city on the Missouri River but which turns out to be empty of any amenities—as well as of Grandpa who has disappeared leaving only a disheveled steamboat in the weeds. False rumors of gold and business and building boom abound and the rascals almost win—but Grandpa shows up just in time, bringing riches and rescue. A tall tale spun with ingenuity, with larger-than-life characters and improbabilities too much to be believed and not meant to be, this tomfoolery is fun. And the story, told through the boy's eyes, shows people growing and gaining strength during adversity and runs deeper than it at first appears.

Marjorie Lewis, in a review of "Humbug Mountain," in School Library Journal, *Vol. 25, No. 1, September, 1978, p. 136.*

Sid Fleischman's zest for frontier foolishment and humbug is at full steam in this story of an itinerant newspaperman's family. . . . A summary would be unfair as Fleischman's lively incidentals dovetail too neatly to be abstracted . . . Tarnatious fun all the way.

A review of "Humbug Mountain," in Kirkus Reviews, *Vol. XLVI, No. 19, October 1, 1978, p. 1071.*

The language is peppery and picturesque, the storytelling irresistibly paced, and the elaborate plot worked out with consummate precision. To the rich vein of American tall-tale frontier humor, the author has added his own mercurial, ever-ready wit in a book that appropriately crowns his earlier achievements.

Ethel L. Heins, in a review of "Humbug Mountain," in The Horn Book Magazine, *Vol. LIV, No. 6, December, 1978, p. 640.*

As one would expect from Sid Fleischman's other books, the tone of this one is partly satirical, with its assemblage of such stock Western stage-properties as gold dust and card-sharpers, with a ghost-town background and plenty of old-timer idiom. This is not entirely parody, though, for the bizarre sequence of events is slanted in one direction, towards the fears, the bewilderment and the tenacity of a boy of twelve or so. . . . The humour and slapstick action of the story (the revelation of the author of the Quickshot comics not the least of its surprises) are balanced by the sober portrayal of the boy's feelings.

Margery Fisher, in a review of "Humbug Mountain," in Growing Point, *Vol. 19, No. 6, March, 1981, p. 3834.*

It is rare to find hilarity and ingenuity so happily combined as in Sid Fleischman's tale of a family's adventures in a 'wild' West setting, a sort of Swiss Family Robinson marooned beyond Cripple Creek. If Bret Harte, writing for children, had chosen to lighten his irony and limit his pathos, he might well have produced something similar. The tale abounds in characters, some wild, others just woolly (though not always as woolly as they seem). . . . The fun never loses touch with reality but there is no end to its possibilities. It is not surprising that the book won the Boston Globe/Horn Book Award.

A. R. Williams, in a review of "Humbug Mountain," in The Junior Bookshelf, *Vol. 45, No. 2, April, 1981, p. 79.*

JIM BRIDGER'S ALARM CLOCK AND OTHER TALL TALES (1978)

Fleischman is among the few bona fide humorists who write for young readers and they're sure to make his new book warmly welcome. . . . ***Jim Bridger's Alarm Clock*** is the tale of a mountain man so tall it takes six minutes for him to feel the "ouch" when he stubs his toe. But he's not famous for height or other impossible deeds. What makes his name a legend is that he saved his life in a blizzard by making a distant mountain his alarm clock. Before nestling into his bedroll, Jim bellows at the mountain and sleeps until the echo rouses him—eight hours later. Two more tales so tall they're almost out of sight make a total of three infectious amusements.

A review of "Jim Bridger's Alarm Clock and Other Tall Tales," in Publishers Weekly, *Vol. 214, No. 25, December 25, 1978, p. 60.*

Three short, related tall tales told as straight adventure stories. . . . Funny stories are always needed, and this one has really subtle humor. Older readers looking for a short book will also enjoy these episodes.

Annette C. Blank, in a review of "Jim Bridger's Alarm Clock and Other Tall Tales," in Children's Book Review Service, *Vol. 7, No. 7, February, 1979, p. 64.*

The American tall-tale has seldom been rendered . . . as effectively as it is in these marvelously funny tales of the legendary mountain man, Jim Bridger. Three tales, each distinct, yet all linked by a common motif—the amazing flat-topped mountain Jim discovered in his wanderings—reveal Fleischman's humor at its best, outrageous exaggeration delivered in a cool, laconic style. . . . This is a treat for any audience.

Stephen Roxburgh, in a review of "Jim Bridger's Alarm Clock and Other Tall Tales," in School Library Journal, *Vol. 25, No. 8, April, 1979, p. 55.*

THE HEY HEY MAN (1979)

A prankish tree spirit, *The Hey Hey Man,* outwits a thief who steals the farmer's gold. The Hey Hey Man turns the robber's nose into a horseradish root, his ears into cabbage leaves, and causes all sorts of trouble until the rascal finally gives up in disgust. Again Fleischman has written a humorous and colorful tale, full of mischief, that children will enjoy reading as well as telling. . . . Children who have read other books by Fleischman will not want to miss this one. (pp. 135-36)

Blair Christolon, in a review of "The Hey Hey Man," in School Library Journal, *Vol. 26, No. 1, September, 1979, pp. 135-36.*

As in the marvelous chronicles of the McBroom family, the style and rhythm of American tall tales dominate the story. . . . [The Hey Hey Man] becomes a distinctive personality in the hilarious comedy as he uses his magical powers to help the farmer. . . . Artfully composed, the tale would be a natural vehicle for storytellers.

Mary M. Burns, in a review of "The Hey Hey Man," in The Horn Book Magazine, *Vol. LV, No. 5, October, 1979, p. 527.*

Sid Fleischman can put more action into 32 pages than some authors of "explosive best sellers" can put into 75 turgid chapters. . . .

[The story has] a highly satisfactory ending. I can't say I was greatly taken with the [illustrations by Nadine Bernard Westcott], . . . but this defect is more than compensated by Mr. Fleischman's rightly colorful language and absurd inventiveness.

Georgess McHargue, in a review of "The Hey Hey Man," in The New York Times Book Review, *January 20, 1980, p. 30.*

McBROOM AND THE GREAT RACE (1980)

Fun seekers, here's Fleischman's most uproarious invention yet about the marvels yielded by the rich topsoil on the tiny acreage described in ***McBroom and the Beanstalk*** and its companions. . . . Again, miserly Heck Jones plots to grab McBroom's lush farm, especially after a chick hatched there grows to the size of a horse. Jones challenges the farmer to a footrace, with the McBroom land the stakes, and the nonsense—as well as the tensions—accelerates into a frenzied finale.

A review of "McBroom and the Great Race," in Publisher's Weekly, *Vol. 217, No. 16, April 25, 1980, p. 80.*

Although the tall-tale exaggerations and far-fetched situations may seem familiar, the latest of McBroom's escapades is longer than its predecessors and benefits from a stronger plot. Smoothly told in the author's inimitable style. . . .

Kate M. Flanagan, in a review of "McBroom and the Great Race," in The Horn Book Magazine, *Vol. LVI, No. 4, August, 1980, p. 405.*

I read half of ***McBroom and the Great Race*** and put it aside—a non-starter. I tried again. Children, if necessary, must try again. This is a book I recommend urgently for all junior libraries (and senior ones too, why not?). It is a book full of fast-moving, jerky, irrepressible humour, a book of incident and detail and joke, in which the language will be enjoyed by many for its own sake. . . .

Banana skin and sophistication all in one.

Will Harris, "Rolling in the Aisles," in The Times Educational Supplement, *No. 3422, January 29, 1982, p. 30.*

THE BLOODHOUND GANG IN THE CASE OF THE CACKLING GHOST; THE BLOODHOUND GANG IN THE CASE OF PRINCESS TOMORROW **(1981)**

[***The Case of the Cackling Ghost***] is the first of the Bloodhound Gang Books, an easy-to-read mystery based on the "3-2-1 Contact" TV show. The detective trio—Vikki, Ricardo and Zach—go to the stately residence of wealthy Mrs. Fairbanks, a widow of 70 confined to a wheelchair. She assigns the Bloodhound Gang to solve the mystery of the cackling ghost, an apparition she beholds in her garden nightly and hears via her stereo. Mrs. Fairbanks's nephew Edmund pooh-poohs the ghost story, but the lady believes the spirit is connected somehow to the curse on her fabulous Darjeeling necklace. . . . Fleischman's mystery is as easy to read as claimed, but just as easy to solve and regrettably lacking in the humor that usually salts his stories.

A review of "The Case of the Cackling Ghost," in Publishers Weekly, *Vol. 219, No. 9, February 27, 1981, p. 150.*

Based on a series created by the author for the Children's Television Workshop, [***The Bloodhound Gang in the Case of Princess Tomorrow***] is a not very convincing detective story that has some superficial but colorful characters and a good bit of action, as one might expect in a book adapted from a visual medium. What it lacks, in addition to credibility, is the robust flavor of Fleischman's usual writing style. The three detectives are Vikki (sixteen), who has been employed by the Bloodhound Detective Agency for three years, Ricardo (fifteen), and Zach (ten) and they solve the puzzle of the medium Princess Tomorrow's ability to forecast race results by a combination of Vikki's acumen and Zach's dog whistle.

Zena Sutherland, in a review of "The Bloodhound Gang in the Case of Princess Tomorrow," in Bulletin of the Center for Children's Books, *Vol. 34, No. 8, April, 1981, p. 150.*

These spin-offs [***The Bloodhound Gang in the Case of the Cackling Ghost*** and ***The Bloodhound Gang in the Case of Princess Tomorrow***] from a Children's Television Workshop series have the advantage of being written by the creator of the TV script. As a result there is some substance to them, and the writing, while undistinguished, isn't hackneyed either. In each, a neatly worked out plot is based on simple, believable gimmicks. . . .

Judith Goldberger, in a review of "The Bloodhound Gang in the Case of the Cackling Ghost," and "The Bloodhound Gang in the Case of Princess Tomorrow," in Booklist, *Vol. 77, No. 16, April 15, 1981, p. 1159.*

THE BLOODHOUND GANG IN THE CASE OF THE FLYING CLOCK; THE BLOODHOUND GANG IN THE CASE OF THE SECRET MESSAGE **(1981)**

These latest adventures of the Bloodhound Gang . . . have a little more zip than the dismally perfunctory first two [***The Bloodhound Gang in the Case of the Cackling Ghost*** and ***The Bloodhound Gang in the Case of Princess Tomorrow***], but there is still little evidence of the Fleischman wit, inventiveness, and high spirits. And of course the idea of three kids investigating for an insurance company is too far-fetched for any nine-year-old's reality meter. But that's the situation in ***The Case of the Flying Clock,*** when Vikki, Ricardo, and Zach check out the theft of a snobbish horologist's flying pendulum clock. "Once belonged to Louis," says pompous Mr. Keefe—Louis XVI, that is. But because they know that steam will fog a mirror and salty water makes objects more buoyant, the Gang deduces that Mr. Keefe did not see a red-haired robber, as he claimed, but instead dumped his plastic-wrapped clock in his wishing-well pending future removal. ***The Case of the Secret Message*** brings the Bloodhounds up against a purse snatcher, a smuggler called Mr. Big, his bodyguard Muscles, and a little old lady who seems first a victim, then a cohort, and at last reveals herself as a young policewoman. Perhaps the point of the series is that the TV tie-in will lead habitual viewers to print. In any case, these belong with the merchandise mysteries. (pp. 1235-36)

A review of "The Case of the Flying Clock" and "The Case of the Secret Message," in Kirkus Reviews, *Vol. XLIX, No. 19, October 1, 1981, pp. 1235-36.*

Sid Fleischman's new additions to his Bloodhound Gang series are an improvement over his previous two. . . . Reluctant readers will be attracted to the large print, short chapters and simple style, although the plots are still contrived.

A review of "The Case of the Secret Message" and "The Case of the Flying Clock," in School Library Journal, *Vol. 28, No. 4, December, 1981, p. 81.*

Fleischman adds two more workable mysteries to his series as he continues to give poor readers a mild challenge to their problem-solving skills without overtaxing their decoding abilities. . . . The stories are more or less plausible, if thin, and are kept simple.

Judith Goldberger, in a review of "The Bloodhound Gang in the Case of the Flying Clock" and "The Bloodhound Gang in the Case of the Secret Message," in Booklist, *Vol. 78, No. 8, December 15, 1981, p. 553.*

THE BLOODHOUND GANG IN THE CASE OF THE 264-POUND BURGLAR **(1982)**

[Vikki, Ricardo and Zach] return for their fifth print appearance in ***The Case of the 264-Pound Burglar.*** The Bloodhounds are investigating the theft of an old woman's life savings, hidden in her attic. The only clue is a card from a weight machine (reading 264 pounds) on the floor of the attic. The gang proves that the woman's thin twin nephews weighed themselves together and left the card to confuse the authorities. With its large print, short chapters and fast action, the book will make good reluctant reader bait. But this slim paperback reads like a television segment in book form. (pp. 83-4)

A review of "The Case of the 264-Pound Burglar," in School Library Journal, *Vol. 28, No. 9, May, 1982, pp. 83-4.*

As before, in the series based on a Children's Television Workshop program, Fleischman offers a fast-reading, simply plotted mystery—a good combination for slow or reluctant readers. The story is spare, with dialogue as the prime ingredient, and, while personae are neither developed nor portrayed as credible people, the roles in the mystery and its solution are played out in character. Sentences tend to be lengthy, but vocabulary is accessible.

Judith Goldberger, in a review of "The Bloodhound Gang in the Case of the 264-Pound Burglar," in Booklist, *Vol. 78, No. 20, June 15, 1982, p. 1371.*

There's a heavy dose of coincidence in the way the children solve the problem: the text is breezy in style, weak in characterization and dialogue. Lots of action, the element of mystery, and the solution of a problem by young people may appeal to readers, but the adaptation from television to print has produced a mediocre book.

Zena Sutherland, in a review of "The Case of the 264-Pound Burglar, in Bulletin of the Center for Children's Books, *Vol. 36, No. 2, October, 1982, p. 25.*

***McBROOM'S ALMANAC* (1984)**

A hilarious compendium of tall tales, useful information, homespun advice, notes on natural history, and handy tips for the farmer. Starting with "McBroom's Calendar of Important Dates," the book is divided into twelve months, each of which has a motto, a McBroom story, and all the various bits and pieces expected in an almanac. For example: "McProverb—He who leaves no stone unturned will have a sore back." One of the best McBroom stories tells the tale of how a corkscrew carrot was used to dig a well, which went so deep that it took a tornado to get the carrot out. Extending the fun and humor are an abundance of lively, comical line drawings [by Walter Lorraine] . . . , which exactly match the exuberance of the stories. (pp. 465-66)

Ann A. Flowers, in a review of "McBroom's Almanac," in The Horn Book Magazine, *Vol. LX, No. 4, August, 1984, pp. 465-66.*

Sid Fleischman has done it again! . . . A good introduction to longer McBroom stories and fun for browsers as well, ***McBroom's Almanac*** will be appreciated by older children for its humorous use of the almanac form, while other children will simply enjoy Fleischman's riproarious humor.

Louise L. Sherman, in a review of "McBroom's Almanac," in School Library Journal, *Vol. 31, No. 1, September, 1984, p. 116.*

[A] compendium of pseudo-advice and humor that is often hilarious. As in other McBroom books, there are tales that depend, in tall-tale style, on exaggeration for their humor; there is word-play ("Freeze & thaw & sunshine fickle—Mercury rides a Pogo stickle" is the October motto) and there are ridiculous farming tips, proverbs ("Birds of a feather that flock together make a good target") and assorted bits of nonsensical nature hints and household lore. It's all great fun, and the fact that there are many short bits indicate a potential usefulness for slow or reluctant readers who will find the humor as appealing as do their more proficient peers.

Zena Sutherland, in a review of "McBroom's Almanac," in Bulletin of the Center for Children's Books, *Vol. 38, No. 3, November, 1984, p. 44.*

***THE WHIPPING BOY* (1986)**

A fabricator of tall tales about McBroom and his wonderful farm, and of zesty early frontier extravaganzas . . . , Fleischman now tries his hand at a story that has all the trappings of a fairy tale. Jemmy, an orphan plucked from the streets, is the designated whipping boy for all the bad things that spoiled Prince Brat does, such as refusing to learn to read and write and removing the wigs from the assembled court nobles. When Prince Brat decides to run away because he is bored, he takes Jemmy with him, but the boys' roles are reversed when they encounter the villains Cut-Water and Hold-Your-Nose-Billy. After a climactic pursuit through a rat-infested city sewers, the boys escape, and it is a chastened prince who escorts his former whipping boy back to the castle. There is no indication of locale, but the tale . . . has a Dickensian flavor. There's plenty of fast action for the adventure lover, and although no magic is used, readers will find the happy ending eminently satisfying.

Mary Lathrope, in a review of "The Whipping Boy," in Booklist, *Vol. 82, No. 13, March 1, 1986, p. 1018.*

A rollicking tale of adventure and mistaken identity, written in a style reminiscent of 19th-century melodrama. . . .

Short chapters and a rapid pace make this slight tale easy to read, despite an occasionally complex style. Language is well-chosen and the robust scenes and characters are vividly, if sketchily, evoked. . . . Thin at times, this comic adventure story does offer readers a nice change of pace.

A review of "The Whipping Boy," in Kirkus Reviews, *Vol. LIV, No. 9, May 1, 1986, p. 715.*

Forsaking the American tall-tale humor and the elaborate plotting of his other novels, the author has written another kind of broadly comic tale and characteristically seasoned it with trickery, villainy, and hairsbreadth escapes. In the manner of Joan Aiken and Lloyd Alexander, he sets the story in an undefined time and place. . . . Sid Fleischman once remarked that his books are improvisations, and the new story rings changes on the theme of *The Prince and the Pauper*. It is populated with some time-honored stock characters of low comedy and peppered with nimble-witted repartee; but like much of the author's writing, beneath the surface entertainment the story also speaks of courage, friendship, and trust. (pp. 325-26)

Ethel L. Heins, in a review of "The Whipping Boy," in The Horn Book Magazine, *Vol. LXII, No. 3, May-June, 1986, pp. 325-26.*

This comic adventure is old in the manner of the earlier time in which it is set, complete with chapter titles like "Of assorted events in which the plot thickens thicker." Besides its lively entertainment value and stylistic polish, the story has much to say about human nature and the vagaries of justice. Short chapters, a strong beginning, and humorous dialogue add audience appeal.

Janet Hickman, in a review of "The Whipping Boy," in Language Arts, *Vol. 63, No. 8, December, 1986, p. 822.*

[***The Whipping Boy***] is full of adventure, suspense, humor and lively characters. . . .

This is indisputably a good, rollicking adventure, but in its characterizations ***The Whipping Boy*** offers something special. Jemmy learns to sympathize with the Prince's isolation, boredom and constricted life. He learns to admire his courage in facing dangers, including a frightening chase through a rat-filled sewer. In a memorable turnabout Horace takes a whipping for Jemmy, the presumed Prince, without a whimper. The street-smart lad discovers in his life at the palace an appetite for knowledge. And, in his journey with Horace, he tastes a friendship based on more than struggle and deprivation.

Horace, on the other hand, arrives at an altered sense of his own life after living it without protective batting for a while. Once he experiences his own strength, he can admire Jemmy's without seeing it as a taunt. When he discovers that the people in his kingdom refer to him as Prince Brat and fear the day when he will become king, he has traveled far enough on his own to admit both the pain and the justice of the appellation. He is able to do so because he has grown strong enough to change.

Martha Saxton, in a review of "The Whipping Boy," in The New York Times Book Review, *February 22, 1987, p. 23.*

Based on the fairy tale traditions of good overcoming evil, a child learning his lesson before it is too late, and the poor being rescued from poverty because of good deeds, this delightful book will entrance the most reluctant child. . . .

Sid Fleischman and the Newbery committee have offered us a value-packed selection in easy-access guise. Hilariously funny, ***The Whipping Boy*** will catch and hold even the most reluctant reader. . . . And the subtle lessons within the story will not be lost on children of all ages or abilities. The importance of education, the true meaning of friendship, and the need for understanding and compassion for all people in all walks of life are enclosed within the covers of this book—but not so obviously that children will find them offensive. Rather, they are such an integral part of the story that there would be no story without them.

Frances Bradburn, in a review of "The Whipping Boy," in Wilson Library Bulletin, *Vol. 61, No. 8, April, 1987, p. 48.*

Jaap ter Haar

1922-

Dutch author of fiction, nonfiction, and picture books; reteller; playwright; and scriptwriter.

An internationally acclaimed author, ter Haar is recognized for creating gripping stories characterized by their vivid writing, absorbing plots, meaningful themes, and moralism. He gained worldwide attention with *Boris* (1966), a work of historical fiction for middle graders noted for its emotional power, suspense, and message of benevolence towards enemies. Set in Leningrad during World War II, the book centers on a starving Russian youth who is captured and befriended by the Germans. Ter Haar's English-language fiction for adolescents includes a retelling of the King Arthur legend and the well-received novel *Het wereldje van Beer Ligthart* (1973; *The World of Ben Lighthart*), which depicts a teenage boy who adjusts to his recent blindness by accepting an altered lifestyle. In addition to *De geschiedenis van Noord-Amerika* (1959; *The Story of America*), a narrative history of the United States and ter Haar's only nonfiction work translated into English, he has written extensive historical coverage on such topics as the French Revolution, the Dutch Red Cross, Russia, and the Benelux countries. A prolific writer for younger children as well as older ones, ter Haar began producing picture books in the early 1950s. He based his first picture book on his twins, who were also the featured characters in one of ter Haar's radio plays. Since then, he has created several series of picture books which total over forty titles, of which three have been published in English.

Highly regarded in Europe, ter Haar receives mixed reviews from English-speaking critics. While pointing out his tendency to be didactic, sentimental, and too consciously literary, most reviewers commend ter Haar for the compassion, vigor, and factual accuracy of his writings.

Ter Haar has won many European awards for his books, including the Bijenkorf Award in 1961 for his total body of work and the Het Kinderboek van het Jaar Award in 1974 for *The World of Ben Lighthart*.

(See also *Something about the Author*, Vol. 6 and *Contemporary Authors*, Vols. 37-40, rev. ed.)

NOODWEER OP DE WEISSHORN [*DANGER ON THE MOUNTAIN*] **(1957)**

It is hard to look at this as a "juvenile"; actually it belongs in the young adult bracket, since the characters are all adults, chiefly young men and mature men, qualified guides in the Zermatt area. It is an exciting story of a guide who was involved—through no fault of his own—in a disaster on the Matterhorn and who had lost his nerve. And of the challenge that restored his self respect and confidence. Good mountaineering details—written with assurance of practical knowledge. A boys' best seller in Holland.

A review of "Danger on the Mountain," in Virginia Kirkus' Service, *Vol. XXVIII, No. 15, August 1, 1960, p. 628.*

Photograph by Ronald Hoeben

ERNSTJAN EN SNABBELTJE [*DUCK DUTCH*] **(1958)**

"Quack-quack" in Duck Dutch can mean many things as little Ernst Jan learns when he becomes the owner of a duckling with quaint manners and winsome spirit. The manners become apparent on a public bus when Snapper escapes to the luggage rack and proceeds to perform anti-social acts on an innocent lady, much to the hilarity of Ernst Jan's seat companion. The special spirit comes through when Snapper makes a deliberate choice between a group of pond ducks and his scolding, lovable master. No fragile duckling this! Snapper survives the interior of a garbage truck and a thunderstorm, though he is not foolhardy enough to retrieve Ernst Jan's shoes from the plank carrying them off to sea. A set of amusing stories suitable for family sharing or independent entertainment.

A review of "Duck Dutch," in Virginia Kirkus' Service, *Vol. XXX, No. 9, May 1, 1962, p. 424.*

DE GESCHIEDENIS VAN NOORD-AMERICA [*THE STORY OF AMERICA*] **(1959)**

This should more accurately have been entitled *The Story of the U.S.A.* It is a narrative history written in a curiously episodic, even anecdotal, style. After every few paragraphs of narrative is inset a passage in italics describing an incident in the life of a person of the time. Some of these cameos are undoubtedly based on real events; others seem to have come from the author's imagination, and in some cases it is not clear which is which. Even what is evidently intended as straightforward narrative is not always free from anecdote, and the style is emotional. The basic facts of American history appear, however, to be accurate and clearly arranged. It may be that some children will benefit from the unusual approach, for there is no doubt that it evokes a feeling of almost personal involvement.

A review of "The Story of America," in The Junior Bookshelf, *Vol. 31, No. 4, August, 1967, p. 263.*

***BORIS* (1966)**

[***Boris*** is set] in the city—Leningrad in 1942, besieged by German troops, racked with disease and weakened by starvation. Boris is only twelve but since his father's death he has assumed responsibility for his sick mother, and would like to do the same for his friend Nadia; but when the two children make a perilous journey to the front lines in search of buried potatoes it is a German patrol that rescues them from the snow and takes them safely back to the city. This piece of human kindness, and Nadia's death of malnutrition, turn Boris's thoughts towards international understanding; the moral is enforced by quotations from the girl's diary which too obviously echo Anne Frank—the reader could have been trusted to see the point, and feel the poignancy, without this. The story exists for its message, however, and has been planned to this end. (pp. 1442-43)

Margery Fisher, in a review of "Boris," in Growing Point, *Vol. 8, No. 6, December, 1969, pp. 1442-43.*

This is a moving book with all the issues filed down to the essential problem of what is necessary for survival. . . . The writing is straightforward, almost naive, but never sentimental, which speaks well for the translation [by Martha Mearns].

"Growing Up in Wartime," in The Times Literary Supplement, *No. 3536, December 4, 1969, p. 1385.*

Perilous as it was, the London blitz comes nowhere near the siege of Leningrad in the scale of human suffering. So perhaps it's natural that Jaap ter Haar's novel of Leningrad, ***Boris,*** is higher-keyed and much more strained than *Fireweed* [by Jill Paton Walsh]. . . . There are haunting accounts of a search for a clump of potatoes buried in no-man's-land; of a children's theatre show where the one thought in every child's mind is whether there will be food to follow. The theme is survival, the suspense is harrowing, and the relief of the city is a relief to the reader's nerves.

But Boris is just a little too good to be true; and the high-mindedness, the awareness of heroism, the message of war's futility and the need to forgive, come across a little too strongly. Now and then one has a sense of celestial music in the background. This doesn't seem to me to be a good novel, but it does have value, does stretch the imagination, and perhaps is best seen as a moving piece of fictionalised documentary.

John Rowe Townsend, "Growing Up," in Punch, *Vol. 257, December 17, 1969, p. 1016.*

The Dutch author of this book wrote it after a visit to Leningrad where he saw the mass graves of the victims of the siege. So deeply did he feel that this must never happen again that he wrote this testimony to the people of Leningrad.

The book is deeply moving and beautifully written. It is too sombre for the average child today, for Nadia and Boris are so overwhelmed by their situation that they do not react as normal children, and the reader will have difficulty in associating himself with them. In spite of this the more sensitive reader will see that it is circumstances which have made Boris too adult and his understanding too deep for their comprehension. (p. 109)

A review of "Boris," in The Junior Bookshelf, *Vol. 34, No. 2, April, 1970, pp. 108-09.*

From disturbing dust jacket to hopeful conclusion this translation [***Boris***] . . . held my interest and emotion. . . . The horrors of hate and starvation and the imminence of death are communicated, but so too are the strengths of character of unheroic people that enable them to survive with dignity. For boys this book might be what *Anne Frank* has been to many girls. It should certainly be offered to boys from eleven or twelve onwards. ***Boris*** is an outstanding book. (pp. 215-16)

David Churchill, in a review of "Boris," in The School Librarian, *Vol. 18, No. 2, June, 1970, pp. 215-16.*

This brief, intensely compassionate novella . . . is more than a realistic children's book—it is a beautifully realized parable of war, death, kindness, and endurance. . . . Boris lives to realize the essential humanity of all peoples, and his beloved Leningrad survives as a remarkable memorial to the persistence and nobility of the human spirit. Simply written, well translated from the Dutch original, and enormously effective.

Rosemary Neiswender, in a review of "Boris," in School Library Journal, *an appendix to* Library Journal, *Vol. 17, No. 5, January, 1971, p. 63.*

***KONING ARTHUR* [*KING ARTHUR*] (1967)**

The Arthurian story can stand retelling: this version relies for its success on the recurring impetus of action rather than on subtle characterisation. Swords are frequently out; intrigue festers into bloodshed as Modred plays Iago to Arthur's Othello; Lancelot's agonising dilemma resolves itself in a daring snatch as Guinevere faces trial by ordeal; Arthur's consciousness of the fidelity and treachery that surround him heralds the final great battle and his own death.

The historical truth about Arthur is blurred by centuries of legend but the excitement of his adventures and the validity of his ideals still speak to the young of 1974 through the pages of this adroitly fashioned narrative.

G. Bott, in a review of "King Arthur," in The Junior Bookshelf, *Vol. 38, No. 2, April, 1974, p. 113.*

A self-conscious treatment of the life of King Arthur, with all the symbolism on the surface and explained to death. . . . The author does pare away the late medieval varnish, giving readers a late Roman Arthur, with only a few touches of chivalry thrown in. However, the story is already familiar from Malory and dozens of retellings, films, etc. and this version is burdened with some tiresome literary trappings.

Donald K. Fry, in a review of "King Arthur," in School Library Journal, *Vol. 24, No. 1, September, 1977, p. 144.*

From the opening sentence, the reader knows this has to be a new version of the ancient legend, and it is. . . . [The] book eschews all of the chivalric trappings and language usually associated with King Arthur and his Knights of the Round Table. Here, he is a man of his time. . . . Absent are Morgan Le Faye, Guinevere and Lancelot's love affair, and other well-known segments of the saga. Strong characterizations, vivid descriptions, and a sense of immediacy make this an earthy historical novel, rather than the legendary romance it has tended to be. Told from Merlin's viewpoint on two different levels, the book should draw readers back to the "classics," at least to the Arthurian epics. (p. 215)

Ruth M. Stein, in a review of "King Arthur," in Language Arts, *Vol. 55, No. 2, February, 1978, pp. 214-15.*

The three novels to be discussed, J. T. Haar's ***King Arthur,*** Victor Cunning's *The Crimson Chalice,* and Vera Chapman's *The Green Knight,* reflect three contemporary interests—the historical, the mystical, and . . . romantic idealisation. . . . The least successful of the three is ***King Arthur***. . . . Like Henry Treece in *The Eagles Have Flown* and Rosemary Sutcliff in *Sword at Sunset,* Haar sets the action in that period of the Dark Ages with which the historical Arthur—if, indeed, he existed—must be associated. The story opens clumsily with an unnecessarily brutal description of a young murderer's death at the stake. Neither character nor event is linked to subsequent development but perhaps the scene is intended to characterise a Tennysonian "land of beasts" which Arthur will civilise. We are whisked quickly through the events of Arthur's life. . . . As one might expect in a realistic treatment, the marvels are rationalized; for example, Arthur succeeds in the sword test because Merlin has shown him how to give the sword a downward thrust that will release the secret steel catches holding it in the stone.

To avoid inflaming the sensibilities of youth (are Dutch teenagers more Puritanical than ours?), Haar has treated the Lancelot-Guenevere romance in a *Woman's Own* style that in terms of the medieval setting is extraordinarily silly. Mordred, traditionally the result of Arthur's incestuous liaison with his half-sister, here becomes Arthur's plausible, power-hungry brother-in-law, a change in relationship that works rather well. Arthur himself is a high-minded prig.

Aside from an infelicitous style, the chief weaknesses are two. The attempt to recreate the barbarous milieu of sixth-century Britain is marred by introducing the knights, jesters, and tournaments of the high middle ages six hundred years later. And the attempt to create credible characters is marred by a lack of psychological realism. The Haar version is faithful neither to medieval romance nor to modern concepts of reality. (pp. 3-4)

Muriel Whitaker, "Enduring Knights," in The World of Children's Books, *Vol. III, 1978, pp. 3-5.*

***LOTJE, DE KLEINE OLIFANT* [*JUDY AND THE BABY ELEPHANT*] (1972)**

Judy and the Baby Elephant, sequel to ***Judy at the Zoo,*** offers more anecdotes of a small girl whose father is a vet attached to a Dutch zoo. The arrival of the baby elephant is the high spot of a book in which Judy also helps to persuade an Alsatian bitch to adopt orphan lion cubs, watches an operation on a fish with an abscess and shrinks from the crocodile whose owner has at last found it too big for a town flat. A good deal of information about the behaviour and needs of zoo animals is conveyed through the artless questions of a child of six or so.

Margery Fisher, in a review of "Judy and the Baby Elephant," in Growing Point, *Vol. 9, No. 2, July, 1970, p. 1555.*

[Any] child who shares [Judy's] enthusiasm for animals should enjoy this collection of stories. . . . Excitements and emergencies abound and they are always satisfactorily resolved. The stories are necessarily simple, but appear to be factually correct.

"Themes for Under Nines: For Beginners and Listeners," in The Times Literary Supplement, *No. 3572, August 14, 1970, p. 909.*

So that Judy may exploit the opportunities provided by her zoo vet father for coming and going behind the zoo scene, the author makes her pre-school age but her conversation is unconvincingly precocious. Eight- to ten-year-olds may be able to forgive this for the sake of the rescue of the lost seals whose lives were saved by forcible feeding with 'a fine mixture of herrings, eggs, milk, liver' or the adoption by Bella, the Alsatian bitch, of four abandoned lion cubs.

Most children will reject the silliness of the account of the two gossiping ladies who failed to notice the elephant (out walking with a keeper and Judy) nudging against them. I found the chapter 'Trouble with Friends' unsatisfactory, too, but the young may be less critical of its mild gang quarrel though some will, I hope, find Judy's part in it unattractive.

Eleanor Phillips, in a review of "Judy and the Baby Elephant," in The School Librarian, *Vol. 18, No. 4, December, 1970, p. 488.*

***HET WERELDJE VAN BEER LIGTHART* [*THE WORLD OF BEN LIGHTHART*] (1973)**

Ben wakes in a hospital bed to find he has suddenly lost his sight. By struggling with himself, he learns not only the skills needed for survival, but also to "see" people without being distracted by appearance; the reader is to believe that seeing may be viewed as a handicap since it distracts one from the true nature of things. Such lofty sentiments may be beyond young adolescents. The book is also maudlin and preachy; characters, regardless of their station speak in the same polite, stuffy tones.

Marilyn Darch, in a review of "The World of Ben Lighthart," in Children's Book Review Service, *Vol. 5, No. 11, June, 1977, p. 112.*

Knowledgeable older readers may be puzzled at the meager counseling and training afforded Ben and note the corresponding largesse of family encouragement and brisk progress toward compensatory skills and independence. But the characters are no less liable to despair, anger, and fear of the future—are, in short, recognizably human.

Sharon Spredemann Dreyer, "Annotations: 'The World of Ben Lighthart'," in her The Bookfinder: A Guide to Children's Literature about the Needs and Problems of Youth Aged 2-15, Vol. 2, *American Guidance Service, Inc., 1981, p. 287.*

Although there are some scenes in this work that deal effectively with the emotional trauma attendant upon adventitious blindness, the absurdity of the events and the fatuousness of their interpretation render this effort unacceptable. In addition to the many grammatical lapses, the story is replete with literary clichés, such as the name "Lighthart" for the brave, blind boy, the name "Win" for a nurse who urges the hero to struggle and win his battle for independence, a watch given to Ben by a dying young man whose time has run out. Among the seemingly endless supply of platitudes, those asserting that loss of sight can be a boon are the most ludicrous: Ben is advised that "our eyes often distract us from the important things . . . that mistake won't be yours from now on. Can you understand that it can be an advantage?" and "Because if death can be a loving friend, blindness can certainly grow to be a good companion." By so extravagantly overstating his claim, the author inevitably calls into question the validity of his judgment. (p. 440)

Barbara H. Baskin and Karen H. Harris, "An Annotated Guide to Juvenile Fiction Portraying the Disabled, 1976-1981: 'The World of Ben Lighthart'," in their More Notes from a Different Drummer: A Guide to Juvenile Fiction Portraying the Disabled, *R. R. Bowker Company, 1984, pp. 439-40.*

Shirley Hughes

1929-

English author/illustrator and illustrator of picture books and fiction.

One of England's foremost contemporary author/illustrators, Hughes is primarily known for creating books which capture the universal fears and joys of childhood by realistically and humorously depicting ordinary preschool children and their families. She is also acknowledged for bridging the gap between picture books and books with chapters through her inventive mixture of cartoon strips, speech balloons, and straight narratives, characteristics of several of her works. The prolific illustrator of approximately two hundred books by other authors, Hughes began writing and designing stories for her own children with the popular *Lucy and Tom's Day* (1960) and its sequels, which describe the everyday activities of two youngsters in multiethnic London. Many of her other works describe real situations with which small children can easily identify, most notably the *Alfie* series, an affectionate glimpse at the experiences of a delightful four-year-old. The reassurance of Hughes's tales, which portray common situations like the first day of school, the joys of new boots, or a disastrous birthday party, enable her preschool audience to recognize both themselves and a comfortably familiar world. Acclaimed for its nonstereotypical approach, *Helpers* (1975, published in the United States as *George, the Babysitter*) describes the hilarious bedlam that occurs when a mother leaves three small children with the babysitter, a teenaged male. The prizewinning *Dogger* (1977, published in the United States as *David and Dog*) won attention for its sensitive portrayal of a little boy who loses and regains a beloved toy. Executed in expressive black-and-white and watercolor drawings, Hughes's illustrations are noted for their accurate representations of chubby, rumpled children, unpretentious homes, and fascinating backgrounds filled with people and activity. With *Up and Up* (1979), a wordless fantasy about a mischievous girl who learns to fly, Hughes established her mastery of the comic-book form and created a work which is often considered a truly original contribution to the picture book genre. For primary-grade readers and hesitant middle-grade readers, she has written and illustrated the *Charlie Moon* and *Chips and Jessie* series, which combine droll illustrations in a variety of styles with exciting texts. Hughes has also created a series of basic concept books for the nursery which introduce children to such principles as counting, shapes, colors, and sounds as well as providing illustrations for a compilation of classic metaphors.

Critics praise Hughes for her honest, loving recreation of contemporary urban family life, her ability to find drama in the familiar, and her technical virtuosity. They admire her cadenced prose, the expressive faces and gestures of her characters, and her sure understanding of the concerns and feelings of children from two to twelve. Although a few reviewers pointed to some weak plots and found instances of stereotypical male and female roles in Hughes's early books, most critics agree that her engaging observations of childhood and her original attempts to transform lookers into readers have provided introductions to reading and literature which both educate and entertain.

Photograph by Carole Cutner. Courtesy of Shirley Hughes.

Hughes has won several awards, both for her own books and for the illustrations she has done for other authors. *Flute and Cymbals,* a book of poems compiled by Leonard Clark and illustrated by Hughes, was a Kate Greenaway Honor Book in 1969. *Helpers* won the 1976 Children's Rights Workshop Other Award and was also a runner-up for the 1976 Kate Greenaway Medal. *Dogger* won the Kate Greenaway Medal in 1978 and the Silver Slate Pencil in Holland in 1980.

(See also *Something about the Author,* Vol. 16 and *Contemporary Authors,* Vols. 85-88.)

AUTHOR'S COMMENTARY

The skills studied by the Mock Turtle in his youth are most appropriate to anyone trying to be a working illustrator. Reading, writing and painting in oils (except that I do it in gouache) is how I spend most of my time, with a lot of reeling and writhing thrown in (not to mention, after a heavy day, fainting in coils). In a professional capacity, I probably read fewer children's books than anyone else in the book business. (How do librarians and reviewers find time to read all those books without staying up all night?) Now that I am increasingly involved with doing my own books, I read fewer manuscripts than when I was largely employed as an interpretative illustrator. It's a matter of pressure of time which, in some ways, I regret.

Reading a story with a view to doing illustrations for it is a situation of promise. You read the manuscript many times, but in various ways. The first time you're absorbed with the plot, dying to know what happens next, like everybody else. The next time you're sorting out the pictures which have filled your head at the first reading and already deciding what shape they might make on the page: half-page, drop-ins or double-page spreads. The placing of these is dictated by the high points of the narrative and the drama of the relationships, close-ups, chases, detailed interiors and so forth, rather like a film. The publisher has told you how much space is allotted for this, and the trusting ones let you break it up as you wish. Oddly enough, the most difficult shape of all is the conventional full-page plate. Whoever decided that novels were going to be the shape they are clearly wasn't an illustrator. When you think of it, what interior, group of figures or landscape fits well into an upright rectangle? One is forever trying to invent interesting things to do with the bit at the top. Of course all the great masters of our trade, from Ardizzone and Shepard to Rackham and Heath Robinson, found marvellously inventive answers to this one.

In subsequent readings you are checking details, with particular attention to bits of description. There is always the fear that the pictures in the head are so strong that they will by mistake contradict something which the author has written. My favourite kind of book is scattered with seemingly inconsequential but cunningly placed little visual clues which you can piece together into a vivid picture, rather than long passages of descriptive prose. (p. 308)

Sometimes authors kindly furnish you with extra details after you have been commissioned. If the plot is set, for instance, on a canal barge or in a Birmingham suburb before the planners yanked it all down; or hinges on a piece of Minoan pottery or a belamine bottle (these have all come my way over the years), then some good references are more than welcome. But, on the whole, the essentials are all in the manuscript. Like a hound-dog being given somebody's old slipper, you're getting the scent, the feeling of the author's imagination. It's like a shadow of himself, left unconsciously in the whole like the letters inside a stick of sea-side rock. The way the drawings come out, their style, has a lot to do with considering the audience who will receive them, of course. In a book for young children the pictures will be more accessible and simpler than those for a sophisticated adult novel, but that doesn't mean (for me at any rate) cutting down on detail.

Dickens wrote, presumably, on the assumption that he would have an illustrator. I wonder if this affected the way he described things? Today, children's writers are the only ones who can make this assumption and, with older fiction, it's far from a safe one. If illustrated adult fiction is due for a big come-back, and I think it is, this may mean a writer and an artist working very closely together from the word go, and emerging as a duo whose style is recognisable as such. (Any publisher reading this piece, please note.) A text of any length would have to be illustrated in black and white, for economic reasons. The talent to meet such a challenge will always be thrown up, but if thirty-two-page full-colour picture books get most of the attention and illustrator awards it is natural for young artists to deploy their talent in this form.

Which brings me to painting in oils, which is something of a cheat because I've never been able to get the hang of it. For colour work, I use water-colour gouache, a bit of chalk and some very fine brushes. I also love black-and-white line. Looking at my fellow illustrators' work, I find myself most impressed and seduced by this aspect of their expertise.

Soon I'll be getting down to the finished drawings for ***Chips and Jessie***. . . . It's going to be a sort of plum-pudding mixture (in black-and-white line, of course) of strip-cartoon, illustrations with speech balloons, and some 'proper' text. I had to write it myself because how else could I engineer such a golden opportunity to have as much visual comment as I want mixed up with the narrative? Or allow a nine-year-old hero, Chips, to step down to the footlights like Hamlet and address the audience directly? Or invent ordinary domestic animals whose observations about life can be read in bubbles coming out of their heads? And who, come to that, would have the patience to put up with all this and keep on sending me little bits of type all ready set in the exact size for me to draw round but my old friends, the editors at The Bodley Head? But that's another story, and nothing to do with the Mock Turtle at all. (p. 309)

Shirley Hughes, "Reeling and Writhing and Fainting in Coils," in The School Librarian, *Vol. 32, No. 4, December, 1984, pp. 308-09.*

GENERAL COMMENTARY

ANNE WOOD

Shirley Hughes has been illustrating books for children since 1970. For a long time she was best known for her illustrations to Dorothy Edward's brilliant stories for preschool children, especially ***My Naughty Little Sister.*** Her slightly romantic, nostalgic style is best seen in her essentially warm and loving evocation of the domestic scene; little girls in dresses and ankle socks trailing skipping ropes, tousle-haired small boys in jerseys and shorts with rounded kindly adults always somewhere in the background. Our favourites are Lucy and Tom in ***Lucy & Tom's Day*** and ***Lucy and Tom Go To the Seaside.***

But Shirley Hughes also has the ability to evoke fantasy and beauty as seen in her pictures for fairy stories, especially ***Cinderella*** by Perrault. Her own story telling ability is considerable. ***It's Too Frightening for Me*** is a triumph of publishing in providing a book that is just right for tempting those slow or reluctant readers of seven and eight. Then there is her newest creation—a kind of liberated Shirley Hughes has appeared with her latest picture books ***Helpers***—about the trials of babysitters and ***Dogger***—last year's well deserved Greenaway Medal winner for the best picture book for children in 1977. . . . ***Dogger***—a soft toy of indeterminate species—certainly unique and of irreplaceable value to his owner, is accidentally given away to a jumble sale. The story of his eventual recovery is told entirely from the child's point of view with utter sympathy—and there is every single thing to be seen and pondered over again and again in the pictures. There are very few better books than this for two and three and four-year-olds entirely on the child's side and besides that it's unashamedly on the side of love and teddies. We are looking forward to many more for generations of children to come.

Anne Wood, "Cover Artist," in Books for Your Children, *Vol. 14, No. 2, Spring, 1979, p. 3.*

JOHN HORDER

[***Alfie Gets in First*** and ***Lucy & Tom's Christmas***] remind me of Eve Garnett's *The Family From One End Street,* which I read years ago as a Puffin. . . . Lovable though Miss Hughes's characters all are, they seem insulated from other worlds. This is despite the black child on a skate-board in the street where Alfie lives and all of Lucy and Tom's family actually hugging one another on Christmas Day. Both books are more élitist than [Eric Carle's] *The Honeybee and the Robber,* which won't prevent them from being extremely popular with children who want to be read to rather than have the bother of making up stories for themselves. (p. 1023)

John Horder, "For the Kids," in Punch, *Vol. 281, No. 7360, December 2, 1981, pp. 1023-24.*

MARY GORDON

There seem to be two genres of books for young children, each catering to a particular fantasy. For the precious-memory school there are, of course, the classics. We like to believe that one day our own children will look back upon the same Pooh, the same Alice in Wonderland, the same Peter Rabbit as we do. But then, ambivalent about concentrating entirely on the past, most of us are also willing to welcome the other type of children's book, the more realistic, contemporary type with characters and situations the children are supposed to, God help us, identify with.

But what do the children like? They don't come to books with the same baggage as we do. Many a cultivated adult has been distressed at a child's rejecting Beatrix Potter's *Tailor of Gloucester* for the book about the little girl and the wet kitten, with its execrable illustrations, purchased at the supermarket for 59 cents. Children do like situations that are familiar; they particularly like to see examples of children behaving badly or in distress. To please a child, yet introduce him to beautiful things, the Alfie books are a happy solution. Alfie is a kind and well meaning little boy, but also insecure and a bit rash. He has a younger sister named Annie Rose and a mother who seems attentive, understanding, cheerful and attractively disorganized.

In ***Alfie Gets in First,*** Alfie runs in the door before his mother and sister and locks himself in and them out. His mother tries to enlist help from everyone on the block—the neighbors, the mailman, a window cleaner with a long ladder. All their solutions are unacceptable in one way or another, but finally Alfie discovers that if he stands on a chair he can reach the lock (his mother initially suggested he try that, but he was crying too hard to listen). So, with half of London on the doorstep proffering help, Alfie opens the door. Finally, everyone sits at Alfie's table and has tea. No one is mad at him and, miraculously, no one is mad at his mother.

The new book, ***Alfie Gives a Hand*** is a charming account of a birthday party—an event adults think children will love, but which is often terrifying to them. Alfie is invited to his first birthday party. He's scared because his mother and baby sister aren't coming with him; he insists upon bringing his own blanket. At the party Bernard, the birthday boy, behaves badly. He throws Alfie's present of crayons all around the yard, he is cruel to a little girl and bossy to everyone. The little girl, Min, finds solace only in Alfie. Finally, he has to decide to put down his blanket in order to hold Min's hand while they play a game. He makes the painful choice and discovers he may not have needed his blanket in the first place.

The least of the series is ***Alfie's Feet,*** in which Alfie puts his boots on the wrong feet, his parents don't notice it and he discovers for himself what the source of his discomfort is.

To say that one of these books is less engaging than the others, however, is not to imply that any of them is short of delightful. The illustrations are deft—realistic yet dreamy. They depict a world of blissfully disheveled kids in catch-as-catch-can clothing. There are wonderful ducks in Alfie's pond, and beautiful bubbles at Bernard's birthday party. Shirley Hughes's rendering of flats and back gardens will be a delight to anyone with fond memories of particular residential sections of London that have no glamour but the domestic kind. These are books that children will love, because the situations are clear, familiar and pressing to them, and adults will enjoy reading to children because of the sensitivity of Mrs. Hughes's treatment, and the enchantment of her drawing.

Mary Gordon, in a review of "Alfie Gives a Hand," in The New York Times Book Review, *June 24, 1984, p. 33.*

LUCY AND TOM'S DAY (1960)

There's a pleasant time to be spent with a couple of English children in ***Lucy and Tom's Day***. . . . In a calm, unhurried visit we follow two preschoolers from sun-up, through meals, play, naps, "helping" mother, to evening tuck-in time. The English background notwithstanding, our boys and girls will see their own antics and activities mirrored in Lucy's and Tom's. The book's sketches have zest and handsomeness. (p. 58)

George A. Woods, "A Child's Best Friend Can Be a Picture Book," in The New York Times Book Review, *Part II, November 13, 1960, pp. 58-9.*

Shirley Hughes is a new author-artist as far as I am concerned, but one I hope who will continue with the good work. ***Lucy and Tom's Day*** is a quite outstanding picture book describing the very ordinary events in the lives of two pre-school children with much charm and realism. The pictures are excellent, both those in full colour and the ones in black and white. Every nursery school should have a copy of this book.

G. Taylor, in a review of "Lucy and Tom's Day," in The School Librarian and School Library Review, *Vol. 10, No. 4, March, 1961, p. 383.*

In this pleasant little story, the daily activities of two English children are presented. These activities are quite like those of young children in America, but the illustrations give the reader a feeling and appreciation for life in another land. American children will be pleased by this tale and feel a real closeness to Lucy and Tom.

Jane Ann Flynn, in a review of "Lucy and Tom's Day," in Social Education, *Vol. XXV, No. 5, May, 1961, p. 266.*

[***Lucy and Tom's Day***] is an unpretentious chronicle and avoids the sentimentality that sometimes finds its way into books about a preschooler's daily life. Although Lucy and Tom are English and the neighborhood scenes slightly different from those of America, there are dozens of familiar objects that a child can identify on each page. The text is simply a caption for each picture, yet it is apt and childlike: "Lucy is scraping the last bit of cereal out of her bowl. Tom has finished his and is waving his spoon for some more."

In using books like this, one finds that half the fun is the child's excitement about his own family and his eagerness to talk about it. In fact story hours using this kind of book end up being a continuous series of conversations with the audience, and sometimes the book is forgotten altogether. (pp. 109-10)

Donnarae MacCann and Olga Richard, "Specialized Texts: 'Lucy and Tom's Day'," in their The Child's First Books: A Critical Study of Pictures and Texts, *The H. W. Wilson Company, 1973, pp. 109-10.*

THE TROUBLE WITH JACK (1970)

Shirley Hughes has hardly created an individual world in ***The trouble with Jack.*** This extended picture-book could be read in one session to a four- or five-year-old or could be put into the hands of a beginner-reader. She would find a recognisable situation here—the havoc made in a tidy child's life by a mischievous and riotous younger brother; she would find a middle-class setting with what one might call television-attributes (balloons, jelly for a party, standard furnishings and standard Mum). Nancy's birthday passes happily, after Jack has been given an unbirthday-present, until the party table is left unattended for a few moments; then Jack seizes his chances and last-minute repairs are needed to bring about a happy ending. Cosy pictures in blurred bright colour, cosy words, present not a special, one-time-only world but a cheerfully typical one. (p. 1497)

Margery Fisher, in a review of "The Trouble with Jack," in Growing Point, *Vol. 8, No. 9, April, 1970, pp. 1496-98.*

From realms of magic and fantasy in which it most often delightfully roams Shirley Hughes brings home the picture-book to the minor pleasures and disasters of everyday life. Jack is the younger brother, just a little more horrid than most of his kind. (p. 80)

Miss Hughes draws him and his setting with remorseless accuracy, with no trace of sentimentality. She has a passion for sticky mustard colours which not all her readers will share, but this is professional reporting and no more designed to please the eye than the newsman's camera. Real-life Nancies will recognise themselves here; maybe the Jacks will too and learn to be a little less beastly. (pp. 80-1)

A review of "The Trouble with Jack," in The Junior Bookshelf, *Vol. 34, No. 2, April, 1970, pp. 80-1.*

The beauty of the story is in the pictures. In how many books can children look at the illustrations (such good design, so little depth) and tell the story for themselves? This is one of the rare occasions when non-readers aren't left behind and for all the others there is a finely unified experience. A fitting successor to ***Lucy and Tom's Day*** and likely to be a great favourite in nursery and infant schools. (p. 254)

Elizabeth Crawthorne, in a review of "The Trouble with Jack," in The School Librarian, *Vol. 18, No. 2, June, 1970, pp. 253-54.*

[The Trouble with Jack *was published in the United States in 1986.*]

[***The Trouble with Jack***] was published in England in 1970, which shows how stereotypical depiction of sex roles was lingering and how far Hughes has come as an author in the intervening years, for the stiff writing is nothing like the easy and humorous flow of the author's current Alfie stories. The realistic and deft line-and-wash pictures, on the other hand, show that she had already reached her potential as an artist.

A review of "The Trouble with Jack," in Bulletin of the Center for Children's Books, *Vol. 39, No. 7, March, 1986, p. 129.*

SALLY'S SECRET (1973)

[***Sally's Secret***], is a book that small children, especially girls, will want to hear frequently, and they will readily identify with its heroine. Sally's favourite game is making houses for herself, but all too often her houses are tidied away before she has finished playing with them. The game reaches perfection when she finds a hidden space among the bushes in the garden where she can arrange everything as she likes and then invite a friend to tea in her own secret house. The comfortable realism of Shirley Hughes's illustrations is nicely edged with fantasy, so that we see not just a child playing, but what she imagines as she plays.

"Entertaining Flights of Fancy," in The Times Literary Supplement, *No. 3734, September 28, 1973, p. 1120.*

Shirley Hughes has produced a picture book for little girls which should provoke an outcry from even the mildest Women's Lib. supporter but will no doubt be snapped up by countless old-fashioned parents. . . .

Shirley Hughes has chosen a subject which tempts her to the brink of sentimentality in a series of studies of Sally engaged in earnest domesticity. Full colour beguiles the eye on every page with pretty pinks predominating. Great care has been taken with the design of page openings, text and illustration are enclosed in a cosy oval frame often made of foliage and flowers.

The text abounds in those little details that delight many small girls: 'Sally brought her own little chair. Then she brought her best rose-patterned teaset with all the handles still on. She swept the floor with a branch, and made a little path of stones up to the front door'.

Many teachers and librarians as well as parents will be grateful to Shirley Hughes for serving up such a popular mixture in the acceptable guise of a 'quality' picture book.

Eleanor von Schweinitz, in a review of "Sally's Secret," in Children's Book Review, *Vol. III, No. 5, October, 1973, p. 138.*

This tiny snatch of childhood, gently and economically described, is shown visually in beautiful scenes, many of them enclosed in an oval with richly entwined borders of flowers and leaves. Shirley Hughes's talent for domestic vignettes has never been used to better purpose. (p. 2245)

Margery Fisher, in a review of "Sally's Secret," in Growing Point, *Vol. 12, No. 4, October, 1973, p. 2245.*

The story is told with simplicity. The illustrations are full of ovals: oval flower frames, oval vignetted pictures, oval objects and many flowers. It is a very female book, with implications of nesting and nurture; not "cute" or "girly," it is earthy and comfortable.

Mary B. Nickerson, in a review of "Sally's Secret," in School Library Journal, *Vol. 27, No. 10, August, 1981, p. 56.*

LUCY AND TOM GO TO SCHOOL **(1973)**

In ***Lucy and Tom go to School*** Shirley Hughes gives a lot of visual and written detail about what goes on at school (and rather less about playgroup). We hear about the delights of playing shop, dressing up and acting, listening to stories, and music and movement. But, although she does not dwell on them, Shirley Hughes does not hide the less pleasant aspects of school life—the strangeness of it at first, the wrench of parting with your mother, the noise and crowds in the playground, and the bullying. Her assessment of Lucy's overall reaction to primary school is confident without being irresponsibly optimistic:

> Some days Lucy looked forward to going to school and some days she did not want to go very much, but she soon got used to it.

The attractive, colourful pictures make school look a very interesting place to be. (p. 1437)

> *"Grandmother's Footsteps and Some Progressive Games," in* The Times Literary Supplement, *No. 3742, November 23, 1973, pp. 1436-37.*

There are many anxieties and fears which all children share and which once overcome, remain so for always. . . . One hurdle which all children have to overcome is their first day at school and in writing about Lucy and Tom's experiences at this critical time, Shirley Hughes has produced a book which should render every mother with this approaching problem, eternally grateful to her. It is not just the subject, but the way she handles it that makes this sequel to ***Lucy and Tom's Day,*** an attractive, immensely practical aid for mothers and teachers at playgroup and infant school level. Shirley Hughes's healthy, cherubic children with their mussy hair, rolled down socks and untidy clothes are drawn straight from life, with an authenticity which instantly communicates with the reader. Here are the night-before preparations of clothes and satchel, the tight hand-hold as Mother takes Lucy into school for the first time, the clothes peg, the teacher and the newly-made friends. The whole range of a child's first impressions of school are illustrated with warmth and feeling and many teachers will recognise their own school playground in one of Shirley Hughes's double-page spreads. Her mastery of childish expression, particularly, shows in the one of children listening to a story; they really are listening! One could go on adding plaudits about each page. Tom, still too young to go to school, joins a playgroup and gets his first taste of group activities as the book ends. Shirley Hughes has filled a long-felt need in a superlative way with a book of universal appeal.

> *Edward Hudson, in a review of "Lucy and Tom Go to School," in* Children's Book Review, *Vol. III, No. 6, December, 1973, p. 170.*

No artist is less affected by contemporary fashions than Shirley Hughes. She has been going her own way for a long time now, and a very sensible way it is, too. Not for her the heady essences of fantasy. She draws the everyday world, peopled by ordinary mums and dads and kids doing ordinary things. In her new book she examines the crises of school and play-group. The drawing is beautifully free of exaggeration and sentimentality, the writing utterly without pretentiousness. There is an honoured place for such books, and Shirley Hughes fills it precisely. (pp. 13-14)

> *M. Crouch, in a review of "Lucy and Tom Go to School," in* The Junior Bookshelf, *Vol. 38, No. 1, February, 1974, pp. 13-14.*

For many children the picture book in which they first found themselves was ***Lucy and Tom's Day.*** Now Lucy and Tom go to school. The stages are instantly recognisable so that the book will be a boon to all those parents who are faced with separation and to teachers who are settling their reception classes. The neighbourhood is a multiracial one, the fathers take their children to school and not everyone is pleased all the time. The playground has its bully; the anxiety is not minimised, but allayed.

The drawings are an absolute delight. Here is a flesh and blood situation with real people who must have names and problems, fun and games. Lots of children are difficult to draw, but Shirley Hughes can draw classrooms full of them, all different, and never frozen on the page. Tom goes to a playgroup which is honestly crowded. From cover to cover a gem.

> *Elisabeth Crawthorne, in a review of "Lucy and Tom Go to School," in* The School Librarian, *Vol. 22, No. 2, June, 1974, p. 204.*

HELPERS **(1975; U.S. edition as *George, the Babysitter*)**

Shirley Hughes has a talent for taking the really ordinary and particularising it through a multiplicity of detail and a pleasant range of colour. ***Helpers*** describes simply and directly the day when Mother goes out and George, lanky, long-haired and

From Helpers, *written and illustrated by Shirley Hughes. The Bodley Head, 1975. Copyright © 1975 by Shirley Hughes. Reproduced by permission of The Bodley Head Ltd., on behalf of the author.*

'teen-aged, comes to look after the three small children. To start with, all is energy and goodwill; all four tidy the toy-cupboard (though Jenny retrieves some of the throw-outs from the dustbin) and lunch passes peacefully. Then George hopefully sits down with a magazine—but time off is not a concept known to the inexhaustible children, and the day gathers tempo again with shopping and television. The illustrations, with their delicate, subtle range of colour, are mainly composed within lightly suggested circular frames which lend to the book the authenticity and charm of a family album. (p. 2733)

Margery Fisher, in a review of "Helpers," in Growing Point, *Vol. 14, No. 5, November, 1975, pp. 2733-34.*

Among the small band of picture book artists who choose to depict the real world Shirley Hughes is supreme. She sees the beauty and the humour of ordinary everyday things and presents them without a veneer of sentimentality. The three kids left in George the baby-sitter's care are neither pretty nor cute, but their naughtiness and messiness are beautifully observed. Miss Hughes' draughtsmanship and design are as always quietly immaculate. An important part of a child's development is his recognition of the environment in which he grows, and here it is seen through the eyes of a master.

M. Crouch, in a review of "Helpers," in The Junior Bookshelf, *Vol. 40, No. 1, February, 1976, p. 16.*

Adults admire artistry; children look at pictures. Here both can be pleased. . . . The pictures are superbly detailed (look at the inside of the toy cupboard and the social comment of the 'rec' scene, for instance) and deeply textured. Solidly bound and beautifully spaced, this is a treasure of a book, not only for the young but for a sympathetic teenager who has shared this problem and would be glad to read about it.

Margaret Meek, in review of "Helpers," in The School Librarian, *Vol. 24, No. 1, March, 1976, p. 32.*

The main attraction here is Hughes' illustrations—warm, true-to-life drawings of children who make mistakes, drop things, and live in a house that is not very neat. . . . There isn't much plot but it's sufficient to hold the pictures together, and children will readily identify with a familiar family situation.

Ann Hanst, in a review of "Helpers," in School Library Journal, *Vol. 24, No. 9, May, 1978, p. 56.*

LUCY AND TOM AT THE SEASIDE (1976)

A new picture book of an everyday family situation from this delightful author-artist is always welcome, and her account of a day, preparing the picnic, travelling in the train, paddling, building sand-castles, playing games, collecting seaweed, and having a donkey-ride is no exception. Although it "has been a lovely day", the author paints a realistic picture—"They walk down a rather long road carrying all the picnic things and bathing bags and buckets and spades", and then later "They settle down to their picnic. Several wasps try to join in". Full marks to the author for trying to get across the idea that one or two disadvantages do not matter.

B. Clark, in a review of "Lucy and Tom at the Seaside," in The Junior Bookshelf, *Vol. 40, No. 5, October, 1976, p. 263.*

Lucy and Tom at the Seaside is . . . less good than Shirley Hughes's last picture-book, the prizewinning ***Helpers,*** although it has a great deal to recommend it—the feel of a day out by the sea, the journey, the sandwiches, the wasps, the wind, sand, waves and donkey rides. The busy full colour pictures are a delight but the use of sepia and black on the alternate openings is disappointing in that the colours have been used separately, black for text, sepia without black for illustrations; this throws text and illustrations away from one another. (p. 1244)

Elaine Moss, "Protecting the Innocent," in The Times Literary Supplement, *No. 3890, October 1, 1976, pp. 1244-45.*

A pleasantly unusual combination of alternate soft colour and sepia gives the book a reposeful quality saved from blandness by Shirley Hughes's talent for suggesting movement and activity. As Lucy and Tom ride on donkeys, bury their father in the sand, build a sandcastle and see it undermined by the tide and leave their names in huge letters on the beach, their enjoyment is expressed unmistakably in gesture and attitude.

Margery Fisher, in a review of "Lucy and Tom at the Seaside," in Growing Point, *Vol. 15, No. 6, December, 1976, p. 3030.*

IT'S TOO FRIGHTENING FOR ME! (1977; U.S. edition as *Haunted House*)

Shirley Hughes's ***It's Too Frightening for Me!*** begins with a touch of the Gothic horrors. What is the secret of Hardlock House; what are the wailings that Jim and Arthur hear when they creep up the drive; whose is the face at the window? All these troubling questions are soon resolved in a down-to-earth fashion; the two boys make friends with Mary and her granny, caretakers at Hardlock House, and in the second part of the book help to unmask the fake Captain Grimthorpe who is passing himself off as the owner of the house. As a picture book for older children this is an ambitious but slightly uneasy production. Designed to help the narrative, the pictures tend, on the whole, to interrupt it. They are meant to have a key function, to supplement a rather slim story and to help build up the atmosphere. But Shirley Hughes's very detailed and naturalistic style of drawing does not altogether fit the jokey tone of her story: the speech balloons in some of the pictures seem positively out of place, while the placing of the pictures often makes for a rather hiccuping progress through the text.

Myra Barrs, "Comic Horrors: Myra Barrs on Junior Adventure," in The Times Educational Supplement, *No. 3258, November 18, 1977, p. 32.*

Part of the transition from picture books to full-text stories and information books relies on children being able to retain interest in events and characters. Moving from pictorial to text narrative is a long and gradual process, helped by books like ***It's Too Frightening For Me*** . . . , with its realistic literal (highly imaginative!) drawings, its immediately arresting storyline (a haunted house and a mysterious trapped girl), and its invitation to get involved in associated activities after the book has been put down (in this case dressing up). The story is a full 'proper' story, respectable for six-up, maturer than a mere picture book which many children feel they have outgrown as a form by about seven. It is also an exercise in looking, since the pictures are angled variously, like TV shots, working with text to extend the storyline and the reactions of the reader. Identification is easy. Through such books the emphasis is on the way the children feel and react: that is the dominant feature of the book, and it draws on a substantial enough story to keep it up in the air. (p. 125)

Stuart Hannabuss, "Beyond the Formula: Ways of Extending the Obvious for Children & Young People," in The Junior Bookshelf, *Vol. 46, No. 4, August, 1982, pp. 123-27.*

DOGGER **(1977; U.S. edition as *David and Dog*)**

Children will recognise a familiar situation when Dave's battered stuffed dog, mislaid in the town, turns up as junk at the Summer Fair and is retrieved by generous sister Bella, who sacrifices a raffle prize in a swap. How naturally Shirley Hughes suggests mood and action in her warm, active pictures! With crowds and individuals, in bedroom or street, her acuteness of vision and obvious sympathy are as notable as ever in this new picture-book.

Margery Fisher, in a review of "Dogger," in Growing Point, *Vol. 16, No. 7, January, 1978, p. 3250.*

Shirley Hughes draws the real world as only she can. This is a world of children and grownups living and sharing, of summer fairs and small personal disasters. A little cosy? Not really. It is no bad thing to show that unselfishness still exists among children and that families stick together. Lovely drawing, fine printing.

From Dogger, *written and illustrated by Shirley Hughes. The Bodley Head, 1977. Copyright © 1977 by Shirley Hughes. Reproduced by permission of The Bodley Head Ltd., on behalf of the author.*

M. Crouch, in a review of "Dogger," in The Junior Bookshelf, *Vol. 42, No. 1, February, 1978, p. 16.*

Pure coin of the realm is ***David and Dog***. . . . Sweet but not cloying, it relates a homely adventure about a small boy's favorite "soft brown toy called Dog." With nary a false note, it captures the small-scale triumphs and despairs of childhood, as well as the near miraculous empathy young children sometimes exhibit toward one another. Its pictures have a messy verisimilitude that small viewers will both recognize and appreciate, and the tale itself is sure to hold spellbound any four- or five-year-old who ever cherished a special toy.

Selma Lanes, "When Showing Really Tells," in Book World—The Washington Post, *November 12, 1978, p. E3.*

Young children can readily comprehend a passionate attachment to a stuffed animal, and the story contains a blend of suspense and satisfaction. . . . The action is comfortably realistic. . . . Dramatic intensity is scaled to a preschooler's emotions; the backdrop of the story's climax is a busy panorama of side shows, costume parades, and amateur athletic events. As the economical text develops the relationship between the central characters, the detailed full-color illustrations delineate the urban English setting and complement the homely plot. A subtle, balanced, and loving portrayal which touches the core of family relationships without sounding forced or contrived.

Mary M. Burns, in a review of "Dogger," in The Horn Book Magazine, *Vol. LIV, No. 6, December, 1978, p. 632.*

With a great deal of care and concern, Shirley Hughes has written and illustrated a story about a lost toy. . . . With simple prose and detailed pictures that every child will wish to explore, Ms. Hughes has skillfully dealt with a real family situation that evokes sympathy from the reader. She is as good a storyteller as she is an artist. When David loses his much-loved, soft, brown toy dog, you really want to help him find it—and when he does but can't get it back, you REALLY empathize. It's a touching book and well worth keeping in a special place in one's library. One of the best of 1978.

Barbara Ann Kyle, in a review of "Dogger," in The Babbling Bookworm, *Vol. 7, No. 2, March, 1979, p. 1.*

MOVING MOLLY **(1978)**

Successive framed circles or squares show the small girl performing sequential actions, so that the pictures have a strong narrative quality that directs and expands the brief text. The reactions of a child to a new home in the country, where everyone is busy and imagination must for a time supply playfellows, is illustrated with an unerring sense of a child's movements and expressions. Molly's old pram, later converted to a go-kart, provides continuity for scenes that are attractive and entertaining in their glossy colour and neat ink line.

Margery Fisher, in a review of "Moving Molly," in Growing Point, *Vol. 17, No. 5, January, 1979, p. 3449.*

Life in a town basement flat, the family's removal day and the new life in the country are depicted at a small child's eyelevel, in a text to which younger readers will easily relate. . . . Shirley

Hughes' amusing illustrations, full of detail and charm, depict the family's dreams as well as accurately observed real scenes.

M. Hobbs, in a review of "Moving Molly," in The Junior Bookshelf, *Vol. 43, No. 1, February, 1979, p. 18.*

I think that I have found another book for adults to give to children. It is Shirley Hughes' latest effort called ***Moving Molly.*** Over twenty-five, you'll love it; under ten, you'll never read it twice. The illustrations are so good, you almost want to cry—Ms. Hughes uses natural everyday settings and gestures to make you feel a part of the story—little Molly watching her mom paint walls while clutching the rungs of a ladder—the look of the cats in the overgrown garden next door. The story is good, too: a youngster, moved from the bustle of a city house to the country house and loneliness. But somehow the whole thing is too sad and uninteresting to a child, even if, from an adult viewpoint, it is sensitive, poetic and wonderful. You know what? I keep it in my bookcase and read it—the heck with the kids!

Barbara Ann Kyle, in a review of "Moving Molly," in The Babbling Bookworm, *Vol. 7, No. 7, August, 1979, p. 1.*

This is an old-fashioned book with a completely predictable plot. The very fact that it *is* so clichéd makes the story utterly safe; there are no unexpected surprises. If reassurance is being sought, especially around the question of moving, then ***Molly*** will answer needs. The skill of the drawings exceeds the text. They are comfortably cluttered and richly colored; there are two or more on every spread and all of the people are nice. (pp. 65-6)

Joan W. Blos, in a review of "Moving Molly," in School Library Journal, *Vol. 26, No. 3, November, 1979, pp. 65-6.*

UP AND UP (1979)

The strong narrative line of ***Up and Up*** needs not a single syllable to help it on its hilarious way. Shirley Hughes gets better and better. The many drawings of her comic strip are done with great confidence and technical virtuosity. A little girl, having observed a bird in flight, tries various ways of achieving the same. At last the gift of an enormous chocolate egg produces, surprisingly, the right result. She eats the lot and acquires a total loss of gravity. Weightlessness may have its problems, but it offers endless opportunities for mischief and anti-social behaviour. At length she reverts to normal, returns home, and we leave her contemplating her breakfast egg! The drawings, monochrome on a sepia ground, are beautifully done and meet all the problems of a bird's-eye view easily. In its smaller way, ***Up and Up*** may enjoy some of the popularity of Raymond Briggs' Father Christmas, and anxious parents and teachers may find in it an answer to the 'comic' problem. The children will accept it gratefully for what it is, a very good joke. (p. 16)

M. Crouch, in a review of "Up and Up," in The Junior Bookshelf, *Vol. 44, No. 1, February, 1980, pp. 15-16.*

Shirley Hughes's exquisitely detailed drawings carry the story unhesitantly through to its wholly satisfying conclusion without the aid of words or colour—no mean feat. Picture books without words very often fail to hold the attention, but here the combination of sympathetic detail with the twists and turns of the narrative in strip-cartoon format will surely make all but the most reluctant 'reader' turn the pages again and again.

Linda Yeatman, in a review of "Up and Up," in British Book News, *Children's Supplement, Spring, 1980, p. 8.*

Shirley Hughes, a recent Greenaway Medal winner, is an illustrator who inspires affection as well as admiration. Her first picture book, ***Lucy and Tom's Day,*** pictured the world she seems most to enjoy in her work, the busy, happy occasions of ordinary child and adult life, naturalistically and humorously presented against backgrounds full of enlivening detail. Essentially a dramatist—she has said that she thinks of the words in her picture books as being the captions for silent films—Hughes does the kind of illustrations that make you smile because the artist so clearly loves people and possesses that best of all gifts, the ability to show what is extraordinary and absorbing about everyday life.

Ever since her first work was published in 1952, she has been a sought-after illustrator; but in the seventies she flowered as an author as well, and her work has developed significantly. The change began with ***George the Babysitter*** and continued in ***David and Dog,*** but I doubt that anyone could have predicted the latest book, for in it Shirley Hughes makes her first substantial graphic statement, fully orchestrated and entirely personal, which places her firmly among our leading picture-book artists. ***Up and Up*** is a masterpiece in the true, craftsman sense of the word—the work that establishes her as a master of her art—and leaves one eager to see what she will do next.

The comic-strip form is currently much employed by our picture-book artists because so many of those now in their maturity were brought up on comic books as children. ***Up and Up*** uses that form, too, but transcends it to become something of Shirley Hughes's own, just as Sendak transcended the form and made it his own in *In the Night Kitchen* and Briggs did in *Father Christmas* and in *Fungus the Bogeyman.*

Up and Up is also a wordless picture book, another current fad, about a perky little girl who wants to fly. Finding that she can fly with the unexpected aid of an enormous chocolate egg, she spends a glorious, airborne morning flitting mischievously about, causing panic among the adults below and hilarity among the children; eventually she is brought back to earth with a cushioned bump and returns home to a late breakfast. The English edition opens with a double-page spread showing an aerial view of the city streets in and over which this comic fantasy is to be enacted. Many of the places involved in the story can be found here if you look carefully enough—but, of course, you do not realize this till you've "read" the story; and then you want to start all over again. The pictures themselves are in black line set against a delicate, light yellowish-brown tint which picks out each frame of the design. Bravo to this courageous and confident decision. Full color would somehow have diminished, not enhanced, the book, and the tint gives it visual distinction. I dread to think, though, what will happen if the success of this idea puts sloppy illustrators and publishers up to trying the same effect: The muddy, inappropriate washes and the inaccurate registration of tint to picture will be offensive. Like so many simple ideas in art, this one needs considerable skill and refined taste if it is to come off.

Some books seem to recall the child reader you used to be. ***Up and Up*** does this to me. I'm seven once again, slumped com-

From Up and Up, *by Shirley Hughes. Lothrop, Lee & Shepard Books, 1986. Copyright © 1979 by Shirley Hughes. All rights reserved. By permission of Lothrop, Lee & Shepard Books (A Division of William Morrow & Company, Inc.). In Canada by The Bodley Head Ltd., on behalf of the author.*

fortably on the floor, utterly mesmerized by a book so filled with details of people, places, and events, all lorded over by a protagonist of such commanding personality and charm that I search each page for hours on end. Now, of course, there is the extra pleasure of also being an adult reader, who welcomes the irony that avoids the sentimental and gives a sharp edge to the humor; who admires the pantomime inventiveness, the precision of the draftsmanship, and the discipline with which the comic strip has been used to suggest space and time and movement all in shifting, interrelated sequences on the same page. ***Up and Up*** is a vibrant work—generous, energetic, highly finished, and also promising much more to come. (pp. 211-12)

Aidan Chambers, "Letter from England: Hughes in Flight," in The Horn Book Magazine, *Vol. LVI, No. 2, April, 1980, pp. 211-14.*

Like *The Snowman,* . . . ***Up and Up*** is a wordless picture book which attracts all ages. Shirley Hughes is much concerned about the decline in the art of patient absorbed looking. This cartoon story, about a girl who finally manages to *fly* round her town causing havoc and having fun, demands of the 'reader' the closest possible attention. For the story is told not in bursts of exclamation (as is customary in lesser comic strips) but in the subtle changes of facial expression that accompany the action. Delight (I'm going to take off); astonishment (I have taken off); panic (Will I fall?). Perspectives change, as with a zoom lens: people, landscape features are seen huge in close-up or tiny in the distance. There is no colour (other than a warm beige wash) but, a triumph for Shirley Hughes, 'readers' contentedly supply their own in their mind's eye.

Elaine Moss, in a review of "Up and Up," in her Picture Books for Young People 9-13, *second edition, edited by Nancy Chambers, The Thimble Press, 1985, p. 35.*

[Up and Up *was revised in 1986.*]

Employing an elegant version of the comic-book style, Shirley Hughes develops the narrative and the characters in sharp, incisive black drawings contained within buff-colored blocks, strips, and panels of varying sizes. When Prentice published the book in this country, they curiously omitted the opening double-page spread—a splendid panoramic aerial view of the story's setting—which in the new edition has fortunately been restored.

Ethel L. Heins, in a review of "Up and Up," in The Horn Book Magazine, *Vol. LXII, No. 4, July-August, 1986, p. 442.*

OVER THE MOON: A BOOK OF SAYINGS (1980)

The one way to revive a metaphor once it has died is to take it literally, which is what Shirley Hughes has done to some fifty or more exanimate English sayings in ***Over the Moon.*** She has picked her clichés shrewdly, and made them into amusing pictures. It is comical to watch language being brought down to earth: to see someone actually casting pearls before swine, or keeping their nose to the grindstone, or being born with a silver spoon in their mouth. The style of the drawings is early-*Punch,* strongly naturalistic everywhere except for the human faces, which are furiously expressive. On Shirley Hughes's first page it rains worryingly lifelike cats and dogs on to two cowering pedestrians; overleaf a revoltingly meek young man is visibly tied to his shrewish mother's apron-strings. There is an edge of unpleasantness to these two drawings that will please any child, and which too many of the remaining pages lack. But this is a simple and engaging book that might prompt its readers to have fun of their own visualizing the merely verbal.

J. S., "Literally Speaking," in The Times Literary Supplement, *No. 4042, September 25, 1980, p. 1025.*

Deft, realistic drawings by the former winner of the Greenaway Award add action and humor to a collection of interpreted sayings. . . . A few of the sayings may be unfamiliar to American children ("This won't buy the baby a new bonnet," or, "Up a gum tree") but they should be perfectly comprehensible. Not outstanding, but a mildly interesting and probably useful collection.

Zena Sutherland, in a review of "Over the Moon: A Book of Sayings," in Bulletin of the Center for Children's Books, *Vol. 34, No. 8, April, 1981, p. 152.*

Shirley Hughes has selected fifty-eight well-known sayings, given simple definitions, and provided meaningful illustrations in black and white. The formula is ideal for her and the detailed pictures communicate a sense of fun through their depiction of a wide range of characters. . . . The draughtsmanship is first class and this alone ought to make it a popular browsing book in any library.

Peter Kennerley, in a review of "Over the Moon: A Book of Sayings," in The School Librarian, *Vol. 29, No. 2, June, 1981, p. 146.*

HERE COMES CHARLIE MOON (1980)

[***Here Comes Charlie Moon***] will arouse no strong feelings. Charlie, staying in his Auntie Jean's joke shop, gets involved with rich, careless Mrs Cadwallader and her sour sister-in-law, and helps to protect Mr Cornetto's Crazy Castle from hooligans and bankruptcy. The plot is complex, incorporating lost jewelery, comic masks and stink bombs. Narrow line-drawings run across the top of every page, providing an effect like that of a strip cartoon parallel to the text. But the necessarily small size of the drawings robs them of impact and individual flavour and similarly the story, although it is competently told, lacks any memorable characters or distinctive atmosphere.

That is sad, since Shirley Hughes is capable of the most exuberant and joyful originality, as is shown in her illustrations to Mary Welfare's ***Witchdust.***

Gillian Cross, "Foul but Funny," in The Times Literary Supplement, *No. 4051, November 21, 1980, p. 1330.*

Sundry excitements—romance, sabotage, lost jewellery—are extended from a breathless historic-present text by vignettes which establish the characters through facial expression and attitude and provide a shrewd, amusing and swift second narrative. Technique is triumphant in establishing a special kind of veracity for the hyperbolic tale; the artist has devised her own kind of counterpoint narrative.

Margery Fisher, in a review of "Here Comes Charlie Moon," in Growing Point, *Vol. 19, No. 6, March, 1981, p. 3853.*

The best feature of this book is the illustrations. The line drawings, little more than an inch high, run in a band across the tops of the pages and they portray character and incident in miniature with humour and verve. There is an interesting combination of picture and text and the pictures are a necessary part of the whole, particularly where character portrayal is concerned. The story has some of the crazy ingredients children enjoy—slightly eccentric adults, a couple of obvious baddies, mystery, and the bizarre qualities which seaside hotel, joke shop and amusement arcade provide. There is plenty of dialogue though the speakers are without subtlety or depth. It is an unpretentious book but fun to read. (pp. 133-34)

Peter Kennerley, in a review of "Here Comes Charlie Moon," in The School Librarian, *Vol. 29, No. 2, June, 1981, pp. 133-34.*

Full of Briticisms and British ambience, this novel will not appeal to every American child. Nevertheless, Charlie's spirited adventures and earnest personality span the continents, making this engaging fare. Hughes' simple pen-and-ink drawings illustrate the fun.

Ilene Cooper, in a review of "Here Comes Charlie Moon," in Booklist, *Vol. 82, No. 21, July, 1986, p. 1612.*

LUCY AND TOM'S CHRISTMAS (1981)

A thoroughly conventional family Christmas. Brother and sister count the days as they stir the pudding, colour cards and arrange the crib, post letters up the chimney to Father Christmas and listen to carols. Shirley Hughes has put down all the details with grace and colour and a measure of humour, arranging her direct text to fit descriptive scenes which spell out the atmosphere of a family festival. But conventional? Perhaps not, if one looks at the expressions on some of the faces. This is an author who draws individuals, not types, and when you look at her serene pictures you find yourself wondering what Grandma is thinking, whether Dad's relaxed air is genuine and just what made little Tom suddenly feel the anti-climax we all have to learn to cope with. A discerning piece of domestic embellishment.

Margery Fisher, in a review of "Lucy and Tom's Christmas," in Growing Point, *Vol. 20, No. 4, November, 1981, p. 3972.*

[Shirley Hughes's new Lucy and Tom story is] written in the present tense . . . [and] the effect is to draw readers in, making them feel involved with the family preparations and the gradually mounting excitement as Christmas Day draws near. Everything about this book—from the glowing, red endpapers to its final message 'On earth peace, good will toward men'—epitomises Christmas as we'd like it to be. Warmth and homeliness are hallmarks of all Shirley Hughes's books, and this one positively overflows with both. (p. 27)

Jill Bennett, in a review of "Lucy and Tom's Christmas," in The School Librarian, *Vol. 30, No. 1, March, 1982, pp. 26-7.*

Lucy and Tom's Christmas is very much of today but with all the warmth and traditional patterns of the ideal family Christmas. There's a lot of love and friendship in Shirley Hughes' beautifully observed pictures which exactly capture the way people are. Look at the superb sequence of drawings of the baby more interested in the wrapping paper than the present, or at Tom, leaning back secure and calm again between Grandpa's legs; the two lovingly entwined figures in Shirley Hughes' drawing express far more than words.

"Christmas Stories," in Books for Keeps, *No. 35, November, 1985, p. 8.*

There are a great many Christmas books dealing with families preparing for and celebrating Christmas. This British import is particularly good as it seems fuller and more expansive in presenting the many details of the celebration, albeit with a British slant. It is also one of the few titles to touch on the religious aspects of the holiday. Hughes even shows the stressful aspects. A teary-eyed Tom is shown over-excited from all of the presents and rather cross. Like a special Christmas treat, this is a story chockful of delights. Warmly colored detailed paintings add an extra glow.

Judith Gloyer, "Celebrate the Season!" in School Library Journal, *Vol. 33, No. 2, October, 1986, p. 110.*

***ALFIE GETS IN FIRST* (1981)**

An entirely believable domestic problem . . . is exploited with demure humour and with that attention to individual features that gives Shirley Hughes's neighbourhood scenes complete validity. . . . Neat, blithe and engagingly realistic.

Margery Fisher, in a review of "Alfie Gets In First," in Growing Point, *Vol. 20, No. 6, March, 1982, p. 4037.*

A small boy reaches home just before his mother (and baby sister) and slams the door shut. The key is inside the house with Alfie, however, and a small excitement ensues. With elements of the cumulative tale—as neighbors and milkmen offer assistance—the story reaches a very happy end in which no one is any way blamed. Inventive use of the double spreads establishes the simultaneous display of indoor and outdoor actions. The setting is English and the prose understated, and the illustrations, in full color, manage to be pleasing in a slightly scruffy way. The blurb on the back of the jacket suggests that this is the first title in a projected series of Alfie books. If so, it's an auspicious beginning by an accomplished author-artist. (pp. 134-35)

Joan W. Blos, in a review of "Alfie Gets In First," in School Library Journal, *Vol. 28, No. 7, March, 1982, pp. 134-35.*

The realistic, full-color pictures capture the British quality of the row houses on the street as well as that of the people involved; many of the pages facing each other ingeniously show Alfie in his isolation from the outside world and enhance the dramatic give-and-take between the boy and his would-be rescuers. Both the text and the pictures unassumingly but delightfully present a situation that is universal in its humor. (pp. 155-56)

Paul Heins, in a review of "Alfie Gets In First," in The Horn Book Magazine, *Vol. LVIII, No. 2, April, 1982, pp. 155-56.*

Clever layout takes Alfie's story, already highly appropriate for this age group, and lifts it out of the ordinary. . . . [Hughes'] four-color artwork offers a nice slice of British life (though setting is not integral to the story); her faces are extremely expressive, but at times very old heads seem to be sitting on young shoulders. A recognizable situation presented with inventiveness and energy.

Ilene Cooper, in a review of "Alfie Gets In First," in Booklist, *Vol. 78, No. 16, April 15, 1982, p. 1096.*

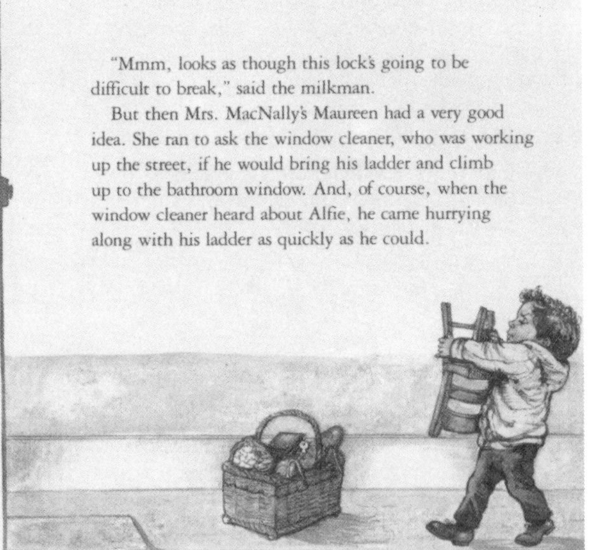

From Alfie Gets in First, *written and illustrated by Shirley Hughes. Lothrop, Lee & Shepard Books, 1982. Copyright © 1981 by Shirley Hughes. All rights reserved. By permission of Lothrop, Lee & Shepard Books (A Division of William Morrow & Company, Inc.). In Canada by The Bodley Head Ltd., on behalf of the author.*

CHARLIE MOON AND THE BIG BONANZA BUST-UP **(1982)**

The Lady Illustrator down on her knees drawing the outline of a huge dragon and pushing stray wisps of hair back into her bun sounds like—and indeed looks like—Shirley Hughes herself, who doubles here as Lady Writer of her second Charlie Moon book. The integration of pictures with text is more ambitious than in ***Here comes Charlie Moon*** and works particularly well at some of the most active moments of the plot. Best of all are the beautifully composed prelims, complete with cast list, and the final toast to Mr Bowen the painter. However, the paragraph which accompanies this illustration seems excessively moralistic. As the story itself implicitly commends art and artists of all kinds and condemns property merchants, harassment of tenants, glossy television images, and so on, it scarcely seems necessary to overstate the case for art in this way. Indeed, common to both Charlie Moon books is the portrayal of imaginative, artistic, slightly mad people as sympathetic and more worldly types as unsympathetic.

The book opens with Charlie in pitch darkness, stumbling about inside the back legs of a horse as he practises with his friend Dodger for the Book Bonanza organized by Linda, the children's librarian. They end in a heap on the floor, intertwined with a robot—otherwise Charlie's cousin, Ariadne. With Charlie's young uncle, Norman, they all visit Linda's uncle, Owen Bowen, the sitting tenant on the top floor of an old house owned by crafty Mr Dix. It transpires that the landlord has been trying to get his tenant out by making smells in the hallways (with mouldy kippers under the floorboards) and then complaining about them. He is also keen to get his hands on a valuable old chalk drawing of Owen Bowen's grandmother. When he does so, he is followed by two ham-handed antique shop owners, one a toughy, the other a hypochondriac, who want the drawing for themselves. In a somewhat far-fetched plot which ends up with the magician at the Book Bonanza, TV personality Duggie Bubbles, being the younger brother of Mr Dix, the theft is exposed and the drawing returned to its owner.

Perhaps more impressive than the plot itself is the speed with which it moves. Shirley Hughes obviously has a firm grasp of the concentration spans of her potential readers and she packs each chapter with so much incident that even the wilder coincidences of the plot are forgiveable. ***Charlie Moon*** is great fun as a quick read for eight to eleven year olds.

Josephine Karavasil, "Packing It In," in The Times Literary Supplement, *No. 4146, September 17, 1982, p. 1002.*

Charlie Moon is a new comic figure in children's books. He and his bookish cousin, Ariadne, provide for primary school children the romping kind of adventure that stories should be made of at that stage; lots of plotting, adventure with the possibility of surprise, and memorable characters. Here these are Linda, the library lady, and her uncle Mr Owen Bowen, the artist who lives in a flat overlooking the Thames from which the villain Mr Dix is trying to evict him. . . .

The text and the drawings make an artistic unity that reminds one of Ardizzone. There is also a sub-plot about painting and pictures, all firmly rooted in Thames-side London, that carries a more serious intent. But the fun is the thing, and the story with pictures keeps the reader going, from first to last.

Margaret Meek, in a review of "Charlie Moon and the Big Bonanza Bust-Up," in The School Librarian, *Vol. 31, No. 1, March, 1983, p. 37.*

This is the literary equivalent of a comic strip story; that is, the emphasis is on swift, ever-changing action, a fleeting resemblance to real life, and basic, boldly coloured characterisation. That having been said, I will readily admit that Shirley Hughes' second story about Charlie Moon is an excellent read, full of high spirits and incredible excitement. . . . [There] are some funny set-pieces before the mystery is—not very convincingly—resolved.

If Miss Hughes is not the best maker of plots she is one of the most professional of today's illustrators, and almost every page is enriched with an elegant, evocative or comic example of her work. They alone are worth the price.

M. Crouch, in a review of "Charlie Moon and the Big Bonanza Bust-Up," in The Junior Bookshelf, *Vol. 47, No. 2, April, 1983, p. 76.*

Hughes, who is best known in America for her picture books about that universal child, Alfie, reaches out to an older audience with her character Charlie Moon. Charlie, a London kid of about 9 or 10, is quite engaging himself; and despite the definite British tone and setting, kids in this part of the world should find him a kindred spirit. Hughes pulls off a good one here—a finely tuned mystery so full of complexities it would make Agatha Christie smile. . . . Perhaps British children read better than American; it does seem as if Hughes is writing a bit above her intended age group. Fortunately, she strings her delightful pen-and-ink drawings across the pages, and readers will probably become thoroughly involved with the story before they realize it contains some difficult words.

Ilene Cooper, in a review of "Charlie Moon and the Big Bonanza Bust-Up," in Booklist, *Vol. 81, No. 14, March 15, 1985, p. 1059.*

ALFIE'S FEET **(1982)**

The success of ***Alfie's Feet*** must surely be attributed to Shirley Hughes's understanding of children. Alfie is every little boy, splashing and stamping through puddles in his old brown shoes. Could he be envious of his sister Annie Rose's new red shoes? The joy of a trip to the shoe shop for a pair of shiny yellow wellington boots is perfectly conveyed in the lively, detailed, yet warm and cosy illustrations we have come to expect from this author. In childlike eagerness Alfie makes the mistake of putting his boots on the wrong feet. The discovery of why he felt uncomfortable and his mother's action to ensure it doesn't happen again is so sensitively dealt with that every little boy may identify with the situation without losing face. This is a book to read to three- to six-year-olds and to be enjoyed by young readers.

Maisie Roberts, in a review of "Alfie's Feet," in British Book News, *Children's Supplement, Autumn, 1982, p. 12.*

[Shirley Hughes] is good at identifying the realities of an infant's life. There is a small story in ***Alfie's Feet.*** Alfie enjoys walking in puddles, so Mum buys him some wellies. . . . These are . . . sophisticated, professional drawings, but they . . . are firmly based in reality. Cute Alfie and his sister may be, but there is no trace of sentimentality in these portraits. Mum and Dad are presented without glamour, and so is the cosy muddle of their home. Here and in the High Street and the park the young observer will recognise a world which is most clearly his own, but, seeing it through such candid eyes, will find his own observation sharpened.

M. Crouch, in a review of "Alfie's Feet," in The Junior Bookshelf, *Vol. 47, No. 1, February, 1983, p. 7.*

Once again, with affection and skill the author-artist shows her understanding of the minor dilemmas of the very young and glorifies the everyday life of ordinary people. A matter-of-fact text recounts the events, while handsome full-color paintings—wonderfully unromanticized—offer little children a wealth of fascinating activities and details to pore over.

Ethel L. Heins, in a review of "Alfie's Feet," in The Horn Book Magazine, *Vol. LIX, No. 2, April, 1983, p. 160.*

The clever blending of text and illustrations adds zest and vitality to Alfie's everyday happenings. Children relate well to these action-oriented episodes. The endearing scenes share a sense of warm realism particularly in the calm acceptance of the parents—perhaps they have been through this before! A great empathy is established between father and son since the dad's nonchalant attitude is caring rather than impatient or scolding. Shirley Hughes captures the treasured moments of childhood: being big enough to carry your own boots home in a box, the enjoyment of splashing in huge puddles of water, and the joy of being securely comfortable with one's parents. The humorous images of Alfie stamping around in his new yellow rubber boots and his sister skimming around the floor in her potty will delight the young reader. (pp. 395-96)

Ronald A. Jobe, "Books and Children: The Reader's Connexion!" in Language Arts, *Vol. 61, No. 4, April, 1984, pp. 395-96.*

***ALFIE GIVES A HAND* (1983)**

We all know Alfie, through his first two books and in real life. He is the small boy who finds adventure in the most ordinary events of daily life. This time he goes to Bernard's birthday party. Without the support of Mum and Annie Rose Alfie feels shy, and so it is necessary for him to take his old blanket with him as a Mum-substitute. It gets a bit messy at tea-time, but time, and the need to give his support to Min—who will hold no hand but his—give him the confidence to put his blanket on one side. Alfie's exemplary behaviour shows up Bernard who, as host, could hardly be more objectionable. Word and picture march together in this model of a story of everyday happenings. Notice how Shirley Hughes gives character to each child-face, and how each face reflects the passions of fright, grief, amazement. Enjoying this story the four-year-old finds his own experience confirmed in the most satisfactory and comforting way. (pp. 13-14)

M. Crouch, in a review of "Alfie Gives a Hand," in The Junior Bookshelf, *Vol. 48, No. 1, February, 1984, pp. 13-14.*

In her picture books the author-artist provides a marvelous mirror of the concerns of young children. . . . Honest, forthright, and engaging, the story—like its predecessors—is a gem, a successful blending of twentieth-century genre painting with a brisk, matter-of-fact text.

Mary M. Burns, in a review of "Alfie Gives a Hand," in The Horn Book Magazine, *Vol. LX, No. 3, June, 1984, p. 320.*

As in two earlier books, ***Alfie Gets in First*** and ***Alfie's Feet,*** Alfie faces a familiar preschool predicament. He is invited to playmate Bernard's birthday party—but Mom isn't. . . . The text is as natural and unadorned as the characters it describes. As in the earlier books, Hughes' realistic, stocky figures come alive in colorful line and wash settings. This one is sure to find a place among children's favorite birthday stories.

Heide Piehler, in a review of "Alfie Gives a Hand," in School Library Journal, *Vol. 30, No. 10, August, 1984, p. 61.*

***LUCY AND TOM'S A.B.C.* (1984)**

Lucy and Tom are already familiar from four of Shirley Hughes's earlier picture books. Here, vignettes of their everyday activities—shopping with their mother, going to the play-ground, having a bedtime story read to them—are used to illustrate each letter of the alphabet. Thus the first page shows them self-referentially absorbed in their own book, identifying aunts, acrobats and artists while munching apples and apricots. Finally, "z is for zoo, of course".

The "of course" highlights some of the book's problems. On the one hand, some children are bound to find a comforting familiarity in the paintpots and brickblocks of the nursery school, in the packets of biscuits and honey pot on the tea table, in the trains and teddy bears. Others may find this well-equipped home, with its tasteful pastel walls, its dresser and chesterfield, it forays into Conran-land, decidedly unlike their own. There is plenty of stress on activity, from colouring in and skipping to dressing up (girls) and sailing yachts on the pond (largely boys), but there is also a decided stress on consumer durables. Perhaps those who identify less readily with the life depicted will suffer most strongly from the unintended implications of that "of course". For the book is dully uninventive. Even the odd twitches of naughtiness on the part of Lucy and Tom—surprising their father with an empty eggshell at breakfast, Tom's jumping on the furniture, having tactfully taken off his shoes, are tame. Where are the aardvarks and anteaters, the goats and gnats and gnus which make other alphabet books fun?

Who, indeed, is this alphabet book intended for? Hughes carefully gives children unfamiliar with their letters large upper and lower-case characters, yet there is, on most pages, a solid ratio of prose to pictures. Those already conversant with the alphabet are hardly going to have their vocabulary extended by learning—only—that "b is for books and bed". Shirley Hughes's watercolours and use of fine brush lines, her eye for detail, are as technically bewitching as ever, particularly in a scene of moonlight over back gardens. But she seems to be appealing to an adult eye, and, what is worse, to a condescending image of child cuteness. Over the last thirty years of excellent illustrative work, her younger children's cheeks have grown chubbier; their heads, with occasional alarming echoes of Atwell, top heavy for their bodies. She seems too often in this book to have forgotten the demand for graphic consistency. It is confusing enough to be asked to discover Lucy and Tom waving from their garden gate in a crowded double-spread of homes and houses, but irritating as well to find that the chimney-stacks on their own house have jumped around from one picture to another.

Kate Flint, "L is for Life-Style," in The Times Literary Supplement, *No. 4237, June 15, 1984, p. 677.*

The child who has a collection of Lucy and Tom books is fortunate indeed. This is an ABC but it works at so many levels that to discuss it merely in terms of the alphabet would be to miss the point.

As with all Shirley Hughes's work, a feature is the skill with which she exploits the shape of a page, and makes each turn of the page lead the reader to the surprise of the next. First we are shown a double-page spread crowded with children and their mums in a park playground, and then we find a simple piece of text with a surround of portraits of Lucy and Tom. This constant shifting of scale and degree of detail keeps the eye lively and the imagination working. Shirley Hughes is a true illustrator and capitalises on the possiblities of text. Here the differences in the typeface help the reader to find the meaning.

The pictures are quite ravishing—acutely observed and full of spontaneity and vigour. A particular pleasure is the weather in the drawings—from cold London rain to gusty days sailing toy boats in the park. A delightful book to introduce children to the pleasures of reading.

Gabrielle Maunder, in a review of "Lucy and Tom's A.B.C.," in The School Librarian, *Vol. 32, No. 4, December, 1984, p. 336.*

While nearly all of the words are readily familiar to preschoolers, one or two may need explanation—for example, "Y is for yachts on the water" shows a group of children sailing toy *boats*; some youngsters may not make the connection unaided. The few Briticisms ("cross" instead of angry, "sweets" instead of candy) are easily understood in context. Hughes' humorous illustrations are cheerfully cluttered and untidy, and Lucy and Tom are a winning, if sometimes mischievous, pair. Too complex to be a first book on the ABCs, this will nonetheless delight listeners who need or want to reinforce their alphabet skills. (p. 69)

Kathleen Brachmann, in a review of "Lucy and Tom's A.B.C.," in School Library Journal, *Vol. 33, No. 6, February, 1987, pp. 68-9.*

AN EVENING AT ALFIE'S (1984)

Shirley Hughes has the enviable gift of capturing childhood in her text and illustrations. She does not indulge in sentimentality for her boys and girls are down-to-earth, sometimes naughty, always full of life. Alfie is sensible—when he hears water dripping he tells Maureen the baby sitter and she in her turn calls for adult help. To Alfie, of course, the flood is exciting and he makes the most of its delights in this eventful story.

The background of the story is one most children know, the home. It is a home where there is affection and neighbours are kind. The adventures are those which a child reader understands and can share in imagination.

Needless to say the illustrations are delightful, a celebration of childhood.

E. Colwell, in a review of "An Evening at Alfie's," in The Junior Bookshelf, *Vol. 48, No. 6, December, 1984, p. 247.*

It could be any ordinary evening at Alfie's snugly helter-skelter house—with Mom and Dad off to a party, "the MacNally's daughter, Maureen," comes to baby-sit, and Alfie and little Annie Rose ready for bed. Hughes so insinuates us into the scene, with her confiding, storyteller's voice and her keenly characterized figures, her vibrantly furnished interior, that any small incident becomes an event. . . . Family feeling, neighborly feeling, the drama of the dripping water, the real-life interest of the burst pipe and the shut-off valve: ***An Evening at Alfie's*** is to relish.

A review of "An Evening at Alfie's," in Kirkus Reviews, *Juvenile Issue, Vol. LIII, Nos. 1-5, March 1, 1985, p. J-6.*

While Alfie's latest adventure is a bit more dramatic than the everyday childhood challenges of the earlier books, Hughes presents it with the same polished execution as the others—a well-developed story, a flowing text and those now-familiar, but always inviting, warm-hued line and wash illustrations. Alfie fans will be delighted with this latest episode and anxiously await the next.

Heide Piehler, in a review of "An Evening at Alfie's," in The School Librarian, *Vol. 33, No. 9, May, 1985, p. 76.*

BATHWATER'S HOT; NOISY; WHEN WE WENT TO THE PARK (NURSERY COLLECTION) (1985)

In her new Nursery Collection series for the very young, Shirley Hughes fulfills a traditional role, teaching numbers, sounds and opposites, with a minimum of fuss. The only extravagance to be found in her unambitious texts with their attachment to everyday scenes is a mild caricaturing of faces. A rather unappetizing mixture, this is all warmed up in a sauce of general good cheer. The hapless appearance of the main character may recall that of Jude the Obscure's eldest child, but Hughes's well-behaved little girl is no trouble to her family, cuddling kittens, acknowledging bed-time, and striking a modest pose in the bath.

Improbable heroine in tow, Hughes sets out to educate and entertain, but originality is lacking. In ***Noisy,*** sounds are named but rarely imitated through language: doors merely slam, telephones ring, cats cat-a-waul. The book becomes a list of wasted opportunities for onomatopoeic invention. To divide the world into contrasts, in a country covered in terraced houses and perpetual twilight, seems yet more misleading, and in ***Bathwater's Hot,*** Hughes stumbles into many foggy issues. "Some things you can throw away, some are nice to keep" is a distinction both adults and children have trouble making. There is some thorough advice on etiquette: "It's kind to be helpful, unkind to tease, rather rude to push and grab, polite to say 'please' "—but Hughes forgets that it is obnoxious to entice the young into a book in order to scold them.

The artificiality of Hughes's impish characters is softened, especially in ***When We Went to the Park,*** by some lovely landscape backgrounds, and more directly altered by the effects of wind and rain.

Lucy Ellman, "Childhood's Image," in The Times Literary Supplement, *No. 4308, October 25, 1985, p. 1218.*

Shirley Hughes's miniatures could be described, pompously, as a mixture of grammar and sociology. Each one shows episodes in the life of a highly paintable average family (father, mother, small girl, baby boy, with shaggy dog and mother cat alongside) and each one offers defining nouns, adjectives and verbs collected in a particular category. ***When we went to the Park*** is a counting book, ***Bathwater's Hot*** illustrates opposites, ***Noisy*** works on a scheme of contrasts. The pictures have the verve and humour we expect from this artist and the firm individuality with which she can always endow her characters. They are Everyman (so they can be accepted by Anychild) yet each one performs a particular action or shows a particular mood in a way that makes them real people. As a bonus this kind of book, given the vivacity of colour and variety of backgrounds, can start and support those bedtime conversations in which early vocabularies grow and flourish. (pp. 4512-13)

Margery Fisher, in a review of "Bathwater's Hot," "Noisy," and "When We Went to the Park," in Growing Point, *Vol. 24, No. 4, November, 1985, pp. 4511-13.*

Hughes' scruffy illustrations have lots of character, which enriches these elementary concept books considerably. . . . The books' slim texts provide just enough substance for the intended concepts to come across. Accompanying illustrations are lovingly done and peopled with characters that look ever so real in their charming imperfection. Hughes has a delightfully unerring eye for the many untidy details that seem to be a permanent fixture when young children are about. A nice trio of concepts imaginatively drawn from real life.

Denise M. Wilms, in a review of "Bathwater's Hot," "Noisy," and "When We Went to the Park," in Booklist, *Vol. 82, No. 7, December 1, 1985, p. 573.*

Three small books by Shirley Hughes are certainly cause for satisfaction. Meant for even younger readers than the Alfie books, they feature one of her harried English families—the kind with less-than-beauty-queen mums and households in cheerful disarray. . . . Particularly pleasing is Hughes's offhand handling of diverse ethnic groups: one illustration shows "three ladies chatting on a bench," where an Indian holds the others spellbound with a story, while their babies rest in their strollers. All three books are a paean to the pleasures and small problems of domestic life, and the author certainly has the gift of entering into the feelings of a small child. Reassurance, education, and amusement are tied together in three small packages. (pp. 48-9)

Ann A. Flowers, in a review of "Bathwater's Hot," "Noisy," and "When We Went to the Park," in The Horn Book Magazine, *Vol. LXII, No. 1, January-February, 1986, pp. 48-9.*

CHIPS AND JESSIE (1985)

No one explores the comedy of ordinary life more accurately and more hilariously than Shirley Hughes, and the fun and the truth spring from the same source. She is a great observer, and also one of those rare artists who write as well as they draw. This little book is surely destined to become a family favourite, and there is a place for its disruptive influence in the classroom too. (p. 259)

M. Crouch, in a review of "Chips and Jessie," in The Junior Bookshelf, *Vol. 49, No. 6, December, 1985, pp. 258-59.*

There are many things to be said about this exceptional book to bring it quickly to the notice of all who teach children to read. It needs a description, but as the operations conducted on its pages are essentially related to sign and symbol systems and the ways in which children learn to operate them, words in a review are not an adequate means of representing the intentions or the effects of the artist and author.

The stories are told by the characters, Chips and Jessie, who introduce themselves, their families and their pets. Each page is a continuous narrative text, a variety of drawing styles—framed or unframed—and different ways of indicating speech, action and thought. For example, the cat and dog are the wise commentators. From the first page the readers are part of the action, 'drawn in' by the characters who perform what the text narrates. When Chips and Jessie plan to have tea together, Jessie is baking on one side of the double spread while Chips is changing his clothes on the other. (Remember the page division of ***Alfie gets in first?***) When there is an argument between Chips and his mother, their faces confront each other while the dialogue sits untagged in the middle of the page. All the skills required for reading, from comics to continuous text, are exercised here while the traditional narrative structure works as well as ever. The last tale, about an up-market jumble sale, has the right degree of subversion in the plot and suspense for the reader.

This is modern reading as the play of the page, learned from TV and advertising. There has to be guessing and puzzling, work in fact, but the fun is uppermost and the children are in charge of the stories. At the start the characters acknowledge Shirley Hughes's help. If ever readers are brought into being, it should be by this book.

Margaret Meek, in a review of "Chips and Jessie," in The School Librarian, *Vol. 34, No. 1, March, 1986, p. 46.*

The format of these four episodes in the lives of Chips and Jessie (who appear to be about seven or eight) will surely attract young readers just moving into chapter books. . . . The children are a likeable lot, and school situations show children of many races. A few Briticisms, such as *vicar, gaoler,* and *maths* are understandable in context. The book's size, a little larger than a standard paperback, will make it just right for children who will undoubtedly want to read the story in tandem. And chuckle.

Susan Hepler, in a review of "Chips and Jessie," in School Library Journal, *Vol. 33, No. 2, October, 1986, p. 162.*

Shirley Hughes has produced a book which deliberately sets out to combine text and illustration in such a way that readers lacking confidence can start with the easy 'bubble' stories and will then move on to the continuous text. It is an original idea which is handled beautifully, giving the feeling that this book really is for children to read to themselves. The characters are lively, the dialogue is crisp and the blend of text and illustration is genuinely inviting. (p. 25)

Julia Eccleshare, "Early Reading," in her Children's Books of the Year 1986, *National Book League, 1986, pp. 24-8.*

ALL SHAPES AND SIZES; COLOURS; TWO SHOES, NEW SHOES (NURSERY COLLECTION) (1986)

[***All Shapes and Sizes*** is a] genuine 'Beginners' book, with pictures of everyday situations matched with the simplest of texts. No one draws ordinary kids better than Shirley Hughes. Technically brilliant, free of extravagance or pretension, these are pictures for baby to gurgle at and parents to marvel at, and there is something for the rest of the family in between. . . . The book is one in this artist's 'Nursery Collection' series. It could not be too highly commended.

Marcus Crouch, in a review of "All Shapes and Sizes," in The Junior Bookshelf, *Vol. 50, No. 4, August, 1986, p. 141.*

Trust Shirley Hughes to turn a simple, small square concept book into something almost magical. Her pictures [in ***Colours***] positively glow by turn with blue, yellow, red, orange, purple, green, not to mention black and white, and feature a small girl and her family in everyday surroundings. There is colour too in the words, a rhyming text with a rhythmic quality, a pleasure both to read and to look at.

Jill Bennett, in a review of "Colours," in The School Librarian, *Vol 34, No. 3, September, 1986, p. 240.*

Each of these concept books has rhyming text and follows the same family of characters, and all art is rendered in watercolor and sepia line. ***All Shapes and Sizes*** compares boxes and balls, high and low, large and small, and narrow and wide. In ***Colors,*** a bright and glowing palette is used to present double pages of objects that are blue, yellow, red, orange, purple, green, black, and white. ***Two Shoes, New Shoes*** shows children wearing or playing dress-up in a variety of shoes, gloves, hats, and other clothes. Young children may need some help in understanding that the British "crown in a cracker" is a party favor, not a snack. Inviting endpaper pictures, an interracial and variously aged cast, plus a winsome, active three or four year old and her lumpy baby brother are just right. These are sure to be popular with children and their parents, and a welcome addition to any preschool collection.

Susan Hepler, in a review of "All Shapes and Sizes," in School Library Journal, *Vol. 33, No. 4, December, 1986, p. 90.*

Simply rhymed text and good humored drawings explore the everyday world of a preschool child and her baby brother and convey traditional sets of concepts in these new additions to Hughes's Nursery Collection Series. As in ***Bathwater's Hot*** each book is filled with cluttered, homey scenes of children happily at play in many inviting situations. . . . While the structure of each book is episodic, character, story, and continuity run through this collection of vignettes. A favorite stuffed dog in varied dress, the jolly baby, the happy mess, and numerous details in the watercolor drawings provide lingering enjoyment for parent and child.

Margaret A. Bush, in a review of "Two Shoes, New Shoes," in The Horn Book Magazine, *Vol. LXIII, No. 1, January, 1987, p. 48.*

ANOTHER HELPING OF CHIPS (1986)

Following on from ***Chips and Jessie*** are four short stories employing the previously successful variety of presentation. The first and last are in strip-cartoon form, while the middle two have paragraphs of print interspersed with drawings of the characters, their thoughts and speech shown in balloons. First impressions of this layout suggest a busy look which might seem confusing, but closer acquaintance reveals many merits. There is provision for different levels of reading ability. In the stories containing large blocks of unrelieved print, the story-line could be followed from the pictures with direct speech. The eight-year-old for whom the printed word is still daunting

From Another Helping of Chips, *written and illustrated by Shirley Hughes. Lothrop, Lee and Shepard Books, 1987. Copyright © 1986 by Shirley Hughes. All rights reserved. By permission of Lothrop, Lee & Shepard Books (A Division of William Morrow & Company, Inc.). In Canada by The Bodley Head Ltd., on behalf of the author.*

would not be insulted by the content. There is a wealth of humour in the tales of warm relationships, human and animal. The black-and-white line-drawings are superb in portraying exactly the feelings and situations in the stories. Would it be greedy to ask for yet another helping of Chips?

Maisie Roberts, in a review of "Another Helping of Chips," in British Book News Children's Books, *December, 1986, p. 14.*

In her second book about Chips and his best friend, Jessie, Hughes again mixes short stories and comic-strip art to tell four stories in a humorously inviting format.

The focus is primarily on Chips as he, by turns, deals with the inconveniences of his mother's spring cleaning; the visit of a particularly obnoxious middle-aged cousin; the reaction of his cat, Albert, to a small but cute feline invader; and the attempts of Barkis (Jessie's dog) to join the neighborhood carolers, attempts which have surprisingly profitable results. The first story, **"Spring Fever,"** and the last, **"We Wish You a Merry Christmas,"** are done entirely as comic strips and bracket the two longer, interior stories, which artfully mix illustration and witty text to add texture to basically predictable plots. Especially well done is Cousin Waldo, a health-nut done in by his affection for apple pie and spaghetti and Chip's clever work with the bathroom scale. Also memorable are Albert's Machiavellian tactics against a kitten who deflects Chips' attention and threatens to take his place in the household.

Hughes' eye for illustrative detail and her ear for humor carry the day; and her inventive format will draw even the most reluctant reader into the slightly British but very funny neighborhood at Mallard Street.

A review of "Another Helping of Chips," in Kirkus Reviews, *Vol. LV, No. 4, February 15, 1987, p. 302.*

At first glance, ***Another helping of Chips*** is almost indistinguishable from its predecessor, ***Chips and Jessie.*** There is the same ingenious integration of pictures and written text; the same range of illustrative modes from comic strip to deep-perspective drawing and, of course, the same two characters. . . . The stories themselves are not especially remarkable. Indeed the first of the longer stories, **'Cousin Waldo's visit'**, draws upon a theme familiar to all comic readers and cartoon viewers: the arrival of an unwanted relative who shatters domestic routines and is eventually routed by the ingenuity of the hero or heroine. The excitement and challenge for the reader lie in charting a course that takes in the various images and icons that have been strategically placed on every page. One could read the printed text only and try to ignore the pictures, but it would be very difficult and besides, one would miss half the pleasure and most of the point.

'The ghost in the shopping-bag' is the most effective story in the collection, telling of Chips finding a stray kitten and of the subsequent defection of Albert, the family cat. Here we find a collection of the kinds of illustration that Shirley Hughes draws so well, including short, wordless sequences in the manner of ***Up and up.*** Although ***Another helping of Chips*** doesn't quite match up to the previous collection in terms of narrative richness and variety, it is none the less clearly the work of an illustrator and storyteller on the top of her form. (pp. 135-36)

David Lewis, in a review of "Another Helping of Chips," in The School Librarian, *Vol. 35, No. 2, May, 1987, pp. 135-36.*

Chips and Jessie are back in another quartet of engaging stories that get an extra boost from Hughes' rumpled but ever-so-apt illustrations. . . . The illustrations are as important as the text. . . . There is a British flavor to the book, but Chips is definitely *not* dissimilar from American children his age. A humorous slice of child life served up by an author-artist whose knack for depicting the funnier foibles of families is undeniable.

Denise M. Wilms, in a review of "Another Helping of Chips," in Booklist, *Vol. 83, No. 22, August, 1987, p. 1748.*

LUCY AND TOM'S 1, 2, 3 **(1987)**

Again, what's-only-to-be-expected presented so freshly it takes a while to persuade yourself you won't be smudging the ink as you turn over the pages. Shirley Hughes is our foremost chronicler of the life of ordinary households and every detail here *counts*—which is what she's after—from ornamental ducks on the mantelpiece to the marking of family heights on Mum and Dad's bedroom wall. There's much opportunity for Maths work but so cunningly crafted into the storyline it comes across as maths-play. Who needs Nuffield or Harold Fletcher? Clearly the Lucy and Tom show will run and run . . . all the way to GCSE if I had my way.

Chris Powling, in a review of "Lucy and Tom's 1.2.3.," in Books for Keeps, *No. 44, May, 1987, p. 27.*

This counting book with a difference wends its way delightfully from one little Lucy fast asleep in bed to ten kisses on sixty-year-old Granny's birthday card. Lucy and Tom make two of course and Mopsa has five kittens but this story introduces numbers in an irregular way therefore inviting children to work out where, when and how the next might occur. The houses in the street also demonstrate odds and evens in sequence—a good way to open up discussion with young children. As usual Shirley Hughes's illustrations complement the text admirably and her detailed style continues to intrigue and captivate.

Cliff Moon, in a review of "Lucy and Tom's 1.2.3.," in British Book News Children's Books, *June, 1987, p. 13.*

[***Lucy and Tom's 1.2.3***] is technically as competent as [Eric Carle's *Papa, Please Get the Moon for Me*], and its 'message' is unequivocally one of love. Lucy and Tom have a busy day culminating in Granny's birthday party. The unassuming text and the warm and amusing drawings both press home gently a lesson in counting, but you would hardly be aware that you were being 'got at'. It is all good fun and sound observation.

M. Crouch, in a review of "Lucy and Tom's 1.2.3.," in The Junior Bookshelf, *Vol. 51, No. 4, August, 1987, p. 159.*

Lilian Moore

19??-

American poet; author of fiction, nonfiction, and picture books; reteller; and editor.

Moore is the creator of a wide variety of poetry collections and easy readers which are distinguished by her simplicity, wit, and understanding of young children. Best known for her poetry, which ranges from droll Halloween verse to thoughtful reflections on both the natural world and contemporary urban life, she writes brief, perceptive lyrics in flowing, occasionally rhyming lines which are unrestricted by meter and characterized by their fresh images and consistent metaphors. Acknowledged for her skillful craftsmanship, discriminating ear for sounds, and graceful restraint, Moore focuses on the universal experiences and feelings of childhood and enables her audience to find beauty in familiar and unexpected places. A former teacher, reading specialist, and editor, she has written more than forty beginning readers with easy language and lively plots to encourage the primary grade reader. Moore began her literary career with books which are noted for their humor, depiction of warm family relationships, and ingenious use of repetition. A versatile writer, she has authored such diverse tales as a story about a French taxi driver which includes an appended glossary useful for foreign language classes, a mood piece about a farmer's concern for ecological balance, and a series of animal fantasies about engaging Little Raccoon, who also serves as the subject of a book of poetry. Moore has also produced concept books on numbers and words, created a storyless picture book with Remy Charlip which celebrates self-identity, and faithfully retold a Hans Christian Andersen fairy tale in her typically simple but rich English.

Critics praise Moore for her economy of language, evocative imagery, and natural unforced style. They admire the variety, humor, and accessibility of her stories for the early independent reader. Although some reviewers point out that her plots lack originality and that her poems tend to be similar, most agree that Moore's accurate observations of nature, her sensitivity to children's feelings, and her ability to distill the essence of experience in a few carefully chosen words have established her works as an excellent introduction to poetry and reading.

Moore received the National Council of Teachers of English Award for excellence in poetry for children in 1985.

(See also *Contemporary Authors,* Vol. 103).

AUTHOR'S COMMENTARY

[*The following excerpt is from an interview by Joan I. Glazer.*]

"Poems should be like fireworks, packed carefully and artfully, ready to explode with unpredictable effects," says Lilian Moore. . . . "When people asked Robert Frost—as they did by the hundreds—what he meant by 'But I have promises to keep / And miles to go before I sleep / And miles to go before I sleep,' he always turned the question aside with a joke. Maybe he couldn't answer it, and maybe he was glad that the lines exploded in so many different colors in so many people's minds."

Courtesy of Joan Glazer

Lilian Moore's poems have exploded in the minds of children and adults alike, causing them to visualize wind "wrinkling" the water, or sense something, "slinkety-sly," coming down the stairs. Her works of poetry include ***I Feel the Same Way, I Thought I Heard the City, Sam's Place, See My Lovely Poison Ivy, Think of Shadows,*** and ***Something New Begins.*** She has also authored many picture books and compiled several collections of poems for children.

She was living in New York when her first book of poems was published, but laughs when the idea of her being a "city person" is questioned. "I started out with a flower pot, then I had a window box, then I had a back yard, then I came here. So I've always wanted things that grow, and the light of the sky in the country." "Here" is a farm in Kerhonkson, New York, where she and her husband, Sam Reavin, live, and which is the setting for ***Sam's Place.*** It was also the setting for this interview. The visitor can step out the back door to where deer approached the house, see the chestnut tree and what now remains of the old apple orchard, look across the pond, see those aspects of nature which were observed so carefully and written about so lovingly.

What does Ms. Moore see as the outstanding characteristic of her work? "I try to tell the truth." It is the truth of accurate observations, without sentimentality. "The equivalent of doing research for a book when you're writing about a willow, let's say, as I did in **'Yellow Willow,'** is to live with that willow the whole year round. I watched those willows, and they're all kinds of yellow—spring yellow, summer yellow-green. But it took me some time to realize that they were yellow all through the winter too, that those "brassy boughs" do stay yellow. Now, Sam was a terrific help, because I was always asking questions about how things grew, how the land changed, checking to see if I was precise—telling the truth."

Does she see any of her writing as being fantasy, or is it all the real world and how she perceives it? "Well, this is a poem of mine I happen to like," she responds. "Is this real or is it fantasy?"

"Mural on Second Avenue"

Someone
stood here
tall on a ladder,
dreaming
to the slap of a
wet brush,

painting
on the blank
unwindowed wall of
this old house.

Now the wall is a
field of wild
grass,
bending to a wind.

A unicorn's grazing there
beside a zebra.

A giraffe is nibbling a
tree top
and in a sky of
eye-blinking
blue
A horse is flying.
All
right at home in the
neighborhood.

She continues. "One day, when I walked down Second Avenue, I saw a wall which had been painted. And what was on it was a pond with a duck on it, and a tree. I was very much taken with the idea that in the city somebody wanted to paint this kind of dream. When I tried to write a poem that told exactly what I saw, it was klunky. It didn't work. I didn't capture what I thought the painter felt or what I felt when I saw the wall. A flying horse and a unicorn were necessary. I don't know whether that answers your question or not. To get the truth of how I felt, and the truth of what I saw, I had to have some magic, the same magic that person had while painting what to me was a dead duck."

The "truth of how I felt" permeates the writing of Ms. Moore. Some poems, such as **"Mural on Second Avenue"** and the ones in ***Sam's Place,*** reflect her experiences as an adult. Others, such as many of those in ***I Feel the Same Way,*** recall memories of her childhood. She describes the way she always felt when looking at the sea, her feeling in the fog as if it were wrapping her up, her memories of walking to and from school in the third grade on days so cold that she blew "dragon smoke" with her breath. When a poem is completed, she has a different feeling about the subject. "Once I have the poem done, I don't feel the same intensity." Is that a disappointment? "Oh, no. There are others ways of looking."

"When I'm writing a poem," Ms. Moore says, "I feel as if I'm working all the time. I think I wrote **'Until I Saw the Sea'** on the subway on the way to work." She concentrates on the imagery she's seeking and on the play of words—"I like the *echo* of words more than rhyme"—until she has the poem under control. "I once wrote a poem while at the dentist's. I withdrew completely into myself, with a real absorption, trying to solve a problem. Much testing and revising seems to be done in my head when I'm working on a poem.

"As I'm working on a version I've done, I read the poem to myself but not aloud. I hear it. I hear everything that's wrong with a line inside my head. You know the most autobiographical poem I ever wrote? That's a little lighthearted one in ***See My Lovely Poison Ivy.*** It's very apt.

"I Left My Head"

I left my head
somewhere
today.
Put it down for
just
a minute.
Under the
table?
On a chair?
Wish I were
able
to say
where.
Everything I need
is
in it!

That's my head! I could never use a computer, but don't tell anybody that. I love polishing. I can do a line twenty-five times trying to get it right. I edit my own things constantly.

"I believe that editing is a kind of sculpture. If there's a line with a bump in it and you have a sense of form, you smooth it and give it shape. When I was an editor, I was able to help people do that with their manuscripts. I was able to do that with my own stories. And possibly that's what happens with my poetry.

"Do you know who helps the most?" she asks. "Other poets. When I need a response, I turn to my friends—Judith Thurman, or Eve Merriam. I would ask Valerie Worth if she lived closer. We know each other only through letters. Poets help each other wonderfully. For instance, we'd been through a severe dry spell here and the line came to me, 'Roots have forgotten the taste of rain.' I told a poet friend, 'I'm really stuck on this line. I can't go forward.' She said, 'Why don't you back into it?' I said, 'Of course!' And that's what I did, backed into it. It worked as the last line of **'Dry Spell.'** That's how poets help one another—by listening seriously and taking seriously the problems in structuring a poem." It is on this level that Ms. Moore responds to the poetry of her son Jonathan, a published adult poet. Sharing a poem of his about the growth, both plant and animal, in the pond, she says, "It speaks to me, not as son to mother, but as poet to poet."

Ms. Moore has been a teacher and a reading specialist, and was the editor at Scholastic who established the Arrow Book

Club. As a child she was a voracious reader. She would go to the library, leave with an armful of books, and have read two of them before she got home. She simply assumed that she would be a writer when she grew up, and often created stories which she would tell to friends. With utter confidence in the loyalty of her audience, she would stop midway through the tale and announce that it was "to be continued tomorrow."

When her son was young, she wrote many light verses. "Feet that wear shoes can walk and have fun / Feet that wear sneakers want only to run," was inspired by her three year old with his first pair of sneakers. Jean Karl suggested that she collect some of the verses for a book. When she started writing the book, she found herself tapping her own childhood memories, rather than writing exclusively about the experiences of her son or other children whom she had observed.

She describes herself as being conscious of the limited experience of children and wanting her poetry to be accessible. However, if a poem works, she does not "censor" it, hoping that someone will help the child to "take in" the poem, or that the poem may become a "deposit" that the child can draw upon. She suggests that teachers not "bear down too hard" on a poem. They should begin with children's experience, then present the poem. Looking at **"Recess"** from ***Think of Shadows,*** Ms. Moore says she believes that children who have observed their own shadows on the playground can then be encouraged to talk about "scribbling their shadows on the school yard," and can deal with such figurative language as "till a cloud moving across the morning sun wipes out all scribbles like a giant eraser." She says ruefully that her poem **"Telling Time"** may be becoming old-fashioned, and an unfamiliar experience, for children with digital watches. They may not know what was meant when she wrote that "time . . . ticks, whispers, rings."

Ms. Moore does see her work evolving. Talking again of ***Think of Shadows,*** she comments, "I decided that although this book was aimed for the young school child, whatever I put in it, whatever idea or language or imagery I needed, I was going to include, not fight. To me a poem is like a balloon on a string. What you get out of it depends on how tall you are, how long the string is. Something there for everyone!"

The need to make books and poetry available to children has motivated many of Ms. Moore's activities. She was delighted with her task at Scholastic of setting up a paperback book club, for she was able to select good books and bring them to children inexpensively. "The whole process of learning to read comes from reading. After all, you can't learn to swim in a bathtub." Her own picture books have been widely translated, particularly the Little Raccoon books.

The most recent request for publication rights, however, has been refused. Ms. Moore's letter to the South African publisher concluded with a succinct statement of her reasons for refusal: "It has always been a source of deepest pleasure to me to know how much children have loved these books. Some day, when apartheid is only a terrible memory, when all children can freely have access to these books, I should be proud and happy to have you publish them."

The Russian translations of the Little Raccoon books sold over 375,000 copies. In 1967, when Ms. Moore was in the Soviet Union, she made a special request of the editors she met. What she really wanted was to meet Kornei Chukovsky, the noted Russian author, editor, translator, and critic. As well as writing for children himself, he had observed and recorded young children's own uses of language. Ms. Moore had read his book, *From Two to Five,* and it spoke to her own interest in the speech and expressions of children. "To hear young children as they explore experiences—everything being observed and responded to for the first time—well, it's like the morning of the world," she marvels. The editors arranged a visit, and she was driven to Peredelkino to meet Chukovsky. He was then eighty-five years old, "a tall, vital, handsome man with a mane of white hair." She told him about her son, who when quite young, looked at the new moon and cried out, "Look! The moon is broke!" Chukovsky was going to write it down, but there was no need for that. It was already in his book—a young Russian child had said the same thing.

Then he turned to her and said that he'd been told she wrote poetry for children. "Tell me one."

After what she describes as feeling like a child being asked to recite, and after recovering from a "moment of total amnesia," she said this poem for him.

"Until I Saw the Sea"

Until I saw the sea
I did not know
that wind
could wrinkle water so.
I never knew
that sun
could splinter a whole sea of blue.

Nor
did I know before
a sea breathes in and out
upon a shore.

"Beautiful," he said, and kissed her on the cheek.

The NCTE Award for Excellence in Poetry for Children is our kiss on Lilian Moore's cheek, and as we read her poetry, we too say, "Beautiful!" (pp. 647-51)

Joan I. Glazer, "Profile: Lilian Moore," in Language Arts, *Vol. 62, No. 6, October, 1985, pp. 647-52.*

GENERAL COMMENTARY

MAY HILL ARBUTHNOT AND ZENA SUTHERLAND

Lilian Moore decided, in her capacity as an editor, that writers often use too many words. This knowledge and her years of experience as a specialist in reading problems have influenced her poetry, which is simple and direct, yet fluent and witty in a way that younger children can comprehend and appreciate. In **"Winter Cardinal"** she creates a vivid image with elegance and restraint:

Fat
and elegantly
crested,
clinging to the branch
of the stripped tree
like
one bright leaf that
bested
every wind and lived to
show
its red
against
the astonished snow.

Moore has written several stories for children and compiled some poetry anthologies, but it is her own poetry that makes a unique contribution. Children respond to the humor and incongruity of the lighthearted poems in ***See My Lovely Poison Ivy,*** especially those in which there is a surprising turn. . . . (p. 287)

May Hill Arbuthnot and Zena Sutherland, "Poetry," in their Children and Books, *fifth edition, Scott, Foresman and Company, 1977, pp. 244-301.*

CHARLOTTE S. HUCK

Lilian Moore has captured the changing moods of both the city and the country in her books ***I Thought I Heard the City*** and ***Sam's Place.*** Her earlier book ***I Feel the Same Way*** identifies some of the thoughts and feelings of the young child. Her most recent book, ***See My Lovely Poison Ivy,*** contains some delightful shivery poems about witches, ghosts, and goblins. Moore's poems are simple and frequently appealing to the senses, as in this poem from her book about the city:

"Foghorns"

The foghorns moaned
  in the bay last night
so sad
so deep
I thought I heard the city
  crying in its sleep.

Her images of country scenes are clear and evocative, as can be seen in the description of the "Winter Cardinal" or an "Encounter" with a deer. (p. 348)

Charlotte S. Huck, "Selecting Poetry for Children," in her Children's Literature in the Elementary School, *third edition, updated, Holt, Rinehart and Winston, 1979, pp. 324-52.*

JUDITH GLEASON

Lilian Moore's [***I Feel the Same Way***] presents a series of forthright responses to natural phenomena: (wind) "When the wind blows / The quiet things speak" and (rain) "The outside world / is melting / upon my / window pane." Such responses are at the opposite pole from gratuitous aestheticism. Theirs is the urgency of the unpretentious. Before the outside world can be "seen" it must melt and an inner image formed upon the blurry pane. Become poetically aware, this quiet voice seems in effect to be saying to the complicit child-reader, and nature, which to the talkative denizens of the social world seems mute, will in turn disclose the way things really are. Such awareness, in the simplicity of solitude, will cut through the lies significant others are propagating in prose. Their noisy gaze—be it vacant, clouded, riveting, or askance—cannot be trusted. However, "When / the green eyes / of a cat / look deep into / you You know that / whatever it is / they are saying / is / true." And suddenly, reading over the child's shoulder, one realizes that Lilian Moore, for all her prudent ingenuousness, has presented us with nothing less than the prime paradox of the poetic enterprise with which Mallarmé in modern times has become notably associated as its most recondite victim, practitioner, exponent. Pure speech inevitably differentiates itself into silence, a song for the inner ear. The crafted presence of the image spells its literal absence. "Green is good for the eyes," says Hans Christian Andersen in *The Ugly Duckling,* but when in a beautiful creature the eyes themselves are green, their thought is eclipsed, or, as Marvell put it, "annihilated" by their own proper virtue: that unspeakable, transcendental integrity which they impeccably reflect back upon itself. Nature's eyes are green; they see without deceptive blinking, and therefore are as silent "as a mirror is believed."

No doubt Lilian Moore will find such Parnassian invocations of great ghosts suspiciously pretentious. Her own **"Bridge"** (in ***I Thought I Heard the City***), spun of stoic rather than orphic strings, goes straight across the bay in two short stanzas: one by day, one by night. Yet therein lies its mystery. For in the dark what was "steel and might" becomes temporarily "spun of light." A rift has occurred in the everyday reality of things; we have moved across the visible and at the same time been forced to take the invisible as its luminous surrogate. Again, the mirror-image prying us off the superficial surface of the quotidian. Such gazing, whether in water or glass, is the beginning of levitation.

Further to quote Hart Crane, "moth / bends no more than the still / imploring flame." When the two are held simultaneously in focus we have plunged again into the matrix of poetry. Two important poems in her . . . city volume make Lilian Moore's awareness of this weaning from the obvious quite clear. In **"Rain Pools"** mirror splinters glitter, silver and brown with (disintegrated) "sky / cloud / tree / upside down." And in the haunting **"Reflections"** we witness the liquefaction of the material sidewalk world into its true (silent and cruel) opposite:

On this street
of windowed stores
see, in the glass
shadow people meet
and pass
and glide to
secret places.

Ghostly mothers
hold
the hands of grim gray children,
scold
them silently
and melt away.

And
now and then,
before
the window mirror
of a store,
phantom faces
stop
and window shop.

There is nothing sentimental about Lilian Moore's view of nature-as-is. A child in [***I Feel the Same Way***] makes a sand castle: "In rolled the sea / 'All sand castles / belong to me . . .'" To which the stalwart child responds by snatching her by-now floating bucket: "'My sand pail / belongs to me . . .'" To which the sententious critic responds by meditating upon container and contained: what does it mean to salvage a bucketful of tamed angry sea? A mere dose of salt water . . .? Far from being unable to bear bucketsful of reality, T. S. Eliot notwithstanding, humankind, once having broken through the garrulous illusions of culture, will thereafter stop at nothing short of the terror of process. Inner eyes once opened cannot be pried shut. The poet in the city observes all shades of spurious seasonal leafage, concludes with the cold wind that "you really do not see / a tree / until you see / its bones" and moves out into the country for more of that sweet punishment.

As reckless in her unobtrusive way and as irrevocable in direction as Monet pursuing light, Lilian Moore, coming closer and closer to nature's flaming sun, has ended up glowing splendidly as a poet not for children but for herself. Because "adults" of our youth culture have given senior citizens a half-fare ride to periphery, they project the myth that children are frightened by old age, by intimations of death. If this talk be true, then when children come to apple trees wearing "their thinning blossoms / like white hair," they'll turn away from ***Sam's Place***. But if it be false, then a few pages more and they'll be captive of that symbiotic process Lilian Moore calls **"Arson"**:

Slowly
in the long hot days
Virginia creeper
reaches out and
roots and
winds
around a tree.

Reaches,
roots
and
winds
till even dead tree trunks
wear summer green.

A late
September day
the creeper
turns
erupts
to sudden red,
ignites
each captive tree
in ivy flame,
and sets the fires of autumn
burning
in these hills.

Like the weathered wood of the old barn, "not yet done with ice, with sun," Lilian Moore grows taut. Her setting sun bleeds into the pond.

Although she lived for years in New York, Lilian Moore . . . is not poetically a city person, never was. Her city cries in its sleep (**"Foghorns"**). And before she grew taut she wrote fourteen lines on **"Pigeons"** from which this exigent critic would delete all but the following six: "A pigeon never sings / of hill / and flowering hedge, but busily commutes / from sidewalk / to his ledge." (pp. 66-70)

Judith Gleason, "That Lingering Child of Air," in Parnassus: Poetry in Review, *Vol. 8, No. 2, 1980, pp. 63-82.*

A CHILD'S FIRST PICTURE DICTIONARY (1946)

While the title ***A Child's First Picture Dictionary*** suggests some usefulness, it does not correctly describe what is presented in this book. . . . The words are not defined; they are simply used in extraordinarily uninteresting sentences.

A review of "A Child's First Picture Dictionary," in School Library Journal, *an appendix to* Library Journal, *Vol. 14, No. 4, December, 1967, p. 88.*

My First Dictionary, by Laura Oftedal and Nina Jacob and ***A Child's First Picture Dictionary*** by Lilian Moore may appear to be attractive because of their modest prices, but don't be misled. Both dictionaries are written in that stilted style so favored by reading specialists. The latter one may be a good buy, however, if you want to teach your child some history. The word "up" is illustrated with a plane writing BUY BONDS in the sky. I haven't seen that since 1947, which is about when both of them should have been taken off the market. (pp. 36-7)

Jack McGarvey, "Dictionaries: From Delightful Definitions to the Deadly Didactic," in The New York Times Book Review, *May 6, 1973, pp. 36-7.*

OLD ROSIE, THE HORSE NOBODY UNDERSTOOD (with Leone Adelson, 1952)

Rosie, a retired milk wagon horse, was lonesome but whenever she tried to find her friends she got into trouble and made the farmer and his wife angry. Then one night she tried to make friends with a robber, frightened him away, and became the family heroine. Not an original plot but the story has humor and is easy enough for third grade readers to handle alone.

A review of "Old Rosie, the Horse Nobody Understood," in Bulletin of the Children's Book Center, *Vol V, No. 9, May, 1952, p. 67.*

THE SNAKE THAT WENT TO SCHOOL (1957)

Thoroughly spontaneous story of fourth-grade boys and girls who are responsible for their school's science room and of Hank's summer-camp snake that becomes its central attraction. Excitement rises to an amusing climax when the hog-nosed snake disappears. Natural children with credible enthusiasms, something in the style of the popular Henry Huggins and Little Eddie.

Virginia Haviland, in a review of "The Snake That Went to School," in The Horn Book Magazine, *Vol. XXXIII, No. 5, October, 1957, p. 395.*

Hank Jenkins returned from summer camp with a new pet, a hog-nosed snake, much to the delight of his younger brother and the dismay of his mother. When she refused to allow him to keep it at home, he solved the problem by presenting it to the science museum at school. There it caused mixed reactions on the part of teachers and students alike, but was finally accepted. There are occasional flashes of humor to the story in spite of its rather didactic treatment of Hank's relationship with his younger brother.

Zena Sutherland, in a review of "The Snake That Went to School," in Bulletin of the Children's Book Center, *Vol. XI, No. 6, February, 1958, p. 62.*

ONCE UPON A HOLIDAY (1959)

Twelve selections which revolve about holidays, told in simple language and based on familiar themes. Using material well within the young reader's experience, the author, . . . recognizing the child's limited attention span, writes in a concentrated manner with the emphasis placed largely on plot. . . . [This book] will find its niche both at home and in the school room.

A review of "Once Upon a Holiday," in Virginia Kirkus' Service, *Vol. XXVII, No. 3, February 1, 1959, p. 88.*

TONY THE PONY **(1959)**

Tony belonged to Mr. Luke, who had a stand in the park; children who came for pony rides talked about the zoo, and one day Tony walked right out of his yard and went to the zoo. He saw all the things the children had talked about, and he was then content to go back to work. A useful, easy-to-read tale for beginning readers, but one that is neither original nor exciting.

A review of "Tony the Pony," in Bulletin of the Center for Children's Books, *Vol. XIII, No. 5, January, 1960, p. 87.*

EVERYTHING HAPPENS TO STUEY **(1960)**

There is nothing in the world Stuey wants more than a big new chemistry set. But his parents are skeptical about their son's ability to cope with the high powered ingredients of such a kit. How Stuey proves his worth and at the same time saves his little sister from trauma make up the core of this lively story of home life and diminutive adventure. Well written, the language is simple but evocative.

A review of "Everything Happens to Stuey," in Virginia Kirkus' Service, *Vol. XXVIII, No. 12, June 15, 1960, p. 452.*

Family relationships are good, especially that of Stuey's bond with his grandmother. Slightly exaggerated but believable; Stuey is a bit of a stereotype, but his episodic story is told with a casual humor. A weakness of the book is in the failure to rectify a concept held by Stuey, the concept that it is acceptable to combine chemicals in haphazard fashion.

Zena Sutherland, in a review of "Everything Happens to Stuey," in Bulletin of the Center for Children's Books, *Vol. XV, No. 3, November, 1961, p. 47.*

BEAR TROUBLE **(1960)**

Children will get special satisfaction from the fact that it was Smallest Squirrel and Youngest Chipmunk who chased Big Bear away from their woodland pond, when all the grown-up animals were afraid to try. And they'll be tickled by the clever way they did it. If old sleepy Bear had seemed more of a real menace, there'd have been greater excitement. Still there are more action, conversation and humor than in many primers. . . .

This "Read-It-Yourself" book has short sentences—each a separate paragraph. Second graders will proudly read it to themselves and to their younger brothers and sisters. The story itself makes one almost forget the vocabulary control, though unnecessary repetition of words does create thinness and slowness.

Elizabeth Minot Graves, "The Harder They Fall," in The New York Times Book Review, *November 13, 1960, p. 52.*

A PICKLE FOR A NICKEL **(1961)**

With limited vocabulary for beginning independent readers, a slight story about a quiet man who had a quiet parrot. A small boy taught the parrot to talk and he was delighted when he was given the parrot, since it had now become too noisy for Mr. Bumble, the owner. . . . [The] text is rather abrupt in style and inconsequential in plot but has some humor.

Zena Sutherland, in a review of "A Pickle for a Nickel," in Bulletin of the Center for Children's Books, *Vol. XV, No. 9, May, 1962, p. 146.*

LITTLE RACCOON AND THE THING IN THE POOL **(1963)**

While this story has the repetition helpful to new and slow readers, it is never monotonous. (It has the fun of Chicken Little's kind of repetition). Little Raccoon has to cross the pool on a moonlit night and his reflection, seen for the first time, is almost too much for him. He has to run back past all his friends and ask his mother for advice before he can make it across. She advises him to smile at the thing and on his second try he makes it. Mother Raccoon breaks up as she breaks down and finally tells him what it was he saw. Young readers will be tickled, too.

A review of "Little Raccoon and the Thing in the Pool," in Virginia Kirkus' Service, *Vol. XXXI, No. 3, February 1, 1963, p. 108.*

PAPA ALBERT **(1964)**

A picture book [which is] . . . not a bilingual text, but a story in which French words are ingeniously introduced via a shopping list and assorted street signs. Papa, a Parisian taxi driver, prepares to take his four children to the Chantilly Woods for a picnic. He takes the small twins with him on his rounds, presumably to shop for food; business is so good there is not time, so the shopping has to be done early and quickly on the day of the picnic. Not a strong story, but lightly humorous and enjoyably Parisian; those French words used (two dozen) are repeated in a glossary with illustration, definition, and phonetic pronunciation. The glossary need not be restricted to readers studying French, but it does require independent readers; it is possible that the picture-book format therefore may, in one way, limit the use of the book. (pp. 37-8)

Zena Sutherland, in a review of "Papa Albert," in Bulletin of the Center for Children's Books, *Vol. 19, No. 2, October, 1965, pp. 37-8.*

This charming book presumably has its origins in the United States, but it is wholly French in spirit. It is the thoroughly delightful story of how Papa Albert took his children for a picnic in the family taxi. . . . The simple story is told with easy grace and natural fun. . . . The "Frenchness" of the story is carried over most satisfactorily into [Gioia Fiammenghi's] pictures, but I wish the author had not appended a glossary which includes execrable "phonetic" renderings of the French words appearing in text and illustrations. On the whole, however, a most pleasing book.

A review of "Papa Albert," in The Junior Bookshelf, *Vol. 30, No. 3, June, 1966, p. 169.*

LITTLE RACCOON AND THE OUTSIDE WORLD **(1965)**

The humor here comes from Little Raccoon's first experience of such ordinary human equipment as a shower ("hot rain"), a clothes rack ("a tree that goes around"), and spaghetti ("long, long things to eat"). It all happened the first time Little Raccoon ventured past the point where his woods ended. He leaves his timid pals, twin skunks, parked on the edge of the woods, which allows him to run back and report his various finds and also allows the necessary word repetition of the easy reader to happen most naturally.

A review of "Little Raccoon and the Outside World," in Virginia Kirkus' Service, *Vol. XXXIII, No. 13, July 1, 1965, p. 624.*

[***Little Raccoon and the Outside World,*** *Johnny Lion's Book,* by Edith Thatcher Hurd, and *The Good Tiger* by Elizabeth Bowen] are all nicely written. . . . They all have animals caught up in adventure—a sure-fire hit with the younger set you'd think—but they all have one vital ingredient missing.

There is no climax. No moment of drama. They all build up to a letdown, and what a shame, because they could have done otherwise so easily.

Cynthia Parsons, "Grab That Reader!" in The Christian Science Monitor, *November 4, 1965, p. B2.*

THE MAGIC SPECTACLES AND OTHER EASY-TO-READ STORIES (1966)

There are seven easy reading stories included, all of which first appeared in *Humpty Dumpty's Magazine*. Read one and you'll want to read them all. They offer variety, are all slightly silly, and all deal with situations which pull ready recognition and interest. **"The Silver Bird Express"** is a boy's dream of glory about rescuing a train which had ground to a halt because an elephant had plunked down on the tracks; in **"Janey's Boss"** a pet crow who liked to say "stop that" became a neighborhood pest and then a hero; **"The 'Now Really' Time"** is the wintertime when mothers crossly scold their children for their lost objects; and so on. As in the "Little Raccoon" stories and others by this author, the necessary repetition of phrases is handled as an integral and enjoyable aspect of the stories.

A review of "The Magic Spectacles and Other Easy-to-Read Stories," in Virginia Kirkus' Service, *Vol. XXXIV, No. 6, March 15, 1966, p. 301.*

"Easy-To-Read" with all its euphemisms, has become a suspect phrase in the last few years, for, too often for comfort, it has been used as a cloak to hide an emaciated story. But these seven easy-to-read stories are a welcome surprise—they are real stories, with meat on their bones, entertaining stories that will entertain beginning readers.

A review of "The Magic Spectacles and Other Easy-to-Read Stories," in Publishers Weekly, *Vol. 189, No. 17, April 25, 1966, p. 122.*

Each of the seven short stories in this collection for beginning readers has a gentle conflict which resolves itself in a satisfactory, and often clever, way. The range is wide: humor, suspense, adventure, realism, fantasy, and a bit of wisdom thrown in for good measure. Less original than the rest is the title story, whose kernel for thought hinges on the trite idea of owls' wearing spectacles. Text and [Arnold Lobel's] illustrations have vitality and verve, however, and the whole seems free of restrictions except for the "easy-to-read" label, which must irk beginning readers.

Mary Silva Cosgrave, in a review of "The Magic Spectacles and Other Easy-to-Read Stories," in The Horn Book Magazine, *Vol. XLII, No. 4, August, 1966, p. 428.*

The literary quality of the stories is minimal, but they have some humor that alleviates the static writing. The stories are varied: some are animal tales, one is a fantasy in the form of a dream, one is a realistic but pat story of a boy choosing a pet.

Zena Sutherland, in a review of "The Magic Spectacles and Other Easy-to-Read Stories," in Bulletin of the Center for Children's Books, *Vol. 20, No. 9, May, 1967, p. 143.*

I FEEL THE SAME WAY (1967)

Rain: "The outside world is melting upon my window pane." The sea: "a sea breathes in and out upon a shore." . . . In short lines, in varied rhymes—an experience crystallized, a perception delineated, sound or movement evoked: at times reminiscent of Haiku, at all times fresh and subtle. . . . [The poems] transcend and illuminate reality. . . .

A review of "I Feel the Same Way," in Kirkus Service, *Vol. XXXV, No. 13, July 1, 1967, p. 737.*

The title suggests that the experiences of child confronting environment are universal. The poems themselves speak of the environment of both the suburban and city child: the wind and rain on a street, a geranium on a window sill, fog along the river, fire-flies, a sunlit doorstep, the ocean. Many of the poems have the flavor of haiku and capture the very essence of experience. **"Rain Rivers"** with its image of "little twig boats . . . towing leaf barges" is a fine example of word imagery which should appeal to first- and second-graders who enjoy conjuring up their own interpretations of the world around them. **"Until I Saw the Sea"** and **"Wind Song"** will speak to slightly older children who are verbally more agile and introspective. . . . Excellent language arts material, especially for the urban child, the poems and illustrations emphasize the importance of looking beyond the drabness of one's surroundings to discover the truth of the old maxim that beauty is where you find it.

Barbara Gibson, in a review of "I Feel the Same Way," in School Library Journal, *an appendix to* Library Journal, *Vol. 14, No. 1, September, 1967, p. 111.*

A precious few free-flowing verses tell of the fog and the sea, of ants and spiders, of twig boats and leaf barges, and the wind—"Go wind, blow / Push things—wheee / No, wind, no. / Not me— / not *me*." Simple, intimate, and childlike, the words ring true. Author and [Robert Quackenbush the] artist meet in perfect harmony to fling out a moment's abandon to anyone old or young.

Mary Silva Cosgrave, in a review of "I Feel the Same Way," in The Horn Book Magazine, *Vol. XLIII, No. 5, October, 1967, p. 587.*

[A small] collection of poems about a child's reactions to such everyday phenomena as wind and rain, or to the awareness of his own patterns. The pictures capture the moods of season and weather that are so frequently the settings of the poems, which are short, bright, perceptive, and simply written—neither too long nor too complex for the read-aloud audience.

Zena Sutherland, in a review of "I Feel the Same Way," in Bulletin of the Center for Children's Books, *Vol. 21, No. 6, February, 1968, p. 98.*

***JUST RIGHT* (1968)**

This one isn't really a book, it's a mood—a fine tranquil mood. There *is* a story, and a pleasant, keyed-to-the-mood story it is, of a farmer and the farm he loves and hates to lose, one with a happy ending (he keeps the farm). But the pastoral mood it is written in and the pastoral mood it leaves the reader in, is the interesting story about this story.

A review of "Just Right," in Publishers Weekly, *Vol. 194, No. 1, July 1, 1968, p. 55.*

A well written, though contrived, story about a farmer who wants to sell his farm but can't find the proper buyer—someone who will keep it the way it is. . . . [The] book could prove helpful in a first- or second-grade study of farm life.

Joan Lear Sher, in a review of "Just Right," in School Library Journal, *an appendix to* Library Journal, *Vol. 15, No. 1, September, 1968, p. 124.*

***JUNK DAY ON JUNIPER STREET AND OTHER EASY-TO-READ STORIES* (1969)**

This hasn't nearly the sparkle of ***Magic Spectacles.*** In the title story, one man's refuse becomes another man's find—and friends of *Dear Garbage Man* know there's more to it than that. **"A Fish Story"** *is* fishy: Kenny hooks mother's gold bracelet (not even reported missing here) when he reluctantly goes fishing in Raccoon Pond. Another resurrects the disobedient-donkey-knows-best theme (complete with poor sombreroed peasants and a silver lode); still another is a long runaround involving a silly dog and a duckling who—wonder of wonders—can swim. The last is strictly nursery school level and some of the others are pretty thin for independent readers: e.g. a dog who stops following his mistress to school when she switches from peanut butter sandwiches. Seven in all, and no strain—that's about all that can be said about them. (pp. 437-38)

A review of "Junk Day on Juniper Street and Other Easy-to-Read Stories," in Kirkus Reviews, *Vol. XXXVII, No. 8, April 15, 1969, pp. 437-38.*

[***Junk Day on Juniper Street***] is a collection of seven stories that are uneven in quality. The first has the same theme as Gene Zion's *Dear Garbage Man* and is the most fun of the group. A couple lack action or surprise and are flat and slow. . . . It's easy second-grade reading, but all in all, it's a usable but mediocre item.

A review of "Junk Day on Juniper Street and Other Easy-to-Read Stories," in School Library Journal, *an appendix to* Library Journal, *Vol. 16, No. 4, December, 1969, p. 62.*

Moore's good-humored stories are bound to please beginners who will have no trouble understanding the crisp, rollicking sentences relating unusual happenings. Clean-up time means getting rid of things nobody needs on Juniper Street. On the appointed day, all the families roll up their sleeves and deposit old chairs, bird cages, toys, pictures, books, etc., outside where a junk man will pick them up. But he gets nothing except a big rocking chair, since all the neighbors have discovered things they must have among the cast-offs. The five other adventures are just as twisty and funny as the first. . . .

A review of "Junk Day on Juniper Street and Other Easy-to-Read Stories," in Publishers Weekly, *Vol. 226, No. 21, November 23, 1984, p. 75.*

***I THOUGHT I HEARD THE CITY* (1969)**

Although a few of these poems deal with primarily urban phenomena (pigeons, roofscapes) many are city properties by association (window shopping, a construction site) and just as many belong to no particular setting (rain pools, forsythia). The poems themselves are pleasant to the ear and frequently to the mind's eye and contain some fresh and simple ideas which younger readers can handle: "you really do not see / a tree / until you see / its bones" or "from my window / I can see / how roofs / design a sky." The seamier sides of city life are absent, although the attitudes are emotionally selective rather than ultra-sanitary (e.g., the silence after a snowfall, not the slush). . . . Lightweight but not lackluster.

A review of "I Thought I Heard the City," in Kirkus Reviews, *Vol. XXXVII, No. 17, September 1, 1969, p. 934.*

A brief collection of poems that make quiet comments about some of the magic and some of the moods of city life: "A bridge / at night / is spun of light". . . . It is poetry that encourages the listener to consider familiar objects with fresh attention.

Diane Farrell, in a review of "I Thought I Heard the City," in The Horn Book Magazine, *Vol. XLV, No. 6, December, 1969, p. 681.*

Seventeen original, successful poems about urban scenes and sounds. Brief, flexibly but carefully structured, occasionally rhyming, the poems reveal the author's talent for terse verse and unmixed metaphors, as well as her observant eye. A wistful pastoral emotion is heard in [some] verses . . . ; particularly evocative are the poems entitled **"Foghorns"** and **"The Bridge."**

Ginger Brauer, in a review of "I Thought I Heard the City," in School Library Journal, *an appendix to* Library Journal, *Vol. 15, No. 4, December, 1969, p. 54.*

The subjects are not out of ordinary (summer rain, foghorns, pigeons, a snowy morning; no element of people, their problems, relationships, or urban pastimes) but the poems are all agreeable, quite deft, and occasionally vivid in imagery.

Zena Sutherland, in a review of "I Thought I Heard the City," in Bulletin of the Center for Children's Books, *Vol. 23, No. 6, February, 1970, p. 102.*

***LITTLE RACCOON AND NO TROUBLE AT ALL* (1972)**

Bouncy drawings [by Gioia Fiammenghi] echo the humor of an engaging animal story. The two little chipmunks would be no trouble at all, their mother said, as she prepared to go off with Little Raccoon's mother on an excursion to the outside world. The two little chipmunks are ready to fall in with any suggestion, but Little Raccoon cannot keep up with their vigorous play. Finally he has an idea: he assures them that crayfish are the most delicious food there is, escorts them to the water's edge and gets them a lift on a beaver. Marooned on the beaver's mound, the chipmunks sit, bored and frustrated, while Little Raccoon gorges on crayfish. When it's time to go home, the charges are meek and obedient; when their mother returns, Little Raccoon assures her that the chipmunks *were* no trouble at all. The animals and the situation are appealing; the raccoon solves his problem without damaging the chipmunks, and there is a tacit understanding that out-ployed children can understand very well indeed.

Zena Sutherland, in a review of "Little Raccoon and No Trouble at All," in Bulletin of the Center for Children's Books, *Vol. 26, No. 1, September, 1972, p. 12.*

Beginning readers who are hooked on Moore's earlier ***Little Raccoon and the Thing in the Pool*** will respond favorably to the further adventures of Little Raccoon. . . . [This] is an easy reading, low-keyed animal story based on very plausible and humorous misadventures of a lovable hero. As a read-aloud this is a natural for pre-schoolers.

A review of "Little Raccoon and No Trouble at All," in School Library Journal, *an appendix to* Library Journal, *Vol. 19, No. 4, December 15, 1972, p. 4082.*

SAM'S PLACE: POEMS FROM THE COUNTRY (1973)

An appealing collection of 20 nature poems which evoke an unspoiled mountain setting. A winter cardinal ("Fat / and elegantly crested, / clinging to the branch / of the stripped tree"), a squirrel "all quiver and scurry," a dry spell, a sunset, the falling of chestnuts, and other tableaux of nature powerfully and effectively convey images, sounds, and physical sensations. . . . [This has a] sparse, skillfully crafted text.

Daisy Kouzel, in a review of "Sam's Place: Poems from the Country," in School Library Journal, *an appendix to* Library Journal, *Vol. 20, No. 2, October, 1973, p. 119.*

Homely, plainspoken country images are fluently eased out one word at a time to simulate the oozing of **"Wet"**—"everything / dripping / slipping / gushing / slushing / and listen to that brook / rushing / like a puppy loosed from its leash"—or the aridity of a **"Dry Spell"**. . . . The absence of forced cleverness and attenuated metaphors is certainly praiseworthy, though by the time September rolls around with the red leaves falling—"something is bleeding / into the / pond, / the stains are freshly / red"—one wonders whether Moore is practicing simplicity or indolence. It's worth waiting for those occasional wake-up moments (like the beginning of **"Flight"** when "A hound sound / comes out of the sky") that are sprinkled throughout these neat, restrained translations from the natural world—otherwise more admirable than exciting.

A review of "Sam's Place: Poems from the Country," in Kirkus Reviews, *Vol. XLI, No. 20, October 15, 1973, p. 1168.*

Twenty descriptive nature poems that reach into the hearts of seasons and cycles. A natural quality graces the poet's skill in combining words, using them sparingly and meaningfully to give impact, and shaping them into lines that flow down a page. . . . Lovely, subtle free verse for the quiet in heart.

A review of "Sam's Place: Poems from the Country," in The Booklist, *Vol. 70, No. 5, November 1, 1973, p. 294.*

HOORAY FOR ME! (with Remy Charlip, 1975)

[***Hooray for Me!*** tells] about a great variety of people all giving answers to the question: "Who are you?" "I'm me," all answer in a book which is an original and lighthearted way to help girls and boys identify themselves. The text and [Vera B. Williams's] pictures also point out relationships within the family and within society. And we see roles filled: "That's not all I am: I'm my cat's pillow. I'm my dog's walker. I'm my shadow's body, I am my best friend's best friend. . . ." The creators of ***Hooray for Me!*** will make many best friends.

A review of "Hooray for Me!" in Publishers Weekly, *Vol. 207, No. 12, March 24, 1975, p. 48.*

This book could be a bright spot in anyone's day. . . . There is no real story, just a happy celebration of the "me" in each of us. The book lightly explores our relationships to one another. . . . The text might . . . be slightly confusing in spots for the young so an adult nearby to clarify might be helpful. Recommended for setting a happy "hooray" tone at the beginning or end of a story hour.

Marilyn Darch, in a review of "Hooray for Me!" in Children's Book Review Service, *Vol. 3, No. 9, April, 1975, p. 65.*

Much rereading of ***Hooray for Me*** could drive an adult bonkers. But it is nonetheless a winsome book for the very youngest. A child would soon make the words his own and "read" the book himself. . . . The unusual bright watercolors and word play mesh to give a feeling of flatout celebration, making it no wonder adults like to read children's books—at least once.

June Goodwin, "Getting Martha to Eat Her Spaghetti," in The Christian Science Monitor, *May 7, 1975, p. B3.*

This is a warm, witty, social and enjoyable romp for young and old. Children appear in all colors and fathers (of all colors) are nurturing. Stepfathers, too.

The marvelous watercolor illustrations echo the celebration of life and human interdependence. *Every* day-care center, kindergarten and home should have this book.

"Pre-School and Early Years: 'Hooray for Me!'" in Human and Anti-Human Values in Children's Books, *Racism and Sexism Resource Center for Educators, 1976, p. 57.*

SEE MY LOVELY POISON IVY AND OTHER VERSES ABOUT WITCHES, GHOSTS, AND THINGS (1975)

Whimsical witchery so slight it could melt under a full moon. Lilian Moore gives us some metrical surprises and a few funny limericks (including one about a very long crocodile: "I know I should diet / But each time I try it / I'm hungry for more than a mile"). But mostly these are small free-verse speculations—on an urban witch who rides a vacuum cleaner, a skeleton pursued by a dog who only wants a bone to chew on, ghouls wearing "ghoul-oshes," even a "teeny, tiny ghost no bigger than a mouse." While nothing here is as memorable, or as wicked, as the nonsense verse in X. J. Kennedy's *One Winter Night in August,* Moore delights in sounds . . . and there's just enough unselfconscious kookiness here to make reading aloud worthwhile. (pp. 775-76)

A review of "See My Lovely Poison Ivy and Other Verses about Witches, Ghosts, and Things," in Kirkus Reviews, *Vol. XLIII, No. 14, July 15, 1975, pp. 775-76.*

A rollicking collection of poems, some of which have a wistful touch, is illustrated with black and white drawings [by Diane Dawson] that capture the eerie-merry mood of the writing very nicely. The poetry is fresh, deft, and imaginative. (pp. 115-16)

Zena Sutherland, in a review of "See My Lovely Poison Ivy and Other Verses about Witches, Ghosts, and Things," in Bulletin of the Center for Children's Books, *Vol. 29, No. 7, March, 1976, pp. 115-16.*

Good poetry for the Halloween season is sometimes a bit hard to find, but for those who wish new, clever and original verses—take note! Lilian Moore's poetry—some humorous, some thoughtful, but all delightful—can stand by itself, but when combined with the. . . . [drawings] we have a masterpiece. Highly recommended. . . .

James Norsworthy, in a review of "See My Lovely Poison Ivy and Other Verses about Witches, Ghosts, and Things," in Catholic Library World, *Vol. 47, No. 10, May-June, 1976, p. 452.*

Lilian Moore writes simple, intimate, and skillfully crafted poems about familiar things. A favorite among teachers and their students is ***See My Lovely Poison Ivy, and Other Verses about Witches, Ghosts and Things.*** Both funny and slightly scary, these poems are delightful for listening or for reading to oneself, whether at Halloween time or in other seasons. (p. 282)

Joan Mason, "A Librarian Looks at Poetry for Children," in Language Arts, *Vol. 59, No. 3, March, 1982, pp. 280-83.*

LITTLE RACCOON AND POEMS FROM THE WOODS (1975)

[The words] dribble down the page, one or two to the line. Moore has few enough ideas; even in this handful of tiny poems some of her devices begin to pall, particularly the "surprise" last verse. But she uses sounds quite effectively—best of all in a rain poem that flows "wet fur / wet feather / weather." And Little Raccoon's reactions to "bug burly bumble bee," snake and porcupine will be sure to evoke ah's of recognition.

A review of "Little Raccoon and Poems from the Woods," in Kirkus Reviews, *Vol. XLIII, No. 23, December 1, 1975, p. 1333.*

Lilian Moore's poems are gentle, fresh and enticing. . . . Try "Friend: When / he wills / his quills / to stand on / end / I'm very glad / that / I'm a friend / of / Porcupine." . . . Other lyrics are addressed to a spider, a weed, a toad, to new sounds, to night and day in a lovely introduction to poetry for little ones who can feel the music and understand the meanings.

A review of "Little Raccoon and Poems from the Woods," in Publishers Weekly, *Vol. 208, No. 22, December 1, 1975, p. 66.*

Through brief rhymed but not heavily metered verse, the reader becomes aware of the forest activities from an animal's-eye view. . . . Useful in nature study units or as short fillers for story hour, these poems should also be popular with beginning readers.

Barbara Dill, "Picturely Books for Children," in Wilson Library Bulletin, *Vol. 50, No. 6, February, 1976, p. 485.*

This fourth in the series of Little Raccoon books presents little poems mostly about animals. Too much of the poetry is perfunctory: word play and imagery is often too sweet, too cute. The poems are not clever; offer no new perceptions; and neither meter nor rhyme provides any redemption. . . . Even its status as part of a series should not rescue this one.

Michele Woggon, in a review of "Little Raccoon and Poems from the Woods," in School Library Journal, *Vol. 22, No. 7, March, 1976, p. 95.*

THINK OF SHADOWS (1980)

Freewheeling in form but often cast in rhyme, Lilian Moore's ***Think of Shadows*** . . . tells of a sundial, a groundhog, the first man on the moon, and other shadow-casters. If, like their subjects, the poems seem insubstantial, the slightest things by Lilian Moore still outweigh most other children's poets. (p. 62)

Karla Kuskin, "Storyteller's Voice," in The New York Times Book Review, *November 9, 1980, pp. 51, 62.*

Each of 17 short poems describes a different aspect of our interactions with shadows. Each is a succinct, concise comment on our world. Almost every one is a perfect blend of sound and sense and, therefore, an excellent introduction to poetry for children. Following in the tradition of McCord's *Take Sky* and Merriam's *There Is no Rhyme for Silver,* most are fun to read aloud or memorize.

Meryl Silverstein, in a review of "Think of Shadows," in School Library Journal, *Vol. 27, No. 5, January, 1981, p. 53.*

SOMETHING NEW BEGINS: NEW AND SELECTED POEMS (1982)

Lilian Moore's ***Something New Begins: New and Selected Poems*** has the sort of title that gives poetry a bad name, and her subjects—nature and the weather—have too often adorned the leftover spaces in grade school readers. Never mind. Here is a poet who writes with a child's-eye view that is keen, accurate and full of vitality. Whether Miss Moore is noticing how wet stones you pick up at the seashore lose their luster when you get them home, or reminding us that we can tell a snowy city morning before we see it by the lack of street sounds, or recreating the buffeting of a windy day, she captures experience. She sees advancing rainclouds

> butting like old gray
> goats.

After a hurricane, "stunned" trees look down on the wreckage of

> battered
> branches
> crossed like
> swords.

Miss Moore sustains metaphors through whole poems, and her subtle timing makes use of both traditional stanza and free-verse techniques. Like Theodore Roethke and May Swenson, whom in her way she resembles, she is often funny. (p. 45)

Alicia Ostriker, "Tulip, Julep, Sloshes, Galoshes," in The New York Times Book Review, *November 14, 1982, pp. 45, 57.*

Creative, reflective, full of imagery, and accessible, this splendid collection will delight young readers as well as adults looking to stretch children's minds and imaginations. Fifteen new verses, along with selections from previously published books such as ***I Thought I Heard a City, See My Lovely Poison Ivy,*** and ***Think of Shadows,*** provide a wide range of topics that stimulate, amuse, and challenge.

Barbara Elleman, in a review of "Something New Begins: New and Selected Poems," in Booklist, *Vol. 79, No. 9, January 1, 1983, p. 620.*

Lilian Moore is a fine poet of moments observed. She has an alert eye for nature, and a sensitive ear. At times she is nimble, as in **"Winding Road,"** where the poem mimics the action playfully. Moore can be humorous too, as in the section titled **"See My Lovely Poison Ivy."** At the same time, there is much of a sameness here. One-hundred-and-eleven pages of the same poetical pattern, whether for tree frogs, ducklings, apple trees or witches, is soporific. Oddly, in the entire book there is scarcely one mention of a human being conversing or having anything to do with another. The narrow, timid bounds of this collection make it distinctly unexciting. (pp. 181-82)

Peter Neumeyer, in a review of "Something New Begins: New and Selected Poems," in School Library Journal, *Vol. 29, No. 7, March, 1983, pp. 181-82.*

Fifteen new poems precede selections from six earlier collections of the poet's work. Four of these—***See My Lovely Poison Ivy, Think of Shadows, I Feel the Way,*** and ***Little Raccoon and Poems from the Woods***—are still available; ***I Thought I Heard the City*** and ***Sam's Place*** are out of print. Consequently, the present volume offers an overview of the author's versatility, style, and range of themes which might otherwise be difficult to obtain and demonstrates to young readers the wonder which poetic vision can extract from ordinary objects and events. Nature and the elements are recurring motifs evoked in a kaleidoscope of images, from "icicles weeping themselves away / on the eaves" to the marvels of a sea that "breathes in and out / upon a shore." Personification is deftly handled—much as a child might endow the environment with sense and feeling. Yet the phrases, never clichés, are finely honed and fresh. In Lilian Moore's world a witch's child logically requests a bedtime story "'About a monster / Crawly-creepy, / Something nice / To make me sleepy,'" and children "scribble their shadows / on the school yard" until a cloud "wipes out all / scribbles / like a giant eraser." It is a world which children can readily enter, understand, and appreciate. (pp. 179-80)

Mary M. Burns, in a review of "Something New Begins: New and Selected Poems," in The Horn Book Magazine, *Vol. LIX, No. 2, April, 1983, pp. 179-80.*

THE UGLY DUCKLING (1987)

This is a faithful and lively retelling: still rather lengthy for reading aloud, but with large type and simplified sentence structure to make it accessible to good readers in second or third grade. The typical Andersen blend of satire and sentiment has lost only a bit of its sweet-and-sour pungence.

Patricia Dooley, in a review of "The Ugly Duckling," in School Library Journal, *Vol. 33, No. 11, August, 1987, p. 72.*

Two new editions of one of Andersen's best-known stories [***The Ugly Duckling,*** as retold by Marianna Mayer and Lilian Moore], will provide ready comparison material for children who are encouraged to look carefully at picture books. There are interesting differences in the language, with Mayer's text using a more formal phrasing. When the ugly duckling runs off to the swamp and finds two wild ducks, Moore says: "'How ugly you are!' they said. 'Just don't try to marry into our family.'" Mayer's version reads: "'But you can remain with us, if you wish,' the leader of the flock said, 'so long as you don't try to get above your station.'" Mayer's retelling omits one incident from Andersen's story, while Moore's is very close to the original in both detail and language, though Moore provides a context for words like "moat," which younger readers might find puzzling. (pp. 543-44)

Janet Hickman, in a review of "The Ugly Duckling," in Language Arts, *Vol. 64, No. 5, September, 1987, pp. 543-44.*

Richard Peck

1934-

American author of fiction and editor.

Considered one of the most popular creators of young adult literature, Peck is also regarded as one of the best writers of the genre for his versatility, consistency, insight, honesty, and skill as a literary stylist. Formerly a high school English teacher and textbook editor, he is often lauded for his understanding of contemporary adolescents as well as for his awareness of their changing needs and interests. Peck's works, mysteries and family stories which are directed to a junior high through late teenage audience, become increasingly serious in subject matter and tone as their age levels increase. Chief among his books for preteen and early teenage readers are a series of slapstick adventures set in the late nineteenth century about Blossom Culp, a spunky young psychic who is often seen as Peck's most engaging character. The majority of Peck's works consist of realistic fiction, both for younger and older teenagers, which focuses on the trials involved in reaching maturity by overcoming social obstacles and peer pressure. Peck tells his stories through the first-person narratives of his adolescent protagonists, average teenagers with whom his readers can easily identify. By addressing such sober issues as stormy family relationships, teenage pregnancy, rape, suicide, and murder, these works have achieved a controversial reputation; two of them, *Are You in the House Alone?* (1976) and *Father Figure* (1978), have been removed occasionally from school library shelves. *Are You in the House Alone?* is perhaps Peck's most publicized book. Depicting the trauma of a sixteen-year-old girl who is pursued and eventually raped by a classmate, the novel was praised for Peck's restrained handling of his subject as well as for his indictment of the American legal system and the stigma regarding the victims of rape. Despite their controversy, the novels are praised as morally challenging, thought-provoking, and moving works which fortify the self-confidence of young readers through Peck's positive and supportive approach. The books have also generated enthusiasm among teenagers, who respond to Peck's inclusion of pertinent topics and familiar settings, use of drama and suspense, and examples of humor and sharp wit. Peck is respected as a craftsmanlike author who is adept at constructing quality works—realistic stories which are intense without being sensational, and light fiction which is acknowledged as interesting and entertaining. He has also written *Monster Night at Grandma's House* (1977), a picture book about a boy who conquers his fear of the dark.

Peck receives consistent praise for his perceptive assessments of the preoccupations, pleasures, and literary requirements of his adolescent readers. Regarded as an author who is proficient with both suspense and humor, he is applauded for the emotional depth, meaningful themes, gripping plots, appealing characters, lively dialogues, vivid settings, and vitality with which he invests his works. While reviewers sometimes find his characters superficial or stereotyped and state that the thoughts of his protagonists are occasionally incongruent with their ages and personalities, most critics acclaim Peck as a talented writer of books which are relevant as well as enjoyable.

Photograph by Don Lewis. Courtesy of Richard Peck.

Peck received an Edgar Allan Poe Award runner-up in 1974 for *Dreamland Lake* and the Edgar Allan Poe Award for *Are You in the House Alone?* in 1976.

(See also *Contemporary Literary Criticism*, Vol. 21; *Something about the Author Autobiography Series*, Vol. 2; *Something about the Author*, Vol. 18; *Contemporary Authors New Revision Series*, Vol. 19; and *Contemporary Authors*, Vols. 85-88.)

AUTHOR'S COMMENTARY

[*The following excerpt is from a speech presented to the Arkansas Library Association in October, 1981.*]

[We are gathered here today] in the *educationally* wrecked 1980's.

But we are here because we like books, because we like young people. And because we know something . . . : the young will live in as small a world as they can unless they get a nudging from the nest and that if they do not start early to read about a wider world, they will never be a part of it.

You and I are people of the word. As our life's work, we have decided to try to bring the ideas in books and young people closer together. To give them in books—not in films or audiovisual aids hardware, but in books—the survival skills to help them cope with a world they never made.

We must take them where we find them, living in the narrow world of the 1980's—a dark time for being young. We may think we are still young ourselves. But we are not. Time's winged chariot had done its work, and we find that being young means not being able to remember President . . . Carter.

Our readers of the 1980's are citizens of the moment not only because they are very young, but because they are no longer taught much history or foreign language or geography or cartography or scripture, which combines history, geography, poetry, and faith. You and I, we people of the word, spend our lives hollering across the famous generation gap, hoping to hear an answering echo.

Occasionally we hear one. Just the other day I had a letter from one of my young readers.

"Are you old?" she inquired. "I want to know because I like your books, and I wonder how many more there will be."

I wonder myself.

You and I are in the communications business. For me that means sitting in an empty room, staring at a blank sheet of paper in the typewriter. Trying to carve out one little corner of reality to shape in the form of a novel—a young adult novel—that will make some youngster somewhere say, "Why that's the way it is."

I want to hook them every bit as much as their local drug dealer does. And like him, I want to hook them for life.

But how do you do that? I have written twelve novels and I still do not know how to write a novel. Do you start early? I hope not. I never wrote a line of fiction until I was 37 years old. Do you take a course in creative writing? I doubt it.

But how? In our society, we find that an astonishing percentage of novelists came from three professions: journalism, advertising, and teaching. What have these three fields in common as a seedbed for novelists? I expect two things: they all depend upon dealing persuasively with strangers and they all depend upon deadlines. Two skills notably absent from our school and college curricula.

I came from teaching, where I learned things about the private life of the young their parents need never know. Ironically, it was my students who taught me to be a writer, though I had been hired to teach *them*.

They taught me that a novel must entertain first before it can be anything else. I learned that there is no such thing as a "grade reading level"; a young person's "reading level" and attention span will rise and fall according to his degree of interest. I learned that if you do not have a happy ending for the young, you had better do some fast talking. I saw in the classroom how little time the young have left for anything else after they have paid their tremendous debt to peer-group approval. I learned from my students that the young have no taste for realism in their reading; they want reassurance from their books, not reality. I learned just how little the English teacher can do in the absence of the only real colleague he ever had—the Latin teacher. And I learned what every teacher learns. That when a problem arose that required parental cooperation, I never got it. But that when a parent wanted to find me, he knew where to look.

All that was a good beginning, but I believe I was set on a writer's course long years before; thirty years ago in fact, and it was on the first day of senior year in Stephen Decatur High School in Decatur, Illinois. And it was a teacher who set me on this fatal course.

Her name was Miss Franklin; she taught senior English to the college-bound. We had all heard about her, but if you aspired to college, there was no avoiding her.

On the first day of class, she drew herself up exceedingly tall and said, "I can get all of you in this room into the colleges of your choice. Or I can keep you out."

There was not a non-believer in the bunch. Certainly not me, but I had more to learn from Miss Franklin.

I had fallen into bad habits as a student. I had grown accustomed to getting A's, on my English compositions. And A's, as we now know from the sad experiences of our children are the end of education, not the beginning. Nobody ever learned anything from an A.

When I got my first paper back from Miss Franklin, it had no grade on it of any sort. Instead, she had written words across the page I still have reason to remember: "Never express yourself again on my time. Find a more interesting topic."

Well, I was seventeen years old. I did not know what a more interesting topic than me would be. I actually went to the woman and said, "What would a more interesting topic be?"

And she said, "Almost *anything*."

That sent me to the library in search of subject matter that was not me. I am still in search of it.

Miss Franklin was my first real reader because she taught me that the needs of the reader take precedence over the needs of the writer, *every time*. That writing is the craft of communicating with strangers, and on *their* terms.

One way of communicating with the young of the 1980's is a form of growing popularity called the "young adult novel." What is a "YA novel?" I can only speak for myself. Judy Blume does not consult me. Robert Cormier manages on his own. S. E. Hinton, at the age of seventeen, beat me to it.

For me a YA novel is about coming of age. In it the reader meets a worthy young character who takes one step nearer maturity, and he or she takes that step independently.

After twelve novels, I find I have only one theme. And since no reviewer has ever discovered what that theme is, I will tell you. It is simply that you will never grow up until you begin to think and act independently of your peers.

My message is not, you will notice, to think and act independently of your *parents*. The young do not need that message. In the 1980's they have already won all their battles with their parents and their teachers, with all the adult world, and they have turned upon each other.

My single theme is not likely to convert them, but then the young like advice in books you do not have to take. And they are reading those books mainly to find friends—friends they can look up to—better friends than they have or are.

People are forever asking authors where they get their ideas. I get mine from the young. I have come to see that *their* ideas are better than mine. My newest book is from an idea handed to me in a library in Toronto.

I was talking with a group of 7th-graders in a library. At one point, I turned to the boys and asked them to tell me the topics they wanted to read about. They told me, in no uncertain terms, they wanted books on the lives of sports figures, on customized cars, and on World War II. As you know, by World War II, they mean the Nazi party. I have heard this laundry list of topics before, and I will hear it again. And I believe them up to a point.

After the meeting, I lingered because there is often a private citizen with a private message that should not be overheard by his peers. And so there was.

I thought I was in the room alone, but I looked down below my elbow to see a boy looking up. He checked the room to make sure we were not going to be overheard, and then he said, "Say, listen, have you written anything on dating?"

"Dating?" I said. "You mean non-fiction?"

"What's that?" he said.

"A how-to-do-it book?" I ventured.

"Oh no," he said, looking away. "I mean, you know, a story."

"You mean a love story," I said, and he nodded.

I did not have a love story, and I was sorry since he was brave enough to ask. Love stories delight the young. Dame Barbara Cartland, Rosemary Rogers, Gothic novels, Harlequins, and Candelights out-perform us YA authors to our own readers. Could I write a love story at all unlike the millions already in print?

Yes, I could. I could write a love story *told by a boy*. It might please some boys to be given this voice. It might surprise some girls that boys have emotions too. Mother never told them. Mothers are still telling daughters that boys only want one thing. How wrong they are. Boys want a great deal.

I have written a novel told by a boy who loses the first girl he ever loves. He loses her in a particularly final way: not to another boy, but to death. He thinks what he would think: that there will never be another. He is right in a way. There never will be another first one. He has not been taught to deal with grief, particularly his own. He is a boy. He thinks he must hide behind a strong facade.

This boy has a father who would lay down his life to spare his son's pain. But he is a man without an emotional vocabulary to solace his son. If it were not for the reader of the book, this boy would not have anyone to turn to. The reader is expected to suffer with him, and then can share in his reward.

There is no sexual content in this book. This is a novel about the emotions, not the senses.

It is called ***Close Enough to Touch.*** (pp. 13-15)

You can hardly mention Young Adult novels in this decade without raising the ghost of that ancient evil—censorship. The 1980's is a new golden age of censorship. This is one of those odd, irrational turns that history takes, reminding us that we have not really made much progress, or learned from the past.

Being censored and condemned puts an author in some pretty distinguished company, of course—with writers of our own country's past and of the present of Soviet Russia. Besides, a bit of banning never hurt a book. It is free and effective advertising. Today, a book can not even be banned. A book, especially for the young, that is expunged from home and school and library is readily available just down the road at the paperback bookstore of the shopping mall, a place better attended than the home, school, or library.

A young adult book, in the minds of those who have never read many, is almost by definition a single-problem shocker on some harsh issue such as racial conflict, the drug culture, suicide, insanity, obesity, running away or some other psychological, sociological, or sexual issue. Most of our books are neither that simple nor that easy. Growing up is not just one problem at a time. It is a great many, often quiet problems. Our books are mainly about human relationships, friendships, family life, and trying to grow up the best way you know how.

I wrote a book once that got mislabeled as a single-problem shocker, apparently by people who had not read it. While I was writing it, I thought it would end my career. It turned out to be my best-seller, translated into five languages and a television movie. Now I learn it is being used in, of all places, social studies classrooms.

The book is called ***Are You In The House Alone?*** It is about a high school girl who suffers the crime of rape. I wrote it not because I wanted to but because the typical victim of this crime is a teen-aged girl—one of my readers perhaps.

I did not write the novel to tell the young about rape. They already know what that is. I wrote it because in our society we have developed a tremendous contempt for the victims of crime and a great respect for the criminals.

I wrote it to tell the young that life is not a television show, that in real life the guilty are rarely caught and never rehabilitated. The victim of a crime bears the full burden of it for the rest of their life.

I did not write ***Are You Alone In The House?*** on a sexual subject. I wrote it on a worse problem than that. In the book, the young victim is rejected by her own peer group. There is no one more contemptuous of a victim, of a loser, than an adolescent. That is why I wrote the book: to ask the young to evaluate the standards of their own peers.

Our books teach very little sex education, if any. In a way, this is a bad thing because the young are in desperate need of it. The young of the 1980's are not sexually sophisticated. In their homes they are not taught to be responsible for the consequences of their actions. Many of them—perhaps a majority—are illiterate. They cannot read responsible information on the subject, and so they are at the mercy of the lies and rumors circulated by their peers.

But what of that other problem, the *language* in our books? The book-banners are now underlining isolated words in our pages, and their followers read only those words and not the books.

I for one do not know any language I have not already heard from junior high school students. It is true. I may not have first heard some of that language until I was in the army, but I hear it now from people passing through puberty.

I do not use coarse language in my books because my young readers do not like it there. In a book, they want to look up to the main character as a role-model. Our main characters are more resourceful, more compassionate, more articulate than our readers.

What worries me is not that young people use dirty language but that they do not use any language at all. They cannot get through a sentence without using the three loneliest words in the English language: "like" and "you know," They are verbally anorexic.

They do not learn language usage at home in front of the television set. Nor in classrooms where they are lulled by the remedial reading teacher or that hopelessly optimistic figure in charge of the "academically gifted." Today, in the standards of our schools, to be *literate* is to be "gifted."

In Russia a child must be able to read before he *goes* to school. In England a 7-year-old child must pass a strict reading-and-writing test before he goes a step beyond. In Cuba there are mandatory literacy exams, not just in Spanish, but in English as well.

In America, millions of high school graduates cannot read the diplomas automatically handed to them. This could not happen in a country with a future and it should cause a national scandal far worse than any sexual one. But that is the world as it should be, not as it is.

Our children are not being corrupted by *books*. They are being corrupted by anti-intellectual parents, political school administrators, elective courses, colleges hungry for tuition, and by a society in which the *librarian* would be *fired* for using the kind of language a *coach* uses every day.

You and I pursue our careers against this backdrop. Usually we are permitted to function because nobody cares enough to stop us. But that is no solution to this age in which adults have turned on books and librarians as scapegoats.

Why do they do it? I suppose that families are at their wit's end now, and must find someone, something to blame. Families have been in retreat for many years. They fled from cities to suburbs, in retreat from urban problems. Now they are heading for the hills and for censorship, never knowing that *they* are the problems they flee.

A thing has happened in our country that could not possibly have happened. Our famous public school system lies in expensive ruins, and no parent wants to send his child there. We have withdrawn into private schools, parochial schools, Christian schools, whose standards are rarely challenged. When a child is sent to a private school for social, racial, or religious reasons or for reasons of bare, physical safety, *education* is the first casualty, and the *child* is the second. There is no place to hide, and even when parents do, their *children* cannot.

You and I, we people of the word, are in the business of communicating with those children. We would like to offer them some alternatives in their lives—alternatives to conformity, to mindless following, to smug provincialism. We are also in the business of spotting for survivors. We are looking for them in the rubble of a collapsed order. We are looking in the ruins of the American public school system that once promised a start in life for every citizen, native-and foreign-born. We are looking in the ruins of a society that had begun to rise out of its virulent anti-intellectualism, and then fell back. We are spotting for the survivors of the permissive home and there are very few. There is not anywhere you can go from a permissive home. The rest of the world has rules.

There is another America, of course, beyond this somber landscape. An America revealed chiefly by books—by novels: of the past, on this year's list, of novels yet to be written.

This America is one of self-reliance and coming from behind; of characters who learn to accept the consequences of their actions; of happy endings worked for and almost achieved; of being young in an old world and finding your way in it; of a nation of people hasty and forgetful but full still of hope; of limitless distances and new beginnings and starting over; of dreams like mountaintops, and rivers that run to the sea.

We owe our young this record of our dreams, and if you and I do not put that record into their hands, who will? (pp. 15-16)

Richard Peck, "People of the Word," in Arkansas Libraries, *Vol. 38, No. 4, December, 1981, pp. 13-16.*

GENERAL COMMENTARY

MAY HILL ARBUTHNOT AND ZENA SUTHERLAND

In ***Representing Super Doll*** a beautiful but not very astute girl, Darlene, goes to New York for one round of a teenage beauty contest. Her ambitious mother convinces Verna, Darlene's classmate, to go along as companion. Verna, level-headed and intelligent, scorns the whole proceeding and goes home—and Darlene does the same. To her mother's fury, she has quit just before the final round. The message is firmly feminist, but Peck does not let the message obscure the story; the plot is solid, the characters strong, and the treatment of adolescent concerns balanced.

Dreamland Lake has a wry humor in the classroom scenes to offset the somberness of a story in which two boys, finding a vagrant's corpse in an amusement park, become so engrossed in making a mystery of a natural death that they carelessly bring about another death. Another story of suspense is ***Through a Brief Darkness,*** in which a sixteen-year-old girl discovers that her father is a prominent underworld figure. While this has some conventional mystery story elements, it also has good pace and dialogue that is natural. Dialogue is one of the strong aspects in all Peck's stories, and his books are notable for their fresh viewpoints and their vitality.

May Hill Arbuthnot and Zena Sutherland, "Modern Fiction: Richard Peck," in their Children and Books, *fifth edition, Scott, Foresman and Company, 1977, p. 337.*

GEORGE NICHOLSON

[The following excerpt is from an interview by Roni Natov and Geraldine DeLuca with Peck's publisher, George Nicholson, who is Editorial Director of Books for Young Readers at Dell Publishing Company.]

I think Richard Peck is an extraordinarily gifted writer. I think he has a tendency to be slick, but he is probably the most thoughtful novelist in terms of being able to explain exactly why he does what he does, of anybody I work with. And I think he will write a great novel one of these days. His sensibilities are deep enough. (p. 105)

George Nicholson, in an interview with Roni Natov and Geraldine DeLuca, in The Lion and the Unicorn, *Vol. 5, 1981, pp. 89-107.*

ALLEEN PACE NILSEN AND KENNETH L. DONELSON

In a similar way to how William Wharton told most of Birdy's story through the eyes of his best friend [in *Birdy*], authors may look around for a relatively minor character to tell the story. Richard Peck has explained that he chooses to do this because the interesting stories are at the extreme ends of the normal curve. The exciting things are happening to the brilliant and successful students such as those that Ursula Le Guin wrote about in *Very Far Away from Anywhere Else*. Or they are happening to the kids at the other end of the scale as in Fran Arrick's *Steffie Can't Come Out to Play* and S. E. Hinton's *That Was Then, This Is Now*. Peck says that these extreme characters are wonderful to write about, but they aren't the ones who will read his books. They are too busy, too involved in their own lives. Readers are most likely to come from the large group of students in between whose lives aren't full of such highs and lows. Therefore, what Peck does is to choose for a narrator someone from the middle group with whom readers can identify. He then tells the story through this person's eyes. For example in ***Don't Look and It Won't Hurt,*** it is the fifteen-year-old sister who tells the story of the pregnant and unmarried Ellen who goes to Chicago to have her baby. And in ***Representing Super Doll,*** it is the beauty queen's friend Verna who relates the story and who, in an example of wish fulfillment, is shown to be the real winner. (p. 60)

Supernatural books usually ignore the comic, so it is a relief occasionally to turn to Richard Peck's ***The Ghost Belonged to Me, Ghosts I Have Been,*** and ***The Dreadful Future of Blossom Culp.*** In the first book, Alexander Armsworth uses his gift of second sight to contact a young ghost. In the second, Blossom Culp, one of the spunkiest characters in American fiction, uses her talents with the supernatural to become more and more compassionate, not to hurt others. The last book is the least satisfying, but a slightly older Blossom who projects herself into a 1980s world of video games is still entertaining. (pp. 153-54)

Alleen Pace Nilsen and Kenneth L. Donelson, "Literary Aspects of Young Adult Books" and "Excitement and Suspense: Of Sudden Shadows," in their Literature for Today's Young Adults, *second edition, Scott, Foresman and Company, 1985, pp. 34-76, 136-71.*

HILARY CREW

In a speech given to the American Association of School Librarians, Richard Peck says that "in reaching for a book, the young are looking for characters they can befriend, characters they can become." This confirms one of Peck's greatest strengths as a writer—the portrayal of character. His young adult books are peopled with a wealth of diverse characters from singular old ladies to independent and sometimes lonely teenage protagonists, including the intrepid Blossom Culp and her reluctant sweetheart, the more conservative Alexander in his argyle sweater. Peck portrays widowed or divorced fathers suddenly faced with the bewildering task of parental responsibilities, snobby mothers, working mothers, cruel mothers, and Blossom Culp's mother, who, with her gypsy blood, fortune-telling cards, and "gambler's dice" earrings, is in a class of her own. Some of his protagonists are boys coping with the finality of death; others, girls having to face up to rape and teenage pregnancy. There are ghosts—very much "alive" ghosts—each with his or her own personality, and teachers, lots of teachers, who alternately triumph over or crumble under their charges. They are part of Peck's vast array of secondary characters. He is adept at the quick character sketch. In very few words he is able to conjure up distinct, credible personalities.

Although Peck says that one of his main themes is that fathers, brothers, and sons have emotions too (and Peck does write about emotions and friendship rather than sex per se), and although the main characters in ***Father Figure, Close Enough to Touch,*** and ***Remembering the Good Times*** are boys whose feelings are sensitively drawn, there is an emphasis in his work on the independent, female character. The girl-woman waitress in ***Father Figure*** plays "mama for three lost souls" and attempts to weld Jim, his younger brother, and his father into "a family." Margaret, in ***Close Enough to Touch,*** unconventional and self-assured, loosens Matt from grief and self-pity. In ***Remembering the Good Times,*** it is Kate who holds together the trio of friends. All three female characters are vital, warm, and magnetic, stepping with assurance into the lives of boys who feel inadequate as they experience feelings of love, grief, and guilt. Through their strength of character, these women assume dominating roles in these novels. Peck's books feature resourceful, resilient, and independent girls who not only take the responsibility for their own lives but are also supportive of others. Carol, in ***Don't Look and It Won't Hurt,*** takes her mother's place in her relationship with her sisters, one younger and dependent on Carol for love and attention, the other facing teenage pregnancy and dependent on Carol for moral support and caring. When Karen, in ***Through a Brief Darkness,*** realizes how her father has kept her from him in order to protect her from the knowledge of his criminal activities, she decides to "determine the distance between them herself. And to measure it in truth." Gail, in ***Are You in the House Alone?*** rejects her mother's plan to send her away after being raped. She goes back to school because she has "a right to go back." She, more than her parents, understands the responsibility that falls to the victim of a rapist. And in a lighter vein, there is the incomparable Blossom Culp, who introduces herself, "My name is Blossom Culp, and I live by rules of my own." Using the more cautious Alexander as a foil, Peck endows Blossom with the feisty spirit necessary to survive, with humor and old-fashioned "spunk," and with a less-than-advantageous home environment. As Blossom says, "advantages . . . tend to kill your initiative"—a sentiment echoed by the author throughout his books.

Blossom can be a scheming little minx; she is outrageous, but she has the courage and bravado to cover the real loneliness that lies underneath. The theme of isolation runs through much of Peck's work. Blossom is "used to going it alone." Her independence and resourcefulness both protect and separate her from the Letty Shambaughs of this world, who are "as alike as gingerbread figures in skirts." Poignancy breaks through Blossom's breezy self-assertiveness as the reader is made aware of her alienation among her own age group in the stratified society of Bluff City and her need for love and companionship. In ***The Dreadful Future of Blossom Culp,*** she travels from 1914 through time to meet a real friend, the "forlorn and friendless" Jeremy, as much an outcast in his society as Blossom is in hers.

The "future" Blossom notes, "was a lonely place," and the prevailing mood in the novel ***Don't Look and It Won't Hurt*** is one of silence and isolation. The "empty black asphalt" of the road "stretched out between" Ellen and her sister symbolizes the void that exists in the relationships between each of the sisters and her mother. The fear of loneliness is a tangible one. Carol walks away from her mother afraid that "we were all starting to drift away from the little we had together to the nothing we'd have without each other." In ***Through a Brief Darkness,*** Karen learns to protect herself through a silence that "began to lead to independence." Gail in ***Are You in the House Alone?*** is "sealed . . . off" from family and friends as she faces alone the anonymous threats of a rapist, and Trav in ***Remembering the Good Times*** sees suicide as the ultimate solution to isolation. Love and understanding are achieved through communication—a communication that Peck infers is painfully lacking with adolescents in many families today. Of central concern in his books are family relationships—distances between mothers and daughters, fathers and sons groping their way to loving relationships, single parents struggling to provide home and security—and divorce, separation, bereavement, and love.

In ***Remembering the Good Times,*** Peck emphasizes the need to establish one's roots in a community in order to foster a feeling of belonging and solidity. When Trav commits suicide his father complains that "We aren't a community. We are all strangers here." It is Polly, the "third oldest woman in Slocum" who points out the need for students, parents, and teachers to make a commitment to care about and for others. She is one of several singular, perceptive, elderly characters in Peck's books who intuitively understands young people, offering them friendship, love, and connections with the past.

Blossom's far-from-ghostly ghosts function as credible secondary characters who do more than add a whiff of the supernatural to conventional Bluff City. They bring a consciousness of history of places far from small-town America. And as Blossom finds out, ghosts, like herself, need a place to belong. Seemingly isolated and self-contained, Bluff City has its own submerged connections. This continuity with the past is brought into many of Peck's books. Margaret in ***Close Enough to Touch,*** explains why she rides sidesaddle. "It's a linking up of the present with the past. Who wants to be locked into anything—even a time?" Certainly not Blossom, who travels back and forth through time with her psychic powers. For along with a need to belong, there is also the need for independence and an escape from limiting backgrounds.

In an interview in *English Journal* Peck says that in all his novels the "main character takes a trip, a geographic trip. They all slip the bonds of peer group and family for an independent look at the world. Then they return, a bit more able to cope" [see Author's Commentary for *The Ghost Belonged to Me*]. Peck's characters come from a wide range of social and economic backgrounds. In his novels, he consciously contrasts these backgrounds. Many of his independent teenagers come from working-class families and make friends from the "other" part of town. Carol's home in ***Don't Look and It Won't Hurt,*** with its peeling wall-paper, is contrasted with the pale beige carpet and uncluttered look of a friend's home, which exemplifies "gracious living." Blossom's "two-room dwelling by the streetcar tracks" lies opposite the Armsworth Mansion, Alexander's home. In Peck's work, it is frequently the teenage protagonist who often bridges, if only temporarily, the socio-economic gap between "those who have arrived and those who never will." In ***Remembering the Good Times,*** Trav, a "complete sub," unable "to grasp the concept of [Buck's] trailer living," traverses "party lines" in his friendship with Buck and Kate. But it is Kate, Blossom, and Carol who are the survivors, who gain their independence and maturity from coping with a life-style minus both economic advantages and one parent. Buck notes that "Kate—she was in charge around her house. Anything that got done, she did it." Marietta, with her "Mrs. Got-Rocks daydreams," is "nobody's easy convenience" but is "queen of her little world and dreaming of a better one," and Margaret in ***Close Enough to Touch*** runs her own antique business. These independent females are contrasted with ineffectual girls and sometimes snobby mothers seemingly locked behind wide, curving drives and imposing front doors.

Feminist issues are raised in Peck's work. He relates with humor the attitude toward the vote held by some of the town's worthy mothers in ***Blossom Culp and the Sleep Of Death.*** They do not see the need to vote for it is "a woman's destiny to convince her husband to vote the way she sees fit. Women are put on this earth to tell men what to do." An admirable sentiment and one that Blossom Culp (who else?) forces them to translate into more positive action. That advocate of the suffragette movement, "dangerous agitator," and teacher Miss Fairweather is finally accepted and points the way toward political independence for Bluff City women. In ***Representing Super Doll,*** Moon gives the feminist point of view on beauty contests. "It's *exploitive* . . . of the female body to pander to chauvinist male lust in the name of crass commercialism." It's a tongue-in-cheek look at the world of beauty contests, but Peck deals sensitively with Darlene, beauty queen of the Hybird Seed Corn Company, whose story is told from the point of view of her friend, Verna. The "superdoll" image of women is contrasted with Verna's future sister-in-law and mother, both of whom work and wish to be equal partners in a marriage. Verna's hopes and dreams and those of her friends include not romance and marriage but travel, education, and community service. Perhaps the most truly liberated woman in Peck's books is Blossom Culp's mother. She does her gardening and harvesting in other people's gardens and drives Blossom out at night to raid the neighbors' chicken pens. How can you help but have a sneaking admiration for a woman who does not one jot of housework, reads her future in tea leaves, throws the dregs on the floor, puts her feet upon the table, and goes to sleep? No stereotyped housewife here!

The variety of characters in Peck's books and his use of history can extend the horizons of an adolescent. Add a dash of the supernatural, a great sense of humour, and a real interest in and understanding of the problems of adolescents and you have a successful writer for young adults. One, moreover, who believes in the feminist movement and creates resourceful, intelligent, independent female characters in books that appeal to young people of both sexes. (pp. 297-300)

Hilary Crew, "Blossom Culp and Her Ilk: The Independent Female in Richard Peck's YA Fiction," in Top of the News, *Vol. 43, No. 3, Spring, 1987. pp. 297-301.*

DON'T LOOK AND IT WON'T HURT **(1972)**

AUTHOR'S COMMENTARY

A writer of whatever kind works against continual deadlines. And I have no recollection of what gives form to the lives of non-writers. But to write to these youngsters who are only with us a moment is a deadline in itself. It hones you to a fine point and makes you aware of your priorities. Fortunately I was a teacher. So I have some notion of how quickly the young grow up and how original they find this process. I'd be a teacher still if I'd been able to teach as I'd been taught.

And where do I find myself today? Still back at the same old post. Still trying to devise subject matter of immediate and manifest relevance. Still working against the shrinking attention span of the permissively reared. Trying to make common cause with a group of young people who have not yet paid their dues or tested their opinions or lived on their own incomes. Still trying to bring home the idea that reading and of course writing are not pastimes, but essentials.

From the very beginning writing was for me 90% eavesdropping. And my head rang with information I'd gathered in the classroom and in student compositions. The writer's first tool is a listening ear. Attuned to the rhymes and patterns of speech. I'm not talking about the still, small voice crying in one's own heart; I'm talking about other voices in other rooms. For the very reason that my readers live imprisoned by the present in a world without a history, I have to keep moving among the young for clues to their latest ways. But I can only use pinches of their reality in a stew of my own brewing.

If I photographed the lifestyle of the young and handed them back a print of it, they'd recoil in disbelief and disgust. I'm always listening for the latest turn of phrase. But I can only use the odd word. No one can tell me how long the word TURKEY will be current in slang parlance. And of course, if my book characters were as inarticulate as my readers, my stories would never proceed.

If I could use true speech patterns, my course would be clear. I'd hide tape recorders in the boys' and girls' washrooms of any school, retrieve them at the end of any day, and transcribe them into a plot. And what would happen? Parents would condemn my books for teaching their children filth. (pp. 18-19)

In most of my novels, morals and themes lurk beneath the window-dressing of suspense or humor or local color or wish-fulfillment or melodrama or escapism or fantasy or the supernatural. And here I practice a compromise so familiar to a teacher. I choose the morals and themes. But my young readers choose the window-dressing.

I write in the forms popular to them. When it comes to the look of the book, I bury my taste in reading and salute theirs. (p. 19)

I began with a novel called ***Don't Look and It Won't Hurt.*** It's a story about a girl who goes to a home for unwed mothers. And I was not off the 1st page before I was in more trouble than she was.

I couldn't make that unwed mother the central figure. I'd spent too much time in school, seeing how much attention is lavished on the youngster who's already in the kind of trouble adults can no longer overlook. And all this attention to the exclusion of the quieter, probably more desperate and undoubtedly more literate child. And so I couldn't put the unwed mother at center stage, nor portray her in the chic liberal manner as society's wretched victim. Instead, I restarted from the viewpoint of her younger brother, but he didn't survive the opening chapter. He was a young boy, looking up at an older sister with a sentimentality that blurred the issue.

Third time around, I found my narrator. A younger sister who can regard the situation of a fellow-female with a clear and near pitiless eye. And she grew on the page to become the protagonist, very nearly thrusting the unwed mother off the stage. I remembered from teaching that my readership, if any, would not be made up largely of unwed mothers. It would be that vast and silent majority who sit quietly on the fringe of the famous Youth Culture and in a corner of the library, waiting without hope for the exhibitionists to shut up. In the third draft, I finally located my reader and tried to reflect that reader in the protagonist. And I'm still trying.

In all our books, the main characters are encouraging portrayals of the reader, or they go unread. The young will not accept a negative protagonist and will not identify with losers. And here lies a vast difference between writing for the young and writing for adults. The young seem not to like to feel superior to the protagonists; they want to be them. And they identify in ways that you and I have lost over the years.

In that first novel, a young girl has to pull her collapsed family together after they've been dealt a blow. And she's only 15. Significantly she's able to do things her own mother cannot. So I stumble onto role-reversal, a topic of apparently unlimited interest to the young. I learned too that I'm only comfortable in telling a story in first person through a young character's voice. It keeps me, the alien adult, out of the picture. My narrators are never passive, though they begin by standing at the edge of the action, wondering what they can do. That's where most of my readers are, standing and wondering. (pp. 19-20)

Richard Peck, "What Turns Them On!" in Kentucky Library Association Bulletin, *Vol. 41, No. 3, Summer, 1977, pp. 15-25.*

Life on the wrong side of the tracks when the tracks are in Claypitts the "Pearl of the Prairie" isn't much to brag about, and Carol, with her ready self-deprecating wit would be the first to admit it. But when older, wilder sister Ellen falls for a pot dealer (disguised as anti-draft organizer) and uses her resulting pregnancy as a not unwelcome excuse to get away to Chicago, Carol is determined to go up there and convince her that at least one member of the family still cares enough to want her back. Don't look and it won't hurt—Carol's advice to Ellen who's wondering how she can bear to give her baby up for adoption—is neither true nor very comforting, but Claypitt's teenage characters bend themselves to cheerfully hard-boiled sarcasm—particularly tough Mitsy Decker . . . and the precociously poised minister's daughter Shirley Gage. It won't hurt if you read if for the humor, but don't look for any hidden profundity.

A review of "Don't Look and It Won't Hurt," in Kirkus Reviews, *Vol. 40, No. 16, August 15, 1972, p. 949.*

This successful first novel by Mr. Peck . . . will touch girls with its honesty and sensitivity. . . . [Carol's] tribulations at home when her eldest sister becomes pregnant, and her struggles to grow up are offered with a wry style and the bite of a young girl trying to cut through superfluity to an understanding of herself and her family. Not a great book, but one that will be popular and will reassure. They'll be hooked by the first sentence: "Welcome to CLAYPITTS, PEARL OF THE PRAIRIE and if you'd believe that, you'd believe anything."

A review of "Don't Look and It Won't Hurt," in Children's Book Review Service, *Vol. 1, No. 2, October, 1972, p. 14.*

Mr. Peck's is a textured story of three daughters in a desperately poor home headed by a mother who is both defeated and proud. Through the insightful eyes of the middle child we come to understand the complex forces that lead to the eldest girl's pregnancy. There are no absolutes: abject poverty is tempered by humor; a ne'er-do-well father is allowed an unlikely streak of compassion; and the pregnant sister gives her baby up for adoption only after the subtleties of her predicament are seen and felt.

Rather than arousing judgemental passions, ***Don't Look and It Won't Hurt*** leaves the reader empathic and terribly moved. (pp. 8, 10)

Letty Cottin Pogrebin, in a review of "Don't Look and It Won't Hurt," in The New York Times Book Review, *November 12, 1972, pp. 8, 10.*

[The advice in the title] typifies the bitter wisdom of this family of losers. . . . [The story] is well written but concludes with few solutions and only sketchy plot development. Nevertheless, as a slice of none-too-enjoyable life, Peck's first novel will interest many readers.

Peggy Sullivan, in a review of "Don't Look and It Won't Hurt," in School Library Journal, *an appendix to* Library Journal, *Vol. 19, No. 4, December, 1972, p. 68.*

DREAMLAND LAKE (1973)

Not once, but three different times, Brian Bishop finds himself staring into the "Awful Face of Death." Brian's stunned reactions to the suddenness of death and the ultimate incomprehensibility of a corpse are in stark counterpoint to his other memories of his thirteenth summer. He and his friend Flip subsist largely on sly adolescent wit—chuckling over the inept efforts of English teacher Mabel Klimer to introduce them to POETRY, Brian's mother's fondness for Bacharach, and the frumpish gentility of an old local history book produced by one Estella Winkler Bates; they also fantasize together about their hero, the YMCA swimming teacher whom they nickname Ralph The Free. After the two boys find the body of an old tramp in the woods Flip, who lives up to his name and has a cruel streak besides, encourages Brian in another illusion: perhaps the pathetic fat boy Elvan, who has been trying to interest them in his collection of Nazi souvenirs, knows something more about the tramp's death? Their efforts to build their discovery into a full-scale mystery eventually leads to a real tragedy—a startlingly convincing freak accident which sets the seal to Brian's chronicle of innocence remembered and lost. Less convincing, however, is the implication that Flip is actually responsible for what happens to Elvan. This assignment of guilt by hindsight adds an unsettling dimension to an otherwise finely tuned shocker. Though the fraternal naivete of boarding school life in another generation has been replaced with a kind of wry public school prescience, this ambiguous mixture of nostalgia and guilt is invariably reminiscent of *A Separate Peace*. The message is somewhat less than meets the eye, but for boys at a certain stage of growing up, ***Dreamland Lake*** projects a firm reality.

A review of "Dreamland Lake," in Kirkus Reviews, *Vol. 41, No. 12, June 15, 1973, p. 648.*

Beautifully told, the story has just enough foreshadowing to heighten the sense of impending doom. Everything rings true—the dialogue, the minor characters as well as Flip and Brian, small scenes of English class and of the boys' newspaper route, and, most of all, Brian's painful coming of age. Even slower readers will grab this book, captivated first by the mystery, and then by its deeper levels of meaning.

Alice H. Yucht, in a review of "Dreamland Lake," in School Library Journal, *an appendix to* Library Journal, *Vol. 20, No. 3, November, 1973, p. 53.*

A subtle and provocative novel. . . . There is some humor in the rather caustic depiction of classroom scenes, but the story is serious; it is not grim, however, despite the fact that it begins and ends with death, because the skilful construction, the sound characterization and dialogue, and the realistic fluctuation and conflict in the relationships outweigh the fact that the boys are reacting to death. (pp. 83-4)

Zena Sutherland, in a review of "Dreamland Lake," in Bulletin of the Center for Children's Books, *Vol. 27, No. 5, January, 1974, pp. 83-4.*

Ending with a sudden and shattering tragedy, this is more somber perhaps than the usual teenage mystery. Yet the author has a light, controlled touch, and an emotional depth to his narrative that turns it into an unusually strong and subtle novel of early adolescence.

A review of "Dreamland Lake," in The New York Times Book Review, *January 13, 1974, p. 10.*

THROUGH A BRIEF DARKNESS (1973)

In his third YA novel Peck wisely relinquishes any pretense to relevance or depth and comes out with a tightly drawn romantic melodrama about sixteen year-old Karen, protected daughter of a big time crook, who is suddenly pulled out of boarding school and hustled off to "relatives" in England, there to discover gradually that she has actually been kidnapped by ruthless members of a rival syndicate. The unconvincing presence of a handsome young Etonian (remembered companion of an idyllic childhood summer) who comes to Karen's rescue makes it impossible to take the adventure seriously, but Karen's gradual admission of the illegality of her father's activities gives it what little ballast is needed, and—most important—the shocks and terrors of Karen's captivity and flight and the unexpected reversals when "nice" people turn out villains and vice versa are handled by a calculating mastermind who knows just how to maximize suspense.

A review of "Through a Brief Darkness," in Kirkus Reviews, *Vol. 41, No. 23, December 1, 1973, p. 1314.*

A suspense story that has good pace and construction. . . . The story ends with a smashing chase sequence that is a natural for motion pictures, with Karen pursued by members of the gang and helped by a childhood friend who's at Eton and by a grande dame meant to be played by Margaret Rutherford. Karen's reunion with her father is a tentative conclusion, but the story as a whole is strong: an unusual heroine, a touch of mystery, a credible outcome, and lashes of action and suspense. (pp. 116-17)

Zena Sutherland, in a review of "Through a Brief Darkness," in Bulletin of the Center for Children's Books, *Vol. 27, No. 7, March, 1974, pp. 116-17.*

This is one of those old-fashioned crime and mystery stories in which things are so often not what they purport to be that you end up trusting nothing and nobody. . . . In the first two chapters, Karen goes through a succession of schools and introspections which are pretty pointless as she never develops as a character anyway. . . . The occasional bits of pseudo-psychology and superficial glances at Karen's relationship with ever-absent, busy, crooked Daddy, only get in the way of an otherwise fast-moving, fairly enjoyable piece of hokum. But to be successful a thriller of this sort needs to be worked out more carefully and to show its derivations much less obviously. The book could have been much worse and much better.

M. H. Miller, in a review of "Through a Brief Darkness," in Children's Book Review, *Vol. VI, October, 1976, p. 20.*

Kidnapping, like hi-jacking, is very much the thing, so it is not surprising to find the theme occurring several times in this issue's selection. Mr. Peck at least manages a flourish of novelty in having Rachel kidnapped in a very elaborate way. . . . [In Rachel's escape], a modest element of romance (the blurb calls it 'tingling'!) plays a part when Rachel makes use of an old holiday pal, Jay, . . . to prise her out of her phoney home, planting her, fortuitously, in the hands of a deliciously eccentric aunt of a friend. Unfortunately, Rachel's father really is a crook and one is not, at the end of the story, too happy about her future. The yarn certainly moves rapidly—in terms of locale as well; Mr. Peck seems to make use of places he once knew. It is a pity that a slight taint of cynicism seems to colour the whole. It is such a good novel that one feels like reading it all over again once one has reached the end.

A. R. Williams, in a review of "Through a Brief Darkness," in The Junior Bookshelf, *Vol. 40, No. 5, October, 1976, p. 283.*

REPRESENTING SUPER DOLL (1974)

Verna is a wholesome farm girl who finds being bused to high school in industrial Dunthorpe a bit of a culture shock, but before long she is in with the girls she had aimed for and even accompanies one of them, beautiful though stupid Darlene, to her appearances in New York City as Central U.S. Teen Super Doll. How Velma helps Darlene to resist her divorced mother's determination to groom her as Miss America doesn't seem all that significant, nor does older brother Hal's decision to let Sheri, his nice stewardess wife-to-be, support him through medical school. But here it's the scenes and encounters and experiences along the way that make the trip worthwhile: Verna's mother's proud company dinner when her school friends come to visit, sour Aunt Eunice's self-conscious pleasure upon winning some perfume at the county fair, and above all Verna's reactions to New York, where TV panelists vote her "the real Super Doll" and Darlene a "well chosen and well endowed imposter." Any visitor to the city will recognize the inflections of chaperone Miss Teal, who talks as though "she's mad at us" (really it's "the way almost everybody talked there") and arranges dinner at Mama Minestrone's, "the noisiest place on earth," where Velma's blind date yells above the din that "I always stick with Super Doll's friend. You meet a more interesting class of women that way." Velma indeed is a likable girl and, as Sheri says, she doesn't miss much.

A review of "Representing Super Doll," in Kirkus Reviews, *Vol. 42, No. 20, October 15, 1974, p. 1110.*

Peck's writing is admirable. It has vitality and flow, vivid characterization and dialogue, a fresh viewpoint that makes the story convincingly that of an intelligent adolescent, and a deeper treatment of a theme than most beauty contest books achieve.

Zena Sutherland, in a review of "Representing Super Doll," in Bulletin of the Center for Children's Books, *Vol. 28, No. 3, November, 1974, p. 51.*

[The older characters in ***Representing Super Doll***], for the most part, are stereotype adults; the teasing father, the devoted mother, the English teacher who wears straight skirts and gives assignments on "Your hopes, your dreams."

Bernice is a midwestern farm girl attending a small-town high school after her earlier years in a country school. Once there she quickly forsakes her country ways (there is an interesting passage in the book about how her mother killed a chicken by whirling it around and around until its head broke off) for those of the small town. She becomes friends with three town girls, one of whom is the beautiful but stupid Darlene Hoffmeister.

Mrs. Hoffmeister, a divorcee living on alimony, enters her daughter in several beauty contests, one of which is Miss Teen Super Doll. When Darlene wins the regional contest she gets to travel to New York City and compete in the national event, and Bernice is given the chance to go along with her as a chaperone.

In New York the two of them meet up with more stereotypes and Darlene bungles her chances in the big contest by her vague confused answers to all questions. Bernice begins to learn that she herself is attractive and, unlike Darlene, is able to answer questions. When the chance comes on a television quiz show to guess who is the real Miss Super Doll, Bernice is asked to participate because one of the contestants fails to appear. Guess who everyone thinks is the Miss Super Doll?

The author fails to make his point. The beautiful Darlene is really the heroine of this novel although Mr. Peck maybe didn't intend it that way. She makes her own choices. She will not be the beauty queen that her mother insists she be. Perhaps in her own fumbling, inarticulate way she found the only way out of her mother's plans. Unfortunately we see this person, an early teenage Marilyn Monroe, through the eyes of smug Bernice, whose only goal was to become what Darlene chose not to be.

Jean Alexander, "Girls Growing Up," in Book World—The Washington Post, *November 10, 1974, p. 8.*

THE GHOST BELONGED TO ME (1975)

AUTHOR'S COMMENTARY

[The following excerpt is taken from an interview by Paul Janeczko.]

[*English Journal*]: The biographical blurb on your latest novel, ***The Ghost Belonged to Me,*** said that your previous novels were "highly successful." What are the ingredients of a "highly successful" young adult, YA, novel?

[Richard Peck]: If I knew them, I'd be in that room writing a novel now. But I think the signal feature of a YA novel is that it is unreality masked as realism. One way or another, the protagonist has to do something that the reader cannot do. This can range from the deadly serious to the melodramatically absurd. Perhaps the protagonist rises up at a strategic moment to make a decision or to influence others. Or perhaps he/she is simply able to have a little more freedom and fun than the reader has in his life. No matter what, in a YA novel the protagonist acts on behalf of the reader in a particularly direct way. (p. 97)

In all of my novels, the main character takes a trip, a geographic trip. They all slip the bonds of peer group and family for an independent look at the world. Then they return, a bit more able to cope. We have to remember that our readers are institutionalized twice—in homes and in schools. They set great store in mobility.

In ***The Ghost Belonged to Me,*** a boy is stifled by a pompous small-town family. Suddenly, through unlikely, even supernatural circumstances, he finds himself on an odyssey down the Mississippi River to New Orleans. And he is accompanied by the only adult in his life whom he looks up to and wants to emulate. It's too nearly ideal to happen in the lives of most readers. And that's one more reason for reading.

EJ: In ***The Ghost Belonged to Me*** why did you switch from a contemporary setting to an early 20th-century setting?

RP: In part, to make a break from the contemporary settings and situations of the previous four novels. Before I start a new novel, I always make up a list of ways in which it will differ from the previous ones. The differences may be only cosmetic or they may exist only in my mind, but they spur me on and get me writing.

There's an element of the past in an earlier novel, though. In ***Dreamland Lake*** two boys who keep looking into local history have the idea that there was more excitement in the past than in their dull present.

An early draft of ***The Ghost Belonged to Me*** was much in the same vein, shifting back and forth from past to present. Originally, the novel was to be a love story between a contemporary New York baseball-playing boy and the ghost of a girl who was killed on the Titanic. He lives in a brownstone in Brooklyn Heights. Her shade haunts the carriage house at the end of the garden. The two alternate in telling their stories. Not quite aware that she's dead, she speaks of her Edwardian girlhood. Not quite willing to confront a ghost in the garden, the boy clings to his literal present. When they finally confronted each other, the story fell apart.

And so I started over, setting the story entirely in the past for local color and because it's a convention of ghost stories to have period settings. And I quickly dumped the love story for a comic tale. I'm not naturally drawn to the supernatural, but the young very clearly are. And the supernatural turns out to be a very useful device for pointing up certain odd bits of human nature.

We have had plenty of novels of grim contemporary realism and social problems. We overlook the fact that kids are reading in large part for escape. And if we followed the leads of our reviewers we would draw farther from the tastes of our readers. If we're going to vie with television, even in a limited way, we need to think more of entertaining and less about edifying.

I think we have a problem in leading adolescent readers into the past in any kind of story. They don't study much history any more. It was replaced by a non-course called Social Studies that often depends upon no reading at all. But I think the young have a curiosity about the past, particularly if they find the present youth culture stultifying. Novels with period settings are no substitutes for an orderly study of history. Still, for some readers, they may be a start. (pp. 97-8)

Richard Peck, in an interview with Paul Janeczko, in English Journal, *Vol. 65, No. 2, February, 1976, pp. 97-9.*

At the turn of the century, in a barn loft in Bluff City, Middle America, the ghost of the drowned Inez Dumaine—a benign and pitiable apparition—appears to young Alex Armsworth and makes a cryptic request: "To be among my own people . . . above the ground, but at rest." She tells Alex to find other "true believers" to assist him. And he does. The enlisted—outspoken 85-year-old Uncle Miles and Blossom Culp, Alex's realiable and credulous classmate—set off to lay Inez's wandering soul and skeletal remains to rest in New Orleans.

The journey is humorous and Peck is reminiscent of Twain; but for the most part, the droll intimations of a Twain are in Alex's perceptive glimpses of family and friends. For example, Alex on his mother's social aspirations: "We have given up being Baptists in favor of being Episcopalians, which is one step up socially but a step down when it comes to hymn singing."

Such sophisticated humor could easily come from Uncle Miles, the town gadfly, but coming from Alex it exemplifies the problem with this book. Alex is supposedly an adult looking back to his 13th year, "when he was long in the leg but short on experience . . . a difficult age to sort out or live through." But the voice is unsteady, rarely evoking the feelings of a child. The voice of a child is distinctly missing except, ironically, in the encounters with the soggy spirit of the dead child, Inez Dumaine.

Joan Goldman Levine, in a review of "The Ghost Belonged to Me," in The New York Times Book Review, *July 27, 1975, p. 8.*

Richard Peck has written a fast novel for young people. . . . (p. 11)

All ghost stories turn on the question of whether the ghost is real or not. This disappearing girl in the long green dress who carries a dog and leaves wet footprints: is she real—an independent element in the story, a creature who will contend for control of events—or is she something happening in the hero's head, a sign of illness or desire or genius? If she's a projection, her story is likely to become his case history. If she's real, the writer has to be very good to keep the story from becoming melodramatic clap-trap.

Peck is very good. His ghost is believable and affecting, and so is his hero. Alexander is direct, he knows what he wants, he's not too embarrassed by his faults, he's observant, he's honest. And he has an elegant style, at once down-to-earth and courtly.

Alexander's most impressive quality is his sense of justice, the care he takes to report honestly what he saw and felt and to give everyone, with the unfortunate exception of his family, a fair hearing. He talks eagerly about his adventures with Inez but in a style that reflects his reluctance to believe in her. The evidence of her reality accumulates slowly; avenues of scientific or medical explanation are shut off gently, carefully, clearly, one by one. As a result, the reader believes in the ghost before Alexander does and inwardly urges him to accept her. We become evangelists in her behalf.

Peck does a few things that are unpleasant and don't work. For comic purposes, and to add a little of the mandatory sex, he gives Alexander a silly older sister and allows her more freedom by far than her class or her parents would ever have permitted her. Her big scene, a coming-out party destroyed by a drunken suitor, is believable but it's not important and it's not funny. A second comic female also bombs. She's the kitchen-maid, Gladys, and every time she comes on the scene it's like watching a rerun of *The Brady Bunch*.

In place of a mother and father we get cartoons: flat, predictable, failed people, one hysterical and the other given to sardonic one-liners. They would be easier to accept if Alexander weren't telling the story, if we were listening to someone less intelligent and fair.

After Inez has found rest, Alexander loses his gift. He knows, he says, that there will be "no place for being receptive to the Spirit World in my future." So the notion that childhood is a time of revelation is given another ride, probably for the usual purpose, to permit us to praise openness without feeling that we ought to try to imitate it.

Why should Peck, having written such a neat story, feel the need to reassure young readers that they will soon be grown-up, happy, and narrow? It's an odd, unnecessary and unpleasant way to end a well-told story. (pp. 11, 75)

Bruce Clements, "Believable Ghosts and Heroes," in Psychology Today, *Vol. 9, No. 4, September, 1975, pp. 11, 75.*

Both these books [***The Ghost Belonged to Me*** and *Tuck Everlasting* by Natalie Babbitt] have a similar approach to traditional story telling, and both have the added advantage of being part of an increasingly American phenomenon; the stylish, casual, well-written, and well-told story. There seems to be a widening gap between the kind of story-telling in these books and that of much current British fiction. There is a good-humoured ease, even in the most serious moments, which is far more in tune with the way twelve to fifteen-year-olds actually think and speak, even on this side of the Atlantic.

The Ghost Belonged To Me is a conventional ghost story, of a drowned girl and her dog. . . . The circumstances of the apparition, Alexander's relations and the whole small-town, turn-of-the-century atmosphere in Middle America is conveyed with an easy, enviable skill. The bizarre machinations of a New Orleans reporter, a strange girl whose mother has second sight, a madman who chops down and burns a wooden bridge; these are only a few of the events and characters effortlessly packed into the short story. There are more witty asides on each page than in the whole of many British books.

Brian Hall, "New Haunts," in The Times Literary Supplement, *No. 3915, March 25, 1977, p. 348.*

This multilevel adventure tale is a quixotic mix. On the surface, it is an exciting ghost story. Fundamentally, however, it is about a youngster's growing sense of his own adequacy because of the increasing unity between his imagination and his perception of reality. There are historical strands from the Civil War, geographical, of the Mississippi and the old quarters of New Orleans, social, of a Midwest town at the turn of the century, as well as deftly presented observations about human nature. The vivid touches that describe a boy's and girl's awareness of each other are human. Even the generation span between uncle Miles and Alexander accounts for a large measure of the growing awareness of a boy. (p. 189)

Diana L. Spirt, "Identifying Adult Roles: Richard Peck, 'The Ghost Belonged to Me'," in her Introducing More Books: A Guide for the Middle Grades, *R. R. Bowker Company, 1978, pp. 187-90.*

ARE YOU IN THE HOUSE ALONE? (1976)

AUTHOR'S COMMENTARY

Not long ago I had a reasonably satisfying experience, as writers' experiences go. I'd written a novel, ***Are You in the House Alone?,*** to alert young teens to a serious sexual/legal/medical/social problem: the crime of rape, for which adolescents are the prime victims.

I was sitting in the living room of a woman who was explaining to me in fairly benevolent terms why she could not allow her fourteen-year-old daughter to read my book. Midway through the one-sided conversation, her daughter drifted down the hallway past the living room carrying a copy of ***Are You in the House Alone?***—with a bookmark in it.

For several generations now we've been a nation of parents anguishing over the proper guidance and home environment for children who will not be guided and are rarely at home. For the rest of our lives, splinter groups and vigilante committees will be fighting rearguard actions, trying to purify their children's reading matter and textbooks. This is very likely an inevitable venting of frustration against untouchable television and an unmanageable outside world full of assaults on the standards of families unsure of what their standards really are.

Thus, books for children and adolescents on controversial topics—all the *Show Me*'s and *Why Me*'s—play curious roles today in a society that gives lip service to frankness even as it tries to withdraw from reality. The central irony is that there are no books, fiction or nonfiction, for adolescent readers on topics that are not more blatantly aired on TV. My book is about rape. There is hardly a current police-suspense drama or a soap opera that hasn't dealt with that problem far more graphically and in sensational, exploitative, sometimes strangely sentimental ways—all this plus the evening TV news broadcast.

The main problem with books that ask the young to consider their attitudes toward sexual problems, drugs, crime, mental illness, intolerance, dehumanizing role-playing is not that these books are vulnerable to censorship. . . . The central problem is that while the young are receptive to the fiction form, they won't be preached to. Another is that a didactic novel is always in danger of deteriorating into a tract, distorting the strengths of characterization, motivation, plot, and pacing that make a novel, regardless of its theme.

I was once determined to stay away from the single-problem novel. Too many "young adult" novels are based on the premise that a young character's entire fate turns upon a single issue. Real life, even in the eighth grade, is more complex than this, unmasking the narrowed novel as life in a slice too thin. Adolescence is a tangled skein of problems, all apparently unsolvable. It's a rare teenager who has only one worry. And I'd entered the YA field when the single-problem novel was in full cry: subjects always seemed to be drugs, political revolt, or racial identity.

In response to my early novels, I never had a letter from a reader who mentioned drugs, revealed the slightest awareness of politics, or mentioned his/her race. Thus I was poorly prepared to write a novel on a problem that consumes a young character and alters her life in a single moment.

While the young are prudish about sex, they're less breathless in the face of sexual topics than the librarians and teachers attending convention workshops on "outspoken realism." And adolescent readers seem relatively unawed by seeing the same language in a book that they've seen scrawled on the tile in the school washroom.

I hesitated more than a while over a novel about a high school junior who is raped by one of her classmates. The topic crept up on me. I'd received review copies of several nonfiction adult books on rape: its political significance, its legal status, society's attitudes, the effect on its victims and on the rest of us.

They all mentioned in early chapters that the typical victim of this fastest-growing, least-reported crime is the adolescent girl; this target victim was my potential reader. Yet each one of these adult-oriented books dropped the typical victim like a stone and discussed the victim as if she were always an adult woman, living independently in an urban setting, a victim, I thought, less vulnerable in many ways than the characteristic one: a young girl living—perhaps trapped—in the narrow circle of family and school and neighborhood and inexperience.

I began to think somebody ought to write a book to alert young people to this crime, to the legal posture that favors the criminal at the victim's expense, the *necessity* for follow-up medical treatment that few rape victims seek, the attitude of a society that refuses to come to grips with this clear and present danger, the situation that a victim with a previous sexual history encounters in our courts of law. And when a writer begins to think, "*Somebody ought to write a book on . . .* ," he's just signed himself up.

The form I chose was the novel, in the hope it would find young readers who wouldn't have been attracted to long nonfiction books that grew shrill through 300 pages after snubbing the same young readers in the first chapter. I found myself writing a single-problem didactic novel, largely bereft of the techniques that had seen me through earlier novels.

If young people who dream of being novelists knew the amount of research involved in writing fiction, they might be given pause. For me, writing about a rape victim was no exercise in self-expression, and I had to go beyond the books that had alerted me to the crime. I worked closely with Dr. Richard L. Hughes of the Northwestern University Medical Center. I did my best to follow the legalese of legislation, both current and proposed. I did time in a planned parenthood center serving teenagers.

In each step toward the novel, I was more sickened by the crime and its disposition by law enforcement and the law; much more research and I would have been heading for yet another nonfiction book on the subject. I had to give my notes a final sorting and begin a novel, peopled with credible characters, not nameless statistics and faceless testimonials.

The setting of the story was an important first consideration, even though the crime strikes in every locale every day. The novel is set among the middle classes of a snug, smug suburb because I wanted to bring the situation home to those many young people who equate most kinds of crime with the inner city and the poor.

My victim-protagonist, who tells her story in her own voice, is the articulate daughter of a middle-class, recession-ridden, professional, decent, uncertain, emotionally frozen family.

The reader walks in her shoes and is given all the opportunities to identify with her that I could manage before she becomes a victim. Building tension in the early chapters was no problem, given the pending issue. But making sure my protagonist, a girl named Gail Osburne, did and said nothing to encourage the rapist was crucial. There's still an ugly bigotry afoot in our society that something within the rape victim basically wants the attack.

The rape occurs at midpoint in the book. Gail is overpowered, knocked unconscious, and raped. I didn't portray the graphic details of the rape, and not merely because I hoped to short-circuit the book-burners.

I have immense respect for my readers' imaginations. To depict the rape would be to create a gratuitous horror story; such a scene would pale in contrast to my readers' visualizing of it in their own minds.

Instead of the execution of the crime, the most explicit scene is a pelvic examination the victim receives soon after, and I wanted nothing to eclipse this sequence. Research indicated that the typical rape victim never goes for medical treatment and attention. I wanted my readers to know what this treatment is and why it's vital.

There were some other sequences that had to go unwritten. I very much wanted a courtroom scene, but that would have raised false hopes in my readers. The typical rape case is never reported, much less brought to trial. And I wanted to include a rape crisis center in the story. But again, this might well be dabbling in wish-fulfillment for readers in communities where no such centers exist, as well as in schools and families where the locations of existing centers are unknown and unmentioned.

Recently a review of ***Are You in the House Alone?*** in *The Berkshire Eagle* (Pittsfield, Massachusetts) by Marjorie N. Allen included the name and address of the local rape crisis center and the work of the local police rape squad. Would that more reviews recognized the needs of their own readers in the relating of books to them.

There comes the time in the writing of any sort of novel when the book rises up, turns on its author, and walks off independently in a direction of its own. This happened in ***Are You in the House Alone?*** The second half of the book is *not* a single-problem novel. It's about the consequences of being a young victim, regardless of the crime, a young victim in a society filling up with them. In an age of daily papers and late news bulletins, we rarely learn how life does and does not go on for former victims.

So the burden of the novel shifts to those suddenly silent days when the ex-victim has to go on living with her traumatized family, her former friends, the rumors in her school, and with the rapist who is going free and is often very near. In the way of victims, she ends up reassuring others, though she cannot reassure herself, or her reader.

To write for adolescents omitting wish-fulfillment, an optimistic ending, and escapism is to deny them what they most want. I can only hope they will read this book to learn how the laws—and, more important, the *implementation* of the laws—favor the criminal at the expense of the victim. I hope they will change this situation in their time, as we do not seem able to in ours. I hope too that they read this novel because they like the protagonist, who is in many ways a model of behavior for the reader. She refuses to languish, to become an invalid, to go crazy—options too easy in fiction and often enough impossible in life. She even has to battle her own parents in order to go back to the school their taxes support and which she has every right to attend.

After a novel is finished and walks away, the chief problem is the reviewer—that adult standing between the book and the intended reader. The great hazard of a single-problem novel is that the problem is reviewed at the expense of the novel. And the novel is too neatly typed, categorized, and unexamined.

To offset my own misgivings about the single-problem book, I tried to texture the story as much as I could without blurring its central issue. Rape is a community's problem, as well as the victim's. And a community is full of people living on the peripheries of other people's problems and at the centers of their own. Too many YA novels leave the impression that the whole world revolves upon the plight of the teenager. The whole world doesn't. And so I include a school guidance counselor who neither guides nor counsels; young readers will recognize this figure, and not from their reading. I include a woman too frightened at the thought of rape to allow the victim ever again to come near her children. I include a father unmanned in the face of a legal establishment that denies him and his daughter ordinary justice. And I include a teacher gifted in many human ways who can see deeply into her students' lives but is powerless to lead them or to protect them from each other because she's a teacher in an American school today.

Any novelist who believes he or she can raise the consciousness of the young above the level of television is tilting at windmills. But the young have a dangerously distorted view of the accessibility of justice. They are betrayed by all those television melodramas wherein the guilty are apprehended just before the final commercial, every hour, every night. They need a lot more books to prepare them for a world that refuses to conform to the shoddy strictures of that tiny, flickering screen. (pp. 173-77)

Richard Peck, "Rape and the Teenage Victim," in Top of the News, *Vol. 34, No. 2, Winter, 1978, pp. 173-77.*

Gail Osburne's ordeal begins with an obscene note pinned to her school locker, builds until she is raped and beaten by her best friend's disturbed steady, and is intensified throughout by her isolation—first, when family, friends, and counselors are indifferent or incapable of reacting to the anonymous threats, and, later, when a sneering police chief and timid hypocritical townspeople dissuade her from prosecuting a boy from a prominent family. The rough stuff is discreetly elided from both the notes and the attack itself. But Peck's view of affluent Connecticut, and of Gail's snobbish, self-centered parents in particular, is harsh enough. Distortingly harsh, and insofar as Peck presents this as an accurate profile of rape and its aftermath, readers might conclude that it's futile for any victim to seek protection or justice. As we expect this to be read as a chiller rather than a case study, we'll rate it medium cool—fast-paced and frighteningly accurate but without the quality of inevitability that keeps one awake after lights out.

A review of "Are You in the House Alone?" in Kirkus Reviews, *Vol. 44, No. 17, September 1, 1976, p. 982.*

[The author's] purpose is to show how rape victims are further victimized by society and the law. As a feminist, as the mother of two daughters, and as one who was sexually assaulted at the age of 11, I think all children should be warned and wary; however, I'm not sure it serves a function to do so in melodramatic terms.

Mr. Peck has chosen just such a format, building up a sense of mystery and terror preceding the attack by the use of menacing, obscene phone calls and anonymous threatening notes, and by having the rapist be a psychopath who stalks the girl as she baby-sits alone at night. Although he knocks her unconscious prior to the actual rape—so the event itself is neither experienced directly by the victim or the reader—I wouldn't want my 12-year-old to read this book: The fear that foreshadows the encounter seems far worse than its realization (fear of the dark, of being alone, of being watched at every turn). Nonetheless, my 15-year-old read it, empathized, wept, became incensed at the legal inequities, appreciated the complexity of the issue and its social and medical aftermath, didn't object to the way the deck was stacked to serve the thesis (the rapist is the son of the richest and most powerful local family, thus ruling out prosecution as a feasible option—leaving the boy free to attack again, which he does), and found the victim's plight and courage subsequent to the attack edifying and convincing. As for the Hitchcock kind of hysteria that comes before it, she thought that made it more interesting and gave one a reason for turning the page.

My reservation, therefore, should be viewed merely as my own bias, and Mr. Peck ought to be congratulated for connecting with, and raising the consciousness of, his target audience (14 and up) on a subject most people shun.

Alix Nelson, "Ah, Not to Be Sixteen Again," in The New York Times Book Review, *November 14, 1976, p. 29.*

Peck brings the story to a logical, tragic conclusion . . . but it isn't *what* happens that gives the story impact, although that is handled with conviction, and although the style, dialogue, and characters are equally impressive—it is the honest and perceptive way that the author treats the problem of rape. For Peck sees clearly both the society's problem and the victim's: the range of attitudes, the awful indignity, the ramifications of fear and shame. (p. 112)

Zena Sutherland, in a review of "Are You in the House Alone?" in Bulletin of the Center for Children's Books, *Vol. 30, No. 7, March, 1977, pp. 111-12.*

In a remarkable fictionalized treatment of the subject of rape, Peck has created a moving drama full of suspense. Peck's settings are detailed carefully: the high school, the babysitting job, the hospital, the small Connecticut town with its rigidly structured society. This background for the incidents which occur, including the rape, makes these events immediate and believable. Gail, the victim, is a sound, ordinary high school student whose first-person-narrative quickly is accepted by the reader who shares her shock not only in the humiliation of the rape but in the fact that the rapist will go unpunished. It is first of all a successful novel, but in the reading, one examines the crime of rape in all its emotional and legal complexities.

A review of "Are You in the House Alone?" in Kliatt Young Adult Paperback Book Guide, *Vol. 12, No. 1, Winter, 1978, p. 11.*

There is a good deal in Peck's novel to justify its critical acclaim. Peck deals sympathetically with adolescent alienation and does not criticize Gail for "beginning to feel pretty cut off from everybody." His novel recognizes that not all adults are *ipso facto* villainous—though even his most candid adults are misfits (like Mme. Malevich) or temporizers (like Naylor, the sympathetic attorney who advises Gail not to seek legal redress against Phil)—and that not all adolescents are trustworthy (Phil is Gail's contemporary; Gail's good friend, Alison, is no less determined than Gail's mother to pretend "it never happened"). Peck hints at Gail's limitations . . . , while insisting on the shortcomings of her parents . . . and the community. . . . It is Gail's discovery of what lies beneath the surface that gives the novel its thematic richness. In its own way, Gail's story is a kind of mid-seventies *Paradise Lost*, an account of the loss of innocence; her story is prefaced with an idyllic memory of a moonlight swim with her first love . . . , and ends with Gail confronting a world in which human compromise and human weakness are the real facts of life. . . . (pp. 47-8)

Peck's account of the fall of Gail Osburne, however, has its weaknesses too—weaknesses which are typical of so much modern fiction for adolescents. At times Peck cannot resist the temptation to fall into the kind of cliché likely to appeal to teen-age readers: a contemporary of Gail's "sounds real normal. Kind of like a teacher"; Gail wonders "if there's such a thing as a bright spot in a school day" (guess what the answer is); a typical attempt to talk with her mother "sounded weirdly like my mother practicing ventriloquism with me as the dummy." One might benignly ignore such cheap shots as a way of establishing *rapport* with the reader, but for the fact that they indicate a general shallowness, a glibness which oversimplifies the problems Peck apparently addresses so fearlessly. "The whole point in living in Oldfield Village," Gail informs the reader, "was to play the social game by the rules"—as if this lust for conformity were the sole reason why big-city parents might want to move to a small town. In the obligatory confrontation on the issue of birth-control pills, Gail tells her mother: "You take them. . . . The only difference is that yours are in the medicine cabinet in the bathroom, and I keep mine under my scrapbook in that drawer over there where you must have found them." It is true that Gail's mother is not being candid at this point, but it is also true that candor is not "the only difference" between the two cases. A similar shallowness is evident in Naylor's sweeping assertion that the law protects the rapist instead of the victim because "the law is wrong." There can be no doubt that Gail is the victim of a bitter injustice, but Peck should be able to show this without glibly denouncing the entire legal system and blithely ignoring the problems involved in seeing that justice is done. In short, the strength of Peck's novel lies in the sympathetic frankness with which it presents the adolescent protagonist and acknowledges her point of view; its weakness lies in its readiness to achieve that sympathy by the sacrifice of complexity and in its failure to provide an adequate context for its adolescent readers. (p. 48)

An author is, of course, at liberty to present the loss of childhood innocence without any accompanying consolation. (p. 52)

In a work which does not provide consolation, the impulse to criticism and recrimination is dominant. . . . Peck's ***Are You in the House Alone?,*** like its numerous and inferior imitations, is more inclined to recrimination than consolation. . . . Of course, a writer ought to tell the truth, but to offer young people little more than a confirmation of their suspicion that adults have messed everything up, and that the world is invariably a nasty place, is to cheat those readers. Such fiction encourages, not mature strength, but only snide cynicism. The problem is one of balance and emphasis and of providing a context in which the reader can make some sense of human evil and human shortcomings. Only when writers are willing to refrain from a trendy sensationalism and to attempt to grapple honestly with the moral complexities of life . . . , can they hope to produce the kind of literature that our young people so desperately need. (pp. 52-3)

William Blackburn, "'Peter Pan' and the Contemporary Adolescent Novel," in Proceedings of the Ninth Annual Conference of the Children's Literature Association, *Vol. 9, 1982, pp. 47-53.*

***MONSTER NIGHT AT GRANDMA'S HOUSE* (1977)**

Peck's first story for younger children takes Toby through a scary summer night at his grandmother's Victorian house. "Just as he did every August night, Toby climbed the tall stairs"—with trepidation—and listened to the night bugs hitting the window screen "like tapping fingers." But "on this worst night of all" Toby also hears the floorboard squeak, hears a Monster breathing in his room, and then sees something gray—the Monster's tail?—moving in the hall. Because Toby is brave, he gets out of bed to investigate, following the noises down the stairs and out onto the porch, where he falls asleep on the swing confident that he's chased the THING off Grandma's property. Toby is a likely stand-in for any frightened child and, in his response, a properly encouraging model. Young readers might recognize every detail of Toby's vigil—but, as Peck doesn't make them share the terrors, their emotional involvement is minimal.

A review of "Monster Night at Grandma's House," in Kirkus Reviews, *Vol. 45, No. 9, May 1, 1977, p. 485.*

The story is a bit long for the small amount of action it carries, and the ratio of imagination to fact is not quite clearly enough delineated in text or illustration [the illustrations are by Don Freeman]. . . . Presumably it's all meant to be in Toby's mind, but the pictures offer little clue. (p. 24)

Zena Sutherland, in a review of "Monster Night at Grandma's House," in Bulletin of the Center for Children's Books, *Vol. 31, No. 1, September, 1977, pp. 23-4.*

Toby pulls a switch on this universal experience when ***he*** decides to track down the monster. Written in narrative style with minimum conversation, the amusing tale reads well silently or aloud. Short words and sentences build suspense. (pp. 45-6)

Ruth M. Stein, in a review of "Monster Night at Grandma's House," in Language Arts, *Vol. 55, No. 1, January, 1978, pp. 45-6.*

***GHOSTS I HAVE BEEN* (1977)**

Fourteen-year-old Blossom Culp, Alexander Armsworth's erstwhile companion in ***The Ghost Belonged to Me,*** is the heroine and narrator of a first-class psychic action tale. Ever the master of style and construction, Peck rebuilds a view of small-town Bluff City, with its unique incidental characters, from the other side of the tracks. Blossom is an indigent but inventive survivor; when she accidentally discovers her "second sight," it leads to involvement in a number of humorous minor incidents and presence at a child's tragic drowning on the *Titanic*. In the process, the recess bully gets a seatful of rock salt, the school snob gets put in her deserved place, the perceptive school principal gets more attention than she wants, Alexander gets reluctantly involved (to his acute discomfort), Blossom's peculiar friend Miss Dabney gets to meet the queen of England, and Blossom's peculiar mother gets some business. An outrageous sequence of events charmed together by skillful wordwork.

Betsy Hearne, in a review of "Ghosts I Have Been," in Booklist, *Vol. 74, No. 3, October 1, 1977, p. 300.*

[***Ghosts I Have Been*** is a] throroughly engrossing story. . . . There is comedy as well as suspense and intrigue in this well-written novel. Plot and characters are expertly developed, and both are enhanced by Peck's keen, unfailing ear for dialogue. Highly recommended.

Glenda Broughton, in a review of "Ghosts I Have Been," in Children's Book Review Service, *Vol. 6, No. 4, December, 1977, p. 39.*

Blossom Culp, the doughty and persistent ghost's companion of ***The Ghost Belonged to Me,*** now fourteen, tells her own story here, and she's completely convincing. . . . She gets involved in strange dramatic situations, becomes famous when her prescience is proven accurate, and takes it all in her stride. Somehow, in this melange of eccentric characters and dramatic, fantastic events, Peck instills in Blossom and her story a sturdy, lively believability.

Zena Sutherland, in a review of "Ghosts I Have Been," in Bulletin of the Center for Children's Books, *Vol. 31, No. 7, March, 1978, p. 117.*

The narrative gets a bit heavy-handed when Blossom foresees World War I and moralizes on the futility of war, but in general the story is an engrossing adventure and Blossom an engaging narrator. A blurb on the jacket accurately compares Peck's style to Mark Twain's; as in some of Twain's books, the wit and insight of the narrator will be missed by most of the audience the book is intended for. But the story alone should make it popular with YA readers. (p. 12)

Jane B. Jackson, in a review of "Ghosts I Have Been," in Kliatt Young Adult Paperback Book Guide, *Vol. 13, No. 6, Fall, 1979, pp. 10, 12.*

FATHER FIGURE (1978)

AUTHOR'S COMMENTARY

I met her last fall. In an abstract way I'd known she was out there, but for long stretches I'd thought she wasn't there for me. She was though, and waiting, even eager in her controlled way. She's a book censor, and she'd recently banished a book of mine from her daughter's junior high library.

She lives in a picture-perfect town; 18th-century church spires punctuating brilliant foliage. . . . Boys on battle-fields have dreamed of coming home to towns like this.

I went to this town to speak to a group of junior high students. I heard of her almost before I was out of the airport, but I didn't expect to meet her. My clichéd view of successful censors is that they neither read the book in question nor let you see them. I was about to be wrong twice. My guard wasn't up either. You'd have to give my collected young adult works a close reading if you were scanning for rough language or sexual content. Even then, you'd come up disappointingly short in the sensation department. I've never thought you could build a faithful constituency of young readers with shock value. I've always believed they read to be reassured and recognized.

As it happened, there'd been earlier rumblings of censorship about a novel of mine called ***Are You in the House Alone?*** I'd even heard of librarians who wouldn't give it shelf space for fear it might occasion trouble. It's my best seller. Evidently the censor I was about to meet had never heard of that book. The book she'd efficiently purged is ***Father Figure.***

This news struck me (almost) dumb. ***Father Figure*** is my best book. It may be the best book I can do. It's the story of a defensive 17-year-old boy who has to make an unthinkable sacrifice before he can begin to grow up. The book is devoid of sexual content because the boy's passions are directed elsewhere. He's clinging ardently to role-playing the part of father to his small eight-year-old brother. When their mother dies, these brothers are reunited with their own, unknown father. The novel chronicles a rocky father-son relationship. It wonders if the members of a suddenly all-male family can move beyond macho posturing to a shared commitment. In the end the teenaged son is able to surrender his little brother to their real father. In this, his first mature act, he rids himself of anger.

Father Figure is no longer available in a certain junior high library. I was forewarned that the book-banner would attend my meeting with students, though she wouldn't allow her own daughter to be present. This situation was novel enough to be disorienting. (pp. 37-8)

Thanks to teachers and the librarian, every student at our program had read at least one of my books. Real readers had been singled out and given an extra event for themselves. . . . Even the principal and his assistant were present, though perhaps more in honor of the solitary parent at the back of the room than of the occasion. I tried not be more aware of her than anyone else in the group. But when a youngster made a good comment, I glanced back to see if she'd caught it, and I began to wonder if I was censoring myself. Was I trying to tailor these 45 minutes to keep her from gathering more evidence against me? Was I, God help me, trying to win her over? Fortunately, in a single class period, time is short for wondering. When the bell rang and the students streamed out into the hall, I half-expected the censorial mother to slip away too. Wrong again.

While the administrators and the librarian stood back, she came forth: a handsome woman, well-dressed. She was a prominent doctor's wife in fact, with an air of cool command. Quite a bit younger than I am too. All expectation of seeing her as an illiterate crank withered within me. . . . She knew I knew who she was. From the first moment I marveled at how completely she appeared to be in control of her universe—and a corner of mine.

After finding a copy of ***Father Figure*** in her daughter's possession, she'd read it herself. I know because she booktalked my own book to me from start to finish with admirable economy. She'd disliked it from beginning to end.

Father Figure begins with the death of a mother. Worse, this character takes her own life because she's suffering a terminal illness. The removal of a maternal character so early was clearly repugnant to this reader, however, she spoke mainly of the immorality of suicide. She harped on nothing and moved swiftly to the central issues of the book. All were equally unsuitable: another book about divorced parents; the angry disrespect of a son for his father; the inability of a parent to shape his child.

Her tone was so reasoned that there seemed promise of dialogue. I pointed out that nearly half of my potential readers are the children of divorced parents, that their special problems are meant to be recognized in this book.

"That isn't my daughter's situation," she said, "nor her friends'. They have been drawn mainly from our church."

Another mother, implying she was able to choose, even screen, her 13-year-old child's friends, would have made me gravely skeptical. I was less sure about this one. For a sentence or so I clung to the argument that attention must be paid to the needs of readers from broken homes. She wasn't interested. She was even less interested in the particular problems of emotional communication between fathers and sons. She had no sons, and referred to her husband only obliquely with the pronoun *we*: "We set a good standard for our daughter, and we don't want to be undermined."

It was several days before I took serious offense to the suggestion that any book of mine undermines parental authority. Until this moment, I hadn't thought that parents had enough authority to be undermined. Had I wished other parents were more like this one? I was sinking fast. And it was useless to suggest a larger view. She didn't have to be reminded that her daughter attends a public school with classmates from all backgrounds, and that the girl couldn't live as circumscribed a life as her own mother.

Because her interest was limited to her daughter, I cited which of my books she might find more suitable for her. Her face began to close; she'd given my work all the attention it deserves. She turned to go. There was nothing whatever wrong with her timing.

"I can respect any parent who cares enough to oversee her child's reading," I said, "but I think that no parent has the right to withhold a book from other readers."

She almost smiled at this impertinence. She hadn't come here to be criticized. But at the door she spoke again, with the first note of uncertainty in her voice. "I am able to direct my daughter now," she said, "but I don't know about the future."

There, I thought, I could reassure her. "If you can dominate her at puberty," I said, "I expect you can hold her for life."

She seemed to take that more kindly than it was meant and walked away down the empty hallway of the school.

And so, I have met and faced my first censor. In the way of adversaries she wasn't at all what I'd expected. She hadn't clothed her arguments in religion or politics; she was clearly no joiner. She was interested in power of her own. I sensed that power early on, from across a crowded room. She didn't need to follow any prescribed procedure to have a book eliminated from a library. She removed it with the force of her personality, augmented by her position in the community. My only faint hope lies in the librarian quietly reshelving the book once the daughter moves on to high school. (pp. 38-9)

And so, in a picture-perfect town and an orderly schoolhouse, I've met my first censor, but she hasn't met her first writer, though she went out of her way to do so. She was deaf to the notion that I cared as much in my way for a group of young readers as she cared in her way about only one. She was proof against any suggestion I may have made that books are meant to ready young readers for the world. Prisoners of civilization both, we didn't raise our voices, and neither of us budged from who we'd been. Each thought the other immoral. Each wouldn't mind running the other out of the community, though only one of us succeeded in that.

There's another offstage character in this squalid, genteel little drama. It's the daughter, that young stranger finding her way through a school day not yet completely monitored by her mother. If she finished reading my book, she either reacted to it or not. If she hadn't been allowed to finish it, my book may lay a greater claim upon her than it deserves to have. (p. 39)

Richard Peck, "The Genteel Unshelving of a Book," in School Library Journal, *Vol. 32, No. 9, May, 1986, pp. 37-9.*

Count Peck's new novel as the best of many that have won him honors, and assuredly one of the best for all ages in many a moon. When Jim Atwater is 17 and devoted to his eight-year-old brother Byron, their mother takes her life to escape the ravages of cancer. The boys have had no father since Mr. Atwater had deserted them when Byron was a baby. After the funeral, a crisis forces their imperious maternal grandmother to send them from her stiff Brooklyn Heights home to their father in Florida. Jim, as Byron's "father figure," resents the little boy's attachment to dad. Jim also gets a crush on a perfect love of a woman, Marietta, his father's friend and, the youth suspects, his mistress. Callowness and vanity make Jim mess up somewhat but he learns some poignant truths. Peck makes everyone so human and interesting that readers believe in and care about one and all.

A review of "Father Figure," in Publishers Weekly, *Vol. 214, No. 3, July 17, 1978, p. 168.*

Peck's tough-minded, uncompromising view of things dominates a novel as intense and charged as its high concentration of strong characters: Marietta, Southern poor-white waitress with a definite mind of her own; self-contained Byron, with his lizard collection "on lettuce leaves like a weird salad," who chooses a father over a ***Father Figure***; and Jim, who loses his paternal/protector status, doesn't lose his virginity, doesn't gain a father, but muddles through to maturity after all.

Pamela D. Pollack, in a review of "Father Figure," in School Library Journal, *Vol. 25, No. 2, October, 1978, p. 158.*

James Atwater, a sensitive 17-year-old stranded on the shoals of adolescence, narrates the latest addition to Richard Peck's notable list of titles for young adults. As he tells it, ***Father Figure*** is more a situation than a story, since its pivotal dramatic events take place outside the narrator's range of vision. But it is a situation dramatic enough in itself to seize and hold our attention. And, in the end, we admire the restraint with which it is described.

Although told in the vernacular of today, the novel's stark setting and strangled emotional atmosphere give the tale a Victorian quality. As it opens, James' mother has just died from purposely inhaling carbon monoxide fumes in her car following a long and fatal illness (presumably cancer). Her children are now virtually orphans—since their father had disappeared eight years before, leaving his pregnant wife and two children at the home of James' conservative grandmother in Brooklyn Heights. James, already an overanxious father figure, now finds himself more responsible than ever for his poetic younger brother, Byron. . . .

What happens is predictable enough. James' father reappears and eventually the boys leave the chilly atmosphere of Brooklyn Heights for the hot climate of Miami. There James' frozen emotions begin to thaw and a reconciliation with his father is gradually achieved. What is remarkable is that the book does not rely on the usual cliché dramatic episode to induce artificially a reversal in the characters' relationships. There are no sudden storms at sea, fires in the condominium or sharks sighted offshore. Only time—the simple, often tediously slow passing of the days—eventually wears down James' resistance, and it is this reliance on time rather than chance which gives the novel's resolution its ring of truth.

On the other hand, it should be noted that the author's restraint, while sometimes an asset, can also be a liability. His narrator's concerns are too cleaned-up to be truly contemporary and seem instead to reflect the concerns of the author's own adolescence. Although Peck never exploits his situation, he never quite gets inside of it either—never really penetrates his characters' skins to connect with their deeper, more private selves. One sometimes suspects that it is the author's reticence which makes it so hard for his characters to get past their own restraints and into a deeper intimacy with each other.

Winifred Rosen, "Pick a Peck of Pickled Pinkwater," in Book World—The Washington Post, *November 12, 1978, p. E4.*

A recent *English Journal* article listed seventeen young adult novels of the 1970's, nearly all realistic, that the writers of the article feel will become "classics of the genre." Classics? Good grief! To how many YA books can even the term *art* be applied, let alone *classic? The English Journal* list includes such works as Judy Blume's *Are You There, God? It's Me, Margaret,* Sue Ellen Bridgers' *Home Before Dark,* Alice Childress' *A Hero Ain't Nothin' But a Sandwich,* Rosa Guy's *Edith Jackson,* and Mildred C. Taylor's *Roll of Thunder, Hear My Cry.* That these works should be acclaimed classics reveals the poverty of literary quality in the whole genre of YA realistic fiction: a poverty sometimes of content, sometimes of craft, often of both. (p. 22)

[Is] there any recent well-crafted YA fiction? Yes. Read or reread, for example, Virginia Hamilton's *M. C. Higgins, the Great*—inexplicably missing from *The English Journal* classics list—and Richard Peck's ***Father Figure***. . . . Each of these novels is rich in narrative and descriptive detail that makes it come alive. The characters, both main and secondary, stand out as individuals. We remember M. C. and the girl who enters his life, and the grandmother and the waitress in Peck's book, long after we finish reading. Each plot is well paced, with peaks and valleys, and contains a cause-effect sequence gradually rising to a climax that is plausible because we have come to know and believe in the protagonist through the author's use of detail, image and tight control of point of view. . . . The writing styles of these two novels are not merely different from that of a Blume or a Guy; they are markedly better. (p. 23)

John Higgins, "All That Glitters Is Not Literature," in The English Record, *Vol. XXXII, No. 1, Winter, 1981, pp. 22-3.*

***SECRETS OF THE SHOPPING MALL* (1979)**

Would you believe a group of runaway children living in the department store of your local shopping mall? No, neither would I, but I'm willing to wager that my students will be lining up to read this book. One of the elements that makes this basically fantastic story fun to read is the characterizations of Teresa and Barnie, two engaging, inner city kids who discover the ***Secrets of the Shopping Mall*** when they run away from the King Korba gang. There is both humor and pathos in their personalities, as they use their streetwise ways to deal with the suburban runaways living in the department store and the "Mouth Breathers," who threaten them from the outside. I may not believe it, but I certainly enjoyed it!

Jennifer Brown, in a review of "Secrets of the Shopping Mall," in Children's Book Review Service, *Vol. 8, No. 2, October, 1979, p. 19.*

One problem with this broad, ham-handed satire is that Peck has no sharp sight on his targets: a mall with Gucci labels and a K mart is hard to place; an outmoded junior miss department buyer promoting the Dale Evans western look is *too* far out even to be a credible figure of fun; and Peck's stereotyped, commodity-oriented runaways are more recognizable as prevailing clichés than as the plastic people he intends to mock. Worse, Teresa and Barnie have no personalities either and their thoughts and conversations no vitality.

A review of "Secrets of the Shopping Mall," in Kirkus Reviews, *Vol. 47, No. 20, October 15, 1979, p. 1213.*

Entry of the Mouth-Breathers strains the story's believability somewhat, and their assault on the Store People, which takes on Marx Brothers overtones, doesn't mesh well with Peck's other, more subtle humor; however, the author's deft handling of dialogue, inventive plot, and action-filled sequences make a highly engrossing and effective combination.

Barbara Elleman, in a review of "Secrets of the Shopping Mall," in Booklist, *Vol. 76, No. 5, November 1, 1979, p. 451.*

[The] intriguing plot is both the book's greatest strength and its greatest weakness. . . . Teresa and Barnie are two junior high drop-outs, yet they speak with all the colorful adjectives and the expressive metaphors of Richard Peck. What Peck was probably aiming for was the ultimate satire on suburbia, but unfortunately where he landed is somewhere beyond realism but short of fantasy. Survival in a shopping mall may be a plausible premise, but for gangs to be able to freeze into realistic mannequins or for Teresa, age thirteen, to be able to assume a job in stemware while living under a bed is a bit much. (pp. 94-5)

Dave Davidson and others, "A Kaleidoscope of Human Relationships," in English Journal, *Vol. 69, No. 5, May, 1980, pp. 91-5.*

***CLOSE ENOUGH TO TOUCH* (1981)**

A tidy package: Matt and Dory fall in love. Just as they're becoming intimate, she dies of an aneurysm. The dilemma is Matt's: how to forget Dory and get back to living. To dramatize a 17-year-old's grief, Peck sensibly chooses first-person narration, but there's a problem. Matt's thoughts and observations structure the book, and they do it economically, because he displays a very mature level of insight. Actually, it belies the immaturity of some of his actions (getting drunk to forget Dory) and expectations (that he'll love Dory forever). In other words, the dramatic problem of grief is undercut by the narrator's worldly wisdom. Readers don't have to grieve long for Dory, because halfway through the book her replacement appears. Margaret has it all over Dory: she's real and witty too, a girl of intellect and determination who deals gracefully with a trying family situation and finances her own future by selling at flea markets. To effect the transition, there are observations that show us Dory's snobbery and Margaret's good sense, as well as an obligatory scene where Matt rejects Dory's old friends, the rich kids on the hill. At the end, Matt takes Margaret to the favorite lake-side place he shared with Dory. Touching bases, yes, but the sense of symmetry is deadening. The other characters (parents, peers) play out social stereotypes: snobbish rich parents, generous but clumsy working-class parents, a hulking football player with a heart of gold. The dialogue is good and the satiric scenes of high school are genuinely funny and touching, but the book as a whole seems to echo Matt's estimation of a day at his factory high school: "already predictable, prepackaged."

Kay Webb O'Connell, in a review of "Close Enough to Touch," in School Library Journal, *Vol. 28, No. 1, September, 1981, p. 140.*

Peck navigates expertly through tricky waters in this story. . . . Dory is never very real to readers; we only meet her in a romantic opening flashback and in a few remarks by and about her friends. But Matt, who has loved her, finds the funeral service difficult (shouldn't he have a more central role in the mourning?) and life without her painful. . . . Then Matt meets Margaret, who appears like an apparition in an old-fashioned long-skirted riding outfit. But Margaret is real. . . . And though she first refuses to be friends—she doesn't want to hear all about Dory—there's enough encouragement between her rebuffs so that Matt does go after her . . . and claim her, in a disarmingly corny climax. Margaret may be romanticized, but cannily so, as her "Jane Eyre" entrance signals. She *is* a dashing character, with most of the best lines, and the lines are in character—with Margaret and the novel, for this is no maudlin chronicle. Early on, a few minutes with Dory's snobbish bereaved mother make an impression neither Matt nor readers forget, and a satiric contemporary-problems classroom scene is wickedly on target without being simplistically typical. None of this makes Matt's grief less serious or real; on the contrary, it only makes the characters and their milieu more distinct, recognizable, and interesting.

A review of "Close Enough to Touch," in Kirkus Reviews, *Vol. 49, No. 18, September 15, 1981, p. 1165.*

Richard Peck announced to applause at the 1980 ALA annual conference that he was writing a male protagonist teen love story, and it is a pleasure to applaud it in print in 1981. . . . The ending, where Matt spirits Margaret away from the senior prom he is ineligible to attend, is perfect.

The sensitivity to male emotions shown in ***Father Figure*** is continued here as is Peck's unerring observance of adolescent mores: e.g., at one point Matt talks about increasing his grades to get better insurance rates as a teen driver. Best of all, the adults in Matt's and Margaret's lives are pretty nice. Only Dory's mother comes off badly, but who wouldn't on the day of her daughter's funeral. The perfect construction of each of the individual chapters makes many of them good booktalk material, and the book is an obvious YASD Best Books candidate. With all the schlock romances flooding the market, it is nice that one of the finest authors of adolescent literature can still make most everybody else look like rank amateurs. Highly recommended with Kleenex. (pp. 36-7)

Mary K. Chelton, in a review of "Close Enough to Touch," in Voice of Youth Advocates, *Vol. 4, No. 4, October, 1981, pp. 36-7.*

[The story] speaks with insight and sensitive perception to the slow adjustment to loss, and later to the confusion and ambivalence [Matt] feels when he first becomes interested in another girl, a very different sort of person. . . . There are no great events here, no dramatic story line, but there is a depth and compassion to Peck's depiction of an adolescent's coping with deep emotional need that make the story compelling and bittersweet.

Zena Sutherland, in a review of "Close Enough to Touch," in Bulletin of the Center for Children's Books, *Vol. 35, No. 3, November, 1981, p. 53.*

THE DREADFUL FUTURE OF BLOSSOM CULP **(1983)**

Blossom Culp and Alexander Armsworth from ***The Ghost Belonged To Me*** and ***Ghosts I Have Been*** are now in their freshmen year at Bluff City High School. Blossom, the narrator of the last novel, also tells this story. The plot centers around Blossom's Second Sight as the second novel did. This time instead of seeing into the past, Blossom travels 70 years into the future and enters 1984 through an eighth grade boy's computer monitor. Blossom is introduced to our world of computers, video games, fast food chains, magnet middle schools, and gifted programs. Blossom, of course, returns back to 1914 in time to stop Alexander and his gang from their annual Halloween harassment of Old Man Leverette and to be the star Gypsy fortune-teller at the freshmen's Haunted House. Peck creates his usual lively, memorable, and interesting characters as well as working in the ever-popular themes of the occult and ghosts. The novel also skillfully blends contemporary scenes with the past, assuring that the novel will not become quickly out-dated. The best in a highly acclaimed trilogy, this is a definite YASD Best Books candidate.

Gayle Keresey, in a review of "Dreadful Future of Blossom Culp," in Voice of Youth Advocates, *Vol. 6, No. 5, December, 1983, p. 280.*

"There is only one Blossom Culp, and I am her," the dauntless heroine of Richard Peck's new Bluff City novel announces, and readers familiar with ***The Ghost Belonged to Me*** and ***Ghosts I Have Been*** know that one Blossom, with her psychic powers and Tom Sawyer ingenuity, is about all one town or even one world can take.

In the earlier books Blossom poked a finger at 1913 pretension of all sorts as she and her friend Alexander took on the Barn Ghost, a phony spiritualist, a Titanic mystery and the Queen of England herself. Nothing or no one seemed too big for Blossom Culp, and that may be why ***The Dreadful Future of Blossom Culp*** seems so small.

Mr. Peck satirically sends Blossom into the future, laying her 1914 adolescent world, with its outhouse pranks and Perils-of-Pauline movies, alongside a slick, computer-game suburbia of 1984. But there is less olden-days detail, more turn-of-the-century cliché, and the range of characters is limited, despite Blossom's spooky mama and colorful Daisy-Rae, a country girl Blossom discovers hiding in the school bathroom.

Moreover, Blossom's concerns seem small—a Halloween Haunted House fund-raiser, Alexander's attention to Blossom's snobbish rival, Letty Shambaugh, and ninth-grade pettiness. This from the character who said "Pshaw" to the Queen of England. Even Blossom's futuristic trip is mainly a sightseeing tour through a 1984 wasteland of McDonald's, middle-school Darth Vaders and Little League suburbs, without real adventure or relationship.

When Blossom tells the tale of the aunt whose finger was bitten off in the San Francisco quake, Mr. Peck is at his mischievous best. But Blossom is too good a character to end up chiefly a vehicle for social commentary on the sterility and loneliness of our contemporary adolescent world.

Patricia Lee Gauch, in a review of "The Dreadful Future of Blossom Culp," in The New York Times Book Review, *December 18, 1983, p. 21.*

[Peck] enhances his reputation as a comic writer in a book that adroitly blends a dash of science fiction into a fast-moving tale. . . . The slapstick is appropriately hackneyed, the well-timed humorous repartee rattles along at a brisk clip, and the element of fantasy adds some fine spoofing of present-day schools and of current educational and technical jargon—while underlying everything is a perceptible human sensitivity.

Ethel L. Heins, in a review of "The Dreadful Future of Blossom Culp," in The Horn Book Magazine, *Vol. LX, No. 1, February, 1984, p. 64.*

Peck has written yet another excellent book for young adults. It is as good, or better, than the other two books in the series, ***The Ghost Belongs to Me*** and ***Ghosts I Have Been***. . . .

Much of the appeal of these novels, and much of their worth, lies in the characters themselves. Peck has a pronounced talent for creating characters that echo both Twain and Tarkington, and he mixes well a kind of "vaudeville lunacy with warmth and affection." Blossom, who appears to have captured the narrator's role from Alexander after the first book, is such a character. Independent, original, proud, intelligent, self-confident, manipulative, and rather unsophisticated, she is sure to become a suffragette if future stories carry her into her twenties.

More importantly, . . . [Blossom] teaches us to dig beneath the surface to find real value and beauty.

The Dreadful Future of Blossom Culp is ultimately a book about values, and though the story is a bit slow in starting, it is carried along quite nicely by its humor and its characters. Peck's book is interesting, entertaining, and perfect for the ten to fourteen year old audience to which it is directed.

Carl B. Yoke, "Third in Series Maintains High Standard," in Fantasy Review, *Vol. 7, No. 7, August, 1984, p. 50.*

REMEMBERING THE GOOD TIMES (1985)

AUTHOR'S COMMENTARY

Most young readers are growing up suburban. Reading remains a middle-class preoccupation, and readers are those with sufficient leisure to spend time with books. Oddly, in our young adult literature we've created for them a cast of outcasts and underdogs, from M. E. Kerr's intellectual misfits to S. E. Hinton's Okie underclass. . . .

We have a literature celebrating precisely the kind of people the reader tries not to notice around school. This marches in the proud, Huck Finn tradition of fiction, for novels have always inclined to the biographies of survivors, of the wretched on the rise, of comers-from-behind. Let's hope there's value in providing a literature of nonconformity to a conformist readership, a literature of the under-valued for a readership of the over-praised. Books may well be the only alternative points of view our readers ever encounter. At our most optimistic, we can even hope the theme puts the readers' feelings of being pressured into some kind of perspective.

Only a very young writer or a crank believes his words will change readers in measurable ways. Not all of our novels championing rebels, independent thinkers, nerds, even, seem to have won readers from their herd instinct and their social distinctions. Still, we know we've given a few isolated readers who feel rejected themselves some much-needed identity because we get heartfelt letters from them.

What we need now are more novels to address the mainstream of readers more directly. (p. 118)

We need more novels that don't trivialize the very real problems of people who aren't supposed to be having any. We live in an age in which both parents often work so their children may enjoy a higher standard of living than their own. There's guilt implicit in that. When parents function as your servants, you'll naturally patronize them, but you may not like yourself the better for it.

There's mounting doubt in the minds of young people who are drifting between the permissive home and the elective school. When parents' demands are only occasional, when teachers' standards are always negotiable, you may suspect there's no value in growing up to play such weak roles as these. You may even panic at the thought. This is the generation being pressed to be competitive and successful in adult life without the necessary stretched attention span, personal disciplines, and communication skills. This is a generation with new reasons to fear the future.

In my latest novel, ***Remembering the Good Times,*** a boy takes his own life. He's a son of the professional suburban class, self-motivated into a downward spiral. He's pressured by his own drive, by the unspoken expectations of his class, and he's nudged over the edge by a slack school and an aimless adolescence that aren't preparing him for the future. He's the quintessential adolescent suicide in that he appears to be living a far too-favored life to elicit anything but admiration. Even if he had an emotional vocabulary with which to cry out for help, he might not be heard.

In the 1980s, suicide is more than a metaphor among the young. It's an epidemic striking heavily at the suburban affluent for whom the permissive home, the elective course, and grade-inflation have, in some tragically ironic way, imposed unbearable pressure as slow-paced adolescence extends into graduate school and beyond.

Even when you spend a lifetime in pursuit of them, adolescents remain the most mysterious of readers. Wherever they live, they regularly confuse the word for the deed, preaching tolerance and practicing exclusion. They are devoted, undependable friends to one another. They believe group identity will solve personal problems. They refuse to accept the consequences of their own actions, and they can project blame any distance. They believe passionately in surfaces: masks, uniforms, poses, and yet when you pierce their defenses, they seem relieved to see you. (pp. 118-19)

We've given our mainstream readers a literature of nonconformity which they've accepted too calmly. We need a new one to question their provincial pieties without belittling the problems or telling them they don't have any. We need a literature that holds out hope to the children of parents who have become so successful in worldly ways that they seem impossible acts to follow.

The unearned advantages won from their parents and the happy endings these young people have promised themselves have edged them near despair. We've given them the success stories of outcasts and opportunities to champion underdogs. Now they need books that invite them to champion themselves, road maps pointing the way out of the subdivision. (p. 119)

Richard Peck, "Growing Up Suburban: 'We Don't Use Slang, We're Gifted'," in School Library Journal, *Vol. 32, No. 2, October, 1985, pp. 118-19.*

With humanity, wit, and a quiet intensity, Peck's novel depicts suicide as a turning inward of the pressures in an alienated and violent society. Sixteen-year-old Buck, who lives in a trailer with his divorced construction worker father, looks back on his close friendship with sensitive, driven Trav and with dynamic Kate and remembers the jealous rivalry he felt for Kate's attention. Kate's family has lived for generations in their midwestern farmhouse, and, though her parents are drifters, she is close to her feisty great-grandmother, Polly. Trav is a suburbanite, part of the affluence that is rapidly transforming the countryside with shopping malls and smart new housing developments: no roots, no tall trees, "not even any shadows." Through Buck's eyes, readers see Trav only from the outside, in flashes: brilliant, pressured; unable to accept himself or the loving, perfectionist parents he so resembles; masking his depression; indirectly asking for help; seeing himself in the disturbed school lout who acts out his violence and receives neither discipline nor caring. School is a wasteland without stimulation or responsibility: pointless classes, blank faces, and incipient violence. When Trav kills himself, the students sensationalize the act; the administration is glad it didn't happen on school property. Peck's acerbic observation has never been funnier; whether it is of fashion or of colloquial idiom ("'Because I'm from California,' she said, 'so I'm flexible.'"). But it is in the emotional moments that ordinary conversation has the concentration of poetry: "Cry with me, Irene. I can't do it alone," Buck's father comforts the wife of his friend murdered in a holdup. Friendship remains—among peers and among generations—and it is possible to build a home in a "strictly temporary" trailer and to run strongly outside the pack. But with the grief for a lost friend, there is also a longing for a whole vanishing way of life, when, as Polly says, "people knew you."

Hazel Rochman, in a review of "Remembering the Good Times," in Booklist, *Vol. 81, No. 13, March 1, 1985, p. 945.*

An author who keeps in touch with young adults, Peck has written his best book so far, a novel based on a symptom of the times, teenage suicide. The story is tragic but it contains moments of joy and high hilarity—like life—and it involves us wholly with recognizable humans. . . .

[After Trav's suicide, the] school board calls a meeting where the principal and parents accuse each other of irresponsibility; the session becomes a mockery rather than a mutually helpful exchange of ideas on preventing tragedies that might follow Trav's death. Then Buck's father and Kate's great-grandmother come forward. In their wisdom, they speak out on issues that could save any troubled community. Peck says he hopes parents will read the novel. We hope everyone will.

A review of "Remembering the Good Times," in Publishers Weekly, *Vol. 227, No. 20, May 17, 1985, p. 118.*

[In ***Remembering the Good Times,*** the] futileness of unexpected and untimely death, no matter what the age or cause, is clearly seen.

This is a quiet novel, making its climactic moments seem more gripping. The action moves not so much to a shattering climax as it does to an end which is also a beginning. The survivors do survive, and life goes on. The problems are not sensationalized or overplayed. Characters, dialogue and action are all believable. Juxtaposition of the adult and adolescent trios is only one indication of the subtle layering of the plot. It's gratifying to see another young adult novel that says so much so well. Neither Peck's readers nor his fans will be disappointed in this one. Highly recommended for all libraries serving adolescents.

Joni Bodart, in a review of "Remembering the Good Times," in Voice of Youth Advocates, *Vol. 8, No. 2, June, 1985, p. 134.*

The epidemic of teenage suicide that is afflicting our society is a notoriously difficult problem to understand. Richard Peck's novel dealing with this subject is subtle, descriptive, and well written but, in the end, still not enlightening. We see the signs but cannot understand the motivation that would impel Trav Kirby—blessed with intelligence, understanding parents, loving friends, and good health—to take his own life. . . . Peck's sympathies obviously lie with the young people, and his descriptions of school life, and even the social life of the parents, are precise and authentic. The author has a quick wit and a sure grip on the preoccupations of adolescence, but we see Buck and Kate more clearly than we do Trav—which may in the end merely reflect the anguish and lack of understanding about suicide which troubles us all. (pp. 457-58)

Ann A. Flowers, in a review of "Remembering the Good Times," in The Horn Book Magazine, *Vol. LXI, No. 4, July-August, 1985, pp. 457-58.*

BLOSSOM CULP AND THE SLEEP OF DEATH (1986)

As fresh and funny as any in the series, this follows the valiant attempts of an unlikely sensitive, high school freshman Blossom Culp, to settle an Egyptian princess, mummified but very restless in spirit, back in the midst of her rightful splendor. Much against his will, Alexander Armsworth finds himself involved again, assigned to an ancient Egypt project by the formidable new suffragette history teacher, who tackles the Daughters of the American Revolution head-on. The Princess seems convincingly capable of carrying out her curses, and Blossom's wayward Mama is always a treat, as is the pre-World War I cast of small town characters. The plot elements are perfectly spliced, the pace carefully metered, the style tongue-in-cheek. A well-crafted, extrasensory mystery with mischievous scenes of high appeal. (p. 156)

A review of "Blossom Culp and the Sleep of Death," in Bulletin of the Center for Children's Books, *Vol. 39, No. 8, April, 1986, pp. 155-56.*

Peck combines adroit plotting with some razor-sharp characterizations and a distinct intolerance for any foolish behavior. Personalities from the other books enhance the plot, and Peck indulges in some wicked slapstick at the expense of pretentious, small-minded figures such as Letty Shambaugh and her towering mother. Comedy and suspense with a bite. (pp. 1226-27)

Denise M. Wilms, in a review of "Blossom Culp and the Sleep of Death," in Booklist, *Vol. 82, No. 16, April 15, 1986, pp. 1226-27.*

Good news for the Blossom Culp cult! Peck's feisty 14-year-old psychic returns for a fourth adventure. . . . As in earlier installments of Blossom's antic autobiography, . . . ***the Sleep of Death*** incorporates elements of both the topical and the occult (women's suffrage and the lively spirit of an ancient Egyptian princess, respectively). Complications abound and Blossom, as usual, is culpable. . . . There is no sting in . . . ***Death,*** but it does seem more contrived in terms of plot and weaker in its setting and use of period than earlier titles in this series. Nevertheless, it is an entertaining and generally well-crafted diversion with moments of inspired humor (the hapless Alexander's fraternity initiation rights) and abundant examples of Peck's gift for turning the humorous phrase ("I was jumpier than turtle parts in a pan").

Michael Cart, in a review of "Blossom Culp and the Sleep of Death," in School Library Journal, *Vol. 32, No. 9, May, 1986, p. 108.*

This fourth book about Blossom and Alexander continues Blossom's adventures with the occult with the humor and small town detail found in the others. There is also some darker humor in Blossom's relationship with her mother. What makes the book of special interest is Blossom's unique character and the way it bounces off Alexander's and Letty's. The memorable characters and intriguing plot make the book a natural for booktalking.

Susan Levine, in a review of "Blossom Culp and the Sleep of Death," in Voice of Youth Advocates, *Vol. 9, No. 2, June, 1986, p. 82.*

PRINCESS ASHLEY (1987)

Here, Chelsea narrates the events in her sophomore and junior years, when she modeled herself on Ashley—lovely, rich, and apparently self-possessed.

Starting Crestwood High at that painful time in early adolescence when self-definition is all-important, Chelsea feels so afflicted by her ambitious mother's new career as guidance counselor that she bitterly rejects her, seeing her insights concerning Chelsea as "witchy" and invasive. Though still feeling close to her ineffectual dog-trainer father, she's ripe for a new role model, and so when, astonishingly, the perfect Ashley taps her as friend, she goes along willingly. Cracks in Ashley's veneer provide early glimpses of the emptiness within—her poems are someone else's, she claims that her stepmother is her father's mistress, she casually drops Chelsea from a long-anticipated fashion show for her own convenience—yet Chelsea remains a loyal follower. Meanwhile, her friend Pod does his own growing from sophomoric poseur to more effective doer; their developing affection provides contrast as well as humor, since with Pod Chelsea is assertive from the beginning. But it takes cataclysmic revelations about both parents and a tragedy involving Ashley's boyfriend, whose glamour masks another debilitating conflict, to get Chelsea to see others clearly and begin to define herself.

One of our finest writers of YA novels, Peck deftly captures the evolving concerns of 15- and 16-year-olds—their speech, anxieties, and shifting relationships with parents and peers. His witty, concise style and a plot full of surprising turns carry the reader quickly along; yet his characters are born of unusual wisdom and empathy for the teen condition. Another winner. (pp. 723-24)

A review of "Princess Ashley," in Kirkus Reviews, *Vol. LV, No. 8, May 1, 1987, pp. 723-24.*

With remarkable consistency, the novels of Richard Peck continue to challenge YAs and the adults who serve them with timely issues, characters of depth and feeling, and life-like scenarios which stun the reader with the power of their reality. . . . Chelsea must learn the difference between friendship and manipulation, between wealth and integrity, between pride and selfishness. The painful price for this knowledge is being paid every day among America's adolescents.

Yet Peck also provides earthy wisdom and rich comic relief in the character of Pod, Chelsea's kind-of boyfriend. In one hilarious scene, as these two dress for a 1960s party with beads and headbands, Pod is described as "kind of a Willie Nelson doll."

Princess Ashley contains such wisdom and caring: the wisdom of an author who travels many miles listening to the kids for whom he writes; the caring of a teacher who knows that the secret to *really* facilitating successful transition to adulthood is to fortify the confidence kids must have in their own instincts and decisions, apart from peer pressures. These are commendable, difficult skills for an author to apply in a novel, without being heavy-handed. Peck offers up these skills with an openness and sincerity whose effectiveness is to a great extent validated by the popularity of his work among today's adolescents. ***Princess Ashley*** is one of his best.

Evie Wilson, in a review of "Princess Ashley," in Voice of Youth Advocates, *Vol. 10, No. 2, June, 1987, p. 82.*

The characters, both adult and adolescent, are expertly drawn and totally believable. Peck obviously knows how teenagers think and feel, and this insight enables him to bring his characters vibrantly to life. Especially compelling is Chelsea, a complex girl longing to fit in with the accepted group. Her offbeat friend Pod is a delightful blend of boyish enthusiasm and mature thoughtfulness. A sensitive and insightful view of teenage life that may cause readers to ponder their own search for identity, Peck's newest book is a must for both school and public library collections.

Denise A. Anton, in a review of "Princess Ashley," in School Library Journal, *Vol. 33, No. 11, August, 1987, p. 97.*

Cynthia Rylant

1954-

American author of fiction, picture books, and short stories; and poet.

A relative newcomer to children's literature, Rylant is already well respected for creating a variety of prizewinning books which are often set in the mountains of West Virginia. Directing her works to an audience ranging from preschool through junior high, she is considered an especially talented literary stylist whose books are characterized by their disarming simplicity, intense feeling, insight, and realistic details. Rylant focuses on interpersonal relationships between young and old, and is particularly noted for her unstereotypical portrayals of the elderly. Thematically, she stresses the importance of family and all living things. Despite the inclusion of such themes as loneliness, fear, or betrayal, her works ultimately convey understanding and hope. Several of Rylant's books reflect the influence of her childhood experiences in Appalachia. In her first work, the nostalgic picture book *When I Was Young in the Mountains* (1982), she communicates the quiet joys of country living. *Waiting to Waltz: A Childhood* (1984), a collection of thirty autobiographical poems which humorously and compassionately depicts growing up in a small town, is regarded as a fine example of free verse as well as an effective expression of heartfelt emotion. In the celebrated picture book *The Relatives Came* (1985), Rylant recounts the visit of a carload of exuberant relations to a lonely mountain family. *A Blue-Eyed Daisy* (1985), her first novel, describes eleven-year-old Ellie's gradual appreciation for her alcoholic father, who had been disabled in the West Virginia coal mines. In *A Fine White Dust* (1986), Rylant relates how a junior high student meets an itinerant evangelist and becomes obsessed with the idea of saving souls. Addressing Pete's inner crisis and growth as he experiences seduction, desertion, and acceptance, Rylant has been acclaimed for her courage in being one of the few children's writers to undertake a religious subject successfully. She has also written collections of short stories, several picture books which recreate the images and sounds of the country, and a lively series of easy readers for beginners to read for themselves about Henry, a small boy, and his large dog Mudge.

Critics laud Rylant for her straightforward approach, economic yet lyrical language, lifelike characterizations, and ability to express powerful emotions with restraint. Although they point to occasional slightness of plot, most reviewers agree that Rylant's poignant tales, well-crafted, rhythmic texts, and evocative poetry have provided young readers with memorable examples of sincere and elegant writing.

In 1982, *When I Was Young in the Mountains* was selected as a nominee for the American Book Award. In 1987, *A Fine White Dust* was named a Newbery Honor Book. Two of Rylant's books were chosen as Caldecott Honor Books for their illustrations: *When I Was Young in the Mountains*, illustrated by Diane Goode, in 1983, and *The Relatives Came*, illustrated by Stephen Gammell, in 1986.

(See also *Something about the Author*, Vol. 44).

Photograph by Margaret Miller. Courtesy of Cynthia Rylant.

AUTHOR'S COMMENTARY

I had this third grade teacher named Miss Evans back in Beaver, West Virginia. She was a short little woman with jet-black hair, tomato-red lipstick, and black-rimmed glasses. I was the new kid in school that year, which is perhaps why my memory of the physical appearance of this woman is so vivid. I never took my eyes off her that first terrifying week.

Miss Evans was the first, and last, person who ever told me stories. I don't mean the reading aloud of books. I mean the spinning of tales. Let me tell you what this very short woman in Beaver, West Virginia created.

It was an ongoing saga entitled *The Journey*. The main characters in *The Journey* were the twenty-five of us sitting in her classroom. Once a week, Miss Evans led us on an adventure into the jungles of Africa or the glaciers of the Antarctic or some equally harrowing place, and she narrated, in a tense, mysterious, breathless voice, the epic battles we won, together and individually.

One time in the Sahara Desert, I was bitten by a rattlesnake. And Randy Meadows carried me to a safe place, slit my flesh into an X, and sucked the poison from my foot. Sitting at my desk, I was nearly overcome with nervous exhaustion before Miss Evans finished this particular installment.

And you know, Randy Meadows and I would spend nine more years together in school. Scrapping over who was next at the water fountain; whispering about who kissed who and when and where; watching each other fall in love, suffer betrayal and shame, struggle with that beast called Adolescence—all this lay ahead for Randy and me. And in those nine years, I never once lost that feeling of immense gratitude toward Randy for saving me from certain death by snakebite, though he sat only three desks away during the entire ordeal.

That is the power of what a story can do to you.

Four years ago, I met a little boy in Cincinnati who had an odd security blanket. It was a copy of *Caps for Sale*. He carried it everywhere and, his mother told me, he slept with it. The boy was extremely shy, overwhelmed by a world he probably found too quick, too noisy, too ready to leap at him. *Caps for Sale* was getting him through.

Again, that is the power of what a story can do for you.

It is that *other life* of a book which makes it important and powerful. Not the medals and applause. It's that other life which makes its author important and its reader important and it creates something else beyond the words and the pictures.

I hope teachers don't forget that when they share books with children. I hope they don't just listen to the pronunciation of the words or the accuracy of their reports.

I hope they, like Miss Evans, look into the faces of those young readers. Because, truly, books alter our hearts.

Once when I was working in a library, pulling old cards from the catalog—records of books that had already seen the incinerator—I came to the title card for a discarded book called *Mrs. Wiggs and the Cabbage Patch*.

And I stood there, for a few minutes, staring at that card and feeling something hopping around inside my stomach and my brain sort of swelling up as it tried to remember. I knew that book from somewhere. That *somewhere* was my childhood, the one lived mostly without books. And I remember the cover of that book, finally, still standing there. All those big green cabbage heads and a skinny old woman wearing a bun, with a hoe in her hands. It was a book club book. I remember because the cover was shiny.

Though I couldn't remember the story, I felt a powerful gratitude toward that book and a sort of love for Mrs. Wiggs. And as I pulled that old brown title card from the library catalog, I felt helpless and ashamed. Because I had not been able to save that book from the fire.

Today, I tend to protect the books I love best like a mother lioness. I have a copy of a book by James Agee. It's called *Let Us Now Praise Famous Men*. It and his other book, *A Death in the Family,* are most responsible, I think, for my writing. How I write, what I write about.

And I often keep one of those books by my bed. When I need solace and there is none, I reach for Agee. And when I can't write and think I won't ever again, I reach for Agee. And though James Agee died a young man in 1955, leaving behind only a few works, he seems as much a part of my life sometimes as my husband or my children.

And it all has something to do with that other life of a book.

I know children experience that in rare moments. And I think they might experience it more often if reading was not so often run like a marathon in their schools and libraries, with activities like Book Bingo or Summer Reading Club. I was approached by children in the library who said, "Give me a fairy tale, a hobby book, a historical fiction, and a family story." And if I offered a book that was too thick, it was refused, for how could the boy or girl expect to win the Bingo game if the books couldn't be read in time? And seeing members of the Summer Reading Club force-feeding themselves books in order to achieve a hamburger coupon. . . .

It seems impossible to me that any of those children ever loved any of the books they read under those circumstances.

It is such a pleasure for me, as an adult, to read Agee again and again. It is such a pleasure to read at a slow pace, or not at all. And like the little boy in Cincinnati, it is such a pleasure to clutch at my own example of *Caps for Sale*. Because I know its power.

I realize children must learn to read. And I know they should be exposed to different types of literature.

Let us never forget, though, the power of what a story can do to them.

If children read my books, I hope it is never in order to achieve a prize. Because my books are worth more than gummed stars or hamburgers.

And I hope that some children will wish my books well, and perhaps, as adults, eulogize them with love if they go into the fire. (pp. 460-62)

Cynthia Rylant, "Thank You, Miss Evans," in Language Arts, *Vol. 62, No. 5, September, 1985, pp. 460-62.*

***WHEN I WAS YOUNG IN THE MOUNTAINS* (1982)**

Rylant's debut proves she knows precisely how to tell a story that brings the reader into the special world of her recollecting. . . . The author simply and poetically describes her childhood in Appalachia where she lived with grandparents. Nothing happens, but everything happens that makes up life: Grandfather coming home from the coal mine to kiss the little ones with his lips, the only part of him that's not begrimed; Grandma taking the girl to the "johnny-house" at midnight, after she had eaten too much okra at supper; heating water to bathe in, poured into a wooden tub before a rousing fire in the stove. These are memories of a way of living that will entrance readers and broaden their outlook. (pp. 70-1)

A review of "When I Was Young in the Mountains," in Publishers Weekly, *Vol. 221, No. 12, March 19, 1982, pp. 70-1.*

[This] is a nostalgic piece as evocatively illustrated [by Diane Goode] as it is told. . . . There is no story line, but a series of memories, each beginning, "When I was young in the mountains . . ." as the author reminisces about the busy, peaceful life of an extended family and their community. Quiet, almost static, this is given appeal by the warmth and contentment that emerge from an account of daily satisfaction and small, occasional joys, described with appropriate simplicity.

Zena Sutherland, in a review of "When I Was Young in the Mountains," in Bulletin of the Center for Children's Books, *Vol. 35, No. 8, April, 1982, p. 157.*

This reminiscence will not have immediate appeal for most children, dealing as it does with a time that seems remote and serene. These snatches of memory do include the kind of details children like to know: what people ate, what games they played; but the dreamy, reflective tone and the detailed drawings signal individual, rather than group, sharing. The people in the story are poor in material things, but rich in family pleasures. The title becomes a pleasing refrain that is used to herald a change in topic.

Holly Sanhuber, in a review of "When I Was Young in the Mountains," in School Library Journal, *Vol. 28, No. 9, May, 1982, p. 56.*

A gently rhythmic text describes the author's youthful days in the Appalachian mountains of Virginia. Repetition of the phrase "when I was young in the mountains" gives the text a poetic quality as it evokes images of mountain pines, home-cooked meals, and country stores. . . . Dedicated to the author's grandparents, the book is a tribute to a childhood when living in the mountains "was always enough." (pp. 282-83)

Karen M. Klockner, in a review of "When I Was Young in the Mountains," in The Horn Book Magazine, *Vol. LVIII, No. 3, June, 1982, pp. 282-83.*

Many of the stories young children enjoy contain repetition of words, phrases, or sentences. Repetition is especially appealing because it encourages children to join in during the reading. It provides a pleasing rhythm in ***When I Was Young in the Mountains***. . . . The author introduces her memories of Grandfather's kisses, Grandmother's cooking, and listening to frogs singing at dusk with "When I was young in the mountains," a phrase that adds an appropriate aura of loving nostalgia to the experiences she describes. (p. 97)

Donna E. Norton, "Evaluating and Selecting Literature for Children," in her Through the Eyes of a Child: An Introduction to Children's Literature, *second edition, Merrill Publishing Company, 1987, pp. 82-109.*

MISS MAGGIE (1983)

The story is slight, but . . . it is in part the economical structure that makes it effective, a vivid fragment. Nat has always been frightened by old Maggie, who lives in a rotting cabin reputed to have a pet snake in the rafters. When his grandmother sent food over, or his grandfather gave old Maggie a lift to town, Nat stayed as far away as possible. Then, one icy day, Nat saw that there was no smoke coming from the cabin chimney; he rushed over, found the old woman mourning over a frozen pet bird, and a friendship began; the story ends with Nat giving Miss Maggie a new pet, a blacksnake that he names "Henry," just like the dead bird. Despite its simplicity, a moving tale about friendship. (pp. 177-78)

Zena Sutherland, in a review of "Miss Maggie," in Bulletin of the Center for Children's Books, *Vol. 36, No. 9, May, 1983, pp. 177-78.*

This sensitive picture-book story benefits from [Thomas] DiGrazia's perceptive soft-focus illustrations, which evoke a mood and a presence that's truly in keeping with the story. . . . The tenderness in the story is refreshing and quite visible in the pictures. Youngsters will have much to think about in watching this unlikely friendship blossom and grow. (pp. 1221-22)

Denise M. Wilms, in a review of "Miss Maggie," in Booklist, *Vol. 79, No. 18, May 15, 1983, pp. 1221-22.*

This is a tender story of age and youth, fear and reality. Nat's growth in mind and spirit is evident as he visits old Miss Maggie, discovering the gossip "Some folks said . . ." as complete fallacy.

The tale is true "country-yarn" in style and text. It is reminiscent of the patchwork storyteller who draws in the audience with "hook, line, and sinker." . . .

Miss Maggie is a fine book to compare with other stories about aging and the aged. (p. 301)

Marilou Sorensen, in a review of "Miss Maggie," in Language Arts, *Vol. 61, No. 3, March, 1984, pp. 300-01.*

This gentle, touching story, simply told, develops mainly through Nat's thoughts and actions. It embodies excellent characterization of Maggie as courageous and fiercely independent, yet vulnerable, and Nat as typical impressionable youngster, who becomes clear-headed and decisive in a crisis.

Inga Kromann-Kelly, in a review of "Miss Maggie," in Language Arts, *Vol. 61, No. 3, March, 1984, p. 301.*

WAITING TO WALTZ: A CHILDHOOD (1984)

Observed if imperfectly understood by the unadulterated senses of a child, Rylant's growing years live on in her poetry. . . . We believe it is a schoolgirl who is elaborating on events in Beaver Creek, where she lives with her mother. The town is so small it has only "a little slip of a street," but still one resident leaves for good and nobody misses him. We feel the narrator's discomfiture and prickly defense as the daughter of a nonmember of the PTA. She's the woman they turn to in crises, though: "Because my mother is a nurse," who doesn't serve popcorn at baseball games "but she could/sure/save their lives, boy." . . . Classmates, friends, confusing adults and everyone in Beaver Creek become as real to the reader as they are to Rylant. Past becomes present, in vivid memories of an adolescent "waiting to waltz," to be a woman.

A review of "Waiting to Waltz: A Childhood," in Publishers Weekly, *Vol. 226, No. 7, August 17, 1984, p. 60.*

There was something effortless, simple, and pure about the first-person narrative language of Ms. Rylant's ***When I Was Young in the Mountains.*** It came, unadulterated, from the heart. ***Waiting to Waltz*** also captures heartfelt, significant recollections of growing up in the speck-of-a-town called Beaver, West Virginia. Portraits of town folks, people just passing through, classmates, family, church . . . and animals known and unknown who did or didn't meet up splat with a car or truck are described in thirty poems. Here, however, her natural writing style has been fussed with, convoluted, and fragmented into a not-quite-found poetic voice. There is no doubt that Ms. Rylant is a very special talent. I wish that she wasn't being rushed into print; I wish she would be allowed to develop and mature and arrive at her own style in her own time.

Leigh Dean, in a review of "Waiting to Waltz: A Childhood," in Children's Book Review Service, *Vol. 13, No. 3, November, 1984, p. 32.*

In this collection of 30 poems, Rylant successfully shows the fears and joys of young adulthood in a small town in Appalachia. The free verse of the poems allows her to express feelings about the death of a dog, the death of a father who had left nine years before and the people and events of the town of Beaver. Cultural items from the 1960s are woven into the poems; there is humor as Rylant compares a boyfriend to a pet rock and pathos in telling about a boy whose dog has died and can no longer run beside his bicycle. These are not easy poems, but rather a quiet yet moving internalization of growing up. As such, they are a fine example for introspective readers of how poetry expresses intense feelings. . . . This book, in its own way, continues the story of Rylant's ***When I Was Young in the Mountains.***

Margaret C. Howell, in a review of "Waiting to Waltz: A Childhood," in School Library Journal, *Vol. 31, No. 3, November, 1984, p. 138.*

Nostalgia and irony, regret and pride, echo through a collection of short, unrhymed poems gleaned from events in the author's childhood. With each poem her story unfolds. Bright images make her experiences—as a naïve child pleased with her small-town surroundings and friends or as a restless teenager—visible to sensitive readers. People and places appear reflected in the unquestioning acceptance of the small child and in the bittersweet appraisal of a mature woman. Humor brightens the dismay of bungling a spelling bee, and regret shadows the passing of her childhood as she finds herself "Forgetting when / I was last time / a child. / Never knowing / when it / ended." . . . For those who have lived long enough to admit to having forsaken a friend—and for a younger audience still seeking to shed the games of childhood and are eagerly "Waiting to shave / and wear nylons / and waltz"—the poems will gently pluck a long forgotten memory or awaken a shared experience.

Ethel R. Twichell, in a review of "Waiting to Waltz: A Childhood," in The Horn Book Magazine, *Vol. LXI, No. 1, January-February, 1985, p. 64.*

THIS YEAR'S GARDEN (1984)

The story transmits a calm feeling of waiting—for time to plant, for the harvest, for the eating; the security of the cycles and the support of family members toiling and playing are of value. However, the book is too slight to warrant staying with or rereading it.

Renee Queen, in a review of "This Year's Garden," in Children's Book Review Service, *Vol. 13, No. 1, September, 1984, p. 4.*

[***This Year's Garden*** contains] a poetic but narrow text about a family's planning of its summer vegetable garden, the seeding and harvesting, and the enjoyment of the preserved crop through the summer and fall—and then the planning again, as the bare brown garden patch waits, like the family, for next year's garden. This is a book that can be used to corroborate a child's concept of the cycle of seasons, or to encourage an interest in gardening, but it's not informative enough to be a useful book about gardening and it's too static to have appeal to some of the read-aloud audience.

Zena Sutherland, in a review of "This Year's Garden," in Bulletin of the Center for Children's Books, *Vol. 38, No. 2, October, 1984, p. 34.*

Rylant follows the life of a garden throughout the seasons of a year. She writes in a flowing style, incorporating sentence fragments to convey the feeling and meaning of the words. The prose carries the story along and truly reveals the gardening cycle—spring planning and planting; summer caretaking and harvesting; autumn harvesting and storing; winter planning and dreaming.

Frances E. Millhouser, in a review of "This Year's Garden," in School Library Journal, *Vol. 31, No. 4, December, 1984, p. 76.*

A poetic sense of sounds and imagery complements the drawn-out, relaxed pace of the text. The homely word choice, variety of phrase length, and underlying dramatic use of the pause punctuates the seasons. (p. 193)

This slick country vignette acknowledges our ecological indebtness to the earth. There is a challenge in abundance. (p. 194)

Ronald A. Jobe, in a review of "This Year's Garden," in Language Arts, *Vol. 62, No. 2, February, 1985, pp. 193-94.*

A BLUE-EYED DAISY (1985; British edition as *Some Year for Ellie*)

[Rylant] tells in lyrical prose the story of Ellie at home in the coal-mining hills of West Virginia.

Okey Farley had lost the use of an arm in an accident and, consequently, his job. Although he drinks, he's a good father to his five daughters and a loving husband to his wife. Ellie, the youngest, is 11 and apprehensive about getting to 12 and then into the teens. Who wants to primp and pose like her big sisters?

Ellie likes to be with Okey and their hound dog, after an outing that brings her deeper appreciation of her father. They are hunting, and Ellie, with an unsuspecting doe in her sights, knows how Okey will brag if she bags a deer her first time out. In agony, she warns the animal off and flinches as it leaps to safety. She hears Okey shout as he runs to her side, and waits for his reproach. But he says, "Now wasn't that the *prettiest* thing you ever seen?" "The prettiest," Ellie says.

Throughout the year, Ellie has other anxious moments and sometimes grave problems, but even they resolve themselves, usually with her help and the cooperation of friends. She has special joys too. In an unforgettable chapter, the author describes an afternoon in town where Ellie and her best pal, Carolyn Oaks, spend their savings from pop-bottle sales. Giggling and sputtering, they take crazy snaps of themselves in the photo booth at the general store, buy each other friendship rings and shiver at a horror movie. No reader will be able to resist Ellie or her kith and kin. Their ability to live life and endure ills is the core of an exquisite novel, written with love.

A review of "A Blue-Eyed Daisy," in Publishers Weekly, *Vol. 227, No. 10, March 8, 1985, p. 91.*

Short, deceptively simple cameos of Ellie's eleventh year, gently strung together with paired themes of fear and hope, death and growth, reveal the metamorphosis of daughter and father. . . . Rylant's spare phrases reveal as much in what they do not state as in what they do say. It is this low-key, evocative style that is the shining quality which sets this book apart. Through her understatedly elegant prose, readers come to know a beautiful person, easy to read about, but hard to forget. There is no dramatic action here to hook readers—but on hearing an excerpt of the book read aloud, they will certainly be captivated.

Katharine Bruner, in a review of "A Blue-Eyed Daisy," in School Library Journal, *Vol. 31, No. 8, April, 1985, p. 92.*

[A] direct, economical style marks each of the 14 short-story-like episodes that sharply illuminate memorable moments in the course of Ellie Farley's eleventh year. . . . Though there is little plot, there is undeniable punch. And if the stories' linkage is not always direct, their connection is resolutely affirmed by the depth of the finished picture.

Denise M. Wilms, in a review of "A Blue-Eyed Daisy," in Booklist, *Vol. 81, No. 20, June 15, 1985, p. 1461.*

The elation of friendship; the recognition of adult unhappiness; television pictures of the war made real when her soldier uncle returns home; getting kissed; ageing, fear and loss, all come Ellie's way in the course of her year of growing up. There are times when the incidents seem to belong too transparently to a primer for the getting of wisdom—a tendency underlined by the otherwise admirable simplicity of Cynthia Rylant's writing. "Ellie Sees a Fit" as a chapter heading strays perilously close to parodied Janet and John or Dick and Jane. For non-American readers, the setting adds a welcome touch of the exotic to the familiar working of family life. It makes its presence felt in elements ranging from the names of Ellie's sisters (there are not too many Wandas and Eunices in the coal-fields of Derbyshire) to her father's Chevy truck and the family attendance at the Church of God. There is, too, a controversial directness in the book's style. Rylant tackles demanding topics—a classmate of Ellie's is shot dead during target practice, her father goes into hospital after driving his truck off the edge of a mountain—in straightforward terms: "Ellie went to the funeral. First one she'd ever gone to. Lester looked just about the same to her dead as he had looked alive. She was ashamed she had found him boring then and still did." The result is a compassionate and reassuring book most likely to appeal to an age group a little younger than that of Ellie herself.

Joanna Motion, "Okey Farley's Girls," in The Times Literary Supplement, *No. 4342, June 20, 1986, p. 691.*

THE RELATIVES CAME **(1985)**

The relatives have come—in an old station wagon that smells "like a real car"—bringing with them hugs and laughs, quiet talk, and, at night when all are asleep hither and yon, "all that new breathing." Rylant has a finely tuned sense for the telling details that capture the essence of an experience. The excitement, fun, love, and joy of a good visit from faraway relatives is crystal clear in her wry text. . . . A memorable experience for all concerned.

Denise M. Wilms, in a review of "The Relatives Came," in Booklist, *Vol. 82, No. 4, October 15, 1985, p. 341.*

You could think of ***The Relatives Came*** as a sort of children's *Lake Wobegon Days*. It has the same air of fond, gentle amusement, the same ability to make readers bounce a little in their seats with the pleasure of recognition. Cynthia Rylant . . . tells her story straightforwardly. The relatives sleep on the floor, filling the house with the sound of their "new breathing," they eat up the strawberries and melons and fix whatever needs fixing, and after several weeks they leave, again at 4 in the morning. . . . Their hosts stand outdoors in pajamas waving goodbye, and then they return to beds that suddenly feel too big and too quiet.

If there's anything more charming than the tone of voice in this story, it's the drawings that go with it [by Stephen Gammell]. . . .

There is no indication near the price on the jacket flap of what ages this book is intended for, but I'd say, oh, about 96 might be a good upper limit.

Anne Tyler, "Disorder at 4 A.M.," in The New York Times Book Review, *November 10, 1985, p. 37.*

Gammell's exuberant, exaggerated color pencil drawings add to the warmth and cheerfulness of the text. Although Rylant's story is thin in plot (relatives come, hug and eat and sleep and work and play, they go) it is robust in every other way: it speaks vividly of the love in an extended family, it speaks humorously of the makeshift arrangements in a crowded household, and it speaks wistfully of the relative pleasures of the familiar scene and the change of scene.

A review of "The Relatives Came," in Bulletin of the Center for Children's Books, *Vol. 39, No. 4, December, 1985, p. 77.*

The most joyous book of the past year certainly must be ***The Relatives Came,*** a perfect blend of Cynthia Rylant's loving homespun recollections and Stephen Gammell's illustrations. . . . Ms. Rylant's narrative has never been cleaner and more lyrical; she distills the essences of this extended family. . . . [This is] a book certain to be treasured by all who make this part of their extended family.

Hughes Moir, in a review of "The Relatives Came," in The Advocates Newsletter, *September, 1986, p. 9.*

EVERY LIVING THING **(1985)**

A collection of simple, elegantly crafted stories about people whose lives are touched by an animal—household pets, a stray puppy, a nesting robin—and how these people are changed and enriched by the experience.

Rylant has attracted attention and acclaim with her earlier works, including ***A Blue-Eyed Daisy*** and ***When I Was Young in the Mountains.*** She has written picture books, poetry and a novel, and now displays her considerable talent in a new form—short stories. There are 12 in all, some just a few pages long. In **"Shells,"** a boy whose parents have been killed finds a way, through his pet hermit crab, to show his aunt that he loves her; in **"Papa's Parrot,"** another boy who has stopped visiting his father's store learns through the store's parrot how much his father misses him; in **"Drying Out,"** a man who drinks too much gets back on his feet with the aid of three squirrels he feeds from his hospital window.

The emotions these stories convey are not simplistic or treacly, but instead are direct and powerful, an impressive feat. Rylant has another winner on her hands. (pp. 1090-91)

A review of "Every Living Thing," in Kirkus Reviews, *Vol. LIII, No. 19, October 1, 1985, pp. 1090-91.*

These are not conventional animal stories. Rylant's deliberate, straightforward style hides a quiet intensity unusual in such short pieces. She builds plot and character simultaneously, with precisely chosen verbs and adverbs; no drawn-out descriptions are needed. A character takes a few steps, says a few words and readers know him. Although the style is not difficult to read, the tone of the stories, the basic sense of human loneliness and isolation which comes through, makes them more suitable for older readers. (One third of the stories have adult protagonists.) Besides being enjoyed for themselves, the stories would make a good classroom read-aloud, generating lots of discussion. They would also be suitable for older reluctant readers.

Ruth S. Vose, in a review of "Every Living Thing," in School Library Journal, *Vol. 32, No. 4, December, 1985, p. 106.*

Twelve deceptively simple contemporary stories explore the relationship between people and animals, and in so doing look also at some of the vagaries of human nature and human relationships. The words are easy, but the emotions aren't; the characters, caught by brief and telling phrases, are memorable and sometimes puzzling. A poet at heart, the author has a spare, understated style and an inclination toward fleeting images and feelings. As a result, some of the selections are vignettes rather than conventional stories. (p. 308)

Sometimes it seems that children's books draw more than their share of characters from a relatively privileged suburban setting; it's a comfort to have someone writing naturally and well about children who mix up their own powdered milk and eat butter sandwiches. (pp. 308-09)

Janet Hickman, in a review of "Every Living Thing," in Language Arts, *Vol. 63, No. 3, March, 1986, pp. 308-09.*

The twelve stories in this volume deal with growth, loss, grief, old age, and beginnings. Rylant's quiet, almost laconic style reminds me of E. B. White at his drollest, or James Thurber in his mellowest mood. She doesn't say much, but the stories *say* a lot.

Most successful are **"Slower Than the Rest, "Planting Things," "Safe,"** and **"Shells."** . . . **"Planting Things,"** deals, as several of the stories do, with older people—in this case a man whose own aging gains meaning when a robin builds its nest on his porch. Rylant is able to depict aging accurately and yet celebrate its achievements, a rare skill. . . .

Rylant's themes are wide-ranging, as are the people whose lives she allows us to glimpse. A thoughtful child or a troubled teen-ager would savor these slices, for they speak directly to the heart. An enthusiastic "A" rating for this completely masterful work.

Loralee MacPike, in a review of "Every Living Thing," in Best Sellers, *Vol. 46, No. 1, April, 1986, p. 40.*

NIGHT IN THE COUNTRY (1986)

[This is] a remarkable picture book that sweeps the reader into the quiet, special world of a country night. Exceptionally beautiful illustrations bring the scenes to life as the text whispers such lines as: "If you lie very still, you may hear an apple fall from the tree in the back yard. Listen." On the next page the apple falls: "Pump!" . . . ***Night in the Country*** is a gentle, soothing story that's perfectly suited for bedtime reading. . . . The combination [of Rylant and illustrator Mary Szilagyi] is auspicious, and we hope there are more treasures to come from them.

A review of "Night in the Country," in Publishers Weekly, *Vol. 229, No. 17, April 25, 1986, p. 69.*

The pairing of Rylant and Szilagyi again results in a graceful blend of evocative prose and exquisite color-pencil drawings. . . . Rich with nuances, the images and sounds evoked by the text have brought forth deeply shadowed drawings by the artist; likewise, the text will conjure up vivid imaginings in the minds of young children. The journey through nighttime fittingly concludes that night animals "will spend a day in the country listening to you." Each page invites children to look, listen and explore. ***Night in the Country*** is a welcome addition to that prized collection of rhythmic, soothing nighttime readings.

Anne E. Mulherkar, in a review of "Night in the Country," in School Library Journal, *Vol. 32, No. 9, May, 1986, p. 84.*

[On] the whole, this is a felicitous mood piece. The quiet text describes the activities, sights, and especially, sounds of night. . . . While each vignette is lyrical, the narrative line from scene to scene seems arbitrary, and occasionally out of sequence.

Roger Sutton, in a review of "Night in the Country," in Bulletin of the Center for Children's Books , *Vol. 40, No. 1, September, 1986, p. 18.*

In the rich and varied world of children's literature there is an entire subcontinent of stories written for the sole purpose of encouraging youngsters to slip from day to night, from wakefulness into sleep. Demystifying the darkness is one of the ways to speed up this process which ***Night in the Country*** does in fine style by focusing on some of the prime actors in the nighttime drama. "There is no night so dark, so black as night in the country," begins Cynthia Rylant's soothing tale with its swooping owls and singing frogs that turn out not to be so scary after all.

Ms. Rylant also has a keen ear for those after dark sounds: the clink of a dog's chain, the distant opening and closing of a screen door, the muted sound of an apple falling from a backyard tree. . . . While within there are the creaks and groans of a house trying to sleep, outside a raccoon licks her babies, a cow nuzzles her calf and an old pig simply rolls over. This country night is a mild and nurturing one. No ghosties or ghoulies lurk to disturb that blissful rural sleep. . . .

Mary Szilagyi's bright illustratioins are as friendly as the text. . . . ***Night in the Country*** is a cheerful way to coax anyone to sleep.

Rollene W. Saal, in a review of "Night in the Country," in The New York Times Book Review, *October 26, 1986, p. 48.*

A FINE WHITE DUST (1986)

An enigmatic, powerful novel about a seventh-grade boy who is enthralled by an itinerant evangelist in the rural South.

Pete, unlike his parents, has been an ardent churchgoer for years, but when the Preacher Man (James W. Carson) arrives, he becomes a born-again Christian and agrees to run away with Carson as his disciple, although he agonizes over abandoning his parents and best friend Rufus, a professed atheist. But the

Biblical parallel suggested by the names is reversed: Carson betrays Pete by skipping town with Darlene, the soda-fountain clerk, while Rufus is the supportive friend who waits patiently for Pete to recover from his infatuation. Pete does; yet although he has lost his enthusiasm for formal religion, his underlying faith in God is unshaken, even strengthened. He discards the "fine white dust" of the ceramic cross broken when the Preacher left because he's "ready for something whole."

Rylant has explored a theme vital to many young people but rare in children's books. By eliminating any description of doctrine beyond Pete's love of Jesus and fear of hell, she leaves the reader free to consider the broader meaning of religion and the nature of a charlatan. Simply but beautifully written, Pete's encounter with the Preacher Man is a tale with enough suspense to hold readers till the end. (pp. 1023-24)

A review of "A Fine White Dust," in Kirkus Reviews, *Vol. LIV, No. 13, July 1, 1986, pp. 1023-24.*

Although the book is more an outline than a fully realized novel, it is strong in delineating the nature of the boy and his intense crisis when the mysterious Preacher Man entices him to run away and then abandons him instead. The characterization of his stable best friend and parents is limited but credible. Neither the Preacher nor his services, however, are vividly enough rendered to make totally convincing Pete's decision to leave a home he loves. The inconsistency in the Preacher's persuading the boy to leave with him and then leaving with a girl instead is baffling without more extensive development of his personality and motivations. The style is spare and rhythmic, sometimes self-consciously so, as in the repetition in the boy's narrative of a phrase "The telling," showing the weight and difficulty of his confession. (pp. 17-18)

Betsy Hearne, in a review of "A Fine White Dust," in Bulletin of the Center for Children's Books, *Vol. 40, No. 1, September, 1986, pp. 17-18.*

Few books have explored young people's fascination with God and their soul. Rylant's subtle telling has a hymn-like quality, sung in a melodic, soulful way which reverberates within the reader's compassion. Although the tone is serious, Peter's recounting is personal and sensitive—like religion and friendships, presumed and assumed. Like Peter, this story has soul.

Julie Cummins, in a review of "A Fine White Dust," in School Library Journal, *Vol. 33, No. 1, September, 1986, p. 138.*

A disarming directness marks this first person novel. . . . The story offers an achingly resonant portrayal of a naive youth. Rylant has captured Pete's tender, honest, searching psyche as it is subjected to the whirlwinds of fierce, raw emotion. Pete's feeling of love is not overtly sexual; rather it is the total idealization of the Preacher Man, who becomes, briefly and devastatingly, a father figure for him. In the aftermath of his shattered emotions, Pete realizes that this figure he has so romanticized is no substitute for the steady, unconditional love and support of his one best friend and his caring parents, who, with painful concern, have watched their son's experience. There is barely a false note to the story's telling. The novel is poignant and perceptive, with almost all of the characters subtly drawn. It's also one of a few but growing number of stories that unabashedly explores a religious theme.

Denise M. Wilms, in a review of "A Fine White Dust," in Booklist, *Vol. 83, No. 1, September 1, 1986, p. 67.*

Stories of friendship and betrayal are common enough in literature, but few authors have the courage to tackle the intense religious feelings that some adolescents experience. Pete's struggle to understand his own heart, told in his own painfully honest voice, rings true.

Janet Hickman, in a review of "A Fine White Dust," in Language Arts, *Vol. 63, No. 8, December, 1986, p. 825.*

HENRY AND MUDGE: THE FIRST BOOK OF THEIR ADVENTURES; HENRY AND MUDGE IN PUDDLE TROUBLE: THE SECOND BOOK OF THEIR ADVENTURES (1987)

A pair of easy readers about a small boy and his very large dog, Mudge, who grows through seven collars before attaining his full 180 pounds.

The first book has the familiar plot: lonely boy gets dog, dog is lost, dog is found; but any dog- or boy-lover will chuckle over this pair. Rylant presents such realistic detail as Mudge drooling, loving dirty socks, and sleeping in Henry's bed in deceptively simple prose—easy to read but vividly evocative. The second book includes three events that take place in the spring: Mudge eats the first blossom, which Henry and his mother had carefully not picked, but is forgiven because it was ". . . just a thing to let grow. And if someone ate it, it was just a thing to let go"; Henry's father decides to jump into a glorious big puddle with Henry and Mudge instead of scolding them; and in the third story, Mudge adopts a litter of kittens. New illustrator [Suçie] Stevenson's . . . drawings are just right, capturing the affection and humor of the text.

Warm, loving, and gently philosophical, these stories about an only child and his closest companion deserve a place in every library collection.

A review of "Henry and Mudge" and "Henry and Mudge in Puddle Trouble," in Kirkus Reviews, *Vol. LV, No. 4, February 15, 1987, p. 300.*

These easy-to-read mini-stories offer a perfect medium for Rylant's style of poetic compression and repetition mixed with sensitive selection of detail. They also have some warmly funny, down-to-earth child appeal. . . . [This] duo has a dynamic future.

Betsy Hearne, in a review of "Henry and Mudge: The First Book of Their Adventures" and "Henry and Mudge in Puddle Trouble," in Bulletin of the Center for Children's Books, *Vol. 40, No. 8, April, 1987, p. 155.*

The galumphing Mudge of these stories has appeal, and there is a knowing warmth in his and Henry's attachment, but the relationship can get a bit precious; the friendship gets a tad *too* dependent ("when Henry was at school, Mudge just lay around and waited. Mudge never went for a walk without Henry again"). The big animal/small person contrast is the draw here. . . . ***Puddle Trouble*** works better than the first book in the series. The stories here . . . have some funny unexpected plot curves and give the pair a chance for some extended interaction. . . . The somewhat flaky emoting that marred parts of the first book is pretty much gone from this round, and it's a good choice for the easy reading shelf.

Nancy Palmer, in a review of "Henry and Mudge: The First Book of Their Adventures" and "Henry and Mudge in Puddle Trouble: The Second Book of

Their Adventures,'' in School Library Journal, *Vol. 33, No. 8, May, 1987, p. 120.*

A welcome debut by a couple of new charmers in the easy reader genre—Henry, a perky little boy, and Mudge, a three-foot tall mutt that looks as if he might be a cross between a Saint Bernard and a Great Dane. The books are lively, reassuring, and comical—just right for newly independent readers. . . . [In the first book, Mudge joins Henry's] family, outgrows seven collars while gaining his adult stature, and becomes Henry's friend and protector. When we join the two again in ***Puddle Trouble,*** the temptations of spring bring Mudge and Henry to odds; Mudge eats a forbidden wildflower, and Henry is mad. Rylant skillfully resolves the conflict with Mudge's woeful expression bringing Henry to realize that it wasn't his flower or anybody's flower: ''Just a thing to let grow. And if someone ate it, it was just a thing to let go.'' Two additional stories involve puddle splashing and kittens and are just as warm and wise as the first.

Elizabeth S. Watson, in a review of ''Henry and Mudge: The First Book of Their Adventures,'' and ''Henry and Mudge in Puddle Trouble: The Second Book of Their Adventures,'' in The Horn Book Magazine, *Vol. LXIII, No. 3, May-June, 1987, p. 339.*

***BIRTHDAY PRESENTS* (1987)**

Seven happy birthdays in the life of one small girl, from the real first one—the day she was born—to the times during her sixth year when she gives presents in return.

Presented as a family album with reminiscences addressed by the parents to the child, each year's mood is a loving celebration of the nuclear family of three, with parents baking a succession of fanciful cakes (star, clown, train, robot) and smiling through the inevitable mishaps—at one, ''you spit up''; at two, ''you were crabby . . . because you needed a nap''; at four, the new toy telephone had to be hidden because all the guests wanted it at once. And every year ''We told you we loved you.'' Then, ''Before you turned six, you gave . . . us for our birthdays flowers . . . You helped bake our birthday cakes . . . You told us you loved us''—thus the loving, giving family produces a loving, giving child. (True, but not always so simple.). . .

A book both parents and children will enjoy—and profit from—this would be fine for a picture-book hour or to share near a birthday. A good companion to Flack's *Ask Mr. Bear,* or to ''The End'' in Milne's *Now We Are Six.*

A review of ''Birthday Presents,'' in Kirkus Reviews, *Vol. LV, No. 13, July 1, 1987, p. 999.*

***CHILDREN OF CHRISTMAS: STORIES FOR THE SEASON* (1987)**

[Six Christmas stories] converge to portray the sensitive moods of togetherness, loss, belonging, privation. Garnet Ash has lived alone in an out-of-the-way house ever since his parents died; his solace is growing Christmas trees, and folks ride out to his place once a year. Francis spends part of Christmas Eve with her father in a diner where a stray cat is fed and sheltered. Philip's grandfather comes for the holiday and misses his dead wife; Philip tries to show him ''you've got us.'' Silvia walks the streets of New York, looking for Christmas in the eyes of strangers. Frankie waits yearly for the Christmas train to arrive in the mountains with a special package for him. And Mae, while hungry and sick, tries to find shelter and instead stumbles across a picture of a woman and a baby and stars in the sky. Rylant's Christmas is a sad and lonely one, but her ability to summon the joys of the season through her writing is extraordinary.

A review of ''Children of Christmas: Stories for the Season,'' in Publishers Weekly, *Vol. 231, No. 27, July 10, 1987, p. 70.*

In her second collection of short stories, Rylant gives her readers a series of vignettes, uneven in their effects but stylish in their execution.

Each of the six stories is a portrait drawn from the Christmas season. The first and fifth (**''Christmas Tree Man''** and **''Silver Packages''**) are descriptions of the role of Christmas in the lives of their subjects—one about a lonely man whose family consists of the Christmas trees he grows and the people who buy them; the other about a boy growing up in poor circumstances who spends each Christmas in expectation of the packages thrown off a train by a philanthropist grateful to his community. The others describe specific incidents occurring during the Christmas season. . . .

As a collection, this often slips into the sentimental, but it's always saved by Rylant's distinctive, sharply concrete prose, placing the reader directly into the experience of the protagonist. The final story, about a bag lady who creeps into a library and learns about wonder, is particularly hard-edged and fine. A high quality addition to any holiday collection.

A review of ''Children of Christmas: Stories for the Season,'' in Kirkus Reviews, *Vol. LV, No. 15, August 1, 1987, p. 1162.*

William Steig

1907-

American author/illustrator of picture books, fiction, and verse.

Considered among the most gifted contemporary creators of books for children, Steig is acclaimed for writing and illustrating joyful tales which explore significant themes in ways that children can understand. Recognized as an author/illustrator whose skills as a storyteller are comparable to his talents as an artist, Steig combines dexterity with words with an ability to capture emotion with precision and humor in his pictures. His gentle stories, which present Steig's view of the world as an exciting, pleasurable, and rewarding place, are hailed for their originality and insight. Commonly focusing on an innocent hero or heroine—generally an anthropomorphic animal—who struggles with and ultimately triumphs over adversity with the help of supportive family and friends and an occasional bit of magic, Steig's fantasies reflect his interest in such philosophical and metaphysical concerns as the nature of existence, self-discovery, and death, while entertaining young readers with magical transformations, ingenious escapes from disaster, touching reconciliations, and tongue-in-cheek humor. Steig structures his works as genial burlesques of folk and fairy tale conventions and such literary forms as the picaresque novel and the Robinsonnade. His prose style, which blends a formal, courtly tone with inventive wordplay, is often praised for its eloquence and for the timeless quality which it gives to the stories. As an illustrator, Steig favors watercolors and swift pen-and-ink lines, demonstrating particular talent in delineating subtle facial expressions and the seasonal changes of nature. Steig began his career as a cartoonist for the *New Yorker* and other periodicals, becoming well known for collections which caricature human neuroses and the world of childhood. In contrast to the often despairing quality of his adult works, Steig's books for children stress such attributes as resourcefulness, bravery, loyalty, self-respect, morality, and regard for fellow creatures, virtues which he presents without pedantry or apology. In addition to his fantasies, Steig has written and illustrated two books of word puzzles and a book of verse for children.

Critics praise Steig for the charm, freshness, and poignancy of his stories of requited love and poetic justice. He is also lauded for his command of language, the expressiveness of his drawings, the vigor of his narratives, the success of his characterizations, and the wry wit which pervades his works. Although reviewers note instances of plot repetition and an overly consistent use of the magical transformation device, most observers agree that Steig's uncommon linguistic and artistic skills have led to the creation of distinctive tales which possess both depth and accessibility.

Steig has received numerous awards for his books, chief among which are the following: *Sylvester and the Magic Pebble* won the Caldecott Medal and was a National Book Award finalist in 1970; it also won the Lewis Carroll Shelf Award in 1978. *Amos and Boris* was a National Book Award finalist in 1972. *Dominic* received the Christopher Award and was a National Book Award finalist in 1973. *Abel's Island* won the Lewis Carroll Shelf Award and was a Newbery Honor Book in 1977. *The Amazing Bone* was a Caldecott Honor Book and a *Boston Globe-Horn Book* Honor Book in 1977. *Caleb and Kate* was a National Book Award finalist in 1978. *Dr. De Soto* won the American Book Award in 1983, was both a *Boston Globe-Horn Book* Honor Book and a Newbery Honor Book in the same year, and an International Board on Books for Young People (IBBY) Honor Book in 1984. Steig was nominated for the Hans Christian Andersen Medal in 1988.

© Nancy Crampton

(See also *CLR*, Vol. 2; *Something about the Author*, Vol. 18; *Contemporary Authors*, Vols. 77-80; *Dictionary of Literary Biography*, Vol. 61: *American Writers for Children since 1960: Poets, Illustrators, and Nonfiction Authors;* and *Authors in the News*, Vol. 1.)

AUTHOR'S COMMENTARY

[*The following excerpt is taken from an interview by James E. Higgins.*]

[James E. Higgins] Bill, you began doing books for children in your later years; do you think you could have written them when you were younger?

[William Steig] No. I don't think so. I'll tell you how I know. In the 50's I made a doll called Pitiful Pearl, and my agent asked me to write a book to go with it. I wrote a terrible book.

So I guess I couldn't have done it. It was really a rotten piece of writing. I don't know how or why I've improved between that time and now. I think it wasn't a good book because I wasn't inspired to write it.

J.E.H. Do you think age had anything to do with it?

W. S. Yes. Perhaps I could have if I sat down to do it. I wrote some adult pieces when I was young that I'm pleased with. I guess I just didn't want to. But also that was a period of my life when I was involved with what's wrong with me. I was still trying to find out who I am. Now I'm not concerned with that—but I guess it's still coming out.

J.E.H. You once said about your cartoon work for adults, like ***Agony in the Kindergarten,*** that despair is a part of the human condition and that your business was to find out what went wrong.

W. S. Did I say that? Well, that has been my lifelong concern as a matter of fact. Why are we the way we are? But that's everybody's concern.

J.E.H. But your children's books seem to be the other side of the coin; they are all filled with hope.

W. S. Yes, somebody else has said that. It's not done intentionally—more unconsciously. Yes, I would never express despair to a kid. It doesn't make sense.

J.E.H. Did you consciously change your writing when you knew children were your audience?

W. S. When you talk to kids you don't talk down to them, but you don't talk to them in the same way that you do to adults. Once you get started you forget that you're writing for them—once you get "into the groove." You don't keep saying to yourself: "I'm doing this for kids."

J.E.H. Do you concretize your audience?

W. S. Probably you write for yourself as a child. I think so.

J.E.H. Do you ever try your manuscripts out on children?

W. S. No. You find the child in yourself and you write out of that. There is one book that didn't turn out right because I forgot I was writing for kids.

J.E.H. You often have your characters ask questions out loud.

W. S. Yes, I think kids do that. I remember the first time I thought about death. I wondered what it would be like. Do dogs go to the same heaven? What would it be like? Things like that.

J.E.H. Has that changed at all for you?

W.S. No. I haven't learned anything since then. I'm still asking the questions. This is one of our human preoccupations. I don't do it consciously. I don't say I'm going to discuss death. It's just something that happens in the story. It's the same sort of subject I would be concerned with if I were writing for adults, but in a different way.

J.E.H. Do you talk to yourself as your characters do?

W.S. Yes, the way everybody does, I suppose. In ***Amos and Boris,*** Amos wonders about where he will go if he drowns, and whether or not there will be other mice there. In ***Abel's Island,*** the mouse asks why God made owls and cats.

J.E.H. Do you believe in God?

W.S. Yes. The way everybody does.

J.E.H. In ***The Real Thief*** you have the king say: "I repent." I haven't seen that notion expressed in many children's books lately.

W.S. That was kind of deliberate. That book started out with a deliberate idea. I was thinking of the way kids sometimes are treated unjustly, and how they feel about it. So I decided to do a story in which someone was treated unjustly, and then I would have the father figure express repentance.

J.E.H. One of the things I most enjoyed in that book was that it demonstrated how easy it is for any of us to go down the path of sin—like Derek, the real thief.

W.S. Yes, that was fun. I enjoyed that. And I really felt that he was a good character. Although I've never been a criminal myself, I stole some sweet potatoes once.

J.E.H. Do you start your stories with a character?

W.S. First of all I decide it's time to write a story. Then I say what shall I draw this time? A pig or a mouse? Or, I did a pig last time; I'll make it a mouse this time. Then I start drawing. ***The Real Thief*** was the only time I really gave myself a theme. Otherwise I just rambled around and discovered for myself what would happen next.

Dominic started this way. I was going to do a trick book for my first publisher. I wanted to make a story wherein a dog started out on a journey, and he had to make a choice between three roads. I was going to follow him along each of the different roads, all of which would end up in the same place. So then I began. Let's see, I'll put in an alligator and I'll make the alligator a witch. I just wrote down a list of characters. And then I never got around to doing it.

And then later Di Capua (Steig's editor at Farrar, Straus & Giroux) said: "Why don't you do a long story for us?" And I said: "I can't do a long story." But anyway, I got out the outline I had for the three roads and the list of characters. And then I began to write.

J.E.H. Did you know where it was going to end up this time?

W.S. No. I thought I'd just have some fun. And then my wife, Jeanne, said: "Hey, this is good! You better keep it up." So I did, with her encouragement.

So when I wrote ***Dominic*** I didn't mean it to be about anything. I feel this way. I have a position—a point of view. But I don't have to think about it to express it. I can write about anything and my point of view will come out. So when I am at work my conscious intention is to tell a story to the reader. All this other stuff takes place automatically.

Dominic is my father by the way. I didn't model the character after him, but as I was writing I became aware of it. I didn't start out thinking about him, but after all I was living with him for a great many years. My father was a very positive man. I liked Dominic because he was a participant in life. I like that. That's one example.

With ***Roland,*** I had an image of a pig hanging on a string. I said that's a nice picture. There's always something that gets me started like that.

Now with ***Sylvester,*** I thought I'd do a book with magic in it because kids like magic.

J.E.H. Is that the only reason for the magic?

W.S. Well, mainly because I like it. I put the magic in a pebble. How does a kid get a pebble? Because he collects them. And then the rest just happens. People ask me how I thought of turning him into a rock. It's just the way you make up anything.

J.E.H. Is there a reason why you always use animals in your stories?

W.S. Yes, I can give you a few reasons. One reason is that they're much easier to draw. To repeat a face is very difficult, but with animals I have only one way to draw a pig or to draw a mouse. So there's no problem. But I think the best reason is that they're *not* animals. They're just people. I think using animals emphasizes the fact that the story is symbolic—about human behavior. And kids get the idea right away that this is not just a story, but that it's saying something about life on earth.

J.E.H. Are you still bothered at all by the controversy that arose about the police in ***Sylvester*** being pigs?

W.S. That was ridiculous! It's such a misunderstanding of my intentions. Why would I bother kids with that? They're sympathetic characters. I could have made them donkeys. They're pigs only because they are different animals in the story. I wouldn't bother kids with that stuff. Besides I would only be hurting myself. I lost a lot of sales because of that. I got a lot of hate mail with that book, but I got the other kind too. The hate mail was really strange. I got angry and started writing angry letters in return.

I think I said in my so-called speech at the Caldecott that in some way the theme related to the theme of *Pinocchio*. Pinocchio is like so many kids who feel locked up inside themselves—misunderstood and armored—trying to be human beings. In ***Sylvester*** the child is unlocked by the love of the parents, which brings him out of himself. These symbols aren't designed. They come out naturally. It works the same way with the reader, doesn't it? People worry about all sorts of things. My first publisher didn't want me to use the word "rotten." He said it reminded him of rotten eggs. So what! What's wrong with rotten eggs?

J.E.H. Did things that happened to you as a child reader have an effect on your work?

W.S. It had a deep effect. Sure. When you read a book don't you think that perhaps behind it all you may find a secret of life or the truth about something? I think the people of my period (Steig is 70) bring that quality to their reading. We grew up, I think, in a more hopeful time before the Second World War struck.

Yes, the kind of books I read have an influence on me now. I like the popular version of *Robinson Crusoe* when I was a kid. And we liked Altsheler. We thought he was the greatest. Just recently I was talking to my local doctor who also read Altsheler, and as we talked he began to remember the villain, Braxton Wyatt,—and how he hated that villain! All of the passion of fifty or so years ago came right up.

We also read *Robin Hood* by Howard Pyle and his *King Arthur* stories. I liked those. We used to go up into the park and beat each other with cudgels. Here were these kids in the Bronx yelling: "I'll smite thee, thou churlish knave." And we thought that was marvelous. We spoke Arthurian language.

J.E.H. You seem always to be having fun with words. What did the king in ***Roland*** ride in?

W.S. Oh, a palanquin. Yes, I looked that up myself. First I drew it and then I looked it up to find the word for it.

J.E.H. And in ***Farmer Palmer*** you used the word *wainwright*.

W.S. Yes, a wainwright is a wagon-wright. There's a wheelwright, a wainwright, and a cooper.

J.E.H. For a city kid, you knew that?

W.S. I do a lot of crossword puzzles.

My books are simple. I feel that if your language is simple in general, and then once in a while you use a phrase in which the readers won't know all the words, they can gloss over it or look it up without losing anything. But if you do it steadily, I think you will lose them.

J.E.H. How do you test the rightness of your language?

W.S. I like words. I think in a sense you hear them even if you don't actually read out loud. I think I can understand something much better by looking at it. But one just doesn't see a line. I think when you look at a line of words you hear them better. I love the physical act of scrivening—making up words. Typing to me is a drag.

J.E.H. Do you write with a pen or pencil?

W.S. Pen.

J.E.H. Do you rewrite much?

W.S. Sure.

J.E.H. How about pictures?

W.S. Pictures are easy. I know right away what I want. I draw quickly.

J.E.H. Do pictures come first or words?

W.S. Sometimes I'll have a series of images—characters. But I think it happens both ways. When I do cartoons, they both happen at the same time, because the idea and the execution are one. So there's no problem.

Cartooning is a much easier profession than writing for kids. After a story you get letters and invitations to attend seminars. As an author you're expected to get involved with selling. I just want to do the books. With cartoons you don't get that response. You may get a few fan letters a year, when someone gets excited about something you did. Nobody ever gives you any awards or asks you to come to Chicago to give a speech. It's a much easier life.

J.E.H. What effect did receiving the Caldecott and the other awards have on you?

W.S. I discovered I like to get medals. Now I think about it. It's something I used to despise, but when you get a medal it feels nice.

J.E.H. What's the hardest part of your work?

W.S. I hate to illustrate. To me it's a real chore. It's the only thing I do that I don't enjoy. I love to draw, and I love to write—but I hate to illustrate.

J.E.H. What's the difference between drawing and illustrating?

W.S. Well, when you draw, you draw anything that wants to come out, but when you illustrate you have to draw someone who has on a polka-dot dress. It has to be the same as the previous picture. You have to remember what it says in the story. It's not the way I want to draw at all.

From Dominic, *written and illustrated by William Steig. Farrar, Straus and Giroux, 1972. Copyright © 1972 by William Steig. All rights reserved. Reproduced by permission of Farrar, Straus and Giroux, Inc.*

J.E.H. Do you think that what you're doing is important?

W.S. I like to think that everything I do is art. But it's hard to tell about your own stuff. I know that the things other people—like Sendak and Zemach—are doing attracts me as art. And I'm doing the same thing that they're doing. (pp. 10-15)

William Steig, in a conversation with James E. Higgins, in Children's literature in education, *Vol. 9, No. 1, Spring, 1978, pp. 10-15.*

GENERAL COMMENTARY

ROBERT KRAUS

[*Kraus is the founder of Windmill Books as well as an author/ illustrator of children's books and a cartoonist for the* New Yorker. *He invited Steig to write his first children's book and later served as his publisher.*]

Ever since [Steig] joined *The New Yorker* he has been delighting Americans with his incisive comments on the human condition. His sympathetic, observant eye has served him well in the production of many adult books—among them ***Small Fry*** and the brilliant ***The Lonely Ones.*** And now, his candid, but uncensorious view has been turned to the service of a new medium for Bill—the writing and illustrating of children's books. Children respond immediately to this kindred soul, whose illustrations display an outlook which is as clear and as fresh as their own. . . .

Bill Steig's work is central to the man. From his myriad *New Yorker* covers and cartoons to his adult books of symbolic drawings and to—most recently—his books for children, his work displays a superb ease of execution and a grace that transcends mastery of technique. It is evident that, in part, Steig works for the sheer love of producing a beautiful drawing. You can see the playfulness, the ease, and the absolute control, and sense the understandably human delight in the virtuoso skill of his performance. Beyond that he has the ability to comprehend the hitherto unimaginable and to make it plain to the rest of us. (p. 362)

Robert Kraus, "William Steig," in The Horn Book Magazine, *Vol. XLVI, No. 4, August, 1970, pp. 361-63.*

KARLA KUSKIN

Since 1930, when his cartoons first began appearing in *Life, Judge* and *The New Yorker,* Steig has been chronicling our emotions; at times humorously, at times bitterly, with an intensity that reaches out from a page. He was always concerned with childhood, depicting its fears and unalloyed joys in the expressionistic drawings of ***Agony in the Kindergarten*** and earlier, in the careful washes of ***Dreams of Glory*** and ***Small Fry*** (the first to apply the latter term to children). However, it was not until 1968, after almost 40 years as one of our most original and influential cartoonists that Steig wrote ***Roland the Minstrel Pig,*** his first book for children.

Some people are self-consciously coy when they talk to children. Others talk down. Steig does neither. There is a sweet, good humor that runs through all his books. The author of **"People are no damn good,"** one of the most famous cartoons of the 1940's, doesn't complain to kids. Giving despair the slip he becomes a benign evangelist for justice, youth and joy. (p. 24)

He doesn't write like an artist. He writes like a writer, projecting his own voice, treasuring the rhythms of words and eccentric phrases. A courtly, almost old-fashioned tone parallels his gentle, poker-faced humor. Steig says he can change his mood by using a thinner pen point. Similarly he seems able to transform his adult version into one suitable for children as effortlessly as if he were trading a "grown-up" pen for a "young" one. ***Dominic,*** his first novel for children, is the story of a high-spirited hound living an artistic life of freedom and action, unencumbered by money. When Dominic inherits a fortune it is so heavy to lug around that he philanthropizes it away.

Softly stated but unswerving moral judgments often resound in the big-flowered hills of Steig country. There are good animals and bad animals. "One could not be happy among the good ones unless one fought the bad ones." Of course the good ones win. Loyal friendship is sure to be rewarded, optimistic energy will prevail and in ***Sylvester and the Magic Pebble*** Steig paeaned family devotion and also won the Cadecott Medal from the American Library Association.

The artlessness of the Steigian line lulls one into forgetting how well he draws. He transfers an uncanny talent for catching human expression to donkey, pigs, a mouse in a smoking jacket and, no matter how the donkey is dressed or how astonished a pig, each retains the essence of its animal self. It all looks perfectly natural and funny. Instead of applauding, we grin.

The uninhibited ego of childhood sings out of these books. In the ideal world Steig has designed for children if you are young and in love with life anything is possible. A mouse can rescue a whale (as in ***Amos and Boris***), a bone can speak Polish and Sylvester, the donkey, can turn into a stone and back into a donkey. "Magic is music for children" says the author, using it, like any good magician, to fulfill youthful fantasies.

Abel's Island, . . . is the most personal and reflective of Steig's storybooks. It is also his favorite. Instead of relying on dialogue and action, the customary building blocks of children's literature, it is primarily a descriptive monologue enhanced by wonderful washes that are threaded so expertly through the text it is hard, at times, to tell the pictures from the words. The ending is perfect: half-suspected, long-awaited, funny and touching. It brought tears to the eyes of a reader. Me. (pp. 24, 34)

"When I'm not working," says Steig, "I feel like I'm not living my right life." The work he likes best is "symbolic drawing" letting his pen and state of mind lead him into love songs, tantrums and laments as he discovers what is "underneath" reality. Relaxed, he works as he listens to music.

His children's books are done very differently. Feeling that it is time to write one he sits down to the task. Until the story is completed he visualizes it in his head. There is a fussiness to book illustration that thwarts his love of freedom. Costumes must match, backgrounds and characters need re-checking. Such details require his complete attention. The music stops. And yet the results have so much spontaneous grace that it is difficult to believe the artist did not dash them off while listening to "Cosi Fan Tutti" or one of Roland the minstrel pig's compositions for lute and tenor.

In 1937 a group of Steig cartoons ran in *The New Yorker* under the heading of "Woe." One of these shows a harassed fellow, head in hands, leaning on a desk, confronting his typewriter. The title is **"Creative Agony."** In 1976 William Steig is still leaning on that desk, still working very hard and making it look very easy as he fills blank sheets with merry pictorial leaps and gracious bends of prose. It's a neat trick turning creative agony into art but the Amazing Steig knows how to do it. (pp. 34, 36)

Karla Kuskin ". . . and William Steig," in The New York Times Book Review, *November 14, 1976, pp. 24, 34, 36.*

JOHN DONOVAN

William Steig has a body of work in children's books and as it seems . . . we are to continue to have work from him, it is instructive to look back over those books he has already given us. (p. 111)

C D B! is a kind of code book, clever in its way, that requires readers to articulate aloud letters or numbers in order to understand the captions on a series of cartoons or situations. The title, with its simple illustration, translates to "See the Bee". While there is not much in ***C D B!*** to suggest the riches that were to follow, some of the codes are accompanied by such antic drawings that they continue to give pleasure. L-C S N X-T-C shows a distant ancestor of Pearl, the pig in ***The Amazing Bone.***

Sylvester and the Magic Pebble . . . is the book that introduces Steig's substantial work for children. His growth after ***Sylvester*** has been astonishing: that first, satisfying book was followed by six more titles, and now . . . by ***Caleb and Kate.*** Each book represents a step forward, if along varied roads. One of the roads relates to his art work; another to storytelling; another to the development of characters; yet another to not wordplay, but word savouring; and a final road that suggests a wholeness and freedom in his work that one infrequently sees in books and that make Steig's work distinctive. As each of these facets of his talents has developed, they have engaged each other so that, now, it is possible beforehand to know that a new Steig book will be a harmonious whole. Steig's plots are alike. ***Sylvester*** has the basic line. An ingenuous creature, both trusting and hopeful, has a misadventure that causes him (and the reader) great anxiety. As this creature's plight becomes more and more desperate, there seems to be no way for him to extricate himself from the frightening situation and, stoically, he not only accepts it but adjusts to it with a kind of bittersweet, humorous resignation. Lo! the seemingly impossible happens and everything comes out all right in the end, where there is customarily a lot of kissing, hugging and affection, or, as in ***Amos & Boris,*** that glorious book, a moving comment on human (animal) relations: "They knew they might never meet again. They knew they would never forget each other."

In bare outline, the plot may appear both simple-minded and trite. With Steig, however, these tales of survival, friendship and love are suffused with such affection—for both the creatures involved and for the reader—that he seems to have discovered, not invented, the stories. This is also true of his pictures. Apparently simple and straightforward, as one looks again and again at his work for children, at least, one appreciates the complexities that have made it possible for him to make these lines. They are direct. They are honest. They tell the reader a story.

There is an interesting element in Steig's children's books that encourages Bettelheimism, i.e., the interpretation of children's literature within a sexual, Freudian framework. This element makes Steig's work all the more fascinating. Without losing their appeal for children, his books appeal to adults for reasons that few would comprehend. For example, what, after all, is "the amazing bone"? A bone? Hardly. And we won't sully these pages with the answer. And as for ***Amos & Boris,*** isn't it really a fantasy about an idealized homosexual relationship? Within the Bettelheim school of criticism, the only thing missing in Steig is that he is—fortunately for us—alive.

It is Steig's strength that he does not illustrate a text. In his longer books, ***Abel's Island,*** for example, the pictures crop up here and there throughout the book and are so fully integrated with the words that it is possible, reflecting on the book long after reading it, not to be able to recollect which scenes were, indeed, read and which were seen. In ***Abel's Island,*** the book's last line—surely a classic, given Abel's adventures—"I've brought you back your scarf," is not the end of the book at all. The story continues in four pictures that take us to the real end. And the pictures are not superfluous; they seem inevitable and necessary. This inevitability of Steig's pictures is also a feature of those books of his—***The Amazing Bone,*** etc.—that are clearly identifiable as picture books. His work, more ebullient yearly, suggests that he is one of a handful of Americans whose contribution to children's books is lasting. (pp. 111-13)

John Donovan, "American Dispatch," in Signal, *No. 24, September, 1977, pp. 111-16.*

GERALDINE DeLUCA AND RONI NATOV

[*The following excerpt is taken from an interview by Geraldine DeLuca and Ron Natov with George Woods, an author of young adult novels who at the time of this conversation was the children's book editor of the* New York Times Book Review.]

I think the three finest people writing today are William Steig, Natalie Babbitt, and Mollie Hunter. All three, come to think of it, have done fantasy. There are others of course. Steig, I think has inherited the mantle of E. B. White: his erudition, his dexterity, his easy grace. Steig gives children food for thought. In the book ***Amos and Boris,*** which is a picture book for the five to nine group, a mouse rolls off the back of a little boat—he's been lying on the fantail of the ship, staring at the stars, thinking about life out there—and falls into the water. And he thinks, "Am I going to die? I wonder what it's like to die? If I die, will I go to heaven? I wonder if there will be other mice in heaven?" These are profound thoughts to offer to a child, and Steig does so in a way that's not didactic; it's not an assault, and it's not incomprehensible. He's just planting tiny seeds.

Children's librarians were suspicious of Steig when he first began publishing because he was an adult cartoonist. Everyone was into children's books. Publishers were expanding, new people were going into it, conglomerates were forming, radio and television stations were buying up publishing—the sky was the limit. And a lot of juvenile editors were going to famous people and asking them to write children's books. Publishers said, "You can do it," or "Just do it with your left hand." So a lot of people did it that way. The name sold the book. Every *New Yorker* cartoonist, virtually, has done a children's book. So there was a lot of resentment among the people more traditionally connected to the field. They felt, here's another of those smart, sophisticated people come to the children's book world to skim the commercial cream off the top. They're in and out of the field. And Steig was thought to be one of them.

The first book that he did was called ***Roland the Minstrel Pig*** and it's almost as good as ***Sylvester and the Magic Pebble.*** But it took ***Sylvester*** and it took a lot of work and support before people began to recognize that Steig's work was good, that it's almost always tongue-in-cheek, that it's colorful, charming, that it has emotion, and that children respond to it. This year (1977), I think he got a bad deal from the Newbery-Caldecott people. ***The Amazing Bone*** is a superb book. (pp. 8-9)

Geraldine DeLuca and Roni Natov, "The State of the Field in Contemporary Children's Fantasy: An Interview with George Woods," in The Lion and the Unicorn, *Vol. 1, No. 2, Fall, 1977, pp. 4-15.*

JAMES E. HIGGINS

For me, reading a new Steig book is like watching Willie Mays play center field. It's a joy—a totally singular experience—something to sing about. In fact it was Steig's first fans, young children, who initially put me onto him, so that my primary intention in writing this piece is to share my good luck with other adults. If what follows wins for Steig some new devotees, I am content. For . . . Steig is a writer of children's books whose work reaches beyond the specific confines of a child audience.

It all began for me when I received a prepublication copy of ***Sylvester and the Magic Pebble.*** . . . I picked it up and read it silently. Though I cannot recall my exact impression, I do remember reading it through again, this time aloud. I was pleased by it. I'm not sure what it was that pleased me, but the words seemed right—whatever that means. The next evening I tried it out on my youngest son, who was six or seven at the time, and he too gave it an "A" rating. This caused me to inspect it a bit more closely to see if I could identify the specific qualities of the story which merited our mutual high regard.

I do think that I was successful in uncovering, for myself at least, several elements of Steig's style that went into making ***Sylvester*** a first-rate book. However, the application of technical analysis takes one only so far in the area of appreciation. At best it only gives hints as to what gives the work its special appeal, which even the author never truly understands. The distinction between a first-rate story and a great one is not so much a matter of quality, but rather the presence in the latter of unique elements that defy analysis. Great works are readily acknowledged, but seldom defined.

A few days later I discovered that ***Sylvester*** was indeed a great picture book, and I also think I discovered why it was so. I took it to a school and read it to several classes of kindergarten children, even though I felt it was probably better suited for a slightly older audience.

To briefly recap the story: Sylvester Duncan is a child donkey who lives with his mother and father at Acorn Road in Oatsdale, and his hobby is collecting pebbles of unusual shape and color. One day, as Steig tells us, Sylvester finds a pebble that is "flaming red, shiny and perfectly round like a marble." He accidentally discovers that anyone who is touching the pebble may have any wish granted that he desires. As he is hurrying home to amaze his parents with his new-found prize, Sylvester is confronted by a mean, hungry lion that suddenly arises from the tall grass on Strawberry Hill. The young donkey becomes so frightened that he forgets the many possible wishes he might make to help him escape his predicament, and he says: "I wish I were a rock."

The reader, or story listener, turns the page to an expansive, two-paged scene of a star-filled night, with the following text:

> And there was Sylvester, a rock on Strawberry Hill, with the magic pebble lying right beside him on the ground, and he was unable to pick it up. "Oh, how I wish I were myself again," he thought, but nothing happened. He had to be touching the pebble to make the magic work, but there was nothing he could to about it.
>
> His thoughts began to race like mad. He was scared and worried. Being helpless, he felt hopeless. He imagined all the possibilities, and eventually he realized that his only chance of becoming himself again was for someone to find the red pebble and to wish that the rock next to it would be a donkey. Someone would surely find the red pebble—it was so bright and shiny—but what on earth would make them wish that a rock were a donkey? The chance was one in a billion at best.
>
> Sylvester fell asleep. What else could he do? Night came with many stars.

Now, by the time I shared the story with those kindergarteners, I practically knew the words from memory, so that I was able to observe the audience closely during the reading. Their comprehension was indeed written all over their faces. They were intensely attending to the story, and it was also evident that they were attending to weighty matters—as St. Exupery would put it ". . . to matters of consequence." They were (their faces were telling me) wrestling with the overwhelming and mysterious concept of eternity. What it would be like to be a rock forever. What it was like to be caught in a situation in which the odds were stacked one billion to one against you. Instantaneously I was pulled back into my own childhood and my own wrestlings with the incomprehensible idea of foreverness. I felt again the impact of the insurmountable odds that seemed to be stacked against my ever being able to enjoy heavenly bliss, but rather the very good odds that I would end up forever in you-know-where.

Through the faces of those children I was able to share in the powerful mythopoeic quality of ***Sylvester.*** They had immediately uncovered the secret essence of the story that is so often missed by the sophisticated adult. From that moment on my reading of ***Sylvester*** was improved; my enjoyment and appreciation was increased. The intenseness and reverence (I can find no better word to describe it) with which those children attended to the story, permitted me to get a glimpse of the basic truth of the tale.

To be sure, this sort of revelation had happened to me before in the thousands of book sharings I've had with children, in the readings of *Ellen Tebbits* and *Charlotte's Web,* to name but two; however, it is nonetheless equally surprising each time it happens. ***Sylvester and the Magic Pebble*** is, as the trite phrase goes, a book on many levels, but the most meaningful level is best recognized by the innocent and the uninitiated, even though they are incapable of verbalizing their response. (pp. 3-5)

Herein lies the basic secret of William Steig's attraction for many young readers, both in his picture books and in his longer works, such as ***Dominic*** and ***Abel's Island.*** When his colleague, Robert Kraus, suggested to Steig that he might join the growing number of veteran illustrators and cartoonists who were writing their own books for the burgeoning children's market, rather than familiarize himself with the work of currently successful writers, Steig chose to sit down and write out of whatever form and substance of story he already possessed, but had never tapped. The result is that he has created stories that have much in common with the tales out of his own childhood. A story like ***The Real Thief*** has a pace and a vernacular that is tuned into and pleasing to the child of the 70's, yet at the same time it has a strong link to the romance stories of past generations.

Steig's fiction for children has naturally been classified as animal fancy, but that is an inadequate description of his narrative signature. To the question: "Why talking animals?"—Steig answers: "I think using animals emphasizes the fact that the story is symbolical—about human behavior. And kids get the idea right away that this is not just a story, but that it's saying something about life on earth" [see Author's Commentary].

His emphasis that his animal characters are symbolic representations should not be interpreted to mean that Steig is a preacher in storyteller's garb, but rather that he had always been the kind of reader who approached stories with the expectation that he would be surprised by some secret revelation; that he would uncover something about life that was already in his experience, but about which he was still unaware. So when he became an author, it was only natural that he would write to please that kind of reader.

All of Steig's work takes an ethical stance without being ponderous or pedantic. He insists that he has always been more interested in universal human problems rather than in current issues. His cartoon work for adults is devastating in its satirical thrust. . . . [***Agony in the Kindergarten***] is penetratingly and sometimes painfully realistic in its honesty.

When he turns to writing for children, Steig is no less honest in his approach. He turns to fancy and romance not to escape reality, but because, for him, it is the most suitable form for expressing those things which he wishes to share with children. As he says: "My lifelong concern has been why are we the way we are." In his work for adults he focuses on how we humans mess up a world that was obviously meant to be a paradise. In his works for children he looks on the other side of the coin; he sets his lens to capture that which is good in life. He shares with children what can happen to humans when we are at our best. In each case he is insightfully perceptive in his art.

As my friend Glenna Davis Sloane points out, Steig's ***Dominic*** is not only a fanciful tale about a gregarious mutt, but it also contains all of the conventions of romance that one finds in myths and legends. The hero is noble, right-thinking, courteous, chivalrous, generous, imaginative, brave and adventurous; all that a romance hero should be. The story is one of adventure, danger, struggle, escape, disaster, and unusual success; all elements common to the romance. All of the conventions of romance are here: touches of sentiment and touches of extravagance, as well as all the rest.

In ***Abel's Island,*** a more recent example, Steig selects a subject that is seldom dealt with in children's literature—that of conjugal love. I'm fairly sure that the love story of Abel and his bride Amanda will not turn up on many sex education supplementary reading lists, and yet I can find no book that can match this one in sharing with children what the world is like for two people in love. The goodness and ecstasy of the first year of married life to be found in ***Abel's Island*** is not moralistic, but rather idyllic in tone and mood. (pp. 5-7)

Abel and Amanda are mice, and yet any grownup who has been in love will recognize the truth and poignancy of Steig's depiction of that time in life, even though later vagaries of life, as described by Steig in his satirical works for adults, may have diminished or extinguished the pleasures of the moment or the ecstatic hopes for the future. Steig agrees with those readers who have recognized that his books for children are filled with hope. He says: "It's not done intentionally—more unconsciously."

While attempting to retrieve Amanda's scarf which is blown away during a hurricane, Abel is also swept away, and he finds himself the next day stranded on a deserted island. The rest of the story is a chronicle of survival, but through it all the love story continues and remains central to the theme. (p. 7)

Also mixed with Abel's adventure of physical survival is his cosmic struggle to find out who he is and what life is all about. His solitary musings, like those of Crusoe and the Indian girl Karana on the Island of Blue Dolphins, give ***Abel's Island*** a quality that is both transcendent and believable. In almost every one of his books Steig effectively uses the soliloquy, because his characters, like the everyday people they represent, are forever wondering about things.

> Was it just an accident that he was here on this uninhabited island? Abel began to wonder. Was

> he being singled out for some reason; was he being tested? If so, why? Didn't it prove his worth that such a one as Amanda loved him?
>
> Did it? Why *did* Amanda love him? He wasn't all that handsome, was he? And he had no particular accomplishments. What sort of mouse was he?

Steig's characters in his children's books also possess the instinctive wisdom of the traditional peasant hero in folk literature. When the realistic pessimism of everyday living overtakes him, and a reasonable inventory of his situation indicates that his plight is hopeless, and melancholia is on the verge of taking over, Abel intuitively takes a gigantic step into the cosmic world of belief.

> . . . He felt the tree knew his feelings, though no words could pass between them.
>
> He believed in his "visits" with Amanda; he had his birch, and his star, and the conviction grew in him that the earth and the sky knew he was there and also felt friendly; so he was not really alone, and not really entirely lonely. At times he'd be overcome by sudden ecstasy and prance about on high rocks, or skip along the limbs of trees, shouting meaningless syllables. He was, after all, in the prime of life.

I strongly surmise that at some time in his own life the author, like most of us, perhaps forgot about this simple technique of psycho-survival used by Abel, which not only pre-dates Freud, but pre-dates history. I also suspect that it was the new audience of children with whom Steig was sharing his stories that brought this way of dealing with reality to the surface. Of one thing we can be sure—Steig did *believe* at the time of the writing, else he would not have written it.

William Steig has the unusual childlike capacity to present incidents of wonder and marvel as if they are but everyday occurrences. He writes not out of a remembrance of childhood, but out of the essence of childhood which no adult can afford to give up or to deny. He reminds us once more that any tale of romance worthy of today's children will be more than a sentimental journey; rather it will be more like the epic quest or the symbolic fairy tale. His stories for children are more than *made-up;* they are truly *make-believe*. Were it not for him, and some others like him, I'm afraid the great romantic tradition in children's literature, so strongly founded by Robert Louis Stevenson a hundred years ago, with an emphasis on narrative and a love for lovely words, would have by now passed from the scene. (pp. 9-10)

James E. Higgins, "William Steig: Champion for Romance," in Children's literature in education, *Vol. 9, No. 1, Spring, 1978, pp. 3-10.*

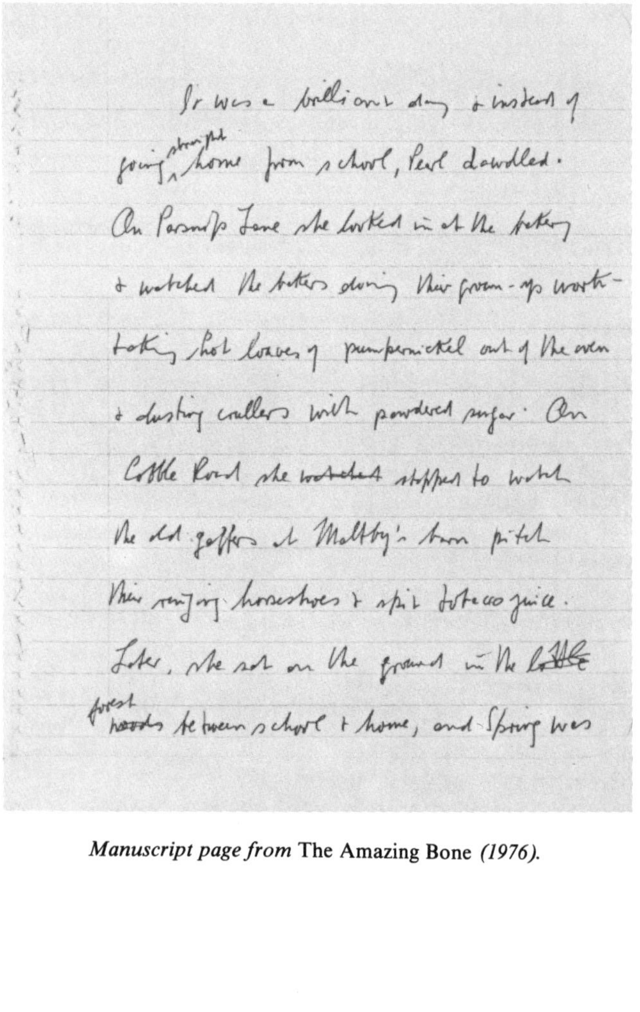
It was a brilliant day & instead of going straight home from school, Pearl dawdled. On Parsnip Lane she looked in at the bakery & watched the bakers doing their grown-up work— taking hot loaves of pumpernickel out of the oven & dusting crullers with powdered sugar. On Cobble Road she ~~watched~~ stopped to watch the old gaffers at Maltby's barn pitch their ringing horseshoes & spit tobacco juice. Later, she sat on the ground in the ~~little~~ forest ~~woods~~ between school & home, and Spring was

Manuscript page from The Amazing Bone *(1976).*

BARBARA BOTTNER

William Steig, the well known *New Yorker* cartoonist, turned to children's books in his seventh decade and brought to his second career a rich and poetic legacy that was already flourishing in his first. What he also brought with him, was a range of themes and concerns that did not suffer diminishing, when they were addressed to a younger, less sophisticated audience. Whereas many picture books concern themselves with the everyday affairs of having a bad day, or the fears of nighttime, or sibling jealousies (and these are just concerns too), Steig paints with a large canvas, no smaller than the universe itself. He travels happily between the cosmic and the mundane, peoples his world with identifiable, sympathetic, sometimes villainous sorts, giving us characters we can easily care about. He embroiders unexpected tales full of magic, searching, death, and love of life; so that thematically his work is classic in scope, yet absolutely accessible in nature.

This happy state of affairs exists no doubt partly because, in one sense, Steig is not writing for children at all. "You probably write for yourself as a child," he has said. The ease with which he does this may itself come from his experience in working for an adult audience. When a writer addresses other adults he is at eye level with his readers, and can usually use contemporary language. But in writing for children, he has to wander through his childhood. He must be willing to recreate who he was and what concerned, feared, or delighted him, and then find a syntax that will invite his readers in. These two different worlds create a duality that some writers span with grace, even genius. But others fail to remember or reinhabit those distant, mistier times of childhood. And thus we get books that make the whole field seem like a secondary art form. This is not true of Steig's books. It is possible, his books remind us, to reach out distantly, deeply and profoundly. It is possible to entertain, ponder the universal order, shiver, long for a friend, wonder what death is, all in as little as thirty-two pages, and satisfy us on all these fronts.

When Steig creates a cartoon, "the idea and the drawing are one . . . you draw what wants to come out." For his children's books, he is often propelled by the visual image. A picture comes to him, and the story grows from that visual moment. Sometimes he gives himself a theme, as in the case of ***The***

Real Thief, where he started with the idea of a child suffering from an injustice. However, he cautions, "it's only when you're consciously aware of what you're doing in a book, that you're in trouble." So it seems that by drawing or picturing something first, Steig reacts to his own unconscious images. He sees them, they stir him in some way, and from them the story comes. By not working from the outset with the idea of accomplishing some "lesson" or theme, but rather from exploring some idea or moment, Steig's stories become freewheeling, liberated from contrived logic, and thus take many unexpected turns.

He uses the unexpected in several ways. One is purely as a plot device. With an almost slapstick sense of timing, Amos, the brave and determined mouse of ***Amos and Boris,*** languishing in a sense of oneness with the universe, is dumped right into the huge ocean. . . . It is just this potentially disastrous event that enables Amos to have his adventure, and make the friendship of his life.

In ***Abel's Island*** the rather foppish, spoiled and indulgent hero, impulsively leaves the shelter of a cave during a "storm that has lost its mind completely," to dash after his wife's gauze scarf. Abel is then not seen again for an entire year, a year that enables him to become a rather mighty mouse. Then, again, in ***Father Palmer's Wagon Ride,*** an enjoyable trip to town almost ends in devastation due to several misfortunes fat Father Palmer and his horse encounter on their way home. And in ***Caleb and Kate,*** Caleb's little snooze in the forest allows Yedida, the witch, to turn up and transform Caleb into a dog.

These plot devices work because Steig so securely grabs our hand at the start of the journey, that should he decide to make a wild turn, a zigzag, or even a leap, his grip on us doesn't falter. He wields us 'round the bend into an entirely new universe, and there we are, maybe just a paragraph or a page later, pondering a whole new set of circumstances. We only have time to catch our breath and tuck in our shirts, before we are worrying with the protagonist about how to cope with the new terrain.

But his use of the unexpected is akin to another motif many of his books have in common, and one that many of his adult drawings dote on, that is the theme of transformation. In his adult collection, ***Male/Female,*** we have shrewish wives railing at their husbands, who have been reduced to the size of small dogs. . . . Indeed, many precursors of Caleb, men tragically transformed into all manner of beasts, can be found in these pages. And maybe a seed or two for ***Sylvester and the Magic Pebble,*** as well. Sylvester, in possession of a magic pebble, panics at the sight of a lion, and recklessly wishes he were a rock. His wish obtained, he spends the rest of the book "hopeless and unhappy", until fate, magic and of course love, release him. (pp. 4-6)

Steig waves his wand (or rather dips his pen), and there is magic. The magic of his adult work is the magic of an absurd glimpse, a crazy insight into gestures and feelings that expose his characters at their most lunatic but lovable moments. In one cartoon, the formally posed body of a man and the demure body of a woman standby while their faces passionately kiss, totally disconnected, a few feet above them both. Steig uses such visual metaphors to encourage us to feel the extreme of situations, for it is only in the extreme that recognition takes place. Through his bizarre exaggerations, the truth hits us like a cold wet rag between the eyes. It is this stretching of reality that makes the spirit of his work so easily grasped. His visual sense of "what if" is the same "what if" of much literature for children, *Alice in Wonderland* to *Stuart Little*. But Steig's "what if's" are not set forth as the very premise to his books; they tend to occur once the story is on its way. Thus his twists and turns have a "fasten-your-seatbelt" kind of excitement.

Yet there is never the sense of using magic gratuitously, or for excitement alone. The invention sits at the center of the tale and enables us to explore familiar territory in a refreshing way. In ***Caleb and Kate,*** might not some of the "odious insults" that Kate utters during the crazy quarrel where Caleb "slammed out of the house hating his wife from top to bottom," be that he would turn into a dog? Couldn't Yedida, the witch, be the very witch of a wife Caleb just left? And couldn't the chatty bone in ***The Amazing Bone,*** also just be the projection of Pearl's magnificent imagination and creativity? Although at first the magic may seem like inventive silliness, purely conjured up for delight, it actually is profoundly related to the tale that Steig unfolds. So although Steig refuses any "real" boundaries to his creations, and thoroughly enjoys making the impossible possible, he does so in a way that is actually embedded in his own organic reality. The feelings in his books, the concerns of his characters, their challenges and worries are as real as "real" can be.

Very often Steig gives us a Homeric journey as the frame for his story. Many of his books involve journeys either chosen or dictated by fate. Dominic, of ***Dominic,*** sets off on his adventure rather jubilantly, as does Amos, who is "full of wonder, full of enterprise, and full of love for life." Father Palmer has to make a journey home, as does Pearl, in ***The Amazing Bone,*** and Abel is forced into a journey, even though it is circumscribed by the island he is abandoned on. The real thief, Derek, forces innocent Gawain, the goose, on an exiled journey full of hurt and isolation, in ***The Real Thief.*** And so, as on many journeys, the hero shifts from soaring feelings of freedom and discovery, to dire, horrible problems, including the threat of death itself.

Here we come to one of the classic concerns of literature, the tension between love of life, and fear of death. Steig doesn't hesitate to throw many of his heroes into the ultimate sphere. On the one hand, many of them display rhapsodic love of life. From Pearl, in the forest: "I love everything," to Dominic: "What a wonderful world. . . . How perfect." Even Caleb, poor unwilling dog that he is, romps in the summer to discover that "being a dog among dogs could be joyous sport." Even in ***The Real Thief*** the fugitive, Gawain, has his moment: "The lake was beautiful, serenely beautiful. The forest was beautiful, greenly beautiful. Lake and forest, the whole shimmering world was painfully beautiful." In Steig's adult cartoons, his creatures also express an almost absurd exuberance for being alive. Lovers frolic in the fields, sing to the moon, or devour each other in lumpish forms of lovemaking. But it is in the midsts of such moments of wanton abandonment that the threats of separation, loneliness, loss, or even death become possibilities too. Sometimes, in the life/death tug of war, Steig intermingles these other themes as well.

Abel's predicament, for instance, includes several morbid dreads come true. Completely abandoned on an island, he longs for his wife, Amanda. He even takes to sending her "mind messages," which he convinces himself she receives. His predicament at times makes him melancholic. He takes to making artistic statues of all his beloved family to dull the pain of separation. But along with the inner threat of trying to preserve a sense of well-being and hope under these circumstances is the real physical threat of the terrible owl who stalks him with proprietary zeal. The threat of death is with Abel for much of his stay on the island. But Steig's way of treating death is rather matter of fact; his heroes might wonder about it, but they never give in to panic or sweeping dread.

> What should he do? Could he possibly kill the obnoxious creature while it slept, so it would die as if in a dream? How? With a rock on the end of a rope? With fire? With a burning javelin of wood?
>
> . . . Was an owl really a bird? What an odd, unheavenly bird. . . . Why did God make owls, snakes, cats, foxes, fleas, and other such loathsome abominable creatures? He felt there had to be a reason.

These are rather calm musings for one whose fate might be sealed by such an aggressive creature. Even Amos, adrift in the ocean, his boat forever lost, philosophically considers his situation: "He began to wonder what it would be like to drown. Would it take very long? Would it feel just awful? Would his soul go to heaven? Would there be other mice there?" As poetic as these musings might be, his thinking is as organized as a church shopping list. And when Pearl in ***The Amazing Bone*** is faced with extinction, she whispers to the bone, "I'm only just beginning to live. I don't want it to end." Later when she hears the sounds of the wood on the stove, and smells the vinegar and oil that is going to dress the salad meant to accompany the main dish, which will be Pearl herself, all she comes up with is a mild, "I hope it won't take too long."

For children separation itself is a kind of death. They often experience separations as devastating mini-deaths, while adults suffer from "separation anxiety." In ***The Real Thief,*** Gawain, outcast, rejected, falsely accused, is thrust into exile, and misunderstood by all those he loved and trusted, and who loved and trusted him. What worse fate could befall a child? A condemned innocent, it looks like he will live out his days to be banned forever. And Sylvester, the donkey cum rock, has some grim moments. "He felt he would be a rock forever and he tried to get used to it." Then,

> Mrs. Duncan sat down on the rock. The warmth of his own mother sitting on him woke Sylvester up from his deep winter sleep. He wanted to shout, Mother! Father! It's me, Sylvester, I'm right Here! But he couldn't talk. He had no voice. He was stone-dumb.

The fear of being invisible, or out of reach, or rendered mute, when so near one's beloved parents, has got to be a tormenting one for a child, an unbearable state, almost as bad as death itself. And in ***Caleb and Kate,*** Caleb as a dog, "got into his rightful place beside Kate, snuggled against her dear body, kissed her sweet neck as he'd always done, and sighed out his sorrows. She welcomed the dog's warmth. With him there, she felt less bereft." Here is another fearful state of affairs. To be punished so as to be made unrecognizable, perhaps just for an evil thought or two—what child has not dreaded this fate? The distortion of guilt that a young person might experience is close to Caleb's fate. He is near his beloved, but unable to be revealed. This is a kind of death too.

But we do not suffer in vain, Steig tells us, thus hitting upon another great literary theme. Facing hardship, we may grow, even discover strengths we did not know we owned. We may learn to appreciate life, our loved ones, even more. We may even find that, if we are open enough to life, imaginative enough, brave enough, we come out quite improved by the whole unpredictable, messy, complicated situation. In a sense, Steig has developed his own style of parable, a very life-giving one at that. As the loquacious bone advises Pearl's parents, "you have an exceptional daughter." We all have it in us to be exceptional if we just face life's difficulties as enthusiastically as Steig's heroes and heroines do. But Steig's protagonists are not only possessed by action, as enthusiastic as they may sometimes be. They can all enjoy a good snooze, a summer day, a pleasant voyage, an hour of enchantment, a bit of music, rest or peace, whenever it happens along. Moments after Dominic, in ***Dominic,*** is imperiled by the Doomsday gang, but then rescued by the trees in the forest, he is ready to join in a lyrical round of music-making in an enchanted garden;

> He touched other flowers and there was orchestration—strings, soft brasses, reeds, light percussion. Dominic felt called upon to join in. Under the golden moon he played his golden piccolo, and he and the flowers understood one another and rose to greater and greater heights of loveliness . . . Dominic did not know how long he played. And when the music was over, there was no stopping him; he had to sit down on his haunches and yield to some deeply felt howling not harsh, pent-up howls this time, but soft yodeling ululations, expressive of feelings that affirmed his presence in an ancient yet young universe.

This sense of the world as pleasureful also permeates Steig's adult cartoons; creatures doze, gaze, eat, paint, make music, wonder, and have a sublime sense of Sunday. So, it comes as no surprise that of all the incomprehensibly lavish array of jewels and wealth that Dominic inherits from Mr. Badger, his favorite possession is the solid gold piccolo. What are diamonds, emeralds, rubies to one who can sing a sweet hymn to life? (pp. 6-15)

Barbara Bottner, "William Steig: The Two Legacies," in The Lion and the Unicorn, *Vol. 2, No. 1, Spring, 1978, pp. 4-16.*

WALTER LORRAINE

There are other story-tellers, but of them all William Steig could be the best illustrator working today. His warmly expressive pig in ***The Amazing Bone*** clearly shows his ability to convey the most subtle nuances of emotion. Most readers of ***Sylvester and the Magic Pebble*** are so caught up in the dilemma of Sylvester that they would never think of separating words and pictures for critical discussion. The story is the thing. A reading of ***Abel's Island*** readily shows that Steig can tell a story with words as well as with pictures. Apparently he makes little separation between the two and though the medium may be different, his intent remains the same. He can communicate equally well with but a few strokes of a pen in black-and-white or by full color paintings. His work has to be considered a true art of illustration. (p. 18)

Walter Lorraine, "Book Illustration: The State of the Art," in Illustrators of Children's Books: 1967-1976, *Lee Kingman, Grace Allen Hogarth, Harriet Quimby, eds., The Horn Book, Inc., 1978, pp. 2-19.*

ANITA MOSS

Author, cartoonist, artist, and sculptor, William Steig has explained why he uses animal characters: "I think using animals emphasizes the fact that the story is symbolical—about human behavior. And kids get the idea right away that this is not just a story, but that it's a way of saying something about life on earth" [see Author's Commentary]. Readers of Steig's fantasies are not surprised to learn that as a child he was deeply impressed by *Grimms' Fairy Tales,* "Hansel and Gretel," Howard Pyle's *King Arthur* and *Robin Hood,* and especially *Pinocchio*. His two longer novels for children, ***Dominic*** and ***Abel's Island,*** reflect these traditions and have been variously described by critics and reviewers as romances, adventure stories, picaresque journeys, and, in the case of ***Abel's Island,*** a Robinsonnade. Indeed, ***Dominic*** and ***Abel's Island*** resemble all of these forms. There is in western literature a long and prestigious tradition of the quest romance which is accented by pastoral interludes; one thinks, for example, of the long pastoral interludes in *Don Quixote* and the world of the shepherds in Book VI of Spenser's *The Faerie Queene*. Blue Calhoun has identified a similar juxtaposition of quest romance and pastoral in William Morris's poem *The Earthly Paradise,* in which the Wanderer's open-ended heroic quest is interrupted by the enclosed structures of idyllic frames, a dialectical balance which Calhoun calls the "mood of energy" and the "mood of idleness." Such a dialectical balance allows the hero to assert his values through the quest and, at the same time, to affirm the value of art and civilization in the garden. True heroes, then, protect community and its values. They are courageous, loyal, resourceful, intelligent, and selfless. Like Virgil's Aeneas, the hero's efforts are devoted to founding and to protecting home and civilization, in contrast to the subversive, anti-social adventurer whose identity is defined wholly in terms of action and whose efforts are in the service of self and and in escape from the categories of duty and obligation. Steig's characters, Abel (a mouse) and Dominic (a dog), are both "pastoral" heroes. Their interests are always those of home and community. They enjoy adventures and prove themselves equal to severe tests of their courage and resourcefulness. But the identities of both are finally defined not only by heroic action but also by pastoral contemplation. Both emerge as artists as well as heroes, and both embrace the companionship of women (unlike the adventurer, who usually remains isolated, unmarried, and outside society).

Leo Marx has observed that the pastoral is an elusive, even confusing term, but that it may appropriately be used "to refer to the motive that lies behind the form, and to the images and themes, even the conception of life associated with it." In this sense, certainly, the underlying impulse in Steig's two longer fantasies is pastoral. The innocence of the characters, their affinity with the natural world, their need for the civilized world of art and companionship, the sophisticated detachment of the narrator, and the elegance of Steig's language are all manifestations that the pastoral is a significant dimension of ***Dominic*** and ***Abel's Island.***

When the reader first meets Dominic, he appears to be an adventurer rather than a hero. Without a definite quest, Dominic is merely bored with home. The restless spirit of adventure seizes him abruptly; he packs his various hats, which he wears not for warmth or shelter, "but for their various effects—rakish, dashing, solemn, or martial." From the outset, however, Dominic's adventurous characteristics are tempered by a pastoral dimension; he also takes along his precious piccolo.

Steig gently burlesques the romance by having Dominic receive guidance from an amiable witch-alligator, who advises him to take the high road to adventure and romance, and to avoid the second road. A possible fate of any hero is lotus-eating indolence and idleness; this second road, the witch-alligator warns Dominic, would lead him to excessive introspection, to "daydreaming and tail-twiddling," absent-mindedness and laziness—the mood of idleness without its counterpart in heroic initiative and energy. Thus Dominic receives a cunning spear, not from the Lady-in-the-Lake but from an affable catfish-in-the-pond. The spear and the piccolo help to define the happy balance of pastoral and heroic qualities in Dominic's nature.

Throughout the fantasy Dominic enjoys pastoral interludes, playing his piccolo in the green world, in tune seemingly with the music and harmony in nature. Dominic is infused with sensuous and spiritual enjoyment of nature. Steig stresses repeatedly Dominic's affinity with the natural world. . . . (pp. 124-26)

In the pastoral interludes of Steig's fantasy, then, Dominic enjoys *otium,* a condition which Thomas Rosenmeyer has described as "something like the American 'liberty,' a soldier's leave from duty . . . vacation, freedom, escape from pressing business, particularly a business with overtones of death." Rosenmeyer further explains that *otium* "is *not* the abolition of energy, not withdrawal and curtailment, but a fullness in its own right." Schiller describes the pastoral ambience of this kind of literature as "calm—the calm of perfection, not merely the calm of idleness." In his moments of solitary pastoral meditation Dominic acquires one quality essential for the serenity of pastoral calm—a sense of the workings of the universe. Dominic thus needs *otium*—life in the golden noon in the green shade—but he also needs the pastoral of melancholy and self-discovery. As he grieves over the death of Bartholomew Badger, the pig whom he has befriended, Dominic gains at least a temporary insight into the nature of things:

> He fell asleep under the vast dome of quivering stars, and just as he was falling asleep, passing over into the phase of dreams, he felt he understood the secret of life. But in the light of morning, when he woke up, his understanding of the secret had disappeared with the stars. The mystery was still there, inspiring his wonder. . . . The moment he stopped being busy, he felt his heart quake. He had to cry. Life was suddenly too sad. And yet it was beautiful. The beauty was dimmed when the sadness welled up. . . . So beauty and sadness belonged together somehow.

Dominic senses the need for wholeness, for the unity of being which all human beings (and maybe dog beings, too) need and yearn for. Pastoral fulfillment, however, demands not only Romantic solitude in nature, but also the companionship of a company of friends. In his communings with nature and in the homes of his good friends along the way, Dominic shores up his energies, assuming and protecting the values of home and community. This core of value and meaning enables him to struggle victoriously against the anarchic force which threatens the pastoral serenity of the community, the evil Doomsday gang.

Heroic initiative is the other important feature in Dominic's character: "Challenges were his delight. Whatever life offered was this way or that, a test of one's skills, one's faculties; and he enjoyed proving equal to the tests." When the Doomsday gang waits for Dominic outside his hole, he tricks them, burrowing away from the hole and surfacing some distance away.

Liberated and exultant, Dominic reminds the reader of Odysseus' boasting to the cyclops, when, as Steig tells us, "Dominic couldn't resist letting out one short bark to announce his liberation."

Subsequently, Dominic nurses the victim of the Doomsday gang's terrorist tactics, the sick and dying pig Bartholomew Badger (who leaves his treasure to Dominic), rescues a yellow jacket in distress, and finally uses the treasure to make the community safe. When he learns that Barney Swain, a friendly but helpless wild boar, has lost all his money to the Doomsday gang and thus cannot wed his beloved, Dominic unselfishly gives his treasure to the young couple. He gives the remainder of the treasure to a poverty stricken, widowed goose and her gaggle of hungry goslings. Finally, the Doomsday gang makes a supreme effort to subvert the community by actually attacking the wedding celebration of Pearl Sweeney and Barney Swain. Dominic is seriously wounded in the ensuing battle, but he defeats the Doomsday gang and protects the love union of the young couple, and hence secures the social values of home and marriage, and the hope for a renewed society.

The fantasy, structured in alternating interludes of pastoral calm on one hand and heroic action on the other, culminates spiritually when Dominic reaches the ideal pastoral garden, in which love, art, and nature blend in perfect harmony. In the prelude to this climax, Dominic has experienced varying moods in nature, including Blakean innocent joy: "The gentle radiance of a rosy sun pervaded the air and little birds sang so lyrically that he took out his golden piccolo and joined them in their music. The world was suffused with peace and warmth." Even Dionysian madness has possessed Dominic. One evening, as Dominic piped for the revels of dancing field mice, he became more and more ecstatic: "the music strove nearer and nearer to the elemental truth of being." In a moment of Romantic agony and ecstasy, Dominic "raised his head, and, straining toward infinity, howled out the burden of his love and longing in sounds more meaningful than words." But Dominic is no solitary Romantic or brooding Byronic hero. Love calls us to the things of this world, and Dominic is called back to a simpler, calmer mood of innocent joy when he finds a worn-out doll lying forgotten in a meadow. His restlessness, his spiritual *angst* vanish when he holds the doll, an emblem of the pastoral pleasure of childhood; the toy inspires an intensely comforting pastoral dream. . . . Dominic's efforts throughout the fantasy have been on the behalf of community and its institutions. He has cared for the sick and dying, presided over and been a good steward of community wealth and property, made the lives of its children safe, and protected the pastoral oasis, the

From Abel's Island, *written and illustrated by William Steig. Farrar, Straus and Giroux, 1976.*

home and marriage of the wild boars, Barney Swain and Pearl Sweeney. He has celebrated nature in all its moods, enjoyed the present, and glimpsed a visionary future. But throughout these heroic endeavors, Dominic has been alone, with only the beneficent natural world to protect him.

Leaving the home he has made secure for the newlyweds, Dominic surrenders to the forest and seems to undergo a form of death and rebirth. Too weak from his wounds to struggle against his enemies, Dominic sleeps, unaware that the Doomsday gang has surrounded him. Suddenly the woods reverberate with Dominic's name as the trees express their love for "the brave generous dog named Dominic." Nature acts in concert against the anarchic malice of the Doomsday gang, and the members of the gang experience a conversion. . . . (pp. 127-31)

Dominic finds himself, finally, in a splendid garden which seems to blend the best of both art and nature; in the garden Dominic finds eternal spring, an illustrious peacock, rainbows of flowers which sound like tinkling bells, and his own sleeping beauty, whom he awakens because the little doll had belonged to her. Evelyn, the sleeping beauteous dog, tells Dominic that the little doll had been hers until she decided one day that she was no longer a child and had thrown the beloved companion away: "I remember I was standing in the field thinking about life and about myself and about growing up. I became eager for the future and I felt that the doll chained me to the past. So I got rid of it."

Dominic helps Evelyn to recover her lost childhood and infuses the present with pastoral joy, which includes art, music, nature, and ultimately, marriage. Dominic represents, then, an ideal condition, a blend of the innocent, childlike, piping shepherd and the valiant, heroic warrior. As a rule, the hero is tamed and domesticated; with the embrace of woman and marriage his adventures cease. Steig, however, gives his readers a new kind of adventure—hero and woman equal in innocence and in spirit. Dominic's adventures will go on, but they will no longer be solitary. Sleeping Beauty no longer has to remain passively waiting in her castle: "Dominic realized he was at the beginning of a great new adventure." Evelyn can embrace her childhood and her womanhood and still go out in the world: "Together they left the little palace."

In ***Abel's Island*** Steig creates an interesting version of a traditional kind of story, the Robinsonnade, in a survival story of an Edwardian mouse, Abelard, who is washed away in a storm while trying to retrieve his wife's kerchief. Once on the island, Abel, previously a mouse who had been at home in drawing rooms, discovers the joys of both the heroic and contemplative moods of the hero. His distinguishing characteristics are chivalry, courage, initiative, resourcefulness, and imagination. On his island he must battle for survival, outwitting an owl who wants to eat him. At the same time he learns the pleasures of communing with nature and the satisfactions of creative work. Abel had left home a pampered mouse with no identity of his own; he returns a wiry-strong artist.

Abelard starts his adventures by accident; like Dominic, he adores his wife and thinks only of home and its domestic comforts. Totally civilized, clinging to his makeshift raft, he thinks:

> When the water subsided, he would descend and go home—and what a story he'd have to tell: Meanwhile, he wished he had something to eat—a mushroom omelet, for example, with buttered garlic toast. Being hungry in addition to being marooned like this was really a bit too much. Absent-mindedly, he nibbled at a twig on his branch. Ah, cherry birch: One of his favorite flavors. The familiar taste made him feel a little more at home on his roost in the middle of nowhere.

Indeed, Abel finds that he is able to make a home from his alien environment. As in traditional versions of pastoral, Abel's island bounteously provides his needs: "He munched on the bark of a tender green shoot, his cheek filled with the pulp and juice. He sat there, vaguely smug, convinced that he had the strength, the courage, the intelligence to survive."

Abel reveals his heroic initiative in various attempts to escape the island: he builds a boat, a raft, tries to build a bridge, and finally tries to catapult himself across the stream with his suspenders. Although each attempt fails, he is not discouraged, realizing that the island has indeed become the place where he lives. On the island Abel recovers a lost sense of childhood reciprocity with the natural world:

> He was suddenly thrilled to see his private, personal star arise in the East. This was a particular star his nanny had chosen for him when he was a child. As a child, he would sometimes talk to this star, but only when he was his most serious, real self, and not being any sort of show-off or clown. As he grew up, the practice had worn off.

Abel's experience on the island, then, helps him to recover this "serious real self." Like a benevolent parent, the island itself provides abundant food in the harvest season: ripe raspberries, groundnuts, mulberries, wild mustard, wild onions, new kinds of mushrooms, spearmint, peppermint, and milkweed, all of which comes to Abel without excessive work. He has ample time for contemplation and meditation. Leo Marx has remarked that nature's abundance without labor is a significant dimension of traditional pastoral. Nature also provides Abel shelter in a hollow log. Asleep in his log, the melancholy rains cause him to reflect on the "poignant parts of life." Abel is sustained by his dreams of home: "The castaway dreamed all night of Amanda. They were together again in their home. But their home was not 89 Bank Street, in Mossville; it was a garden, something like the island, and full of flowers." Thus Abel's experience on his island gives him a new vision of home as a pastoral garden, rather than as the constraints of a house on Bank Street.

As Abel grows in his understanding of nature and as his response to it intensifies, he observes the eternal patterns in the natural world. As he watches the great plan and design of creation at work, he feels "a strong need to participate in the arranging and designing of things." Artistic creation demands the mood of idleness, of leisure, and Steig depicts his animal heroes at work—imaginative work—in their contemplative moments. In these times of leisure Abel transforms the pain of homesickness into statues of his family and friends. Through art he creates the familiar. His world is improved by his artistic efforts, and he searches for other ways to civilize the island and to make a home of an alien environment. Abel maintains a strong connection to the civilized world through art and through two items which he finds on the island—a clock and a book about bears.

Traditional pastoral poems, shepherds' calendars, are organized according to the seasons of the year. Accordingly, in

Abel's Island pastoral pleasance is interrupted by winter and by the terrifying appearance of an owl. The battle with the owl provides a test of Abel's courage, heroic anger, and resourcefulness as he fashions a spear with which to challenge and put to flight the bewildered owl. As winter closes in, Abel retreats into his log. Physically and spiritually ill, Abel survives by remembering the comforts of home. In his cold log, he reflects upon Amanda, the firelight, lentil soup on the stove—domestic pleasures and human companionship. Still he feels isolated, convinced that he is the only living thing in a wintry waste land. Spring, however, brings hope and the renewal of body and spirit. By April, Abel is certain that he and Amanda are no longer isolated from each other; his faith that he will return safely to her grows stronger. At the same time nature has given him much-needed independence: "Abel ate grass and young violet greens, fresh food with the juice of life. . . . At times he felt that he had no need of others."

While Abel stills dreams of Amanda and loves her, he has come through an initiation. He has sloughed off the old, spoiled, and pampered self and has been reborn. Renato Poggioli has remarked that European writers of the seventeenth century liberated pastoral from an exclusive concern with sexuality by developing "the pastoral of the self, which in the end transcended all previous traditions of the genre." Abel, the reader is told, had lived on his mother's wealth; apparently his wife has served primarily as a mother surrogate. Secure in his snug urban home, Abel had not really lived. His pastoral sojourn on the island has given him an identity: "He was a wiry-strong mouse after his rugged year in the wilds. The Abel who was leaving was in better fettle, in all ways, than the Abel who had arrived in a hurricane, desperately clinging to a nail. . . . He was imagining ahead to Amanda, and beyond her to his family, his friends, and a renewed life in society, that would include productive work, his art." At last, as a result of his resourceful efforts, Abel's dream of home comes true. Home and Amanda are just the same; only Abel has changed and has found himself embarrassed and uncomfortable in an elegant velvet jacket. While Steig does not resolve Abel's new problem, the reader is left with a sure sense that Abel's abiding love for Amanda, coupled with his newly discovered strength, will insure their future happiness.

In ***Dominic*** and ***Abel's Island,*** Steig has created a tension between the pastoral and the heroic interludes, between the spear and the piccolo, a balance which suggests that his heroes, Dominic the Indomitable Dog and Abel the Miraculous Mouse, achieve two characteristics which Rosenmeyer considers essential to the serenity of the pastoral frame of mind: a perspective with the benign universe and fellowship with a goodly company. Their lives are filled with possibility because they know when to play, when to work, when to create, and when to meditate. Their lives are enriched by their affinity with nature, a quality which is blended harmoniously with their love of art and the best of the civilized world. Unlike regressive expressions of the pastoral impulse, such as that of James Barrie's *Peter Pan,* Dominic and Abel willingly face the darker layers of existence—predation, old age, sickness, and death. They infuse the present and the future with the pastoral values of childhood while embracing the pleasures of maturity. Even in maturity they retain their innocence, as well as their imaginations and their sensuous joy in the sights, sounds, and smells of the natural world. Ursula Le Guin has written that fantasy helps to provide the internal exploration necessary to produce a whole, integrated human being—to allow emotional growth and healthy maturity. For Le Guin, "maturity is not an outgrowing, but a growing up: . . . an adult is not a dead child, but a child who survived." So it is with Abel and Dominic.

An important way in which Steig expresses the pastoral in ***Abel's Island*** and ***Dominic*** is through his formal, elegant language. Theorists on the nature of pastoral have often remarked upon its civilized and sophisticated qualities, the "double-vision" of a narrator. Blue Calhoun comments on the pastoral narrator's dual perspective: "The pastoral world is a civilized creation. Simple life in a green garden is necessarily the vision of a sophisticated writer, one who is committed by history and temperament to the complexities of city life but who questions its basic assumption." In Steig's fantasies, the elegant language and the gentle burlesque of fairy tale and romance conventions underscore the artifice of the fantasy world. The courtly manners of Dominic and Abel, their serene restraint, suggest not romantic primitivism but a life in nature improved by art, social grace, and civilization. In ***Dominic*** the image of the ideal garden at the end, replete with gorgeous artifice, combines the best of the pastoral and the urban worlds. In ***Abel's Island*** the island itself becomes an aesthetic construct which similarly combines attributes of nature and art. Steig draws upon the language of civilization to depict the natural world—the light in the forest is like a stained-glass window; the sounds of nature are like a symphony orchestra. In fact Steig has spoken of his own long-time delight in courtly language. Having grown up in the Bronx, far from green pastoral bowers, Steig and his playmates created their own linguistic make-believe world of romance. They had read *Robinson Crusoe, King Arthur,* and *Robin Hood* and incorporated the language of these stories into their play. Steig explains: "Here were these kids in the Bronx yelling: 'I'll smite thee, thou churlish knave.' And we thought that was marvelous. We spoke Arthurian language" [see Author's Commentary]. Dominic's language is equally courtly. After rescuing goose-in-distress Matilda Fox from a Doomsday deathtrap, Dominic gallantly declares; "Your life is my reward. . . . With you in the world, the world is a better place, I'm sure. My name is Dominic. I am at your service, madam." This gallant statement is accompanied by a graceful bow, and the amused narrator adds, "Dominic was exceptionally attentive to ladies." Steig, a child of the city, has acquired his own visions of pastoral, romance, and heroic adventure through stories and their linguistic conventions. The pastoral sensibility in his fantasies is expressed, then, through his playful burlesque of conventions, and his witty play with language. He obviously enjoys naming the pastoral lovers in ***Dominic***—the two affectionate wild boars—Barney Swain and Pearl Sweeney, just as he whimsically reverses the names of several animals: the pig is "Bartholomew Badger"; the artistic mouse is "Manfred Lyon"; and the plump, widowed goose is "Matilda Fox." Steig's elegant language and his playful use of conventions help to define the fantasies as artifice, in sharp contrast to the random world of disordered and chaotic experience. His sophisticated tone and detachment, however, convey amused affection, not contempt, for the pastoral world. The knowing, urbane writer is keenly aware that he is not creating the world as it is actually experienced. The green world of pastoral, the ideal garden—its innocence, heroism, beauty, art, joy, its freedom from greed, ignorance, and cupidity—is an emblem of mankind's possibility, of what the poet dreams in his "deep heart's core," of civilized life as it might be lived. It expresses the wish that human beings may someday attain the fullness of experience and yet retain the innocent sense of newness which assures them that they are at the beginning of a great new adventure. (pp. 131-40)

Anita Moss, "The Spear and the Piccolo: Heroic and Pastoral Dimensions of William Steig's 'Dominic' and 'Abel's Island'," in Children's Literature: Annual of the Modern Language Association Division on Children's Literature and The Children's Literature Association, *Vol. 10, 1982, pp. 124-40.*

JONATHAN COTT

[Steig] has shaped a career as one of the finest cartoonists and creators of children's books of our time. (p. 88)

Steig didn't turn to children's literature until he was sixty years old. Throughout the preceding four decades—and continuing to the present—he was contributing regularly to *The New Yorker* . . . and was working on ten of his twelve collections of cartoons. The most remarkable of these—***About People, The Lonely Ones, All Embarrassed,*** and ***The Rejected Lovers***—present faces with sardonic grins, helpless grimaces, and embittered smiles, as if smile and frown had intermixed and had become inextricably locked together in oxymoronic perplexity. In this world of characterological distress, each of Steig's figures seems to be an almost allegorical representation of an unhappy body and consciousness—the actual implication of these drawings being that a happy consciousness is a function of a happy body and incapable of existing independently of a fulfilled sense of life. As Steig later wrote in the preface to *Dreams of Glory*: "I believe that people are basically good and beautiful, and that neurosis is the biggest obstacle to peace and happiness. In my symbolical drawings I try to make neurotic behavior more manifest."

At first glance, however, many observers assumed that famous cartoons such as **"I Mind My Own Business," "People Are No Damn Good,"** and **"I Do Not Forget To Be Angry"**—included in ***The Lonely Ones*** and widely reproduced for many years on paper napkins, coasters, and ashtrays—were simply scornful tauntings of neurotic behavior. Many people, moreover, expected and wanted sickness to be made fun of. And because Steig embodied, rather than exploited, this sickness, his work was often thought of as being cruel. In fact, the intense and expressive lines of his "symbolical drawings" allowed Steig instinctively to discover and render the frozen movements of suffering humanity; what people often took to be negative statements about existence were actually brilliantly acute revelations and mirrorings of armored consciousness.

Unbeknownst to Steig, the psychiatrist Wilhelm Reich had also, in the twenties and thirties, been observing and analyzing the distorted expression of the emotions in human beings. (pp. 88-9)

[In 1946,] the artist first met the psychiatrist, becoming his patient and, later, his collaborator and friend. Rarely has a deeper affinity between a psychologist and an artist existed than between Wilhelm Reich and William Steig. . . . For, working independently, and unknown to each other, both Reich and Steig seemed to be connected by the same concerns, the same focus of attention. (p. 90)

Inspired by Reich's fortitude and ideas, William Steig irreversibly chose the path of creation. (p. 92)

As a cartoonist Steig has always confronted the various manifestations of armored human life, depicting those epiphanic moments and situations that reflect the ways in which people stunt the growth of both themselves and their children. . . . (p. 95)

[If] in his earlier work, Steig embodied the characterological attributes of unhappy individuals, in his children's books he created and tested the possibilities of an unarmored life. For it is axiomatic that one has to be in touch with one's unarmored feelings to create lasting, meaningful, and enjoyable books for children.

"The expression of the armored organism," Reich stated in *Character Analysis,* "is one of 'holding back.' . . . Literally defined, the word 'emotion' means 'moving outwards' or 'pushing out'." It is interesting that one of Steig's cartoons for ***Listen, Little Man!*** simply contrasts these two antithetical character attitudes in the figures of a walled-in human and a lively, unbounded dog. And it is this dog that seems to have jumped out of the cartoon into Steig's ***Dominic,*** one of the most inspired and inspiring children's books of recent times.

"Dominic was a lively one, always up to something" is the way the text begins. After picking up his piccolo, bandanna, and an assortment of hats, we see the hound hero taking off on his life journey. Meeting a witch-alligator at the crossroads, she advises him:

> That road there on the right goes nowhere. There's not a bit of magic up that road, no adventure, no surprise, nothing to discover or wonder at. Even the scenery is humdrum. You'd soon grow much too introspective. You'd take to daydreaming and tail-twiddling, get absent-minded and lazy, forget where you are and what you're about, sleep more than one should, and be wretchedly bored. Furthermore, after a while, you'd reach a dead end and you'd have to come all that dreary way back to right here where we're standing now, only it wouldn't be now, it would be some woefully wasted time later.

Needless to say, Dominic chooses the path of adventure and wonder. (pp. 95-7)

[At the end of the book] we understand that to find someone's "doll" is to rediscover that person's childhood self, and also, in the process, one's own childhood; and that to be truly like a child is not to regress, like Peter Pan, but to "be out in the world again" and on that road which, as St. Augustine knew, was a path not from place to place, but of the affections.

"Originally," Steig explains, "I had the idea of doing a book in which a dog, going to visit his cousin or some other relative, comes to a fork where there are three roads. And I was going to try to have included in the book some kind of spinning toy that would determine which road the dog would take. Each road was going to have a different set of adventures, and each was to have been represented by a separate strip of color on the same page, so that the dog would have followed the red, blue, or green path. And at the end, the roads came together and ended up in the same place.

"I quickly wrote down a list of characters the dog would meet: a witch-alligator, a rich pig, a goose, a boar, an elephant that loses its memory. And when I decided to do ***Dominic*** a couple of years later, I just used every animal I had originally written down, as if they belonged together because they had all come to me at the same moment."

"Why talking animals?" someone once asked Steig, who responded: "I think using animals emphasizes the fact that the story is symbolic—about human behavior. And kids get the idea right away that this is not just a story, but that it's saying something about life on earth'' . . . adding, ''When you write about a dog, you're really writing about a child, because a dog's mature when it's only a year old.''

''The terrible cuteness and triteness of most children's books,'' writes Roger Sale in *Fairy Tales and After,* ''sometimes seems little more than the result of ignorance or incomprehension or carelessness about the materials being used, most of which concern animals in one way or another.'' As with the greatest creators of animal tales, Steig's carefulness about the materials being used can be seen in the way he respects the doglike nature of Dominic, that passionate lover of liberty who leaves the path to sniff and explore, always to return to it—howling and yodeling (the original primal screamer!) in sorrow and joy.

But, standing erect on his hind legs, Dominic is obviously, as Steig says, a symbolical human being. (pp. 104-05)

In many ways, of course, Dominic is a prototypical picaresque hero who shares the Odyssean qualities of agility, courage, persistence, and inventiveness; the Whitmanesque celebration of ''health, defiance, gayety, self-esteem, curiosity'' . . . ; the Emersonian sense of self-reliance and nonconformity; and the Tolstoyan notions of loving-kindness and openheartedness. . . .

Dominic is also a classic children's literature protagonist, like Kipling's Kim or Dorothy in *The Wizard Oz*. . . . And with his Sleeping Beauty princess, Dominic also takes on the role of a classic fairy-tale hero. . . . (p. 105)

It would, of course, be egregiously reductive and slighting of Steig's remarkable literary and pictoral style—which combines the rough-hewn, the gentle, the comic, and the noble—to see ***Dominic*** simply as some kind of mouthpiece for Wilhelm Reich's social and ethical ideas. As Steig once told James E. Higgins [see Author's Commentary], ''When I wrote ***Dominic*** I didn't mean it to be about anything. . . . I have a position—a point of view. But I don't have to think about it to express it. I can write about anything and my point of view will come out. So when I am at work my conscious intention is to tell a story to the reader. All this other stuff takes place automatically.'' But it is fascinating to realize that the character of Dominic perfectly exemplifies what Reich at various times, and often interchangeably, called the ''self-governing,'' ''genital,'' or ''unarmored'' character, which he saw and valued as the pinnacle of health and the optimum of human functioning.

In *The Murder of Christ,* Reich interprets and portrays Jesus—and in a sense Dominic himself—as exactly this type of character,

> knowing and yet naïve . . . streaming with love and kindness, and yet able to hit hard; gentle and yet strong, just as the child of the future is. . . . The more he gives off in strength and love, the more new strength he gains from the universe, the greater and closer is his own contact with nature around him, the sharper his awareness of God, Nature, the air, the birds, the flowers, the animals, to all of whom he is close. . . . Christ did not like to remain sitting in the home with his brothers and sisters and his mother, though he loved them dearly. He liked to wander about the beautiful countryside, to greet the sun when it rose over the horizon in glaring pink.

''Aglow with energy'' and opposed to all forms of acedia, Dominic, Steig tells us, is ''master of himself and in accord with the world. . . . He never debated these impulses, hemming and hawing over what he should do. Thought and action were not separate with Dominic; the moment he thought to do something, he was already doing it.''

As mentioned before, Dominic even respects the Doomsday Gang more than he does the rabbits because the former ''had plenty of brass.'' The Gang, of course, is an apt embodiment of what Reich called the ''emotional plague''—a term he first used to describe the kind of group irrationalism and group sadism that manifested itself in, for example, the Inquisition, the Salem witch trials, and the Third Reich. . . . But as Dominic knows, ''one could not be happy among the good ones unless one fought the bad ones.'' (pp. 105-07)

In his most popular children's book, ***Sylvester and the Magic Pebble,*** . . . Steig presents in picture-book form the story of a donkey named Sylvester Duncan who lives with his parents in Oatsdale. One rainy day, the hero, who collects unusual and beautifully colored pebbles, comes across a special one—''flaming red, shiny, and perfectly round, like a marble.'' Shivering from excitement he wishes it would stop raining . . . and the rain ceases. He rushes home to show his parents his magic pebble; but, coming across a lion, he feels afraid:

> If he hadn't been so frightened, he could have made the lion disappear, or he could have wished himself safe at home with his father and mother.
>
> He could have wished the lion would turn into a butterfly or a daisy or a gnat. He could have wished many things, but he panicked and couldn't think carefully.
>
> ''I wish I were a rock,'' he said, and he became a rock.

Having armored himself—''a Quartz contentment, like a stone''—he wishes he were *himself* again, but nothing happens because he can't touch the pebble—which is lying by his side—to make the magic work. He is alone and feeling hopeless (''I made a connection,'' Steig says, ''with the fact that I'd read *Pinocchio* in my youth, and that it's a similar case of a real boy being locked up in a piece of wood, inside himself, misunderstood, and armored.'') (pp. 118-19)

Back in Oatsdale, the Duncans are miserable. ''Life had no meaning for them any more.'' In a series of three beautiful double-page spreads, we see the stone in autumn, leaves blowing over and around it (''Night followed day and day followed night over and over again. Sylvester on the hill woke up less and less often. When he was awake, he was only hopeless and unhappy. He felt he would be a rock forever and he tried to get used to it. He went into an endless sleep''); then the stone in winter, covered with snow and with a wolf sitting on top of him and howling in hunger; and then in spring, under blue skies and blossoming flowers. As Steig says: ''I think kids are interested in the weather, day and night, winter and summer. I feel it's important. Moonlight and snow and wind.''

In spring things come alive, and the Duncans decide to take a picnic. Naturally, they sit down on the rock: ''The warmth of his own mother sitting on him woke Sylvester up from his deep winter sleep.'' Mr. Duncan notices the lovely magic pebble near the rock, goes to pick it up, and as he and his wife sit down to eat, she wishes that Sylvester were with them. ''And in less than an instant, he was!'' In blazing sunlight Sylvester is unlocked and released and embraces his parents with tears of happiness, as they return home and hide the pebble forever.

"To me," says [Steig's son, Jeremy,] in his living room, "the book is about love. When the family gets back together, they put the pebble away because what was important was their being together." (pp. 120-21)

As a child, Steig himself remembers liking adventure books—Howard Pyle's *Robin Hood,* the King Arthur stories . . . , and especially the works of Joseph Altsheler. . . .

But Steig, then or later, must have also absorbed fairy tales and fables—as well as works like *Robinson Crusoe* and *The Golden Ass*—for his children's books take off from these basic plots and situations, although in remarkably inventive ways. His second and first "real" children's book, for example—***Roland the Minstrel Pig***—tells the traditional tale of a lute-playing pig . . . who "sang so sweetly that his friends never had enough of listening to him. He was a natural musician—from his hoofs to his snout." Under starlit skies, he would play at outdoor parties for his friends, many of whom—the donkey, the elephant, the bear, and, of course, the dog—would appear in Steig's later books. (p. 122)

Roland the Minstrel Pig, a charming but hardly major work, was Steig's testing ground as a children's book creator. "I thought that anybody could write for kids when I first started doing the books," he says, "but it's not always that simple. And it's a nice feeling to discover that you can do something new—like Roland's farewell song. . . . I thought, Hey, I can write verse!" And he learned that he could illustrate, much as he says he dislikes to. "I don't like illustrating," he told me, "because it's very unspontaneous. When I'm illustrating, I know that a character has to walk in a certain way, and I have a hard time doing it. I'm incapable of making the drawing conform to the requirements of telling a story, making the pig look like the pig on the previous page." But despite himself, his gouache illustrations for ***Roland*** are ardent and witty—especially his double-page spread showing the masked dancers under magic lanterns and the stars; and also his drawings of Roland leaning on a rock, lute nearby, contemplating the possibilities of fame and wealth; and of Roland, purple beret on his head, singing a lonesome plaint in the moonlight.

Steig's next major work, after the audacious ***The Bad Island*** and the now-classic ***Sylvester and the Magic Pebble,*** was another picture book, ***Amos and Boris***—a brilliant variation on the fable about the lion and the mouse. (p. 123)

Not since Edward Lear's Owl and Pussy-Cat or Kipling's Mowgli and Baloo have the love of characters so different from each other been so totally accepted and perfectly portrayed in children's literature.

With ***Dominic,*** Steig presented his first work for older children, a short novel that featured some of his greatest line drawings, and showed him developing a prose style combining grace and muscularity, lyricism and drama, one that moved from scene to scene like an inspired jazz improvisation. He must have been delighted by his newly realized powers, for a year later he published another long story, ***The Real Thief,*** which revealed the author in complete possession of a spare, unadorned style that was the appropriate match for its dark theme of injustice and betrayal. An unfairly underrated work, ***The Real Thief*** is, in fact, the only one of Steig's books that started out with what he calls a "deliberate idea." (pp. 124-25)

Gawain the goose is Chief Guard of the Royal Treasury and totally devoted to King Basil the bear: "His heart warmed in the King's presence. He admired his strength. He loved the smell of honey on him, on his fur, on his robes, on his breath. He wanted to please him, to stay forever in his gruff, good graces." Only Basil and Gawain have the keys to the treasury, so when rubies, gold ducats, silver ornaments, and then the prized Kalikak diamond disappears, Gawain is accused of the thefts. He stands trial, and is attacked with mechanistic logic and uncorroborated evidence; excoriated by the king himself, he is found guilty and is about to be imprisoned.

Caleb the carpenter and Kate the weaver loved each other, but not every single minute. Once in a while they'd differ about this or that and wind up in such a fierce quarrel you'd never believe they were husband and wife.

From Caleb and Kate, *written and illustrated by William Steig. Farrar, Straus and Giroux, 1977. Copyright © 1977 by William Steig. All rights reserved. Reproduced by permission of Farrar, Straus and Giroux, Inc.*

One of Steig's greatest talents is the way he enters into and conveys the experience of his characters' sensations and feelings (think of Sylvester "shivering with excitement" as he studies his pebble for the first time). And now upon hearing the sentence of imprisonment, Gawain, Steig tells us, "stared at the ground and saw his own yellow feet. They, at least seemed real. He could feel no compassion from anyone around him. He felt leaden, benumbed." So, seeing the wide blue sky outside the courtroom, he honks loudly and escapes through the open window.

In the second part of the book, we learn the story of the real thief, Derek the mouse. (p. 125)

Hearing about Gawain's plight, he comes to realize what it means to be a thief. . . . So he decides to vindicate Gawain by continuing to steal from the treasury and then, later, returning the treasure. Realizing that he had accused the goose unjustly, Basil is devastated. Everyone is devastated. (p. 126)

One day [Gawain] is discovered by Derek, who has been searching for him everywhere. "He felt so many emotions—

joy at having been vindicated and at being with Derek, anger at what had happened, misery that such things *could* happen, pity for Derek, bitterness toward his faithless friends and toward the King he had loved, longing for a good life, sweetness at thinking how beautiful it could be, and sorrow that it wasn't so. It was all too much for him." . . . Gawain gradually comes to forgive Derek and his former friends, and he returns home in honor. "He was able to love them again," Steig writes, "but he loved them now in a wiser way, knowing their weakness."

In 1974, Steig left this bittersweet kingdom and brought out ***Farmer Palmer's Wagon Ride***—a Buster Keatonesque tale about Palmer the pig and his hired hand, Ebenezer the donkey. . . . (pp. 126-27)

This divertissement was followed by Steig's most ambitious work, ***Abel's Island.*** And nowhere else are Steig's verbal and illustrative gifts so beautifully matched as in this novel that takes its inspiration from *The Odyssey* and *Robinson Crusoe,* and which tells how Abel the mouse, picnicking with his new wife Amanda, gets caught in a violent thunderstorm. While attempting to retrieve his wife's scarf, Abel gets carried off in a torrential stream and winds up on an island, from which he tries unsuccessfully to escape by means of boats, makeshift bridges, and catapults. Filled with loneliness and self-pity, he is befriended by his personal star, which tells him, "You will do what you will do."

The rest of this novel narrates the ways in which Abel makes himself a home inside a hollow log and learns, like Robinson Crusoe, to accept his solitary existence and to turn the chance of isolation into an occasion of spiritual realization. As Jeremy Steig comments: "When Abel's finally in touch with himself for the first time in his life, he realizes he can learn to do everything. That's my father—having Abel do what he'd see himself doing in that situation." (p. 127)

Since 1976, William Steig has published five additional picture books. ***The Amazing Bone,*** like ***Roland,*** is about a pig, but for the first time in Steig's children's books he presents us with a heroine ("I guess it's easier for a boy to write about a boy than about a girl," Steig says, smiling). . . .

Caleb and Kate is a more complex transformation tale and the first of Steig's children's books in which he talks about and draws adult human beings. And one is reminded that children's books—certainly picture books—are usually read by adults to and with children, and that the best of these books must therefore be meant for and significant to adults as well as to their supposed audience. What makes ***Caleb and Kate*** so interesting is the way in which it undoubtedly speaks to parents who may find themselves at odds with each other, and to children who may be upset by their parents' arguments. As with all the best children's books, there are thus "two" versions of ***Caleb and Kate***—one for adults, one for children—both read simultaneously.

"Caleb the carpenter and Kate the weaver loved each other," the book begins, "but not every single minute. Once in a while they'd differ about this or that and wind up in such a fierce quarrel you'd never believe they were husband and wife." After one especially crazy quarrel, Caleb walks out of the house and into the nearby woods, where, like Gower the frog, he immediately forgets what the fight was about. (p. 129)

Instead of returning home immediately, however, he takes a nap, during which time Yedida the witch discovers Caleb and decides to test out her latest spell. When Caleb wakes up he realizes he has been transformed not, like Sylvester, into a rock but into a dog. And with this *donnée,* Steig turns the table on the positive notions of animal faith and animal happiness that he had promulgated in ***Dominic.*** For Caleb, returning home as a dog, is no longer able to communicate with his wife. Unlike Dominic, he is not a "symbolical human being"—he walks on all fours like the "dog" (despicable fellow) he has been to his wife and has now turned into. (pp. 129-30)

Trailing Kate, Caleb the dog follows her into the gray, lifeless woods (another characteristically powerful double-page illustration), past a group of rocks that remind us of Sylvester's fate. "There was no finding Caleb because there he was behind his wife, with the shape and the shadow of a dog." In a sense, then, we might see in this hopeless search the loss of intimacy and understanding that must have provoked Caleb's and Kate's original quarrel. . . . (p. 130)

Neither dog nor man, [Caleb] returns sorrowfully to the woods, hoping to find "in that luckless spot some clue to the secret of his transformation. . . . He watched Kate move through the house, hopeless now about ever being able to reveal his true self."

At this static point, something has to change. . . . Then one night, fighting off some robbers who have entered the house, Caleb gets wounded—which breaks the spell—and magically turns into *himself.* And having scared off the thieves, "Caleb and Kate leaped into each other's arms and cleaved together for a long time."

As Jeremy Steig says about the book: "I like the fact that it's about a middle-aged couple and that you can feel the physical relationship between them (Kate does take the dog to bed with her). In most stories you have Wrigley's chewing gum people, and in movies you hardly ever seen a couple like Caleb and Kate. But love goes on a very long time, it's not just for twenty-year-olds."

In 1978 Steig published his picture book ***Tiffky Doofky,*** which depicts the adventures of a garbage-collector hound who, after consulting a fortune-telling goose, excitedly anticipates a meeting with the female of his dreams that very day. (pp. 130-31)

Although it contains some of the wittiest of his picture-book illustrations, ***Tiffky Doofky,*** as Steig admits, is not one of his most successful works. "I labored over it too long, and it wasn't inspired enough," he says. "People think that writing or painting is hard work, but that's because of our armor. When we function naturally, it becomes a joy. If we fail, it's because we're not functioning well."

Steig was certainly functioning at the height of his powers when he created his recent picture book, ***Gorky Rises,*** which tells of Gorky the frog's attempt to concoct a magic potion in the kitchen sink. . . . As he lies stretched out on the grass—the bottle resting on his hip—an entranced Gorky seems at one with all aspects of the universe ("The wide, open sky outside him was bright with brilliant sun, but the sky inside him shimmered with stars"). And as we turn the page, we see Gorky's slumbering body floating up into the gentle blue sky "like a bubble rising in water."

Just as Amos on the deck of his little boat in ***Amos and Boris*** stares up in wonder at the immense starry sky, so Gorky sails through the air in some of Steig's most spacious drawings, feeling the "brilliant bubbles flow into his arm from the bottle he held in his hand," soaring past kites and passing over creatures and towns. But just as Amos gets thrown into the open sea, so Gorky finds himself caught in the midst of storms, and he escapes to the heights of the sky where we see him, in an extraordinary illustration, limned helplessly against the cold, starlit heavens, looking for all the world like one of Steig's Lonely Ones, as he clutches in terror onto what now seems to be a baby's bottle. Like Sylvester, he feels motherless, fatherless, homeless. But finally he decides to remove the bottle's stopper and to release the magic liquid drop by drop, thereby allowing him to fall gradually down to earth. He lands on Elephant Rock—which, in a very childlike turn of events, turns into a real elephant—where Gorky's anxious parents find him at last and take their much-adventured son home to bed.

Rarely have the ecstasies and terrors of flying been so simply and beautifully suggested as in Steig's illustrations for ***Gorky Rises.*** Connected to the freedom of flying is, of course, the fantasy of sexual potency, suggested in Steig's depiction of the slumbering Gorky with the magic bottle on his hips. (pp. 131-32)

Also connected to the freedom of flying is the freedom of drawing. . . . (p. 132)

When I ask him which of his children's books are his favorites, he mentions ***Sylvester and the Magic Pebble*** and ***Abel's Island*** because "I remember doing them with excitement." It is the *doing* of things that excites Steig and reveals him to be a true Reichian. And it is this sense of doing—along with Steig's Reichian notion that "the artistic activity of human beings is creative, form-making energy exercising its fullest powers, just as it does throughout the universe—without 'practical' intention"—that suggests an affinity between Reich's ideas and the work of some of the greatest creative artists of the century: Igor Stravinsky . . . ; Charlie Chaplin . . . ; George Balanchine . . . ; and Pablo Picasso. . . .

Steig's children's books are filled with shining suns. And it was Picasso who said: "Any man can make the sun into a yellow ball. Ah, but to make a yellow ball into a sun!" (p. 133)

Jonathan Cott, "William Steig and His Path," in his Pipers at the Gates of Dawn: The Wisdom of Children's Literature, *Random House, 1983, pp. 87-136.*

THE AMAZING BONE **(1976)**

Of the thousands of books published annually, none is more certain of lasting life than one of Steig's. This year he has created two classics, ***Abel's Island*** and now the story of a pretty pig, Pearl. Again, Steig's precise and inspired language is a miraculous match for his color-filled pictures, lovely as well as funny, like the story. Pearl dawdles on her way home from school on a spring day and happens upon a magic bone; it can speak in any language. The two become friends and the bone agrees to live with Pearl and her family. They are attacked by muggers in the forest but the bone scares them off. They're not so lucky, however, when a fox which can't be intimidated grabs them and drags them to his house where he plans to roast Pearl for dinner. The story sizzles with suspense until an unexpected twist and a happy end.

A review of "The Amazing Bone," in Publishers Weekly, *Vol. 210, No. 23, December 6, 1976, p. 62.*

About halfway through ***The Amazing Bone*** Mr. Fox, the villain, asks "Why should I be ashamed? I can't help being the way I am. I didn't make the world." William Steig the author-illustrator of this book can't claim to be as innocent as Mr. Fox. He seems to make a new world every time he makes a new book. . . .

In ***The Amazing Bone*** the author and the illustrator seem to be two different people. The illustrator at least at first glance appears to be a fluffy young thing just out of Pratt Institute, while the author comes on as a retired professor of literature turning his hand to writing a children's book. The interaction between these two gives the book its special, piquant character. . . .

Possibly the most remarkable thing about the book is the drawing of Pearl's eyes. The fact that such economical and casual lines can produce such explicit characterization is a miracle.

Alvin Eisenman, in a review of "The Amazing Bone," in Children's Book Showcase 1977 *by Barbara Bader, Betty Binns, and Alvin Eisenman, The Children's Book Council, 1977, p. 6.*

In watercolor illustrations of outlined shapes, in the style of Steig's 1970 Medal Book [***Sylvester and the Magic Pebble***], the animal characters of this tale assist the author-illustrator in presenting the human emotions which provide the story's universal appeal. The audience can easily sense the euphoria Pearl experiences as she strolls along the water and chats with her newfound companion, who is tucked inside her opened pocketbook. The impressionistic environment, dabs of light spring hues and vibrant violets, reinforces Pearl's attitudes and communicates them to the audience.

As the innocent piglet is confronted by the sharp-toothed fox, the wickedness of the fox's intent is contrasted by Pearl's horrified expression, as well as by the innocent activity of the mother bird feeding her babies in a tree of the background.

Steig, in his inimitable cartoonlike style, has produced a tale of the young overpowering the grips of Fate, with a little magic and a little luck. (p. 366)

Linda Kauffman Peterson, "The Caldecott Medal and Honor Books, 1938-1981: 'The Amazing Bone'," in Newbery and Caldecott Medal and Honor Books: An Annotated Bibliography, *by Linda Kauffman Peterson and Marilyn Leathers Solt, G. K. Hall & Co., 1982, pp. 365-66.*

ABEL'S ISLAND **(1976)**

This is a remarkable, I would venture to say a great, book, absorbing on any level but beneath all, a fable for our times. Abel, a rich idle mouse, finds himself, like so many today brought up to a well-ordered secure life, faced with the humiliations of a situation where familiar assumptions and conditioning are useless, but having to swallow all pride and face his true self in order to survive. In 1907 (the date is doubtless significant as a climax of luxury and security for the rich), a hurricane has the bad taste to spoil Abel's picnic with his lovely wife Amanda, and sweep him away to an island while rescuing Amanda's silk scarf. Confidently he tries the time-honoured methods of escape, but each time the river is too strong for him. Gradually, his defences are destroyed, his image in his friends' eyes can no longer console him, and he has to accept the life of a castaway. At once he begins to put into effect all his passive knowledge and the instinctive rodent behaviour under his cultured exterior. He discovers a talent for sculpture, he learns to enjoy everything in nature, he has time to think—

he is even convinced he can communicate telepathically with Amanda. An owl and extreme cold provide danger to keep him alert, a frog becomes a temporary friend, and he imagines a special guardian star. After a year, he dares to swim the now drought-shrunken river by stages, inspired, as always, by his almost unbearably deep love for Amanda, though it has passed through only-too-believable stages of resentment and fears. Yet all he says is "I've brought you back your scarf". It is the wonderful line-and-wash drawings which develop further the poignancy of the story, here and throughout. A book which will grow with the reader. (pp. 49-50)

M. Hobbs, in a review of "Abel's Island," in The Junior Bookshelf, *Vol. 42, No. 1, February, 1978, pp. 49-50.*

[Steig has, as well as his] talent for equating animal and human characters, a disarming air of easy, civilised enjoyment. ***Abel's Island*** is told with a beautifully sustained urbanity well suited to the tale of a prosperous socialite coping with sudden adversity. The piquant situation of Abelard Hassam di Chirico Flint . . . , a mouse marooned on a desolate islet after a storm, is described in stately, comic and circumstantial terms. . . . The illustrations are excitingly explicit in scenes of action and they complement the accounts of Abel's moods, gay or grim, with exactly the kind of mild caricature which this ironic piece demands. A story as good as this, with its hints of seriousness and its versatility in narrative, deserves a very wide readership, young and old. (pp. 3291-92)

Margery Fisher, in a review of "Abel's Island," in Growing Point, *Vol. 16, No. 9, April, 1978, pp. 3291-92.*

Famous for his many award-winning masterpieces, . . . William Steig has produced one more. In a beautifully told and illustrated morality tale, he relates the thoughts and events that thrust a contented and secure mouse on his own for a full year as he struggles to survive and fight his way back home. This timeless story about finding oneself is for all seasons and ages. It is straightforward and simple truth expressed and portrayed gloriously. More than 50 drawings—many full-page or half-page—are done in this illustrator's inimitable style in ink wash with pen outline. . . .

Young readers of ages 7 to 11, as well as thoughtful adults, will savor it. Reading it to older elementary and junior high age children will not be amiss. (p. 66)

One of the most important values of life—harmoniously balancing work and play—is subtly explained in this story. It shows that one must know her or his capabilities and be willing and able to work with them. It also shows that one must be able to let recreation be a part of existence. The combination of artistic imagination and practical rationality, is exalted. Industriousness, determination, and the ability to implement learning are stressed.

Throughout runs an excellent discourse on nature and the weather cycle of a river in the temperate zone. (p. 68)

Diana L. Spirt, "Developing Values: William Steig, 'Abel's Island'," in her Introducing More Books: A Guide for the Middle Grades, *R. R. Bowker Company, 1978, pp. 66-9.*

The primary strain of the beast tale, with its emphasis on moralistic parable, softened in the first half of the twentieth century, as children's literature in general softened, only to resurface in a harsh and misanthropic form in recent years. It is the thunder of the moralist that is most strongly heard in such talking-animal stories as Richard Adams's *The Plague Dogs,* John Donovan's *Family,* Russel Hoban's *The Mouse and His Child,* Alan Arkin's *The Lemming Condition,* William Steig's ***Abel's Island,*** and, to a lesser degree, Adams's *Watership Down,* and Robert O'Brien's *Mrs. Frisby and the Rats of NIMH.*

The secondary strain can more truly be called animal fantasy as opposed to the tradition of the beast tale. It is almost a parvenu, its genesis rooted in the Edwardian period and its characteristics akin to those of classic fantasy. Writers in this subgenre, who number only a few, have used animals to create another secondary reality and to comment broadly and compassionately on the human condition, as distinct from the specific pointed attack on humanity in the beast tales. The writing styles of the fantasists frequently reflect a poetic and imaginative vision of life, the language enriched with beautiful diction and subtle images. This is opposed to the more naturalistic, mundane style of the moralists. (p. 107)

William Steig's ***Abel's Island,*** [a] condensed fable, is unique to the new wave in that the central protagonist wishes to remain in his present society but is forced out of it and finally reverts to his true animal nature. Abel is a dandified Edwardian mouse, who is so extremely self-centered that although "the sky was overcast . . . Abel didn't think it would be so inconsiderate as to rain when he and his lovely wife were in the mood for an outing."

Abel's placid life of privilege, comfort, and security is shattered when those very rains sweep him away to an uninhabited island. Thus begins Abel's rite of passage, wherein his determination and courage are tested. Like Odysseus, Abel eventually returns home to his Penelope-like wife, Amanda, but in mythic fashion, his heroic trials and quests have made a better mouse of him. In a moment of revelation during a life-and-death conflict with a cat, "Abel realized that the cat had to do what she did. She was being a cat. It was up to him to be the mouse." Abel has discovered his true animal identity. What a long way from *Wind in the Willows*! If Toad had ever discovered his real animal nature, he would have sat out half the book under a rock. (p. 117)

Sheila A. Egoff, "The New Fantasy," in her Thursday's Child: Trends and Patterns in Contemporary Children's Literature, *American Library Association, 1981, pp. 80-129.*

William Steig's ***Abel's Island*** tells somewhat the same story [as Tove Jansson's *Moominpappa at Sea*]. But there are differences, chiefly that Abel is alone and capable of effective action and that his island is more life-threatening than the Moomins'. These differences, indicating a further displacement of myth toward romance, are important. ***Abel's Island*** is more about heroism in the conventional sense than *Moominpappa at Sea;* it is largely typical of the adventure story usually told when an island is a book's setting. Since the publication of *Robinson Crusoe,* there have been more robinsonnades than any other type of books about islands. As a robinsonnade, Steig's book is, however, unique because it is also an animal story and thereby fantasy rather than mimetic fiction. It serves as a bridge between stories like the three already discussed, [Kenneth Grahame's *Wind in the Willows,* J. M. Barrie's *Peter Pan,* and Jansson's *Moominpappa at Sea,*] and more realistic and frightening stories like *Robinson Crusoe, Swiss Family Robinson,* and *Island of the Blue Dolphins.*

Abel is a mouse, a fact which Steig uses to his fullest advantage. There are the incongruity and consequent humor of there being a mouse named Abelard Hassam Di Chirico Flint, a name indicating his aristocratic background and behavior as the story opens. There are all the incongruities and humor resulting from his being characterized as human, worrying about his dress and reading a human book by running back and forth across the page. There is also Abel's animal nature, allowing him to be more at home in the wild than a human could be. All of these effects of Abel's dual nature function to distance the reader. Even young children identifying because of Abel's smallness and inexperience in an uncivilized environment do not measure distance in tails or dream of their wives. Their differences are their cushion against excessive fear when Abel's life is at risk as well as their reason for laughter. For adults the differences are additionally a source of irony—what Anita Moss calls "the gentle burlesque of fairy tale and romance conventions."

And this burlesque is, on the whole, very gentle. The survival story is not parodied as it is in *Moominpappa at Sea*. Its conventions are, in fact, all present. Abel arrives on the island as a result of an accident. His first efforts are all attempts to leave the island. Then he makes a home on the island. . . . He becomes strong and self-possessed in the process of transforming his island into something like a garden; he learns his vocation. Someone does eventually arrive on his island, only to renew his dissatisfaction with the island after his new found friend's departure. Now ready to return home, he finds a way. Back home he is a new person or mouse. He has learned to appreciate nature, strengthened his body, and discovered his artistic talent.

The robinsonnade formula has immense potential, primarily because it taps the emotional and intellectual significance of the myth of earthly paradise. The island here functions again as a symbol of the self, its transformation signaling Abel's integration and growth at the end of the book. His dreaming and sculpting enable his psychological survival and teach him the value of art, leading to his decision to become an artist. In every way, this romance celebrates transformation—of the self, of nature, and of reality. Abel becomes a better person than he was, the island becomes a loved place, and Steig's story offers us reality as it can be imagined. Earthly paradise becomes a goal rather than a gift, something one can achieve rather than something one merely possesses. Action—adventure—rather than a state of mind is thus the principal feature of the book, the emphasis shifting from the lovely place one has to the lovely place one may create. (pp. 54-5)

Virginia L. Wolf, "Paradise Lost?: The Displacement of Myth in Children's Novels Set on Islands," in Studies in the Literary Imagination, *Vol. XVIII, No. 2, Fall, 1985, pp. 47-63.*

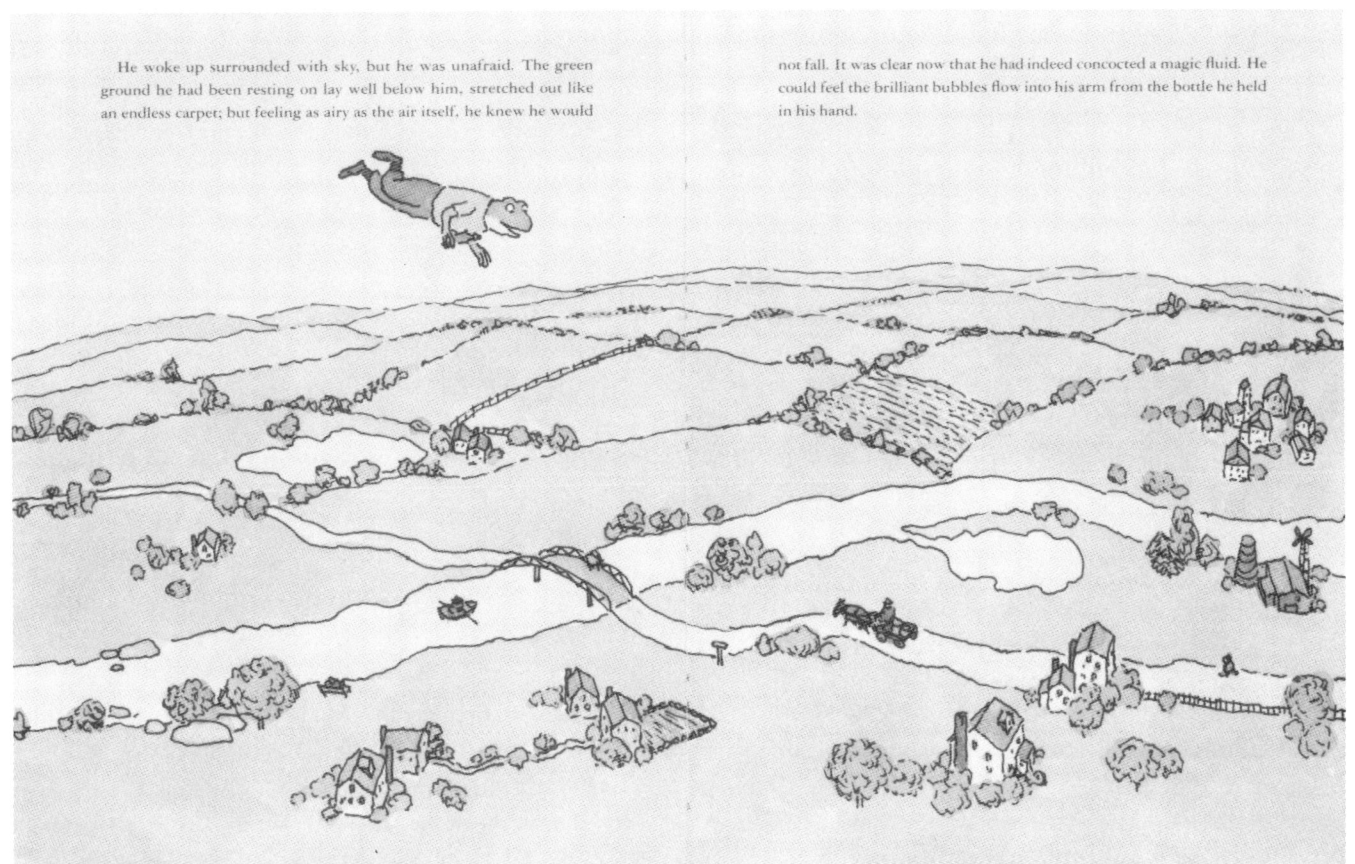

From Gorky Rises, *written and illustrated by William Steig. Farrar, Straus and Giroux, 1980. Copyright © 1980 by William Steig. All rights reserved. Reproduced by permission of Farrar, Straus and Giroux, Inc.*

***CALEB AND KATE* (1977)**

The illustrations in William Steig's newest children's tale, ***Caleb & Kate,*** are exactly right—inspired drawings for a fairytale world inhabited by old-fashioned folks. Kate, the weaver, is a comic-bosomed wife in her apron, shawls and a variety of daffy bonnets. Caleb, the carpenter, her barrel-chested husband with lank red mustache and hair, is transformed during the course of the story into Steig's approximation of a stunted golden retriever bewildered by his doggy fate. The hand-drawn circle of the moon is charming in its wavery imperfection. In Kate's kitchen the cupboard is stocked with bourgeois crockery—dangling cups, the good teapot and a beflowered oval platter for the Sunday roast: here's a world of comfort suggested in the single line (forming a stack of yellow plates) that squiggles down to rest on the top shelf. The ancestor portraits that hang on the walls are not half so witty as the laces of Caleb's boots.

Yes, as a parent I'd buy this book by the well-known cartoonist for *The New Yorker* on the strength of William Steig's humorous and humane art. But on one page we find poor Kate in her downtown hat inquiring after Caleb, her lost husband. The sympathetic villagers are truly wonderful to behold in their expressions of concern—all worried brows and sorrowful long noses. And there, in front of the Bakery and the Pharmacy just off the curb, march a half-dozen white ducks neither chic nor whimsical. They are simply there, where they belong, at the bottom of the picture. William Steig seems to be one of those rare grown-ups who come easily to the world of fantasy. Those rather serious parading ducks are the real clue to why both parents and children will read and reread ***Caleb & Kate:*** they are as unforced and inexplicable as Steig's talent.

The story opens with a fight: "Caleb the carpenter and Kate the weaver loved each other, but not every single moment." Stopping in the woods, Caleb can hardly remember the cause of their argument. As characters will in stories, he lies down to rest, and an amiable witch appears, smoking a corncob pipe. She's anxious to try a new incantation: and there is Caleb, who has "slipped into a green sleep." He is turned into a dog, not as a consequence of his anger at Kate but by happenstance, which can only be reasonable in fairy tales. We know not to dread his transformation because the witch crows "What a darling spell!" We know, too, that the spell will be broken, but there is an element of suspense and a nice unfolding of Kate's steadfast faith in the lost Caleb and her growing affection for the reddish dog that so mysteriously enters her life. The mute Caleb, licking and slobbering, gives what comfort he can to his wife. (p. 33)

Whatever trouble I had at first with the story of ***Caleb & Kate*** I attribute to my rusty adult imagination. When I read the story to younger children, I knew from the pure satisfaction on their faces that it would have been a mortal sin to question their belief. Another of Steig's children's books, ***Sylvester and the Magic Pebble,*** is a great favorite. In that story a donkey makes an unfortunate wish and turns into a stone. Again there is the loyalty motif—his parents, like Kate, are bereft, but never cease to hope for his return. I don't think there is any harm in Steig repeating the formula of a magic transformation. In one story the child is separated from his parents, and in the other the husband and wife are kept apart by fate. ***Caleb & Kate*** is more elaborate in its details. The language is richer, more knowing: "Night fell and there was a simple moon." Steig admits us to the world of make-believe that is natural to him. The simplicity of ***Sylvester*** makes it a classic tale; the fine points and minor complications of ***Caleb & Kate*** may make it just a joy to have on the bookshelf. . . .

Caleb & Kate is a reassuring story about two grownups who fight but care for each other deeply. The frightening aspect of parents quarreling must haunt us all: the reasonable world dissolves; Daddy is a dog and mother's in tears. Even the most faithful dog cannot replace a darling though difficult man. True love breaks the evil spell; but enough—I'm not a spoiler. ***Caleb & Kate*** is a terrific children's book, beautifully drawn, written and produced. The ducks are marching up Main Street. (p. 64)

Maureen Howard, "Daddy in the Dog House," in The New York Times Book Review, *November 13, 1977, pp. 33, 64.*

The resolution arrives through coincidence, which is too bad because the conflict touches on the deep-seated fear of losing a loved one by losing one's temper. Steig's talent shows up best in the art: the sympathetically drawn Caleb, afraid of his own animal nature, is the most personable of beasts. The story (un)hinges on the accidental nature of all that occurs in it. Although there is something to be said for happenstance, it's oversold here to an age group [grades 1-3] known for its attachment to cause and effect.

Pamela D. Pollack, in a review of "Caleb & Kate," in School Library Journal, *Vol. 24, No. 5, January, 1978, p. 82.*

Steig refurbishes his recycled plot with an inimitable wit that marks both incident and writing style: "Whenever their friends came calling, Kate would show off her dog. He enjoyed these gatherings, the human conversation, but he didn't like to have his head patted by his old cronies." Pen and wash drawings are familiar in style, their hues this time dominated by earthy browns, greens, and ochers. Facial expressions, human or animal, are not to be missed.

Denise M. Wilms, in a review of "Caleb & Kate," in Booklist, *Vol. 74, No. 10, January 15, 1978, p. 815.*

The well-cadenced storytelling has a certain old-fashioned elegance of language, and the humor is emphasized by an atmosphere of mock-pathos. William Steig is a superb artist with the literary ingenuity to produce durable, energetic stories; the result is another unified picture book in which text and illustrations are fully worthy of each other. (pp. 38-9)

Ethel L. Heins, in a review of "Caleb and Kate," in The Horn Book Magazine, *Vol. LIV, No. 1, February, 1978, pp. 38-9.*

***TIFFKY DOOFKY* (1978)**

One is invariably surprised by joy when a new book by Steig appears. Here he again blends comedy, suspense and adventure into a story, with the telling rivaling his paintings in originality, not to mention enchantment. The dog, Tiffky Doofky, likes his role as garbage collector in the town of Popville. One day, he feels that something welcome awaits him and consults the local fortune-teller, the goose, Madame Tarsal. She vows nothing will keep Tiffky from meeting the girl of his dreams, his future bride, before the sun sets. On his rounds, Tiffky meets a mean chicken, a magician. Jealous of the seer's powers, the biddy sends Tiffky on a fool's errand, into weird territory to be disappointed and buffeted by misfortunes. They are so jolly you don't want them to end, even though it's a relief to find Madame Tarsal right and Tiffky happy.

A review of "Tiffky Doofky," in Publishers Weekly, *Vol. 214, No. 19, November 6, 1978, p. 78.*

Steig can dress a floppy-eared, benign-looking dog in vest, armbands, and bow tie, give him the somehow perfectly suitable name of Tiffky Doofky, make him a jolly garbage collector on his way to a picnic—and who can resist going along? Tiffky Doofky is even more eager to get to the picnic after a visit to Madam Tarsal the fortuneteller, a duck who predicts that "This very day before the sun goes down, you will fall in love with the one you are going to marry. Nothing you can do can keep it from happening." But Tiffky Doofky never does make the party, for on the way he runs into a bike-riding biddy in baboushka who sends him off to a strange landscape and a series of dreamlike encounters. (The hen, it seems, is an evil rival of Madam Tarsal, maliciously enchanting Tiffky Doofky until she loses interest and he wakes up back in familiar territory—but Steig puts this information in parentheses as if scorning the pretense of working it into the story.) The duck's prophecy is fulfilled delightfully when Tiffky Doofky, dreaming of a gentle, sinuous caress, wakes to find himself in the coils of a boa constrictor—but the snake's carnival trainer, following close behind, is the pink-frocked poodle he's been waiting for. She might, however, disappoint readers with her pale, prissy appearance. But who's to quibble, when the whole is as good-naturedly loose as Tiffky Doofky himself, as arbitrary as vindictive magic—or falling in love.

A review of "Tiffky Doofky," in Kirkus Reviews, *Vol. XLVI, No. 24, December 15, 1978, p. 1354.*

You know what the pictures are like: Steig's personified charmers. But the deep, gentle humanity that audiences have learned to expect from his exemplary animal tales is missing here. It is the text that is at fault. Causes snatched from nowhere have effects snatched from someplace else; what might have been silly and funny turns out to be silly and unfunny.

Marjorie Lewis, in a review of "Tiffky Doofky," in School Library Journal, *Vol. 25, No. 5, January, 1979, p. 48.*

[***Tiffky Doofky*** is] a droll tale which parodies the structure of a sentimental novel—including a last view of the canine couple in the afterglow of the setting sun. The descriptive, witty text is finely honed to complement the extraordinarily articulate line with which the characters are limned. The illustrations further extend the parody in the contrast between the beauty of the watercolors and the absurdity of the concept. The picture storybook will probably be most appreciated by an audience slightly older than that which enjoys ***Sylvester and the Magic Pebble*** or ***Amos and Boris.*** (p. 55)

Mary M. Burns, in a review of "Tiffky Doofky," in The Horn Book Magazine, *Vol. LV, No. 1, February, 1979, pp. 54-5.*

GORKY RISES (1980)

[The illustrations in ***Gorky Rises***] have a buoyancy and ease that charm far more than the slight story does. A young frog makes and swallows a magic potion, falls asleep in a field, and wakes up in midair. He flies all over the countryside and eventually—after a thunderstorm and a night aloft—comes down. Mr. Steig's vision of the frog amidst the starry sky or floating lazily over a rolling New England landscape has a pastoral quality that is most attractive. There's lots of simple space and air in the book, appropriately enough; it's not so tangled and cluttered as many of his recent works have been. (p. 64)

Harold C. K. Rice, "A Potpourri of Picture Books," in The New York Times Book Review, *November 9, 1980, pp. 49, 64-5.*

The story loses momentum by the finish. . . . The plot's being a pastiche of previously seen Steig story elements takes away a degree of freshness, but the text is marvelously dry and the pictures hold a full measure of comedy. Not Steig at his best, but definitely not bad, either.

Denise M. Wilms, in a review of "Gorky Rises," in Booklist, *Vol. 77, No. 8, December 15, 1980, p. 576.*

This might not be the most psychologically resonant of Steig's picture books, but who can resist his unlikely transformations, flatly related marvels, and dabs of elementary humor? . . . There's no telling how Steig arrived at Gorky's name—or that of his cousin Gogol, who is "goggle-eyed" as Gorky comes rolling by. "He tore after his cousin yelling 'Gorky! Gorky! What's up?' " To which Gorky, of course, replies "I am," and laughs at his cousin's "look of stupid wonder." There are more wonders when Gorky lands, and more puns, with no need for questions and answers. Like Gorky, who seems to float inertly through the clouds, Steig treats the most remarkable events with aplomb, tossing them off as all in a day's dreamwork. (pp. 3-4)

A review of "Gorky Rises," in Kirkus Reviews, *Vol. XLIX, No. 1, January 1, 1981, pp. 3-4.*

Steig's paintings have a freshness and a bland translation of nonsense-into-fact that are appealing, with a cartoonist's use of deft, economical line. His story is lightly told, the vocabulary making few concessions to the picture book audience; in this story of a young frog who mixes a magic potion and goes flying, the incidents are stronger than the story line, however, and the ending—Gorky's parents don't believe him until he shows them the hole in the ground where Elephant Rock used to be and thus convinces them that it really did turn into an elephant he rode home after his flight—is a bit of a letdown.

Zena Sutherland, in a review of "Gorky Rises," in Bulletin of the Center for Children's Books, *Vol. 34, No. 6, February, 1981, p. 121.*

DOCTOR DE SOTO (1982)

In this captivating story of a mouse dentist, Steig sets his stage according to the ludicrous logic of size discrepancy that intrigues children: to treat large animals . . . , Dr. De Soto stands on a ladder; and for extra-large animals . . . , he is hoisted up on a pulley contraption by his wife/assistant. Then he gets right into his patients' mouths, "wearing rubbers to keep his feet dry." Understandably, Dr. De Soto refuses to treat animals dangerous to mice—not even "the most timid-looking cat." But one day when a well-dressed fox comes pleading with him to ease his pain, the De Sotos relent. And as the dentist works inside the fox's mouth, the patient goes from a lip-smacking dream under gas ("How I love them raw, with just a pinch of salt, and a dry white wine") . . . to wondering, after the first visit, "if it would be shabby of him to eat the De Sotos when the job was done" . . . to "I really shouldn't eat them. On the other hand, how can I resist?" . . . to "definitely" making up his mind to eat them. But the De Sotos, though compassionate, are no fools, and so they outfox the fox—coating his teeth with a final preventive treatment that is really glue. And so, with his jaw stuck shut (for just a day or two, the dentist assures him), the defeated fox stumbles down the stairs—which Steig, as a parting reference to the arrangements set forth at the beginning, has divided into the regular flight the fox is using and a narrower one of smaller steps. Simple but sly, a mischievously imaginative rendition of the classic theme.

A review of "Doctor De Soto," in Kirkus Reviews, *Vol. L, No. 21, November 1, 1982, p. 1191.*

The Newbery Honor book goes beyond the usual tale of wit versus might; the story achieves comic heights partly through the delightful irony of the situation—how often is a dentist at the mercy of his patient?—as well as through the orchestration of text and illustration. Watercolor paintings, with the artist's firm line and luscious color, depict with aplomb the eminently dentistlike mouse as he goes about his business, whether dangling above a donkey with a quiver of tools on his belt or cheerfully standing up to the sly fox.

Kate M. Flanagan, in a review of "Doctor De Soto," in The Horn Book Magazine, *Vol. LIX, No. 2, April, 1983, p. 162.*

The genius of William Steig is not, in my view, fully appreciated in this country. His use of language is quite brilliant, and his pictures underline the wit of his words. A picture book which should be put in the way of readers over eight, who are likely to appreciate its subtleties, particularly if shared with an enthusiastic adult. (p. 54)

Jill Bennett, in a review of "Doctor De Soto," in The School Librarian, *Vol. 32, No. 1, March, 1984, pp. 53-4.*

From Doctor De Soto, *written and illustrated by William Steig. Farrar, Straus and Giroux, 1982. Copyright © 1982 by William Steig. All rights reserved. Reproduced by permission of Farrar, Straus and Giroux, Inc.*

A novel and thoroughly contemporary treatment of a traditional theme—the outwitting of the strong and wily by the small and weak—lies at the heart of this deliciously funny tale set in a dentist's surgery. Steig's slightly crude but gloriously detailed illustrations show the ingenuity required and the risks run when a mouse is the dentist and a hungry fox has [a] toothache. A judicious blend of comedy, chills, and an unexpectedly civilized conclusion.

Elizabeth Hammill, "Picture Books & Illustrated Stories 6 to 9: 'Dr. De Soto'," in The Signal Review of Children's Books, 2, *1984, p. 12.*

***YELLOW AND PINK* (1984)**

In Steig's latest dazzler, exquisitely understated writing meshes with the sophisticated, witty pictures that emphasize again the scope of his ingenuity. Two little wooden figures—one pink, the other yellow—lie under the sun in the grass in front of a country house. Cows, chickens, trees and everything else are depicted in ink drawings, including possibilities that Yellow talks about as the story unfolds. Pink wonders who they are, how they got here; "Someone must have made us." But Yellow claims they are a mere accident. He goes into elaborate surmises on how they could have been formed by a tree branch, splitting in just the right way to make legs. He suggests ever more preposterous explanations for how they acquired mouths, eyes, hands, etc. Pink argues vainly against Yellow's elaborate theories and the discussion rolls on until a man comes from the house, tests the dolls and finds their paint is dry. As he takes them into the house, Yellow whispers, "Who is this guy?" Pink doesn't know. With this skillful thrust, Steig concludes a comic fable that has more clout than the most fervent homily.

A review of "Yellow & Pink," in Publishers Weekly, *Vol. 225, No. 20, May 18, 1984, p. 152.*

Ontologists, cosmologists, epistemologists, metaphysicans and theologians have continued through the centuries to ponder these central, compelling questions of human existence: who are we? why are we here? who or what made us? why do people of all races share physical similarities, except for pigmentation? Steig, in words and pictures made familiar by his many *New Yorker* cartoons over the years and his fewer and much better books for children, thoroughly trivializes these concerns by way of a sophomoric joke nearly as old as the questions. A series of actionless illustrations follow the conversation of two jointed, wooden puppets . . . as they struggle to arrive at the purpose and nature of their existence. Just as they decide that, "Some things will have to remain a mystery," a man walks up, checks them over and decides that the puppets he's made and painted are "Nice and dry." Hence, no purpose, no answers, no self-will safe from the frivolous interference of uncaring forces. . . . The publishers' jacket copy labels this for all ages, always a sure sign that something either overly sentimental (such as Buscaglia's *The Fall of Freddie the Leaf*) or something cheaply cynical is being dumped on the children's book market when, in fact, it isn't good enough for children.

Lillian N. Gerhardt, in a review of "Yellow & Pink," in School Library Journal, *Vol. 30, No. 10, August, 1984, p. 66.*

Most people love stories in which something magical occurs as if it were entirely ordinary—horses fly, animals talk, or inanimate objects like stones or puppets speak as if they were alive. And not only alive, of course, but just like us. In William Steig's new book, ***Yellow & Pink,*** a pair of small wood figures are lying on a newspaper out in a grassy field where the cows are "dreamy," the chickens "busy," and the pair are "wondering." What they are wondering about is the creation of their lives.

Yellow, who, with his hat, round, small, "gimlet" eyes and trim mustache, looks remarkably like James Joyce, is the first to sit up and ask, "Do I know you?" Pink doesn't think so. Yellow is the fellow who will ask all the questions: What are we doing here? How did we get here? Who are we? Pink doesn't know. Instead, he looks Yellow over. "He found Yellow's color, his well-chiseled head, his whole form, admirable. 'Someone must have made us,' he said." But Yellow will have none of it. "How could anyone make something like me, so intricate, so perfect? . . . Or, for that matter, like you." For Yellow, thin and testy, has decided they're an accident of nature. Plump, easygoing Pink is incredulous and laughs. How could anything as wonderful as they are be a "fluke"?

"Don't laugh," Yellow says. "Just stop and reflect. With enough time, a thousand, a million, maybe two and a half million years, lots of unusual things could happen. Why not us?"

Yellow believes in evolution. Pink does not. But he does want Yellow to explain. Yellow tries and tries. Maybe a piece of wood fell from a tree, got struck by lightning "in such a way as to make arms, fingers, toes." Maybe eyes and ears are made by insects boring or hailstones striking. But he can never answer to Pink's satisfaction. Because Yellow, however inventive and even hopeful he may be, is also clearly wrong, and children will have known this from the first. Finally, exasperated by Pink, he resorts to name-calling, never the tactic of the sure: Pink's a "dummy."

And yet is this not, dear children, just the way life is? In any pair, there is always one who can neither ask nor answer but who can always find objections to the other fellow's attempt. For all of Yellow's fancy surmises, he is in the end silenced. "I can't answer all the questions. . . . But why are we arguing on such a fine day?"

They aren't arguing; they are questing. Then out shambles their maker, "humming out of tune." We're back in the real world, where puppets get made and painted by someone else. But maybe this gentleman is the real dummy, for how can he not notice that Yellow is standing up, leaning against a tree stump instead of being where he left him to dry? And how can he not overhear Yellow's last question, addressed, of course, to Pink (who else will there ever be for Yellow to talk to?): "Who is this guy?"

This guy's Geppetto. And if the youngsters in your life are short philosophers, this book's for them. If not, not.

Nancy Milford, in a review of "Yellow & Pink," in The New York Times Book Review, *August 12, 1984, p. 28.*

Abstractions can go to the heart of a problem. ***Yellow and Pink*** is a somewhat sardonic account of two wooden figures . . . who lie on an old newspaper idly chatting about how they got there. . . . The two colours of the pictures, hatched, splashed, outlined and shaded, exploit woodenness in the postures of the figures; humour and a touch of melancholy make this Lear-ish fable reverberate in the mind, as the pictures in their total simplicity point to universal truths.

Margery Fisher, in a review of "Yellow and Pink," in Growing Point, *Vol. 25, No. 4, November, 1986, p. 4703.*

ROTTEN ISLAND **(1984)**

Issued in 1969 and long out of print, ***The Bad Island*** as reproduced disappointed Steig, who worked with the publisher of this renamed, revised edition to ensure that the illustrations were effectively reproduced. Now the undimmed, coruscating, deliberately clashing colors in the paintings appropriately portray the thoroughly hideous and hilarious creatures on the rotten island. Integrated with the marvelous scenes is the story that one assimilates like music or poetry, in Steig's inimitable telling. The ugly beasts are perfectly at home in the place that offers nothing but spiny plants and gravel to eat. They exult in fighting each other and all-round misery. Then comes the day when the sight of a single, fragile flower on the rotten island terrifies the inhabitants. They go raving mad, leap into the sea and vanish forever. Then the flowers proliferate, the place becomes edenic: "It wasn't long before the first birds came to the new, beautiful island." The book can be taken as an analogue or just for fun. (pp. 99-100)

A review of "Rotten Island," in Publishers Weekly, *Vol. 225, No. 25, June 22, 1984, pp. 99-100.*

This slight allegory remains a situation rather than a story partly because no characters emerge to engage readers' sympathy. Instead, the monsters act out the conflict *en masse,* and the illustrations—here reproduced in fluorescent inks—lack the subtlety of Steig's later work. Nonetheless, a few gems appear. There's a glorious night sky scene plus several double-page spreads of creatures drawn in deliciously monstrous detail. Also, the vocabulary contributes some quirky delights. This is not Steig at his best, and most libraries can easily pass it by, but some may want to have it as a not-unworthy exhibit in one writer/illustrator's development.

Ellen D. Warwick, in a review of "Rotten Island," in School Library Journal, *Vol. 31, No. 2, October, 1984, p. 152.*

Rotten Island is like the world before the Flood: "From cursing and blaming, scratching and shoving, they took to serious fighting, and all their deepest demons of hate tore loose. . . . It was every rotten one for his own rotten self against every rotten one else." In visual terms this is a nonthreatening world. The childish tantrums are similar to the tantrums of the Princess in [Mordecai Gerstein's] *Prince Sparrow.* Like Steig, children enjoy devising creatures that are amazingly creative in their design. No matter that the jagged teeth suggest a hideous persona. A gorgeous geometric surface treatment, as in Steig's goggle-eyed insect with chopping mandibles, turns a monster into an object of fun. And the incongruities and strings of adjectives set the same tone in the text. . . .

The structure of the allegory is so simple that teachers could use the book as an antiwar, antipollution, anticommunism, anticapitalism, antiracism fable. . . .

As in Steig's *New Yorker* drawings, there is a commentary here in relation to our times, but Steig lets the viewer sort out the implications. An alien world is paradoxically fascinating and incredible. To a child the closest analogy may be an elementary school playground at recess time: at the peak of a competitive game, children sometimes shove, shriek, and glare almost as senselessly as Steig's seriocomic monsters. Then they take pens in hand (like Steig and their other artist friends) and create rich, harmonious, other-worldly designs. (p. 129)

Donnarae MacCann and Olga Richard, "Picture Books for Children," in Wilson Library Bulletin, *Vol. 59, No. 2, October, 1984, pp. 128-29.*

***CDC?* (1984)**

This companion volume to the ever-popular brainteaser ***CDB!*** . . . is every bit as ingenious and twice as challenging as its predecessor. As in ***CDB!***, Steig has devised letter and number sequences, with a few figures like $ and ¢ thrown in for good measure, which, when pronounced aloud, translate roughly into captions for the accompanying cartoon drawings. The cartoons also contain helpful clues to the words' meanings, as in the title phrase, which is matched with a drawing of a man and boy looking out at the sea. Some of these quips contain references that children will have difficulty interpreting: the drawing of two ladies in a garden will bewilder kids trying to decipher "S A R-D N-U-L" (It's a hardy annual). Also, as in this example, the vocabulary is often demanding. Not many children tackling this book are likely to recognize words like *asinine, odious,* and *exhilarating* when properly spelled out, let alone in Steig's shorthand phonetic renditions. Still, collections where demand for the original puzzler runs high will surely want to add this stimulating sequel.

Karen Stang Hanley, in a review of "CDC?" in Booklist, *Vol. 81, No. 10, January 15, 1985, p. 724.*

Steig's latest compilation of puzzlers defies age- or grade-level classification; larger, longer, somewhat more sophisticated in content than its predecessor, the book has a transgenerational appeal—provided that children are willing to share it with adults. As in the earlier book, letters and numbers which suggest the sounds of words or phrases are printed as captions for interpretive cartoons. The combination is irresistible, luring the reader from riddle to riddle until "D N." But translating the text is only half the fun, for the illustrations are more than helpful clues. Characterized by a marvelously fluid, expressive line—finer than that used for ***C D B!***—they gently satirize familiar situations and clichés or hint of a story about to begin. . . . Flawlessly executed, purely pleasurable, the book is definitely "D Q-R" for doldrums at any season.

Mary M. Burns, in a review of "CDC?" in The Horn Book Magazine, *Vol. LXI, No. 1, January-February, 1985, p. 56.*

Steig has created a collection of comic, cartoon-like black-and-white line drawings captioned with cryptic phrases in code. . . . For sophisticated readers who discern the meaning, the message may well raise a chuckle or at least stir a groan. The humor of both illustration and "text," however, presumes knowledge well beyond what the picture book format indicates. For example, an obviously unhappy, withdrawn man is pictured in a fetal position crouched in a stuffed chair. The caption reads, "M-N-U-L S N-C-Q-R." Translation: Emanuel is insecure. . . . Even a "F-N" (Heaven) is juxtaposed to a fiery "L" on a double-page spread. (Steig's background as a cartoonist is evident in this book; some of these would be better placed in the *New Yorker*.) Steig's humor and language is consistently mature, even in books appreciated by young audiences. Yet because each vignette here is intended to stand on its own and contains little contextual clue as to its meaning, it will be best understood by mature readers. Certainly children will quickly understand some of these, but even adults may struggle with others. In any case, this adult sequel to ***CDB!*** will be fun for those who like word play and puzzles. Enough said: D N!

Maria Salvadore, in a review of "CDC?" in School Library Journal, *Vol. 31, No. 6, February, 1985, p. 87.*

***SOLOMON THE RUSTY NAIL* (1985)**

In yet another delightfully inventive picture book, Steig combines a tale of uncanny transformation with his distinctively animated illustrations.

By coincidence, Solomon the rabbit scratches his nose and wiggles his toes simultaneously—and a marvelous metamorphosis occurs: he discovers that he's capable of turning himself into a nail. (p. 1399)

One summer day, while Solomon is searching for rare butterfly specimens in a meadow, he meets a most unpleasant stranger—Ambrose, a one-eyed cat. Armed with a knife, Ambrose is ready to march Solomon home to cook for supper. It's a frightful predicament but suddenly Solomon remembers his magic trick and vanishes. Ambrose, whose surly demeanor would frighten anyone, marches off in a rather confused state. Solomon reappears prematurely and is spotted by the cat, who pockets him as a nail and takes him away, not quite understanding the strange turn of events. Clorinda, his portly wife, doesn't really believe Ambrose's tale, but they put the nail in a padlocked cage in anticipation of fresh rabbit stew. As the days pass, the two become increasingly frustrated, and Ambrose eventually hammers Solomon into the side of the house in a fit of rage.

Being a nail imbedded in a wall is a new experience for Solomon and he copes as best he can, though a pervading sense of loneliness permeates his reverie. A stroke of good fortune luckily occurs and Solomon returns home to his astounded family.

Children will love this bizarre tale with its humorous drawings and lively sense of fun. Steig continues to create enchanting pictures in the style that has brought him international popularity. (pp. 1399-1400)

A review of "Solomon the Rusty Nail," in Kirkus Reviews, *Vol. LIII, No. 24, December 15, 1985, pp. 1399-1400.*

Steig's transformation motif is at work again in this story of Solomon, an ordinary rabbit but for the power to turn into a rusty nail anytime he pleases. . . . While the freshness of Steig's theme has faded, children who have enjoyed the author's other tales may relish the familiarity to be found here. The art is the familiar pen-and-wash drawings, which, like the text, are practiced and appealing but break no new ground.

From Brave Irene, *written and illustrated by William Steig. Farrar, Straus and Giroux, 1986. Copyright © 1986 by William Steig. All rights reserved. Reproduced by permission of Farrar, Straus and Giroux, Inc.*

Denise M. Wilms, in a review of "Solomon the Rusty Nail," in Booklist, *Vol. 82, No. 9, January 1, 1986, p. 687.*

Steig's watercolors are, as always, uniquely expressive, ranging from wryly witty to luminescently lovely. However, there is more than a hint of *déjà vu* to the story line: echoes of ***Sylvester and the Magic Pebble*** mix with overtones of ***The Amazing Bone*** conjuring up earlier—and better—fantasies. In the process of pasting together elements from other fantasies, Steig has created a world leaking at its logical seams. If Solomon can "still hear though he had no ears, and see though he had no eyes," why can he not also talk, though he has no mouth, and thus save himself at once? Furthermore, Solomon discovers his magical power while sitting on a green, flower-sprinkled lawn, then proceeds to mystify his friends, "starting the next day," as they all frolic with sleds on a snow-covered hillside. Now really! Quibbles, perhaps, but ones that glare like errors in this less-than-masterful performance by a master storyteller. (pp. 78-9)

Kristi Thomas Beavin, in a review of "Solomon the Rusty Nail," in School Library Journal, *Vol. 32, No. 6, February, 1986, pp. 78-9.*

William Steig is one of a few remarkable illustrators whose use of language can be compared to his artistic talents. Many examples of this ability adorn his new book, which will inevitably remind readers of ***Sylvester and the Magic Pebble***. . . . The felicities of language are numerous: the cat, a rather Bogart-style gangster, addresses his wife as Pussykins; when he is enraged beyond all endurance and yells at Solomon to turn himself back into a rabbit, "Solomon chose not to." The illustrations are inimitably Steig, although a trifle quieter in color than his work usually is. But the book is, without a doubt, a prize pazoozle of a picture book. (pp. 197-98)

Ann A. Flowers, in a review of "Solomon the Rusty Nail," in The Horn Book Magazine, *Vol. LXII, No. 2, March-April, 1986, pp. 197-98.*

BRAVE IRENE **(1986)**

Each new picture book by William Steig is met with eager anticipation. His latest, a heroic fable, stands as a testament to the magical power of love. Hardworking Mrs. Bobbin has just finished a beautiful ballgown for the duchess, but she has a headache and can't deliver it. Brave and devoted daughter Irene takes charge, tucking her mother snugly into bed and determinedly marching out into a raging snowstorm with the dress. Howling "GO HO-WO-WOME" at poor Irene, the fierce wind rips the box open and the gown sails out, "waltzing through the powdered air with tissue-paper attendants." "How could anything so terribly wrong be allowed to happen?" the girl wonders miserably. She trudges on through the snowy night, ready to tell her sad story to the duchess. But in Steig's universe, miracles *do* happen: when Irene arrives at the palace, having defeated the blizzard, there is the gown, wrapped around a tree. She tells the duchess her amazing story, attends the ball and arrives home in triumph, greeted joyously by her mother. Bleak winter landscapes, in gray and white washes, contrast with the warmth and cheer of vibrant colors inside the two houses. Story and art are in perfect concord here; ***Brave Irene*** has the timeless quality of a classic fairy tale.

A review of "Brave Irene," in Publishers Weekly, *Vol. 230, No. 13, September 26, 1986, p. 80.*

Steig, who tells his uncomplicated story in a disarmingly breezy style, is a master of the perfect unexpected word, the startlingly right phrase. Mrs. Bobbin calls her wholesome daughter "cupcake," "dumpling," and "pudding." The ill-tempered wind [is] a feisty character in itself. . . . The illustrations showing Irene's indomitable struggle on her way between comfortable home and welcoming castle complement the text admirably, deftly charting the passage on Irene's expressive face of determination, discouragement, surprise and jubilation; the illustrations are also interesting as a series of subtly changing paintings of girl and yellow box in a gradually darkening winter landscape.

A thoroughly satisfying picture book. . . .

A review of "Brave Irene," in Kirkus Reviews, *Vol. LIV, No. 20, October 15, 1986, p. 1580.*

Somehow, magically, the world has been made safe for Brave Irene and [Patricia C. McKissack's Flossie Finley in *Flossie & the Fox*]. They represent a new archetype we may have to call Junior Ms. A girl who can match wits with a bushy-tailed bandit, or a dark and stormy night, or fear itself. A girl so game and street (or dirt road) smart, she might grow up into one of those career viragoes now striding across our television and movie screens. Out of Africa and into space. Saving the farm, the orphan, the marines, the galaxy. Irene and Flossie may fly over a Rambo, armed only with spunk, upper-body strength and a salty vocabulary. These are not the little girls Maurice Chevalier thanked heaven for. Thank Heaven.

To be sure, William Steig's and Patricia McKissack's heroines need every survival skill they can muster—or what's a folk tale for? Poor but precious only children, in the classic mold, both are bursting with old-fashioned goodness. . . .

Though Mr. Steig's artistry makes us love her most when she's angry, Irene's finest moment comes not in the wonderful, life-saving rage she feels when all seems lost. It's when she decides to face the duchess, and poor Mama, with that soggy empty box. When was the last time a hero, regardless of age or gender, risked life and limb to deliver an *apology*? Hurray for Irene; this delightful tale has a perfect ending—even for the ball gown.

Lois Gould, "Junior Ms., Tough and Smart," in The New York Times Book Review, *November 9, 1986, p. 41.*

Sometimes one could imagine that William Steig uses books to illustrate the various virtues—***Sylvester and the Magic Pebble*** might demonstrate steadfastness; ***Amos and Boris,*** loyalty; ***Doctor De Soto,*** resourcefulness and devotion to duty. In ***Brave Irene*** bravery is certainly a major theme. . . . In this book Steig pictures humans instead of animal surrogates, a rather unusual departure for him, and the snow scenes at nightfall have a blue duskiness that is very effective. Not only does Irene show bravery, she also shows the qualities of steadfastness, loyalty, resourcefulness, and devotion to duty. The book indicates that Steig has a general view of humanity that esteems all the virtues, and his beliefs are expressed with such a felicitous combination of gifts, verbal and artistic, that we are the more fortunate for it. (pp. 740-41)

Ann A. Flowers, in a review of "Brave Irene," in The Horn Book Magazine, *Vol. LXII, No. 6, November-December, 1986, pp. 740-41.*

Mildred Pitts Walter

1922-

Black American author of fiction and picture books.

Walter is respected as an accomplished author of works which, although written almost exclusively from the viewpoint of black characters, are considered universally appealing. She is noted for providing the preschool through high school audience with books which capture atmosphere and maintain story interest, for expertly presenting and integrating themes which range from the simple to the complex, and for creating interesting, believable characters. Formerly an elementary school teacher, Walter is often acclaimed for her understanding of children and their problems. Her works address such topics as race relations, family life, and the struggles of growing up. While centering on situations which revolve around the home and school, Walter's books reflect such diverse locations as urban Los Angeles, the Louisiana Bayou, the rural South, and Africa.

Walter began her career with two works, *Lillie of Watts: A Birthday Discovery* (1969) and *Lillie of Watts Takes a Giant Step* (1971), which were written for the older elementary school audience. Although these books include a realistic assessment of ghetto life, their emphasis is on the everyday disappointments and accomplishments that bring Lillie's values—which include a growing involvement with black consciousness—into perspective. *Justin and the Best Biscuits in the World* (1986), which is also for the elementary school reader, explores sex-role stereotyping as ten-year-old Justin learns that housework can be satisfying from his grandfather, who also tells the boy inspiring stories about their cowboy ancestors. This book exemplifies one of Walter's characteristic features, the inclusion of examples of black history in her works. *The Girl on the Outside* (1982), a fictionalized version of the first attempt to integrate a high school in Little Rock, Arkansas in 1954, is a more straightforward historical account. Directing this work to junior high and high school readers, Walter uses semi-alternating chapters to provide insight into the characters of her two protagonists, a white girl enveloped by racism and a black girl who volunteers to be bused. *Because We Are* (1983) and *Trouble's Child* (1985) examine adolescent maturation within the challenges of inhibiting environments: in the first book, Walter describes how high school senior Emma overcomes classroom racism and difficulties at home, while *Trouble's Child* depicts fifteen-year-old Martha's dilemma whether to stay on a small Louisiana island or go to school on the mainland. Walter has also written three picture books: *Ty's One-Man Band* (1980), the story of a mysterious musician and the boy who observes him; *My Mama Needs Me* (1983), which describes how Jason adjusts to his new baby sister; and *Brother to the Wind* (1985), a fantasy about a young African who yearns to fly.

Walter is praised for creating relevant works which attract a wide variety of young readers through their warmth, vivid settings, and insightful explorations of self-discovery. While reviewers are divided as to the success of her low-keyed writing style and also state that she summarizes with unrealistic endings, most agree that Walter is a sensitive author of stories which accurately reflect the feelings and concerns of her audience.

Reproduced by permission of Mildred Walter

Walter received the Coretta Scott King Award honorable mention in 1984 for *Because We Are;* she won the Coretta Scott King Award in 1987 for *Justin and the Best Biscuits in the World.*

(See also *Something about the Author*, Vol. 45.)

LILLIE OF WATTS: A BIRTHDAY DISCOVERY **(1969)**

If the name *Watts* had no overtones, this would still be a good book. And Lillie's ups and downs would be appealing no matter what her color. But Watts is here what it is—a blend of crowded housing and scarred storefronts and sturdy palm trees, a place where people are forebearing like Lillie's mother (who works as a domestic in Malibu) or restive like her older sister Evelyn. . . . The story centers on Lillie's three bad days. The first, her birthday, starts well: Mama lets her wear her best sweater and skirt, (black) teacher Mr. Knox plays "Happy Birthday" on his violin. Then a classmate spills paint on her sweater and Lillie, trying to wash out the stain, ruins it altogether. In disgrace, she is denied a trip to Malibu and further disheartened when Mama brings her employer's cat to stay overnight. Terrified by Grandma's tales of death-dealing cats, Lillie lets it out, is told the next morning to "find that cat (or) don't come back." But before the cat turns up (near home), Lillie, prompted by Mama, realizes that "people are more important than cats, sweaters and (money for) cars." The narrative neither minces nor wastes words. . . . The only thing that may hamper the book (besides its blatant title) is the picture book sizing; it's about a credible eleven-year-old though written on the third-fourth grade level.

A review of "Lillie of Watts: A Birthday Discovery," in Kirkus Reviews, *Vol. XXXVII, No. 7, April 1, 1969, p. 379.*

Here is a beguiling story of a small black girl's birthday in the ghetto of Watts. Here is another genuine book written by a black author to add to the growing—not fast enough but still growing—list of juvenile books with black characters that are genuine stories. It is a gentle, disarming story that will not join the too-fast growing list of books with black characters that are being written today by the opportunist group of juvenile writers; but it will be enjoyed by all young readers because its author knew what she was writing about. And knew how to write it.

A review of "Lillie of Watts: A Birthday Discovery," in Publishers Weekly, *Vol. 195, No. 15, April 14, 1969, p. 97.*

A low-keyed story with . . . a weak story line and an interesting setting. Over the weekend of Lillie's eleventh birthday, a series of small, personal disasters trouble her; some are solved and some, realistically, are not. The candid, simple writing is a bit flat, but the book's appeal is not in dramatic events and the style is little of a handicap. Appeal is vested in the very ordinariness of Lillie's day-to-day life: the busy, crowded household, the accepted scarcity of material goods, a small girl's desire to be admired and her struggle to overcome fear.

Zena Sutherland, in a review of "Lillie of Watts: A Birthday Discovery," in Bulletin of the Center for Children's Books, *Vol. 22, No. 10, June, 1969, p. 166.*

When [Lillie's 11th birthday] arrives, it is marred by a series of unfortunate incidents which culminate during the night: frightened by the cat that her mother is taking care of for her employer, Lillie lets it escape. As she wanders about the streets the next morning in search of the cat, the sights and sounds of the ghetto provide an accompaniment; as translated for the reader, they give a realistic picture of what life in Watts is really like. The strength of this book, however, lies in its believable, warm portrait of Lillie and her family. Poor they are, but rich in love (which Lillie finally learns to appreciate) and self-respect. Deftly written, a low-keyed story with well-realized characters . . . , this should win friends among little girls, both white and black.

Barbara S. Miller, in a review of "Lillie of Watts: A Birthday Discovery," in School Library Journal, *an appendix to* Library Journal, *Vol. 16, No. 6, February, 1970, p. 82.*

LILLIE OF WATTS TAKES A GIANT STEP (1971)

The little girl who made a *Birthday Discovery* in 1969 is ready for junior high school, and this longer, more mature novel covers a crucial year in her incipient sense of identity. In September Lillie is annoyed because Mama is still picking out her school clothes and mortified because she can't afford to buy lunch like the other children; the lunch issue becomes so important that she throws away her sandwich every day and goes hungry, falls down in all her subjects (even volleyball), and becomes "just plain evil" at home. By May she's a core member of the school's new African-American Culture Club and a leader of the movement to boycott classes on Malcolm X's birthday—much to the distress of Mama, who thinks Malcolm X "ain't done nothing but teach hate and violence" and doesn't like Lillie's natural hairdo either: "Never thought I'd live to see the day. We going backwards." Lillie's older sisters, too, emerge as personalities: regarding Lillie's Africa bag, mini-skirted Evelyn says "I'll take America"—to which the heavy college student Joyce remarks, "And that's the only way you're going to get America too, is take it." It's too bad the last page cops out, with Mama suddenly converted to the need for black heroes, the vice-principal agreeing to discuss an in-school Malcolm X assembly, and the militant students compliantly defused; until then Lillie's small agonies and her growing involvement with black consciousness are vividly and affectingly handled.

A review of "Lillie of Watts Takes a Giant Step," in Kirkus Reviews, *Vol. XXXIX, No. 20, October 15, 1971, p. 1124.*

Like the first book, this is a quiet and realistic portrayal of small events, although Lillie's first move away from maternal jurisdiction and her growing sense of black identity give it more impact. The writing style is adequate, marred by occasional awkwardness; for example, when there is a boycott of classes on the occasion of the birthday of Malcolm X, the vice-principal says, "I didn't say I'd call the police." "Oh yes you did!" one girl replies, and the author continues, redundantly, "Deborah said, disagreeing with the vice-principal."

Zena Sutherland, in a review of "Lillie of Watts Takes a Giant Step," in Bulletin of the Center for Children's Books, *Vol. 25, No. 5, January, 1972, p. 82.*

Mildred Pitts Walter writes with authority. She knows the children about whom she writes because she has taught for many years in the schools of Los Angeles. When Lillie Stevens enters Pelham Junior High School for the first time in ***Lillie of Watts Takes a Giant Step,*** her anxiety and uncertainty is authentic; Mildred Walter projects her major character into a real school situation. . . .

The author explores many anxieties of a thirteen-year-old girl: friendship with other girls, a growing interest in the opposite sex, the awfulness of deceit, the struggle to find out what is right. . . .

I believe that a younger adolescent reader will be deeply interested in Lillie and her attempts to find out what is right for her. ***Lillie of Watts Takes a Giant Step*** is easy but thoughtful reading.

John W. Conner, in a review of "Lillie of Watts Takes a Giant Step," in English Journal, *Vol. 61, No. 3, March, 1972, p. 435.*

[Lillie's] most important "giant step" is her beginning interest and eventual involvement in the black social revolution. Unfortunately, the story is somewhat dated by the use of such terms as "groovy" and "African American" (the latter never having been used by blacks), and Walter does not discuss Martin Luther King's assassination and its effect on kids in the Watts community during the summer of '68 when this story is set. Nevertheless, Walter does create believable characters, correctly identifies the problems confronting young blacks, and uses a simple vocabulary to advantage.

Rosalind K. Goddard, in a review of "Lillie of Watts Takes a Giant Step," in School Library Journal, *an appendix to* Library Journal, *Vol. 18, No. 8, April, 1972, p. 141.*

TY'S ONE-MAN BAND **(1980)**

From out of the still, summer heat, a peg-leg man appears. To Ty, this man, Andro, is a miracle; he juggles his tin plate, spoon, and cup and makes wonderful rhythms with them. Then Andro sparks Ty's curiosity even further: he says he's a one-man band and will prove it if Ty brings a washboard, wooden spoons, a tin pail, and a comb at sundown. Ty's family and friends are nonbelievers—no one could make music from such dull, practical items. But Andro brings music to town, the people dance joyfully to his irresistible beat, and only Ty notices Andro slip away in the dark. The episode has a magical quality; the mystery of the man stays cloaked while his bold music steps forward in the sound-sensitive words of the text. . . . A fine work, with music of its own. (pp. 122, 124)

Judith Goldberger, in a review of "Ty's One-Man Band," in Booklist, *Vol. 77, No. 2, September 15, 1980, pp. 122, 124.*

What is significant about this book is the evocation of a single episode in Southern life of an age gone by. In fact, Mildred Pitts Walter remembered it from her own Louisiana childhood. Her text is filled with rhythms: the sound of the pegged-legged man walking, the freight train passing, drumming fingers and stamping feet.

George A. Woods, in a review of "Ty's One-Man Band," in The New York Times Book Review, *October 12, 1980, p. 39.*

[***Ty's One-Man Band***] takes place in a small Southern community on a hot summer day about 50 years ago. Both Ty and Andro are black. Despite some idealized integration in [Margot Tomes's] illustrations, the words and pictures work nicely together to project the special atmosphere of the time and place and the special occasion created by the stranger's drifting through. (pp. 1353-54)

A review of "Ty's One-Man Band," in Kirkus Reviews, *Vol. XLVIII, No. 20, October 15, 1980, pp. 1353-54.*

Margot Tomes' imaginative illustrations are interesting in their subdued tonalities and their 1920s milieu. But there is a problem with the book, the text. It is far too long for the picturebook age and nearly impossible to read, as it tries to recreate the rhythms of the one-man band's plate, cup and spoon routines: "Tink-ki-tink-ki-ki-tink-ki-tink . . ." and so on—for what appear to readers to be endless lines.

Jane Bickel, in a review of "Ty's One-Man Band," in School Library Journal, *Vol. 27, No. 7, March, 1981, p. 153.*

THE GIRL ON THE OUTSIDE **(1982)**

Based on an incident that occurred during the 1954 desegregation of a Little Rock high school, this follows two girls through the last few days of summer vacation and the opening of school. Sophia, a white senior, is fearful and resentful of the coming invasion of her high school by nine black students. Ending her summer job at the dime store, she keeps a black girl waiting while she waits on whites who come in later. Atypically, Sophia has a journalist older brother and an incipient beau, a college boy, both of whom favor integration—but Sophia does not soften. . . . Eva, one of the nine students designated to switch from Carver to the white school, is a sophomore with average marks but a firm understanding of what she's doing. She is also the girl Sophia kept waiting at the store. Eva prepares for school calmly, sewing a dress for the first day; but she becomes uneasy and uncertain as the Governor's speech, the judge's decision, the arrival of the Guard (and of ugly out-of-town whites), and the advice of NAACP lawyers keep changing the plans of her group. The only one of the nine without a phone, Eva misses the last change of plans and shows up at school . . . to be barred by the soldiers she thought were there to protect her, and then surrounded by the angry crowd. At that point Sophia comes to her defense and, though both girls are spit upon, helps her escape by bus. In reality, as Walter's afterword notes, it was a nonsouthern white teacher from a Little Rock black college who befriended the trapped girl. The change makes a better idea for a YA novel, and Walter shows some understanding of both girls' feelings and situations. She never goes beyond predictable portrayals of either, though, and she doesn't handle the tension of the situation nearly as compellingly as have non-fiction chroniclers of desegregation struggles. So, if subject-interest suggests a fictional version, this will serve—but it's not a strong novel. (pp. 681-82)

A review of "The Girl on the Outside," in Kirkus Reviews, *Vol. L, No. 12, June 15, 1982, pp. 681-82.*

The chapters more or less alternate, so that readers can see the attitudes of both girls: Sophia angry, fearful, but increasingly ashamed and eventually sympathetic; Eva fearful but courageous. In the aftermath of the final, shameful incident of mob hatred, it is Sophia who benefits most by the joint departure from the scene; Eva has simply gotten away from a hostile mob, but for Sophia, the book concludes, "What she had gained was the beginning to the end of her pain." A vivid story is written with insight and compassion, its characters fully developed, its converging lines nicely controlled.

Zena Sutherland, in a review of "The Girl on the Outside," in Bulletin of the Center for Children's Books, *Vol. 36, No. 3, November, 1982, p. 58.*

The frenzy that seizes the town as [the integration] becomes a media event attracting hundreds of strangers produces anxiety in the reader as we think of the coming confrontation. We are moved also by the courage required of these children and their parents as they try to exercise the right granted them in a Supreme Court decision. The novel portrays the contrast in the daily lives of these two young women and the tension both feel as the first day of school approaches. In a dramatic finale Sophia does herself, her brother and Arnold proud even at the cost of behaving in a manner totally unexpected by her parents.

Lillian L. Shapiro, in a review of "The Girl on the Outside," in School Library Journal, *Vol. 29, No. 5, January, 1983, p. 89.*

***MY MAMA NEEDS ME* (1983)**

The arrival of a new baby—portrayed with fidelity and feeling, if no imaginative reach. When Mama comes home with his new baby sister, Jason wants so much to be helpful, to be needed, that he keeps saying "My mama needs me"—to his friends, asking him out to play; to neighbor Mrs. Luby, offering him some "spicy brown cookies." Even after he relents and goes to the duck pond with Mr. Pomeroy, the thought that his little sister might awaken sends him home again. But he's discovering that babies sleep a lot; also, was his mama "that tired when I was born?" But there comes a chance to help bathe the baby, then a chance to hold her on his lap. And finally, with a hug from his mama (*"That's what I needed to do"*), Jason is off to play with his friends. The details of baby care, related with tender gravity, keep this from being hackneyed. . . . And the situation is inexhaustible when it is indeed true to life.

A review of "My Mama Needs Me," in Kirkus Reviews, *Vol. LI, No. 2, January 15, 1983, p. 62.*

The characters are members of a black family—father, mother, little Jason and his baby sister—but they could be of any race. . . . Walter's rhythmic prose and understanding convey meaning as well as empathy in her quietly appealing book.

A review of "My Mama Needs Me," in Publishers Weekly, *Vol. 223, No. 6, February 11, 1983, p. 71.*

My Mama Needs Me deals nicely with important themes. One is the welcome of a new baby by a sister or brother and the older child's subsequent adjustment to the new baby. A second theme is the help and concern young children can learn to express for the new baby in a positive family setting. This straightforward, uncomplicated text conveys Jason's welcome and concern for a new sister, as well as his concern for his mother. We see the worry Jason feels when he's away from home for even a brief while. (pp. 26-7)

Geraldine L. Wilson, in a review of "My Mama Needs Me," in Interracial Books for Children Bulletin, *Vol. 14, No. 5, 1983, pp. 26-7.*

***BECAUSE WE ARE* (1983)**

An African proverb that Emma learns from a teacher is "Because we are, I am." Black, bright, and beautiful, Emma is a high school student who is evicted from a "good" school because of her insolence to a teacher and is sent to Manning, where most of her classmates resent her because they feel she's snobbish. Emma's problems are adjusting to her father's absence and to his second wife, who's white, getting along with

Walter at her desk. Reproduced by permission of Mildred Walter.

her mother, keeping her old boyfriend (although she resents the way he treats her), getting into a good university (she does), getting along in her new school, and solving an unsatisfactory relationship with an arrogant teacher. All of these situations are ones that many readers share, and Walter handles them capably except for one thing: in almost every case, Emma overreacts, often drenched with self-pity or anger or despair. Characterization otherwise is adequate, and the writing style is capable if not polished, the flaw in Emma reflected in the treatment of ordinary problems as dramatic crises.

Zena Sutherland, in a review of "Because We Are," in Bulletin of the Center for Children's Books, *Vol. 37, No. 3, November, 1983, p. 60.*

Walter draws readers into a complex situation with finely paced writing, a good integration of themes and an understanding of the feelings of young men and women. Themes of racial understanding are developed expertly; other themes such as teenage sexuality, language and subculture are also well executed. The author's use of simple language makes this a title that will be accessible to most teens.

Gale P. Jackson, in a review of "Because We Are," in School Library Journal, *Vol. 30, No. 7, March, 1984, p. 176.*

Any effort to deal with the complex dynamics of class, race and sex from an African American perspective in a work of adolescent fiction is important and ambitious. So, too, is the main theme of this book. . . .

The book deals with a myriad of complex issues—racist white teachers, the materialistic values of upwardly mobile Blacks, divorce, a single-parent home, interracial marriage, male-female friendships, seeking adolescent peer approval and unequal education for Blacks. Some of these many issues—such as the racist teachers and the seemingly non-supportive, but deeply protective and caring divorced mother—are well-handled. However, Emma's father's interracial marriage is not presented clearly, a problem complicated by the fact that his white wife, who is not a well-realized character, plays a major supportive role in Emma's ultimate challenge of the system. (Some of Emma's friends are also underdeveloped as characters.) As Emma's values change, she becomes more concerned with the welfare of her people than with a debutante ball—a change that comes about because of her friendship with two boys. It is strange that a teenaged girl does not find *one* female friend to share her deep concerns.

Despite some flaws, I recommend the book because the topics presented are so vital to young people. As in life, the topics discussed are complex, and resolution is no simple matter.

Suzanne C. Carothers, in a review of "Because We Are," in Interracial Books for Children Bulletin, *Vol. 15, No. 3, 1984, p. 19.*

This excellent book is directed to any ethnic group. It deals with the feelings any senior high school teenager experiences in the process of growing up. In this book, we see the comparison between ethnic and racial groups and their thoughts and feelings in dealing with their problems. I think the subject is treated in an unassuming manner because the author came to know the thoughts of the age group. This book will appeal to black and white students alike at all high school age levels.

Vicki F. Bell, in a review of "Because We Are," in The Book Report, *Vol. 3, No. 1, May-June, 1984, p. 36.*

BROTHER TO THE WIND (1985)

Jeered at by his peers because he wants to fly and plans to ask Good Snake to make his wish come true, Emeke joins a throng of animals and has a chance to inform Good Snake of his desire. He is told how to make a kite and how to wait until the wind tells him the time is right. Then, gliding on his huge kite, Emeke floats through the sky. The tale then ends abruptly, having the appeals of achievement and adventure, but weakened by the juxtaposition of fantasy and reality that never become a blend.

Zena Sutherland, in a review of "Brother to the Wind," in Bulletin of the Center for Children's Books, *Vol. 38, No. 7, March, 1985, p. 136.*

Emeke, a goat herder, wishes to fly. His grandmother tells him that if he reaches Good Snake, he will grant his wish. After some difficulties, Emeke gets his wish and becomes "brother to the wind." An original African-American tale that manages to incorporate both cultures effectively. It is easier to read and less didactic than many of the African stories, and overcomes some of the large cultural differences between Black Americans, Americans, and Africans. (pp. 105-06)

Leila Davenport Pettyjohn, in a review of "Brother to the Wind," in Children's Book Review Service, *Vol. 13, No. 10, May, 1985, pp. 105-06.*

Brother to the Wind is a gem. The collaboration of a fine storyteller and two gifted illustrators [Diane and Leo Dillon] has produced an incredibly beautiful book that shines with its creators' love of story. . . . The story is compelling in its presentation of the virtues of faith and the preservation of heritage. Walter's writing is imaginative, engaging and filled with metaphors of flight and fancy and the infinite wonders of life. . . . This story of a boy's quest for, and eventual, flight, does in fact give readers room to soar. (pp. 84-5)

Gale P. Jackson, in a review of "Brother to the Wind," in School Library Journal, *Vol. 31, No. 9, May, 1985, pp. 84-5.*

TROUBLE'S CHILD (1985)

Caught between her desire to go on to high school and pressure from her peers and elderly grandmother to stay on their small Louisiana island and accept its ways and life style, 15-year-old Martha must struggle with this excruciatingly painful decision. She finds it difficult to adopt the ways and rituals that rule the lives of the island's people. Her yearning to see more of the world is dismissed constantly by her grandmother, her only family, who has guided and trained her to follow in her footsteps as the island's midwife. Martha, who has delayed the island tradition whereby girls announce their readiness to marry, knowing that by going through with it she'd be forsaking her longings for knowledge and adventure, eventually shows the strength to make the difficult decision. Walter immerses readers in Martha's internal struggle, holding their attention to the last page. The quickly paced text utilizes the native dialect, further adding to the aura of the isolated island setting as Walter shows how ritual and superstition dominate. The only noticeable weakness in the text is the lack of substantial development of the secondary characters. While Martha's particular problems are unique, adolescent readers will easily empathize with her predicament of feeling confused by the pull from so many different directions at this stage of life.

Tom S. Hurlburt, in a review of "Trouble's Child," in School Library Journal, *Vol. 32, No. 2, October, 1985, p. 188.*

In the present dearth of novels exploring facets of Black culture, this book is a welcome account of the Louisiana bayou community of Blue Isle. Martha, now finished with school at fourteen, is expected like the other island girls to announce her readiness for marriage by displaying a special quilt pattern. Her grandmother Titay, with whom she has lived since her parents' deaths, is ready to train Martha to follow in her footsteps as midwife. But Martha, without quite understanding her own recalcitrance, is not ready to fulfill these expectations. Despite her aptitude for nursing, she longs to continue her education off-island. "'I don't like sayin' this, but you's a child bo'ned t'trouble,'" Titay intones, invoking a local superstition that a child born during a storm will lead a tempestuous life. . . . Uttered in the soft cadence of bayou speech, the women's chorus of condemnation of Martha's eccentric attitude serves to codify the island's rigid social conventions. Details of dress, domestic arrangements, superstitions, and folklore further enrich the novel—which draws strength and universality from Martha's growing recognition that the island code defines and sustains, even as it restricts her. Her efforts to assess her place in the society that bred her provides a fine regional version of a dilemma faced by adolescents everywhere.

Charlotte W. Draper, in a review of "Trouble's Child," in The Horn Book Magazine, *Vol. LXI, No. 6, November-December, 1985, p. 744.*

Although the characters are clearly delineated here, the real protagonist is an island off the coast of Louisiana, where an isolated society resists change in any form. . . . The characters as a whole are stock types, though the grandmother is a believable mix of starch and sensitivity. The strong dialect is confined to a limited amount of dialogue. Ultimately, this is more descriptive than emotionally involving, but both the setting and the situation are unusual enough to overcome some lack of spark.

Zena Sutherland, in a review of "Trouble's Child," in Bulletin of the Center for Children's Books, *Vol. 39, No. 5, January, 1986, p. 99.*

Picking up right where [*The Dream Keeper* by Margery Evernden] left off, at least in the use of worn-out devices and unrealistic resolutions, is ***Trouble's Child***. . . . [Martha is] caught between loyalty to her own desires and commitment to the community. This could have been used for a good look at adolescent values and the problem of the individual versus society, but unfortunately it becomes a catalog of tormented days without relevance. There is, however, some very nice prose here detailing the customs, rituals and taboos of this highly superstitious island culture. Characterization is strong, but motivational elements are sometimes lacking, with the reader then having to supply causal links.

Sydney's charge to all authors, to delight and to instruct, should be a touchstone for Kidlit. Ms. Evernden and Ms. Walter have both created sugar-coated soap bubbles here. When the coating wears off, there is nothing left but air. What appears on the surface to be fraught with meaning is nothing more than unrealistic answers for faceless children in reheated situations. (pp. 435-36)

Joe Pellegrino, S.J., in a review of "Trouble's Child," in Best Sellers, *Vol. 45, No. 11, February, 1986, pp. 435-36.*

JUSTIN AND THE BEST BISCUITS IN THE WORLD (1986)

The value of having someone to look up to is pointed out in this brief novel, though not explored deeply.

Justin, 10, feels frustrated and put-upon, both by his inability to keep a neat bedroom and by a pair of older sisters who pressure him continually to help around the house. He tries to save his self-respect by convincing himself that housework and cooking are women's work, but a visit to his beloved grandfather sets him straight: Justin learns to make his own bed, wash dishes properly and prepare biscuits according to Grandpa's private recipe. Later, the author injects a healthy shot of self-validation into the story, having Justin win several prizes at a local fair/rodeo, then return home to clean his room and to make dinner for his mother and sisters. Justin learns these new skills with reassuring but unrealistic rapidity—like Leo, he is a Late Bloomer. But why his immediate family could not instruct him is left unclear.

Some young readers may find their preconceptions bent by Walter's intriguing if tangential discussion of black cowboys and rodeo stars.

A review of "Justin and the Best Biscuits in the World," in Kirkus Reviews, *Vol. LIV, No. 19, October 1, 1986, p. 1513.*

Walter's story is simple but effective and all the richer because her characters are black. Besides watching the tender relationship between Justin and his grandfather, readers also get a slice of black history as Grandpa reminisces about his ancestors and how they came west and also fills Justin in on black cowboys and the role they played in settling the land. A warm story welcome for its positive portrayal of black family life.

Denise M. Wilms, in a review of "Justin and the Best Biscuits in the World," in Booklist, *Vol. 83, No. 4, October 15, 1986, p. 358.*

Grandpa is loving, understanding, and patient, so Justin's refusals to help are treated with gentle humor. . . . The inclusion of history of a family who headed West after the Civil War and information about some of the famous black cowboys who helped settle the West and create events still used in rodeos is wonderfully woven in, sure to make readers seek additional information. The same love between a grandfather and son occurs in Virginia Hamilton's *Junius Over Far,* which is for older readers. . . . The strong, well-developed characters and humorous situations in this warm family story will appeal to intermediate readers; the large print will draw slow or reluctant readers.

JoAnn Butler Henry, in a review of "Justin and the Best Biscuits in the World," in School Library Journal, *Vol. 33, No. 3, November, 1986, p. 94.*

[***Justin and the Best Biscuits in the World***] offers a rare (for [the 8 to 12] age group) look at the history of slavery in this country, and the proud heritage of the black cowboys and cattlemen who helped to settle the American West. It also has a lot to say about the warm friendships that young boys and granddads often share, including their secret recipes for "best biscuits." While "delightful" may be an overused word, it fits this title nicely. (p. B5)

Diane Manuel, "A Sleigh Full of Novels and Picture Books," in The Christian Science Monitor, *December 5, 1986, pp. B4-B6.*

APPENDIX

The following is a listing of all sources used in Volume 15 of *Children's Literature Review*. Included in this list are all copyright and reprint rights and acknowledgments for those essays for which permission was obtained. Every effort has been made to trace copyright, but if omissions have been made, please let us know.

THE EXCERPTS IN CLR, VOLUME 15, WERE REPRINTED FROM THE FOLLOWING PERIODICALS:

The Advance, August 19, 1909.

The Advocates Newsletter, September, 1986. Reprinted by permission of the publisher.

American Artist, v. 37, May, 1973. Copyright © 1973 by Billboard Publications, Inc. Reprinted by permission of the publisher.

American Quarterly, v. XVI, Spring, 1964 for "'The Wizard of Oz': Parable on Populism" by Henry M. Littlefield; v. XX, Fall, 1968 for "L. Frank Baum and the Progressive Dilemma" by Fred Erisman. Copyright 1964, 1968, American Studies Association. Both reprinted by permission of American Studies Association and the respective authors.

Appraisal: Children's Science Books, v. 13, Winter, 1980; v. 13, Fall, 1980; v. 15, Fall, 1982; v. 16, Spring-Summer, 1983; v. 17, Winter, 1984; v. 18, Summer, 1985; v. 19, Summer, 1986; v. 20, Winter, 1986. Copyright © 1980, 1982, 1983, 1984, 1985, 1986 by the Children's Science Book Review Committee. All reprinted by permission of the publisher.

Arkansas Libraries, v. 38, December, 1981. Copyright © 1981 Arkansas Library Association. Reprinted by permission of the publisher.

The Babbling Bookworm, v. 7, March, 1979; v. 7, August, 1979. Copyright 1979 The Babbling Bookworm Newsletter. Both reprinted by permission of the publisher.

The Baum Bugle, Christmas, 1971 for "Oz and the Fifth Criterion" by C. Warren Hollister. Reprinted by permission of the publisher and the author./ v. 7, Autumn, 1963; v. 8, Spring, 1964. Both reprinted by permission of the publisher.

Best Sellers, v. 36, March, 1977; v. 45, February, 1986; v. 46, April, 1986. Copyright © 1977, 1986 Helen Dwight Reid Educational Foundation. All reprinted by permission of the publisher.

Book News, v. XIX, October, 1900.

The Book Report, v. 3, May-June, 1984. © copyright 1984 by Linworth Publishing Co. Reprinted by permission of the publisher.

Book World—The Washington Post, November 10, 1974; November 12, 1978; November 9, 1980; September 13, 1981; April 27, 1986. © 1974, 1978, 1980, 1981, 1986, *The Washington Post.* All reprinted by permission of the publisher.

Booklist, v. 72, September 1, 1975; v. 73, September 15, 1976; v. 73, April 15, 1977; v. 74, January 15, 1978; v. 74, May 15, 1978; v. 75, May 1, 1979; v. 76, September 1, 1979; v. 76, May 1, 1980; v. 77, December 15, 1980; v. 77, April 15, 1981; v. 78, December 15, 1981; v. 78, April 15, 1982; v. 78, June 15, 1982; v. 78, July, 1982; v. 79, November 1, 1982; v. 79, January 1, 1983; v. 79, May 15, 1983; v. 81, January 15, 1985; v. 81, March 1, 1985; v. 81, March 15, 1985; v. 81, April 15, 1985; v. 81, June 15, 1985; v. 82, October 15, 1985; v. 82, December 1, 1985; v. 82, January 1, 1986; v. 82, March 1, 1986; v. 82, April 1, 1986; v. 82, April 15, 1986; v. 82, July, 1986; v. 83, September 1, 1986; v. 83, October 15, 1986; v. 83, August, 1987; v. 84, September 1, 1987. Copyright © 1975, 1976, 1977, 1978, 1979, 1980, 1981, 1982, 1983, 1985, 1986, 1987 by the American Library Association. All reprinted by permission of the publisher.

The Booklist, v. 70, November 1, 1973; v. 74, October 1, 1977; v. 76, November 1, 1979; v. 77, September 15, 1980. Copyright © 1973, 1977, 1979, 1980 by the American Library Association. All reprinted by permission of the publisher.

Books for Keeps, n. 35, November, 1985; n. 44, May, 1987. © School Bookshop Association 1985, 1987. Both reprinted by permission of the publisher.

Books for Your Children, v. 14, Spring, 1979; v. 19, Autumn-Winter, 1984. © *Books for Your Children* 1979, 1984. Both reprinted by permission of the publisher.

Books in Canada, v. 8, December, 1979 for an interview with Ann Blades by Eleanor Wachtel. Reprinted by permission of Eleanor Wachtel.

British Book News, Children's Supplement, Spring, 1980; Autumn, 1982. © *British Book News*, 1980, 1982. Both courtesy of *British Book News*.

British Book News Children's Books, December, 1986; June, 1987. © The British Council 1986, 1987. Both reprinted by permission of the publisher.

Brush and Pencil, v. XII, September, 1903.

Bulletin of the Center for Children's Books, v. XIII, January, 1960; v. XV, November, 1961; v. XV, May, 1962; v. 19, October, 1965; v. 20, May, 1967; v. 21, February, 1968; v. 22, June, 1969; v. 23, February, 1970; v. 23, April, 1970; v. 23, May, 1970; v. 25, January, 1972; v. 25, May, 1972; v. 26, September, 1972; v. 27, January, 1974; v. 27, March, 1974; v. 28, November, 1974; v. 28, December, 1974; v. 29, March, 1976; v. 30, March, 1977; v. 30, June, 1977; v. 31, September, 1977; v. 31, March, 1978; v. 31, July-August, 1978; v. 33, July-August, 1980; v. 34, February, 1981; v. 34, April, 1981; v. 35, November, 1981; v. 35, April, 1982; v. 36, October, 1982; v. 36, November, 1982; v. 36, May, 1983; v. 37, November, 1983; v. 38, October, 1984; v. 38, November, 1984; v. 38, March, 1985; v. 39, December, 1985; v. 39, January, 1986; v. 39, March, 1986; v. 39, April, 1986; v. 40, September, 1986; v. 40, April, 1987. Copyright © 1960, 1961, 1962, 1965, 1967, 1968, 1969, 1970, 1972, 1974, 1976, 1977, 1978, 1980, 1981, 1982, 1983, 1984, 1985, 1986, 1987 by The University of Chicago. All rights reserved. All reprinted by permission of The University of Chicago Press.

Bulletin of the Children's Book Center, v. V, May, 1952; v. XI, February, 1958.

Canadian Children's Literature: A Journal of Criticism and Review, n. 39-40, 1985 for "Northern Children" by Mary Ellen Binder. Reprinted by permission of the author./ v. 1, Spring, 1975; n. 21, 1981. Both reprinted by permission of the publisher.

Catholic Library World, v. 47, May-June, 1976; v. 52, November, 1980. Both reprinted by permission of the publisher.

Chicago Sunday Tribune Magazine of Books, May 2, 1954.

Children's Book News, Toronto, v. 8, December, 1985. Reprinted by permission of The Children's Book Centre, Toronto, Canada.

Children's Book Review, v. III, October, 1973; v. III, December, 1973; v. VI, October, 1976. © 1973, 1976 by Five Owls Press Ltd. All rights reserved. All reprinted by permission of the publisher.

Children's Book Review Service, v. 1, October, 1972; v. 3, April, 1975; v. 5, June, 1977; v. 6, December, 1977; v. 7, February, 1979; v. 8, October, 1979; v. 10, August, 1982; v. 13, September, 1984; v. 13, November, 1984; v. 13, May, 1985. Copyright © 1972, 1975, 1977, 1979, 1982, 1984, 1985 Children's Book Review Service Inc. All reprinted by permission of the publisher.

Children's Literature: Annual of the Modern Language Association Division on Children's Literature and The Children's Literature Association, v. 10, 1982. © 1982 by Francelia Butler. All rights reserved. Reprinted by permission of Yale University Press.

Children's Literature: Annual of the Modern Language Association Seminar on Children's Literature and The Children's Literature Association, v. 4, 1975. © 1975 by Francelia Butler. All rights reserved. Reprinted by permission of Francelia Butler.

Children's literature in education, v. 9, Spring, 1978. © 1978, Agathon Press, Inc. Both reprinted by permission of the publisher.

The Christian Science Monitor, April 6, 1984 for "Animal Books for Information and Pleasure" by Franja C. Bryant; December 5, 1986 for "A Sleigh Full of Novels and Picture Books" by Diane Manuel. © 1984, 1986 by the respective authors. All rights reserved. Both reprinted by permission of the respective authors./ November 4, 1965; May 7, 1975; November 3, 1976. © 1965, 1975, 1976 The Christian Science Publishing Society. All rights reserved. All reprinted by permission from *The Christian Science Monitor*.

Columbia Library Columns, v. IV, May, 1955.

Commentary, v. 69, March, 1980 for "Judy Blume's Children" by Naomi Decter. Copyright © 1980 by American Jewish Committee. All rights reserved. Reprinted by permission of the publisher and the author.

Commonweal, v. CVII, July 4, 1980. Copyright © 1980 Commonweal Publishing Co., Inc. Reprinted by permission of Commonweal Foundation.

The Detroit News, September 13, 1903.

The Dial, v. XXIX, December 1, 1900.

Elementary English, v. 51, September, 1974 for "Books That Blume: An Appreciation" by Richard W. Jackson. Copyright © 1974 by the National Council of Teachers of English. Reprinted by permission of the publisher and the author.

English Journal, v. 61, March, 1972 for a review of "Lillie of Watts Takes a Giant Step" by John W. Conner; v. 65, February, 1976 for an interview with Richard Peck by Paul Janeczko; v. 69, May, 1980 for "A Kaleidoscope of Human Relationships" by David Davidson and others. Copyright © 1972, 1976, 1980 by the National Council of Teachers of English. All reprinted by permission of the publisher and the respective authors.

The English Record, v. XXXII, Winter, 1981. Copyright New York State English Council 1981. Reprinted by permission of the publisher.

Fantasy Review, v. 7, August, 1984 for "Third in Series Maintains High Standard" by Carl B. Yoke. Copyright © 1984 by the author. Reprinted by permission of the author.

The Five Owls, v. 1, July-August, 1987. Copyright © 1987 by The Five Owls, Inc. Reprinted by permission of the publisher.

The Georgia Review, v. XIV, Fall, 1960. Copyright, 1960, by the University of Georgia. Reprinted by permission of the publisher.

Growing Point, v. 8, December, 1969; v. 8, April, 1970; v. 9, July, 1970; v. 12, October, 1973; v. 14, November, 1975; v. 15, December, 1976; v. 16, January, 1978; v. 16, April, 1978; v. 17, January, 1979; v. 19, March, 1981; v. 20, November, 1981; v. 20, March, 1982; v. 21, July, 1982; v. 24, November, 1985; v. 25, November, 1986. All reprinted by permission of the publisher.

Hobbies, v. 64, May, 1959. Reprinted by permission of the publisher.

The Horn Book Magazine, v. LVI, April, 1980 for "Letter from England: Hughes in Flight" by Aidan Chambers. Copyright © by the author. Reprinted by permission of the author./ v. XLII, August, 1966; v. XLIII, October, 1967; v. XLV, December, 1969; v. XLVI, April, 1970; v. XLVI, August, 1970; v. L, August, 1974; v. LI, October, 1975; v. LII, October, 1976; v. LIII, October, 1977; v. LIV, February, 1978; v. LIV, December, 1978; v. LV, February, 1979; v. LV, October, 1979; v. LVI, August, 1980; v. LVIII, April 1982; v. LVIII, June, 1982; v. LVIII, October, 1982; v. LIX, April, 1983; v. LX, February, 1984; v. LX, June, 1984; v. LX, August, 1984; v. LX, September-October, 1984; v. LXI, January-February, 1985; v. LXI, July-August, 1985; v. LXI, November-December, 1985; v. LXII, January-February, 1986; v. LXII, March-April, 1986; v. LXII, May-June, 1986; v. LXII, July-August, 1986; v. LXII, November-December, 1986; v. LXIII, January, 1987; v. LXIII, May-June, 1987; v. LXIII, July-August, 1987. Copyright, 1966, 1967, 1969, 1970, 1974, 1975, 1976, 1977, 1978, 1979, 1980, 1982, 1983, 1984, 1985, 1986, 1987, by The Horn Book, Inc., Boston. All rights reserved. All reprinted by permission of the publisher./ v. XXXIII, October, 1957. Copyright, 1957, renewed 1985, by The Horn Book, Inc., Boston. All rights reserved. Reprinted by permission of the publisher.

In Review: Canadian Books for Children, v. 7, Autumn, 1973; v. 8, Spring, 1974. Both reprinted by permission of the publisher.

Interracial Books for Children Bulletin, v. 7, 1977; v. 14, 1983; v. 15, 1984. All reprinted by permission of the Council on Interracial Books for Children, 1841 Broadway, New York, NY 10023.

Journal of Popular Culture, v. VII, Summer, 1973. Copyright © 1973 by Ray B. Browne. Reprinted by permission of the publisher.

Journal of Reading, v. 28, January, 1985. Copyright 1985 by the International Reading Association, Inc.

The Junior Bookshelf, v. 30, June, 1966; v. 31, August, 1967; v. 34, April, 1970; v. 38, February, 1974; v. 38, April, 1974; v. 40, February, 1976; v. 40, October, 1976; v. 40, December, 1976; v. 41, February, 1977; v. 42, February, 1978; v. 43, February, 1979; v. 44, February, 1980; v. 45, April, 1981; v. 46, August, 1982; v. 46, October, 1982; v. 47, February, 1983; v. 47, April, 1983; v. 47, August, 1983; v. 48, February, 1984; v. 48, December, 1984; v. 49, December, 1985; v. 50, February, 1986; v. 50, August, 1986; v. 51, August, 1987. All reprinted by permission of the publisher.

Junior Libraries, an appendix to *Library Journal*, v. 4, October, 1957.

Kentucky Library Association Bulletin, v. 41, Summer, 1977. Reprinted by permission of the publisher.

Kirkus Reviews, v. XXXVII, April 1, 1969; v. XXXVII, April 15, 1969; v. XXXVII, September 1, 1969; v. XXXVIII, July 1, 1970; v. XXXIX, October 15, 1971; v. XL, August 15, 1972; v. XLI, June 15, 1973; v. XLI, October 15, 1973; v. XLI, December 1, 1973; v. XLII, May 15, 1974; v. XLII, October 15, 1974; v. XLIII, July 15, 1975; v. XLIII, December 1, 1975; v. XLIV, September 1, 1976; v. XLIV, December 1, 1976; v. XLV, February 15, 1977; v. XLV, May 1, 1977; v. XLVI, February 1, 1978; v. XLVI; April 1, 1978; v. XLVI, October 1, 1978; v. XLVI, December 15, 1978; v. XLVII, April 1, 1979; v. XLVII, October 15, 1979; v. XLVIII, May 1, 1980; v. XLVIII, October 15, 1980; v. XLIX, January 1, 1981; v. XLIX, September 15, 1981; v. XLIX, October 1, 1981; v. L, June 15, 1982; v. L, November 1, 1982; v. LI, January 15, 1983; v. LIII, October 1, 1985; v. LIII, December 15, 1985; v. LIV, April 15, 1986; v. LIV, May 1, 1986; v. LIV, July 1, 1986; v. LIV, October 1, 1986; LIV, October 15, 1986; v. LV, February 15, 1987; v. LV, May 1, 1987; v. LV, July 1, 1987; v. LV, August 1, 1987; v. LV, August 15, 1987. Copyright © 1969, 1970, 1971, 1972, 1973, 1974, 1975, 1976, 1977, 1978, 1979, 1980, 1981, 1982, 1983, 1985, 1986, 1987 The Kirkus Service, Inc. All rights reserved. All reprinted by permission of the publisher.

Kirkus Reviews, Juvenile Issue, v. LIII, March 1, 1985. Copyright © 1985 The Kirkus Service, Inc. All rights reserved. Reprinted by permission of the publisher.

Kirkus Service, v. XXXV, July 1, 1967. Copyright © 1967 The Kirkus Service, Inc. Reprinted by permission of the publisher.

Kliatt Young Adult Paperback Book Guide, v. 12, Winter, 1978; v. 13, Fall, 1979. Copyright © 1978, 1979 by Kliatt Paperback Book Guide. Both reprinted by permission of the publisher.

Kulchur, n. 4, Fall, 1961. Copyright © 1961, by Kulchur Press, Inc. Reprinted by permission of the publisher.

Language Arts, v. 55, January, 1978 for a review of "Monster Night at Grandma's House" by Ruth M. Stein; v. 55, February, 1978 for a review of "King Arthur" by Ruth M. Stein; v. 59, March, 1982 for "A Librarian Looks at Poetry for Children" by Joan Mason; v. 59, October, 1982 for "Profile: Sid Fleischman" by Emily R. Johnson; v. 61, March, 1984 for a review of "Mouse Writing" by Ronald A. Jobe; v. 61, March, 1984 for a review of "Miss Maggie" by Marilou Sorensen; v. 61, March, 1984 for a review of "Miss Maggie" by Inga Kromann-Kelly; v. 61, April, 1984 for "Books and Children: The Readers Connexion!" by Ronald A. Jobe; v. 62, February, 1985 for a review of "This Year's Garden" by Ronald A. Jobe; v. 62, September, 1985 for "Thank You, Miss Evans" by Cynthia Rylant; v. 62, October, 1985 for "Profile: Lilian Moore" by Joan I. Glazer; v. 63, March, 1986 for a review of "Every Living Thing" by Janet Hickman; v. 63; December, 1986 for a review of "The Whipping Boy" by Janet Hickman; v. 63, December, 1986 for a review of "A Fine White Dust" by Janet Hickman; v. 64, September, 1987 for a review of "The Ugly Duckling" by Janet Hickman. Copyright © 1978, 1982, 1984, 1985, 1986, 1987 by the National Council of Teachers of English. All reprinted by permission of the publisher and the respective authors.

Library Journal, v. 92, June 15, 1967. Copyright © 1967 by Reed Publishing, USA, Division of Reed Holdings, Inc. Reprinted from *Library Journal,* published by R. R. Bowker, Co., Division of Reed Publishing, USA, by permission of the publisher.

The Lion and the Unicorn, v. 1, Fall, 1977; v. 2, Spring, 1978; v. 2, Fall, 1978; v. 5, 1981. Copyright © 1977, 1978, 1981 *The Lion and the Unicorn.* All reprinted by permission of the publisher.

Maclean's Magazine, v. 98, December 9, 1985. © 1985 by *Maclean's Magazine.* Reprinted by permission of the publisher.

The Nation, New York, v. 233, November 21, 1981. Copyright 1981 *The Nation* magazine, The Nation Company, Inc. Reprinted by permission of the publisher.

The New Republic, v. LXXXI, December 12, 1934.

The New York Review of Books, v. XXIV, September 29, 1977 and October 13, 1977. Copyright © 1977 Nyrev, Inc. Reprinted with permission from *The New York Review of Books.*

The New York Times, May 11, 1919. Copyright 1919 by The New York Times Company. Reprinted by permission of the publisher.

The New York Times Book Review, September 8, 1900./ November 13, 1960; November 12, 1972; May 6, 1973; January 13, 1974; July 27, 1975; November 14, 1976; May 1, 1977; September 11, 1977; November 13, 1977; January 20, 1980; October 12, 1980; November 9, 1980; November 23, 1980; November 15, 1981; November 14, 1982; October 9, 1983; December 18, 1983; June 24, 1984; August 12, 1984; November 10, 1985; October 26, 1986; November 9, 1986; February 22, 1987; November 8, 1987. Copyright © 1960, 1972, 1973, 1974, 1975, 1976, 1977, 1980, 1981, 1982, 1983, 1984, 1985, 1986, 1987 by The New York Times Company. All reprinted by permission of the publisher.

The New Yorker, v. LIX, December 5, 1983 for "Children's Books for Christmas" by Faith McNulty. © 1983 by the author. Reprinted by permission of the publisher.

Newsletter on Intellectual Freedom, v. XXX, May, 1981. Reprinted by permission of the publisher.

Parnassus: Poetry in Review, v. 8, 1980. Copyright © 1980 Poetry in Review Foundation. Reprinted by permission of the publisher.

Proceedings of the Ninth Annual Conference of the Children's Literature Association, v. 9, 1982. Copyright © 1982 by The Children's Literature Association. Reprinted by permission of the publisher.

Psychology Today, v. 9, September, 1975. Copyright © 1975 (American Psychological Association). Reprinted with permission from *Psychology Today* magazine.

Publishers Weekly, v. 189, April 25, 1966; v. 191, May 22, 1967. Copyright © 1966, 1967 by R. R. Bowker Company. Both reprinted from *Publishers Weekly*, published by R. R. Bowker Company, by permission./ v. 194, July 1, 1968; v. 195, April 14, 1969; v. 198, September 14, 1970; v. 207, March 24, 1975; v. 208, December 1, 1975; v. 210, December 6, 1976; v. 211, May 16, 1977; v. 213, February 27, 1978; v. 213, March 27, 1978; v. 214, July 17, 1978; v. 214, November 6, 1978; v. 214, December 25, 1978; v. 217, April 25, 1980; v. 219, February 27, 1981; v. 221, March 19, 1982; v. 223, February 11, 1983; v. 225, May 18, 1984; v. 225, June 22, 1984; v. 226, August 17, 1984; v. 226, November 23, 1984; v. 227, March 8, 1985; v. 227, May 17, 1985. Copyright © 1968, 1969, 1970, 1975, 1976, 1977, 1978, 1980, 1981, 1982, 1983, 1984, 1985 by Xerox Corporation. All reprinted from *Publishers Weekly*, published by R. R. Bowker Company, a Xerox company, by permission./ v. 229, April 25, 1986; v. 230, September 26, 1986; v. 231, March 20, 1987; v. 231, May 29, 1987; v. 231, July 10, 1987; v. 232, August 14, 1987. Copyright 1986, 1987 by Reed Publishing USA. All reprinted from *Publishers Weekly*, published by the Bowker Magazine Group of Cahners Publishing Co., a division of Reed Publishing USA.

Punch, v. CCLVII, December 17, 1969; v. CCLXXXI, December 2, 1981. © 1969, 1981 by Punch Publications Ltd. All rights reserved. May not be reprinted without permission.

Quill and Quire, v. 51, August, 1985 for a review of "By the Sea: An Alphabet Book" by Celia Lottridge. Reprinted by permission of *Quill and Quire* and the author.

Reading Time, v. 31, 1987 for a review of "Letters to Judy: What Kids Wish They Could Tell You" by Elizabeth McCardell. Copyright 1987 by the author. Reprinted by permission of the publisher.

School Arts, v. 85, February, 1986. Copyright 1986 by Davis Publications, Inc. Reprinted by permission of the publisher.

The School Librarian, v. 18, June, 1970; v. 18, December, 1970; v. 22, June, 1974; v. 24, March, 1976; v. 25, March, 1977; v. 29, June, 1981; v. 30, March, 1982; v. 31, March, 1983; v. 32, March, 1984; v. 32, December, 1984; v. 33, May, 1985; v. 34, March, 1986; v. 34, September, 1986; v. 35, May, 1987. All reprinted by permission of the publisher.

The School Librarian and School Library Review, v. 10, March, 1961. Reprinted by permission of the publisher.

School Library Journal, v. 22, November, 1975; v. 22, March, 1976; v. 23, February, 1977, v. 23, March, 1977; v. 23, May, 1977; v. 24, September, 1977; v. 24, January, 1978; v. 24, May, 1978, v. 25, September, 1978; v. 25, October, 1978; v. 25, January, 1979; v. 25, April, 1979; v. 25, May, 1979; v. 26, September, 1979; v. 26, November, 1979; v. 26, August, 1980; v. 27, January, 1981; v. 27, March, 1981; v. 27, August, 1981; v. 28, September, 1981; v. 28, December, 1981; v. 28, March, 1982, v. 28, April, 1982; v. 28, May, 1982; v. 29, January, 1983; v. 29, March, 1983; v. 30, December, 1983; v. 30, March, 1984; v. 30, August, 1984; v. 31, September, 1984; v. 31, October, 1984; v. 31, November, 1984; v. 31, December, 1984; v. 31, February, 1985; v. 31, April, 1985; v. 31, May, 1985; v. 31, August, 1985; v. 32, October, 1985; v. 32, December, 1985, v. 32, February, 1986; v. 32, May, 1986; v. 32, August, 1986, v. 33, September, 1986; v. 33, October, 1986; v. 33, November, 1986; v. 33, December, 1986; v. 33, February, 1987; v. 33, May, 1987; v. 33, August, 1987. Copyright © 1975, 1976, 1977, 1978, 1979, 1980, 1981, 1982, 1983, 1984, 1985, 1986, 1987. All reprinted from *School Library Journal*, a Cahners/R. R. Bowker Publication, by permission.

School Library Journal, an appendix to *Library Journal*, v. 14, September, 1967; v. 14, December, 1967; v. 15, September, 1968; v. 16, December, 1969; v. 16, February, 1970; v. 17, January, 1971; v. 18, January, 1972; v. 18, April, 1972; v. 19, December, 1972; v. 19, December, 1972; v. 20, October, 1973; v. 20, November, 1973; v. 20, March, 1974; v. 20, April, 1974. Copyright © 1967, 1968, 1969, 1970, 1971, 1972, 1973, 1974. All reprinted from *School Library Journal*, a Cahners/R. R. Bowker Publications, by permission.

Science Books & Films, v. XIII, December, 1977; v. XIV, March, 1979; v. XV, December, 1979; v. 22, November-December, 1986. Copyright 1977, 1979, 1986 by AAAS. All reprinted by permission of the publisher.

Signal, n. 24, September, 1977 for "American Dispatch" by John Donovan. Copyright © 1977 by the author. Reprinted by permission of the author./ n. 30, September, 1979; n. 34, January, 1981; n. 41, May, 1983. Copyright © 1979, 1981, 1983 The Thimble Press. All reprinted by permission of The Thimble Press, Lockwood, Station Road, South Woodchester, Glos., GL5 5EQ, England.

The Signal Review of Children's Books, 2, 1984. Copyright © 1984 The Thimble Press, Lockwood, Station Road, South Woodchester, Glos. GL5 5EQ, England.

Social Education, v. XXV, May, 1961. Copyright, 1961, by the National Council for the Social Studies. Reprinted with permission of the National Council for the Social Studies.

Studies in the Literary Imagination, v. XVIII, Fall, 1985. Copyright 1985 Department of English, Georgia State University. Reprinted by permission of the publisher.

The Times Educational Supplement, n. 3258, November 18, 1977; n. 3422, January 29, 1982. © Times Newspapers Ltd. (London) 1977, 1982. Both reproduced from *The Times Educational Supplement* by permission.

The Times Literary Supplement, n. 3536, December 4, 1969; n. 3572, August 14, 1970; n. 3734, September 28, 1973; n. 3742, November 23, 1973; n. 3890, October 1, 1976; n. 3915, March 25, 1977; n. 4042, September 25, 1980; n. 4051, November 21, 1980; n. 4146, September 17, 1982; n. 4237, June 15, 1984; n. 4308, October 25, 1985; n. 4324, February 14, 1986; n. 4342, June 20, 1986; n. 4365, November 28, 1986. © Times Newspapers Ltd. (London) 1969, 1970, 1973, 1976, 1977, 1980, 1982, 1984, 1985, 1986. All reproduced from *The Times Literary Supplement* by permission.

Top of the News, v. 34, Winter, 1978; v. 39, Winter, 1983; v. 43, Spring, 1987. Copyright © 1978, 1983, 1987 by the American Library Association. All reprinted by permission of the publisher.

The Use of English, v. 36, Spring, 1985. © Granada Publishing Limited 1985.

Virginia Kirkus' Service, v. XXVII, February 1, 1959; v. XXVIII, June 15, 1960; v. XXVIII, August 1, 1960; v. XXX, May 1, 1962; v. XXXI, February 1, 1963; v. XXXIII, July 1, 1965; v. XXXIV, March 15, 1966. Copyright © 1959, 1960, 1962, 1963, 1965, 1966 Virginia Kirkus' Service, Inc. All reprinted by permission of the publisher.

Voice of Youth Advocates, v. 4, October, 1981; v. 6, December, 1983; v. 8, June, 1985; v. 9, June, 1986; v. 9, August-October, 1986; v. 10, June, 1987. Copyrighted 1981, 1983, 1985, 1986, 1987 by *Voice of Youth Advocates*. All reprinted by permission of Scarecrow Press, Inc.

Wilson Library Bulletin, v. 50, February, 1976; v. 51, February, 1977; v. 59, October, 1984; v. 61, April, 1987. Copyright © 1976, 1977, 1984, 1987 by the H. W. Wilson Company. All reprinted by permission of the publisher.

The World of Children's Books, v. III, 1978. © 1978 by Jon C. Stott. Both reprinted by permission of the publisher.

THE EXCERPTS IN CLR, VOLUME 15, WERE REPRINTED FROM THE FOLLOWING BOOKS:

Arbuthnot, May Hill and Zena Sutherland. From *Children and Books.* Fifth edition. Scott, Foresman, 1977. Copyright © 1977, 1972, 1964, 1957, 1947 by Scott, Foresman and Company. All rights reserved. Reprinted by permission of the publisher.

Attebery, Brian. From *The Fantasy Tradition in American Literature: From Irving to Le Guin.* Indiana University Press, 1980. Copyright © 1980 by Brian Attebery. All rights reserved. Reprinted by permission of the publisher.

Bader, Barbara. From *American Picturebooks from Noah's Ark to the Beast Within.* Macmillan, 1976. Copyright © 1976 Barbara Bader. All rights reserved. Reprinted with permission of Macmillan Publishing Company.

Baskin, Barbara H. and Karen H. Harris. From *More Notes from a Different Drummer: A Guide to Juvenile Fiction Portraying the Disabled.* Bowker, 1984. Copyright © 1984 by Barbara H. Baskin and Karen H. Harris. All rights reserved. Reprinted by permission of R. R. Bowker Company, Division of Reed Publishing, USA.

Baum, L. Frank. From *The Wonderful Wizard of Oz.* G. M. Hill Co., 1900.

Bewley, Marius. From *Masks & Mirrors: Essays in Criticism.* Atheneum, 1970. Copyright © 1964, 1970 Marius Bewley. All rights reserved. Reprinted with the permission of Atheneum Publishers, an imprint of Macmillan Publishing Company.

Bradbury, Ray. From "Because, Because, Because . . . . .," in *Wonderful Wizard, Marvelous Land.* By Raylyn Moore. Bowling Green University Popular Press, 1974. Copyright © 1974 by Raylyn Moore. Reprinted by permission of the publisher.

Cott, Jonathan. From *Pipers at the Gates of Dawn: The Wisdom of Children's Literature.* Random House, 1983. Copyright © 1981, 1983 by Jonathan Cott. All rights reserved. Reprinted by permission of Random House, Inc.

Cutler, May. From "Ah, Publishing!" in *One Ocean Touching: Papers from the First Pacific Rim Conference on Children's Literature.* Edited by Sheila A. Egoff. The Scarecrow Press Inc., 1979. Copyright © 1979 by Sheila A. Egoff. Reprinted by permission of the publisher.

Donelson, Kenneth L., and Alleen Pace Nilsen. From *Literature for Today's Young Adults.* Scott, Foresman, 1980. Copyright © 1980 Scott, Foresman and Company. All rights reserved. Reprinted by permission of the publisher.

Dreyer, Sharon Spredemann. From *The Bookfinder: A Guide to Children's Literature about the Needs and Problems of Youth Aged 2-15, Vol. 2.* American Guidance Service, 1981. © 1981 American Guidance Service, Inc. All rights reserved. Reprinted by permission of the publisher.

Eccleshare, Julia. From *Children's Books of the Year 1986.* National Book League, 1986. © National Book League 1986. Reprinted by permission of the publisher.

Egoff, Sheila. From *The Republic of Childhood: A Critical Guide to Canadian Children's Literature in English.* Second edition. Oxford University Press, Canadian Branch, 1975. © Oxford University Press 1975. Reprinted by permission of the publisher.

Egoff, Sheila A. From *Thursday's Child: Trends and Patterns in Contemporary Children's Literature.* American Library Association, 1981. Copyright © 1981 by the American Library Association. All rights reserved. Reprinted by permission of the publisher.

Eisenman, Alvin. From a review of "The Amazing Bone," in *Children's Book Showcase 1977.* By Barbara Bader, Betty Binns, and Alvin Eisenman. Children's Book Council, 1977. © 1977 The Children's Book Council, Inc. Reprinted by permission of the publisher.

Gardner, Martin. From "The Royal Historian of Oz," in *The Wizard of Oz & Who He Was.* By L. Frank Baum, edited by Martin Gardner and Russel B. Nye. Michigan State University Press, 1957.

Greene, David L., and Dick Martin. From *The Oz Scrapbook.* Random House, 1977. Copyright © 1977 by David L. Greene and Dick Martin. All rights reserved. Reprinted by permission of Random House, Inc.

Greene, Douglas G., and Michael Patrick Hearn. From *W. W. Denslow.* Clarke Historical Library, 1976. Copyright 1976 Clarke Historical Library. Reprinted by permission of the publisher.

Hearn, Michael Patrick. From an introduction to *The Annotated Wizard of Oz: The Wonderful Wizard of Oz*. By L. Frank Baum. Potter, 1973. Copyright © 1973 by Michael Patrick Hearn. All rights reserved. Used by permission of Clarkson N. Potter, Inc.

Huck, Charlotte S. From *Children's Literature in the Elementary School*. Third edition, updated. Holt, Rinehart and Winston, 1979. Copyright © 1961, 1968 by Holt, Rinehart and Winston, Inc. Copyright © 1976, 1979 by Charlotte S. Huck. All rights reserved. Reprinted by permission of Holt, Rinehart and Winston, Inc.

Huck, Charlotte S. and Doris Young Kuhn. From *Children's Literature in the Elementary School*. Second edition. Holt, Rinehart and Winston, 1968. Copyright © 1961, 1968 by Holt, Rinehart and Winston, Inc. All rights reserved. Reprinted by permission of Holt, Rinehart and Winston, Inc.

From *Human and Anti-Human Values in Children's Books*. Racism and Sexism Resource Center for Educators, 1976. Copyright © 1976 by the Council on Interracial Books for Children, Inc. All rights reserved. Reprinted by permission of the publisher.

Israel, Callie. From "Ann Blades," in *Profiles*. Edited by Irma McDonough. Revised edition. Canadian Library Association, 1975. Copyright © 1975 by Canadian Library Association. All rights reserved. Reprinted by permission of the publisher and the editor.

Lorraine, Walter. From "Book Illustration: The State of the Art," in *Illustrators of Children's Books: 1967-1976*. Lee Kingman, Grace Allen Hogarth, Harriet Quimby, eds. Horn Book, 1978. Copyright © 1978 by The Horn Book, Inc. All rights reserved. Reprinted by permission of the publisher.

MacCann, Donnarae and Olga Richard. From *The Child's First Books: A Critical Study of Pictures and Texts*. Wilson, 1973. Copyright © 1973 by Donnarae MacCann and Olga Richard. Reprinted by permission of The H. W. Wilson Company.

Moore, Raylyn. From *Wonderful Wizard, Marvelous Land*. Bowling Green University Popular Press, 1974. Copyright © 1974 by Raylyn Moore. Reprinted by permission of the publisher.

Moss, Elaine. From *Picture Books for Young People 9-13*. Second edition. Edited by Nancy Chambers. The Thimble Press, 1985. Copyright © 1981, 1985 Elaine Moss. Reprinted by permission of the publisher.

Nilsen, Alleen Pace, and Kenneth L. Donelson. From *Literature for Today's Young Adults*. Second edition. Scott, Foresman, 1985. Copyright © 1985, 1980 Scott, Foresman and Company. All rights reserved. Reprinted by permission of the publisher.

Norton, Donna E. From *Through the Eyes of a Child: An Introduction to Children's Literature*. Second edition. Merrill Publishing Company, 1987. Copyright © 1987, 1983 by Merrill Publishing Company, Columbus, OH. All rights reserved. Reprinted by permission of the publisher.

Nye, Russel B. From "An Appreciation," in *The Wizard of Oz & Who He Was*. By L. Frank Baum, edited by Martin Gardner and Russel B. Nye. Michigan State University Press, 1957.

Peterson, Linda Kauffman. From "The Caldecott Medal and Honor Books, 1938-1981: 'The Amazing Bone'," in *Newbery and Caldecott Medal and Honor Books: An Annotated Bibliography*. By Linda Kauffman Peterson and Marilyn Leathers Solt. Hall, 1982. Copyright 1982 by G. K. Hall & Co. Reprinted with the permission of the publisher.

Rees, David. From *The Marble in the Water*. The Horn Book, Inc., 1980. Copyright © 1979, 1980 by David Rees. All rights reserved. Reprinted by permission of the publisher.

Sadker, Myra Pollack and David Miller Sadker. From *Now upon a Time: A Contemporary View of Children's Literature*. Harper & Row, 1977. Copyright © 1977 by Myra Pollack Sadker and David Miller Sadker. All rights reserved.

Sale, Roger. From *Fairy Tales and After: From Snow White to E. B. White*. Cambridge, Mass.: Harvard University Press, 1978. Copyright © 1978 by the President and Fellows of Harvard College. All rights reserved. Excerpted by permission of the publishers.

Schiller, Justin G. From an appreciation to *The Wonderful Wizard of Oz*. By L. Frank Baum. University of California Press, 1986. Copyright © 1986 by The Pennyroyal Press. All rights reserved. Reprinted by permission of Pennyroyal Press, Inc.

Spirt, Diana L. From *Introducing More Books: A Guide for the Middle Grades*. R. R. Bowker Company, 1978. Copyright © 1978 by Diana L. Spirt. All rights reserved. Reprinted by permission of the author.

Stott, Jon C. From *Children's Literature from A to Z: A Guide for Parents and Teachers*. McGraw-Hill Book Company, 1984. Copyright © 1984 by McGraw-Hill, Inc. All rights reserved. Reproduced with permission.

Thompson, Ruth Plumly. From "Concerning 'The Wonderful Wizard of Oz'," in *The Wizard of Oz*. By L. Frank Baum, edited by Michael

Patrick Hearn. Schocken Books, 1983. Copyright © 1983 by Dorothy Curtiss Maryott. Reprinted by permission of the Literary Estate of Ruth Plumly Thompson.

Viguers, Ruth Hill. From "Golden Years and Time of Tumult, 1920-1967: Quests, Survival, and the Romance of History, Adventure Tales and Historical Fiction," in *A Critical History of Children's Literature*. By Cornelia Meigs and others, edited by Cornelia Meigs. Revised edition. Macmillan, 1969. Copyright 1953, 1969 by Macmillan Publishing Company. Copyright renewed 1981 by Charles H. Eaton. All rights reserved. Reprinted with permission of the publisher.

Wagenknecht, Edward. From *Utopia Americana*. University of Washington Book Store, 1929. Copyright, 1929, renewed 1957, by Edward Wagenknecht. Reprinted by permission of the University of Washington Press.

CUMULATIVE INDEX TO AUTHORS

This index lists all author entries in *Children's Literature Review* and includes cross-references to them in other Gale sources. References in the index are identified as follows:

AITN: *Authors in the News,* Volumes 1-2
CA: *Contemporary Authors* (original series), Volumes 1-122
CANR: *Contemporary Authors New Revision Series,* Volumes 1-20
CAP: *Contemporary Authors Permanent Series,* Volumes 1-2
CA-R: *Contemporary Authors* (revised editions), Volumes 1-44
CLC: *Contemporary Literary Criticism,* Volumes 1-46
CLR: *Children's Literature Review,* Volumes 1-15
DLB: *Dictionary of Literary Biography,* Volumes 1-67
DLB-DS: *Dictionary of Literary Biography Documentary Series,* Volumes 1-4
DLB-Y: *Dictionary of Literary Biography Yearbook,* Volumes 1980-1986
NCLC: *Nineteenth-Century Literature Criticism,* Volumes 1-17
SAAS: *Something about the Author Autobiography Series,* Volume 1-5
SATA: *Something about the Author,* Volumes 1-50
TCLC: *Twentieth-Century Literary Criticism,* Volumes 1-27
YABC: *Yesterday's Authors of Books for Children,* Volumes 1-2

CUMULATIVE INDEX TO NATIONALITIES

Title Index

CUMULATIVE INDEX TO TITLES

Title Index

Title Index

Title Index

Title Index